ACCOUNTING PRINCIPLES

SIXTH EDITION

by

HOWARD S. NOBLE

Certified Public Accountant, Professor of Accounting
School of Business Administration
University of California, Los Angeles

and

C. ROLLIN NISWONGER

Certified Public Accountant, Professor of Accounting
School of Business Administration
Miami University, Oxford, Ohio

PUBLISHED BY

SOUTH-WESTERN PUBLISHING COMPANY

CINCINNATI 27   CHICAGO 5
SAN FRANCISCO 3   DALLAS 2   NEW ROCHELLE, N. Y.

A10

COPYRIGHT, 1953

by

SOUTH-WESTERN PUBLISHING COMPANY
CINCINNATI, OHIO

All Rights Reserved

The text of this publication, or any part thereof,
may not be reproduced in any manner whatsoever
without permission in writing from the publisher.

K856

Printed in the United States of America

PREFACE

An understanding of principles of accounting is essential for those who study our modern economic system. In accounting is found the basic language of business. The present day complexity of economic problems and their interrelationship with social and political developments have made an appreciation of accounting principles of paramount importance. The study of accounting enhances the ability of college and university students to comprehend the functions of the many phases of business activity.

As in previous editions, this sixth edition is planned to serve as a basic course for the following groups: (1) those who plan to continue the study of accounting and to seek a career in public or private accounting; (2) those who plan to enter other areas of business activity and will need an understanding of accounting as a tool of business management; (3) those whose major interest is in economics, political science, or law and who seek a sounder understanding through a knowledge of principles of accounting; (4) those who anticipate entering other professions and will need accounting to measure their financial progress in professional practice.

The continued use of previous editions by colleges and universities throughout the country is evidence of the effectiveness of this text in teaching students the principles of accounting. Basic features of the earlier editions have been retained in this edition. The approach is through the analysis of the effect of business transactions upon the financial statements. A service business is first used in developing the accounting cycle, which is completed in the first six chapters. Journals are introduced earlier than heretofore and greater stress has been placed upon their flexibility in design to meet the needs of the particular enterprise. There is less emphasis upon the use of explanatory data in the journals and the accounts, in keeping with the modern practice of using business papers as the authority for and the explanation of entries, thus avoiding needless work in recording information.

Much new material has been added, particularly in the chapters dealing with corporations. There are many new charts, diagrams, and outlines to assist in the development of the subject matter and in summarizing the more complex and difficult procedures. Alternate methods of accounting are developed in such a way as to avoid confusing the student. Throughout the text there is an emphasis upon the usefulness of accounting to those engaged in managing a business, to owners, to creditors, and to other interested parties.

Questions and problems at the end of each chapter provide ample material for class discussion and practice assignments. Supplementary problems for each chapter are given in an appendix. They may be used when problems in addition to those given at the end of the chapter are desired or when the instructor desires to vary the assignments from year to year. Some of the supplementary problems are longer than those in the main body of the text. Bound books of working papers containing the ruled forms needed in solving the problems are available.

Three optional practice sets are provided. The narratives of transactions for Practice Sets Nos. 1 and 2 are given in the textbook, but that for Practice Set No. 3 is provided in a pamphlet included with the blanks required for the set. Business papers are available for use with Practice Set No. 1. The first set deals with a mercantile business conducted as a sole proprietorship. The second is a trading enterprise conducted initially as a partnership and later incorporated. The third set provides practice in general manufacturing accounting and job order cost accounting. Each of the three practice sets is divided into parts and is integrated with the text material in such a way as to permit the alternation of chapter assignments with work assignments.

In anticipation of the writing of this edition, the opinions and the preferences of accounting teachers were sought by means of a questionnaire. A summary of the opinions and the suggestions received served as an invaluable guide to the authors. A draft of the manuscript was then submitted to a number of experienced teachers for review and criticism. Thus the present book is the result of the cooperative effort of many persons.

The authors wish to acknowledge their indebtedness to all those who assisted in the preparation of this new edition. Limitations of space do not permit the personal recognition of every person. The authors particularly appreciate the assistance of the following professors who read the manuscript and gave suggestions for its improvement: Conley R. Addington, University of Miami; John Woodward FitzGerald, Ithaca College; Ernest A. Heilman, University of Minnesota; T. C. Hilliard, De Paul University; Christian Oehler, Fordham University; Ralph C. Russell, Texas College of Arts and Industries.

H. S. N.
C. R. N.

CONTENTS

*Questions and problems are given at the end of each chapter.

PART XII — USING ACCOUNTING INFORMATION

Chapter 1

Meaning and Purpose of Accounting

STUDY OF ACCOUNTING Accounting principles are concerned with business transactions and their effect on the various economic units in society. Economic units include business units; political units, such as cities and school districts; consumer units, such as families and individuals; and other social units, such as churches, hospitals, and clubs. In this text the emphasis will be placed on accounting principles applied to business enterprises. It should be kept in mind, however, that accounting principles can be applied to each unit in economic society.

Accounting always applies to a unit. It cannot be spread over a group of units. It is a particular automobile manufacturer, not the automobile industry, that has transactions to be accounted for. Each business enterprise has its own business transactions and its own accounting.

As a study, accounting is never-ending. Capable scholars devote their lives and their intellectual energies to analyzing its phenomena. Experienced professional accountants contribute their best thinking to the satisfactory solution of accounting problems. Organizations of accountants have established permanent committees for continuous study in certain areas. Their investigations and conclusions form the basis for recommendations concerning specific policies and procedures.

BUSINESS TRANSACTIONS A business transaction is an exchange of goods or services at a particular price. The purchase of a package of gum for 5 cents, the payment of a 12-cent bus fare, and the acquisition of a new home for $15,000 are illustrative of the variety of business transactions. The first two transactions are simple, being an exchange of money for a commodity in the first example and of money for a service in the second. The purchase of a house may be more complex, as it may involve an arrangement to spread the payment of a substantial part of the price over a period of years, the payment of interest, an agreement as to the payment of taxes on the property, and provisions designed to safeguard the seller until the full price has been received.

It can readily be seen that the study of a business transaction does not always end with the purchase or the sale of a commodity or a service. If payment is not made at the time of the exchange, both the buyer and the seller should have records that will provide information about the obligations of the buyer. If goods or services that are purchased are to be used at some time in the future, the accounting records should keep track of them until they are used or exchanged.

The basic raw materials of accounting are business transactions. But the persons who actually complete the transactions are not necessarily the ones responsible for the accounting; and, if they are, they may not immediately make the entries in the accounting records. It is necessary, therefore, that some evidence of the transactions be provided so that the details can be recorded. The form that this evidence takes varies with the nature of the transaction and the medium used. For example, a sale of merchandise or services for cash may be evidenced by a handwritten sales ticket or by pushing the proper keys on a cash register or other recording device.

PROPERTY AND   The use of property is essential to the conduct
BUSINESS OPERATIONS   of business. A place for the business must be
provided in a building that is owned or rented; equipment adapted to the activities of the business must be owned or leased; if goods are sold, they must be purchased or manufactured and kept in stock prior to sale; if services are rendered, the equipment and supplies used in rendering the services must be available for use. Wherever there is business, property is found.

Through the sale of commodities or services, business operations produce funds that may be used to purchase additional property as the business expands. These funds constitute an important element in the total property of the business. If a business is conducted in such a way that its total property increases, the business is said to be successful. In contrast, if its operations result in a decrease in its property, the business is considered to be unsuccessful.

An automobile-manufacturing business that grew from a one-man shop in the back lot of a Detroit residence to a huge corporation employing hundreds of thousands of people is an example of successful business operations and the accompanying increase in property. A five-and-ten-cent business that grew from a small store in a small town in Pennsylvania to a world-wide enterprise with departmentalized stores in every large city is another instance of expansion in business and property. Many of the large business firms in existence today began years ago as small enterprises. It should not be concluded, however, that only the giant enterprises are successful. Moderate-sized and small business enterprises also render valuable services and often earn substantial profits for their owners.

TRANSACTIONS AND   The business transaction determines the value
ACCOUNTING VALUES   to be used in accounting. This value is the
price agreed upon between the buyer and the seller in the transaction; it measures the amount shown on the accounting record. For example, if a building is purchased by a businessman for $50,000, that amount is used in the accounting records. The seller may have held the building at $60,000 up to the time of sale; the buyer may have planned to pay $40,000 for it; the building may have been assessed at $35,000 for property tax purposes, and another buyer may offer the purchaser $75,000 for it the day after he buys it. These values have no effect on the accounting records. The transaction price, $50,000, sets the value of the building in the accounting records of the purchaser.

If the purchaser should decide that it is better for him to sell the building at $75,000 to the new buyer than to use it himself, then there is a new transaction that sets a new accounting value for the new buyer. The building appears on the accounting records of the new buyer at $75,000 because that is the price he paid for it.

Or, assume the purchase in 1940 of 1,000 shares of stock at $8 and the purchase in 1950 of 1,000 shares of the same stock at $42. Assume also that the stock may be sold at $60 a share on December 31, 1952. On the accounting summary of December 31, 1952, the 2,000 shares would be listed at the actual cost of $50,000 ($8,000+$42,000). It is true that the 2,000 shares could have been purchased in 1940 for $16,000, that they would have cost $84,000 if all had been purchased at the same time in 1950, and that they could have been sold for $120,000 at December 31, 1952; nevertheless, the amounts actually paid are the values used in the accounting records.

It is only by recording the prices of the actual transactions of the owner that accounting records can have satisfactory stability. In this way a true record of the owner's transactions and the effect of his transactions on his financial condition is obtained.

PURPOSE OF   In a general way, the purpose of accounting
ACCOUNTING   may be said to be to provide information con-
cerning property and the rights to property and to show how property and the rights to it have been affected by business operations. More specifically, accounting has been described as:

... the art of recording, classifying and summarizing in a significant manner and in terms of money, transactions and events which are, in part at least, of a financial character, and interpreting the results thereof.[1]

Recording commits the transactions and events to writing. It is important that consideration always be given to methods to be used in recording, to the end that the cost involved be kept as low as possible.

Classifying involves sorting the mass of transactions in an orderly and systematic manner. Special forms and procedures are devised to facilitate this process. Many isolated transactions are of little significance when viewed individually. The information becomes useful when arranged according to predetermined classes. Accounting records are justified only insofar as they are useful to management. Obviously, transactions must be analyzed before they can be classified. An understanding of the effect of each transaction upon property and property rights is therefore of paramount importance.

Summarizing brings the accounting data together in a form that further enhances their usefulness. As indicated above, it is not the single business act but the sum of all of the operations of a day, a week, a month, or a year that has the greatest significance. Therefore, summaries of operations and their effect on property and rights to property are prepared at intervals. These reports are made to the managers of the enterprise and to others who need the information. Some reports must be made frequently; others, only at longer intervals. For example, it may be desirable to have a daily summary of transactions affecting cash, while an annual report of transactions affecting buildings may be satisfactory.

Interpreting the results of operations, as summarized in the various reports, is an essential part of accounting. Interpretation is frequently in the form of percentage analyses and ratios. Comparison of operations for different periods may indicate important trends. By these and other means the most significant developments in the affairs of a business may be explained and emphasized.

PROPERTY AND PROPERTY RIGHTS The use of property in the operation of a business has been emphasized. It has also been pointed out that accounting deals with property and rights to property. For every business enterprise the sum of the properties owned must be equal to the sum of the rights to the properties.

---

[1]*Accounting Research Bulletin No. 9*, "Report of Committee on Terminology," May, 1941 (New York: American Institute of Accountants), p. 67.

The properties owned by a business are called *assets*. The right or interest of the proprietor in the assets of the business is called his *proprietorship, capital,* or *net worth*. If there are no claims against the assets of a business other than that of the proprietor, the relationship of the assets to the claim of the proprietor is expressed by the following equation:

$$\text{ASSETS} = \text{PROPRIETORSHIP}$$

For example, assume that John Field decides to engage in the business of operating a gift and novelty store. He begins operations by depositing $6,000 cash in a bank account in the name of the business, the Field Gift Shop. His assets and his proprietorship in the Field Gift Shop are shown by the following equation:

	ASSETS	=	PROPRIETORSHIP
Transaction (a)	Cash	=	John Field
	$6,000		$6,000

It should be noted that the equation applies only to the business enterprise. Field may own his home, stocks in various companies, and other assets not connected with the business. But he now has $6,000 of cash in the business and his proprietorship in the business is $6,000.

The effect of various transactions on the equation will be shown in a series of illustrations.

Field's next step in establishing his business is to purchase counters and showcases for which he pays $1,000 in cash. This decreases his asset cash by $1,000, but he acquires other assets called store equipment. The transaction changes the nature of the assets, but it does not alter the total value of the assets nor the amount of the proprietorship. The effect of the transaction, in terms of the equation, is as follows:

	ASSETS	
		Store
Transaction (b)	Cash	Equipment
	−$1,000	+$1,000

After giving effect to these changes in the original equation, the new equation now appears as follows:

	ASSETS		=	PROPRIETORSHIP
		Store		
	Cash +	Equipment	=	John Field
	$5,000	$1,000		$6,000

Field purchases merchandise for resale, paying $3,500 in cash. This transaction is like the preceding one in that one type of asset is exchanged for another type of asset. Cash of $3,500 is exchanged for merchandise worth $3,500, which is shown as follows:

ASSETS

Transaction (c)   Cash   Merchandise
                        − $3,500   + $3,500

Incorporating the transaction into the equation yields the following:

ASSETS   = PROPRIETORSHIP

Store
Cash + Merchandise + Equipment = John Field
$1,500 $3,500 $1,000 $6,000

Businessmen frequently find that, in order to conduct their businesses satisfactorily, they need property in addition to that provided by their own proprietorship. They can obtain the use of additional property in either of two ways: (1) they can borrow money and use it to purchase assets or (2) they can purchase property *on account*, that is, they can procure the property by giving a promise to pay at some future date.

Those from whom businessmen borrow or purchase on account are known as *creditors*. The creditors of a business have a claim on the entire assets of that business until the proprietor pays them in accordance with their agreement. The rights of the creditors in the assets of a business are known as the *liabilities* of the business.

Needing additional stock, Field purchases $1,400 of merchandise from Ace Gift Co. and promises to pay for it later. This transaction increases his merchandise by $1,400 and, because he is not making immediate payment, increases the total of his assets by the same amount. As a part of the transaction, however, he grants Ace Gift Co. a claim against his assets, creating a liability of $1,400. The amount of Field's proprietorship is not affected. In terms of the fundamental equation, this is what happens:

                        ASSETS   LIABILITIES
Transaction (d)   Merchandise   Ace Gift Co.
                        + $1,400   + $1,400

After giving effect to these changes in the equation as it appeared just prior to this transaction, the new equation appears as follows:

ASSETS   = LIABILITIES + PROPRIETORSHIP

Store
Cash + Merchandise + Equipment = Ace Gift Co. +   John Field
$1,500 $4,900 $1,000 $1,400 $6,000

Inasmuch as Field would use nearly all of the cash remaining in the business if he paid Ace Gift Co. the total amount of the liability, he decides to pay $500 on account at this time. The effect of the transaction is as follows:

	ASSETS	LIABILITIES
Transaction (e)	Cash	Ace Gift Co.
	−$500	−$500

Incorporating the foregoing transaction into the equation yields the following:

ASSETS			= LIABILITIES	+ PROPRIETORSHIP
		Store		
Cash +	Merchandise +	Equipment =	Ace Gift Co. +	John Field
$1,000	$4,900	$1,000	$900	$6,000

CHANGES IN PROPRIETORSHIP AS A RESULT OF BUSINESS OPERATIONS The primary objective of the proprietor of a business is to increase his proprietorship by earning a profit. This may be accomplished by selling commodities or services at a price above cost and by keeping the expenses of operating the business at an amount that is less than the difference between the sales price and the cost. For instance, if goods that cost $400 are sold for $600, there is an excess of selling price over cost, or a *margin*, of $200. If the expenses incurred in making the sale are *less* than $200, the proprietor has earned a profit; if the expenses are *more* than $200, he has suffered a loss.

In actual practice it is not always feasible or necessary to determine the margin on each sale of merchandise nor to determine the amount of expense incurred in making the sale. Ordinarily the profit earned or the loss incurred is calculated for all sales and all expenses of a particular period of time. The period selected is arbitrary; it may be a week, a month, a year, or some other period.

During the first month of operations, Field, whose transactions we have been studying, sells for $1,800 in cash merchandise that cost him $1,100, leaving a margin of $700. This represents the sum of numerous individual sales to various customers. The effect of these transactions is to increase cash by $1,800, to decrease merchandise by $1,100, and to increase proprietorship by $700.

	ASSETS		PROPRIETORSHIP
Transaction (f)	Cash	Merchandise	John Field
	+$1,800	−$1,100	+$700

After giving effect to these changes in the equation, the new equation appears as follows:

ASSETS			= LIABILITIES	+ PROPRIETORSHIP
		Store		
Cash +	Merchandise +	Equipment =	Ace Gift Co. +	John Field
$2,800	$3,800	$1,000	$900	$6,700

Various expenses in the amount of $400 have been incurred and paid during the month. The effect of expenses is to reduce proprietorship. The increase in proprietorship by the amount of the $700 excess of selling price over cost is now reduced by $400; thus the profit earned by the proprietor is $300. The effect of the expenses on cash and proprietorship is shown as follows:

	ASSETS	PROPRIETORSHIP
Transaction (g)	Cash	John Field
	−$400	−$400

Revising the preceding equation to give effect to the payment of expenses results in the following equation:

$$\text{ASSETS} = \text{LIABILITIES} + \text{PROPRIETORSHIP}$$

Cash +	Merchandise +	Store Equipment =	Ace Gift Co. +	John Field
$2,400	$3,800	$1,000	$900	$6,300

SUMMARY OF ILLUSTRATION The transactions of the Field Gift Shop discussed in the two preceding sections are summarized in tabular form at the top of the opposite page. The letters correspond to the transaction numbers. After each transaction, the balance of each item in the equation is shown. In studying the illustration the following points should be noted:

(1) Regardless of the nature of the transaction, its effect may always be stated in terms of increases and decreases in assets, liabilities, and proprietorship.
(2) Equality between the two sides of the equation is always maintained. This is true for each particular transaction and also for the complete equation that reflects the financial condition of the business.
(3) No particular relationship can be observed between the amount of the profit earned and the changes in the amount of any one asset or of the total assets. During the month the cash decreased from $6,000 to $2,400 and the total assets increased from $6,000 to $7,200; but the profit, as shown by the increase in the proprietorship, was $300.

ACCOUNTING STATEMENTS There are two principal accounting summaries: one lists the kinds and the amounts of property of the business, together with the ownership rights in the property; the other reports the effects of the operations of the business on the owner's equity or right in the property. The first of these summaries is known as the *balance sheet;* it shows the assets, the liabilities, and the proprietorship. The second summary is known as the *profit and loss statement;* it lists the income and the costs of operation for the period, which result in an increase or a decrease in proprietorship. The *balance sheet* gives a picture of financial condition at a given

	Cash	+	Merchandise	+	Store Equipment	=	Ace Gift Co.	+	John Field
			ASSETS			= LIABILITIES + PROPRIETORSHIP			
(a)	$6,000					=			$6,000
(b)	−1,000				+$1,000				
Balances	$5,000			+	$1,000	=			$6,000
(c)	−3,500		+$3,500						
Balances	$1,500	+	$3,500	+	$1,000	=			$6,000
(d)			+1,400				+$1,400		
Balances	$1,500	+	$4,900	+	$1,000	=	$1,400	+	$6,000
(e)	− 500						− 500		
Balances	$1,000	+	$4,900	+	$1,000	=	$ 900	+	$6,000
(f)	+1,800		−1,100					+	700
Balances	$2,800	+	$3,800	+	$1,000	=	$ 900	+	$6,700
(g)	− 400							−	400
Balances	$2,400	+	$3,800	+	$1,000	=	$ 900	+	$6,300

moment of time; the *profit and loss statement* covers the period of time between two balance sheets.

For example, the information needed to prepare a balance sheet for the Field Gift Shop after transaction (g) appears on the last line of the tabulation shown above. The profit and loss statement for the period would report the amount of the sales, the cost of the goods that were sold, the various expenses, and the net profit or loss.

From an accounting point of view, the life of any business enterprise is a succession of balance sheets, usually prepared annually and tied together by profit and loss statements, each covering one year. When statements are prepared annually, the profit and loss statement covers the year beginning with the previous balance sheet and ending with the date of the present balance sheet. If the life of a business enterprise is represented by a line starting at point X and moving toward the right, accounting statements may be diagrammed as follows:

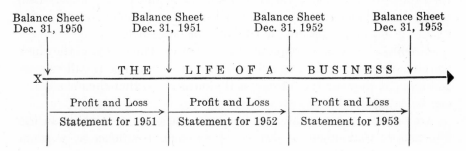

NEED FOR BUSINESS RECORDS If the proprietor is to conduct his business in such a manner that his proprietorship will be increased and if he is to make satisfactory decisions with regard to future operations, he must know the effect of his business transactions on his assets, liabilities, and proprietorship.

If he is considering the desirability of employing additional sales clerks, he should consider the results obtained from the employment of his present clerks and should try to judge from this experience what probable results will be obtained from employing additional clerks. If he is considering the purchase of additional equipment or additional store space, he should give careful attention to the results obtained from the present equipment and space.

If the proprietor is contemplating the purchase of additional property by increasing his liabilities, he must consider (1) whether his past experience indicates that this property can be used profitably, that is, whether it can be used so that it will result in an increase in proprietorship, and (2) whether he will be able to pay his creditors in accordance with the terms under which he can obtain the property from them. Creditors will usually accept only cash in payment of their claims. If the proprietor invests too much of his property in land, buildings, equipment, and other assets of a similar nature, he may not have the cash needed to pay his creditors at the proper time. He must have information that will show him the amount of his liabilities and he must know whether he will have the cash to pay them when they are due.

There are persons other than the proprietor who are interested in the operations of the business and who are entitled to information about these operations. If the proprietor wishes to borrow money from a bank, the officers of the bank may require him to give information that will enable them to judge his ability to repay the loan. This information will probably include the amounts and the nature of his assets and liabilities, the amounts of the profits earned in previous years, and a detailed explanation of how the profits were earned. If the profits were earned in the regular operation of the business, a much better condition might be indicated than if they were unusual gains resulting from transactions that might not occur again.

Creditors may also request similar information before they sell merchandise on account to a business. The government will require a statement showing the income of the business so that the income tax can be ascertained and assessed.

Obviously, in controlling his business, the proprietor needs all the information that might be desired by anyone else; hence accounting records that meet the needs of the proprietor will ordinarily meet the needs of all others. The proprietor, however, frequently needs information about many details in which outsiders are not interested. Statistics showing the amounts of different expenses, the cost of selling certain kinds of merchandise, the ratio of returned goods to goods sold, and many similar types of information are important to the proprietor but are ordinarily not needed by others. In the following chapters attention will be given primarily to the needs of the proprietor, but the needs of others will not be ignored.

RECORDS FOR NONCOMMERCIAL ENTERPRISES　　Records are often needed by those not engaged in business operations in the technical sense. For example, records are used by professional men and by those who have retired from active participation in business. The physician, the lawyer, and the accountant must maintain records to show at least (1) the amounts owed them by their clients so that they can take the necessary steps to procure collection and (2) the amount of income earned so that they can make their income tax returns to the government. Governmental units, such as cities and states, need information concerning past operations in planning their future activities. The same is true of lodges, clubs, and churches. Every individual or organization that uses property in the conduct of operations should maintain a record of this property and the effect of operations on the property. Emphasis will be placed primarily on the records needed by those carrying on commercial operations for profit, but much of this discussion will be applicable to the needs of all those requiring the services of accounting records.

THE PROFESSION OF ACCOUNTANCY　　The tremendous development of accounting theory and technique during the current century has been accompanied by an ever-increasing number of professionally trained accountants. Among the factors contributing to this growth have been the increase in number, size, and complexity of business corporations; the imposition of new and more complex taxes, especially since the adoption of the Federal Income Tax Amendment in 1913; and the restrictions imposed on business operations by governmental regulations.

Accountants who render accounting services to clients on a fee basis are said to be engaged in *public accounting*. Similarly, their employees to whom they assign portions of the work may be termed public accountants. Accountants serving a particular employer, perhaps as chief accountant or controller, are said to be engaged in *private accounting*.

Recognizing the need for reliable professional accounting service, all the states have enacted laws providing for the licensing of certified public accountants, commonly called C.P.A.'s. Only those who have met the qualifications and received a license may designate themselves as C.P.A.'s. Some states provide for the licensing of all public accountants. In other states there are no restrictions as to the practice of public accounting. Public accountants who do not hold the C.P.A. certificate are sometimes designated as P.A.'s.

The qualifications required for the C.P.A. certificate differ among the various states. In most states the applicant must be a high-school graduate, or have equivalent education, and must have had at least two or three years' experience in public accounting or accounting work considered equivalent. In some states accounting education may be substituted for all or part of the experience requirement. Some states require the completion of a course of study in accounting that is approved by the respective state boards of education. In all states candidates must successfully pass a series of examinations on the subjects of auditing, commercial law, theory of accounts, and accounting practice. All states use the uniform examination, prepared by the American Institute of Accountants, the national organization of C.P.A.'s. A few states also require candidates to pass an examination in an additional subject, such as business economics, governmental accounting, or taxation. Details regarding the requirements of any specific state can be obtained from the state board of accountancy or from a local C.P.A. association.

One indication of the recent rapid growth of the accounting profession is that the number of C.P.A.'s more than doubled between 1940 and 1951. But the growth in the number of persons engaged in private accounting has exceeded the increase in public accountants during the past half century.

The scope of activities and responsibilities of private accountants varies quite widely. Private accountants are concerned with the financial records of a particular business enterprise or nonprofit organization. They are frequently referred to as administrative or executive accountants, but they are sometimes called industrial accountants when they are employed by a manufacturing concern. Various branches of federal, state, and local governments also employ accountants. There are a number of national organizations of private accountants that seek to improve accounting service through periodic meetings and publications.

SPECIALIZED ACCOUNTING FIELDS　　The accounting that has been referred to in previous pages is sometimes called *general accounting*. It has to do with the recording of transactions for a business or other economic unit and the periodic preparation of statements from these records. It provides accounting information for management, for creditors, for the government, and for any others who have use for such information.

In addition to general accounting, a number of specialized accounting fields have developed, especially during the past fifty years. Among these specialized fields attention may be given briefly to the following:

Auditing and investigations represent a field of accounting activity that reviews independently the general accounting. Auditing is usually done by public accountants. These accountants examine records and reports and issue a statement of opinion regarding accuracy, together with a report containing confidential advice to the management. Large corporations frequently employ their own staff of internal auditors. In such cases the work programs of the public accountant and the internal audit staff are dovetailed so as to avoid needless duplication of effort.

Cost accounting emphasizes accounting for costs, particularly manufacturing costs. It stresses costs of products and processes rather than the proprietorship of the enterprise as a whole.

Tax accounting work includes the preparation of tax returns and the consideration of the tax consequences of proposed business transactions. Accountants specializing in this field must not only be familiar with the tax statutes affecting their employer or clients, but must also keep up to date on administrative regulations and court decisions.

Accounting systems is the special field concerned with the creation of accounting forms and office procedures for particular enterprises or groups of similar enterprises. It seeks to devise the most efficient means of recording and reporting financial data.

Budgetary accounting presents the plan of financial operations for a period and, through accounts and summaries, provides comparisons of actual operations with the predetermined plan. It is a combination of planning and controlling future operations.

Governmental accounting specializes in the transactions of political units, such as states and municipalities. It seeks to provide useful accounting information with regard to the business aspect of public administration.

QUESTIONS

1. Name five different kinds of assets that each of the following is likely to own: (a) a college student, (b) a retail grocery store, (c) an automobile manufacturer, (d) a practicing attorney, (e) a hospital.

2. Of the five units mentioned above, (a) which requires the greatest total amount of assets? (b) which requires the least?

3. George Meredith sold for $10,000 some shares of stock that he had originally purchased for $6,500. How did this transaction affect the total amount of (a) his assets? (b) his proprietorship?

4. When a business incurs a liability, what effect does it have on proprietorship? Explain.

5. The Star Electric Company manufactures various kinds of electrical equipment. Describe a transaction that will (a) increase an asset and decrease another asset, (b) increase an asset and increase a liability (c) increase an asset and increase proprietorship, (d) decrease an asset and decrease a liability, (e) decrease an asset and decrease proprietorship.

6. Robert Clair purchases for $2,000 used store equipment that he is certain is worth $3,000. At what amount should the equipment be recorded by Clair?

7. "Accounting is an indispensable tool of management." Do you agree? Explain.

8. Describe in general terms the requirements that an individual must meet to become a C.P.A.

9. Edward Black's proprietorship on November 1 is shown by the first equation given below. Each line designated by a letter indicates the effect on the equation of a particular transaction. Describe each of the transactions.

	CASH	+	MERCHANDISE	+	STORE FIXTURES	=	LIABILITIES	+	PROPRIETORSHIP
	$4,000	+	$6,000	+	$1,500	=	$1,500	+	$10,000
(a)	−500		+500						
	$3,500	+	$6,500	+	$1,500	=	$1,500	+	$10,000
(b)	+300				−300				
	$3,800	+	$6,500	+	$1,200	=	$1,500	+	$10,000
(c)			+1,000				+1,000		
	$3,800	+	$7,500	+	$1,200	=	$2,500	+	$10,000
(d)	+1,500		−1,000						+500
	$5,300	+	$6,500	+	$1,200	=	$2,500	+	$10,500
(e)	−100								−100
	$5,200	+	$6,500	+	$1,200	=	$2,500	+	$10,400
(f)	−1,000						−1,000		
	$4,200	+	$6,500	+	$1,200	=	$1,500	+	$10,400

10. Summary financial data of the village of Fairview on July 1 are shown by the first equation given below. Each line designated by a letter indicates the effect on the equation of a particular transaction. Describe each of the transactions.

	CASH	+	TAXES RECEIVABLE	+	BLDG.	+	LAND	+	EQUIP.	=	LIAB.	+	PROP.
	$14,000	+	$ 8,000	+	$20,000	+	$ 6,500	+	$12,000	=	$10,500	+	$50,000
(a)	+5,000		−5,000										
	$19,000	+	$ 3,000	+	$20,000	+	$ 6,500	+	$12,000	=	$10,500	+	$50,000
(b)	+4,000								−4,000				
	$23,000	+	$ 3,000	+	$20,000	+	$ 6,500	+	$ 8,000	=	$10,500	+	$50,000
(c)	−5,500										−5,500		
	$17,500	+	$ 3,000	+	$20,000	+	$ 6,500	+	$ 8,000	=	$ 5,000	+	$50,000
(d)	+13,000				−10,000		−1,000						+2,000
	$30,500	+	$ 3,000	+	$10,000	+	$ 5,500	+	$ 8,000	=	$ 5,000	+	$52,000
(e)			+8,000										+8,000
	$30,500	+	$11,000	+	$10,000	+	$ 5,500	+	$ 8,000	=	$ 5,000	+	$60,000
(f)	−11,000												−11,000
	$19,500	+	$11,000	+	$10,000	+	$ 5,500	+	$ 8,000	=	$ 5,000	+	$49,000

PROBLEMS

1-1. Frank Hurst has organized a dance band to play for various community organizations on Friday and Saturday nights. Record the following transactions in tabular form similar to that used in Question 9 in this chapter, using the following headings:

ASSETS	=	LIABILITIES	+	PROPRIETORSHIP
Cash+Equipment+Music		Miller's Music Co.		Frank Hurst

(a) Invested cash, $200, and equipment (music stands), $70.
(b) Purchased sheet music on account, $25, from Miller's Music Company.
(c) Received $170 from the Friday Night Club for services rendered.
(d) Paid $125 to members of the band.
(e) Purchased an amplifier on account from Miller's Music Company, $85.
(f) Received $180 from Kenton Country Club for services rendered.
(g) Paid $125 to members of the band.
(h) Paid Miller's Music Company in full of account.

1-2. Lee Smith is the owner of Lee's Men's Shop, selling men's clothing. Record the following transactions for July in tabular form similar to that used in Question 9 in this chapter. The headings to be used are:

ASSETS	=	LIABILITIES	+	PROPRIETORSHIP
Cash+Mdse.+Store Equip.		Lions, Inc.		Lee Smith

(a) Invested $18,000 in cash.
(b) Purchased store equipment for $4,500 in cash.
(c) Bought merchandise — shirts, coats, etc. — on account from Lions, Inc., $17,500.
(d) Sold merchandise costing $12,000 for $15,000 cash.
(e) Paid salesmen's salaries and miscellaneous expenses, $1,750.
(f) Paid Lions, Inc. $15,000 on account.

At the end of July, Mr. Smith decided to enlarge his business to include men's shoes. He rearranged his store to accommodate the new department and hired more salesmen. Record the following transactions for August:

(g) Purchased additional equipment for $3,000 cash.
(h) Purchased a stock of men's shoes on account from Lions, Inc., $5,000.
(i) Sold merchandise costing $8,000 for $10,000 cash.
(j) Paid Lions, Inc. in full of account.
(k) Paid salesmen's salaries and miscellaneous expenses, $2,500.

1-3. On June 1, R. A. Chapman opened a dry cleaning agency known as Varsity Cleaners. Record the following transactions for June in tabular form similar to that used in Question 9 in this chapter, using the following headings:

ASSETS	=	LIABILITIES	+	PROPRIETORSHIP
Cash + Century + Store + Truck Club Equip.		Xpert Cleaners, Inc.		R. A. Chapman

(a) Mr. Chapman deposited $2,000 in a bank account that is to be used in the business.
(b) Purchased counter and racks, $400, and used truck, $750, paying cash.
(c) Billed the Century Club $50 for cleaning draperies, allowing them two weeks to pay.
(d) Received $200 from cash customers during first week.
(e) Paid rent for month, $75.
(f) Received balance due from Century Club.
(g) Received $250 from cash customers during second week.
(h) Received bill from Xpert Cleaners, Inc. for cleaning and pressing during first half of month, $285.
(i) Reimbursed a customer $10 for a garment lost by Xpert Cleaners, Inc. Xpert Cleaners agreed to deduct this amount from bill received and recorded in transaction (h).
(j) Received $240 from cash customers during third week.
(k) Paid balance due Xpert Cleaners, Inc.
(l) Paid $30 for advertising.
(m) Withdrew $150 for personal use.
(n) Received $270 from cash customers during remainder of month.
(o) Received bill from Xpert Cleaners, Inc. for cleaning and pressing during second half of month, $300.
(p) Paid $50 for gas, oil, and repairs for delivery truck.

Submit answers to the following questions:

(1) What is the total of Chapman's assets after transaction (p)?
(2) What is the net amount of Chapman's increase in capital from transaction (a) through transaction (p)?
(3) Can the increase in capital be identified with any particular asset?
(4) What is the amount of Chapman's net profit for the month?

Chapter 2

The Balance Sheet

**PURPOSE OF THE
BALANCE SHEET** For the intelligent conduct of business activity, the manager of a business must know at appropriate intervals the financial condition of his enterprise and the changes in the financial condition that have taken place. It would be virtually impossible for him to obtain such information by a direct inspection of the hundreds and thousands of transactions completed by the business. If he is to have this information in a usable form, many transactions must be summarized so that he can see the effect of all of them together. These periodic summaries are usually prepared annually, quarterly, or monthly. They are designed to provide the proprietor and others with useful information about the financial condition of the business. The summary or report that shows the assets, the liabilities, and the proprietorship of a business at a particular time is known as a *balance sheet*.

**FORM OF THE
BALANCE SHEET** The form of the balance sheet is derived from the basic accounting equation. The relationship of the equation and the balance sheet may be shown by a simple illustration. If Joseph Brown, a retail merchant, is using $22,000 of assets in his business and there are claims of creditors amounting to $7,000, his financial condition may be shown by the equation:

$$\text{Assets} = \text{Liabilities} + \text{Proprietorship}$$
$$\$22,000 \qquad \$7,000 \qquad \$15,000$$

In preparing a balance sheet it is customary to present the assets on the left and the liabilities and the proprietorship on the right, as in the equation, but with the equation symbol omitted. Thus, the balance sheet of Joseph Brown's business might appear as follows:

Assets................... $22,000 Liabilities................ $ 7,000
Proprietorship........... 15,000

Such a statement would obviously not fulfill the needs of the proprietor or of others entitled to information about his business. It does not disclose the nature of his properties or of the claims of his creditors. It does not show whether he has sufficient cash to meet his needs and his obligations or sufficient merchandise to satisfy the wants of his customers. Nor does it list the value of the store and delivery equipment he uses in rendering service to his customers. It does not indicate whether he owns the building in which his business is conducted or how much of his capital is invested in his various assets. His balance sheet should show the amount he has invested in each kind of asset. It should also show the nature of his obligations.

An examination reveals that the assets of Brown's business enterprise are composed of the following: cash, $1,800; merchandise inventory, $5,300; store supplies, $300; office supplies, $100; store equipment, $3,000; office equipment, $1,500; building, $8,000; and land, $2,000. He owes $4,000 on his note at the bank and he owes various suppliers $3,000 for goods he has purchased. The details of his financial condition can be studied more readily if they are arranged in columns in the following manner:

ASSETS		LIABILITIES	
Cash....................	$ 1,800	Notes Payable...........	$ 4,000
Merchandise Inventory....	5,300	Accounts Payable........	3,000
Store Supplies...........	300		
Office Supplies..........	100	Total Liabilities..........	$ 7,000
Store Equipment.........	3,000		
Office Equipment........	1,500		
Building................	8,000	PROPRIETORSHIP	
Land...................	2,000	Joseph Brown, Capital.....	15,000
		Total Liabilities and	
Total Assets.............	$22,000	Proprietorship..........	$22,000

The details set forth in the balance sheet reflect the financial condition as of a particular date. A new balance sheet could be prepared after each transaction. For example, if Joseph Brown purchased additional store supplies for $20, paying cash, his new balance sheet would differ from the one above with respect to cash and store supplies; the former would decrease by $20 and the latter would increase by $20. The effect of other transactions could be shown by preparing a series of balance sheets, much as was done with the accounting equation in Chapter 1.

CLASSIFICATION AND DEFINITION OF ASSETS In dealing with a large number of asset items on a balance sheet, it is helpful to have them grouped in significant classes. For example, one class may include cash and other items, such as amounts due from customers, that will ordinarily be converted into cash within a short time. Another class may include desks used in the office, a truck used to deliver merchandise, and other items that were acquired for use in the business rather than for sale.

The number of groups into which assets are divided varies with the type of enterprise. There are also differences of opinion among accountants as to the criteria to be followed in classifying certain assets. Finally, there is not complete uniformity in the terms used to describe particular subgroups.

The asset classifications frequently found on balance sheets are (1) *current assets* and (2) *fixed assets*. Certain assets that are known as prepaid expenses are often included with the current assets, but some accountants prefer to present them as a distinct class under the heading *prepaid expenses* or *deferred charges to expense*. The assets most commonly owned by business enterprises are described in the following paragraphs:

1. Current Assets. Cash and other assets that may reasonably be expected to be realized in cash, sold, or consumed in the near future through the normal operations of the business are called *current assets*. This group is also sometimes referred to as *circulating* or *working assets*. In addition to Cash, the assets usually found in this group are Notes Receivable, Accounts Receivable, Merchandise Inventory, and Prepaid Expenses. They are customarily listed in that order, which, in general, is the order of liquidity or probable conversion into cash.

Cash. Cash includes currency, checks, bank drafts, and money orders. Any medium of exchange that a bank will accept at face value on deposit may usually be shown on the balance sheet as cash. The cash that a business uses in its operations may be partly in its cash drawer or safe and partly on deposit at the bank.

Notes Receivable. A note receivable is a promissory note received from a debtor. A promissory note is a written promise to pay a certain sum in money at a definite time to the order of a specified person or to the bearer. This note may be transferred by the business to some other person, or it may be transferred to a bank for cash. It represents a type of asset very readily convertible into cash.

Accounts Receivable. An account receivable is a claim, not based on a note, against a certain person or other concern. Usually an account receivable arises from the sale of merchandise on account. The granting of credit for goods sold results, not in an increase in cash, but in an asset called Accounts Receivable on the seller's accounting records.

Merchandise Inventory. Merchandise consists of goods purchased or produced for sale. Food offered for sale in a grocery store and clothing produced for sale in a clothing factory are examples of merchandise. The merchandise on hand at any specific time is referred to as the *merchandise inventory*. The inventory is usually determined by a physical count of the merchandise on hand. Such a count of merchandise is known as a *physical inventory*.

Prepaid Expenses. Supplies on hand and prepayments of expenses of a subsequent period are assets. Unlike the current assets described above, prepaid expenses are not expected to be sold or realized in cash in the normal course of business operations. Those who limit the definition of current assets to those assets that will be *realized in cash* consider prepaid expenses to be a distinct category and hence exclude them from the current group. Other accountants broaden the definition of current assets to include prepaid expenses that are to be *consumed* during the normal operating cycle, which is usually a year. It is argued that if an expense had not been incurred in advance, it would require the use of other current assets in a subsequent period. The present trend is toward classifying prepaid expenses as current assets.[1] Three of the more common types of prepaid expenses are described below.

Store Supplies. Store supplies include paper, twine, and similar items used in selling. They are consumed in the operation of the business and are considered as assets until they are consumed. The amount of such supplies on hand may be ascertained by taking a physical inventory on the date of the balance sheet.

Office Supplies. Office supplies include stationery, stamps, and similar items not used in selling but needed for the general operation of the business. Like store supplies, the amount on hand must be ascertained on the date of each balance sheet.

Prepaid Insurance. Insurance premiums are paid in advance and become an expense with the passage of time. The unexpired portion of the premiums at the balance sheet date represents a prepaid expense. Included are such types of property and casualty insurance as fire, windstorm, theft, compensation, and liability insurance.

2. Fixed Assets. Assets used in the business that are of a relatively fixed or permanent nature are called *fixed assets* or *plant and equipment*. It is expected that such assets, with the exception of land, will be worn out through use, although they may be sold when they no longer serve the purpose for which they were acquired.

The order of fixed asset items within the classification is not uniform in practice. In some cases the most permanent of these are listed first

---

[1]Recommended by *Accounting Research Bulletin No. 30*, "Current Assets and Current Liabilities," August, 1947 (New York: American Institute of Accountants), p. 248.

in the fixed assets section; at other times the least fixed are reported first. In this book those assets with the shortest life will be shown first.

Delivery Equipment. Delivery equipment includes trucks and other equipment used in delivering goods to customers.

Store Equipment. Store equipment includes such long-lived assets as counters, showcases, window decorations, and any other items of furniture used directly in selling the goods.

Office Equipment. Office equipment includes such assets as desks, typewriters, adding machines, and other items not used directly in selling the goods but needed for the general operation of the business.

Building. A building owned by a business may be used as a factory, a warehouse, a store, or an office. When a building is not owned by the business, it is rented or leased from its owner. In that case the value of the building does not appear on the balance sheet of the business because the building is not property of the enterprise.

Land. The value of the land on which a building is located is usually shown as a separate item on the balance sheet. Although a building may no longer be valuable because of its age or its condition, the land still remains. Because of this difference, it is desirable to show the land value separately.

3. Deferred Charges to Expense. As indicated above, prepaid expenses such as insurance and supplies may be classified either as current assets or as *deferred charges to expense* (frequently shortened to *deferred charges*). Prepayments that are chargeable to operations of a number of years, such as bonus payments to secure a long-term lease, should be classified as deferred charges rather than as current assets. There is no rigid rule that can be used to differentiate between prepayments that are properly classifiable as current assets and those that should be shown as deferred charges. Although the normal operating cycle of most enterprises is a year, it is not customary to segregate prepayments of insurance that extend beyond a year from the date of the balance sheet from those that will be used up within a year from such date. In this book all supplies and prepaid operating expenses will be classified as current assets unless otherwise indicated.

CLASSIFICATION AND DEFINITON OF LIABILITIES The number of liability items on the balance sheet is usually less than the number of asset items but is sufficiently large to justify classification. The classification used for liabilities is similar to that used for assets, usually consisting of (1) current liabilities and (2) fixed liabilities. A third category, composed of collections received in advance of the delivery of goods or the performance of services, may be included with current liabilities or may be shown separately under the heading *deferred credits to income*.

1. Current Liabilities. Liabilities that will be due within a short time and that are to be liquidated out of current funds are called *current liabilities*. For example, when a merchant purchases merchandise on account with the agreement that he will pay for it within 30, 60, or 90 days, he incurs a current liability. The general rule is that liabilities payable within one year of the balance sheet date are classified as current liabilities.

Notes Payable. A note payable is a promissory note given by the business to someone to whom it owes money. The business may give a note to a creditor from whom it has purchased merchandise or to a bank from which it borrows money.

Accounts Payable. An account payable is a financial obligation for which a note has not been given. Usually an account payable arises from a purchase on account. A purchase in which the buyer gives his promise to pay at some future time for the goods he receives results in a liability called Accounts Payable on his accounting records.

Accrued Liabilities. Amounts that are not yet due but that are owed to the government for taxes, to employees for salaries, or to creditors for interest on notes are called accrued liabilities. When income tax rates are high, Taxes Payable is often the largest single current liability item on a corporation balance sheet. More complete explanations of accrued liabilities will be given in later chapters.

Unearned Income. Collections received in advance for which goods or services will have to be given in the next fiscal period may be classified as current liabilities[2] or may be shown in a separate category. For example, when a magazine publishing company receives in one fiscal period payments for subscriptions that extend into a future fiscal period, the unearned portion of the subscriptions is a liability that may be listed on the balance sheet as a current liability entitled "Unearned Subscriptions Income." Similarly, tickets or tokens may be sold that require delivery of services or commodities in the future; they also may be reported as current liabilities.

2. Fixed Liabilities. Liabilities that will not be due for a comparatively long time are called *fixed liabilities* or *long-term liabilities*. Such lia-

---

[2]Recommended by *Accounting Research Bulletin No. 30*, "Current Assets and Current Liabilities," August, 1947 (New York: American Institute of Accountants), p. 250.

bilities usually arise in connection with the purchase of items of plant equipment. Inasmuch as obligations due and payable within a year are classed as current liabilities, it follows that obligations not payable within a year are classed as fixed liabilities. When the maturity of a liability that formerly was a fixed liability falls within the one-year limitation, it becomes a current liability. For example, an obligation that is due and payable twenty years after it is incurred will be classed as a fixed liability until the end of the nineteenth year, when it will become a current liability.

When a long-term liability is to be renewed at maturity rather than paid, it should continue to be classed as a fixed liability. In the interest of complete information, the maturity date of the obligation and other essential descriptive data should be shown on the balance sheet. When an obligation is required to be paid in installments, that portion due within a year should be listed with the current liabilities and the remainder should be listed as a fixed liability.

Mortgage Payable. A mortgage payable represents a debt owed by a business for which the creditor possesses a secured claim through a mortgage on some particular asset. If the amount owed is not paid by the debtor, this secured claim gives the creditor the right to bring court action that may result in the sale of the asset to satisfy the claim.

Bonds Payable. Long-term obligations of corporations are commonly evidenced by formal papers known as bonds. Bonds may be secured by mortgages on fixed assets as described in the previous paragraph or may be based on the general credit standing of the corporation. In any case, they represent a debt to be paid more than one year hence and are therefore included under fixed liabilities.

3. Deferred Credits to Income. Incomes received but not yet earned are sometimes reported on the balance sheet as *deferred credits to income* (frequently shortened to *deferred credits*). Obligations that represent long-term deferments, such as the receipt of rent for a long-term lease, are properly reported as deferred credits to income. On the other hand, obligations that will be satisfied in the near future by the delivery of goods or services in the ordinary course of business operations are properly reported as current liabilities.

DEFINITION AND ILLUSTRATION OF PROPRIETORSHIP   Proprietorship is the interest of the owner in the assets of the business. If a business has no liabilities, the proprietorship is equal to the total of the assets; otherwise, it is the difference between the assets and the liabilities.

Proprietorship, capital, and *net worth* are synonymous terms. All of these terms are used by businessmen and accountants. The first two are, perhaps, more accurate terms than the third, since the term "net worth" may seem to imply that accounting values are all based on present market values. As was stated in Chapter 1, accounting values are determined by the prices agreed upon in the recorded transactions. These may be above or below the present market prices.

Sometimes the proprietorship is vested in two or more persons. Then the business is known as a *partnership* or a *corporation* according to the method of ownership. The capital interests of partners in a partnership are shown separately on the balance sheet. The sum of the interests of the various partners represents the proprietorship of the partnership. The interest of each stockholder in a corporation is not shown on the balance sheet. The interest of the stockholders as a group is shown in two amounts, the original investment and the accumulated earnings or losses of the corporation since the beginning of operations. The manner of reporting the different types of ownership interest on the balance sheet is illustrated below:

SOLE PROPRIETORSHIP

Harry Logan, Capital...............................	$24,400

PARTNERSHIP

George Adams, Capital......................	$17,500	
John Becker, Capital........................	15,100	
Total Capital......................................		$32,600

CORPORATION

Capital Stock...............................	$200,000	
Surplus......................................	86,400	
Total Capital......................................		$286,400

In the sole proprietorship and the partnership the interests of the owners are designated by the names of the owners. In the corporation the stockholders' interests are represented by the sum of the *capital stock* (capital contributed) and the *surplus* (accumulated earnings) items. The nature of partnerships and corporations will be considered in later chapters.

Each time a balance sheet is prepared, it is desirable to report the changes that have occurred in proprietorship since the previous balance sheet. This practice gives a more complete report of financial condition by showing the additions through profits and additional investments and the subtractions through losses or withdrawals. The form of statement for a sole proprietorship is illustrated on the following page.

Harry Logan, Capital, January 1, 1953......... $15,000
Additional Investment, July 1, 1953............   5,000

Total Investment............................... $20,000
Net Profit in 1953..................... $8,000
 Less Withdrawals in 1953.............   3,600

Increase in Capital...........................   4,400

Harry Logan, Capital, December 31, 1953........ $24,400

If Harry Logan's withdrawals had exceeded the amount of his profit in 1953, the excess would have been deducted from the total investment of $20,000. If he had suffered a loss in 1953, the amount of the loss would have been added to the withdrawals and the sum of the two items would have been subtracted from the total investment of $20,000.

The details of the changes in proprietorship may be set forth in the proprietorship section of the balance sheet or they may be presented in a separate report entitled "Statement of Proprietor's Capital." When a separate statement is prepared, the proprietorship section of the balance sheet will show only the final balance of capital.

STANDARD FORMS OF THE BALANCE SHEET   One of the most commonly used forms for the balance sheet is called the *account* form. Patterned after the equation $A = L + P$, the various assets are listed in tabular form on the left side of the page and the liabilities and the proprietorship items are listed in similar fashion on the right side of the page.

In another form, usually referred to as the *report* form, the liability and the proprietorship sections appear immediately below the asset section rather than to the right of the asset section. In both the account and the report forms the total of the assets is balanced by the total of the liabilities and the proprietorship.

Regardless of the variations in form, the purpose of the balance sheet is to show the financial condition of the business on a specific date. A balance sheet would not be complete if it did not disclose the date and the identity of the particular business. It is customary to use a three-line heading that states (1) the name of the business or of the proprietor, (2) the name of the statement, "Balance Sheet," and (3) the date, as in the illustration on pages 26 and 27. The particular time of the day need not be indicated in the heading as it is always understood as of the close of business.

<u>Assets</u>

Current Assets:
Cash. $ 8,500.00
Accounts Receivable 14,000.00
Merchandise Inventory 28,200.00
Store Supplies. 300.00
Office Supplies 250.00
Prepaid Insurance 1,300.00
Total Current Assets. $52,550.00

Fixed Assets:
Store Equipment . . . . $ 8,000.00
Office Equipment. 3,800.00
Building. 12,000.00
Land.   3,000.00
Total Fixed Assets. 26,800.00

Total Assets $79,350.00

Balance Sheet—

BALANCE SHEET ILLUSTRATED AND ANALYZED For purposes of illustration assume that Robert Bell has been engaged in a retail furniture business for several years and that he maintains adequate accounting records. The balance sheet prepared from his records on December 31, 1953, is illustrated above. If, because of accompanying statements or physical space limitations, it were inconvenient to present liabilities and proprietorship at the right, they would be listed below the assets section in the report form.

The various assets and liabilities in the balance sheet are grouped under the headings *current* and *fixed* as an aid in understanding and interpreting the data. A balance sheet in which these or other headings are employed is called a *classified* balance sheet.

In studying the balance sheet illustrated above, particular attention should be given to the manner in which capital letters, spacing, and indentations are employed. The use of single-line and double-line rulings and of dollar signs should also be noted. Such matters of style are important devices to aid the reader.

The significance of any one item on the balance sheet considered alone is frequently quite limited. For example, it cannot be said that a business with $1,000,000 in current assets is in better financial condition than one with half that sum invested in current assets. The one with the larger amount of current assets may have $2,000,000 of current liabilities while the other has only $100,000 of current liabilities. Relationships between different amounts on the financial statements

Liabilities

Current Liabilities:
Notes Payable . . . . $ 5,000.00
Accounts Payable. 16,350.00
Taxes Payable 250.00
Salaries Payable. 300.00
Total Current Liabilities $21,900.00

Fixed Liabilities:
Mortgage Payable (Due 1960) 5,000.00

Total Liabilities. $26,900.00

Proprietorship

Robert Bell, Capital, January 1, 1953. . . . . $44,250.00
Net Profit for the Year. $15,400.00
Less Withdrawals. 7,200.00
Increase in Capital. 8,200.00
Robert Bell, Capital, December 31, 1953. . . . 52,450.00

Total Liabilities and Proprietorship $79,350.00

Account Form

can be more easily understood through the use of ratios and percentages.

One of the most frequently quoted and most useful financial ratios
is that of current assets to current liabilities, or the *current ratio*. The
current ratio for Bell Home Furniture on December 31, 1953, is $52,550
(current assets) divided by $21,900 (current liabilities), or 2.4 to 1.
This ratio gives some indication of the ability of the firm to pay its current liabilities as they come due. In the normal course of operations,
merchandise inventory is converted to accounts receivable and thence
to cash. Although there are no definite criteria for judging the ex-
cellence of a current ratio, 2 to 1 has long been considered satisfactory.

The difference between current assets and current liabilities is
called *working capital*. Mr. Bell's working capital is $52,550 minus
$21,900, or $30,650. Working capital shows in dollars the amount
available for current use in the operation of the business.

A later chapter is devoted to methods of analyzing and interpreting
financial statements. The subject has been introduced here in order to
emphasize its importance and to indicate the desirability of classifying
items on the balance sheet.

The report form of balance sheet, with an accompanying statement
of proprietor's capital, is illustrated on page 28. When a separate statement of capital is prepared, only the final balance of capital is shown on
the balance sheet. The use of the separate statement is optional and is
not restricted to any particular form of the balance sheet.

A. C. RICHARDS
Balance Sheet
October 31, 1953

Assets

Current Assets:
Cash	$6,700.00	
Notes Receivable	1,200.00	
Accounts Receivable.	4,000.00	
Supplies	900.00	
Prepaid Insurance.	460.00	
Total Current Assets		$13,260.00

Fixed Assets:
Delivery Equipment	$3,000.00	
Store Equipment.	1,500.00	
Office Equipment	900.00	
Total Fixed Assets		5,400.00

Total Assets.		$18,660.00

Liabilities

Current Liabilities:
Accounts Payable	$3,840.00	
Salaries Payable	750.00	
Taxes Payable.	320.00	
Total Current Liabilities.		$ 4,910.00

Proprietorship

A. C. Richards, Capital	13,750.00

Total Liabilities and Proprietorship.	$18,660.00

Balance Sheet — Report Form

A. C. RICHARDS
Statement of Proprietor's Capital
For Year Ended October 31, 1953

A. C. Richards, Capital, November 1, 1952		$14,450.00
Net Profit for the Year	$7,600.00	
Less Withdrawals	8,300.00	
Decrease in Capital		700.00
A. C. Richards, Capital, October 31, 1953 . . .		$13,750.00

Statement of Proprietor's Capital

One of the ever-present problems confronting accountants is that of communicating financial data to persons not trained in accounting. In recent years there has been much discussion of this problem. It has been accompanied by experimentation in terminology and the form of statements. As an example, "Statement of Financial Position" (or "Condition") has been proposed as a more descriptive title than "Balance Sheet." The newer title identifies the statement of assets, liabilities, and proprietorship in terms of its purpose, namely, to depict financial position. whereas the traditional title does not.

QUESTIONS

1. Of the following items in the cash drawer of R. M. Bogan, a retail merchant, on September 30, state which ones can properly be included under the heading of "Cash" in Bogan's balance sheet of September 30: (a) postage stamps, $10; (b) a postal money order for $25; (c) an IOU for $5 from G. Carr, an employee; (d) a check from John Wagner, dated October 8, for $50; (e) currency, $45; (f) a check for $70 from B. J. Cromer, dated September 29, which has not yet been presented to the bank; (g) a check for $15 from A. C. Johnston, dated July 2, which has been returned from the bank marked "Not Sufficient Funds."

2. One transaction was completed before each of the following balance sheets was prepared. (The balance sheet headings and classifications of assets and liabilities have been omitted to conserve space.) Explain the nature of each transaction.

(a)
Cash	$ 2,000	Arthur Carr, Capital	$ 6,000
Merchandise Inventory	4,000		
	$ 6,000		$ 6,000

(b)
Cash	$ 2,000	Davis Equipment Co.	$ 3,000
Merchandise Inventory	4,000	Arthur Carr, Capital	6,000
Store Equipment	3,000		
	$ 9,000		$ 9,000

(c)
Cash	$ 3,000	Davis Equipment Co.	$ 3,000
Merchandise Inventory	4,000	Arthur Carr, Capital	7,000
Store Equipment	3,000		
	$10,000		$10,000

(d)
Cash	$ 2,800	Davis Equipment Co.	$ 3,000
Merchandise Inventory	4,000	Arthur Carr, Capital	7,000
Store Equipment	3,000		
Prepaid Insurance	200		
	$10,000		$10,000

(e)
Cash	$ 1,300	Davis Equipment Co.	$ 1,500
Merchandise Inventory	4,000	Arthur Carr, Capital	7,000
Store Equipment	3,000		
Prepaid Insurance	200		
	$ 8,500		$ 8,500

3. How would each of the following be shown on a balance sheet: (a) adding machines held for sale by an office equipment company; (b) adding machines owned by a retail dry goods store; (c) stationery on the counters of a drugstore; (d) stationery owned for its own use by a grocery store; (e) stamps in a C.P.A.'s office; (f) a truck used by a furniture store to deliver merchandise; (g) trucks in the showrooms of an automobile sales company.

4. There are twelve errors in the following balance sheet. Make a list of the errors.

BALANCE SHEET
B. T. LITTLE

ASSETS			LIABILITIES		
Current Assets:			Current Liabilities:		
Cash	$ 500		Notes Payable	$1,000	
Accounts Receivable	4,000		Accounts Payable	3,500	
Delivery Equipment	1,800		Mortgage Payable	3,000	
Purchases	3,000				
Total Current Assets		$ 9,200	Total Liabilities		$ 7,500
Fixed Assets:					
Store Equipment	$1,500		PROPRIETORSHIP		
Store Supplies	400				
Building	8,000		B. T. Little, Capital	$9,550	
Land	2,000		Sales	3,950	
Total Fixed Assets		11,900	Total Proprietorship		13,500
Total Assets		$21,100	Total Liabilities & Prop.		21,100

5. The proprietorship of George Porter increased $7,000 during the past fiscal year. Compute the amount of the profit or the loss of his business enterprise under each of the following assumptions:

(a) No additional investments or withdrawals were made.
(b) Only additional investments of $1,000 were made.
(c) Only additional investments of $2,000 were made.
(d) Only withdrawals of $2,000 were made.
(e) Additional investments of $1,000 and withdrawals of $3,000 were made.
(f) Additional investments of $2,000 and withdrawals of $6,000 were made.

6. What types of information should be presented in the heading of (a) the balance sheet? (b) the statement of proprietor's capital?

7. A. C. Nash incurred a debt of $10,000 secured by a mortgage on business assets. The agreement provided that the debt be paid in monthly installments of $200 each. How should this liability be classified on his balance sheet on December 31 of the current year, at which time the amount still owed is $6,000?

8. What is the essential difference between the account form of balance sheet and the report form?

9. George Harris has current assets of $20,000 and current liabilities of $8,000. (a) What is his current ratio? (b) What is the amount of his working capital?

10. George Harris (see Question 9) borrows $7,000 from his bank, payable in 90 days. Assuming that there have been no other transactions, (a) what is his current ratio? (b) the amount of his working capital?

PROBLEMS

2-1. On May 31 of the current year Earl Holmes deposited $20,000 cash in a bank account to be used in the operation of a retail hardware store. The following transactions took place before opening the store on the first of June:

    (a) Purchased a building for $15,000, paying half in cash and giving a mortgage for the balance.

    (b) Purchased store equipment for $3,500, paying $2,000 cash and giving a six-month note payable for the balance.

    (c) Purchased merchandise for $7,500, paying $2,500 cash and the balance on account.

    (d) Paid cash for store supplies, $250.

Instructions: (1) Record the above transactions in an equation form similar to that used in Question 9, page 14. Use the following headings: Assets — Cash, Merchandise Inventory, Store Supplies, Store Equipment, Building; Liabilities — Notes Payable, Accounts Payable, Mortgage Payable; Proprietorship — Earl Holmes, Capital.

(2) Prepare a classified balance sheet in account form as of May 31 of the current year.

    In the recording processes of bookkeeping and accounting, dollar signs are not used with amounts when the amounts are entered on paper that is ruled to indicate dollars and cents. But dollar signs are commonly used with typewritten or printed balance sheets in the manner shown in the illustrations on pages 26, 27, and 28. It is customary, therefore, to include dollar signs in handwritten balance sheets even though they may be prepared on paper with columnar rulings. It is desirable for these handwritten balance sheets to be prepared in a form that can be followed without any variations by a typist or a printer.

2-2. On December 31 the assets and the liabilities of R. H. McNeil were as follows:

Accounts Payable	$ 8,000
Accounts Receivable	17,000
Building	15,000
Cash	4,500
Land	3,000
Merchandise Inventory	7,500
Mortgage Payable (due Jan. 1, 1963)	5,000
Notes Payable	2,000
Office Equipment	1,000
Prepaid Insurance	1,000
Store Equipment	1,500

On January 1 at the beginning of the year, R. H. McNeil's capital had been $32,500. He made withdrawals of $750 a month. The business showed a net profit for the year of $12,000.

Instructions: (1) Prepare a classified balance sheet in report form as of December 31 of the current year. Include the details of changes in proprietorship as a part of the balance sheet.

(2) Compute the following: (a) working capital and (b) current ratio.

2-3. On December 31 the assets and the liabilities of Paul Marshall were as follows:

Accounts Payable	$ 2,060
Accounts Receivable	4,620
Buildings	10,000
Cash	3,410
Furniture and Fixtures	3,500
Land	1,500
Merchandise Inventory	10,540
Mortgage Payable (due Feb. 1, 1961)	5,000
Salaries Payable	600
Supplies	1,130
Taxes Payable	550

At the beginning of the year, Mr. Marshall's capital had been $22,090. On August 1 he invested an additional $2,100 cash in the business, and during the entire year he made weekly withdrawals of $100. As a result of operations for the year, the business earned a net profit of $7,500.

Instructions: (1) Prepare a classified balance sheet in account form as of December 31 of the current year.

(2) Prepare a statement of proprietor's capital for the year ended December 31.

2-4. On June 30 of the current year the assets and the liabilities of John Sanders were as follows:

Accounts Payable	$ 3,625
Accounts Receivable	5,122
Buildings	12,450
Cash	4,739
Land	800
Merchandise Inventory	13,200
Mortgage Payable (due April 1, 1958)	6,000
Notes Payable	1,200
Notes Receivable	750
Office Equipment	1,424
Prepaid Insurance	296
Prepaid Rent	300
Salaries Payable	338
Store Equipment	3,540
Supplies	853
Taxes Payable	461

On January 1, Mr. Sanders' capital had been $29,728. During the six-month period ended June 30 he made total withdrawals of $6,000. As a result of operations for the six months, the business earned a net profit of $8,122.

Instructions: (1) Prepare a classified balance sheet in report form as of June 30 of the current year.

(2) Prepare a statement of proprietor's capital for the six months ended June 30.

(3) Compute the following: (a) working capital and (b) current ratio.

Chapter 3

The Profit and Loss Statement

PURPOSE OF THE PROFIT AND LOSS STATEMENT
The proprietor of a business hopes to operate in such a way that he will increase his proprietorship. His accounting records should provide the information that will aid him in accomplishing this purpose. Each balance sheet shows the proprietor the amount of his proprietorship at the date of the balance sheet. By comparing the amount of his proprietorship as shown by balance sheets prepared on successive dates, he can ascertain whether his proprietorship is increasing or decreasing, as well as the amount of the increase or the decrease; but he cannot determine the cause of the increase or the decrease.

The proprietor needs to know at frequent intervals the amount and the causes of his profit or loss in order that he may intelligently plan his future operations. In a mercantile business, profit or loss results from the buying and selling of commodities. The proprietor needs a report showing the amount of his sales, the cost of procuring and selling the goods, and the difference, which is the profit or the loss. The statement that gives this information is known as the *profit and loss statement*. Other names given to this statement include *income statement, operating statement, income account,* and *income summary*.

FORM OF THE PROFIT AND LOSS STATEMENT
A profit and loss statement showing the results of the purchase and the sale of a single unit of property is the simplest to explain, since it involves very few transactions. For example, if John Borden purchased a house and lot for $12,000 and immediately sold them for $14,000, he could show the effect of the two transactions by the following statement:

Sale Price of House and Lot	$14,000
Cost of House and Lot	12,000
Profit	$ 2,000

If he paid a real-estate agent a commission of $700 for selling the house and lot, his profit would be shown in the following manner:

Sale Price of House and Lot....................	$14,000
Cost of House and Lot........................	12,000
Gross Profit.................................	$ 2,000
Commission Expense.........................	700
Net Profit..................................	$ 1,300

In this summary only three transactions are involved: (1) the purchase of the property; (2) the sale of the property; and (3) the payment of the commission. But in the average business there may be many purchases, hundreds or even thousands of sales, and a variety of expenses that are necessary in making the sales. It is not practicable for a business to determine the gross and the net profit on each sale. Moreover, information about the exact profit on each sale is usually not needed. The needs of the businessman are served satisfactorily by periodic summaries of transactions. The profit and loss statement provides the summary.

THE ACCOUNTING PERIOD The accounting period covered by a profit and loss statement is ordinarily a month, three months, six months, nine months, or a year. The maximum length of the accounting period is ordinarily a year because the year represents a recurring cycle of business activities. The twelve-month period adopted by an enterprise is known as its *fiscal year*. The fiscal year need not coincide with the calendar year; it may begin with the first day of any particular month and end with the last day of the twelfth month. Any accounting period for which a profit and loss statement is prepared, regardless of whether it is a year or some fraction of a year, may be referred to as a *fiscal period*.

Some transactions come within the limits of the accounting period and have effects pertaining to that period only. The effects of other transactions are carried over from previous periods or may continue into future periods. For example, the payment of a premium of $180 on a three-year fire insurance policy results in an expense of $5 a month; this transaction affects 35 future monthly periods. Office supplies bought during a period that are left over at the end of the period represent another type of carry-over. In all cases the amounts shown on the profit and loss statement must conform to the length of the accounting period. Thus on a profit and loss statement for the month of May, sales, purchases, cost of goods sold, rent, and all other items must apply to that month alone; none may apply to April, which has passed, or to June, which is to come.

Ordinarily the amount of goods sold in a given accounting period does not correspond to the amount of goods purchased during that period. A portion of the goods purchased during the previous period is sold during the current period. Similarly, a portion of the goods purchased during the current period may still be on hand at the end of the period. It is necessary, therefore, in determining the cost of the goods sold, to take into consideration the lag between purchases and sales.

DEFINITION OF ITEMS ON THE PROFIT AND LOSS STATEMENT The items shown on the profit and loss statement of Bell Home Furniture, page 39, are those that are commonly included in the simple form of that statement. A discussion of each follows:

Sales. In a mercantile business the total amount customers have paid or have agreed to pay for the merchandise sold is called *sales*. Various other types of businesses make sales of numerous commodities and services that are designated by different terms. For example, the sales of railroad services are called freight revenue and passenger revenue; the income of professional men is known as fees; the income of investment trusts is called interest income and dividend income. In any case, the first item listed on the profit and loss statement represents the selling price of the goods or the services sold.

Cost of Goods Sold. The *cost of goods sold* is the total price the business has paid for the merchandise it has sold. A merchant ordinarily carries a stock of goods on hand at all times. If there is an inventory at the beginning of the fiscal period and one at the end of the fiscal period, both inventories must be taken into consideration in order to determine the cost of the goods sold.

The cost of merchandise acquired by a merchant is made up of two different items: (1) the price charged by the vendor as shown on the invoice of sale; and (2) the transportation charges for the delivery of the goods. On the profit and loss statement the amount of the transportation charges is added to the invoice cost of purchases in order to show the cost of goods delivered at the merchant's place of business.

For example, Bell Home Furniture began its fiscal year on January 1 with an inventory of $26,000. During the year it purchased merchandise amounting to $85,000, incurring transportation charges of $3,100. The total cost of the goods it had available for sale was therefore the sum of these three items, or $114,100. Since the merchandise on hand on December 31 was $28,200, the cost of goods sold was the difference between $114,100 and $28,200, or $85,900.

This information would be shown on the profit and loss statement for the year ended December 31 in the following manner:

Cost of Goods Sold:

Merchandise Inventory, Jan. 1, 1953...		$ 26,000
Purchases.............................	$85,000	
Transportation on Purchases..........	3,100	
Delivered Cost of Purchases..........		88,100
Merchandise Available for Sale........		$114,100
Less Merchandise Inventory, Dec. 31, 1953.............................		28,200
Cost of Goods Sold...................		$85,900

Gross Profit on Sales. When the cost of merchandise sold is subtracted from the total sales, the difference represents the profit that would be made if no expenses were incurred in conducting the business. Expenses are always incurred, however, in the operation of a business, and they must be considered in determining the net profit. Consequently, the difference between the amount received from sales and the cost of the merchandise sold is termed *gross profit on sales.* It is called *gross* profit because the expenses of operating the business must be deducted to obtain the final or *net* profit.

Operating Expenses. Commodities and services of various kinds are consumed in the operation of a business. The services of salesclerks are used in selling merchandise to customers, and the services of other employees may be used in delivering to customers the merchandise sold. Paper and twine are consumed in wrapping the merchandise to prepare it for delivery. Coal is consumed in heating the building in which the business is conducted. Stationery and stamps are consumed in carrying on the correspondence between the business and its creditors and customers.

The operating expenses of a business could be shown as one item on the profit and loss statement, but this method would not provide adequate information concerning their nature. A proprietor desires to know the amount of each expense so that he can ascertain whether the amount is too large and, if it is, take measures to reduce it. He wishes the profit and loss statement to be made in such a form that he can see the amount of each expense. Large firms need a very detailed analysis of expenses for control purposes. In subsequent chapters attention will be given to the method of providing this analysis.

CLASSIFICATION OF OPERATING EXPENSE ITEMS The extent to which the classification of operating expenses is carried depends on the degree to which information on the profit and loss statement is used to measure business activities. The operating expenses of a large business will probably be classified in a large number of groups, but those of a small business can usually be classified under one or two major heads. In a small retail business of the kind that has been used for illustrative purposes, it is usually satisfactory to classify the operating expenses in two main groups. In a service business, like a repair shop, operating expenses may be shown in a single group.

Selling Expenses. Expenses that are incurred directly and entirely in connection with the sale of merchandise are known as *selling expenses.* They include such things as salaries of the sales force, store supplies used, and advertising.

Selling expenses that are not of sufficient importance to make it desirable to show them as separate items on the profit and loss statement are reported under the heading "Miscellaneous Selling Expense." In general the best classification of expenses is one that keeps at a minimum the amount representing miscellaneous selling expense. Whenever the total of the miscellaneous selling expense account is a considerable amount, this total should be analyzed and new expense classifications should be set up.

The order in which the selling expenses are presented on the profit and loss statement varies among businesses. One of the arrangements commonly followed is to list them approximately in the order of size, beginning with the larger items. Miscellaneous selling expense is usually shown as the last item regardless of amount.

General Expenses. Expenses incurred in the general operation of the business are known as *general expenses.* They include office salaries and office supplies used.

Expenses that are partly connected with selling and partly connected with the general operation of the business may be analyzed and reported in part as selling expenses and in part as general expenses. In a small business, however, such mixed expenses are commonly reported as general expenses. Examples of such expenses are rent, insurance, and taxes.

General expense items that are not of sufficient importance to justify their being reported separately are reported under the heading "Miscellaneous General Expense." If the amount of the miscellaneous general expense account becomes large, the total should be analyzed and new expense classifications should be set up.

As in the case of selling expenses, the order in which the general expenses may be listed is subject to considerable variation. Any particular system adopted is ordinarily applied to both classes, that is, to selling expenses and to general expenses.

It is customary to employ this classification of expenses on the profit and loss statement in the manner shown below:

Gross Profit on Sales				$36,100
Operating Expenses:				
Selling Expenses:				
Sales Salary Expense	$11,200			
Advertising Expense	1,400			
Delivery Expense	500			
Store Supplies Expense	350			
Miscellaneous Selling Expense	250			
Total Selling Expenses		$13,700		
General Expenses:				
Office Salary Expense	$ 3,600			
Rent Expense	1,200			
Taxes Expense	600			
Insurance Expense	550			
Utilities Expense	400			
Office Supplies Expense	200			
Miscellaneous General Expense	450			
Total General Expenses		7,000		
Total Operating Expenses			20,700	
Net Profit from Operations				$15,400

NET PROFIT FROM OPERATIONS   The difference between the gross profit on sales and the total operating expenses is shown on the profit and loss statement as the *net profit* or the *net profit from operations*. The latter term is preferred because a business sometimes has incomes and expenses not directly connected with the usual operations. These incomes and expenses are reported after the net operating profit is obtained. The nature of these nonoperating incomes and expenses is discussed in later chapters.

If the total operating expenses are greater than the gross profit on sales, the difference between the two amounts is reported as *net loss from operations*.

PROFIT AND LOSS STATEMENT ILLUSTRATED   As in the case of the balance sheet, the profit and loss statement should be properly identified. The heading should state (1) the name of the business or of the proprietor, (2) the name of the statement, and

BELL HOME FURNITURE
Profit and Loss Statement
For Year Ended December 31, 1953

Sales.			$122,000.00
Cost of Goods Sold:			
Merchandise Inventory, January 1, 1953. .		$ 26,000.00	
Purchases $85,000.00			
Transportation on Purchases . 3,100.00			
Delivered Cost of Purchases		88,100.00	
Merchandise Available for Sale.		$114,100.00	
Less Merchandise Inventory, Dec. 31, 1953		28,200.00	
Cost of Goods Sold.			85,900.00
Gross Profit on Sales.			$ 36,100.00
Operating Expenses:			
Selling Expenses:			
Sales Salary Expense . . . $11,200.00			
Advertising Expense. . . . 1,400.00			
Delivery Expense 500.00			
Store Supplies Expense . . 350.00			
Misc. Selling Expense. . . 250.00			
Total Selling Expenses . .	$ 13,700.00		
General Expenses:			
Office Salary Expense. . . $ 3,600.00			
Rent Expense 1,200.00			
Taxes Expense. 600.00			
Insurance Expense. 550.00			
Utilities Expense. 400.00			
Office Supplies Expense. . 200.00			
Misc. General Expense. . . 450.00			
Total General Expenses . .	7,000.00		
Total Operating Expenses.			20,700.00
Net Profit from Operations			$ 15,400.00

Profit and Loss Statement for a Mercantile Business

(3) the exact period of time covered by the statement. The data appearing in a profit and loss statement have little meaning unless the reader is informed of the particular period that is being reported. One must know not only the length of the period, such as a month or a year, but also the particular month or year.

The profit and loss statement for Bell Home Furniture for the year ended December 31, 1953, is shown above. As in the balance sheet, indentations, dollar signs, and rulings are employed to accentuate the several distinct sections and subsections of the statement.

Although the analysis and the interpretation of financial statements is discussed in a later chapter, its importance may be indicated here by a brief introduction. The management of a business enterprise is always vitally interested in comparing results of operations of the current period with those of previous periods. For example, Robert Bell would compare the profit and loss statement above with the statements for earlier years. If monthly statements were also prepared, the results for December, 1953, would be compared with those for November, 1953, and for December, 1952.

In making such comparisons between different periods, it is well to know the relationship of various items on the profit and loss statement to sales. For example, Bell Home Furniture's gross profit on sales for 1953 is 36,100/122,000 or 29.6 per cent of sales. If this percentage margin has materially changed from the previous year, Bell should give serious consideration to his pricing policies. The percentage of sales salary expense to sales is 11,200/122,000 or 9.2 per cent; that of advertising expense to sales is 1,400/122,000 or 1.1 per cent. The other expense items should be related to sales in similar fashion, and the resulting percentages should be compared with those of the preceding year.

The net profit is 15,400/122,000 or 12.6 per cent of sales. If this is an increase or a decrease as compared with the previous period, it is advisable for the proprietor to make a careful inquiry into all the factors. Most of these factors are shown on the two profit and loss statements, and a study of them should provide information for more intelligent operation in the future.

In a service type of business there are no inventory and purchases of merchandise; therefore the profit and loss statement has to report only the sales and the expenses. If the business is small, it is probable that the operating expenses will not be classified and that the profit and loss statement will be prepared in a form similar to the following:

A. C. RICHARDS
Profit and Loss Statement
For Year Ended October 31, 1953

Sales		$20,200.00
Operating Expenses:		
Salary Expense	$8,400.00	
Supplies Expense	1,500.00	
Rent Expense	1,200.00	
Taxes Expense.	600.00	
Miscellaneous Expense.	900.00	
Total Operating Expenses		12,600.00
Net Profit from Operations.		$ 7,600.00

Profit and Loss Statement for a Service Business

RELATION OF THE PROFIT AND LOSS STATEMENT TO THE BALANCE SHEET The profit and loss statement of Bell Home Furniture on page 39 covers the period of a year since January 1, 1953. This profit and loss statement accompanies the balance sheet shown on pages 26 and 27. Both statements report the net profit from operations for the year. On the balance sheet the withdrawals of the proprietor during the year are deducted from the net profit to yield the net increase in proprietorship since the date of the last balance sheet. The profit and loss statement expands the idea of proprietorship increase shown in the balance sheet by summarizing the details of the business operations of the period.

The profit and loss statement that accompanies a balance sheet measures the effect of the operations of the accounting period just preceding the date of the balance sheet. The balance sheet is cumulative; that is, it shows the financial position resulting from all previous activities. The profit and loss statement is limited to a particular accounting period; it is one of many such statements that, taken together, would show the net profit or the net loss resulting from the total volume of activities since the enterprise began.

QUESTIONS

1. What type of information should be given in the heading of the profit and loss statement?

2. On July 1, George Grant paid a premium of $126 for a three-year fire insurance policy on his store equipment. How much of this premium should be shown on his profit and loss statement for the six-month period ended on the following December 31?

3. During the month of November Louis Beeler purchased merchandise at a cost of $10,000, including transportation charges. During the same period his sales amounted to $11,000. Does it necessarily follow that his gross profit on sales for the period amounted to $1,000?

4. John Andersen purchased a particular item of merchandise for $100 including transportation charges. He added 50% to the cost, establishing a selling price of $150. Assuming that he sells the item for $150, what will be the percentage of the gross profit to the selling price?

5. William Osborn's profit and loss statement for the month of August shows a net profit of $1,000. During the same period Osborn withdrew $1,200 in cash from the business for personal use. Would it be correct to say that he incurred a *loss* of $200 during the month?

6. If the purchases of The Acme Food Company were $95,000 during the fiscal period, what was the cost of goods sold during the period:

    (a) If there was no merchandise on hand at either the beginning or the end of the period?

    (b) If the beginning inventory was $40,000 and there was no ending inventory?

    (c) If there was no beginning inventory and the ending inventory was $10,000?

    (d) If the beginning inventory was $30,000 and the inventory at the close of the period was $45,000?

7. Which of the following expenses should be classified on the profit and loss statement as selling expenses? as general expenses?

(a) Salaries of salesmen.
(b) Salary of a stenographer.
(c) Postage.
(d) Cost of pamphlets mailed to customers.
(e) Payments to salesmen to reimburse them for their traveling expenses.
(f) Taxes on office equipment.
(g) License fee for truck used to deliver merchandise.
(h) Fee paid to C.P.A. to audit the financial records.
(i) Insurance on store equipment.

8. The profit and loss statement presents a detailed analysis of what single figure in the statement of proprietor's capital?

9. There are nine errors in the following profit and loss statement. List the errors.

PROFIT AND LOSS STATEMENT
DECEMBER 31, 1954

Sales		$20,000
Operating Expenses:		
Salary Expense	4,000	
Notes Payable	100	
Advertising Expense	600	
Payments to Reduce Mortgage	1,000	
Office Equipment Purchased	300	
Supplies Expense	400	
Withdrawals by Proprietor	5,000	
Total Operating Expenses		12,400
Net Profit from Operations		$ 7,600

PROBLEMS

3-1. The records of Jiffy Automotive Laundry show the following items of income and expense for the current fiscal year ended June 30:

Advertising Expense	$ 500	Salary Expense	$ 4,800
Electricity Expense	1,000	Sales	20,000
Insurance Expense	200	Supplies Expense	1,400
Miscellaneous Expense	520	Taxes Expense	180
Rent Expense	4,200	Telephone Expense	100
Repair Expense	600	Water Expense	700

Instructions: Prepare a profit and loss statement for the fiscal year ended June 30 of the current year. Show the percentage of each item to sales in a column to the right of the dollar amounts.

As was suggested in connection with the preparation of the balance sheet on page 31, use needed dollar signs in the profit and loss statement even though your copy is handwritten. The copy will then be in a satisfactory form to be given to a typist or a printer.

3-2. On January 1 of the current year, David Allen's merchandise inventory amounted to $25,000; on December 31, the end of the current year, the inventory was $28,000. His accounting records for the current year show the following additional information:

Advertising Expense	$3,000	Purchases	$120,000
Insurance Expense	250	Rent Expense	2,400
Misc. General Expense	400	Sales	160,000
Misc. Selling Expense	500	Sales Salary Expense	11,000
Office Salary Expense	3,700	Store Supplies Expense	1,500
Office Supplies Expense	1,250	Transportation on Purchases	3,000

Instructions: (1) Prepare a classified profit and loss statement for the current year.

(2) Compute the percentage of the following items to sales: (a) cost of goods sold, (b) gross profit on sales, (c) total selling expenses, (d) total general expenses, (e) total operating expenses, (f) net profit from operations.

3-3. W. L. Slade, owner of the Slade Products Co., had a capital balance of $15,500 on January 1 of the current year. On May 1 he invested an additional $5,000 in cash. The following asset and liability balances are as of December 31 of the current year; the income and expense figures are for the current year ended on that date.

Accounts Payable	$6,200	Prepaid Insurance	$ 250
Accounts Receivable	5,500	Purchases	80,000
Advertising Expense	700	Rent Expense	4,000
Cash	7,300	Sales	125,000
Commissions Payable	1,850	Sales Commission Expense	15,000
Insurance Expense	875	Store Equipment	4,225
Office Equipment	1,500	Store Supplies	600
Office Salary Expense	3,900	Store Supplies Expense	1,250
Office Supplies	300	Transportation on Purchases	900
Office Supplies Expense	750		

The merchandise inventories were: January 1, $17,500; December 31, $22,000. Withdrawals of $9,000 were made by Mr. Slade during the current year.

Instructions: (1) Prepare a classified profit and loss statement for the current year.

(2) Prepare (a) a classified balance sheet as of December 31 of the current year in report form and (b) a statement of proprietor's capital for the current year.

(3) Compute the percentage of the following items to sales: (a) cost of goods sold, (b) gross profit on sales, (c) total selling expenses, (d) total general expenses, (e) total operating expenses, (f) net profit from operations.

(4) Compute the following: (a) working capital and (b) current ratio.

Chapter 4

Accounts and the Trial Balance

RECORDING TRANSACTIONS   During any fiscal period the number of transactions completed by an ordinary business is large and results in many changes in assets, liabilities, and proprietorship. If an accurate balance sheet and profit and loss statement are to be prepared, the results of all transactions must be recorded. It is the purpose of this chapter to discuss and illustrate an effective method of recording individual transactions. This method makes use of the account, which gives the subject of accounting its name.

THE ACCOUNTING CYCLE   In the life of a going business, time periods are set up in which a standard accounting process takes place. The periodic repetition of this accounting process is referred to as the *accounting cycle*. It consists of a standardized procedure in recording and analyzing transactions and reporting their effect on the accounting statements.

THE NATURE OF THE ACCOUNT   The effect of each transaction might be shown by the preparation of a new balance sheet and a new profit and loss statement after the completion of the transaction. Since hundreds of transactions are performed during each fiscal period, and in many businesses during each day, this plan would result in an unreasonable amount of detailed work. Furthermore, new statements are not desired after each transaction, since the manager does not have time to observe the effect of each of a great number of transactions. Information showing him the effects of groups of similar transactions is sufficient for his purpose. It is therefore convenient and satisfactory to maintain a separate record for each item that appears on the balance sheet and on the profit and loss statement.

The form of record kept for each item is called an *account*. A group of accounts is known as a *ledger*. For example, an enterprise might have thirty *accounts*, each one being a record of a particular asset, liability, proprietorship, income, or expense item. The thirty accounts, which would ordinarily be kept together in a binder, would be referred to as the *ledger*.

The simplest form of an account provides for three things: (1) a title, which is the name of the item recorded in the account; (2) a space for recording increases in the amount of the item, in terms of money; and (3) a space for recording decreases in the amount of the item, also in monetary terms. This form of the account, illustrated at the left, is known as a "T" account because of its similarity to the letter T. There are other forms of the account that provide spaces for recording additional information. More complete forms are illustrated later. Regardless of form, however, the three basic parts of the account are the title, a section for increases, and a section for decreases.

TITLE	
Debit	Credit

The left side of the account is called the *debit* side and the right side is called the *credit* side. The word *charge* is frequently used as a synonym for debit. Amounts entered on the left side of an account, regardless of the account title, are called *debits* or *charges* to the account, and the account is said to be *debited* or *charged*. Amounts entered on the right side of an account are called *credits*, and the account is said to be *credited*.

CASH		
	4,000	600
	1,500	1,000
	2,000	1,500
3,600	*7,500*	200
		600
		3,900

In the illustration that appears at the left, the receipts of cash have been listed in vertical order on the debit side of the cash account. The cash payments have been listed in similar fashion on the credit side of the account. This arrangement of the increases and the decreases in cash facilitates the determination of the totals of each. The total of the cash receipts, $7,500, is shown in small figures to distinguish it from debits to the account. The total of the cash payments, $3,900, is also shown in small figures so that it will not be confused with the credits to the account. Finally, by subtracting the credits from the debits ($7,500 − $3,900), the *balance* of the cash account, $3,600, is obtained. If a balance sheet were prepared at this time, the amount of cash to be shown thereon would be $3,600.

ACCOUNTS AND THE BALANCE SHEET   The relationship of accounts to the *account form of the balance sheet* can be observed from a study of the following illustrations:

(a) On September 21, 1953, Henry Baker deposits $3,200 cash in a bank account for use in a business venture to be known as Quality

Shoe Repairs. Immediately after depositing the money, the balance sheet for the business would appear as follows:

QUALITY SHOE REPAIRS
BALANCE SHEET
SEPTEMBER 21, 1953

Cash................	$3,200	Henry Baker, Capital...	$3,200

The information could be recorded in accounts by debiting Cash and crediting Henry Baker, Capital, as follows:

CASH		HENRY BAKER, CAPITAL	
(a)	3,200	(a)	3,200

Note that the title of each account is written above the horizontal line. The title is descriptive of the data to be recorded in the account. It is not necessary to label the two sides of the accounts, inasmuch as the left side is always the debit side and the right side is always the credit side.

The amount of the asset Cash, which is on the left side of the account form of balance sheet, is recorded on the left or debit side of the cash account. The amount of the proprietorship, Henry Baker, Capital, which is on the right side of the account form of balance sheet, is recorded on the right or credit side of the account. Similarly, all other assets are entered on the left or debit side of appropriate accounts; all other proprietorship items and all liabilities are entered on the right or credit side of appropriate accounts. All the accounts can then be conveniently brought together to form a balance sheet with the assets on the left and the liabilities and the proprietorship on the right.

(b) Quality Shoe Repairs purchases supplies for $600 in cash. This transaction results in the acquisition of a new asset, Supplies. The cost of this new asset, like that of any other asset, is recorded on the left or debit side of an account. The transaction also results in a decrease in the asset Cash. This decrease is entered on the right or credit side of the cash account. When all increases are entered on the debit side of the cash account and all decreases are entered on the credit side, the total of the receipts, the total of the payments, and the balance of the account may be found at any time in the manner illustrated on page 45. After this transaction is recorded, the ledger appears as follows:

CASH				HENRY BAKER, CAPITAL		
(a)	3,200	(b)	600		(a)	3,200

SUPPLIES	
(b)	600

(c) Quality Shoe Repairs wishes to purchase equipment from Miller & Co. for $2,500, but reference to the cash account reveals that payment of the entire amount would reduce the cash balance to $100. The business therefore arranges with Miller & Co. to pay $1,500 in cash and the balance in 90 days. The effect of this transaction is to increase the asset Equipment by $2,500, to reduce the asset Cash by $1,500, and to increase the liability Accounts Payable by $1,000.

Liability accounts appear on the right side of the account form of balance sheet; similarly, increases in liabilities are recorded on the right or credit side of appropriate accounts. This transaction is therefore recorded as follows: Equipment is debited for $2,500 to record the cost of this new asset; Cash is credited for $1,500 to record the decrease in this asset; and Accounts Payable is credited for $1,000 to record this new liability.[1] The ledger of Quality Shoe Repairs now appears as follows:

CASH				ACCOUNTS PAYABLE		
(a)	3,200	(b)	600		(c)	1,000
		(c)	1,500			

SUPPLIES				HENRY BAKER, CAPITAL		
(b)	600				(a)	3,200

EQUIPMENT	
(c)	$2,500

---

[1]It is apparent that if there are a number of accounts payable, it would be necessary to maintain a separate record for each creditor. The method of accounting for each individual account payable will be presented in Chapter 8.

At this time the following balance sheet could be prepared from the accounts of Quality Shoe Repairs:

QUALITY SHOE REPAIRS
BALANCE SHEET
SEPTEMBER 22, 1953

Cash	$1,100	Accounts Payable	$1,000
Supplies	600	Henry Baker, Capital	3,200
Equipment	2,500		
Total Assets	$4,200	Total Liab. and Prop.	$4,200

THE THEORY OF DEBIT AND CREDIT

Balance Sheet Accounts. It has been observed that for *asset* accounts the *left* side is used for recording *increases* and the *right* side is used for recording *decreases*. For *liability* and *proprietorship* accounts the procedure is just the reverse, the *right* side being used to record *increases* and the *left* side to record *decreases*. It has also been emphasized that for all accounts, whether asset, liability, or proprietorship, the *left* side is called the *debit* side and the right side is called the *credit* side. It may therefore be said that:

Debit means: *increase* in *asset* accounts
decrease in *liability* accounts
decrease in *proprietorship* accounts

Credit means: *decrease* in *asset* accounts
increase in *liability* accounts
increase in *proprietorship* accounts

The effect of transactions is ordinarily stated in terms of debit and credit rather than in terms of left and right, or increase and decrease. For example, the effect of the purchase of $600 of supplies for cash is stated as follows: debit Supplies for $600 and credit Cash for $600.

The following diagram illustrates the theory of debit and credit in relationship to the fundamental equation:

ASSETS	=	LIABILITIES	+	PROPRIETORSHIP
ASSET ACCOUNTS		LIABILITY ACCOUNTS		PROP. ACCOUNTS
Debit +	Credit −	Debit −	Credit +	Debit −	Credit +

A business transaction always affects at least two accounts. If only two accounts are affected, one of them must be debited and the other must be credited for a like amount. If more than two accounts are affected, the sum of the debits must equal the sum of the credits.

This was demonstrated by the transaction involving the purchase of equipment, partly for cash and partly on account. The $2,500 debit to Equipment was equaled by the $1,500 credit to Cash plus the $1,000 credit to Accounts Payable. This equality of debit and credit for each transaction is inherent in the fundamental equation. It naturally follows that the sum of all the debit entries in the ledger equals the sum of all the credit entries.

Profit and Loss Statement Accounts. The theory of debit and credit in its application to income and expense accounts is based on the relationship of these accounts to proprietorship. The net income or the net loss of a period, as revealed by the profit and loss statement, is the net increase or decrease in proprietorship resulting from operations. In order to collect efficiently the data that are needed to prepare the profit and loss statement, accounts are maintained in the ledger for each type of income and expense.

Income increases proprietorship; hence, increases in income are recorded as credits. The titles used for income accounts vary according to the source of the income. Income from the sale of merchandise or business services is usually termed "Sales"; income from professional services may be called "Professional Fees"; the principal income of a bank may be "Interest Income." From the sale price or income, all expenses must be subtracted. Expenses decrease proprietorship and are therefore recorded as debits to such accounts as Rent Expense, Salary Expense, and Miscellaneous Expense. Although debits to expense accounts indicate decreases in proprietorship, they may also be spoken of as increases in expense. It is customary to consider debits to expense accounts in the positive sense (increases in expense) rather than in the negative sense (decreases in proprietorship). The rules of debit and credit as applied to income and expense accounts are shown in the diagram above.

PROPRIETORSHIP ACCOUNTS	
Debit −	Credit +

INCOME ACCOUNTS	
Debit −	Credit +

EXPENSE ACCOUNTS	
Debit +	Credit −

Income and expense accounts are periodically summarized on the profit and loss statement. Their balances are then transferred to a proprietorship account. Because the balances of the income and the expense accounts are transferred out of these accounts at the end of each fiscal period, these accounts are sometimes called *temporary proprietorship accounts.*

Normal Balances. The account serves as a mathematical device for recording increases and decreases in values. Increases are placed on one side of the account and decreases are placed on the opposite side. The total of the increases can easily be found by adding all the items on the increase side; the total of the decreases can be similarly determined. When the balance of the account is to be determined, the smaller of the two totals is subtracted from the larger. Obviously the sum of the amounts entered on the decrease side of an account will normally be smaller than the sum of the items on the increase side.

For example, the total debits (increases) in an asset account will ordinarily be greater than the total credits (decreases); thus, asset accounts normally have debit balances. It is entirely possible, of course, for the debits and the credits in an account to be equal, in which case the account is said to be *in balance.* The various types of accounts and their normal balances are as follows:

ACCOUNT	NORMAL BALANCE
Asset	Debit
Liability	Credit
Proprietorship	Credit
Income	Credit
Expense	Debit

When an account that normally has a debit balance actually has a credit balance, or vice versa, it is an indication of an error in recording or of an unusual transaction. A credit balance in the office equipment account, for example, could occur only through erroneous entries. On the other hand, a debit balance in an account payable account could result from paying an amount greater than that owed.

ARRANGEMENT OF ACCOUNTS IN THE LEDGER It is customary to arrange accounts in the ledger in the same order in which they are listed on the accounting statements. Current asset accounts precede fixed asset accounts; all asset accounts come before liability accounts; proprietorship accounts are last in order. If a loose-leaf ledger is used, any new account needed as the result of any transaction can be readily inserted into its correct place.

ILLUSTRATION OF A COMPLETE LEDGER L. D. Hart, C.P.A., who prepared the financial statements for Bell Home Furniture shown in the two preceding chapters, opened a public accounting office in October, 1953. Although he is engaged in professional practice, his activities, like those of lawyers, doctors, and dentists, have their business aspects. The application of the theory of debit and credit will be illustrated by recording the transactions of L. D. Hart, C.P.A., for the month of October. In the illustration the arrangement of the accounts will conform to the account form of the balance sheet, and the increase and decrease sides of each account will be indicated by + and − signs. The letters used to identify the transaction will be recorded in the accounts to facilitate cross-referencing. As an additional aid in identifying the related debits and credits, they will be shown initially in bold type.

(a) L. D. Hart, C.P.A., in opening a public accounting practice, invested $3,000 in cash, office equipment costing $300, and a library costing $900.

Analysis: The three asset accounts, Cash, Office Equipment, and Library, increase by the amounts indicated and are debited for $3,000, $300, and $900 respectively. Hart's claim against these assets is equal to the total of the three amounts; hence his capital account is credited for $4,200.

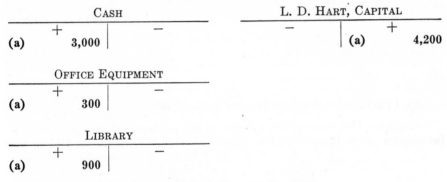

(b) Hart paid office rent for the month, $150.

Analysis: Rent is usually paid at the beginning of the month and is therefore an asset at the time of payment. But if the payment is made for one month only, at the end of the month it will be an expense. It is customary, therefore, to treat it as an expense at the time of payment. Expense accounts are subdivisions of proprietorship. Increases in expense are decreases in proprietorship; hence the rent expense account is debited for $150. The asset Cash is reduced by the transaction; therefore that account is credited for $150.

CASH				RENT EXPENSE		
+		−		+		−
(a)	3,000	(b)	150	(b)	150	

(c) Purchased on account from Gordon Equipment Co. additional office equipment for $800.

Analysis: Office Equipment increases and, in accordance with the rules of debit and credit, is debited for $800. The liability Accounts Payable increases and is credited for $800.

OFFICE EQUIPMENT			ACCOUNTS PAYABLE	
+	**−**		**−**	**+**
(a) 300				(c) 800
(c) 800				

(d) Purchased an automobile for business use from Superior Motors Corp., $2,050, paying $730 in cash and agreeing to pay the remainder in twelve monthly installments of $110 each.

Analysis: The asset account Automobile increases as a result of the transaction and is debited for $2,050. Another asset, Cash, decreases by $730 and is credited for $730. Superior Motors Corp. acquires a claim of $1,320 ($2,050−$730) against the business; hence Accounts Payable, a liability account, increases by $1,320 and is credited. The recording of the transaction may be expressed as follows: debit Automobile, $2,050; credit Cash, $730, and credit Accounts Payable, $1,320. Note that the one debit ($2,050) is equal to the sum of the two credits ($730+$1,320=$2,050).

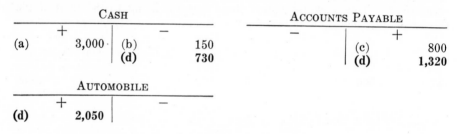

CASH			ACCOUNTS PAYABLE	
+	**−**		**−**	**+**
(a) 3,000	(b) 150			(c) 800
	(d) 730			(d) 1,320

AUTOMOBILE	
+	**−**
(d) 2,050	

(e) Purchased office supplies for cash, $200.

Analysis: This transaction represents the exchange of one asset, Cash, for another asset, Office Supplies. The office supplies account is debited for $200 to record the increase, and Cash is credited for $200 to record the decrease. Although the supplies will become an expense as they are used, it is proper to record them as an asset at the time of purchase. The problem of accounting for supplies consumed will be discussed in a subsequent chapter.

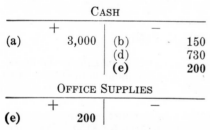

CASH		
+	**−**	
(a) 3,000	(b) 150	
	(d) 730	
	(e) 200	

OFFICE SUPPLIES	
+	**−**
(e) 200	

(f) Paid Gordon Equipment Co. $600 on account.

Analysis: This payment reduces the liability account Accounts Payable, and that account is debited for $600. It also reduces the asset account Cash. which is credited for $600.

CASH			ACCOUNTS PAYABLE	
+	**−**		**−**	**+**
(a) 3,000	(b) 150		(f) 600	(c) 800
	(d) 730			(d) 1,320
	(e) 200			
	(f) 600			

(g) Received $175 in payment of professional fees for services rendered a client.

Analysis: Cash is increased and is debited for $175. The income account Professional Fees, which is a subdivision of proprietorship, is increased and is credited for $175.

CASH				PROFESSIONAL FEES			
+		–		–		+	
(a)	3,000	(b)	150			(g)	175
(g)	175	(d)	730				
		(e)	200				
		(f)	600				

(h) Paid the premium for a three-year insurance policy on the equipment and the library, $90.

CASH			
+		–	
(a)	3,000	(b)	150
(g)	175	(d)	730
		(e)	200
		(f)	600
		(h)	90

Analysis: In this transaction the asset Prepaid Insurance is increased and the asset Cash is decreased by $90; Prepaid Insurance is debited for $90 and Cash is credited for $90. Consideration will be given in a later chapter to the problem of the gradual expiration of the prepaid insurance.

PREPAID INSURANCE			
+		–	
(h)	90		

(i) Paid biweekly salaries, $400.

Analysis: This transaction results in an increase in expense (decrease in proprietorship) and a decrease in cash; therefore Salary Expense is debited for $400 and Cash is credited for $400.

CASH				SALARY EXPENSE			
+		–		+		–	
(a)	3,000	(b)	150	(i)	400		
(g)	175	(d)	730				
		(e)	200				
		(f)	600				
		(h)	90				
		(i)	400				

Transactions (j) through (p) are similar to those that have been analyzed and recorded above. Although each is not illustrated separately, the effect of all are shown in the accounts on page 55.

(j) Received $300 for professional services. [See transaction (g).]

Analysis: Debit Cash, $300; credit Professional Fees, $300.

(k) Paid a one-year insurance premium on the automobile, $80. [See transaction (h).]
Analysis: Debit Prepaid Insurance, $80; credit Cash, $80.

(l) Received a $250 fee for services. [See transaction (g).]
Analysis: Debit Cash, $250; credit Professional Fees, $250.

(m) Paid telephone and other miscellaneous expense bills, $280. [See transaction (b).]
Analysis: Debit Miscellaneous Expense, $280; credit Cash, $280.

(n) Paid biweekly salaries, $400. [See transaction (i).]
Analysis: Debit Salary Expense, $400; credit Cash, $400.

(o) Received a $200 fee for services. [See transaction (g).]
Analysis: Debit Cash, $200; credit Professional Fees, $200.

(p) Paid automobile expenses, $70. [See transaction (b).]
Analysis: Debit Automobile Expense, $70; credit Cash, $70.

(q) Hart withdrew $350 cash for personal use.
Analysis: This transaction results in a decrease in proprietorship and a decrease in cash. Withdrawals of cash or other assets by the proprietor are recorded in a separate proprietorship account in order that the total may easily be determined at the end of the accounting period. This special account is called the proprietor's *drawing* or *personal* account. The transaction is recorded by a debit to L. D. Hart, Drawing and a credit to Cash of $350. Note entries (q) in the accounts Cash and L. D. Hart, Drawing on the opposite page.

(r) Sent bills to clients for services rendered in October, $1,200.
Analysis: These bills represent charges to clients for work done up to the end of the month for which payment has not yet been received. The transaction is recorded by a debit to Accounts Receivable, as this asset is increased, and by a credit to Professional Fees, as this income is increased.

ACCOUNTS RECEIVABLE				PROFESSIONAL FEES			
	+		−		−		+
(r)	1,200					(g)	175
						(j)	300
						(l)	250
						(o)	200
						(r)	1,200

The complete ledger of L. D. Hart, after all transactions for October have been recorded, is shown on the opposite page. In order to emphasize their nature, the accounts are grouped under the three major classifications of the fundamental accounting equation, with income and expense accounts appearing as subdivisions of proprietorship. Each transaction should be reviewed and the entry should be traced to the ledger. The small figures in italics are memorandum totals and balances. Note that they are written in only when they serve a purpose. For example, the $1,100 total is sufficient to indicate the balance of the account Office Equipment, as the account has no credits; similarly, memorandum figures in Accounts Receivable would be superfluous, as the account has only one entry.

Assets	**=**	**Liabilities**	**+**	**Proprietorship**

CASH

					ACCOUNTS PAYABLE			**L. D. HART, CAPITAL**	
(a)	3,000	(b)	150	(f)	600	(c)	800	(a)	4,200
(g)	175	(d)	730			(d)	1,320		
(j)	300	(e)	200			*1,520*	*2,120*		
(l)	250	(f)	600						
(o)	200	(h)	90					**L. D. HART, DRAWING**	
575	*3,925*	(i)	400						
		(k)	80					(q)	350
		(m)	280						
		(n)	400						
		(p)	70						
		(q)	350						
			3,350						

Income

PROFESSIONAL FEES

(g)	175
(j)	300
(l)	250
(o)	200
(r)	1,200
	2,125

ACCOUNTS RECEIVABLE

(r)	1,200

OFFICE SUPPLIES

(e)	200

Expenses

SALARY EXPENSE

(i)	400
(n)	400
	800

PREPAID INSURANCE

(h)	90
(k)	80
	170

AUTOMOBILE

(d)	2,050

RENT EXPENSE

(b)	150

OFFICE EQUIPMENT

(a)	300
(c)	800
	1,100

AUTOMOBILE EXPENSE

(p)	70

LIBRARY

(a)	900

MISCELLANEOUS EXP.

(m)	280

THE TRIAL BALANCE   The debits resulting from each transaction are equal to the credits from each transaction. This equality of debits and credits has been observed in recording the transactions in the preceding illustration; consequently, the sum of all the debits in the ledger should be equal to the sum of all the credits. A test of this equality is made at intervals, usually at the end of each month. Such a test is known as a *trial balance*.

The trial balance serves to summarize the information shown in detail in the ledger. This summary is always prepared at the end of a fiscal period and provides much of the information needed to prepare the balance sheet and the profit and loss statement.

A trial balance of totals could be taken by listing in parallel columns the total of the debits and the total of the credits of each account in the ledger and then adding the two columns. If the equality of debits and credits had been maintained for each transaction and there were no arithmetical errors, the sum of the column of debit totals would equal the sum of the column of credit totals.

In preparing financial statements, however, it is the balance of each account that is needed rather than the total debits and the total credits of each account. Referring to the cash account in the ledger of L. D. Hart, for example, it is the balance of $575 that will appear on the balance sheet, not the total debits of $3,925 and the total credits of $3,350. Therefore, a trial balance of balances is usually preferable to a trial balance of totals. If the sum of the debit balances equals the sum of the credit balances, it is evident that the debits and the credits in the ledger are equal. The trial balance of the ledger of L. D. Hart, prepared according to the latter method, is illustrated at the top of the following page.

PROOF PROVIDED BY   The trial balance does not give a complete
THE TRIAL BALANCE   proof of the bookkeeper's work. It shows only that the debits and the credits are equal. This is valuable information, however, since errors frequently affect the equality of the debits and the credits and are indicated by a trial balance that is out of balance. The trial balance does not, of course, prove that the proper account has been debited or credited or that the debits and the credits are for the proper amounts. It is therefore important that the accuracy of the figures be determined before they are entered in the bookkeeping record and that care be taken to record the entries in the proper accounts.

L. D. Hart, C. P. A.
Trial Balance
October 31, 1953

Cash	575 00	
Accounts Receivable	1200 00	
Office Supplies	200 00	
Prepaid Insurance	170 00	
Automobile	2050 00	
Office Equipment	1100 00	
Library	900 00	
Accounts Payable		1520 00
L D Hart, Capital		4200 00
L D Hart, Drawing	350 00	
Professional Fees		2125 00
Salary Expense	800 00	
Rent Expense	150 00	
Automobile Expense	70 00	
Miscellaneous Expense	280 00	
	7845 00	7845 00

Trial Balance

QUESTIONS

1. Distinguish between the terms *account* and *ledger*.

2. Identify each of the following accounts as asset, liability, proprietorship, income, or expense, and state in each case whether the normal balance is a debit or a credit: (a) Cash, (b) T. A. Adams, Drawing, (c) Accounts Receivable, (d) Accounts Payable, (e) Salary Expense, (f) Delivery Equipment, (g) T. A. Adams, Capital, (h) Rent Income, (i) Office Supplies.

3. James Corcoran, in establishing a ledger for his business, considers the possibility of completely reversing the usual rules of debit and credit. His plan is to record assets and additions to assets on the right side of his accounts, liabilities and additions to liabilities on the left side, etc. (a) Is it possible to follow such a plan? (b) Do you recommend that he do so?

4. Henry Dutton deposits all cash receipts from his business in a bank account and makes all payments by check. In taking a trial balance at the end of the month he discovers that the cash account has a credit balance of $120. (a) Assuming that there are no errors in recording, how would you explain this? (b) What is the actual nature of his cash account at this particular time?

5. Explain how it would be possible for an account receivable account with a customer to have a credit balance. In such a case is the credit balance an asset, a liability, a proprietorship, an income, or an expense?

6. The following accounts contain the record of the investment made by David Martin on October 1 and of six other transactions. List the transactions and give the reason for the debit and the credit for each transaction.

CASH				ACCOUNTS PAYABLE			SERVICE INCOME	
(a)	3,000	(c)	1,000	(c) 1,000	(b) 2,000			(e) 1,200
(e)	1,200	(d)	800	(f) 1,000				
		(f)	1,000					
		(g)	200					

EQUIPMENT		DAVID MARTIN, CAPITAL		OPERATING EXPENSES	
(b) 2,000			(a) 3,000	(d) 800	

DAVID MARTIN, DRAWING	
(g) 200	

7. At the end of the month it is discovered that the payment of rent expense of $100 was debited to Salary Expense rather than to Rent Expense. Would this error have caused the trial balance totals to be unequal?

8. In recording a purchase of $50 of store supplies for cash, the cash account is erroneously debited for $50 instead of being credited. (Store Supplies is debited for the correct amount.) What would be the effect of this error on the totals of the trial balance taken at the end of the month?

9. During November cash amounting to $5,200 was received by Home Laundry. During the same month $5,900 in cash was paid. (a) How were these facts shown in the cash account? (b) Does it follow that November operations resulted in a net loss of $700?

PROBLEMS

4-1. The Zenith Delivery Service was started on June 1 of the current year by Leon S. Brooks. He used the following accounts in his ledger: Cash; Accounts Receivable; Supplies; Prepaid Insurance; Delivery Equipment; Office Equipment; Notes Payable; Accounts Payable; Leon S. Brooks, Capital; Leon S. Brooks, Drawing; Delivery Income; Drivers' Commissions; Rent Expense; Gas, Oil, and Repairs; Miscellaneous Expense.

During the month of June the following transactions were completed:
(a) Invested cash, $2,000.
(b) Paid rent for month, $200.
(c) Purchased delivery equipment for $4,000, paying $500 in cash and giving a note payable for the balance.
(d) Purchased office equipment on account, $425.
(e) Paid cash for miscellaneous expenses, $25.
(f) Withdrew cash for personal use, $100.
(g) Cash receipts for the first half of month, $1,775.
(h) Paid drivers' commissions, $527.
(i) Paid cash for property and public liability insurance on delivery equipment, $220.
(j) Billed customers for services on account, $105.
(k) Paid cash to creditors on account, $310.
(l) Purchased supplies for cash, $80.
(m) Cash receipts for remainder of the month, $1,960.
(n) Paid drivers' commissions, $625.
(o) Paid cash for water, light, and telephone service, $45. (Debit Miscellaneous Expense.)
(p) Paid cash for gas, oil, and repairs, $95.
(q) Withdrew cash for personal use, $200.

Instructions: (1) Record the foregoing transactions in "T" accounts. Identify each debit and each credit by the letter given for that transaction.
(2) Prepare a trial balance as of June 30 of the current year.

4-2. Alan Rinehart is a doctor. The accounts in his ledger are: Cash; Accounts Receivable; Office Equipment; Medical Equipment; Accounts Payable; Alan Rinehart, Capital; Alan Rinehart, Drawing; Professional Fees; and Operating Expenses.

On January 1 of the current year Dr. Rinehart's account balances were as follows:

Cash	$2,000	Medical Equipment	$ 4,500
Accounts Receivable	3,500	Alan Rinehart, Capital	11,000
Office Equipment	1,000		

Instructions: (1) Set up "T" accounts for all of Dr. Rinehart's accounts listed above.
(2) Record the beginning balances in the appropriate accounts. Identify the balances in the accounts by writing "Bal." to the left of the amount.

During January the following transactions were completed:
(a) Purchased medical equipment on account, $400.
(b) Received cash from debtors on account, $1,500.
(c) Withdrew cash for personal use, $1,000.
(d) Paid office rent for January, $300.

(e) Received cash in payment of professional services rendered during January, $1,350.

(f) Paid salaries of receptionist and nurse, $650.

(g) Paid cash for miscellaneous operating expenses, $76.

(h) Paid cash to creditors on account, $300.

(i) Sent bills to patients for services rendered during January, $920, charging Accounts Receivable.

Instructions: (3) Record the transactions in "T" accounts. Identify each debit and each credit by the letter given for that transaction.

(4) Take a trial balance as of January 31 of the current year.

4-3. On July 1 of the current year John Pickett acquired the Palace Theatre. The following accounts are to be used in recording the transactions for his business enterprise: Cash; Supplies; Prepaid Insurance; Theatre Equipment; Office Equipment: Building; Land; Accounts Payable; Mortgage Payable; John Pickett, Capital; John Pickett, Drawing; Admissions Income; Concession Income; Wages Expense; Film Rental Expense; Advertising Expense; Utilities Expense; Miscellaneous Expense.

The following transactions were completed during the month:

(a) Deposited cash in a bank account for use in the business, $25,000.

(b) Purchased the Palace Theatre, including Theatre Equipment, $7,000, Building, $25,000, and Land, $8,000, making a down payment of $20,000 and giving a mortgage for the balance.

(c) Paid for newspaper advertising, $300.

(d) Paid premiums for property and casualty insurance policies, $1,200.

(e) Purchased supplies on account, $450.

(f) Cash receipts from admissions for the week, $1,600.

(g) Paid wages for the week, $315.

(h) Purchased office equipment on account, $562.

(i) Cash receipts from admissions for the week, $1,800.

(j) Paid wages for the week, $315.

(k) Paid miscellaneous expenses, $73.

(l) Granted concession for sale of popcorn, candy, etc. in lobby for 10% of sales, with a minimum of $200 per month collectible in advance. Received $100 cash as advance payment for remainder of July.

(m) Cash receipts from admissions for the week, $2,100.

(n) Paid wages for the week, $340.

(o) Paid cash to creditors on account, $225.

(p) Purchased supplies for cash, $21.

(q) Paid wages for the week, $340.

(r) Paid for advertising, $210.

(s) Cash receipts from admissions for remainder of the month, $2,500.

(t) Paid utilities expenses, $250.

(u) Paid creditors on account, $414.

(v) Received concession income, $23.

(w) Paid film rental, $3,050.

(x) Withdrew cash for personal use, $500.

Instructions: (1) Set up "T" accounts for all of the accounts listed above.

(2) Record the transactions for July in the accounts, identifying each entry by the letter given for that transaction.

(3) Prepare a trial balance as of July 31 of the current year.

Chapter 5

Journalizing and Posting

ACCOUNTING AND BOOKKEEPING   In preceding chapters emphasis has been placed on the analysis and the summary of business transactions. The *recording* phase, sometimes called bookkeeping, will be stressed in this chapter. Through bookkeeping, accounting must provide a complete record so that no financial detail in the history of the business is omitted. In order to accomplish this objective, an additional bookkeeping record must be inserted between transactions and the entries in the accounts.

This additional record is needed for several reasons. In the first place, the information that can be recorded in the account is meager. Furthermore, since the account is a means by which information is summarized and classified, it need not give details. If the account were expanded to show all the details of transactions, it would serve less well as a device for classifying and summarizing, which are its two chief functions.

In addition, if transactions are recorded directly in accounts, errors are likely to occur. As the debit and the credit resulting from a transaction are recorded on different pages of the ledger, a wrong amount may occasionally be entered in an account or a debit or a credit may be recorded on the wrong side of an account. Such errors are difficult to find.

Finally, it is difficult and tedious to enter transactions one by one in accounts. In a large business this method of recording transactions is impossible, for only one person at a time can conveniently work on a ledger and many employees are required to make a record of all the transactions of such a business.

For these reasons it is customary to make a preliminary record of transactions before they are entered in accounts. Such a record is called a *book of original entry* or a *journal*. It shows the debits and the credits resulting from transactions and gives the descriptive data necessary to provide a permanent explanation of the transactions. From time to time the debits and the credits entered in the record are transferred to the accounts in the ledger, which in turn constitute the basis of the accounting reports.

THE GENERAL JOURNAL   There are various kinds of journals. The number and the type used in a particular business will depend upon the size of the business and the nature of its operations. The simplest form of journal is commonly called a *general journal*. It has only two amount columns and may be used for recording all transactions of the business in chronological order.

GENERAL JOURNAL   PAGE 17

DATE	DESCRIPTION	POST. REF.	DEBIT	CREDIT
1953				
June 1	Miscellaneous Expense		10 00	
	Cash			10 00
	Paid telephone bill.			
1	Accounts Payable		250 00	
	Cash			250 00
	Paid Lane Supply			
	Company on account.			
1	Cash		283 00	
	Sales			283 00
	Cash sales for the			
	day.			

Standard Ruling for the General Journal

The procedures followed in *journalizing* an entry in the standard form of general journal are as follows:

(1) The year is written in small figures at the top of the first column. It is not written again on a page unless the year changes.

(2) The month of the first transaction is written on the first line in the first column. The name of the month is entered again only at the top of a new page or at the beginning of a new month.

(3) The day of each transaction is written in the second column on the first line used by each transaction. It is repeated for each transaction regardless of the number of transactions completed on the same day.

(4) The title of the account to be debited is written at the extreme left of the description column, and the amount of the debit is entered in the left-hand or debit amount column.

(5) The title of the account to be credited is written on the following line, indented about one-half inch, and the amount of the credit is entered in the right-hand or credit amount column.

(6) The explanation is written on the next line, with an additional indentation of about one-half inch. The explanation, while not necessarily limited to one line, should be as brief as possible without omitting essential information not readily apparent from reading the entry.

No entry is made in the column headed "Post. Ref." (posting reference) at the time the transaction is recorded in the general journal. The debits and the credits will later be transferred to the proper accounts in the ledger, at which time the numbers of the accounts will be recorded in the posting reference column. The process of transferring the information to the ledger will be explained later in the chapter.

Many bookkeepers prefer to leave a blank line between transactions, as was done in the illustration. While not essential, it has the advantage of clearly segregating each entry on the page from the other entries.

STANDARD FORM OF THE ACCOUNT The "T" accounts used in Chapter 4 are constructed in the simplest form possible. While this form provides the basic elements of the account, it is used primarily for illustrative purposes. By adding special rulings to the basic "T" account form, the following standard form is obtained:

Cash ACCOUNT NO 11

DATE	ITEMS	POST REF	DEBIT	DATE	ITEMS	POST REF	CREDIT
1953 June 1	Balance	✓	1 1 6 5 0 0	1953 June 1		17	1 0 0 0
1		17	2 8 3 0 0	1		17	2 5 0 0 0
2		17	3 1 9 0 0	2		17	1 1 0 0 0
3		17	5 0 0 0	2		17	1 8 0 0
3		17	2 9 1 0 0	3		17	1 2 5 0 0
4		18	3 2 6 0 0	4		18	2 5 0 0
5		18	8 5 0 0	4		18	1 2 0 0
5		18	3 0 4 0 0	4		18	2 0 0 0 0
6		19	3 4 7 0 0	5		18	4 8 5 0 0
				6		18	8 0 0
				6		18	1 1 0 0 0
				6		19	8 0 0 0

Standard Ruling for the Account

The columns on both the debit side and the credit side provide for: (1) the date; (2) a brief explanation of the entry, if it is desired; (3) the page reference to the book of original entry in which the transaction was recorded; and (4) the amount.

Both ledger and journal paper may be purchased either with or without the printed headings shown in the illustrations.

POSTING The process by which the entries in the journal are transferred to accounts is called *posting*. It consists in transferring each amount in the debit column of the journal to the debit side of an account and in transferring each amount in the credit column of the journal to the credit side of an account. The account to which each item is to be posted is determined from the account title stated in the journal. The debits and the credits may be posted in sequence as they appear in the journal or, if a considerable amount of posting is to be done at one time, all of the debits may be posted first, followed by the credits. The use of the latter procedure reduces the likelihood of posting items to the wrong side of accounts.

In some accounting systems much of the posting is done by machines designed for the purpose. When the posting is done manually, it is customary to proceed as follows:

(1) Open the ledger to the account to which the posting is to be made, as indicated by the account title in the journal.

(2) Record in the account the date and the amount in the columns provided. If the item appears as a debit in the journal, the posting will be to the debit side of the account; if it appears as a credit, the posting will be to the credit side of the account. The system of recording dates (year, month, and day) is similar to that employed in the journal. It is illustrated in the accounts on the opposite page.

(3) Record in the posting reference column of the account the number of the journal page from which the posting is made.

(4) Record in the posting reference column of the journal the number of the account to which the posting has been made. This procedure serves two purposes: first, it indicates that the item has been posted; and second, it completes the cross reference between the journal and the ledger.

The foregoing procedures are presented in the diagrams that appear on the opposite page.

CLASSIFICATION OF ACCOUNTS The principal classes of accounts to be found in the ledger have been presented in earlier chapters. The number of accounts to be kept for a particular business will depend upon the nature of its operations, its volume of business, and the extent to which details are desired. In general, the account titles correspond to the descriptions used on the balance sheet and the profit and loss statement. For example, one particular enterprise may maintain separate accounts for light and power expense, heat expense, and telephone and telegraph expense, while another may combine all these expenses into a miscellaneous expense account.

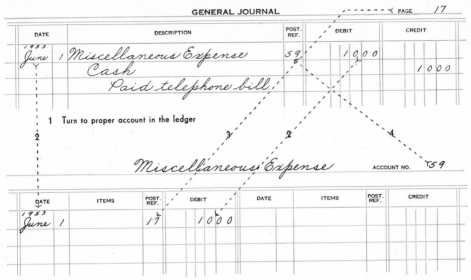

Diagram of the Posting of a Debit

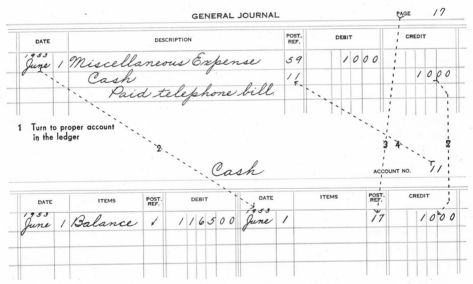

Diagram of the Posting of a Credit

Insofar as possible, the order of the accounts in the ledger should agree with the order of the items on the balance sheet and the profit and loss statement. The accounts are numbered to permit indexing and also for use as posting references in the journal. Accounts may be numbered consecutively like the pages of a book, or a system of indexing major classes and minor classes may be used.

In the chart of accounts reproduced below, all account numbers have two digits, the first digit indicating the major classification. All accounts beginning with 1 represent assets; 2, liabilities; 3, proprietorship; 4, income; and 5, expenses. This system has the further advantage of permitting the insertion of additional accounts in their proper sequence without disturbing the other account numbers. For a large enterprise with a number of departments or branches, it is not unusual for each account number to have four or more digits.

BALANCE SHEET ACCOUNTS

1. Assets

11. Cash
12. Accounts Receivable
14. Supplies
15. Prepaid Rent
18. Repair Equipment

2. Liabilities

21. Accounts Payable
22. Salaries Payable[1]

3. Proprietorship

31. Robert Moore, Capital
32. Robert Moore, Drawing
33. Profit and Loss Summary[1]

PROFIT AND LOSS STATEMENT ACCOUNTS

4. Income

41. Sales

5. Expenses

51. Salary Expense
52. Supplies Expense[1]
53. Rent Expense[1]
59. Miscellaneous Expense

Chart of Accounts for Reliable Repair Shop

ILLUSTRATIONS OF THE GENERAL JOURNAL AND THE LEDGER Robert Moore has operated a repair service in his garage on a part-time basis. He decides to move to rented quarters as of November 1 and to devote his full time to the business, which is to be known as Reliable Repair Shop. The following assets are to be invested in the enterprise: cash, $900; accounts receivable, $400; supplies, $500; and repair equipment, $1,600. This investment may be recorded in the general journal by four separate entries, each debiting one asset account for the value of the asset and crediting Robert Moore, Capital for the same amount. The preferred method, however, is to make a single entry debiting the four asset accounts and crediting the capital account for the total. Such an entry is called a *compound journal entry* and is illustrated at the top of the opposite page.

If there had been any creditors' claims against the assets, such as accounts payable, the appropriate account title and amount would have been included in the opening entry as a credit. The amount of the

---

[1]The use of this account is discussed and illustrated in Chapter 6.

GENERAL JOURNAL   PAGE 1

DATE	DESCRIPTION	POST. REF.	DEBIT	CREDIT
1953 Nov. 2	Cash		9 0 0 0 0	
	Accounts Receivable		4 0 0 0 0	
	Supplies		5 0 0 0 0	
	Repair Equipment		1 6 0 0 0 0	
	Robert Moore, Capital			3 4 0 0 0 0
	Invested assets in			
	Reliable Repair Shop			

Compound Journal Entry

credit to Robert Moore, Capital would have been correspondingly reduced.

Transactions completed by Moore during the month of November are as follows:

Nov. 2. Paid $375 cash on a lease rental contract, the payment representing three months' rental. (As only a part of this payment applied to the month of November, the asset account Prepaid Rent was debited.)

3. Purchased additional repair equipment on account from Johnson Equipment Co. for $1,400.

4. Recorded receipt of $225 from customers in payment of their accounts.

6. Paid $30 for a newspaper advertisement.

10. Paid $400 cash to Johnson Equipment Co. to apply on the $1,400 owed them.

14. Paid assistants $180 for two weeks' salaries.

16. Recorded receipt of $520 cash from sales of services for the first half of November.

17. Paid $250 for additional supplies.

19. Paid $20 for a newspaper advertisement.

28. Paid assistants $180 for two weeks' salaries.

30. Paid $10 for telephone bill for the month.

30. Paid $25 for electric bill for the month.

30. Recorded receipt of $850 cash from sales of services for the second half of November.

30. Withdrew $400 cash for personal use.

The foregoing transactions are recorded in the general journal that appears on pages 68 and 69. Each entry should be studied in connection with the narrative of the transaction. The account numbers appearing in the posting reference column were not placed there at the time the entry was made; they were recorded in the journal as the final step in posting each item to the ledger.

GENERAL JOURNAL

PAGE 1

DATE	DESCRIPTION	POST. REF.	DEBIT	CREDIT
1953 Nov. 2	Cash	11	9 0 0 0 0	
	Accounts Receivable	12	4 0 0 0 0	
	Supplies	14	5 0 0 0 0	
	Repair Equipment	18	1 6 0 0 0 0	
	Robert Moore, Capital	31		3 4 0 0 0 0
	Invested assets in			
	Reliable Repair Shop			
2	Prepaid Rent	15	3 7 5 0 0	
	Cash	11		3 7 5 0 0
	Paid three months' rent			
3	Repair Equipment	18	1 4 0 0 0 0	
	Accounts Payable	21		1 4 0 0 0 0
	On account from			
	Johnson Equipment Co.			
4	Cash	11	2 2 5 0 0	
	Accounts Receivable	12		2 2 5 0 0
	Received cash on acct.			
6	Miscellaneous Expense	59	3 0 0 0	
	Cash	11		3 0 0 0
	Newspaper advertise-			
	ment.			
10	Accounts Payable	21	4 0 0 0 0	
	Cash	11		4 0 0 0 0
	Johnson Equipment Co.			
14	Salary Expense	51	1 8 0 0 0	
	Cash	11		1 8 0 0 0
	Biweekly salary.			
16	Cash	11	5 2 0 0 0	
	Sales	41		5 2 0 0 0
	Cash sales for first			
	half of month.			
17	Supplies	14	2 5 0 0 0	
	Cash	11		2 5 0 0 0
	Purchased supplies			
	for cash.			

General Journal — Reliable Repair Shop

GENERAL JOURNAL   PAGE 2

DATE	DESCRIPTION	POST. REF.	DEBIT	CREDIT
1953 Nov. 19	Miscellaneous Expense	59	20 00	
	Cash	11		20 00
	Newspaper advertisement.			
28	Salary Expense	51	180 00	
	Cash	11		180 00
	Biweekly salary.			
30	Miscellaneous Expense	59	10 00	
	Cash	11		10 00
	November telephone bill.			
30	Miscellaneous Expense	59	25 00	
	Cash	11		25 00
	November electric bill.			
30	Cash	11	850 00	
	Sales	41		850 00
	Cash sales for second half of month.			
30	Robert Moore, Drawing	32	400 00	
	Cash	11		400 00
	Withdrew cash.			

General Journal — Reliable Repair Shop (concluded)

After all of the entries for the month have been posted, the ledger will appear as shown on pages 70 and 71. Tracing each entry from the journal to the accounts in the ledger will give a clear understanding of the posting process.

Each account is on a separate page in the ledger. The accounts are numbered in accordance with the chart of accounts shown on page 66. Four accounts listed in the chart do not appear in the illustration of the ledger. They will be required in completing the work of the accounting cycle, which will be discussed in the next chapter.

Cash

ACCOUNT NO 11

DATE	ITEMS	POST REF	DEBIT	DATE	ITEMS	POST REF	CREDIT
1953 Nov 2		1	900 00	1953 Nov 2		1	375 00
4		1	225 00	6		1	30 00
16		1	520 00	10		1	400 00
30	6250 0	2	850 00	14		1	180 00
				17		1	250 00
				19		2	20 00
				28		2	180 00
				30		2	10 00
				30		2	25 00
				30		2	400 00

Accounts Receivable

ACCOUNT NO 12

DATE	ITEMS	POST REF	DEBIT	DATE	ITEMS	POST REF	CREDIT
1953 Nov. 2	17500	1	400 00	1953 Nov 4		1	225 00

Supplies

ACCOUNT NO 14

DATE	ITEMS	POST REF	DEBIT	DATE	ITEMS	POST REF	CREDIT
1953 Nov 2		1	500 00				
17		1	250 00				

Prepaid Rent

ACCOUNT NO 15

DATE	ITEMS	POST REF	DEBIT	DATE	ITEMS	POST REF	CREDIT
1953 Nov 2		1	375 00				

Repair Equipment

ACCOUNT NO 18

DATE	ITEMS	POST REF	DEBIT	DATE	ITEMS	POST REF	CREDIT
1953 Nov 2		1	1600 00				
3		1	1400 00				

Ledger — Reliable Repair Shop

Accounts Payable　　　　ACCOUNT NO 21

DATE	ITEMS	POST REF	DEBIT	DATE	ITEMS	POST REF	CREDIT
1953 Nov. 10		1	400 00	1953 Nov. 3	1000.00	1	1400 00

Robert Moore, Capital　　　　ACCOUNT NO 31

DATE	ITEMS	POST REF	DEBIT	DATE	ITEMS	POST REF	CREDIT
				1953 Nov. 2		1	3400 00

Robert Moore, Drawing　　　　ACCOUNT NO 32

DATE	ITEMS	POST REF	DEBIT	DATE	ITEMS	POST REF.	CREDIT
1953 Nov. 30		2	400 00				

Sales　　　　ACCOUNT NO 41

DATE	ITEMS	POST REF	DEBIT	DATE	ITEMS	POST REF	CREDIT
				1953 Nov. 16		1	520 00
				30		2	850 00

Salary Expense　　　　ACCOUNT NO 51

DATE	ITEMS	POST REF	DEBIT	DATE	ITEMS	POST REF	CREDIT
1953 Nov. 14		1	180 00				
28		2	180 00				

Miscellaneous Expense　　　　ACCOUNT NO 59

DATE	ITEMS	POST REF	DEBIT	DATE	ITEMS	POST REF	CREDIT
1953 Nov. 6		1	30 00				
19		2	20 00				
30		2	10 00				
30		2	25 00				

Ledger — Reliable Repair Shop (concluded)

THE TRIAL BALANCE As the first step in preparing the trial balance, the accounts having two or more debits or credits are footed. For accounts having both debits and credits, the balance is entered. Observe in the illustration on page 70 that in the cash account the debit and the credit amount columns are totaled. The totals, called *pencil footings*, are entered in small pencil figures immediately below the last entry on each side so that they will not interfere with an entry made on the following line. The balance is entered in small pencil figures in the items column of the account on a line with and on the same side as the larger of the two footings. Observe that in the cash account the debit footing is larger than the credit footing and therefore the balance of $625 is entered in the items column on the debit side. This balance is the amount that is to be entered on the trial balance.

The supplies, repair equipment, sales, salary expense, and miscellaneous expense accounts are also footed, but the balances are not entered in the items columns as each account contains entries on one side of the account only and therefore the footing is the balance. Accounts having only one debit and one credit, such as the accounts receivable account on page 70, are not footed, but the balance is entered in the items column. Accounts that contain only one entry, such as the prepaid rent account, are not footed, and the balance is not entered in the items column because the amount of the entry is the amount of the balance.

The trial balance taken from the ledger of Reliable Repair Shop on November 30 is shown on the opposite page.

OTHER JOURNAL FORMS The two-column general journal provides for a chronological record of transactions. Its use also eliminates, for the most part, any need for explanations in the ledger accounts. It does not reduce the number of entries in the accounts, however, as each debit and each credit is posted individually to the ledger. Some of the unnecessary detail in the ledger can be eliminated by adding special columns to the journal. In any particular case, the number of columns to be added and the manner of their use depends upon the frequency of occurrence of different types of transactions.

For example, examination of the general journal on pages 68 and 69 reveals that, out of a total of fifteen transactions recorded during the month, fourteen involved the receipt or the payment of cash. This means that the account title "Cash" was written in the journal fourteen times and that there were fourteen postings to the cash account. The addition of cash debit and cash credit columns in the general journal

Reliable Repair Shop
Trial Balance
November 30, 1953

Cash	11	625 00		
Accounts Receivable	12	175 00		
Supplies	14	750 00		
Prepaid Rent	15	375 00		
Repair Equipment	18	3000 00		
Accounts Payable	21		1000 00	
Robert Moore, Capital	31		3400 00	
Robert Moore, Drawing	32	400 00		
Sales	41		1370 00	
Salary Expense	51	360 00		
Miscellaneous Expense	59	85 00		
		5770 00	5770 00	

Trial Balance — Reliable Repair Shop

would eliminate the necessity of writing "Cash" in the description column, and the postings to the cash account would be reduced to two a month. Such a four-column journal is illustrated below:

JOURNAL   PAGE *15*

CASH DEBIT	CASH CREDIT	DATE	DESCRIPTION	POST. REF.	GENERAL DEBIT	GENERAL CREDIT
		1953 Sept. 12	Store Supplies		65 00	
			Accounts Payable			65 00
	420 00	14	Office Salary Expense		420 00	
750 00		15	Sales			750 00
	15 00	15	Miscellaneous Expense		15 00	
	150 00	16	Accounts Payable		150 00	
75 00		18	Accounts Receivable			75 00

Four-Column Journal

The two amount columns on the left side of the journal are used exclusively for debits and credits to Cash; the two amount columns on the right side, captioned "General," are used for debits and credits to all other accounts. The description column is used for the titles of accounts that are debited or credited in the general columns.

The procedure for recording a transaction that does not affect Cash is the same as that followed in the two-column journal. The title of the account to be debited is written at the extreme left of the description column and the title of the account to be credited is written on the next line, indented about one-half inch. The amounts are entered in the general debit and credit columns in the usual manner.

Each transaction affecting Cash and another account is recorded on one line. The amount of the debit or the credit to Cash is entered in the proper column at the left, the title of the other account affected is written in the description column, and the amount is entered in the general debit or general credit column at the right. The account title is written at the extreme left of the description column, regardless of whether the account is being debited or credited.

It is customary to omit explanations of routine transactions in multicolumn journals. The advantage of having an explanation after each entry is outweighed by the extra time and space required. In the relatively rare cases in which it becomes necessary to refer back to the explanation of a particular transaction, the details may usually be found in the memorandum used as the basis for the entry. For example, the memorandums supporting disbursements of cash are the check stubs. If payments are made in currency, they are evidenced by "paid out" slips, receipt forms, or other business papers. Invoices and copies of sales tickets are other types of supporting memorandums. In the event explanations are desired in the four-column journal, they are written in the description column immediately below the entry. An additional saving of space is accomplished by using each line rather than leaving a blank line between entries.

FOUR-COLUMN JOURNAL ILLUSTRATED For purposes of illustration, assume that Robert Moore decides to adopt the four-column journal. The journal for March is illustrated on page 75. It has been totaled and all postings have been made. The procedure for posting the items in the general debit and the general credit columns is exactly the same as in the case of the two-column journal illustrated earlier. The procedures for totaling and proving the amount columns and posting to the cash account are as follows:

(1) Draw a single line across the money columns on the line below the last entry of the month.

(2) Foot all four columns, inserting the totals below the ruled line.

(3) Prove the equality of debits and credits. This may be done on an adding machine tape or by a listing similar to the following:

JOURNAL   PAGE 9

CASH DEBIT	CASH CREDIT	DATE	DESCRIPTION	POST. REF.	GENERAL DEBIT	GENERAL CREDIT
		1954				
		Mar. 1	Repair Equipment	18	185 00	
			Accounts Payable	21		185 00
	20 00	2	Supplies	14	20 00	
210 00		5	Accounts Receivable	12		210 00
	180 00	6	Salary Expense	51	180 00	
		9	Accounts Receivable	12	250 00	
			Sales	41		250 00
	350 00	11	Accounts Payable	21	350 00	
	15 00	15	Miscellaneous Expense	59	15 00	
620 00		15	Sales	41		620 00
	150 00	16	Robert Moore, Drawing	32	150 00	
310 00		19	Accounts Receivable	12		310 00
	180 00	20	Salary Expense	51	180 00	
		26	Supplies	14	56 00	
			Accounts Payable	21		56 00
	73 00	29	Accounts Payable	21	73 00	
	32 00	31	Miscellaneous Expense	59	32 00	
	12 00	31	Miscellaneous Expense	59	12 00	
	200 00	31	Robert Moore, Drawing	32	200 00	
728 00		31	Sales	41		728 00
1 868 00	1 212 00	31	Totals	✓	1 703 00	2 359 00
(11)	(11)				(✓)	(✓)

Four-Column Journal — Reliable Repair Shop

	DEBIT	CREDIT
Cash Columns...........	$1,868.00	$1,212.00
General Columns........	1,703.00	2,359.00
Total.................	$3,571.00	$3,571.00

(4) Below the totals draw double lines across all columns except the description column.

(5) Place a check mark in parentheses below the general debit and general credit totals. The check mark indicates that these totals are not to be posted.

(6) Post the total cash debits to the cash account and record the number of the cash account in parentheses below the total. Follow the same routine for posting the total cash credits.

The use of the four-column journal does not alter the postings to any of the accounts except Cash. The savings in time required in posting to the cash account may be observed by tracing the posting of the cash columns to the cash account that appears below. Had the transactions for Reliable Repair Shop for March been recorded in the two-column general journal, there would have been four debit postings and ten credit postings to Cash instead of only one debit and one credit.

Cash   ACCOUNT NO *11*

DATE	ITEMS	POST REF	DEBIT	DATE	ITEMS	POST REF	CREDIT
1954 Mar 1	Balance	✓	1324 00	*1954* Mar 31		9	1212 00
31		9	1868 00				

Cash Account

The foregoing presentation of a four-column combined cash-journal is suggestive of the flexibility in the form of records of original entry. Additional forms will be discussed in later chapters.

FORWARDING JOURNAL TOTALS   When a page of a columnar journal is filled before the end of the month, it is necessary to carry the totals forward to the next page. The procedure for forwarding the totals from one page to the following page is as follows:

(1) Foot the columns and prove the equality of debits and credits.
(2) Enter the date in the date column and write "Carried Forward" in the description column. Place a check mark in the posting reference column to indicate that the totals are not posted.
(3) Finally, enter the totals on the first line of the next page, record the date, write "Brought Forward" in the description column, and place a check mark in the posting reference column.

An illustration of forwarding totals appears on the opposite page. The procedure is the same for all types of multicolumn journals. It is not necessary to forward totals in the two-column general journal, since all items are posted individually and the equality of debits and credits is easily proved for each entry.

JOURNAL　　　　　　　　PAGE 2

| CASH | | DATE | DESCRIPTION | POST REF. | GENERAL | |
DEBIT	CREDIT				DEBIT	CREDIT
	1 05 00	*1953* Dec 1	Supplies	14	1 05 00	
80 00		1	Accounts Receivable	12		80 00
	10 00	2	Miscellaneous Expense	59	10 00	
	23 00	2	Accounts Payable	21	23 00	
		19	Repair Equipment	18	98 00	
			Accounts Payable	21		98 00
	10 00	21	Miscellaneous Expense	59	10 00	3 45 400
1 96 000	1 63 200	21	Carried Forward	✓	3 12 600	3 45 400

JOURNAL　　　　　　　　PAGE 3

| CASH | | DATE | DESCRIPTION | POST REF | GENERAL | |
DEBIT	CREDIT				DEBIT	CREDIT
1 96 00	1 63 200	*1953* Dec 21	Brought Forward	✓	3 12 600	3 45 400

Forwarding the Totals of a Columnar Journal

CORRECTION OF ERRORS　　It is inevitable that errors will occasionally be made in recording transactions in the journal and in posting to the accounts. Such errors should not be corrected by erasures, as erasures may arouse suspicions of dishonesty. The procedure for correcting errors varies with the nature of the error and the time of its discovery. If an incorrect account title or amount in a book of original entry is discovered before the item has been posted, the correction is made by drawing a line through the error and by writing the correct title or amount immediately above. An incorrect amount posted to an account may be corrected in the same manner, by crossing out the incorrect amount and by writing the correct figure above.

When a posting is made to the wrong account, it is usually considered preferable to correct it by an entry in the journal. For example, if a disbursement for miscellaneous expense of $20 was incorrectly recorded and posted as a debit to Salary Expense, the general journal entry to make the correction would be:

```
May 31  Miscellaneous Expense.................... 20.00
            Salary Expense........................        20.00
            To correct entry of May 1 in which a
            payment for Misc. Expense was debited
            to Salary Expense.
```

The effect of the entry is to offset the erroneous debit of $20 to Salary Expense by a credit of like amount and to debit Miscellaneous Expense for the amount that should have been debited originally.

A correcting entry should always be supported by a complete explanation in the journal. In general, the bookkeeper has considerable latitude in the methods used to correct errors. It is important that the corrections and the explanations be so clear that they will be readily understood by anyone examining the records.

DISCOVERY OF ERRORS The existence of errors in the accounts may be ascertained in a variety of ways: through audit procedures, through chance discovery, or through the medium of the trial balance. As was emphasized in Chapter 4, there are some types of errors that are not disclosed by the trial balance. If the debit and the credit totals of the trial balance are unequal, however, the reason for the discrepancy must be found and the error must be corrected.

The general procedure for locating errors revealed by the trial balance is to retrace the various steps in the bookkeeping cycle, beginning with the last step and working back to the original entries in the journal. While there are no rigid rules governing this check or audit, the following plan is suggested:

(1) Prove the totals obtained for the trial balance.
(2) Compare the listings in the trial balance with the balances shown in the ledger, making certain that no accounts have been omitted.
(3) Verify the accuracy of the account footings and balances by recomputing them.
(4) Trace the postings in the ledger back to the book of original entry, placing a small check mark by the item in the ledger and also in the book of original entry. If the error is not found, scrutinize each account to see if there is an entry without a check mark; do the same with the entries in the book of original entry.
(5) Verify the equality of the debits and the credits in the book of original entry.

Ordinarily, errors that affect the trial balance will be revealed before the foregoing procedures have been completed.

QUESTIONS

1. If the same information is to be found in both the journal and the ledger, what distinguishes the two records?

2. (a) What is the general order of sequence of accounts in the ledger? (b) State two reasons for assigning a number to each account in the ledger. (c) State an advantage of a system of indexing accounts by classifications in comparison with numbering them consecutively.

3. If it were necessary to add accounts for Prepaid Insurance, Delivery Trucks, and Utilities Expense to the chart of accounts for Reliable Repair Shop shown on page 66, what number should be assigned to each?

4. Under what circumstances should a payment for rent be debited to: (a) the prepaid rent account? (b) the rent expense account?

5. State in detail the four steps involved in posting the debit portion of the following general journal entry (Prepaid Rent is account number 15):

PAGE 10

Nov.	1	Prepaid Rent		600	
		Cash			600

6. In recording transactions affecting cash in the four-column journal illustrated on page 75, it is unnecessary to write "Cash" in the description column. What is the reason for this?

7. Compare the procedure for posting debits and credits to the cash account from the two-column general journal illustrated on page 68 and from the four-column journal illustrated on page 75.

8. Explain how each of the following errors should have been corrected. In each case the error was discovered before the profit and loss statement and the balance sheet were prepared.

    (a) A disbursement of $320 for salaries was recorded in the journal as a debit to Salary Expense of $320 and a credit to Cash of $230. The error was discovered before the items were posted.

    (b) A $425 credit to Sales was incorrectly posted as $42.50.

    (c) A purchase of $75 of store supplies on account was recorded in the journal as a debit to Store Supplies and a credit to Cash. The error was discovered before the items were posted.

9. Does an error in the trial balance indicate that an error has been made (a) in journalizing? (b) in posting? (c) in summarizing the information recorded in the ledger?

PROBLEMS

5-1. Donald Kramer started the Ace Window Washing Co. on April 14 of the current year. The following account titles and their identifying numbers appear in the chart of accounts for the enterprise: Cash, 11; Accounts Receivable, 12; Supplies, 13; Prepaid Insurance, 14; Truck, 16; Office Equipment, 17; Washing Equipment, 18; Notes Payable, 21; Accounts Payable, 22; Donald Kramer, Capital, 31; Donald Kramer, Drawing, 32; Sales, 41; Salary Expense, 51; Rent Expense, 52; Truck Expense, 53; Miscellaneous Expense, 59.

On April 14 Mr. Kramer deposited $1,250 in a bank account under the name of Ace Window Washing Co. He completed the following business transactions during the remainder of the month:

April 14. Purchased supplies for cash, $45.
    15. Purchased a truck for $1,500, paying $500 cash and giving a note payable for the remainder.
    17. Purchased ladders and other equipment on account, $200.
    18. Collected $40 cash for jobs completed.
    19. Paid rent for period April 14 to end of month, $53.
    20. Billed customers for services rendered, $300.
    21. Purchased office equipment on account, $150.
    22. Purchased supplies on account, $38.
    23. Withdrew $100 for personal use.
    24. Paid creditors on account, $100.
    25. Collected accounts receivable, $240.
    26. Paid insurance premiums on property and casualty insurance, $152.
    27. Billed customers for services rendered, $450.
    28. Collected $25 cash for services rendered. Customer had not been billed previously.
    28. Paid salaries for the two weeks, $250.
    30. Received an invoice for truck expenses for the month, $42. (Credit Accounts Payable.)
    30. Paid miscellaneous expenses, $59.
    30. Collected accounts receivable, $355.
    30. Withdrew $100 for personal use.

Instructions: (1) Open accounts in the ledger in accordance with the list presented above.

(2) Record Mr. Kramer's initial investment and the transactions for April in a two-column general journal.

(3) Post from the journal to the ledger.

(4) Take a trial balance of the ledger.

5-2. Louis Andrews is a real estate broker and rental agent. His income is composed of fees received from acting as an agent in selling and renting property. The trial balance of his ledger on January 31 of the current year follows:

LOUIS ANDREWS
Trial Balance
January 31, 19 - -

Cash	11	$1,450	
Accounts Receivable	12	950	
Office Supplies	14	23	
Prepaid Insurance	15	75	
Automobile	17	2,500	
Office Equipment	18	600	
Accounts Payable	21		$ 120
Louis Andrews, Capital	31		5,146
Louis Andrews, Drawing	32	500	
Fees	41		1,355
Salary Expense	51	300	
Rent Expense	52	125	
Automobile Expense	53	29	
Advertising Expense	54	25	
Miscellaneous Expense	59	44	
		$6,621	$6,621

During the month of February, Mr. Andrews completed the following transactions:

Feb. 1. Paid rent for month, $125.
   3. Collected accounts receivable, $410.
   4. Purchased typewriter on account, $110.
   8. Paid premium on property insurance, $38.
   11. Purchased office supplies on account, $16.
   14. Paid secretary's salary, $150.
   14. Billed fees for first half of month, $830.
   15. Paid $150 to creditors on account.
   18. Purchased office equipment for cash, $40.
   20. Collected accounts receivable, $990.
   22. Discovered that the entry for the transaction of Feb. 11 was incorrectly recorded. The cost of the supplies purchased was $14 rather than $16.
   26. Paid advertising, $36.
   28. Billed fees for second half of month, $670.
   28. Paid automobile expense, $32, and miscellaneous expense, $27.
   28. Paid secretary's salary, $150.
   28. Withdrew cash for personal use, $550.

Instructions: (1) Open an account in the ledger for each item listed in the trial balance of January 31.

(2) Record the balance in each account under the date of Feb. 1, write the word "Balance" in the items column, and place a check mark in the posting reference column.

(3) Record the transactions for February in a two-column general journal.

(4) Post to the ledger.

(5) An error is discovered in billing the fees for the second half of the month. The amount is $620 instead of $670. Journalize the correcting entry and post.

(6) Take a trial balance of the ledger.

5-3. John Reed owns a shoe repair establishment known as Superior Shoe Repairs. The accounts in his ledger on January 1 of the current year, together with the balances of the asset, liability, and capital accounts, are as follows: 11, Cash, $1,423.50; 12, Store Supplies, $210.60; 13, Office Supplies, $24.00; 14, Prepaid Insurance, $29.30; 15, Prepaid Rent; 16, Store Equipment, $6,425.00; 17, Office Equipment, $526.00; 21, Notes Payable, $1,200.00; 22, Accounts Payable, $426.10; 31, John Reed, Capital, $7,012.30; 32, John Reed, Drawing; 41, Sales; 51, Sales Salary Expense; 52, Advertising Expense; 59, Miscellaneous Selling Expense; 61, Office Salary Expense; 69, Miscellaneous General Expense.

During the month of January Mr. Reed completed the following transactions:

Jan. 2. Paid rent for three months, $375. (Debit Prepaid Rent.)
2. Paid cash for advertising, $80.
3. Purchased store supplies on account, $434.76.
4. Paid cash for office supplies, $46.10.
5. Purchased store equipment for $850, giving a note payable for $500 and paying the balance in cash.
6. Cash sales for the week, $470.35.
8. Paid creditors on account, $200.
10. Paid premium on property insurance, $65.
13. Paid cash, $550, for biweekly salaries as follows: sales salaries, $400, and office salaries, $150.
13. Cash sales for the week, $425.10.
16. Withdrew $175 for personal use.
18. Paid cash for miscellaneous selling expenses, $18.50.
20. Cash sales for the week, $437.85.
24. Paid creditors on account, $150.
25. Purchased store supplies on account, $211.04.
27. Cash sales for the week, $415.45.
27. Paid cash, $550, for biweekly salaries as follows: sales salaries, $400, and office salaries, $150.
29. Paid cash for telephone, utilities, and miscellaneous general expense for the month, $87.
30. Withdrew $175 for personal use.
31. Cash sales for the balance of the month, $219.56.

Instructions: (1) Open an account in the ledger for each item listed above.

(2) Record the balances in the accounts under the date of Jan. 1, write "Bal." in the items column, and place a check mark in the posting reference column.

(3) Record the transactions for January in a four-column general journal similar to that illustrated on page 75.

(4) Total and rule the journal.

(5) Post to the ledger.

(6) Take a trial balance of the ledger.

Chapter 6

Completion of the Accounting Cycle

TRIAL BALANCE AND ACCOUNTING STATEMENTS The balance sheet and the profit and loss statement have already been presented as finished products of accounting. The trial balance provides much of the information needed for the preparation of these statements. The items in the trial balance are arranged in the order of the chart of accounts, which in turn follows the sequence of items on the balance sheet and the profit and loss statement.

If all of the amounts listed in the trial balance were the correct amounts for the statements, it would be a simple matter to arrange the asset, liability, and proprietorship items in the proper form for the balance sheet and the income and expense items in the proper form for the profit and loss statement. The amounts would be correct for statement purposes if all transactions recorded in the accounts coincided exactly with the accounting period. For example, if all insurance premiums paid during the period covered by the profit and loss statement applied only to that period, no change in the trial balance amount for insurance would be necessary. The situation with regard to supplies and other prepaid expenses is similar. It is obviously impossible, however, to arrange transactions in such a way as to avoid carry-overs from one accounting period to another. Therefore, it is necessary for accounting to provide a means of meeting this business condition. This chapter deals with the accounting procedures that provide correct data for the balance sheet and the profit and loss statement.

MIXED ACCOUNTS AND BUSINESS OPERATIONS An account with a balance that is partly a balance sheet amount and partly a profit and loss statement amount is called a *mixed account*. For example, the balance of the supplies account, as listed on the trial balance, represents the cost of all supplies on hand at the beginning of the period plus those purchased during the period. It is known that some of the supplies have been used. Therefore, the trial balance amount is composed of two elements, the supplies on hand, which is an asset, and the supplies used, which is an expense. It is for this reason that it is termed a mixed account. Before financial statements are prepared, it is necessary to determine the amount of the asset and the amount of the expense. The former is determined by taking an inventory, which involves counting the various types of supplies, pricing them, and computing the total. The cost of the supplies used is then determined by subtracting the inventory figure from the balance of the supplies account. On the basis of the information thus determined, an *adjustment* to the asset account and the related expense account must be made.

Whether an account is a mixed account sometime during the accounting period need not be considered if it is known in advance that it will become wholly an expense by the end of the period. For example, if rent for March is paid on March 1, it is almost entirely an asset at the time of payment, but it will be wholly expense at the close of business on March 31. It should therefore be debited to Rent Expense at the time of payment, as the true facts will be reflected at the close of the period. On the other hand, if rent is paid in advance beyond the end of the current fiscal period, the payment may be debited to the asset account Prepaid Rent. In this case, at the end of the fiscal period the account Prepaid Rent is adjusted to show the expense for the period and the value of the asset at the end of the period.

**ADJUSTMENTS
ILLUSTRATED
IN ACCOUNTS**
The nature of *adjusting entries* can best be illustrated by the use of "T" accounts. Reliable Repair Shop's accounts with Supplies and Supplies Expense are shown below.. The supplies account has debits of $500 and $250. The balance of the account was listed at $750 in the trial balance at the end of the month. An inventory taken at that time indicates that there are $460 of supplies actually on hand. It follows that of the $750 balance, $460 is asset and $290 is expense. According to the rules of debit and credit, increases in expense accounts are recorded as debits and decreases in asset accounts are recorded as credits. Hence the adjusting entry is a debit to Supplies Expense and a credit to Supplies of $290.

SUPPLIES			SUPPLIES EXPENSE	
Nov. 1	500	Nov. 30 290	Nov. 30 290	
17	250			
	750			

After the $290 has been transferred to the supplies expense account, the asset account has a debit balance of $460 and the expense account has a debit balance of $290.

Prepaid Rent is another mixed account that requires adjustment at the end of the accounting period. The debit balance in this account represents in part an expense of the current period and in part a prepayment of expense of future periods. The portion that is expense should be transferred to the expense account, Rent Expense. After this is done, the prepaid rent account and the rent expense account will accurately reflect the true situation.

The debit of $375 in the prepaid rent account appearing below represents payment of rent for three months, November, December, and January. At the end of November, the rent expense account should be increased (debited) and the prepaid rent account should be decreased (credited) for $125, the rental for one month. The two accounts appear as follows after the adjusting entry has been recorded:

PREPAID RENT				RENT EXPENSE		
Nov. 2	375	Nov. 30	125	Nov. 30	125	

The prepaid rent account now has a debit balance of $250, which is an asset; the rent expense account has a debit balance of $125, which is an expense.

In addition to adjusting mixed accounts at the end of the period, it may be necessary to adjust certain other accounts to bring them up to date. For example, when salaries are paid on a weekly or a biweekly basis, only infrequently will the last day of a pay period coincide with the last day of the month. The salaries that the employees have earned, but that have not been paid, must be recorded in the accounts by an adjusting entry. The accounts presented below were taken from the ledger of Reliable Repair Shop. The first two debits in the salary expense account were the biweekly payments of $180 each. Salaries are paid on alternate Saturdays for the payroll period ended that day; therefore the salaries earned between Saturday, November 28, and the end of the month must be considered in preparing financial statements. The salaries earned on Monday, November 30, amount to $15. As this amount is an increase in salary expense, it is debited to the salary expense account. Since it is not being paid at this time, there is a liability of $15 that is credited to Salaries Payable.

SALARY EXPENSE			SALARIES PAYABLE		
Nov. 14	180				
28	180		Nov. 30	15	
	360				
30	15				

After the adjustment is made, the debit balance of the salary expense account is $375, which is the actual expense for the month; the credit balance of $15 in Salaries Payable is the liability for salaries owed as of November 30.

Business operations, as distinct from business transactions, are continually affecting items recorded in ledger accounts. Supplies are used, insurance expires, wages and salaries accrue. All these effects of operations on account balances are recognized at the time the accounting statements are prepared. This procedure avoids the necessity of recording currently the *internal transactions* that affect account balances.

It is extremely important to note that the rules of debit and credit apply to adjusting entries in exactly the same manner as they apply to regular business transactions. It is necessary first to analyze the facts and then to express the adjustment in terms of debit and credit.

THE WORK SHEET   Adjustments such as those just discussed must be considered in preparing the profit and loss statement and the balance sheet. But before the adjustments are actually recorded in the journal and posted to the ledger, it is usually customary to prepare a form known as a *work sheet*. The work sheet is a device used by accountants as an aid in preparing financial statements and in completing the work of the accounting cycle. Its use lessens the chance of overlooking an adjustment, provides a check on the accuracy of the work, and arranges data in a logical form for the preparation of the statements.

The work sheet for Reliable Repair Shop is presented on page 87. Note that there are three parts to the heading: (1) the name of the enterprise, (2) the title "Work Sheet," and (3) the period of time covered. It has a column for account titles and ten money columns, arranged in five pairs of debit and credit columns. The principal headings of the five sets of money columns are as follows:

1. Trial Balance
2. Adjustments
3. Adjusted Trial Balance
4. Profit and Loss Statement
5. Balance Sheet

Trial Balance Columns. The first step in the preparation of the work sheet is the trial balance. The trial balance may be prepared on another sheet first and then copied on the work sheet or it may be prepared directly on the work sheet in the Trial Balance columns.

Reliable Repair Shop
Work Sheet
For Month Ended November 30, 1953

Account Title	Acct No.	Trial Balance Dr.	Trial Balance Cr.	Adjustments Dr.	Adjustments Cr.	Adjusted Trial Balance Dr.	Adjusted Trial Balance Cr.	Profit & Loss Statement Dr.	Profit & Loss Statement Cr.	Balance Sheet Dr.	Balance Sheet Cr.
Cash	11	62500				62500				62500	
Accounts Receivable	12	17500				17500				17500	
Supplies	14	75000			(a)29000	46000				46000	
Prepaid Rent	15	37500			(b)12500	25000				25000	
Repair Equipment	18	300000				300000				300000	
Accounts Payable	21		100000				100000				100000
Robert Moore, Capital	31		340000				340000				340000
Robert Moore, Drawing	32	40000				40000				40000	
Sales	41		137000				137000		137000		
Salary Expense	51	36000		(c) 1500		37500		37500			
Miscellaneous Expense	59	8500				8500		8500			
		577000	577000								
Supplies Expense	52			(a)29000		29000		29000			
Rent Expense	53			(b)12500		12500		12500			
Salaries Payable	22				(c) 1500		1500				1500
				43000	43000	578500	578500	87500	137000	491000	441500
Net Profit								49500			49500
								137000	137000	491000	491000

Ten-Column Work Sheet

87

Adjustments Columns. The adjustments required at the end of the period are recorded in the Adjustments columns. The order in which the adjustments are made is immaterial. The adjustments applicable to Reliable Repair Shop are as follows:

(a) The cost of the supplies on hand, as determined by an inventory, is $460. Inasmuch as the balance of the supplies account in the trial balance is $750, it follows that the value of the supplies used is $290 ($750 — $460). The adjustment required is a debit to Supplies Expense and a credit to Supplies of $290. As the account Supplies Expense does not appear in the trial balance, it is necessary to write the account title on the first line below the trial balance totals. The adjustment is then made by recording $290 in the Adjustments Dr. column on the line with Supplies Expense and $290 in the Adjustments Cr. column on the line with Supplies. For cross-referencing purposes, the debit and the credit are identified by placing the letter "a" at the left of each of the two items, as shown in the illustration below:

Account Title	Acct. No.	Trial Balance Dr.	Cr.	Adjustments Dr.	Cr.
Cash	11	625 00			
Accounts Receivable	12	175 00			
Supplies	14	750 00			(a) 290 00
		5770 00	5770 00		
Supplies Expense	52			(a) 290 00	

Recording an Adjustment on the Work Sheet

(b) The $375 debit balance in the asset account Prepaid Rent represents a payment for three months, beginning with November 1. On November 30, therefore, one third of the amount, or $125, should be transferred to Rent Expense. Since the account Rent Expense does not appear in the trial balance, it is written on the next available line below. The adjustment is then recorded in the same manner as the adjustment for supplies. The letter "b" is used to identify the related debit and credit of $125.

(c) Salaries owed at the end of the month amount to $15. This is an increase in expense and an increase in liabilities. Salary Expense is therefore debited for $15 in the Adjustments Dr. column and Salaries Payable is credited for $15 in the Adjustments Cr. column, the latter account title being written in on the next available line.

The need for identifying the adjustments by letter is not so apparent in this example, as there are only three entries. The usefulness of the identification will be demonstrated to a greater extent later in work sheets having many adjustments.

The final step in completing the Adjustments columns is to prove the equality of debits and credits by footing and ruling the two columns.

Adjusted Trial Balance Columns. The data in the Trial Balance columns and the Adjustments columns are now combined and entered in the Adjusted Trial Balance columns. This is done for each account title listed, beginning at the top of the sheet and proceeding with each account in order. In the illustration, Cash has a debit balance of $625 in the Trial Balance columns, and the Adjustment columns are blank; hence the $625 amount is carried over as a debit in the Adjusted Trial Balance columns. Similarly, the balance in Accounts Receivable is carried over. Supplies has a debit balance of $750 and a credit adjustment of $290, which yields an adjusted debit balance of $460.

This procedure is continued until all account balances, with or without adjustment as the case may be, have been entered in the Adjusted Trial Balance columns. Note that for accounts listed below the trial balance totals, the amount of the adjustment becomes the adjusted balance of the account. For example, Supplies Expense has an initial balance of zero and a debit adjustment of $290, yielding an adjusted debit balance of $290.

The Adjusted Trial Balance columns are completed by footing and ruling the two columns to prove that the equality of debits and credits has been maintained.

Profit and Loss Statement and Balance Sheet Columns. Each amount entered in the Adjusted Trial Balance columns is extended to one of the remaining four columns. Asset, liability, and proprietorship items are extended to the Balance Sheet columns, and income and expense items are extended over to the Profit and Loss Statement columns. All debit balances in the Adjusted Trial Balance columns will then appear in either the Balance Sheet Dr. column or the Profit and Loss Statement Dr. column, and all credit balances will likewise appear in the appropriate credit columns.

After all of the balances have been extended, the four columns are totaled. The amount of the net profit or the net loss for the period is then determined by ascertaining the amount of the difference between the totals of the two Profit and Loss Statement columns. If the credit column total is greater than the debit column total, the excess is the net profit. For the work sheet presented on page 87, the computation is as follows:

Total of credit column (income)........................ $1,370.00
Total of debit column (expenses)......................   875.00

Net profit (excess of income over expenses)............. $ 495.00

The profit and loss statement accounts are temporary proprietorship accounts that are used to accumulate changes in proprietorship during the fiscal period. At the end of the fiscal period, the balance of all of these accounts is transferred to proprietorship. In this case, the credit balance of $495 is to be transferred to the credit side of a proprietorship account. The transfer is shown on the work sheet by a debit entry in the Profit and Loss Statement Dr. column and a credit entry in the Balance Sheet Cr. column. The words "Net Profit" are written in the Account Title column as an explanation of this transfer.

The columns are then totaled and ruled in the manner shown below. The totals of the two Profit and Loss Statement columns are equal because the net profit, $495, was obtained as the difference between the original totals of these columns. The totals of the Balance Sheet columns are also equal because, after the profit has been transferred to the proprietorship accounts, Assets = Liabilities + Proprietorship.

Account Title	Acct. No.	Profit & Loss Statement Dr.	Cr.	Balance Sheet Dr.	Cr.
Cash	11			6250 0	
Accounts Receivable	12			1750 0	
Supplies	14			4600 0	
Prepaid Rent	15			2500 0	
		8750 0	13700 0	49100 0	44150 0
Net Profit		4950 0			4950 0
		13700 0	13700 0	49100 0	49100 0

Profit and Loss Statement and Balance Sheet Columns
of the Work Sheet Totaled and Ruled

If total expenses of the period should exceed total income, the subtotal of the Profit and Loss Statement Dr. column would be greater than the subtotal of the Cr. column. The difference between the two amounts would be the net loss for the period. Losses decrease proprietorship; therefore the net loss would be entered in the Profit and Loss Statement Cr. column and transferred to the Balance Sheet Dr. column as a decrease in proprietorship.

The work sheet is a device employed by the accountant as the basis for preparing financial statements and recording adjusting and closing entries in the journal. It is not a formal statement and does not take the place of the formal balance sheet and profit and loss statement. Since it is not presented to the proprietor or others interested in the business, it is customarily prepared in pencil.

**FINANCIAL
STATEMENTS**   The profit and loss statement and the balance sheet prepared from the work sheet of Reliable Repair Shop for November are presented below and on page 92. All of the figures for the profit and loss statement are taken from the Profit and Loss Statement columns of the work sheet and those for the balance sheet from the Balance Sheet columns of the work sheet.

There is one item in the proprietorship section of the balance sheet that will not necessarily appear on the work sheet. It is the balance of the capital account at the beginning of the period. If the proprietor invests additional assets in the business during the period, the balance of the capital account shown on the work sheet will be the sum of the beginning balance plus the additional investment. In such cases reference must be made to the capital account in the ledger to obtain these data. In the illustration there were no additional investments; hence the capital balance of $3,400 listed on the work sheet is the capital on November 1.

Reliable Repair Shop
Profit and Loss Statement
For Month Ended November 30, 1953

Sales		$1 370 00
Operating Expenses:		
Salary Expense	$375 00	
Supplies Expense	290 00	
Rent Expense	125 00	
Miscellaneous Expense	85 00	
Total Operating Expenses		875 00
Net Profit from Operations		$495 00

Profit and Loss Statement

Reliable Repair Shop
Balance Sheet
November 30, 1953

Assets		
Current Assets:		
Cash	$ 625 00	
Accounts Receivable	175 00	
Supplies	460 00	
Prepaid Rent	250 00	
Total Current Assets		$ 1 510 00
Fixed Assets:		
Repair Equipment		3 000 00
Total Assets		$ 4 510 00
Liabilities		
Current Liabilities:		
Accounts Payable	$ 1 000 00	
Salaries Payable	15 00	
Total Current Liabilities		$ 1 015 00
Proprietorship		
Robert Moore, Capital, Nov 1, 1953	$ 3 400 00	
Net Profit for Month $495.00		
Less Withdrawals 400.00		
Increase in Capital	95 00	
Robert Moore, Capital, Nov 30, 1953		3 495 00
Total Liabilities and Proprietorship		$ 4 510 00

Balance Sheet

ADJUSTING ENTRIES   At the end of a fiscal period, after the work sheet and the financial statements have been prepared, the accounts in the ledger are adjusted to agree with the statements. The ledger of Reliable Repair Shop was presented on pages 70 and 71. The adjusting entries shown on the work sheet on page 87 must now be recorded in the appropriate accounts.

As in the case of entries for regular business transactions, the adjusting entries must be recorded in the journal and then posted to the ledger. They are copied directly from the Adjustments columns of the work sheet, using the next available space in the journal. Each entry may be supported by an explanation, or the group may be identified by writing "Adjusting Entries" above the first entry in the series. The work sheet and supporting memorandums on adjustment data should be kept on file for future reference. A portion of the general journal of Reliable Repair Shop appears below, showing the adjusting entries:

GENERAL JOURNAL   PAGE 2

DATE	DESCRIPTION	POST REF	DEBIT	CREDIT
	Adjusting Entries			
30	Supplies Expense	52	29 00	
	Supplies	14		29 00
30	Rent Expense	53	1 25 00	
	Prepaid Rent	15		1 25 00
30	Salary Expense	51	15 00	
	Salaries Payable	22		15 00

Adjusting Entries

The ledger accounts affected by the adjusting entries are presented on the following page. Note that the only postings in the three accounts, Salaries Payable, Supplies Expense, and Rent Expense, are those from the adjusting entries.

CLOSING ENTRIES   The process of bringing the ledger into agreement with the financial statements is concluded by a series of transfers that result in a final debit or credit to the capital account. After these transfers are journalized and posted, each of the temporary proprietorship accounts (income, expense, and drawing) will have zero balances, and the balance of the capital account in the ledger will be the same as the amount of capital shown on the balance sheet.

The process by which the balance of an account is transferred to another account is called a *closing entry*, and the account from which the balance has been transferred is said to be *closed*. The first step in the closing procedure is the transfer of the balance of each income and expense account to a summarizing account called *Profit and Loss Summary*. Income accounts have credit balances. Each income account is closed, therefore, by debiting it for an amount equal to the

Supplies
ACCOUNT NO. 1 4

DATE	ITEMS	POST. REF.	DEBIT	DATE	ITEMS	POST. REF.	CREDIT
1953 Nov. 2		1	500 00	1953 Nov. 30		2	290 00
17		1	250 00				

Prepaid Rent
ACCOUNT NO. 1 5

DATE	ITEMS	POST. REF.	DEBIT	DATE	ITEMS	POST. REF.	CREDIT
1953 Nov. 2		1	375 00	1953 Nov. 30		2	125 00

Salaries Payable
ACCOUNT NO. 2 2

DATE	ITEMS	POST. REF.	DEBIT	DATE	ITEMS	POST. REF.	CREDIT
				1953 Nov. 30		2	15 00

Salary Expense
ACCOUNT NO. 5 1

DATE	ITEMS	POST. REF.	DEBIT	DATE	ITEMS	POST. REF.	CREDIT
1953 Nov. 14		1	180 00				
28		2	180 00				
30		2	15 00				

Supplies Expense
ACCOUNT NO. 5 2

DATE	ITEMS	POST. REF.	DEBIT	DATE	ITEMS	POST. REF.	CREDIT
1953 Nov. 30		2	290 00				

Rent Expense
ACCOUNT NO. 5 3

DATE	ITEMS	POST. REF.	DEBIT	DATE	ITEMS	POST. REF.	CREDIT
1953 Nov. 30		2	125 00				

Accounts to Which Adjusting Entries Have Been Posted

balance of the account; the transfer is completed by crediting Profit and Loss Summary. Expense accounts have debit balances. Each expense account is closed, therefore, by crediting it for an amount equal to its balance and debiting Profit and Loss Summary for the same amount.

The amounts shown in the Profit and Loss Statement columns of the work sheet correspond to the balances of the income and expense accounts in the ledger. It is therefore unnecessary to refer to the ledger in formulating the closing entries. The data for the closing entries appearing below were taken from the work sheet for Reliable Repair Shop. Each journal entry may be supported by an explanation, or the group may be identified by writing "Closing Entries" above the first entry in the series.

GENERAL JOURNAL　　　　　　　　　　　　PAGE 3

DATE	DESCRIPTION	POST. REF.	DEBIT	CREDIT
1953	*Closing Entries*			
Nov 30	Sales	41	1 3 7 0 00	
	Profit and Loss Summary	33		1 3 7 0 00
30	Profit and Loss Summary	33	8 7 5 00	
	Salary Expense	51		3 7 5 00
	Miscellaneous Expense	59		8 5 00
	Supplies Expense	52		2 9 0 00
	Rent Expense	53		1 2 5 00

Closing Entries for Income and Expenses

The ledger accounts to which these closing entries are posted are shown on page 96. Examination of the ledger reveals that the income and the expenses of the period are summarized in the profit and loss summary account, and that each individual income and expense account is closed. The sales of $1,370 appear as a credit in Profit and Loss Summary, and the total expenses of $875 appear as a debit in the same account, leaving a credit balance of $495, which is the net profit for the period.

The next temporary account to be closed is Profit and Loss Summary. If operations have resulted in a net profit, the account will have a credit balance; if there has been a net loss, it will have a debit balance. In either case the balance is transferred to the drawing account.

The entry required to close the profit and loss summary account of Reliable Repair Shop is shown on page 97, together with the two accounts affected.

Profit and Loss Summary   ACCOUNT NO. 33

DATE	ITEMS	POST. REF.	DEBIT	DATE	ITEMS	POST. REF.	CREDIT
1953 Nov. 30		3	875 00	1953 Nov. 30		3	1 370 00

Sales   ACCOUNT NO. 41

DATE	ITEMS	POST. REF.	DEBIT	DATE	ITEMS	POST. REF.	CREDIT
1953 Nov. 30		3	1 370 00	1953 Nov. 16		1	520 00
				30		2	850 00

Salary Expense   ACCOUNT NO. 51

DATE	ITEMS	POST. REF.	DEBIT	DATE	ITEMS	POST. REF.	CREDIT
1953 Nov. 14		1	180 00	1953 Nov. 30		3	375 00
28		2	180 00				
30		2	15 00				

Supplies Expense   ACCOUNT NO. 52

DATE	ITEMS	POST. REF.	DEBIT	DATE	ITEMS	POST. REF.	CREDIT
1953 Nov. 30		2	290 00	1953 Nov. 30		3	290 00

Rent Expense   ACCOUNT NO. 53

DATE	ITEMS	POST. REF.	DEBIT	DATE	ITEMS	POST. REF.	CREDIT
1953 Nov. 30		2	125 00	1953 Nov. 30		3	125 00

Miscellaneous Expense   ACCOUNT NO. 59

DATE	ITEMS	POST. REF.	DEBIT	DATE	ITEMS	POST. REF.	CREDIT
1953 Nov. 6		1	30 00	1953 Nov. 30		3	85 00
19		2	20 00				
30		2	10 00				
30		2	25 00				

**Ledger Accounts to Which Closing Entries for
Income and Expenses Have Been Posted**

| | 30 | Profit and Loss Summary | 33 | 4 9 5 0 0 | | | | |
| | | Robert Moore, Drawing | 32 | | | | 4 9 5 0 0 | |

Robert Moore, Drawing   ACCOUNT NO. 32

DATE	ITEMS	POST. REF.	DEBIT	DATE	ITEMS	POST. REF.	CREDIT
1953 Nov. 30		2	4 0 0 0 0	1953 Nov. 30		3	4 9 5 0 0

Profit and Loss Summary   ACCOUNT NO. 33

DATE	ITEMS	POST. REF.	DEBIT	DATE	ITEMS	POST. REF.	CREDIT
1953 Nov. 30		3	8 7 5 0 0	1953 Nov. 30		3	1 3 7 0 0 0
30		3	4 9 5 0 0				

Closing the Profit and Loss Summary Account to the Drawing Account

It should be noted that Profit and Loss Summary is now closed and that the net profit of $495 appears as a credit in the account Robert Moore, Drawing.

The final closing entry transfers the balance of the drawing account to the capital account. It represents the net change in capital for the period, exclusive of any additional investments by the proprietor.

Reference to the account Robert Moore, Drawing, reveals that it has a credit balance of $95 ($495−$400). This same amount appears on the balance sheet as the net increase in capital. The final closing entry is presented below, together with the two accounts affected:

| | 30 | Robert Moore, Drawing | 32 | 9 5 0 0 | | | | |
| | | Robert Moore, Capital | 31 | | | | 9 5 0 0 | |

Robert Moore, Capital   ACCOUNT NO. 31

DATE	ITEMS	POST. REF.	DEBIT	DATE	ITEMS	POST. REF.	CREDIT
				1953 Nov. 2		1	3 4 0 0 0 0
				30		3	9 5 0 0

Robert Moore, Drawing   ACCOUNT NO. 32

DATE	ITEMS	POST. REF.	DEBIT	DATE	ITEMS	POST. REF.	CREDIT
1953 Nov. 30		2	4 0 0 0 0	1953 Nov. 30		3	4 9 5 0 0
30		3	9 5 0 0				

Closing the Drawing Account to the Capital Account

BALANCING AND RULING THE ACCOUNTS After the temporary proprietorship accounts have been closed, the accounts are prepared to receive entries for the next fiscal period. This is done by ruling them in such a way as to segregate entries of the period just closed from entries of the ensuing period. The complete ledger of Reliable Repair Shop with all accounts properly ruled appears on pages 99, 100, and 101. References to certain accounts will be made as the procedures for ruling and balancing the accounts are described.

After the temporary proprietorship accounts have been closed, the debit side and the credit side of each account is totaled. The totals of the two sides of the account are entered on the same line and double rules are drawn under the total and across all columns except the Items columns (see Sales).

If a temporary proprietorship account has only one debit and one credit, there is no need to repeat the same figures as totals; the double lines are drawn immediately under the entries (see Supplies Expense).

When all of the temporary proprietorship accounts have been ruled in the manner indicated, there is no possibility of erroneously combining entries of two or more periods. All entries above the double rulings are ignored in accounting for future periods.

The balance sheet accounts may be balanced and ruled at this time so that they will show only the balance of each account at the beginning of the ensuing period. This is an optional procedure and may be adopted or not, as the bookkeeper prefers. The steps in balancing an account are as follows (see Cash):

(1) Add the balance of the account to the smaller side. To indicate that this amount is not posted from a book of original entry, write the word "Balance" in the items column and place a check mark in the posting reference column.

(2) Record the totals of the two sides, which are now equal, on the same line.

(3) Rule the account as if it had been closed.

(4) Bring down the balance of the account on the side that was originally the larger. To show that this amount is the balance brought down from above and is not a new entry, write the word "Balance" in the items column and place a check mark in the posting reference column. Date the balance as of the first day of the following month.

For accounts with only one entry (see Salaries Payable) there is no need for formal ruling and balancing. Some bookkeepers also prefer to omit ruling and balancing accounts with entries on one side of the account only (see Repair Equipment).

Cash

ACCOUNT NO. 11

DATE		ITEMS	POST. REF.	DEBIT	DATE		ITEMS	POST. REF.	CREDIT
1953					1953				
Nov.	2		1	9 0 0 0 0	Nov.	2		1	3 7 5 0 0
	4		1	2 2 5 0 0		6		1	3 0 0 0
	16		1	5 2 0 0 0		10		1	4 0 0 0 0
	30	625.00	2	8 5 0 0 0		14		1	1 8 0 0 0
						17		1	2 5 0 0 0
						19		2	2 0 0 0
						28		2	1 8 0 0 0
						30		2	1 0 0 0
						30		2	2 5 0 0
						30		2	4 0 0 0 0
						30	Balance	✓	6 2 5 0 0
				2 4 9 5 0 0					2 4 9 5 0 0
1953									
Dec.	1	Balance	✓	6 2 5 0 0					

Accounts Receivable

ACCOUNT NO. 12

DATE		ITEMS	POST. REF.	DEBIT	DATE		ITEMS	POST. REF.	CREDIT
1953					1953				
Nov.	2	175.00	1	4 0 0 0 0	Nov.	4		1	2 2 5 0 0
						30	Balance	✓	1 7 5 0 0
				4 0 0 0 0					4 0 0 0 0
1953									
Dec.	1	Balance	✓	1 7 5 0 0					

Supplies

ACCOUNT NO. 14

DATE		ITEMS	POST. REF.	DEBIT	DATE		ITEMS	POST. REF.	CREDIT
1953					1953				
Nov.	2		1	5 0 0 0 0	Nov.	30		2	2 9 0 0 0
	17		1	2 5 0 0 0		30	Balance	✓	4 6 0 0 0
				7 5 0 0 0					7 5 0 0 0
1953									
Dec.	1	Balance	✓	4 6 0 0 0					

Prepaid Rent

ACCOUNT NO. 15

DATE		ITEMS	POST. REF.	DEBIT	DATE		ITEMS	POST. REF.	CREDIT
1953					1953				
Nov.	2		1	3 7 5 0 0	Nov.	30		2	1 2 5 0 0
						30	Balance	✓	2 5 0 0 0
				3 7 5 0 0					3 7 5 0 0
1953									
Dec.	1	Balance	✓	2 5 0 0 0					

**Ledger After the Accounts Have Been Adjusted, Closed,
Balanced, and Ruled**

Repair Equipment   ACCOUNT NO. 18

DATE	ITEMS	POST. REF.	DEBIT	DATE	ITEMS	POST. REF.	CREDIT
1953 Nov. 2		1	1 600 00				
3		1	1 400 00				

Accounts Payable   ACCOUNT NO. 21

DATE	ITEMS	POST. REF.	DEBIT	DATE	ITEMS	POST. REF.	CREDIT
1953 Nov. 10		1	400 00	1953 Nov. 3	1000.00	1	1 400 00
30	Balance	✓	1 000 00				
			1 400 00				1 400 00
				1953 Dec. 1	Balance	✓	1 000 00

Salaries Payable   ACCOUNT NO. 22

DATE	ITEMS	POST. REF.	DEBIT	DATE	ITEMS	POST. REF.	CREDIT
				1953 Nov. 30		2	15 00

Robert Moore, Capital   ACCOUNT NO. 31

DATE	ITEMS	POST. REF.	DEBIT	DATE	ITEMS	POST. REF.	CREDIT
1953 Nov. 30	Balance	✓	3 495 00	1953 Nov. 2		1	3 400 00
				30		3	95 00
			3 495 00				3 495 00
				1953 Dec. 1	Balance	✓	3 495 00

Robert Moore, Drawing   ACCOUNT NO. 32

DATE	ITEMS	POST. REF.	DEBIT	DATE	ITEMS	POST. REF.	CREDIT
1953 Nov. 30		2	400 00	1953 Nov. 30		3	495 00
30		3	95 00				
			495 00				495 00

**Ledger After the Accounts Have Been Adjusted, Closed,
Balanced, and Ruled — Continued**

Profit and Loss Summary
ACCOUNT NO. 33

DATE	ITEMS	POST. REF.	DEBIT	DATE	ITEMS	POST. REF.	CREDIT
1953 Nov. 30		3	875 00	1953 Nov. 30		3	1370 00
30		3	495 00				
			1370 00				1370 00

Sales
ACCOUNT NO. 41

DATE	ITEMS	POST. REF.	DEBIT	DATE	ITEMS	POST. REF.	CREDIT
1953 Nov. 30		3	1370 00	1953 Nov. 16		1	520 00
				30		2	850 00
			1370 00				1370 00

Salary Expense
ACCOUNT NO. 51

DATE	ITEMS	POST. REF.	DEBIT	DATE	ITEMS	POST. REF.	CREDIT
1953 Nov. 14		1	180 00	1953 Nov. 30		3	375 00
28		2	180 00				
30		2	15 00				
			375 00				375 00

Supplies Expense
ACCOUNT NO. 52

DATE	ITEMS	POST. REF.	DEBIT	DATE	ITEMS	POST. REF.	CREDIT
1953 Nov. 30		2	290 00	1953 Nov. 30		3	290 00

Rent Expense
ACCOUNT NO. 53

DATE	ITEMS	POST. REF.	DEBIT	DATE	ITEMS	POST. REF.	CREDIT
1953 Nov. 30		2	125 00	1953 Nov. 30		3	125 00

Miscellaneous Expense
ACCOUNT NO. 59

DATE	ITEMS	POST. REF.	DEBIT	DATE	ITEMS	POST. REF.	CREDIT
1953 Nov. 6		1	30 00	1953 Nov. 30		3	85 00
19		2	20 00				
30		2	10 00				
30		2	25 00				
			85 00				85 00

**Ledger After the Accounts Have Been Adjusted, Closed,
Balanced, and Ruled — Concluded**

THE POST-CLOSING   The ledger of Reliable Repair Shop has now
TRIAL BALANCE   been adjusted, the temporary proprietorship
accounts have been closed, and the accounts have been ruled. The
proprietor's drawing account, the profit and loss summary account,
and all income and expense accounts have been closed. The amounts
in these closed accounts will not be used in future financial statements. The balances of the accounts remaining open represent assets,
liabilities, and the proprietor's capital. A post-closing trial balance of
the open accounts is prepared at this point to make certain that the
ledger is in balance and ready for the entries of the new fiscal period.
This post-closing trial balance appears below:

Reliable Repair Shop Post-Closing Trial Balance November 30, 1953			
Cash	11	6 2 5 0 0	
Accounts Receivable	12	1 7 5 0 0	
Supplies	14	4 6 0 0 0	
Prepaid Rent	15	2 5 0 0 0	
Repair Equipment	18	3 0 0 0 0 0	
Accounts Payable	21		1 0 0 0 0 0
Salaries Payable	22		1 5 0 0
Robert Moore, Capital	31		3 4 9 5 0 0
		4 5 1 0 0 0	4 5 1 0 0 0

Post-Closing Trial Balance

The accounts and the amounts shown on the post-closing trial
balance are the same as those appearing on the balance sheet. By
means of the closing process, all temporary accounts have been consolidated with the capital account.

THE BOOKKEEPING   In this and the preceding chapter the se-
CYCLE   quence of bookkeeping procedures has been
presented. The sequence of procedures is frequently referred to as
the *bookkeeping cycle* or the *accounting cycle*. It begins with the journalizing of transactions and ends with the post-closing trial balance.
The accounting techniques employed in the various stages of the cycle
will be developed further in subsequent chapters. Although there are
many variations in method, the basic outline of the cycle is a fundamental part of accounting practice.

An appreciation of the steps in the accounting cycle is necessary as
a foundation for further study of accounting principles. The following
outline presents the cycle in terms of eight distinct steps:

1. Journalizing.	Recording transactions in the journal.
2. Posting.	Transferring the entries in the journal to the ledger.
3. Taking a trial balance.	Summarizing the ledger accounts.
4. Determining the necessary adjustments.	Calculating accounting information not recorded currently.
5. Preparing the work sheet.	Classifying information on columnar paper.
6. Preparing the accounting statements.	Preparing the profit and loss statement and the balance sheet from the work sheet.
7. Adjusting and closing the books.	Recording the adjusting and closing entries in the journal and posting them to the ledger; closing, ruling, and balancing the accounts.
8. Taking a post-closing trial balance.	Proving the accuracy of closing the books.

INTERIM STATEMENTS   In the illustrative case of Reliable Repair Shop the accounting cycle was completed in one month. Most business enterprises close their books once a year rather than at the end of each month. Regardless of the length of the period, the procedures for closing the books are the same. A period of a month was used in the illustration in order to keep the number of transactions and the physical space requirements to a minimum.

When the books are closed annually, only the first three steps of the accounting cycle need to be repeated each month. The completion of posting and the preparation of a trial balance at the end of each month is customary regardless of when the books are closed. If *interim* financial statements are to be prepared monthly, Steps 4, 5, and 6 of the accounting cycle must also be completed monthly. These three steps involve the determination of the necessary adjustments, the preparation of the work sheet, and the preparation of the statements.

If the books are not closed each time the statements are prepared, the income and expense data for the interim profit and loss statements will be cumulative. For example, assuming a fiscal year that begins on January 1, the amounts in the profit and loss statement columns of the February work sheet will be the cumulative totals for January and February; the income and expenses on the March work sheet will be the cumulative totals for January, February, and March; and so on. Monthly profit and loss statements may be prepared, however, by determining the difference in the various income and expense items on successive cumulative statements. Thus total sales for the three-month period ended March 31, minus sales for the two-month period ended February 28, yields the sales figure for March. In this way both cumulative and monthly profit and loss statements may be prepared in less time than if the temporary proprietorship accounts were closed each month.

QUESTIONS

1. Expenses are sometimes referred to as "expired assets." Explain this concept by the use of two examples taken from this chapter.

2. Assume that a business pays salaries on Friday for the five-day week ending on Friday. If office salaries total $1,000 weekly, give in general journal form the adjusting entry that would be needed if the fiscal period ended on (a) Monday, (b) Tuesday, (c) Thursday.

3. Give the adjustments indicated by the following information:

	SUPPLIES	PREPAID RENT	PREPAID INSURANCE	SALES SALARY EXPENSE	OFFICE SALARY EXPENSE
Balance, September 1...	$250		$360		
September transactions.	170	$600	205	$600	$300
On hand, September 30.	200	450	490		
Unpaid, September 30..				150	75

4. On April 1, A. M. Stark pays the rent on his store building for the month of April. (a) At the time of payment does he acquire an asset or is he paying an expense? (b) What account should be debited at the time the rent is paid? Explain.

5. William Owens prepares statements at the end of each month but does not adjust and close the accounts until December 31, the end of the fiscal year. In preparing statements at the end of June, he overlooked the fact that he owed salaries of $400 for the last two days of the month. (a) What effect did this error have on the profit reported for the six-month period? (b) What items on his balance sheet for June 30 are overstated or understated?

6. Which of the following accounts should be closed to Profit and Loss Summary at the end of the fiscal year: (a) Advertising Expense, (b) Cash, (c) Insurance Expense, (d) Notes Payable, (e) Office Supplies, (f) Prepaid Rent, (g) Sales, (h) Store Supplies Expense, (i) Taxes Expense.

7. After the income and expense accounts have been closed at the end of the fiscal year, the profit and loss summary, drawing, and capital accounts of Robert Mosley appear as follows:

ROBERT MOSLEY, CAPITAL		ROBERT MOSLEY, DRAWING	
	Jan. 1 29,600	June 30 3,000	
		Dec. 15 4,000	

PROFIT AND LOSS SUMMARY	
Dec. 31 47,100	Dec. 31 59,300

Journalize the following entries: (a) the entry to close the profit and loss summary account to the drawing account, (b) the entry to close the drawing account to the capital account.

8. How can monthly profit and loss statements be prepared if the books are closed only at the end of the year?

PROBLEMS

6-1. The Beeler Automatic Laundry closes its books at the end of each month. Its trial balance on May 31 of the current year was as follows:

BEELER AUTOMATIC LAUNDRY
TRIAL BALANCE
MAY 31, 19 --

Cash	11	$2,190	
Laundry Supplies	14	270	
Prepaid Rent	15	360	
Laundry Equipment	17	3,650	
Accounts Payable	21		$ 460
G. M. Beeler, Capital	31		5,340
G. M. Beeler, Drawing	32	350	
Sales	41		1,960
Salary Expense	51	450	
Miscellaneous General Expense	55	490	
		$7,760	$7,760

Data for end-of-month adjustments were as follows:

Accrued salary expense........... $65
Laundry supplies on hand......... 40
Rent expense for the month....... 90

Instructions: (1) Record the trial balance on a ten-column work sheet.
(2) Complete the work sheet for the month of May.
(3) Prepare a profit and loss statement and a balance sheet in report form.
(4) Record the adjusting entries in a general journal.
(5) Record the closing entries, closing the profit to the drawing account and the drawing account to the capital account.

6-2. The accounts and their balances in the ledger of Martha's Beauty Shoppe on December 31, the end of the current fiscal year, were as follows:

11 Cash	$2,026.65	33 Profit and Loss Summary	$ ......
12 Beauty Supplies	923.18		
13 Office Supplies	85.26	41 Sales	19,653.00
14 Prepaid Insurance	258.50	51 Salary Expense	7,421.00
17 Beauty Equipment	6,250.00	52 Beauty Supplies Expense	......
18 Furniture	1,020.60		
21 Notes Payable	1,500.00	53 Rent Expense	1,200.00
22 Accounts Payable	392.35	54 Utilities Expense	439.43
23 Salaries Payable	......	55 Advertising Expense	361.27
24 Rent Payable	......	56 Insurance Expense	......
31 Martha Mills, Capital	4,736.69	57 Office Supplies Expense	......
32 Martha Mills, Drawing	6,000.00	58 Miscellaneous Expense	296.15

The data for the adjustments on December 31 were as follows:

(a) Inventory of beauty supplies........ $110.50
(b) Inventory of office supplies.......... $ 25.00
(c) Insurance expired.................. $143.20
(d) Salaries payable................... $ 98.00
(e) The lease provides for a rental of 7% of total sales for the year with a minimum of $100 per month, payable monthly.

Instructions: (1) Open an account in the ledger for each account listed. Enter the balances in the appropriate accounts under date of December 31.

(2) Prepare a ten-column work sheet for the year ended December 31.

(3) Prepare a profit and loss statement, a balance sheet in report form, and a statement of proprietor's capital.

(4) Record the adjusting entries in a general journal and post to the ledger accounts.

(5) Record the closing entries and post to the ledger accounts.

(6) Balance and rule the accounts having more than one entry.

(7) Prepare a post-closing trial balance.

If the workbook correlating with this textbook is not used, omit Problem 6-3 or use in its stead Problem 6-A from the supplementary problems in Appendix C.

6-3. John L. Sanders owns and operates the Sanders Repair Service. The ledger after all transactions for June of the current year have been posted is presented in the workbook.

Instructions: (1) Take a trial balance of the ledger as of June 30, using the trial balance columns of a ten-column work sheet.

(2) Complete the ten-column work sheet for the month ended June 30. The data for the adjustments at the end of this month are:

Supplies on hand, $427.00
Insurance expired, $14.85
Salaries payable, $20.00

(3) Prepare a profit and loss statement and a balance sheet in report form.

(4) Record the adjusting and the closing entries in the general journal and post to the ledger.

(5) Rule the temporary accounts. Balance and rule the asset, liability, and proprietorship accounts that contain more than one entry.

(6) Take a post-closing trial balance.

Chapter 7

Accounting for Sales

MERCHANDISING The development of the accounting cycle in preceding chapters has been based on the personal service type of business enterprise. Another type of business activity is that of buying and selling goods, which is known as *merchandising*. In this and succeeding chapters, the accounting cycle will be developed in terms of a merchandising or trading business. Although there are differences between the service type and the merchandising type of business, there are also many obvious similarities. Therefore, many of the accounting techniques to be described in succeeding chapters are applicable to both types of business activity.

Merchandising activities may ordinarily be classified as *retail* or *wholesale*. The retail merchant sells goods to the consumer at retail prices. He may purchase his merchandise directly from the manufacturer or producer, or he may buy from wholesalers, brokers, or other middlemen at wholesale prices. The wholesale merchant sells merchandise to retailers and large consumers. His sources of supply are usually manufacturers, producers, or importers.

We have seen that the principal income account of personal service businesses may be given various titles, such as Fees, Commissions, Service Sales, and Sales. In merchandising enterprises, the account is usually called Sales.

NEED FOR ADDITIONAL JOURNALS All the transactions of a business may be recorded in a single journal, as was demonstrated in Chapter 5. The modification of the two-column journal by adding special columns for cash receipts and cash payments was suggestive of the many variations possible. The recording process and the posting process may be further simplified by the addition of other special columns, such as Accounts Receivable Debit and Sales Credit. But the use of one journal with a number of special columns is not satisfactory for all businesses. In a large business a number of people must record transactions, and all cannot satisfactorily use the same journal.

The customary practice is to classify the transactions of the business according to their nature and to employ special journals for recording the particular classes that occur most frequently. For example, if sales on account are numerous, it is advantageous to use a special journal designed to record this particular type of transaction. On the other hand, if notes payable are issued to creditors only infrequently, no advantage would be derived from using a special journal designed for such transactions.

The number, purpose, and design of the special journals used will of necessity vary, depending upon the needs of the particular enterprise. In the typical merchandising business of moderate size, the transactions that occur most frequently and the special journals employed are as follows:

NATURE OF TRANSACTIONS	SPECIAL JOURNAL
Sales on account	Sales Journal
Purchases on account	Purchases Journal
Cash receipts	Cash Receipts Journal
Cash payments	Cash Payments Journal

Although most of the transactions of the typical business may be recorded in the foregoing special journals, there will always be some transactions that can be recorded only in a general journal.

IMPORTANCE OF SALES The principal income of a business appears as the first item on the profit and loss statement. This principal income is usually designated as Sales, although in some businesses it may be referred to by some other name, such as Commissions or Fees. The amount of sales is an indication of the effectiveness of the enterprise in meeting the needs of its customers. The figure is commonly quoted in business news articles. It is frequently compared with sales of a preceding period. An increase in the volume of sales is ordinarily a good omen and indicates a favorable trend in the fortunes of a business.

The number of sales transactions to be recorded in any business is perhaps largest next to the number of cash transactions. Cash sales are commonly recorded on a cash register and only the total for the day is entered in a journal. Since cash sales involve not only a credit to Sales but also a debit to Cash, it is customary to record them in the cash receipts journal, which is described in a later chapter. In this chapter emphasis will be placed on the recording of sales *on account*.

TRADE DISCOUNTS Manufacturers and wholesalers of certain types of commodities frequently grant substantial reductions from the *list price* quoted in their catalogs. Such reductions in price are called *trade discounts*. Trade discounts are a convenient method of making revisions in prices without the necessity of reprinting catalogs. As prices fluctuate, new schedules of discounts may be issued. Trade discounts may also be used to make price differentials among different classes of customers. For example, the schedule of discounts issued by a manufacturer to wholesalers may differ from that supplied to retailers.

Trade discounts are not recorded in the books of account. For accounting purposes it is the actual price, that is, the list price minus the trade discount, that is significant. For example, the seller of an article listed at $100 with a trade discount of $40 would record the transaction as a sale of $60. Similarly, the buyer would record the cost as $60. Since trade discounts are not recorded in the books of account, they are mentioned here merely to distinguish between them and the cash discounts discussed in later paragraphs.

CREDIT TERMS   The arrangements agreed upon by the seller and the buyer as to payments for merchandise are called the *credit terms*. Payment may be required immediately, in which case the terms are said to be "cash" or "net cash," or the buyer may be allowed a period of time, known as the *credit period*, in which to pay. Credit transactions are numerous in the conduct of business because they tend to increase the total volume of business of the community. The granting of credit also makes payment more convenient for the buyer.

There is considerable variation in credit periods among different types of merchandising activities. Terms may also vary in accordance with the reputation of and the past relations with the particular customer. Retailers frequently require payment by the tenth of the month for all purchases made during the preceding month. They sometimes stipulate that purchases made after the twenty-fifth of the month will not be included in the billing for that month but will be carried over to the succeeding month.

Among manufacturers and wholesalers it is usual for the credit period to begin with the date of the sale as evidenced by the date of the invoice. The credit period may extend to the end of the month in which the goods are sold, 30 days from the date of sale, 60 days from such date, or whatever period of time has become the prevailing practice. If the goods are of a type that tend to be resold within a short time, the credit period is usually short; for slower-moving goods the credit period may be longer.

The expression "n/30," which is read net 30 days, means that payment is to be made in 30 days; "n/60," that payment is to be made in 60 days. To encourage payment before the expiration of the credit period, creditors have developed the practice of offering a special inducement in the form of a cash discount for early payment. Thus, the expression "2/10, n/60" means that, while the credit period is 60 days, the debtor may deduct 2% of the amount of the bill if payment is made in 10 days. This deduction is known as a *cash discount*.

For example, assume a sales invoice totaling $1,000 dated April 15, with credit terms of 2/10, n/30. If the buyer mails his check on or before April 25, he may deduct $20 from the invoice and pay $980. If he wishes to wait the full credit term, payment of the full amount should be made on or before May 15. From the seller's point of view, cash discounts are known as *sales discounts;* the purchaser refers to them as *purchases discounts*.

If the terms of sale call for payment in the following month, incentive for early payment may be expressed "2/10 eom." This means that if the bill is paid during the first ten days following the end of the month (eom), the purchaser is entitled to a 2% cash discount. This cash discount is designed to fit the practices of buyers who wish to accumulate the bills of a month and make payment early in the following month. Payments tend to be concentrated in the first ten days of the month instead of being spread throughout the month.

ACCOUNTING FOR SALES DISCOUNTS   Sales on account are recorded at the full price, no accounting consideration being given to the amount of the cash discount at the time of the sale. The discount allowed to a customer for early payment is recorded at the time payment is received, the amount of the discount being treated as an expense. For example, assume that on April 5 William Gordon, proprietor of Gordon Electric Appliances, sells goods to C. V. Andrews for $450, with terms of 2/10, n/30. The transaction results in an increase in Accounts Receivable and an increase in Sales of $450.

Continuing with the illustration, assume that Andrews pays the account within 10 days, entitling him to a discount of $9. Gordon Electric Appliances will accept $441 in full satisfaction of their $450 claim. Thus, Cash is increased $441, Sales Discount (an expense) is increased $9, and Accounts Receivable is decreased $450.

SELLING OPERATIONS   Every sale is made in response to an order received from a customer. An order given a retail store is usually oral; an order given a manufacturing, a wholesale, or a mail-order business is ordinarily written. There are many methods of handling orders and of recording sales, the routines varying with the type and the size of the business.

In a retail business a *sales ticket* is usually prepared for a sale on account.   This sales ticket is made in duplicate or triplicate.   One copy is given to the customer, one copy is sent to the accounting department for use as the basis of an entry in the sales record, and one copy may be used as the salesman's personal record of his sales or for other purposes as the organization of the business requires.

In a manufacturing, a wholesale, or a mail-order business a written order is received from a customer or from the salesman who obtained the order from the customer.   After the order has been approved by the credit department, it is sent to the billing department, where the invoice is prepared.   At least two copies of a *sales invoice* are made by the billing department.   The original is sent to the customer, and the carbon copy is sent to the accounting department for use as the basis of an entry in the sales record.   Sometimes additional copies of the invoice are made for the use of different departments of the business.   For example, the credit department may desire a copy for use in following up the payment of the invoice, or the shipping department may need a copy as authorization to pack and ship the goods.

One of the sales invoices used by Gordon Electric Appliances is illustrated below:

GORDON ELECTRIC APPLIANCES No. 848.		
WILLIAM GORDON		
1042 RACE STREET • CINCINNATI 2, OHIO		

SOLD TO	Ernest H. Adams	**DATE**	June 1, 1953
	214 Champlain		
	Cincinnati 7, Ohio	**TERMS**	2/10, n/30
		SHIPPED VIA	Express Collect

1 Table Lamp, Model 487J	24.00
1 Floor Lamp, Model 987K	67.50
1 Electric Stove, Model 345J	328.50
1 Exhaust Fan, Model 293	89.00
	509.00

Sales Invoice

THE SALES JOURNAL   A simple form of sales journal is illustrated on page 112.   The use of the columns is, in the main, apparent.   The column headed "Sale No." is used to record the number of each sales invoice (or sales ticket).   The information given on a sales invoice ordinarily includes the description, the quantity,

SALES JOURNAL   PAGE 47

DATE	SALE NO.	ACCOUNT DEBITED	POST. REF.	AMOUNT
1953				
June 1	848	Ernest H. Adams	✓	509 00
3	849	Dorothy L. Case	✓	624 00
5	850	Rogers Restaurant	✓	1 305 00
9	851	George D. Porter	✓	392 00
10	852	Dover Hotel	✓	850 00
17	853	Orchid Beauty School	✓	995 00
23	854	Albert T. Shaw	✓	432 00
26	855	Albert T. Shaw	✓	370 00
29	856	George D. Porter	✓	1 788 00
30		Accounts Rec. Dr — Sales Cr.	113/411	7 265 00

Sales Journal After Posting

and the price of the goods sold. One of the copies of the invoice is used as the basis for the entry in the sales journal, after which it is filed. The number entered in the Sale No. column facilitates future reference to the invoice if the need arises.

The terms of the sale are stated on each invoice for the customer's information. If credit terms vary among classes of customers, an additional column for terms could be inserted in the sales journal and the information posted to the customers' accounts. Gordon Electric Appliances grants uniform terms of 2/10, n/30; hence there is no need to record credit terms in the accounts.

The sales journal, which may also be referred to as the *sales book,* the *sales register,* or the *sales record,* is used solely for recording sales of merchandise on account. Sales of merchandise for cash are recorded in the cash receipts journal, which is discussed in Chapter 9. A sale of a fixed asset or any other asset not a part of the stock in trade is recorded in the cash receipts journal or the general journal; under no circumstances should it be recorded in the sales journal. Each entry in the sales journal is a debit to Accounts Receivable and a credit to Sales.

POSTING THE TOTAL OF THE SALES JOURNAL   The sales on account for Gordon Electric Appliances for the month of June total $7,265, as shown by the sales journal on this page. As indicated by the posting instructions written at the left of the total, the accounts receivable account is debited and the sales account is credited for $7,265. The two accounts appear as follows after posting:

Accounts Receivable

ACCOUNT NO. 113

DATE	ITEMS	POST. REF.	DEBIT	DATE	ITEMS	POST. REF.	CREDIT
1953 June 1	Balance	✓	6 3 7 5 0 0	1953 June 29		J21	7 5 0 0
30		S47	7 2 6 5 0 0				

Sales

ACCOUNT NO. 411

DATE	ITEMS	POST. REF.	DEBIT	DATE	ITEMS	POST. REF.	CREDIT
				1953 June 1	Balance	✓	6 5 3 4 0 0 0
				30		S47	7 2 6 5 0 0

Accounts Receivable and Sales Accounts in the General Ledger

The credit of June 29 to the accounts receivable account is posted from the general journal. This transaction will be discussed later in this chapter.

When two or more journals are used, the posting references in the accounts must identify the particular journal as well as the page number. Thus, the reference "S47" in the posting reference column of the accounts receivable and sales accounts above means "sales journal, page 47." In the sales journal the number of the two accounts to which the postings have been made are written in the posting reference column, separated by a diagonal line.

CONTROLLING ACCOUNTS AND SUBSIDIARY LEDGERS The accounts receivable account records the total amount owed by customers, but it does not reveal the identity of the individual debtors or the amounts owed by each. It is obvious that such details must be recorded. This is customarily done by maintaining a separate account for each debtor to which details of the transactions with that debtor are posted. These individual accounts are kept in a separate ledger, known as the *accounts receivable ledger*.

The ledger containing the balance sheet accounts and the profit and loss statement accounts is known as the *general ledger*. A ledger used for recording the details of a particular account in the general ledger is called a *subsidiary ledger*. The particular account in the general ledger that is supported by a subsidiary ledger is called a *controlling account*.

As applied to the accounting system of Gordon Electric Appliances, the accounts receivable account in the general ledger is a *controlling account*, and the accounts receivable ledger is the related *subsidiary ledger*.

POSTING TO THE   Each item in the sales journal is posted to the
SUBSIDIARY LEDGER   debit of the appropriate account in the
accounts receivable ledger. The postings are made daily so that the
status of all debtors' accounts can be readily determined at all times.
The three-column ledger form used by Gordon Electric Appliances (see
below) is designed to show the balance of the account after each posting. The posting reference placed in the subsidiary accounts is "S"
followed by the page number of the sales journal.

The customers' accounts are ordinarily arranged alphabetically in
a loose-leaf ledger, new accounts being inserted at the proper point.
There is no need to assign numbers to the accounts. As the final step
in posting an item, a check mark ($\sqrt{}$) is placed in the posting reference
column of the sales journal to signify that the account has been posted.

The accounts receivable ledger of Gordon Electric Appliances after
the sales journal has been posted for June appears below and on page
115. It shows the balances at the beginning of the month and the items
posted from the sales journal during the month.

NAME   Ernest H. Adams
ADDRESS   214 Champlain Ave., Cheviot, Ohio

DATE	ITEMS	POST. REF.	DEBIT	CREDIT	BALANCE
1953 May 27		S46	1000 00		1000 00
June 1		S47	509 00		1509 00

NAME   Dorothy L. Case
ADDRESS   747 Barr St., Cincinnati 6, Ohio

DATE	ITEMS	POST. REF.	DEBIT	CREDIT	BALANCE
1953 June 3		S47	624 00		624 00

NAME   Dover Hotel
ADDRESS   2435 Jefferson Ave., Cincinnati 3, Ohio

DATE	ITEMS	POST. REF.	DEBIT	CREDIT	BALANCE
1953 May 29		S46	3600 00		3600 00
June 10		S47	850 00		4450 00

Accounts Receivable Ledger

NAME　S. V. Morton
ADDRESS　143 S. Columbia Ave., Ft. Thomas, Ky.

DATE	ITEMS	POST. REF.	DEBIT	CREDIT	BALANCE
1953 Apr. 24		S45	850 00		850 00

NAME　Orchid Beauty School
ADDRESS　Neave Bldg., Cincinnati 2, Ohio

DATE	ITEMS	POST. REF.	DEBIT	CREDIT	BALANCE
1953 May 19		S46	450 00		450 00
June 17		S47	995 00		1445 00

NAME　George D. Porter
ADDRESS　2131 Lysle Road, Norwood, Ohio

DATE	ITEMS	POST. REF.	DEBIT	CREDIT	BALANCE
1953 June 9		S47	392 00		392 00
29		S47	1788 00		2180 00

NAME　Rogers Restaurant
ADDRESS　681 Kenwood Drive, Deer Park, Ohio

DATE	ITEMS	POST. REF.	DEBIT	CREDIT	BALANCE
1953 June 5		S47	1305 00		1305 00

NAME　Albert T. Shaw
ADDRESS　3744 Observatory St., Cincinnati 9, Ohio

DATE	ITEMS	POST. REF.	DEBIT	CREDIT	BALANCE
1953 June 23		S47	432 00		432 00
26		S47	370 00		802 00

NAME　John B. Wright
ADDRESS　42 Drake Ave., Cincinnati 7, Ohio

DATE	ITEMS	POST. REF.	DEBIT	CREDIT	BALANCE
1953 May 28		S46	475 00		475 00
"					

Accounts Receivable Ledger (Concluded)]

After the posting has been completed at the end of the month, the sum of the balances of the individual accounts in the subsidiary ledger should agree with the balance of the controlling account Accounts Receivable in the general ledger. The following diagram shows this relationship and also indicates the flow of data from the sales journal into the subsidiary and general ledgers.

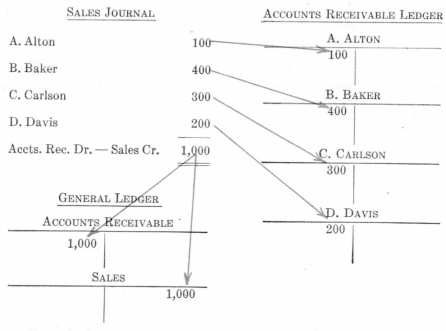

Since the balance of the accounts receivable account is equal to the sum of the balances of the accounts in the accounts receivable ledger, it is apparent that the customers' accounts might be used in the general ledger instead of the accounts receivable account. But the use of the controlling account Accounts Receivable and the subsidiary ledger is generally recommended. Having the customers' accounts in a separate ledger facilitates posting. Furthermore, the use of the controlling account removes detail from the general ledger and facilitates the preparation of the trial balance and the accounting statements.

SALES RETURNS AND ALLOWANCES   Goods sold on account may be returned by the customer or, because of defects or for other reasons, the customer may be allowed a reduction from the original price at which the goods were sold. In such cases the seller usually issues to the customer a *credit memorandum* showing the amount of the credit and the reason therefor. A typical credit memorandum is illustrated at the top of the following page.

Credit Memorandum | No. 32

GORDON ELECTRIC APPLIANCES
WILLIAM GORDON
1042 Race Street
CINCINNATI 2, OHIO

June 29, 1953

Albert T. Shaw
3744 Observatory
Cincinnati 8, Ohio

We credit your account as follows:

1   #18 Vacuum Cleaner returned   75.00

Credit Memorandum

The effect of a sales return or allowance is a reduction in sales and a reduction in accounts receivable. But if Sales is debited, the balance of that account will represent net sales and the total amount of returns and allowances will not be disclosed. It is therefore preferable to debit an account called *Sales Returns and Allowances,* as the additional information thus obtained may be of value in planning future operations. The seller must also credit the accounts receivable (controlling) account in the general ledger and the customer's account in the accounts receivable (subsidiary) ledger.

On June 29, Gordon Electric Appliances issued a credit memorandum for $75 to Albert T. Shaw, a customer, for merchandise returned. The entry could be recorded in a two-column general journal as follows:

General Journal Entry for a Sales Return

Note that both the controlling account and the customer's account are credited. A diagonal line should be placed in the posting reference column at the time the entry is recorded in the journal. It serves as an indication that the amount must be posted to both the general ledger and the subsidiary ledger. When the credit is posted to the customer's account, a check mark is placed to the right of the diagonal line. The number of the accounts receivable controlling account is entered at the left in accordance with the usual routine of posting to the general ledger. After the posting has been completed, the accounts receivable account and the customer's account appear as follows:

Accounts Receivable

ACCOUNT NO. *113*

DATE	ITEMS	POST. REF.	DEBIT	DATE	ITEMS	POST. REF.	CREDIT
1953 June 1	Balance	✓	6 3 7 5 00	*1953* June 29		J29	7 5 0 0

NAME   *Albert T. Shaw*

ADDRESS   *3744 Observatory St., Cincinnati 9, Ohio*

DATE	ITEMS	POST. REF.	DEBIT	CREDIT	BALANCE
1953 June 23		S47	432 00		432 00
26		S47	370 00		802 00
29		J29		75 00	727 00

**Accounts Receivable Account and Customer's Account
After the Posting of a Sales Return**

If sales returns and allowances are of frequent occurrence, special columns for Sales Returns and Allowances Debit and for Accounts Receivable Credit may be inserted in the general journal. The entry in such a journal for a credit given to customer John T. Murray for the return of $96 of merchandise is shown in the following illustration:

GENERAL JOURNAL

PAGE 15

SALES RET. & ALLOW. DR.	GENERAL DR.	DATE		DESCRIPTION	POST. REF.	GENERAL CR.	ACCOUNTS RECEIVABLE CR.
		1953					
96.00			19	John T. Murray	✓		96.00
547.50	1,462.20		30	Totals	✓	1,462.20	547.50
(412)	(✓)					(✓)	(112)

**Journal With Special Columns for Recording
Sales Returns and Allowances**

Each amount in the Accounts Receivable Cr. column is posted to a customer's account in the accounts receivable ledger and the posting is indicated by a check mark in the Post. Ref. column of the journal. The individual amounts in the Sales Returns and Allowances Dr. column and the Accounts Receivable Cr. column are not posted to the general ledger accounts, but only the totals of these columns are posted. Posting of the totals is indicated by the account numbers written below the totals.

Another alternative procedure is to establish a *sales returns and allowances journal* similar to the one illustrated below. The recording and posting routines for this special journal are the same as those that apply to the sales journal.

SALES RETURNS AND ALLOWANCES JOURNAL

PAGE 7

DATE		CR. MEMO. NO.	ACCOUNT CREDITED	POST. REF.	AMOUNT
1953 July	2	147	Edward Norman	√	126.00
	6	148	Wm. T. Hall	√	270.50
	29	169	Frank C. Evans	√	12.00
	31		Sales Ret. and Allow. Dr.—Accts. Rec. Cr.	412/112	1,382.95

Sales Returns and Allowances Journal

All of the alternative systems of recording sales returns and allowances that have been illustrated apply only to transactions involving credits to customers' accounts. If the return or the allowance is granted after the customer has paid for the goods, the settlement may be made by refunding cash. In such a case the transaction would be recorded in the cash payments journal.

USING SALES INVOICES AS A SALES JOURNAL
Businesses that make a large number of sales on account sometimes use duplicate copies of their sales invoices as a sales journal. Under this system, the postings to the customers' accounts are made directly from the duplicate invoices. As they are posted, the invoices are accumulated in a file or a binder. At the end of the month an adding machine listing of all the invoices is made. The total thus obtained is the basis for an entry debiting Accounts Receivable and crediting Sales. For example, if the adding machine list indicates total sales on account for the month as $18,620, the following entry would be recorded in the general journal:

July	31	Accounts Receivable..........	18,620|00	
		Sales.....................		18,620|00
		July sales on account.		

When the volume of transactions is large the use of the invoices as a journal may effect material savings in bookkeeping expenses. The need for writing the name of the customer and the amount of the sale in the sales journal is eliminated. The system also lends itself to a division of labor when there are more postings to customers' accounts than can be handled by one person. The duplicate invoices can be divided alphabetically by customers, and several persons can post to the particular group of accounts assigned to them. In addition, the elimination of the entry in the sales journal reduces the possibility of errors in recording the invoice totals.

It is apparent that this system could be used with equal effectiveness in handling sales returns and allowances. Duplicate copies of the credit memorandums would become, in effect, the sales returns and allowances journal.

QUESTIONS

1. George Collins, a wholesaler, makes a sale of merchandise having a list price of $500 and a trade discount of 40%. The credit terms are 2/10, n/30. (a) At what amount should the sale be recorded? (b) What is the amount of the cash discount allowed for payment within 10 days?

2. James Hansen, a retail hardware merchant, makes about 200 charge sales each month. His bookkeeper records the sales in a two-column general journal. If a sales journal were used, how much work would be saved (a) in recording and (b) in posting these transactions?

3. The Parker Department Store has about 400 customers that buy merchandise on account. If the customers' accounts were kept in the general ledger, how many additional items would appear in the trial balance? Name other disadvantages of keeping customers' accounts in the general ledger.

4. The following errors were made in recording transactions in the sales journal or in posting therefrom. How will each error be discovered?

    (a) A sale of $10 was recorded as $100.
    (b) A sale to Joseph A. Mills was recorded as a sale to Joseph H. Mills.
    (c) An entry of $200 was posted to the customer's account as $20.
    (d) The sales journal for the month was underfooted by $1,000.

5. As an accommodation, Robert Harrod sells some of his store supplies to a customer on account. Should this transaction be recorded in the sales journal or in the general journal?

6. The Dayton Farm Implement Co. maintains a subsidiary ledger for accounts receivable. In posting the journal entry given below, the bookkeeper failed to credit the controlling account. How will this error be brought to the attention of the bookkeeper?

    June 26   Sales Returns and Allowances...... 412   100.00
             Accounts Receivable — Samuel
               Marker.................... √   100.00

7. The Paragon Supply Co. uses carbon copies of its credit memorandums as its sales returns and allowances journal. The total of the credit memorandums for June was $965. Give the journal entry that should be made on the basis of this information.

PROBLEMS

7-1. During March of the current year Ralph Bailey, a plumbing supply merchant, completed the transactions given below. The terms of all sales were 2/10 eom.

March 1. Sold merchandise on account to George Williams, Sale No. 165, $325.

2. Sold merchandise on account to B. D. Cermak, Sale No. 166, $110.

6. Sold merchandise on account to R. G. Meyer, Sale No. 167, $400.

8. Sold merchandise on account to David Gregory, Sale No. 168, $450.

11. Issued Credit Memorandum No. 34 for $10 to B. D. Cermak for merchandise returned by him.

14. Sold merchandise on account to R. G. Meyer, Sale No. 169, $190.

16. Issued Credit Memorandum No. 35 for $60 to George Williams for merchandise returned by him.

19. Sold merchandise on account to Richard Anderson, Sale No. 170, $240.

21. Sold merchandise on account to James Sanford, Sale No. 171, $310.

22. Sold merchandise on account to B. D. Cermak, Sale No. 172, $130.

24. Issued Credit Memorandum No. 36 for $25 to Richard Anderson for damages to merchandise caused by faulty packing.

26. Sold merchandise on account to David Gregory, Sale No. 173, $55.

Instructions: (1) Record the above transactions, using a sales journal similar to the one illustrated on page 112 of the textbook and a four-column general journal similar to the one illustrated on page 118.

(2) Open the following accounts in the general ledger, using the account numbers indicated: Accounts Receivable, 112; Sales, 411; Sales Returns and Allowances, 412.

(3) Open the following accounts in the accounts receivable ledger: Richard Anderson, 2121 Lorain Ave.; B. D. Cermak, 4432 Warner Rd.; David Gregory, 330 Garfield Blvd.; R. G. Meyer, 6700 Marvin Ave.; James Sanford, 8710 Turney Rd.; George Williams, 3456 Miles Ave.

(4) Post from the two journals to the accounts receivable ledger and the general ledger.

(5) (a) What is the sum of the balances of the subsidiary accounts?

(b) What is the balance of the controlling account?

7-2. During August of the current year Edward Kirk, a furniture dealer, issued invoices and credit memorandums for the following charge sales and sales returns. The terms of all sales were 2/10 eom.

Aug. 3. Invoice No. 466, to David Ott, $400.

6. Invoice No. 467, to Robert Hayden, $325.

9. Invoice No. 468, to H. W. Beck, $150.

11. Invoice No. 469, to Herbert Clark, $682.

12. Credit Memo No. 18, to David Ott, $50.

Aug. 15. Invoice No. 470, to Herbert Clark, $320.

17. Invoice No. 471, to T. L. Jackson, $62.

19. Credit Memo No. 19, to Herbert Clark, $100.

20. Invoice No. 472, to Robert Hayden, $524.

23. Credit Memo No. 20, to T. L. Jackson, $62.

24. Invoice No. 473, to N. E. Reed, $263.

26. Invoice No. 474, to H. W. Beck, $170.

29. Invoice No. 475, to T. L. Jackson, $461.

31. Credit Memo No. 21, to N. E. Reed, $45.

Instructions: (1) Record the foregoing transactions in a sales journal and a sales returns and allowances journal similar to the ones illustrated on pages 112 and 119.

(2) Open the following accounts in the general ledger, and enter the following balances as of August 1:

112	Accounts Receivable	$ 1,420
411	Sales	35,625
412	Sales Returns and Allowances	1,692

(3) Open the following accounts in the accounts receivable ledger and enter the balances in the balance columns, as of August 1: H. W. Beck, 914 Euclid Ave., $400; Herbert Clark, 4774 Lee Rd.; Robert Hayden, 9300 Carnegie Ave.; T. L. Jackson, 207 Superior Ave., $350; David Ott, 347 Clifton Blvd.; N. E. Reed, 565 Union Ave., $670.

(4) Post from the two journals to the accounts receivable ledger and the general ledger.

(5) Submit answers to the following questions:

(a) What is the total amount due from customers on August 31, determined by adding the balances in the subsidiary ledger?

(b) What is the balance of the accounts receivable account in the general ledger on August 31?

(c) How much will David Ott need to pay to discharge his obligation within the discount period?

Chapter 8

Accounting for Purchases

PURCHASING PROCEDURES The procedures followed in purchasing activities vary greatly among business firms. In a small retail store the proprietor may do all of the buying, in many cases placing orders with salesmen or by telephone. Large concerns may maintain a purchasing department that is responsible for determining best sources of supply, investigating quality, knowing market prices and their likely trends, placing orders, and doing all other things necessary to assure the efficient operation of all buying activities.

To avoid misunderstanding, all orders for merchandise, equipment, supplies, or other goods should be in writing. The order may be written on a form supplied by the vendor, or the buyer may use his own *purchase order* blank. A purchase order of Gordon Electric Appliances issued to Universal Electric Company is illustrated below.

PURCHASE ORDER

GORDON ELECTRIC APPLIANCES
WILLIAM GORDON

1042 Race Street
CINCINNATI 2, OHIO

MARK ORDER No. ON INVOICE
AND ON ALL PACKAGES

Order No. 693

Universal Electric Company
405 Murray Street
Chicago 15, Illinois

Date   June 4, 1953

Terms   2/10, n/30

Ship Via   Mid-West Trucking Co.

PLEASE ENTER OUR ORDER FOR THE FOLLOWING:

QUANTITY	DESCRIPTION	PRICE
2	R49 Refrigerators	275.25
5	F14 Fans	32.50
6	L37 Floor Lamps	25.00
3	DH1 Dehumidifiers	95.00

DELIVER NO GOODS WITHOUT A WRITTEN ORDER ON THIS FORM

GORDON ELECTRIC APPLIANCES

By _William Gordon_

Purchase Order

The original of the purchase order is sent to the supplier; it is his authorization to deliver the items listed at the prices specified. A duplicate copy of the order is retained by Gordon Electric Appliances as evidence of what was ordered and of the other terms stipulated.

The vendor usually mails an invoice to the buyer at about the time the goods are shipped. From the viewpoint of the seller, the invoice is a sales invoice; the buyer refers to it as a purchase invoice. An invoice should contain the names and the addresses of both the buyer and the seller; the date of the transaction; the terms; the method of shipment; and the quantities, descriptions, and prices of the goods. Additional information may be given. The invoice received from Universal Electric Company in response to the purchase order of Gordon Electric Appliances is shown below:

UNIVERSAL ELECTRIC COMPANY		FOR CUSTOMER'S USE ONLY	
UNIVERSAL ELECTRIC COMPANY 405 Murray Street **CHICAGO 15, ILLINOIS**		Register No.	Voucher No.
		F. O. B. Checked	
Customer's Order No. & Date 693	Refer to Invoice No. 1149-15	Terms Approved	Price Approved *Th.F.*
Requisition No.		Calculations Checked *C.R.S.*	
Contract No.	Invoice Date June 11, 1953	Transportation	
	Vendor's Nos.	Freight Bill No. Amount	
SOLD Gordon Electric Appliances TO 1042 Race Street Cincinnati 2, Ohio		Material Received *6/13* 19*53* *mas.* *Rec. Cl.* Date Signature Title	
Shipped to and Same Destination		Satisfactory and Approved	
Date Shipped June 11, 1953 From Chicago		Adjustments	
Car Initials and No. F. O. B.	Prepaid or Collect? Prepaid	Accounting Distribution	
How Shipped and Route Mid-West Trucking Co.		Audited *GHC*	Final Approval *WF.*
Terms 2/10, n/30			

QUANTITY	DESCRIPTION	UNIT PRICE	AMOUNT
2 ✓	R49 Refrigerators	275.25 ✓	550.50 ✓
5 ✓	F14 Fans	32.50 ✓	162.50 ✓
6 ✓	L37 Floor Lamps	25.00 ✓	150.00 ✓
3 ✓	DH1 Dehumidifiers	95.00 ✓	285.00 ✓
			1,148.00 ✓

Invoice

The invoice illustrated above is a standard form recommended by the National Association of Purchasing Agents. It is divided into three distinct sections: (1) upper left for miscellaneous details of the terms of the transaction; (2) lower section for quantity, description, unit price, and amount; and (3) upper right for use by the purchaser as a record that various comparisons and verifications have been made.

Before a purchase invoice is approved for payment, the following verifications should be made: (1) that the billing is in accordance with the provisions of the purchase order and (2) that the goods have been received in good condition. The invoice usually arrives in advance of the goods. Terms, quantities, prices, and other details on the invoice should be compared with the corresponding items on the copy of the purchase order. When the goods arrive they should be counted and inspected. This work is ordinarily done by the receiving department, which may check the quantities received against those indicated on the invoice or may make an independent report to the purchasing department of quantities received. In the latter case the purchasing department will compare the receiving report with the invoice.

The basis for the entry in the purchases journal is the invoice. The invoices are usually entered as they are received, without waiting for the arrival of the goods. When this is done, adjustments necessitated by errors in shipments are made later. Notification to the vendor of shortages, returns, or other adjustments may be made by letter or by *debit memorandum*. This form, illustrated below, is a convenient medium for informing the vendor of the amount that is being debited to his account on the buyer's books and the reasons therefor.

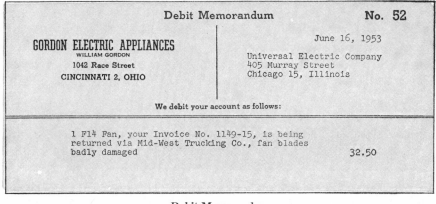

Debit Memorandum	No. 52

GORDON ELECTRIC APPLIANCES
WILLIAM GORDON
1042 Race Street
CINCINNATI 2, OHIO

June 16, 1953

Universal Electric Company
405 Murray Street
Chicago 15, Illinois

We debit your account as follows:

1 F14 Fan, your Invoice No. 1149-15, is being returned via Mid-West Trucking Co., fan blades badly damaged   32.50

Debit Memorandum

CREDIT TERMS AND PURCHASES DISCOUNTS   The credit terms available to a retail merchant ordinarily vary among his suppliers. Some may sell on a net cash basis, others will quote terms of n/30, and still others will grant a discount for payment within a specified time. The payment of accounts as they become due is an important factor in maintaining a good credit rating. When a cash discount is available, it is advantageous to make payment within the discount period, even though it is necessary to borrow money to do so. For example, assume a purchase invoice for $1,500, with terms of 2/10, n/30. The obligation could be discharged within 10 days by payment of $1,470, representing a savings of $30. In contrast, the interest expense incurred by borrowing $1,470 for the remaining 20 days of the credit period would be $4.08, assuming an interest rate of 5%. The net savings accruing to the purchaser would thus be the difference between the cash discount of $30 and the interest expense of $4.08, or $25.92.

There are various systems designed to assure that the payment dates of purchases will not be overlooked. One of the simplest is to file unpaid invoices by the dates when they require attention. The folders in the file are numbered from 1 to 31. For example, assume a purchase invoice dated June 5, with terms of 2/10, n/30. After the invoice has been processed and recorded, it is filed under "15," June 15 being the last date for taking the discount. All other invoices are filed similarly. Each day the invoices are taken from the folder corresponding to the day of the month. If an invoice is not paid at that time, it is refiled according to the date when payment should next be considered. If the June 5 invoice was not paid on June 15 it would be refiled under "5" so that it would be considered for payment on July 5.

THE MULTICOLUMN PURCHASES JOURNAL   The record of purchases is known variously as the *purchases journal*, the *purchases book*, the *purchases register*, and the *purchases record*. Sometimes *invoice* is substituted for *purchases* so that the name becomes *invoice journal*, *invoice book*, etc. A great variety of assets may be purchased by a business. Property most frequently bought by a trading concern may be classified as: (1) merchandise for resale to customers; (2) supplies for use in conducting the business, such as office supplies, store supplies, and advertising supplies; and (3) fixed assets, such as store equipment, office equipment, and delivery equipment.

PAGE 28   PURCHASES JOURNAL

	DATE OF ENTRY	DATE OF INVOICE	ACCOUNT CREDITED	POST. REF.	ACCOUNTS PAYABLE CR.	
	1953	1953				
1	June 2	June 1	American Home Appliance Co.	✓	824 00	1
2	3	2	Queen City Electrical Co.	✓	650 00	2
3	8	8	Ross Supplies, Inc.	✓	38 00	3
4	9	8	Queen City Electrical Co.	✓	358 00	4
5	11	9	Bauer Electric Corp.	✓	923 00	5
6	13	11	Universal Electric Co.	✓	1 148 00	6
7	15	12	Watson Manufacturing Co.	✓	1 110 00	7
8	16	15	Office Equipment Distributors	✓	475 00	8
9	19	17	Tri-State Television Distributors	✓	1 500 00	9
10	22	20	Watson Manufacturing Co.	✓	1 050 00	10
11	25	25	Ross Supplies, Inc.	✓	21 00	11
12	29	27	Bauer Electric Corp.	✓	1 570 00	12
13	30		Totals	✓	7 867 00	13
14					(211)	14
15						15

Columnar Purchases Journal, Left Page

Because of the variety of assets purchased, it is customary to use a multicolumn journal that will accommodate the recording of all purchases on account. The number of columns and the headings used depend to a considerable extent upon the size and the nature of the business. The form used by Gordon Electric Appliances is illustrated below.

For each transaction recorded in the purchases journal, the credit is entered in the Accounts Payable Cr. column. The next three columns are used in accumulating debits to the particular accounts most frequently affected. The Purchases Dr. column is for merchandise bought for resale. A more exact title for the column and the account to which the total is posted would be "Merchandise Purchases." It is customary, however, to refer to goods bought for resale as just "Purchases." The purpose of the Store Supplies Dr. and Office Supplies Dr. columns is readily apparent. If supplies of these two categories were bought only infrequently, the two columns could be eliminated from the purchases journal.

The final set of columns, under the principal heading General Debit, is used to record purchases on account of items not provided for in the special debit columns. The title of the particular account in the general ledger is entered in the Account column, the amount of the debit is recorded in the Amount column, and the number of the account is written in the Post. Ref. column at the time of posting.

PURCHASES·JOURNAL   PAGE 28

| | PURCHASES DR. | STORE SUPPLIES DR. | OFFICE SUPPLIES DR. | GENERAL DEBIT | | | |
				ACCOUNT	POST REF.	AMOUNT	
1	824 00						1
2	650 00						2
3		24 00	14 00				3
4	358 00						4
5	923 00						5
6	1 148 00						6
7	1 110 00						7
8				Office Equipment	122	475 00	8
9	1 500 00						9
10				Store Equipment	121	105 00	10
11		16 00	5 00				11
12	7 175 00	40 00	19 00			580 00	12
13	7 228 00	40 00	19 00			580 00	13
14	(511)	(115)	(116)			(√)	14
15							15

Columnar Purchases Journal, Right Page

CONTROLLING ACCOUNT AND SUBSIDIARY LEDGER   The necessity for maintaining a separate account for each creditor is evident. Although it would be possible to keep these accounts in the general ledger, it is ordinarily preferable to segregate them in a subsidiary ledger. The account in the general ledger that summarizes the debits and credits to the individual accounts is entitled Accounts Payable. It is a *controlling account*. The subsidiary ledger may be referred to as the *accounts payable ledger* or the *creditors' ledger*.

POSTING THE MULTICOLUMN PURCHASES JOURNAL   At frequent intervals, usually daily, throughout the month the amounts in the Accounts Payable Cr. column are posted to the creditors' accounts in the subsidiary ledger. As each posting is completed, a check mark is placed in the posting reference column of the purchases journal at the left of the item.

The three-column account form ordinarily used for the accounts payable ledger is designed to show at all times the balance owed each creditor. The accounts are arranged alphabetically so as to permit easy access. A tray or loose-leaf binder is used to facilitate the insertion of new accounts and the withdrawal of pages that have been completely filled.

As each item is posted to a creditor's account, the source of the entry is recorded in the posting reference column of the account by the letter "P" and the page number of the purchases journal. At the end of June the accounts payable ledger of Gordon Electric Appliances shows the balances at the beginning of the month and the items posted during the month. The ledger then appears as shown below and on page 129.

NAME   *American Home Appliance Co.*
ADDRESS   *1428 Lincoln Ave., Chicago 8, Ill.*

DATE	ITEMS	POST. REF.	DEBIT	CREDIT	BALANCE
1953 May 25		P27		260000	260000
June 2		P28		82400	342400

NAME   *Bauer Electric Corp.*
ADDRESS   *42-46 N. Randolph, Pittsburgh 4, Pa*

DATE	ITEMS	POST. REF.	DEBIT	CREDIT	BALANCE
1953 June 11		P28		92300	92300
29		P28		71500	163800

Accounts Payable Ledger

NAME Moore-Lucas Wholesalers
ADDRESS 3700 Third St., Columbus 2, Ohio

DATE	ITEMS	POST. REF.	DEBIT	CREDIT	BALANCE
1953 May 21		P27		175000	175000

NAME Office Equipment Distributors
ADDRESS 918 Front St., Cincinnati 2, Ohio

DATE	ITEMS	POST. REF.	DEBIT	CREDIT	BALANCE
1953 June 16		P28		47500	47500

NAME Queen City Electrical Co.
ADDRESS 213 Columbia, Cincinnati 5, Ohio

DATE	ITEMS	POST. REF.	DEBIT	CREDIT	BALANCE
1953 June 3		P28		65000	65000
9		P28		35800	100800

NAME Ross Supplies, Inc.
ADDRESS 811 N. High St., Cincinnati 3, Ohio

DATE	ITEMS	POST. REF.	DEBIT	CREDIT	BALANCE
1953 June 8		P28		3800	3800
25		P28		2100	5900

NAME Tri-State Television Distributors
ADDRESS 10231 Fortieth St., Cleveland 13, Ohio

DATE	ITEMS	POST. REF.	DEBIT	CREDIT	BALANCE
1953 May 26		P27		320000	320000
June 19		P28		150000	470000

NAME Universal Electric Company
ADDRESS 415 Murray St., Chicago 15, Ill.

DATE	ITEMS	POST. REF.	DEBIT	CREDIT	BALANCE
1953 June 13		P28		114800	114800

NAME Watson Manufacturing Co.
ADDRESS 136 Chestnut St., Dayton 6, Ohio

DATE	ITEMS	POST. REF.	DEBIT	CREDIT	BALANCE
1953 May 28		P27		52500	52500
June 15		P28		111000	163500
22		P28		10500	174000

Accounts Payable Ledger (Concluded)

At the end of the month the columnar purchases journal is totaled and ruled in the manner illustrated on pages 126 and 127. Before posting, the equality of the debits and the credits should be verified by comparing the total of all of the debit columns with the total of the credit column. This may be done on an adding machine tape or by a listing similar to the following:

DEBIT TOTALS		CREDIT TOTALS	
Purchases.............	$7,228.00	Accounts Payable.....	$7,867.00
Store Supplies.........	40.00		
Office Supplies.........	19.00		
General Ledger........	580.00		
	$7,867.00		$7,867.00

The total of the Accounts Payable Cr. column is posted to the credit of the accounts payable account in the general ledger and the posting references are recorded in the account and below the column total in the usual manner. The totals of the Purchases Dr., Store Supplies Dr., and Office Supplies Dr. columns are posted in a similar manner to the respective accounts in the general ledger. Each individual item in the General Amount column is posted to the appropriate account in the general ledger, the posting reference being entered at the left of the item in the column provided. Since the amounts in this column are posted separately, the total of the column is not posted. A check mark is placed below this total to indicate that it has been properly taken care of.

The general ledger accounts of Gordon Electric Appliances affected by postings from the columnar purchases journal appear as shown on page 131.

After all posting from the purchases journal for June has been completed, the accounts payable account in the general ledger has a credit balance of $15,942 (June 1 balance of $8,075 plus June 30 posting of $7,867). The sum of the balances in the individual accounts in the subsidiary ledger is also $15,942. Since the balance of the accounts payable account is equal to the sum of the balances of the accounts in the accounts payable ledger, it is apparent that the creditors' accounts might be used in the general ledger instead of the accounts payable account. But the use of the controlling account Accounts Payable and the subsidiary ledger is generally recommended. Having the creditors' accounts in a separate ledger facilitates posting. Furthermore, the use of the controlling account removes detail from the general ledger and simplifies the preparation of the trial balance and the accounting statements.

Store Supplies
ACCOUNT NO. 115

DATE	ITEMS	POST. REF.	DEBIT	DATE	ITEMS	POST. REF.	CREDIT
1953 June 1	Balance	✓	750 00				
30		P28	40 00				

Office Supplies
ACCOUNT NO. 116

DATE	ITEMS	POST. REF.	DEBIT	DATE	ITEMS	POST. REF.	CREDIT
1953 June 1	Balance	✓	375 00				
30		P28	19 00				

Store Equipment
ACCOUNT NO. 121

DATE	ITEMS	POST. REF.	DEBIT	DATE	ITEMS	POST. REF.	CREDIT
1953 June 1	Balance	✓	2402500				
22		P28	105 00				

Office Equipment
ACCOUNT NO. 122

DATE	ITEMS	POST. REF.	DEBIT	DATE	ITEMS	POST. REF.	CREDIT
1953 June 1	Balance	✓	520000				
16		P28	475 00				

Accounts Payable
ACCOUNT NO. 211

DATE	ITEMS	POST. REF.	DEBIT	DATE	ITEMS	POST. REF.	CREDIT
				1953 June 1	Balance	✓	807500
				30		P28	786700

Purchases
ACCOUNT NO. 511

DATE	ITEMS	POST. REF.	DEBIT	DATE	ITEMS	POST. REF.	CREDIT
1953 June 1	Balance	✓	5265000				
30		P28	722800				

**General Ledger Accounts After Posting from
Columnar Purchases Journal**

SINGLE-COLUMN PURCHASES JOURNAL   If a business records only purchases of merchandise in its purchases journal, it may use a purchases journal similar to the left-hand side of the columnar purchases journal illustrated on page 126. The heading of the money column will then be "Amount" rather than "Accounts Payable Cr." The total of the column will be posted to Purchases Dr. and to Accounts Payable Cr., and the posting will be indicated in the Posting Reference column of the purchases journal as shown below:

PURCHASES JOURNAL

PAGE 26

DATE OF ENTRY		DATE OF INVOICE		ACCOUNT CREDITED	POST. REF.	AMOUNT	
1953 Aug.	1	1953 July	31	Johnson Mfg. Co.	√	389	10
	3	Aug.	1	Crosby Corp.	√	117	50
	5		4	Black & Fries	√	565	00
	31			Purchases Dr.—Accounts Payable Cr.	511/211	6,342	36

Single-Column Purchases Journal

If this plan is followed, all purchases except the purchases of merchandise will be recorded in the cash payments journal if they are cash purchases or in the general journal if they are purchases on account.

PURCHASES RETURNS AND ALLOWANCES   When merchandise purchased on account is returned or an allowance is requested, the purchaser usually informs the seller of the circumstances in writing. If such transactions are of frequent occurrence, the debtor may use his own *debit memorandum* forms. Regardless of the form in which the request is made, the creditor usually issues a *credit memorandum*. Either form may be used by the debtor as the basis for an entry debiting the creditor's account and crediting *Purchases Returns and Allowances*. A credit to the purchases account would accomplish the same final result, but it is ordinarily preferable to have the books show both the total purchases and the total purchases returns and allowances. The use of the account Purchases Returns and Allowances shows whether the returns and allowances are reasonable in comparison with the total purchases.

On June 16 Gordon Electric Appliances issued a debit memorandum to Universal Electric Company for merchandise returned. The entry could be recorded in a two-column general journal as follows:

General Journal Entry for a Purchases Return

Note that the debit is posted to the accounts payable account, which is Account No. 211 in the general ledger, and to the creditor's account in the subsidiary ledger. The necessity for posting this item twice is indicated by placing the diagonal line in the Posting Reference column when the transaction is recorded; the account number and the check mark are written in when the respective postings are made.

When goods other than merchandise held for resale are returned, or an allowance is granted on such goods, the adjustment is made directly to the account that was originally debited. For example, if office equipment is returned to the vendor, the controlling account and the subsidiary account payable would be debited in the usual manner and Office Equipment would be credited. Similarly, when store supplies are returned to the vendor, Store Supplies would be credited for the amount of the return. The number of such returns is usually so small that no significant information would be obtained by maintaining separate accounts for these returns.

If merchandise purchases returns and allowances are of frequent occurrence, special columns for Accounts Payable Debit and Purchases Returns and Allowances Credit may be added to the general journal. As illustrated below, the posting of individual items to these two accounts would be replaced by total postings at the end of the month.

GENERAL JOURNAL

ACCOUNTS PAYABLE DR.	GENERAL DR.	DATE		DESCRIPTION	POST. REF.	GENERAL CR.	PURCHASES RETURNS & ALLOWANCES CR.
145 00		1953 Oct.	2	Wilson Hardware Co.	√		145 00
876 25	2,326 40					2,326 40	876. 25
(2 11)	(√)					(√)	(513)

Journal With Special Columns for Recording Purchases Returns and Allowances

Sometimes a separate journal, termed a *purchases returns and allowances journal,* is used to record these transactions. Such a journal is illustrated below:

PURCHASES RETURNS AND ALLOWANCES JOURNAL

PAGE 7

DATE		ACCOUNT DEBITED	POST. REF.	AMOUNT
1953 July	1	Standard Paint Corp.	√	33 00
	2	Goodman Hardware Wholesalers	√	93 20
	30	Merkle Builders Supplies, Inc.		229 50
	31	Accts. Pay. Dr.—Pur. Ret. and Allow. Cr.	211/513	923 80

Purchases Returns and Allowances Journal

During the month the individual items in the Amount column are posted to the debit of the creditors' accounts in the subsidiary ledger. At the end of the month the total of the Amount column is debited to Accounts Payable and credited to Purchases Returns and Allowances in the general ledger.

All of the alternative systems of recording purchases returns and allowances that have been illustrated apply only to transactions involving a debit to creditors' accounts. If the return or the allowance is granted after the invoice has been paid, the settlement may be made in cash. In such cases the transaction would be recorded in the cash receipts journal.

USING PURCHASES IN-VOICES AS A PUR-CHASES JOURNAL Sometimes, instead of using one of the forms of purchases journal illustrated in this chapter, a business has its purchases invoices bound together and uses them as a purchases journal. When this is done, the total of each invoice is posted direct to the creditor's account in the subsidiary ledger. At the end of the month an adding machine list may be made of all the invoices. If some of the purchases are for goods other than merchandise, separate adding machine lists are made for each kind of purchase. An entry is then made in the general journal debiting the appropriate general ledger accounts and crediting the accounts payable account. For example, if the adding machine lists show purchases of merchandise, $9,155, of office supplies, $230, of store supplies, $315, and of office equipment, $550, the general journal entry would be as follows:

June	30	Purchases................		9,155	00						
		Office Supplies..............		230	00						
		Store Supplies..............		315	00						
		Office Equipment............		550	00						
		Accounts Payable.........					10,250	00			

While this method saves time in recording in the purchases journal, it is not recommended because invoices from different companies may be of different sizes and shapes and are clumsy and inconvenient for this purpose.

QUESTIONS

1. Explain how an invoice can be both a purchase invoice and a sales invoice.

2. Name two business papers described in this chapter that are used as the basis for bookkeeping entries.

3. Would you recommend the use of sales and purchases journals for the following businesses: (a) a cafeteria, (b) a wholesale drug company, (c) a retail drug store doing a cash business, (d) a gardener who raises vegetables and sells them in a neighboring city?

4. At the end of the month an error is made in footing the single-column purchases journal, with the result that the total is posted as $4,655.20 instead of $4,615.20, the correct amount. (a) What effect will this error have on the trial balance? (b) Will the balance of the accounts payable account in the general ledger agree with the total of the balances in the creditors' ledger?

5. Queen City Motors uses a multicolumn purchases journal. In recording a particular invoice the bookkeeper enters the correct amount of $550 in the Accounts Payable Cr. column and incorrectly enters $500 in the Purchases Dr. column. How will this error be brought to his attention?

6. The Canton Supermarket purchases two cash registers from American Register Co. on account. Where should this transaction be entered if the Canton Supermarket uses a single-column purchases journal?

7. The Canton Supermarket returns one of the cash registers (see Question 6), receiving credit for the purchase price, $900. What general journal entry would be made to record this transaction?

8. Turner Accessory Shop uses its purchases invoices as its purchases journal. At the end of November, adding machine lists show the following totals for the various kinds of purchases on account: merchandise purchases, $2,895; store supplies, $115; office supplies, $65; store equipment, $150. Give the general journal entry that should be made on the basis of this information.

PROBLEMS

8-1. During March of the current year, the Miami Valley Rug House completed the following transactions:

March 3. Purchased merchandise on account from Wearite Linoleum, $800, invoice dated March 1.

5. Purchased merchandise on account from Fine Weave Rug Co., $350, invoice dated March 3.

6. Purchased store supplies on account from Harlow Supply Co., $45, invoice dated March 4.

8. Purchased store equipment on account from Eagle Register Co., $475, invoice dated March 7.

9. Received a credit memorandum for $45 from Wearite Linoleum as an allowance on defective merchandise.

10. Purchased merchandise on account from Imperial Rug Co., $1,550, invoice dated March 9.

13. Purchased office equipment on account from Modern Equipment, Inc., $180, invoice dated March 11.

15. Received a credit memorandum for $15 from Harlow Supply Co. for store supplies returned.

19. Purchased merchandise on account from Fine Weave Rug Co., $580, invoice dated March 17.

21. Purchased merchandise on account from Orient Imports, Inc., $2,475, invoice dated March 19.

23. Received a credit memorandum for $65 from Modern Equipment, Inc. for return of office equipment.

24. Purchased office supplies on account from Shafer Printing Co., $28, invoice dated March 22.

26. Purchased merchandise on account from Fibre Rug Co., $720, invoice dated March 25.

28. Received a credit memorandum for $5 from Shafer Printing Co. for return of office supplies.

29. Purchased merchandise on account from Imperial Rug Co., $200, invoice dated March 27.

30. Purchased store supplies on account from Harlow Supply Co., $21, invoice dated March 29.

Instructions: (1) Record the above transactions, using a purchases journal similar to the one illustrated on pages 126 and 127 of the text and a two-column general journal.

(2) Open the following accounts in the general ledger, using the account numbers indicated:

      114　Store Supplies　　　211　Accounts Payable
      115　Office Supplies　　　511　Purchases
      121　Store Equipment　　512　Purchases Returns and Allowances
      122　Office Equipment

(3) Open the following accounts in the accounts payable ledger: Eagle Register Co., Cleveland; Fibre Rug Co., Cleveland; Fine Weave Rug Co., Cincinnati; Harlow Supply Co., Hamilton; Imperial Rug Co., Chicago; Modern Equipment, Inc., Cincinnati; Orient Imports, Inc., New York; Shafer Printing Co., Cincinnati; Wearite Linoleum, Pittsburgh.

(4) Post from the two journals to the accounts payable ledger and the general ledger.

(5) (a) What is the sum of the balances of the subsidiary accounts?

    (b) What is the balance of the controlling account?

8-2. During July of the current year the Parkway Style Shop completed the following transactions:

July 3. Purchased merchandise on account from Tudor Dress Co., $375.55, invoice dated July 2.

      5. Purchased merchandise on account from Summit Garment Co., $250, invoice dated July 3.

      9. Received a credit memorandum for $95.20 from Tudor Dress Co. for merchandise returned.

   10. Purchased store supplies on account from Premier Supply Co., $35, invoice dated July 9.

   11. Purchased merchandise on account from Glenn Garment Co., $950, invoice dated July 10.

   15. Purchased store equipment on account from Harvard Equipment Co., $415.60, invoice dated July 13.

   16. Purchased merchandise on account from Tudor Dress Co., $640.70, invoice dated July 14.

   17. Purchased merchandise on account from Fashion Frocks, Inc., $360.45, invoice dated July 16.

   18. Received a credit memorandum for $6 from Premier Supply Co. for supplies returned.

   19. Purchased merchandise on account from Glenn Garment Co., $163.50, invoice dated July 17.

   22. Purchased merchandise on account from Hollywood Styles, Inc., $564, invoice dated July 21.

   23. Received a credit memorandum for $15 from Summit Garment Co. as an allowance for defective merchandise.

   24. Purchased office supplies on account from Apex Stationers, $45.10, invoice dated July 23.

   25. Purchased merchandise on account from Fashion Frocks, Inc., $600, invoice dated July 24.

   27. Purchased store supplies on account from Apex Stationers, $21.25, invoice dated July 25.

   30. Purchased store equipment on account from Harvard Equipment Co., $121.60, invoice dated July 28.

Instructions: (1) Record the above transactions, using a purchases journal similar to the one illustrated on pages 126 and 127 of the text and a general journal with special columns for Accounts Payable Dr. and Purchases Returns and Allowances Cr. similar to the one illustrated on page 133 of the text.

(2) Open the following accounts in the general ledger and enter the balances as of July 1:

114 Store Supplies.....	$ 128.75	511 Purchases.........	$12,695.65
115 Office Supplies.....	77.50	512 Purchases Returns	
121 Store Equipment...	4,620.00	and Allowances....	421.50
211 Accounts Payable..	1,044.35		

(3) Open the following accounts in the accounts payable ledger and enter the balances in the balance columns as of July 1: Apex Stationers, Syracuse; Fashion Frocks, Inc., New York, $326.35; Glenn Garment Co., Auburn, $56.15; Harvard Equipment Co., Utica; Hollywood Styles, Inc., New York; Premier Supply Co., Syracuse; Summit Garment Co., New York, $136.20; Tudor Dress Co., Rochester, $525.65.

(4) Post to the accounts payable ledger and the general ledger.

(5) (a) What is the sum of the balances of the accounts in the subsidiary ledger? (b) What is the balance of the controlling account?

8-3. During June of the current year the Swan Stationery Store completed the following transactions:

June 3. Purchased merchandise from Chapman Paper Co., invoice dated June 1, $420.
4. Purchased merchandise from Vernon Novelty Co., invoice dated June 2, $125.
5. Received a credit memorandum for $25 from Chapman Paper Co. for merchandise returned.
7. Purchased store equipment from Jasper Manufacturing Co., invoice dated June 4, $632.
9. Purchased merchandise from Loomis Publishing Co., invoice dated June 7, $315.
11. Purchased office supplies from White and Walker, Inc., invoice dated June 10, $48.
12. Purchased merchandise from Pearl Paper Co., invoice dated June 10, $263.
14. Received a credit memorandum for $15 from Loomis Publishing Co. for an allowance on defective merchandise.
15. Purchased merchandise from Garden City Printing Co., invoice dated June 13, $110.
16. Purchased merchandise from Smith Paper Co., invoice dated June 15, $267.
16. Purchased store supplies from General Supply Co., invoice dated June 15, $18.
19. Received a credit memorandum for $38 from Pearl Paper Co. for merchandise returned.
22. Purchased merchandise from Vernon Novelty Co., invoice dated June 20, $96.
23. Purchased merchandise from Chapman Paper Co., invoice dated June 21, $190.
28. Purchased merchandise from Pearl Paper Co., invoice dated June 26, $316.
30. Purchased merchandise from Banner Printing Co., invoice dated June 28, $87.

Instructions: (1) Record the foregoing transactions, using a single-column purchases journal similar to the one on page 132, a purchases returns and allowances journal similar to the one on page 134, and a two-column general journal.

(2) Open the following accounts in the general ledger, using the account numbers indicated:

114	Store Supplies	211	Accounts Payable
115	Office Supplies	511	Purchases
121	Store Equipment	512	Purchases Returns and Allowances

(3) Open the following accounts in the accounts payable ledger: Banner Printing Co., Glendale; Chapman Paper Co., Fresno; Garden City Printing Co., Sacramento; General Supply Co., Fresno; Jasper Manufacturing Co., Sacramento; Loomis Publishing Co., San Francisco; Pearl Paper Co., Fresno; Smith Paper Co., Sacramento; Vernon Novelty Co., Glendale; White and Walker, Inc., Glendale.

(4) Post to the accounts payable ledger and the general ledger.

(5) (a) What is the sum of the balances of the accounts in the subsidiary ledger? (b) What is the balance of the controlling account?

Chapter 9

Accounting for Cash

NATURE OF CASH More transactions affect the cash account than any other single account. For this reason special journals are used most frequently for cash transactions. This chapter describes the use of two special-column cash journals, the *cash receipts journal* and the *cash payments journal*. In some instances these two journals are combined into a *cashbook*.

Cash is the most liquid of all the assets of a business. Care must be taken in the handling of cash in order to insure a complete accounting for all cash transactions. The generally recommended procedure is to deposit all cash receipts in the bank so that bank deposits will equal cash receipts. When this is done, all payments should be made by checks drawn on the bank. This procedure provides a *double record* of cash; the bank's report of deposits should correspond to cash receipts and the total of checks drawn should agree with cash payments.

SOURCES OF The two chief sources of cash receipts are
CASH RECEIPTS cash sales and collections from customers who have bought on account. When a customer takes advantage of a cash discount, the amount of cash received is less than the amount of the invoice for which payment is received. These facts determine the special columns to be used in the cash receipts journal. By providing special columns for (1) cash, (2) sales, (3) accounts receivable, and (4) sales discount, it is possible to accumulate monthly totals and thereby reduce the amount of labor required to post to the general ledger. If a business frequently receives cash from other sources, other special columns may be added.

THE CASH In the five-column cash receipts journal of
RECEIPTS JOURNAL Gordon Electric Appliances on page 141, each cash receipt is entered in the Cash Dr. column.

The first money column, General Cr., is for miscellaneous credits to general ledger accounts for which no special column is provided. For each entry for which an amount is entered in the General Cr. column, the title of the account credited is written in the Account Credited column.

The Sales Cr. column is used for recording sales of merchandise for cash. Each cash sale is recorded mechanically by the cash register, and the totals thus accumulated are entered in the cash receipts journal each day or at other intervals. In this illustration they are recorded weekly. The account title "Sales" is written in the Account Credited column for each credit entered in the Sales Cr. column. This account title might be omitted, but including it may help to avoid errors.

When an amount is received on account, the transaction is recorded as follows:

(1) The name of the customer to be credited is entered in the Account Credited column.

(2) Cash is debited for the amount of cash actually received.

(3) Sales Discount is debited for the amount of the discount granted. This sales discount may be regarded as an expense of the business.

(4) Accounts Receivable is credited for the amount of the invoice, that is, the sum of the cash received and the sales discount.

At frequent intervals during the month, preferably daily, the amounts entered in the Accounts Receivable Cr. column are posted to the credit of customers' accounts in the accounts receivable ledger. Check marks are placed in the posting reference column opposite these entries to show that they have been posted. During the month, or at the end of the month, the amounts in the General Cr. column are posted to the appropriate accounts in the general ledger, and the posting is indicated by writing the ledger account numbers in the posting reference column of the journal. The items in the Sales Cr. column are not posted individually but are posted only as a total to the sales account. At the time each cash sales item is recorded, a check mark is inserted in the posting reference column to indicate that the item requires no individual posting.

At the end of the month the several columns are footed and ruled as shown in the illustration. To check the accuracy of the footings, the equality of debits and credits should be proved by a listing similar to the following:

DEBIT TOTALS		CREDIT TOTALS	
Sales Discount.........	$ 159.98	General.............	$ 268.60
Cash................	18,220.32	Sales...............	9,162.70
		Accounts Receivable..	8,949.00
	$18,380.30		$18,380.30

Since the items in the General Cr. column have been posted individually to accounts in the general ledger, a check mark is placed

CASH RECEIPTS JOURNAL   PAGE 55

DATE	ACCOUNT CREDITED	POST. REF.	GENERAL CR.	SALES CR.	ACCOUNTS RECEIVABLE CR.	SALES DISCOUNT DR.	CASH DR.
1953							
June 1	Purchases Returns & Allowances	513	6860				6860
4	Ernest H. Adams	✓			100000	2000	98000
6	John B. Wright	✓			47500	950	46550
6	Sales	✓		180000			180000
10	Dover Hotel	✓			360000	7200	352800
13	Dorothy L. Case	✓			62400	1248	61152
13	Sales	✓		235000			235000
15	Rogers Restaurant	✓			130500	2610	127890
19	Orchid Beauty School	✓			45000		45000
20	Sales	✓		212550			212550
22	Notes Receivable	112	20000				20000
24	S. V. Morton	✓			50000		50000
27	Orchid Beauty School	✓			99500	1990	97510
27	Sales	✓		204800			204800
30	Sales	✓		83920			83920
30	Totals	✓	26860	916270	894900	15998	1822032
			(✓)	(411)	(113)	(911)	(111)

Cash Receipts Journal

below the total of this column to indicate that this amount is not to be posted. The totals of the other four money columns are posted to the appropriate accounts in the general ledger. The completion of the posting of each column total is indicated by writing the account number in parentheses immediately below the total.

In terms of posting procedures, there are three distinct types of columns in the cash receipts journal. They may be described as follows:

(1) Items posted individually to general ledger accounts; column total not posted:

General Cr. column

(2) Items not posted individually; column total posted to a general ledger account:

Sales Cr. column
Sales Discount Dr. column
Cash Dr. column

(3) Items posted individually to subsidiary ledger accounts; column total posted to the corresponding general ledger controlling account:

Accounts Receivable Cr. column

**COMPARISON OF
ACCOUNTS RECEIVABLE
CONTROL WITH
SUBSIDIARY LEDGER**
Three postings are made in the month of June to the controlling account Accounts Receivable as a result of the transactions recorded in this and the preceding chapter. They are: (1) June 30, total of sales on account from the sales journal, $7,265; (2) June 29, a sales return and allowance from the general journal, $75; and (3) June 30, the total credits arising from cash received on account, $8,949. The controlling account with its opening balance of $6,375 and these three postings is shown below:

Accounts Receivable   ACCOUNT NO. *113*

DATE	ITEMS	POST. REF.	DEBIT	DATE	ITEMS	POST. REF.	CREDIT
1953 June 1	Balance	✓	6 3 7 5 0 0	*1953* June 29		J29	7 5 0 0
30	*4616.00*	S47	7 2 6 5 0 0	30		CR55	8 9 4 9 0 0

Accounts Receivable Account at the End of the Month

While the posting of column totals from the cash receipts journal to the general ledger must be deferred until the end of the month, postings to the customers' accounts should be made daily. It is advisable to have the exact amount receivable from each customer available currently in the accounts receivable ledger. In approving sales for additional credit, it is useful to know just how much the customer owes; in fact, a review of his paying practices as shown by his account helps materially in credit granting.

The accounts receivable ledger of Gordon Electric Appliances is shown on pages 143 and 144 after the postings from the cash receipts journal have been completed. These accounts also show the postings from the sales journal and from the general journal presented in earlier chapters.

A schedule of accounts receivable, showing the amounts owed by each customer on June 30, 1953, is shown on page 145. The total of the schedule, $4,616, is the same as the balance of the controlling account Accounts Receivable shown above. This equality is evidence that the work has been completed accurately and that the entries in the individual customers' accounts have been correctly summarized in the

NAME **Ernest H. Adams**
ADDRESS **214 Champlain Ave., Cheviot, Ohio**

DATE	ITEMS	POST. REF.	DEBIT	CREDIT	BALANCE
1953					
May 27		S46	100000		100000
June 1		S47	50900		150900
4		CR55		100000	50900

NAME **Dorothy L. Case**
ADDRESS **747 Barr St., Cincinnati 6, Ohio**

DATE	ITEMS	POST. REF.	DEBIT	CREDIT	BALANCE
1953					
June 3		S47	62400		62400
13		CR55		62400	—

NAME **Dover Hotel**
ADDRESS **2435 Jefferson Ave., Cincinnati 3, Ohio**

DATE	ITEMS	POST. REF.	DEBIT	CREDIT	BALANCE
1953					
May 29		S46	360000		360000
June 10		S47	85000		445000
10		CR55		360000	85000

NAME **S. V. Morton**
ADDRESS **143 S. Columbia Ave., Ft. Thomas, Ky.**

DATE	ITEMS	POST. REF.	DEBIT	CREDIT	BALANCE
1953					
Apr. 24		S45	85000		85000
June 24		CR55		50000	35000

Accounts Receivable Ledger at the End of the Month

NAME Orchid Beauty School
ADDRESS Neave Bldg., Cincinnati 2, Ohio

DATE	ITEMS	POST. REF.	DEBIT	CREDIT	BALANCE
1953					
May 19		S46	450 00		450 00
June 17		S47	995 00		1445 00
19		CR55		450 00	995 00
27		CR55		995 00	—

NAME George D. Porter
ADDRESS 2131 Lysle Road, Norwood, Ohio

DATE	ITEMS	POST. REF.	DEBIT	CREDIT	BALANCE
1953					
June 9		S47	392 00		392 00
29		S47	1788 00		2180 00

NAME Rogers Restaurant
ADDRESS 681 Kenwood Drive, Deer Park, Ohio

DATE	ITEMS	POST. REF.	DEBIT	CREDIT	BALANCE
1953					
June 5		S47	1305 00		1305 00
15		CR55		1305 00	—

NAME Albert T. Shaw
ADDRESS 3744 Observatory St., Cincinnati 9, Ohio

DATE	ITEMS	POST. REF.	DEBIT	CREDIT	BALANCE
1953					
June 23		S47	432 00		432 00
26		S47	370 00		802 00
29		J29		75 00	727 00

NAME John B. Wright
ADDRESS 42 Drake Ave., Cincinnati 7, Ohio

DATE	ITEMS	POST. REF.	DEBIT	CREDIT	BALANCE
1953					
May 28		S46	475 00		475 00
June 6		CR55		475 00	—

Accounts Receivable Ledger at the End of the Month (Concluded) controlling account in the general ledger. As in the case of the trial balance, however, the schedule is not an absolute guarantee of correctness. For example, if a collection on account from one customer was credited to the account of another customer, the error would not be disclosed by the comparison of the total of the schedule with the balance of the controlling account.

Gordon Electric Appliances
Schedule of Accounts Receivable
June 30, 1953

Ernest H. Adams	509 00	
Dover Hotel	85 00	
S. V. Morton	35 00	
George D. Porter	218 00	
Albert T. Shaw	727 00	
Total Accounts Receivable		461 6 00

Schedule of Accounts Receivable

THE CASH PAYMENTS JOURNAL   Cash payments are composed primarily of cash paid for operating expenses and for amounts due creditors. In the cash payments journal of Gordon Electric Appliances on page 146, a special column is provided for Cash Cr. as every transaction recorded in this journal includes a credit to Cash. Special columns are also provided for Accounts Payable Dr. and Purchases Discount Cr. as entries are made in these columns frequently. No special columns are provided for expenses. The operating expenses of Gordon Electric Appliances are distributed among many accounts, and no one account is debited frequently enough to justify the use of a special column.

All payments of Gordon Electric Appliances are made by check and the check stubs serve as original memorandums of the transactions. As each transaction is recorded in the cash payments journal, the related check number is entered in the column provided at the immediate right of the date column.

The first money column, General Dr., is for miscellaneous debits to general ledger accounts for which no special column is provided. At the time the entry is made, the title of the account debited is entered in the Account Debited column.

When an amount is paid on account, the transaction is recorded as follows:

CASH PAYMENTS JOURNAL   PAGE 49

DATE	CHK. NO.	ACCOUNT DEBITED	POST. REF.	GENERAL DR.	ACCOUNTS PAYABLE DR.	PURCHASES DISCOUNT CR.	CASH CR.
1953							
June 2	951	Office Supplies	116	650			650
4	952	Store Equipment	121	15000			15000
9	953	Freight In	512	12500			12500
12	954	Queen City Electrical Co.	✓		65000	650	64350
12	955	Sales Salaries	611	32000			32000
12	956	Office Salaries	711	12000			12000
15	957	Miscellaneous General Exp.	715	1420			1420
16	958	Prepaid Insurance	117	9600			9600
18	959	Queen City Electrical Co.	✓		35800	358	35442
20	960	Moore-Lucas Wholesalers	✓		175000		175000
22	961	Sales Returns & Allowances	412	4500			4500
23	962	American Home Appliance Co.	✓		260000		260000
23	963	Purchases	511	6880			6880
24	964	Tri-State Television Distributors	✓		320000		320000
25	965	Watson Manufacturing Co.	✓		52500		52500
26	966	Sales Salaries	611	32000			32000
26	967	Office Salaries	711	12000			12000
26	968	Universal Electric Co.	✓		111550	2231	109319
27	969	Advertising Expense	613	1500			1500
29	970	Miscellaneous Selling Exp.	616	3610			3610
30	971	William Gordon, Drawing	312	60000			60000
30		Totals	✓	209660	1019850	3239	1226271
				(1)	(211)	(811)	(111)

Cash Payments Journal

(1) The name of the creditor to be debited is entered in the Account Debited column.

(2) Cash is credited for the amount of cash actually paid.

(3) Purchases Discount is credited for the amount of the discount granted. This purchases discount may be regarded as an income of the business.

(4) Accounts Payable is debited for the amount of the invoice paid, that is, the sum of the cash paid and the purchases discount.

At frequent intervals during the month, the amounts entered in the Accounts Payable Dr. column are posted to the debit of creditors' accounts in the accounts payable ledger. Check marks are placed in the posting reference columns opposite these entries to show that they have been posted. At the end of the month, or from time to time during the month, the amounts in the General Dr. column are posted to the appropriate accounts in the general ledger, and the posting is indicated by writing the ledger account numbers in the posting reference columns.

At the end of the month the cash payments journal is ruled, each of the money columns is footed, and the equality of debits and credits is determined as follows:

DEBIT TOTALS		CREDIT TOTALS	
General.................	$ 2,096.60	Purchases Discount....	$ 32.39
Accounts Payable......	10,198.50	Cash.................	12,262.71
	$12,295.10		$12,295.10

A check mark is placed below the total of the General Dr. column to indicate that it is not to be posted. As each of the totals of the other three columns is posted to a general ledger account, the appropriate account number is written in parentheses below the double ruling. The presence of the number below the total (1) indicates that it has been posted and (2) identifies the account to which it has been posted.

COMPARISON OF ACCOUNTS PAYABLE CONTROL WITH SUBSIDIARY LEDGER   Three postings are made in the month of June to the controlling account Accounts Payable as a result of the transactions recorded in this and the preceding chapter. They are: (1) June 30, total of purchases on account from the purchases journal, $7,867; (2) June 16, a purchase return and allowance from the general journal, $32.50; and (3) June 30, the total debit resulting from payments on account, $10,198.50. The controlling account with its opening balance of $8,075 and these three postings is shown below:

Accounts Payable   ACCOUNT NO. 211

DATE	ITEMS	POST. REF.	DEBIT	DATE	ITEMS	POST. REF.	CREDIT
1953 June 16		J29	32 50	1953 June 1	Balance	✓	8 0 7 5 00
30		CP49	10 1 9 8 50	30	5711.00	P28	7 8 6 7 00

Accounts Payable Account at the End of the Month

While the posting of column totals from the cash payments journal to the general ledger must be deferred until the end of the month, postings to the creditors' accounts should be made daily. It is advisable to have the exact amount owed to each creditor available currently in the accounts payable ledger.

The accounts payable ledger of Gordon Electric Appliances is shown on pages 148 and 149 after the postings from the cash payments journal have been completed. These accounts also show the postings from the purchases journal and from the general journal presented in earlier chapters.

NAME *American Home Appliance Co.*
ADDRESS *1428 Lincoln Ave., Chicago 8, Ill.*

DATE	ITEMS	POST. REF.	DEBIT	CREDIT	BALANCE
1953 May 25		P27		2600 00	2600 00
June 2		P28		824 00	3424 00
23		CP49	2600 00		824 00

NAME *Bauer Electric Corp.*
ADDRESS *42-46 N. Randolph, Pittsburgh 4, Pa.*

DATE	ITEMS	POST. REF.	DEBIT	CREDIT	BALANCE
1953 June 11		P28		923 00	923 00
29		P28		715 00	1638 00

NAME *Moore-Lucas Wholesalers*
ADDRESS *3700 Third St., Columbus 2, Ohio*

DATE	ITEMS	POST. REF.	DEBIT	CREDIT	BALANCE
1953 May 21		P27		1750 00	1750 00
June 20		CP49	1750 00		—

NAME *Office Equipment Distributors*
ADDRESS *918 Front St., Cincinnati 2, Ohio*

DATE	ITEMS	POST. REF.	DEBIT	CREDIT	BALANCE
1953 June 16		P28		475 00	475 00

NAME *Queen City Electrical Co.*
ADDRESS *213 Columbia, Cincinnati 5, Ohio*

DATE	ITEMS	POST. REF.	DEBIT	CREDIT	BALANCE
1953 June 3		P28		650 00	650 00
9		P28		358 00	1008 00
12		CP49	650 00		358 00
18		CP49	358 00		—

Accounts Payable Ledger at the End of the Month

NAME   Ross Supplies, Inc.
ADDRESS   811 N. High St., Cincinnati 3, Ohio

DATE	ITEMS	POST. REF.	DEBIT	CREDIT	BALANCE
1953					
June 8		P28		3800	3800
25		P28		2100	5900

NAME   Tri-State Television Distributors
ADDRESS   10231 Fortieth St., Cleveland 13, Ohio

DATE	ITEMS	POST. REF.	DEBIT	CREDIT	BALANCE
1953					
May 26		P27		320000	320000
June 19		P28		150000	470000
24		CP49	320000		150000

NAME   Universal Electric Company
ADDRESS   415 Murray St., Chicago 15, Ill.

DATE	ITEMS	POST. REF.	DEBIT	CREDIT	BALANCE
1953					
June 13		P28		114800	114800
16		J29	3250		111550
26		CP49	111550		—

NAME   Watson Manufacturing Co.
ADDRESS   136 Chestnut St., Dayton 6, Ohio

DATE	ITEMS	POST. REF.	DEBIT	CREDIT	BALANCE
1953					
May 28		P27		52500	52500
June 15		P28		111000	163500
22		P28		10500	174000
25		CP49	52500		121500

Accounts Payable at the End of the Month (Concluded)

A schedule of accounts payable, showing the amounts owed to each creditor on June 30, 1953, is shown below. The total of the schedule, $5,711, is the same as the balance of the controlling account Accounts Payable shown on page 147. This equality is an indication that the recording and the posting have been completed accurately.

Gordon Electric Appliances
Schedule of Accounts Payable
June 30, 1953

American Home Appliance Co.	824 00	
Bauer Electric Corp.	1638 00	
Office Equipment Distributors	475 00	
Ross Supplies, Inc.	59 00	
Tri-State Television Distributors	1500 00	
Watson Manufacturing Co.	1215 00	
Total Accounts Payable		5711 00

Schedule of Accounts Payable

REPORTING CASH DISCOUNTS ON THE PROFIT AND LOSS STATEMENT   Purchases discount is usually reported on the profit and loss statement as *other income;* sales discount, as *other expense.*

Items listed on the statement under the headings "Other Income" and "Other Expense" affect the net profit or the net loss of the enterprise. They are considered apart from items representing the ordinary operations of the business and are therefore commonly placed at the end of the statement. A common method of reporting cash discounts on the profit and loss statement is illustrated below:

```
Net Profit from Operations . . . . . . . . . . . . . .        $9,000.00

Other Income:
    Purchases Discount. . . . . . . . . . . . . . . $  650.00

Other Expense:
    Sales Discount. . . . . . . . . . . . . . . . . .    200.00

Net Addition . . . . . . . . . . . . . . . . . . . .          450.00

Net Profit . . . . . . . . . . . . . . . . . . . . .        $9,450.00
```

**Partial Profit and Loss Statement Showing
Purchases Discount and Sales Discount**

In the illustration, the amount of the purchases discount is greater than the amount of the sales discount. When the situation is reversed, Other Income is subtracted from Other Expense and the difference between the two is identified as "Net Deduction." In that case, of course, the net figure would be subtracted from net profit from operations to arrive at net profit.

THE DEPOSITOR'S   Checks have taken the place of currency in
BANK ACCOUNT   the more important transactions involving
receipts and payments; in fact, checks are treated as cash on accounting records. When a businessman uses checks, it is assumed that he has previously made deposits in the bank on which the checks are drawn. The deposits may consist largely of the checks of his customers. This use of a bank account is invariably recommended by accountants. The bank account safeguards and provides a better record of cash.

The forms commonly used by the depositor in dealing with his bank are:

NAME	FUNCTION
1. Signature card.	Provides the bank with the authentic signature of the depositor.
2. Deposit ticket.	Furnishes the bank with the depositor's record of a deposit.
3. Passbook.	Provides the depositor with the bank's record of a deposit.
4. Checkbook.	Furnishes the depositor with a paying medium.
5. Bank statement.	Provides the depositor with a periodic statement showing the condition of his account.

Signature Card. At the time of opening an account, the depositor is required to sign his name on a *signature card.* This card is used by the bank in identifying the depositor's signature on checks presented to it for payment.

Deposit Ticket. The details of a deposit are listed by the depositor on a printed form supplied by the bank. A specimen of this form, which is called a *deposit ticket*, is illustrated at the right. The bills and the coins in the deposit are shown in total in the two spaces provided and the checks are listed individually. Each check should be identified on the deposit ticket by the name or the address of the bank on which it is drawn, or by

Merchants Bank

Cincinnati

Deposited for Account of

Gordon Electric Appliances

1042 Race Street

July 14,   19 *53*

		DOLLARS	CENTS
CASH {	*Bills*	*476*	*00*
	Coin	*32*	*97*
CHECKS:			
1 *13-38*		*475*	*92*
2 *73-16*		*246*	*50*
3 *13-24*		*55*	*75*
4 *13-62*		*436*	*20*
5 *13-10*		*203*	*66*
6			
		1,927	*00*

Deposit Ticket

the code numbers of the American Bankers' Association printed on the check. After the deposit ticket is verified by the bank, it becomes the basis for the bank's entry crediting the depositor.

Passbook. At the time of the first deposit, the bank gives the depositor a *passbook* in which the bank will record the amount of each deposit. The depositor presents his passbook each time a deposit is made, and the teller enters in it the date, the amount, and his signature or initials. This serves as the depositor's receipt. Some banks use a duplicate deposit ticket, signed or initialed by the teller, in place of the passbook.

Checkbook. The depositor orders his bank to make a payment from his account by means of a *check.* When the bank pays a check, it debits the depositor's account. Checks may be obtained in a variety of bound and loose-leaf forms. The name and the address of the depositor may be printed on each check, and the checks may be serially numbered. A record of each check issued is maintained by making a carbon copy or by recording the details on a *stub* such as that shown below. In addition to serving as the basis for entries in the cash payments journal, the check stubs may be used to keep a current account of the bank balance.

Check and Stub

Bank Statement. Banks ordinarily give their depositors a statement of account at the end of each month. The statement gives complete details of the depositor's account during the period, the opening balance, the deposits, the withdrawals, and the balance at the end of the month. A typical bank statement is shown in the illustration on page 153. Accompanying the bank statement are the checks drawn by the depositor that the bank has paid during the period. These *paid* or *canceled* checks are stamped "paid," together with the date of payment. If there have been additions to or deductions from the account other than deposits or checks paid, memorandums describing the items are also sent with the bank statement.

CHECKS AND OTHER DEBITS			DEPOSITS	DATE	BALANCE
		BALANCE BROUGHT FORWARD →		July 1	7,321.18
963.12	122.54			July 2	6,235.52
369.50	732.26	15.35		July 3	5,118.41
293.20	550.00		2,642.35	July 8	6,917.56
126.32	1,791.50			July 10	4,999.74
25.93	160.00		1,927.00	July 14	6,740.81
431.00	315.14			July 15	5,994.67
125.00	862.31	320.00		July 17	4,687.36
475.00	1,332.50		3,122.18	July 21	6,002.04
229.50	28.30	40.72		July 23	5,703.52
56.30	160.00	25.91	1,750.93	July 24	7,212.24
873.10	394.25			July 25	5,944.89
521.10	126.20	DM 2.00	CM 300.00	July 28	5,595.59
468.50			2,896.50	July 29	8,023.59
187.30	19.25			July 31	7,817.04

STATEMENT OF YOUR ACCOUNT WITH

MERCHANTS BANK

Gordon Electric Appliances
1042 Race Street
Cincinnati 2, Ohio

CM—Credit Memorandum   OD—Overdraft   RT—Returned Item
DM—Debit Memorandum   PS—Payment Stopped   SC—Service Charge

The reconcilement of this statement with your records is essential. Any error or exception should be reported immediately.

Bank Statement

**BANK
RECONCILIATION**

The balance indicated on the bank statement usually does not agree with the balance shown on the check stubs or other record maintained by the depositor. One of the reasons for the difference is that some of the checks written by the depositor, probably those issued at the end of the month, have not been presented to the bank for payment. When this is the case, the balance according to the bank statement is greater than the balance in the checkbook. Another reason for disagreement is that a deposit mailed or placed in the night depository on the last day of the month may not have been recorded by the bank until the following day. As a result the bank statement balance is less than the checkbook balance. Additional causes of discrepancies include debits or credits made by the bank (such as service charges and proceeds of notes left for collection) that have not been recorded by the depositor, errors in the check stubs, and errors made by the bank.

In order to discover and correct any errors that may have occurred, the depositor should *reconcile the bank statement* with his own records. The procedure employed in preparing the bank reconciliation is:

(1) Compare deposits listed on the bank statement with the deposits shown on the check stubs. Deposits not recorded by the bank should be added to the balance shown by the bank statement.

(2) Determine whether credit memorandums issued by the bank to the depositor's account have been recorded as deposits in the checkbook. Those unrecorded should be added to the balance shown in the checkbook.

(3) Arrange canceled checks in numerical order and compare them with the check stubs. Indicate those returned by making a check mark on the related check stubs. The total amount of outstanding checks should be deducted from the balance according to the bank statement.

(4) Determine whether debit memorandums issued by the bank to the depositor's account have been recorded as deductions in the checkbook. Those unrecorded should be deducted from the balance shown in the checkbook.

(5) If any errors have been made, they will probably be disclosed during the process of the foregoing comparisons. Appropriate adjustments to the checkbook balance should be made for errors of the depositor, and to the bank statement balance for those made by the bank.

The July bank statement for Gordon Electric Appliances on page 153 shows a balance of $7,817.04 on July 31. The checkbook indicates a bank balance of $7,633.74 as of the same date. Applying the procedures outlined above, the bookkeeper finds that: (1) a deposit of $752.50 entered in the checkbook on July 31 was not taken to the bank until the following day; (2) a credit memorandum dated July 28 for $300, representing proceeds of a note receivable left at the bank for collection, had not been recorded in the checkbook or the cash receipts journal; (3) Check No. 948 for $37, issued in May, and Check No. 1024 for $483.50 and Check No. 1025 for $126.30, issued in July, are outstanding; (4) a debit memorandum dated July 28 for a $2 fee charged by the bank for collecting the $300 note had not been recorded in the checkbook or the cash payments journal; and (5) Check No. 1002 in payment of advertising was written for $43 but was erroneously re-

BANK RECONCILIATION, JULY 31, 1953

Balance in checkbook, 7/31 $7,633.74	Balance on bank statement, 7/31............ $7,817.04
Add:	Add:
Note collected by bank.. 300.00	Deposit of July 31...... 752.50
$7,933.74	$8,569.54
Deduct:	Deduct:
Collection fee..... $2.00	Outstanding checks:
Error on Stub	No. 948...... $ 37.00
No. 1002....... 9.00 11.00	No. 1024..... 483.50
	No. 1025..... 126.30 646.80
Corrected Balance, 7/31.. $7,922.74	Corrected Balance, 7/31.. $7,922.74

corded on the check stub and in the cash payments journal as $34. The bank reconciliation for Gordon Electric Appliances is illustrated on page 154. Note that the reconciliation is completed when the two amounts labeled "Corrected Balance" are in agreement.

Entries that have already been made to the depositor's account in the bank's ledger, but that have not as yet been made to the bank's account in the depositor's ledger, must be recorded in the depositor's ledger and checkbook. If the totaling and the posting of the cash journals is postponed until after the bank statement is reconciled, the necessary entries may be recorded in the usual manner. Assuming that Gordon Electric Appliances follows this practice, the following entries would be made:

CASH RECEIPTS JOURNAL

DATE		ACCOUNT CREDITED	POST. REF.	GENERAL CR.	SALES CR.	ACCTS. REC. CR.	SALES DISC. DR.	CASH DR.
July	31	Notes Receivable		300.00				300.00

CASH PAYMENTS JOURNAL

DATE		CHECK NO.	ACCOUNT DEBITED	POST. REF.	GENERAL DR.	ACCTS. PAY. DR.	PUR. DISC. CR.	CASH CR.
July	31	Memo	Misc. General Expense		2.00			2.00
	31	1002	Advertising		9.00			9.00

If the journals were posted before the statement is reconciled, the necessary entries may be made in the general journal or may be recorded in the usual manner in the cash journals for the following month. The former alternative should be followed if financial statements are to be prepared at the end of the month; otherwise either procedure is satisfactory.

As a final step in the reconciliation procedure, the corrected checkbook balance should be compared with the balance of the cash account after the adjustments have been made. The two records should be in agreement after allowance is made for undeposited cash on hand at the end of the month. A policy frequently followed is to keep a specified sum of cash on hand as a change fund and to deposit all receipts. Thus, if Gordon Electric Appliances maintains a change fund of $200, the balance of the cash account in the ledger as of July 31 should equal the sum of the corrected checkbook balance, $7,922.74, plus the change fund, $200, or $8,122.74.

CASH SHORT   It frequently happens, particularly in a retail
AND OVER   business with many cash sales, that the
amount of cash actually received during a day does not agree with the
cash register tally of cash receipts.   Whenever there is a difference
between the records and the actual cash and no error can be found in
the records, it must be assumed that the mistake occurred in making
change. If the actual cash is less than the balance shown by the cash
records, an entry is made in the cash payments journal debiting an
account entitled *Cash Short and Over* and crediting Cash. If the actual
cash is greater than the balance indicated by the records, an entry is
made in the cash receipts journal debiting Cash and crediting Cash
Short and Over.

If there is a debit balance in the cash short and over account at
the end of the fiscal period, this balance is an expense and may be
included in Miscellaneous General Expense on the profit and loss
statement. If there is a credit balance, it is an income and may be
listed in the other income section as Miscellaneous Income.

QUESTIONS

1. Describe the two related transactions recorded in the "T" accounts
below:

Cash		Accounts Receivable		Sales		Sales Discount	
(b) 1,372		(a) 1,400	(b) 1,400		(a) 1,400	(b) 28	

2. Dan Baird pays several invoices that are subject to a cash discount.
The date of each invoice, the amount, the terms, and the date of payment
are given below. What is the amount of cash paid in each case?

Date of Invoice	Amount	Terms	Date of Payment
(a) November 3	$300.00	2/10, n/30	November 13
(b) November 12	500.00	1/15, n/60	November 27
(c) November 14	200.00	3/10, 1/30, n/60	December 14
(d) November 20	400.00	1/10, n/30	December 20

3. The account at the right is a
controlling account in the ledger of
J. Vincent.

Sept. 10 (1) 50	Sept. 1 Bal. 4,600
30 (3) 4,900	30 (2) 5,200

(a) What is the title of the account?

(b) From what journal was each
of the postings made?

4. List the seven mistakes in the cash payments journal shown below:

CASH PAYMENTS JOURNAL

DATE	POST. REF.	ACCOUNT CREDITED	GENERAL CR.	SALES CR.	ACCTS. REC. DR.	CHECK NO.	SALES DISC. CR.	CASH CR.

5. On November 6 Roy White sells merchandise to George Malloy for $900 on terms of 2/10, n/30. On November 12 he issues a credit memorandum to Malloy for $50 for merchandise returned. On November 16 he receives a check for the account in full. Give the entries to record White's transactions.

6. The cash register indicates cash sales of $1,252.38 for the day. The actual count of cash received from sales for the day totals $1,250.13. No explanation can be found for the discrepancy. Give the entries needed to record these facts.

7. Walter Poole receives notification from his bank that his account has been debited for $50 because of a check deposited by him that had been returned marked "Not Sufficient Funds." The check accompanying the notice had originally been received from John Bronson as a payment on account. What entry should be made by Poole?

8. In reconciling the bank statement with his cash records at the end of the month Walter Harris learns the following facts:

(a) Checks outstanding total $492.

(b) The bank debited his account for a monthly service charge of $3.50.

(c) A deposit of $654 was erroneously recorded in his check stubs as $624. There had been no error in recording the cash receipts.

(d) A deposit of $922 made on the last day of the month did not appear on the bank statement.

(e) A check for $147 in payment of advertising expense had been erroneously entered in the check stubs and the cash payments journal as $47.

Assuming that the special journals have already been posted but that the trial balance has not yet been prepared, give the entries that should be made in Harris' general journal.

9. When reconciling the bank statement with the balance according to the check stubs at the end of the month, Howard Todd's bookkeeper discovers that, in determining the bank balance on Check Stub No. 9321, there had been an arithmetical error of $100. The last check issued for the month is No. 9394. Is it necessary that he correct the balance on each intervening check stub or will the correction of Stub No. 9394 be sufficient?

PROBLEMS

9-1. The following sales, cash receipts, and general journal transactions were completed by Richard Kern during March of the current year. The terms of all sales on account are 1/10, n/30.

Mar. 1. Sold merchandise on account to William Snyder, Invoice No. 676, $3,225.

      5. Sold merchandise on account to Barry King, Invoice No. 677, $1,400.

      7. Kern invested additional cash in the business, $2,500.

    10. Issued to Barry King a credit memorandum for returned merchandise, $200.

    12. Sold merchandise on account to Philip Barker, Invoice No. 678, $4,600.

    14. Received cash for returned purchases, $450.

    14. Sold merchandise on account to Barry King, Invoice No. 679, $2,700.

    15. Cash sales for March 1 to 15, $3,685.

    16. Received cash from Barry King for the $1,200 balance due on Invoice No. 677, less discount.

    20. Sold merchandise on account to Philip Barker, Invoice No. 680, $4,000.

    23. Received cash from Philip Barker for Invoice No. 678, less discount.

    25. Received cash from Barry King for Invoice No. 679, less discount.

    26. Sold merchandise on account to Barry King, Invoice No. 681, $1,753.

    30. Received cash from William Snyder for Invoice No. 676.

    31. Cash sales for March 16 to 31, $5,324.

Instructions: (1) Record the transactions in a sales journal, a cash receipts journal similar to the one illustrated on page 141, and a general journal.

(2) Open the following accounts in the general ledger:

111 Cash	412 Sales Returns and Allowances
112 Accounts Receivable	513 Purchases Returns and Allowances
311 Richard Kern, Capital	911 Sales Discount
411 Sales	

(3) Open the following accounts in the accounts receivable ledger: Philip Barker, Austin; Barry King, Houston; William Snyder, El Paso.

(4) Post from the three journals to the accounts receivable ledger and the general ledger.

(5) Prepare a schedule of accounts receivable.

9-2. The following purchases, cash payments, and general journal transactions were completed by Willis Hood during April of the current year:

Apr. 1. Purchased for cash a three-year insurance policy for $180.

     3. Purchased merchandise on account from Norman Manufacturing Co., invoice dated April 2, $4,600.

     8. Purchased merchandise for cash, $950.

    12. Paid Norman Manufacturing Co. invoice of April 2, deducting 2% discount.

    13. Purchased merchandise on account from Selman & Co., invoice dated April 12, $1,900.

    15. Paid cash for returned sales, $60.

    18. Purchased merchandise on account from Arnold & Wright, Inc., invoice dated April 16, $2,600.

Apr. 20. Received a credit memorandum from Selman & Co. for returned merchandise, $100.

22. Paid Selman & Co. for $1,800 balance due on invoice of April 12, deducting 1% discount.

23. Purchased merchandise from Norman Manufacturing Co., invoice dated April 21, $6,500.

27. Paid for advertising, $250.

28. Paid water and power bills for the month, $320. (Charge Miscellaneous General Expense)

29. Received a credit memorandum from Norman Manufacturing Co., $52.

30. Paid salaries for the month, $620.

30. Withdrew $700 for personal use.

30. Recorded a cash shortage of $9.

Instructions: (1) Record the transactions in a purchases journal similar to the one illustrated on page 132, a cash payments journal similar to the one illustrated on page 146, and a two-column general journal. Number the checks beginning with 788.

(2) Open the following accounts in the general ledger, using the account numbers indicated:

111 Cash	512 Purchases Returns and Allowances
116 Prepaid Insurance	611 Salaries
211 Accounts Payable	613 Advertising Expense
312 Willis Hood, Drawing	714 Cash Short and Over
412 Sales Returns and Allowances	715 Miscellaneous General Expense
511 Purchases	811 Purchases Discount

(3) Open the following accounts in the accounts payable ledger: Arnold & Wright, Inc., Evanston, Ill.; Norman Manufacturing Co., Chicago, Ill.; Selman & Co., South Bend, Ind.

(4) Post from the three journals to the accounts payable ledger and the general ledger.

(5) Prepare a schedule of accounts payable.

9-3. In this problem you are to record and post the transactions of David Baldwin for July, the first month in his current fiscal year.

Instructions: (1) Open the following accounts in the general ledger, entering the balances in the appropriate accounts under date of July 1:

111 Cash	$ 9,620	312 David Baldwin, Drawing	
112 Accounts Receivable	3,121	411 Sales	
113 Notes Receivable	1,200	412 Sales Returns and Allowances	
114 Merchandise Inventory	15,423	511 Purchases	
115 Store Supplies	352	512 Purchases Returns and Allow-	
116 Office Supplies	76	ances	
117 Prepaid Insurance	498	611 Sales Salaries	
118 Prepaid Rent	900	612 Miscellaneous Selling Expense	
121 Store Equipment	4,615	711 Office Salaries	
122 Office Equipment	1,226	712 Miscellaneous General Expense	
211 Accounts Payable	4,600	811 Purchases Discount	
311 David Baldwin, Capital	32,431	911 Sales Discount	

(2) Open the following accounts in the accounts receivable ledger, entering the balances in the balance columns under date of July 1: Frank Arnold, Hannibal, $1,509; Kenneth Kerr, Springfield, $912; Newkirk & Co., Kansas City; Walter Westmore, St. Louis, $700.

(3) Open the following accounts in the accounts payable ledger, entering the balances in the balance columns under date of July 1: Caldwell-Loomis Corp., Chicago, $2,700; W. B. Kizer & Co., Denver, $600; Pearce Manufacturing Co., St. Louis; Reed and Lane, Kansas City, $1,300; Whitney Supply Corp., St. Louis.

(4) Record the transactions listed below, using a purchases journal (as on pages 126 and 127), a sales journal (as on page 112), a cash receipts journal (as on page 141), a cash payments journal (as on page 146), and a four-column general journal (as on page 118). The terms of all sales on account are 2/15, n/60.

July 2. Purchased supplies on account from Whitney Supply Corp., invoice dated July 1, $87. The invoice total should be distributed as follows: store supplies, $62; office supplies, $25.

3. Issued Check No. 896 for a two-year insurance policy, $392.

3. Purchased merchandise on account from Pearce Manufacturing Co., invoice dated July 2, $2,650.

5. Sold merchandise on account to Frank Arnold, Invoice No. 681, $750.

5. Received check from Kenneth Kerr for balance due, $912; no discount.

6. Received credit memorandum from Pearce Manufacturing Co. for merchandise returned to them, $150.

6. Sold merchandise on account to Newkirk & Co., Invoice No. 682, $1,300.
Post from all journals to the accounts receivable ledger and the accounts payable ledger.

8. Issued Check No. 897 in payment of miscellaneous selling expense, $126.

9. Sent Check No. 898 to Caldwell-Loomis Corp. for balance due; no discount.

9. Received check from Walter Westmore for balance due, less discount.

10. Sold merchandise on account to Kenneth Kerr, Invoice No. 683, $1,650.

11. Sent Check No. 899 to W. B. Kizer & Co. for balance due, less 1% discount.

11. Purchased merchandise on account from Caldwell-Loomis Corp., invoice dated July 10, $1,800.

12. Received check from Frank Arnold for $1,509; no discount.

13. Issued Credit Memo No. 46 to Kenneth Kerr for returned merchandise, $100.
Post from all journals to the accounts receivable ledger and the accounts payable ledger.

15. Received check from Kenneth Kerr for balance due, less 2% discount.

15. Purchased merchandise for cash, issuing Check No. 900 for $623.

15. Sent Check No. 901 to Pearce Manufacturing Co. for balance due, less 1% discount.

July 16. Sold Walter Westmore merchandise on account, Invoice No. 684, $900.

16. Cash sales for July 1 through 16, $2,461.

17. Sold merchandise to Kenneth Kerr on account, Invoice No. 685, $1,425.

18. Purchased store equipment from Reed and Lane on account, invoice dated July 16, $450.

19. Purchased merchandise on account from W. B. Kizer & Co., invoice dated July 18, $1,725.

20. Received check from Frank Arnold for balance due, less discount.

20. Issued Credit Memo No. 47 to Walter Westmore for damaged merchandise, $27.
Post from all journals to the accounts receivable ledger and the accounts payable ledger.

22. Sold merchandise on account to Newkirk & Co., Invoice No. 686, $1,126.

23. Received $85 cash for merchandise purchased for cash and later returned.

25. Sent Check No. 902 to Reed and Lane for balance on July 1; no discount.

27. Sent Check No. 903 to Whitney Supply Corp. for balance due; no discount.
Post from all journals to the accounts receivable ledger and the accounts payable ledger.

29. Purchased store supplies on account from Whitney Supply Corp., invoice dated July 27, $53.

30. Paid utility bills, Check No. 904, $124.   (Charge Miscellaneous General Expense.)

31. Issued Check No. 905 for monthly salaries as follows: sales salaries, $650; office salaries, $250.

31. Purchased merchandise on account from Caldwell-Loomis Corp., invoice dated July 30, $2,237.

31. Cash sales for July 17 through 31, $2,515.

31. Withdrew $500 for personal use, Check No. 906.

31. The reconciliation of the bank statement with the balance shown on the check stubs as of July 31 reveals the following transactions that have not been recorded on Baldwin's books:

(a) A note receivable for $250 left with the bank for collection was collected by the bank in July and credited to Baldwin's account.

(b) The bank debited Baldwin's account during July for a collection fee and service charges totaling $3. (Charge to Miscellaneous General Expense.)

Post from all journals to the accounts receivable ledger and the accounts payable ledger.

Instructions: (5) Post from the five journals to the general ledger.

(6) Prepare a trial balance.

(7) Prepare a schedule of accounts receivable and a schedule of accounts payable.

9-4. Charles Warner's bank statement for May of the current year indicates a balance of $1,426.30. His check stubs on that date show a balance of $1,355.48. A comparison of canceled checks and memorandums accompanying the bank statement with the check stubs reveals the following:

(a) Checks outstanding: No. 690, for $115.10; No. 786, for $45.50; No. 787, for $52; No. 788, for $29.34.

(b) Canceled Check No. 765, for $78.50, had been entered in the check stubs and the cash payments journal as $88.50. The check had been issued in payment of advertising expense.

(c) A deposit of $328.80 had been made too late to appear on the bank statement. The cash receipt involved in the deposit had been recorded in the cash receipts journal and the deposit had been recorded in the check stubs as of May 31.

(d) The bank had credited Warner's account for $150 for a note receivable left for collection. No entry had been made in Warner's books or check stubs.

(e) The bank charged $2.32 for collection and service fees for the month. No entry had been made in Warner's books or check stubs.

Instructions: (1) Prepare a reconciliation of the bank statement with the check stubs.

(2) Prepare, in general journal form, the entries necessary to bring the books into agreement with the facts disclosed by the reconciliation. The cash receipts and cash payments journals have been ruled and posted, but the books have not been closed.

9-5. George B. Meeker's bank statement for November of the current year indicates a balance of $3,496.15 on November 30. The bank balance according to his check stubs on that date is $2,870.64. A comparison of the bank statement, the canceled checks, and the memorandums with the check stubs reveals the following:

(a) Checks outstanding: No. 1436, $4.85; No. 1513, $6.28; No. 1635, $462.12; No. 1637, $125.31; No. 1638, $43.90.

(b) A counter check for $100 included with the canceled checks had not been recorded in the check stubs or the cash payments journal. It was a personal withdrawal of cash by the proprietor.

(c) A check for $140 drawn by George C. Meeker was erroneously debited by the bank to George B. Meeker's account and was included with the canceled checks.

(d) A deposit of $450 on November 10 had not been recorded in the check stubs. The receipts included in the deposit had been properly recorded in the cash receipts journal.

(e) A deposit of $225 had been recorded twice in the check stubs.

(f) The bank deducted $1.95 for service charges, which had not been recorded in the cash payments journal or the check stubs.

Instructions: (1) Prepare a reconciliation of the bank statement with the check stubs.

(2) Prepare, in general journal form, the entries necessary to bring the books into agreement with the facts disclosed by the reconciliation. The cash receipts and cash payments journals have been ruled and posted, but the books have not been closed.

Chapter 10

The Periodic Summary

PROCEDURE FOR PREPARING THE PERIODIC SUMMARY The periodic summary for a nontrading business was presented in Chapter 6. A similar summary for a trading business will be presented in this chapter. Although the procedure may be varied in accordance with the preferences of individual accountants, the following outline is typical and will be followed in this and later chapters:

(1) Prepare a trial balance of the general ledger and schedules of the subsidiary ledgers.

(2) Compile the data that will be needed in adjusting the accounts. A good way to insure that none of the data will be omitted is to consider each item in the trial balance in the order in which it appears and to determine if any adjustment will be necessary.

(3) Prepare a work sheet from the trial balance and the data for the adjustments.

(4) Prepare a balance sheet and a profit and loss statement from the data in the work sheet.

(5) Record the adjusting entries in the journal, using the adjustments columns of the work sheet as a basis.

(6) Record the journal entries required to close the income and expense accounts and to transfer the net profit or the net loss to the proprietor's drawing account and the balance of this account to the capital account.

(7) Post the adjusting entries and the closing entries to the accounts in the ledger, rule the accounts that are closed, and balance and rule other accounts as desired.

(8) Prepare a post-closing trial balance of the general ledger.

(9) Record the journal entries required to reverse those adjusting entries that would otherwise need to be referred to in recording transactions of the ensuing accounting period.

(10) Post the reversing entries, and rule the accounts that are in balance.

The outline is similar to that presented in Chapter 6 except for the addition of schedules of subsidiary ledgers in Item 1, and of reversing entries in Item 9. Both procedures apply to nontrading as well as to trading businesses, but they were omitted from the earlier chapter for the sake of simplicity. The illustration of the periodic summary that follows includes two adjusting entries that are different in nature from those previously considered. Both are related to the merchandise inventory and the determination of the cost of the merchandise sold during the period.

MERCHANDISE INVENTORY ADJUSTMENTS   The entry to record a sale of merchandise is a debit to Cash or Accounts Receivable and a credit to Sales. Assuming that the goods are sold at a price in excess of cost, the credit to Sales is composed of two elements: (1) a reduction in merchandise and (2) a gross profit. In most businesses it is impractical to attempt to determine and record these two elements separately. For example, if an item that cost $4.35, including freight, is sold for $6.50, the effect of the transaction is to decrease merchandise by $4.35 and to increase gross profit by $2.15. It is customary to ignore these details for the time being by recording the entire $6.50 as a credit to Sales.

At the end of the accounting period, the balance in Merchandise Inventory represents the inventory of goods at the beginning of the period. It should represent the inventory at the end of the period. Therefore, the beginning inventory is transferred to Profit and Loss Summary, where it is combined with purchases, freight in, and purchases returns and allowances to give the merchandise available for sale. The final inventory is transferred from this merchandise available for sale to the inventory account. These transfers are made by adjusting entries that transfer (1) the beginning inventory from Merchandise Inventory to Profit and Loss Summary, and (2) the ending inventory from Profit and Loss Summary to Merchandise Inventory.

Assuming that the balance of the merchandise inventory account on December 31, 1953, before adjustment, is $21,300 and that, based on a physical count, the inventory on that date is $24,100, the necessary adjusting entries would be as follows:

```
1953
Dec. 31  Profit and Loss Summary................  21,300
             Merchandise Inventory.................          21,300
               To transfer beginning inventory to
               Profit and Loss Summary

Dec. 31  Merchandise Inventory...................  24,100
             Profit and Loss Summary..............          24,100
               To transfer ending inventory to Mer-
               chandise Inventory
```

After the two adjusting entries are posted, the accounts affected would appear as shown in the following accounts:

MERCHANDISE INVENTORY				PROFIT AND LOSS SUMMARY			
1952		1953		1953		1953	
Dec. 31	21,300	Dec. 31	21,300	Dec. 31	21,300	Dec. 31	24,100
1953							
Dec. 31	24,100						

As Sales, Purchases, Purchases Returns and Allowances, Freight In, and the remaining income and expense accounts are closed into Profit and Loss Summary, the latter account will contain all of the items entering into the determination of the net profit or loss for the period.

The balance in Merchandise Inventory, $24,100, represents the cost of the goods on hand on December 31, 1953. This ending inventory for 1953 is naturally the beginning inventory for 1954, and the balance of the account will usually remain unchanged until the books are adjusted and closed at the end of the next accounting period.

ADJUSTMENTS ON THE WORK SHEET   The records of Gordon Electric Appliances will be used in illustrating the various procedures that comprise the periodic summary. As of December 31, 1953, the end of the fiscal year, a trial balance is prepared in the first two columns of a work sheet. The additional data needed in adjusting the accounts are then compiled, as shown in the table below:

DATA FOR ADJUSTMENTS

Merchandise Inventory, December 31, 1953...............		$24,100
Inventories of Supplies:		
Store Supplies......................................		550
Office Supplies.....................................		230
Insurance Expired:		
On Merchandise and Store Equipment............	$410	
On Office Equipment and Building...............	180	590
Salaries Payable:		
Sales Salaries.....................................	$120	
Office Salaries....................................	45	165
Sales Commissions Payable...........................		3,000

The adjustments are entered in the debit and credit Adjustments columns of the work sheet according to whether the amounts are to be posted as debits or credits to the accounts. When an adjustment affects an account that does not appear in the trial balance, the name of the account is written below the trial balance in the Account Title column and the amount is entered on the same line in the proper Adjustments column. (See the work sheet illustrated on page 167.) The debit and the credit for each adjustment are identified on the work sheet by small letters in parentheses. This plan is helpful when the bookkeeper later records the adjusting entries in the journal.

The adjustments are entered on the work sheet in the following manner:

Merchandise Inventory. The merchandise inventory of $21,300 on hand at the beginning of the year has during the year become a part of the cost of goods sold. It is therefore transferred to Profit and Loss Summary by crediting Merchandise Inventory for $21,300 and debiting Profit and Loss Summary for the same amount. (Entry (a) on the work sheet.)

Profit and Loss Summary now has been debited for the beginning inventory and it will be debited for the total amount of the purchases. But goods worth $24,100 remain on hand. This amount is an asset and is not a part of the cost of goods sold. It is therefore transferred to the asset account Merchandise Inventory by a debit to Merchandise Inventory and a credit to Profit and Loss Summary. (Entry (b) on the work sheet.)

Supplies. At the end of the year the inventory of store supplies amounts to $550. Store supplies expense is therefore $610, the difference between the total debits to the account and the value of the inventory. Similarly the office supplies inventory is $230 and the office supplies expense is therefore $290. Adjustments (c) and (d) are made debiting Store Supplies Expense and Office Supplies Expense for the expenses and crediting Store Supplies and Office Supplies to record the decrease in the amount of these assets.

Prepaid Insurance. The value of the asset Prepaid Insurance has decreased $590 and expenses have been incurred for insurance on merchandise, store equipment, office equipment, and building. To record the decrease in the value of the asset Prepaid Insurance, this account is credited for $590. Insurance Expense—Selling is debited for $410, the insurance expense on merchandise and store equipment; Insurance Expense—General is debited for $180, the insurance expense on office equipment and building. (Entry (e) on the work sheet.)

Salaries and Commissions Payable. The liability for the salaries earned but not paid is recorded by a credit of $165 to the liability account Salaries Payable. The appropriate expense accounts are

Gordon Electric Appliances
Work Sheet
For Year Ended December 31, 1953

Account Titles	Acct No	Trial Balance Dr.	Trial Balance Cr.	Adjustments Dr.	Adjustments Cr.	Profit & Loss Statement Dr.	Profit & Loss Statement Cr.	Balance Sheet Dr.	Balance Sheet Cr.
Cash	111	745000						745000	
Accounts Receivable	113	950000						950000	
Merchandise Inv.	114	2130000		(b)2410000	(a)2130000			2410000	
Store Supplies	115	116000			(c)61000			55000	
Office Supplies	116	52000			(d)29000			23000	
Prepaid Insurance	117	147500			(e)59000			88500	
Store Equipment	121	2448000						2448000	
Office Equipment	122	580000						580000	
Building	123	1500000						1500000	
Land	124	300000						300000	
Accounts Payable	211		1035000						1035000
Mortgage Payable	221		600000						600000
William Gordon, Capital	311		5875000						5875000
William Gordon, Drawing	312	800000						800000	
Sales	411		15840000				15840000		
Sales Returns & Allowances	412	260000				260000			
Purchases	511	11520000				11520000			
Freight In	512	365000				365000			
Purchases Ret. & Allowances	513		17500				17500		
Sales Salaries	611	890000		(f)12000		902000			
Advertising Expense	613	165000				165000			
Misc. Selling Expense	616	52500				52500			
Office Salaries	711	320000		(f)4500		324500			
Taxes Expense	712	157000				157000			
Misc. General Expense	715	72000				72000			
Purchases Discount	811		240000				240000		
Sales Discount	911	195000				195000			
		23765000	23765000						
Profit & Loss Summary	313			(a)2130000	(b)2410000	2130000	2410000		
Store Supplies Expense	614			(c)61000		61000			
Office Supplies Expense	713			(d)29000		29000			
Insurance Exp.–Sell.	615			(e)41000		41000			
Insurance Exp.–Gen.	714			(e)18000		18000			
Salaries Payable	212				(f)16500				16500
Sales Commissions	612			(g)300000		300000			
Commissions Payable	213				(g)300000				300000
				5005500	5005500	16592000	18665000	9899500	7826500
Net Profit						2073000			2073000
						18665000	18665000	9899500	9899500

Eight-Column Work Sheet

debited, Sales Salaries for $120 and Office Salaries for $45. (Entry (f) on the work sheet.) Similarly, commissions earned but not paid are recorded by a credit to the liability account Commissions Payable and a debit to the expense account Sales Commissions. (Entry (g) on the work sheet.)

COMPLETING THE   After the adjustments have been entered in
WORK SHEET   the Adjustments columns, the equality of the
adjustment debits and credits is proved by adding the columns.

In the work sheet illustrated on page 87 the amounts in the Trial
Balance columns were combined with the amounts in the Adjustments
columns and were extended into the Adjusted Trial Balance columns.
Many accountants prefer to extend the amounts directly to the Profit
and Loss Statement and Balance Sheet columns, omitting the Adjusted
Trial Balance columns. This latter plan is followed in the
illustration on page 167.

When the amounts in the Trial Balance and the Adjustments
columns are combined and extended, the debit of $21,300 and the
credit of $24,100 to Profit and Loss Summary are both extended into
the Profit and Loss Statement columns. The same amount of net profit
would be obtained at the bottom of the work sheet if the difference
between the two amounts was entered as a credit of $2,800 in the Profit
and Loss Cr. column. But the debit amount of $21,300 is the beginning
inventory and the credit amount of $24,100 is the ending inventory.
Both of these amounts are used in the preparation of the profit and
loss statement; both are therefore extended so that the statement can
be prepared completely from the data in the Profit and Loss Statement
columns of the work sheet.

When all items have been extended into the Profit and Loss Statement and the Balance Sheet columns of the work sheet, the net profit
for the period is determined by subtracting the total of the Profit and
Loss Statement Dr. column from the total of the Profit and Loss Statement Cr. column. This net profit is found to be $20,730. The net
profit is also found by subtracting the Balance Sheet Cr. column from
the Balance Sheet Dr. column. This amount, too, is found to be
$20,730 and is evidence that the work has been completed correctly.
The amount of the net profit is added to the Profit and Loss Statement
Dr. column and to the Balance Sheet Cr. column, and the columns are
ruled in the manner shown in the illustration on page 167.

PREPARATION OF   The balance sheet and the profit and loss
STATEMENTS AND   statement are prepared from the data appear-
SUPPORTING   ing in the work sheet. The order of the items
SCHEDULES   in the work sheet corresponds to the order in
which they appear in the statements, with the exception of those that
are listed below the trial balance. The analysis of changes in capital
during the period may be presented on a separate statement or it may
be incorporated in the proprietorship section of the balance sheet.

GORDON ELECTRIC APPLIANCES   Exhibit A
Balance Sheet
December 31, 1953

Assets

Current Assets:
Cash . . . . $ 7,450
Accounts Receivable - Schedule 1   9,500
Merchandise Inventory. 24,100
Store Supplies   550
Office Supplies.   230
Prepaid Insurance..   885
Total Current Assets $42,715

Fixed Assets:
Store Equipment. $24,480
Office Equipment   5,800
Building 15,000
Land   3,000
Total Fixed Assets   48,280

Total Assets. $90,995

Liabilities

Current Liabilities:
Accounts Payable - Schedule 2. . . . . . . $10,350
Salaries Payable   165
Commissions Payable. 3,000
Total Current Liabilities. $13,515

Fixed Liabilities:
Mortgage Payable (Due 1958). 6,000

Total Liabilities $19,515

Proprietorship

William Gordon, Capital - Exhibit B   71,480

Total Liabilities and Proprietorship. $90,995

Balance Sheet

GORDON ELECTRIC APPLIANCES   Exhibit B
Statement of Proprietor's Capital
For Year Ended December 31, 1953

William Gordon, Capital, January 1, 1953. . . . . . . $58,750
Net Profit for the Year - Exhibit C $20,730
Less Withdrawals   8,000
Increase in Capital   12,730

William Gordon, Capital, December 31, 1953. . . . . . $71,480

Statement of Proprietor's Capital

GORDON ELECTRIC APPLIANCES   Exhibit C
Profit and Loss Statement
For Year Ended December 31, 1953

Income from Sales:
   Sales. $158,400
   Less Sales Returns and Allowances.   2,600
   Net Sales. $155,800

Cost of Goods Sold:
   Merchandise Inventory, January 1, 1953 . . . . . $ 21,300
   Purchases. $115,200
   Add Freight In   3,650
   Delivered Cost of Purchases. $118,850
   Less Purchases Returns and Allowances.   1,750
   Net Purchases. 117,100
   Merchandise Available for Sale $138,400
   Less Merchandise Inventory, December 31, 1953. . 24,100
   Cost of Goods Sold   114,300

Gross Profit on Sales . . . . $ 41,500

Operating Expenses:
   Selling Expenses:
      Sales Salaries. $9,020
      Sales Commissions 3,000
      Advertising Expense 1,650
      Store Supplies Expense.   610
      Insurance Expense--Selling.   410
      Miscellaneous Selling Expense   525
      Total Selling Expenses. . . . . $ 15,215

   General Expenses:
      Office Salaries $3,245
      Taxes Expense 1,570
      Office Supplies Expense   290
      Insurance Expense--General.   180
      Miscellaneous General Expense   720
      Total General Expenses.   6,005
   Total Operating Expenses   21,220

Net Profit from Operations. . . . . $ 20,280

Other Income:
   Purchases Discount . . . . $ 2,400

Other Expense:
   Sales Discount 1,950

Net Addition.   450

Net Profit. . . . . $ 20,730

Profit and Loss Statement

    The schedules of accounts receivable and accounts payable are
prepared from the respective subsidiary ledgers at the time the trial
balance of the general ledger is drawn up. The totals of the schedules
should, of course, be compared with the balances of the related control

accounts at that time and any discrepancies should be corrected before proceeding with the work sheet. In order to facilitate cross referencing between statements and supporting schedules, it is customary to designate each by letter or number. There are variations in the designations employed and in the order in which the various statements are presented. The statements of Gordon Electric Appliances, appearing on pages 169 to 171, follow a pattern that is commonly used.

GORDON ELECTRIC APPLIANCES Schedule of Accounts Receivable December 31, 1953	Exhibit A Schedule 1
Ernest H. Adams	$ 420
Dover Hotel	2,315
Earl A. Jensen	825
S. V. Morton	650
Robert Nelson	1,125
George D. Porter	932
Milton Quinn	128
Rogers Restaurant	1,496
Albert T. Shaw	765
Wright Barber Shop	844
Total Accounts Receivable	$9,500

Schedule of Accounts Receivable

GORDON ELECTRIC APPLIANCES Schedule of Accounts Payable December 31, 1953	Exhibit A Schedule 2
American Home Appliance Company	$ 2,426
Bauer Electric Corporation	1,303
Office Equipment Distributors	325
Parker Manufacturing Company	1,117
Ross Supplies, Inc.	65
Tri-State Television Distributors	1,694
Watson Manufacturing Company	3,420
Total Accounts Payable	$10,350

Schedule of Accounts Payable

ADJUSTING ENTRIES　　　After the financial reports have been prepared, the adjusting entries are journalized and posted. Since all details regarding the adjustments were considered in preparing the work sheet, the entries may be made from the Adjustments columns of the work sheet. After they have been posted to the ledger, the accounts will agree with the details reported in the financial statements. The adjusting entries for Gordon Electric Appliances are presented on the following page.

GENERAL JOURNAL   PAGE 33

DATE	DESCRIPTION	POST. REF.	DEBIT	CREDIT
	Adjusting Entries			
31	Profit and Loss Summary	313	2 1 3 0 0 0	
	Merchandise Inventory	114		2 1 3 0 0 0
31	Merchandise Inventory	114	2 4 1 0 0 0	
	Profit and Loss Summary	313		2 4 1 0 0 0
31	Store Supplies Expense	614	6 1 0 0	
	Store Supplies	115		6 1 0 0
31	Office Supplies Expense	713	2 9 0 0	
	Office Supplies	116		2 9 0 0
31	Insurance Expense–Selling	615	4 1 0 0	
	Insurance Expense–General	714	1 8 0 0	
	Prepaid Insurance	117		5 9 0 0
31	Sales Salaries	611	1 2 0 0 0	
	Office Salaries	711	4 5 0 0	
	Salaries Payable	212		1 6 5 0 0
31	Sales Commissions	612	3 0 0 0 0	
	Commissions Payable	213		3 0 0 0 0

Adjusting Entries

CLOSING ENTRIES   The closing entries are recorded in the general journal, immediately following the adjusting entries. The effect of the closing entries is to reduce the balances of all temporary proprietorship accounts to zero and to transfer the net increase or decrease in proprietorship to the capital account. The four closing entries for Gordon Electric Appliances, which are illustrated on page 173, may be described as follows:

(1) The first entry closes all profit and loss statement accounts with *credit* balances by transferring the total to the *credit* side of Profit and Loss Summary.

(2) The second entry closes all profit and loss statement accounts with *debit* balances by transferring the total to the *debit* side of Profit and Loss Summary.

(3) The third entry closes Profit and Loss Summary by transferring its balance to William Gordon, Drawing.

(4) The fourth entry closes William Gordon, Drawing by transferring its balance to William Gordon, Capital.

GENERAL JOURNAL   PAGE 34

DATE	DESCRIPTION	POST. REF.	DEBIT	CREDIT
	Closing Entries			
1953 Dec. 31	Sales	411	15840000	
	Purchases Returns & Allowances	513	17500	
	Purchases Discount	811	24000	
	Profit and Loss Summary	313		16255000
31	Profit and Loss Summary	313	14462000	
	Sales Returns & Allowances	412		260000
	Purchases	511		11520000
	Freight In	512		365000
	Sales Salaries	611		902000
	Advertising Expense	613		165000
	Misc. Selling Expense	616		52500
	Office Salaries	711		324500
	Taxes Expense	712		157000
	Misc. General Expense	715		72000
	Sales Discount	911		195000
	Store Supplies Expense	614		61000
	Office Supplies Expense	713		29000
	Insurance Expense—Selling	615		41000
	Insurance Expense—General	714		18000
	Sales Commissions	612		300000
31	Profit and Loss Summary	313	2073000	
	William Gordon, Drawing	312		2073000
31	William Gordon, Drawing	312	1273000	
	William Gordon, Capital	311		1273000

Closing Entries

After the foregoing closing entries have been posted, the profit and loss summary account will have three debits and two credits. The first debit and the first credit in the account, which is reproduced below, were posted from the two entries adjusting the merchandise inventory account.

Profit and Loss Summary   ACCOUNT NO. 313

DATE	ITEMS	POST. REF.	DEBIT	DATE	ITEMS	POST. REF.	CREDIT
1953 Dec. 31		J33	2130000	1953 Dec. 31		J33	2410000
31		J34	14462000	31		J34	16255000
31		J34	2073000				
			18665000				18665000

Some accountants, however, prefer to have the profit and loss summary account show the income, costs, and expenses in detail. In such instances the individual items in each entry are posted to the profit and loss summary account. For example, in the first journal entry Sales, Purchases Returns and Allowances, and Purchases Discount are debited, and Profit and Loss Summary is credited for the sum of the three amounts. When the entry is posted to the profit and loss summary account, three credits are entered separately and the source of each credit is indicated in the Items column. Similarly the journal entry shows one debit for all costs and expenses; but when the entry is posted, the various debits making up this total are entered separately and the source of each is indicated in the Items column. This method, illustrated below, has the advantage of showing in the profit and loss summary account all sources of income, cost, and expense instead of totals only.

Profit and Loss Summary   ACCOUNT NO. 313

DATE	ITEMS	POST. REF.	DEBIT	DATE	ITEMS	POST. REF.	CREDIT
1953				1953			
Dec. 31	Beginning Inv.	J33	2 1 3 0 0 0 0	Dec. 31	Ending Inv.	J33	24 1 0 0 0 0
31	Sales Ret & Allow.	J34	2 6 0 0 0 0	31	Sales	J34	158 4 0 0 0 0
31	Purchases	J34	11 5 2 0 0 0 0	31	Pur. Ret. & Allow.	J34	1 7 5 0 0 0
31	Freight In	J34	3 6 5 0 0 0	31	Pur. Discount	J34	2 4 0 0 0 0
31	Sales Salaries	J34	9 0 2 0 0 0				
31	Advertising Ex	J34	1 6 5 0 0 0				
31	Misc. Sell Exp	J34	5 2 5 0 0				
31	Office Salaries	J34	3 2 4 5 0 0				
31	Taxes Exp.	J34	1 5 7 0 0 0				
31	Misc. Gen. Exp	J34	7 2 0 0 0				
31	Sales Disct	J34	1 9 5 0 0 0				
31	Store Sup. Exp	J34	6 1 0 0 0				
31	Office Sup. Exp	J34	2 9 0 0 0				
31	Ins. Exp. Sell	J34	4 1 0 0 0				
31	Ins. Exp. Gen	J34	1 8 0 0 0				
31	Sales Commission	J34	3 0 0 0 0 0				
31	W. Gordon, Draw	J34	20 7 3 0 0 0				
			18 6 6 5 0 0 0				18 6 6 5 0 0 0

Profit and Loss Summary Account with Itemized Entries

After the adjusting entries and the closing entries have been posted to Gordon's ledger, the accounts are balanced and ruled. Only the asset accounts, the liability accounts, and the proprietor's capital account remain open. The balances of these accounts correspond exactly with the amounts on the balance sheet on page 169.

THE POST-CLOSING TRIAL BALANCE   At the end of a fiscal period the equality of the debits and the credits in the ledger is determined by means of a trial balance. The adjusting and the closing entries are then made. If these entries are recorded and posted correctly, the equilibrium of the debits and the credits in the ledger is not disturbed because the entries consist of equal debits and credits. A post-closing trial balance is therefore taken to test the accuracy of these entries. The post-closing trial balance of Gordon Electric Appliances is illustrated below:

Gordon Electric Appliances Post-Closing Trial Balance December 31, 1953			
Cash	111	7450 00	
Accounts Receivable	113	950 00	
Merchandise Inventory	114	24100 00	
Store Supplies	115	550 00	
Office Supplies	116	230 00	
Prepaid Insurance	117	885 00	
Store Equipment	121	2448 00	
Office Equipment	122	580 00	
Building	123	15000 00	
Land	124	3000 00	
Accounts Payable	211		10350 00
Salaries Payable	212		165 00
Commission Payable	213		3000 00
Mortgage Payable	221		6000 00
William Gordon, Capital	311		71480 00
		90995 00	90995 00

Post-Closing Trial Balance

REVERSING ENTRIES   Some types of adjusting entries made at the close of the period affect the entries that will be made for related transactions in the following period. For example, Salaries Payable in Gordon's ledger was credited for $165 on December 31. This represented the liability for sales salaries of $120 and office salaries of $45 that had accrued between the last salary payment date and December 31. Assuming that the salary to be paid to the sales force at the end of the first pay period ending in January amounts to $360, it is evident that $120 of the payment should be debited to Salaries Payable and the remaining $240 should be debited to Sales Salaries. Similarly, of the total payment of $135 to the office staff, $45 should be debited to Salaries Payable and the remaining $90 should be debited to Office Salaries.

It is not necessary to make this analysis at the time the salaries are paid if the balance of the salaries payable account has been previously transferred to the two salary expense accounts. The entry that accomplishes this transfer is exactly the reverse of the original adjusting entry and is called a *reversing entry* or *readjusting entry*. The reversing entries for Gordon Electric Appliances are as follows:

GENERAL JOURNAL   PAGE *34*

DATE		DESCRIPTION	POST. REF.	DEBIT	CREDIT
		Reversing Entries			
1954 Jan. 1		Salaries Payable	212	165 00	
		Sales Salaries	611		120 00
		Office Salaries	711		45 00
	1	Commissions Payable	213	300 00	
		Sales Commissions	612		300 00

Reversing Entries

After the above reversing entries have been posted, the accounts Salaries Payable and Commissions Payable will have a balance of zero and should be ruled. The liability for salaries and commissions will now appear as credits in the respective expense accounts. As salaries and commissions are paid in the new period, the entire amount paid will be debited to the appropriate expense accounts. The balances of the expense accounts will then automatically represent the expense of the new period. This is illustrated in the T account below. After the payment of $360 on January 9, 1954, the balance of the account is $240, which is the amount of the expense to date in the new period.

SALES SALARIES

1953			1953	
Dec. 31 Balance	8,900		Dec. 31 (Closing)	9,020
31 (Adjusting)	120			
	9,020			9,020
1954			1954	
Jan. 9 (Payment)	360		Jan. 1 (Reversing)	120

CORRECTION OF ERRORS   Various procedures used in correcting errors in the accounts were described in Chapter 5. In all of the situations considered, the errors were presumed to have been discovered and corrected in the same period in which they occurred. In some cases the manner in which the correction will be made is affected by the closing of the books in the interim between the occurrence of the error and its discovery. For an error affecting only asset or liability accounts, however, the correcting entry is the same regardless of when it is discovered. A typical example is a debit or credit entry to one customer's account that should have been made to another customer's account.

Errors resulting in a misstatement of net profit of a previous period cannot be corrected by an entry in the appropriate income or expense account of that period but must be corrected, if at all, by an entry in the capital account. This is so because the temporary proprietorship accounts for the earlier period have been closed and the effect of the error has been transferred to the capital account. For example, assume that in adjusting Prepaid Insurance and the two insurance expense accounts at the end of a fiscal year, the former account was understated by $100 and the latter were correspondingly overstated by the same amount. Assume, further, that the error was discovered in the following period. The correcting entry in the general journal would be as follows:

```
Jan. 20  Prepaid Insurance...................... 100.00
             George Adams, Capital................             100.00
             To correct the error in the adjusting
             entry of December 31.
```

There are differences of opinion among accountants as to whether a misstatement of net profit of a period should be corrected through the capital account or whether it should be reflected in the net profit of the subsequent period. To continue the illustration, if the correcting entry had not been made, the understatement of income in the earlier period would have been offset by an overstatement of income in the following period. Factors to be considered in a particular case include the materiality of the error, the feasibility of correcting the financial statements affected by the error, and the manner in which the error is taken care of in determining income taxes.

QUESTIONS

1. Discuss the advantage and the disadvantage of having columns for "Adjusted Trial Balance" in the work sheet.

2. The data for the adjustments on December 31, the end of the fiscal year, are given below. Prepare the necessary adjusting entries.

(a) The merchandise inventories are as follows: January 1, $16,492.30; December 31, $15,120.65.

(b) The balance of the store supplies account on December 31 is $326.15. The inventory of store supplies on hand on that date totals $95.80.

(c) The balance of the prepaid insurance account on January 1, $202.50, was composed of the following items:

POLICY No.	PREPAID AS OF JANUARY 1	NUMBER OF MONTHS	MONTHLY EXPIRATION
14276	$106.50	15	$ 7.10
AC3491	96.00	8	12.00

On September 1 Policy No. AC4763, covering a three-year period from date, was acquired, the premium of $486 being debited to Prepaid Insurance.

(d) Salaries accrued since the last payday amount to $450, of which $340 is owed to sales employees and $110 is owed to office employees.

3. The following relates to the adjustment for accrued salaries in Question 2 above:

(a) Journalize the reversing entry required as of January 1.

(b) On the first payday in January, sales employees are paid $510 and office employees are paid $165, Sales Salaries and Office Salaries being debited for the respective amounts. What is the correct amount of sales and office salaries incurred thus far in January?

4. Discuss the purpose of (a) adjusting entries, (b) closing entries, and (c) reversing entries.

5. Immediately after the work of the periodic summary has been completed at the end of the year, Rent Expense has a *credit* balance of $150. Assuming that there have been no errors, what is the nature of this balance?

6. After the closing entries have been posted and the accounts have been ruled, it is discovered that an advertising expense item of $300 was erroneously debited to Miscellaneous General Expense. Would revision of the profit and loss statement for the period be sufficient to correct this error or should a correcting entry be made in the general journal?

7. The errors listed below were made in the accounts of George Holter during the preceding fiscal year. They were not discovered until after the books had been closed. Journalize the correcting entries that should be made in the current year.

(a) In taking the physical inventory of merchandise at the end of the year, certain items in a rented warehouse were overlooked, with the result that the inventory was understated by $2,600.

(b) In recording a sale of $175 to the White Company on account, the debit was erroneously made to the account of Whitley, Inc.

(c) No adjusting entry had been made for the insurance expired during the year, which amounted to $327.50. All insurance premiums had been charged to Prepaid Insurance.

(d) Routine repairs to the building amounting to $421.36 were erroneously debited to Building.

PROBLEMS

10-1. The account balances in the ledger of Frank Kinley on December 31 of the current year are as follows:

Cash	$ 6,300	Sales Returns and Allowances	$ 1,100
Accounts Receivable	12,500	Purchases	61,400
Merchandise Inventory	18,600	Freight In	950
Store Supplies	400	Purchases Returns and Allowances	700
Prepaid Rent	4,050	Sales Salaries	7,500
Prepaid Insurance	1,300	Advertising Expense	4,100
Store Equipment	2,400	Misc. Selling Expense	1,300
Accounts Payable	8,500	Office Salaries	4,500
Frank Kinley, Capital	22,000	Misc. General Expense	1,300
Sales	96,500		

The data for year-end adjustments on December 31 are as follows:

Merchandise inventory on Dec. 31	$15,500
Store supplies inventory on Dec. 31	50
Rent expense for year	2,700
Insurance expired during year	850

Instructions: (1) Prepare an eight-column work sheet for the fiscal year ended December 31.

(2) Record the adjusting entries in a general journal.

10-2. The accounts and their balances in the ledger of Inland Mercantile Co. on March 31 of the current year are as follows:

111	Cash	$18,763	412	Sales Returns and Allowances	$ 6,440
112	Accounts Receivable	27,955	511	Purchases	156,350
113	Merchandise Inventory	31,500	512	Freight In	3,127
114	Store Supplies	1,166	513	Purchases Returns and Allowances	4,309
115	Office Supplies	1,035	611	Sales Salaries	14,400
116	Prepaid Insurance	2,400	612	Advertising Expense	10,600
121	Store Equipment	3,150	613	Store Supplies Expense	— —
122	Office Equipment	1,275	614	Insurance Expense — Selling	— —
123	Building	18,250	619	Misc. Selling Expense	314
124	Land	12,700	711	Office Salaries	7,200
211	Accounts Payable	17,816	712	Taxes Expense	488
212	Salaries Payable	— —	713	Insurance Expense — General	— —
213	Taxes Payable	— —	714	Office Supplies Expense	— —
221	Mortgage Payable	15,000	719	Misc. General Expense	637
311	Kenneth Thornton, Capital	71,745	811	Purchases Discount	1,870
312	Kenneth Thornton, Drawing	5,400	911	Sales Discount	2,702
313	Profit and Loss Summary	— —			
411	Sales	215,112			

The data for year-end adjustments on March 31 are as follows:

Merchandise inventory on March 31	$40,400
Inventories of supplies on March 31:	
Store Supplies	600
Office Supplies	770

Insurance expired during the year:

Allocable as selling expense....................	$300	
Allocable as general expense...................	520	$820

Salaries payable on March 31:

Sales Salaries..............................	$180	
Office Salaries..............................	90	270
Taxes payable on March 31.....................		75

Instructions: (1) Open an account in the ledger for each account listed, using the account numbers indicated. Enter the balances in the appropriate accounts under date of March 31.

(2) Prepare an eight-column work sheet for the yearly fiscal period.

(3) Prepare a balance sheet in the report form (Exhibit A), a statement of proprietor's capital (Exhibit B), and a profit and loss statement (Exhibit C).

(4) Record the adjusting entries in a general journal and post to the ledger accounts.

(5) Record the closing entries and post to the ledger accounts.

(6) Rule and balance the ledger accounts that have two or more entries.

(7) Prepare a post-closing trial balance.

(8) Record the reversing entries on April 1, post to the ledger, and rule the additional accounts that are now in balance.

10-3. An audit of the accounts of Arthur Hall for the current fiscal year ended September 30 revealed the following errors:

(a) Office equipment costing $420 was erroneously debited to the store equipment account.

(b) In adjusting the prepaid insurance account at the end of the current year, the amount transferred to Insurance Expense was $765. The correct amount was $652.

(c) Three sales returns and allowances totaling $639 were erroneously recorded as purchases of merchandise.

(d) The inventory of store supplies at the end of the current year was overstated by $74.

(e) A payment of $265 to Carson & Co. on account was erroneously debited to Clawson, Inc.

(f) A typewriter purchased for office use at a cost of $110 was erroneously debited to Miscellaneous General Expense.

(g) A payment of $350 for furniture purchased by Mr. Hall for his home was erroneously debited to Store Equipment.

(h) In adjusting the books at the end of the current year, no provision was made for accrued sales salaries of $500 and accrued office salaries of $150.

(i) The merchandise inventory at the end of the current year was understated by $1,200.

Instructions: (1) Assuming that the above errors are discovered before the books are closed, present the necessary correcting entries in general journal form. Identify each entry by the letter given for the error in the list above.

(2) Assuming that the above errors are not discovered until after the books are closed, present the necessary correcting entries in general journal form. Identify each entry by the letter given for the error in the list above.

Trent Wholesale Shoes
Part 1

The transactions in this practice set were completed by Trent Wholesale Shoes, owned and operated by Frank Trent. Although these transactions deal with the operations of a wholesale shoe business, they are intended to illustrate general principles of accounting rather than the technique of the accounting system of a particular business.

Part 1, which is given on the following pages, applies the methods and the principles developed in the first ten chapters. Part 2, which follows Chapter 14, applies the methods and the principles developed in Chapters 11 to 14 also. Both parts of the practice set may be recorded in the same set of books of account.

General Ledger

The general ledger accounts to be used are:

Acct. No.		Acct. No.	
111	Cash	312	Frank Trent, Drawing
112	Notes Receivable	313	Profit and Loss Summary
113	Interest Receivable	411	Sales
114	Accounts Receivable	412	Sales Returns and Allowances
114.1	Allowance for Bad Debts	511	Purchases
115	Merchandise Inventory	512	Freight In
116	Store Supplies	513	Purchases Returns and Allowances
117	Office Supplies		
118	Prepaid Insurance	611	Sales Salaries
119	Prepaid Interest	612	Advertising Expense
121	Store Equipment	613	Store Supplies Expense
121.1	Allowance for Depreciation of Store Equipment	614	Depreciation of Store Equipment
		615	Miscellaneous Selling Expense
122	Office Equipment	711	Office Salaries
122.1	Allowance for Depreciation of Office Equipment	712	Rent Expense
		713	Office Supplies Expense
123	Building	714	Depreciation of Office Equipment
123.1	Allowance for Depreciation of Building	715	Depreciation of Building
124	Land	716	Insurance Expense
211	Notes Payable	717	Bad Debts Expense
212	Interest Payable	718	Miscellaneous General Expense
213	Accounts Payable	811	Purchases Discount
214	Salaries Payable	812	Interest Income
215	Unearned Rent	813	Rent Income
221	Mortgage Payable	911	Sales Discount
311	Frank Trent, Capital	912	Interest Expense

Instructions: (1) The accounts listed above are given in the general ledger in the books of account that may be obtained for this practice set. If these books are not used, open the foregoing general ledger accounts in the order in which they are given, allowing at least twelve lines for each account. Not all of these accounts will be used during the first month of this practice set, but all should be opened at this time.

The post-closing trial balance of Trent Wholesale Shoes as of April 30 of the current year is as follows:

TRENT WHOLESALE SHOES
POST-CLOSING TRIAL BALANCE
APRIL 30, 19 --

Cash.....................	111	6,952 68	
Accounts Receivable.......	114	2,631 23	
Merchandise Inventory.....	115	20,926 87	
Store Supplies............	116	108 67	
Office Supplies...........	117	79 83	
Prepaid Insurance.........	118	125 90	
Accounts Payable.........	213		2,562 90
Frank Trent, Capital......	311		28,262 28
		30,825 18	30,825 18

Instructions: (2) The account balances listed in the post-closing trial balance are already recorded in the general ledger in the books of account that may be obtained for this practice set. If these books are not used, record the foregoing balances in the appropriate accounts as of May 1.

Subsidiary Ledgers

The accounts in the accounts receivable ledger and the balances of those accounts that have balances on April 30 are as follows:

Adams Men's Furnishings, 6230 Broadway, City........	
Decker Department Store, 123 Fairview St., City........	$ 775.80
Paul Eastland, 9251 Sunset Ave., City................	
Greene's Footwear, 465 Bedford St., City..............	
Harvey Bootery, 923 South Main St., City.............	
Lee & Laird, 7862 West Blvd., City..................	526.90
Norton Shoe Store, 29 North Cedar St., City..........	895.78
Ralph Stevens, 3695 First St., City...................	
Waite's Apparel Shop, 629 Grand Ave., City...........	432.75
	$2,631.23

The accounts in the accounts payable ledger and the balances of those accounts that have balances on April 30 are as follows:

Boston Manufacturing Co., Lanesville..................	
Freeman Supply Co., 314 North Main St., City.........	$ 98.00
Horace & Co., 610 River Rd., City....................	
Lite-Tred Shoe Co., 3395 Boyle St., New York..........	782.90
Olds, Penny & Gold, Inc., 4138 Lake St., Chicago.......	
Smart Shoes, Inc., 3679 High St., Denver..............	1,682.00
Turner Shoe Corp., 3616 San Pedro St., Los Angeles.......	
	$2,562.90

Instructions: (3) The accounts and the balances listed above are given in the accounts receivable ledger and the accounts payable ledger in the books of account that may be obtained for this practice set. If these books are not used, open accounts for the accounts receivable and the accounts payable in the order in which they are given, allowing at least twelve lines for each account, and record the balances in the appropriate accounts as of May 1.

Books of Original Entry

The books of original entry consist of a general journal with two amount columns; a purchases journal like that on pages 126 and 127; a purchases returns and allowances journal like that on page 134; a sales journal like that on page 112; a sales returns and allowances journal like that on page 119; a cash receipts journal like that on page 141; and a cash payments journal like that on page 146.

Narrative of Transactions for May

May 1. Issued Check No. 101 for $725 for rent of building and equipment for May.

May 2. Made the following purchases on account:
Lite-Tred Shoe Co., merchandise, $361; invoice dated May 1.
Turner Shoe Corporation, merchandise, $316.80; invoice dated May 1.

May 3. Made the following sales on account:
Sale No. 1081, Paul Eastland, $526.20.
Sale No. 1082, Ralph Stevens, $459.

May 3. Issued checks as follows:
Check No. 102 for $90 for newspaper advertising.
Check No. 103 for $98 to Freeman Supply Co. in payment of its invoice for $98.

May 4. Sale No. 1080 for $775.80 on April 29 was incorrectly charged to the account of Decker Department Store when it should have been charged to the account of Adams Men's Furnishings.

May 4. Issued Check No. 104 for $30 for store supplies.

May 5. Made the following purchases on account:
Freeman Supply Co., office supplies, $24.90, store supplies, $19.80; invoice dated May 4.
Olds, Penny & Gold, Inc., merchandise, $450; invoice dated May 4.

May 5. Issued Check No. 105 for $767.24 to Lite-Tred Shoe Co. in payment of its invoice for $782.90 less a 2% discount.

May 6. Issued Credit Memo No. 201 for $31 to Ralph Stevens for the return of merchandise on the sale of May 3.

May 6. Issued Check No. 106 for $1,648.36 to Smart Shoes, Inc. in payment of its invoice for $1,682 less a 2% discount.

May 6. Received checks as follows:
A check for $516.36 from Lee & Laird in payment of our invoice for $526.90 less a 2% discount.
A check for $877.86 from Norton Shoe Store in payment of our invoice for $895.78 less a 2% discount.

May 6. Made the following sales on account:
Sale No. 1083, Norton Shoe Store, $728.
Sale No. 1084, Greene's Footwear, $1,352.

May 6. Received $1,592.80 from cash sales for May 1–6.

Post from the various journals to the customers' accounts in the accounts receivable ledger and to the creditors' accounts in the accounts payable ledger. In actual practice this posting would be completed daily, but because of the comparatively small number of transactions in this set, the posting will be completed only at the end of each week and of each month.

May 8. Received checks as follows:
A check for $760.28 from Adams Men's Furnishings in payment of our invoice for $775.80 less a 2% discount.
A check for $424.09 from Waite's Apparel Shop in payment of our invoice for $432.75 less a 2% discount.

May 8. Issued Check No. 107 for $62.80 for office supplies.

May 9. Made the following purchases on account:
Smart Shoes, Inc., merchandise, $270; invoice dated May 9.
Turner Shoe Corp., merchandise, $1,400.50; invoice dated May 8.

May 9. Issued Check No. 108 for $42.50 for booklets for the salesmen. (Charge Miscellaneous Selling Expense.)

May 10. Made the following sales on account:
Sale No. 1085, Decker Department Store, $3,220.60.
Sale No. 1086, Lee & Laird, $1,126.32.

May 10. Issued checks as follows:
Check No. 109 for $353.78 to Lite-Tred Shoe Co. in payment of its invoice for $361 less a 2% discount.
Check No. 110 for $310.46 to Turner Shoe Corp. in payment of its invoice for $316.80 less a 2% discount.

May 12. Issued Check No. 111 for $775.25 for a cash purchase of merchandise.

May 13. Received a credit memorandum for $100.50 from Turner Shoe Corp. for the return of merchandise on its invoice of May 8.

May 13. Received checks as follows:
A check for $419.44 from Ralph Stevens in payment of our invoice for $459, less the credit of $31, less a 2% discount.
A check for $515.68 from Paul Eastland in payment of our invoice for $526.20 less a 2% discount.

May 13. Purchased merchandise on account from Boston Manufacturing Co., $2,022; invoice dated May 12.

May 13. Issued checks as follows:
Check No. 112 for $445.50 to Olds, Penny & Gold, Inc. in payment of its invoice for $450 less a 1% discount.
Check No. 113 for $1,100 for biweekly salaries divided as follows: sales salaries, $850; office salaries, $250.

May 13. Received $1,025 from cash sales for May 8–13.
Post to the accounts in the accounts receivable ledger and the accounts payable ledger.

May 15. Issued Check No. 114 for $300 to Frank Trent for personal use.

May 16. Received checks as follows:
A check for $713.44 from Norton's Shoe Store in payment of our invoice for $728 less a 2% discount.

A check for $1,324.96 from Greene's Footwear in payment of our invoice
for $1,352 less a 2% discount.

May 17. Made the following purchases on account:
Freeman Supply Co., office supplies, $50, cleaning supplies (to be charged
to Miscellaneous General Expense), $68.75; invoice dated May 17.
Turner Shoe Corp., merchandise, $3,076.80; invoice dated May 16.

May 17. Issued Check No. 115 for $1,274 to Turner Shoe Corp. in pay-
ment of its invoice for $1,400.50, less the return of $100.50, less a 2% discount.

May 18. Received a check for $42 for the return of merchandise that had
been purchased for cash.

May 18. Issued Check No. 116 for $52 for store supplies.

May 19. Issued Credit Memo No. 202 for $20.60 to Decker Department
Store for merchandise returned on the sale of May 10.

May 20. Made the following sales on account:
Sale No. 1087, Waite's Apparel Shop, $2,076.80.
Sale No. 1088, Greene's Footwear, $982.30.
Sale No. 1089, Harvey Bootery, $700.10.

May 20. Issued Check No. 117 for $1,981.56 to Boston Manufacturing Co.
in payment of its invoice for $2,022 less a 2% discount.

May 20. Received checks as follows:
A check for $3,136 from Decker Department Store in payment of our
invoice for $3,220.60, less the return of $20.60, less a 2% discount.
A check for $1,103.79 from Lee & Laird in payment of our invoice for
$1,126.32 less a 2% discount.

May 20. Received $1,282.89 from cash sales for May 15–20.
Post to the accounts in the accounts receivable ledger and the accounts
payable ledger.

May 24. Made the following sales on account:
Sale No. 1090, Ralph Stevens, $522.
Sale No. 1091, Norton Shoe Store, $892.40.

May 25. Issued Check No. 118 for $3,015.26 to Turner Shoe Corp. in
payment of its invoice for $3,076.80 less a 2% discount.

May 26. Issued Credit Memo No. 203 for $32.40 to Norton Shoe Store
for damaged merchandise returned on the sale of May 24.

May 27. Received a credit memorandum for $130 from Smart Shoes, Inc.
for the return of damaged merchandise on its invoice of May 9.

May 27. Issued Check No. 119 for $1,100 for biweekly salaries divided as
follows: sales salaries, $850; office salaries, $250.

May 27. Purchased merchandise on account from Boston Manufacturing
Co., $3,068.90; invoice dated May 27.

May 27. Received $1,243.25 from cash sales for May 22–27.
Post to the accounts in the accounts receivable ledger and the accounts
payable ledger.

May 29. Purchased store supplies on account from Horace & Co., $85;
invoice dated May 27.

May 30. Issued Credit Memo No. 204 for $42 to Ralph Stevens for the
return of merchandise on the sale of May 24.

May 30. Issued Check No. 120 for $124 in payment of heat, light, and power. (Charge Miscellaneous General Expense.)

May 30. Received a check for $686.10 from Harvey Bootery in payment of our invoice for $700.10 less a 2% discount.

May 31. Sold merchandise on account to Adams Men's Furnishings, $946.20; Sale No. 1092.

May 31. Received a credit memorandum for $48.90 from Boston Manufacturing Co. for merchandise returned on its invoice of May 27.

May 31. Issued checks as follows:
Check No. 121 for $260.35 for freight charges on merchandise purchased.
Check No. 122 for $200 to Frank Trent for personal use.

May 31. Received $982.65 from cash sales for May 29–31.

Cash Proof and Posting

Total all columns of the cash receipts journal and the cash payments journal, entering the totals in small pencil figures. On a separate sheet of paper, add the debit totals and the credit totals for each journal to prove that in each journal the total of the debits is equal to the total of the credits.

Find the cash balance according to the books by adding the beginning balance in the ledger account and the total of the cash receipts and subtracting the total of the cash payments. This balance should be $8,843.21, the cash actually on hand and in the bank. If your balance is not this amount, find the error before proceeding with the posting.

Post to the accounts in the accounts receivable ledger and the accounts payable ledger.

Post to the general ledger accounts from the general columns of the purchases journal, the cash receipts journal, and the cash payments journal.

Total and rule the various special journals and post the totals to the appropriate general ledger accounts.

Periodic Summary

As the proprietor, Frank Trent, considers each month to be a separate fiscal period, the periodic summary must now be completed. The additional data required for this summary are:

Merchandise inventory on May 31	$20,368.92
Inventories of supplies on May 31:	
Store supplies	145.00
Office supplies	125.00
Insurance expired during the month	60.00
Salaries payable on May 31:	
Sales salaries	212.50
Office salaries	62.50

Complete the work at the end of this fiscal period according to the outline on page 163. Also prepare schedules of accounts receivable and accounts payable. Be sure to record and post the reversing entry.

Part 2 of this practice set, containing the narrative of transactions for June, begins on page 261 immediately after Chapter 14. The books of account for May will be needed at that time.

Chapter | 11

Accounting for Notes and Interest

NATURE OF NOTES AND INTEREST
Purchases and sales of goods and services by commercial enterprises are made on either a cash or a credit basis. When goods or services are sold on account, the seller does not receive payment until some time during, or at the end of, the credit period. Ordinarily the agreement between the parties makes no provision for the payment of interest for the credit granted.

There are occasions, however, when *promissory notes* are employed in credit transactions. A promissory note, frequently referred to simply as a *note*, is a written promise to pay a certain sum of money at a fixed or determinable future time. As in the case of a check, it must be payable to the order of a particular person or firm, or to bearer. It must also be signed by the person or firm that makes the promise. The one to whose order the note is payable is called the *payee*, and the one making the promise is called the *maker*. In the illustration below, Robert Reed is the payee and George Harris is the maker.

$ 1,500.00	New Orleans, Louisiana, September 1, _____ 1953
---------------Sixty days--------------- AFTER DATE____I____ PROMISE TO PAY TO	
THE ORDER OF Robert Reed	
One Thousand Five Hundred 00/100--- DOLLARS	
PAYABLE AT First National Bank	
VALUE RECEIVED WITH INTEREST AT --6--- %	
No. 47 DUE October 31, 1953 George Harris	

Interest-Bearing Note

The person or firm owning a note refers to it as a *note receivable* and records it at its face amount in the asset account Notes Receivable. The maker of a note refers to it as a *note payable* and records it at its face amount in the liability account Notes Payable. Thus, the note in the illustration would appear in Reed's notes receivable account at $1,500 and in Harris' notes payable account at $1,500.

A note that provides for the payment of interest for the period between the issuance date and the due date is called an *interest-bearing note*. If no provision is made for interest prior to maturity, the note is said to be *non-interest-bearing*. In such cases, however, interest may be charged at the legal rate for any time that the note remains unpaid after it is due. The interest that a business is obliged to pay is an expense and is called *interest expense*. The interest that a business is entitled to receive is an income and is called *interest income*.

ASCERTAINING   Rates of interest are usually stated in terms
INTEREST   of a period of one year. Thus, the interest on
a $1,500, 1-year, 6% note would amount to 6% of $1,500, or $90. If, instead of one year, the term of the note was half of a year, the interest would amount to one half of $90, or $45.

Notes covering a period of time longer than a year ordinarily provide that the interest be paid annually, semiannually, or at some other stated interval. The time involved in commercial credit transactions is usually less than a year, and the interest provided for by the note is payable at the time the note is paid. In computing interest for a period of less than a year, agencies of the Federal Government use the actual number of days in the year; for example, 90 days is considered to be 90/365 of a year. As a means of simplifying the calculation, the usual commercial practice is to use 360 as the denominator of the fraction; thus 90 days is considered to be 90/360 of a year. The commercial practice will be followed in this book.

The period of time between the issuance date and the maturity date of a short-term note may be expressed either in days or months. When the term of a note is expressed as a specified number of days after the issuance date, the due date may be determined in the following manner:

(1) Subtract the date of the note from the number of days in the month in which it is dated.

(2) Add as many full months as possible without exceeding the number of days in the note, counting the full number of days in these months.

(3) Subtract the total days obtained in (1) and (2) from the number of days in the note.

Assuming a 90-day note dated June 5, the due date is determined as follows:

```
Term of the note..............  90
June (days)...........  30
Date of note..........   5
                        ──
  Remainder.............  25
July (days)...............  31
August (days)............  31
                         ──
  Total......................  87
                              ──
Due date, September.........   3
```

When the term of a note is expressed as a specified number of months after the issuance date, the due date is determined by counting the number of months from the issuance date. Thus, a 3-month note dated June 5 would be due on September 5. In those cases in which there is no date in the month of maturity that corresponds to the issuance date, the due date becomes the last day of the month. For example, a 2-month note dated July 31 would be due on September 30.

When the term of a note is expressed in months, each month may be considered as being 1/12 of a year, or, alternatively, the actual number of days in the term may be counted. For example, the interest on a 3-month note dated June 1 could be calculated on the basis of 3/12 of a year or on the basis of 92/360 of a year. It is the usual commercial practice to employ the first method, while banks usually charge interest for the exact number of days. For the sake of uniformity, the commercial practice will be followed in this book.

The basic formula for computing interest is as follows:

$$\text{Principal} \times \text{Rate} \times \text{Time} = \text{Interest}$$

To illustrate the application of the formula, assume a note for $900, payable 64 days from date, with interest at 6%. The interest would be $9.60, computed as follows:

$$\$900 \times \frac{6}{100} \times \frac{64}{360} = \$9.60 \text{ interest}$$

There are a number of short-cut methods of computing interest. One that is commonly used is called the 60-day, 6% method. This method is based on the fact that interest at the rate of 6% per year is equal to 1% for 60 days or 1/6 of a year. The interest on any amount for 60 days at 6% can be determined, therefore, by moving the decimal point in the principal two places to the left. The interest on $900 for 64 days at 6% may be determined as follows:

$900 for 60 days (1% of $900)................... $9.00
$900 for 4 days (1/15 of $9.00)................   .60
                                                  ─────
Interest for 64 days at 6%..................... $9.60

It is often necessary to compute the interest for a certain period at a rate greater or smaller than 6%. In such a case the interest for the period at 6% is determined first. The proper amount to be added to or subtracted from this amount is then computed, and the interest at the given rate is thus ascertained. For instance, if, in the example given above, the interest rate were 7%, the interest on $900 for 64 days at 6% would be determined first. The interest at an additional 1% would then be found by taking 1/6 of the interest at 6%. The two amounts would then be added. The calculation of the interest in this case is as follows:

$900 for 64 days at 6% (computed on page 189)......	$ 9.60
$900 for 64 days at 1% (1/6 of $9.60)...............	1.60
Interest for 64 days at 7%.........................	$11.20

If the rate of interest in the preceding example were only 4%, 1/3 of the interest at 6% would be determined and this amount would be subtracted from the interest at 6%. The calculation of the interest in this case is as follows:

$900 for 64 days at 6% (computed on page 189).......	$9.60
$900 for 64 days at 2% (1/3 of $9.60)...............	3.20
Interest for 64 days at 4%.........................	$6.40

NOTES PAYABLE   All notes payable are usually recorded in one account in the general ledger. The details of each note issued are kept by preparing a carbon copy at the time the note form is filled in or by maintaining some other type of supplementary record. For this reason there is usually no advantage in maintaining a subsidiary ledger for notes payable.

When a note is issued to a creditor in payment of an account, the liability Accounts Payable is decreased and the liability Notes Payable is increased. These facts are recorded by debiting the accounts payable account and the account of the creditor to whom the note was issued, and by crediting the notes payable account.

For example, if a business requests an extension of time for payment of an invoice, the creditor may require that the debtor issue a note for the period involved. Assume that on October 8 W. L. Camp gave a 30-day, non-interest-bearing note for $1,000 to B. T. Dunbar on account. The transaction was recorded in Camp's general journal as follows:

Oct.	8	Accounts Payable — B. T. Dunbar	213/ √	1,000	
		Notes Payable................	211		1,000
		Issued a 30-day, non-interest-			
		bearing note.			

Dunbar may hold the note until November 7, the due date, or he may transfer it to one of his creditors or to his bank. Regardless of who holds the note at maturity, when Camp makes payment his liability Notes Payable decreases and his asset Cash decreases. The payment of the note was recorded by Camp in his cash payments journal in the following manner:

CASH PAYMENTS JOURNAL PAGE 21

DATE	CHECK NO.	ACCOUNT DEBITED	POST. REF.	GENERAL DR.	ACCTS. PAYABLE DR.	PUR. DISC. CR.	CASH CR.
1953 Nov. 7	596	Notes Payable	211	1,000			1,000

RECORDING INTEREST EXPENSE Like all other expenses, interest expense represents a deduction from proprietorship. It is recorded as a debit in a separate account entitled Interest Expense.

For example, on July 1 C. K. Ramers gave a creditor, R. F. Burdick, a note for $800, due in 60 days and bearing interest at the rate of 6%. On August 30 Ramers gave Burdick a check for $808 in payment of the note and the interest. The issuance of the note was recorded in Ramers' general journal and the payment of the note and the interest was recorded in Ramers' cash payments journal as follows:

July	1	Accounts Payable — R. F. Burdick	213/ √	800	
		Notes Payable..............	211		800
		Issued a 60-day, 6% note.			

CASH PAYMENTS JOURNAL PAGE 16

DATE	CHECK NO.	ACCOUNT DEBITED	POST. REF.	GENERAL DR.	ACCTS. PAYABLE DR.	PUR. DISC. CR.	CASH CR.
1953 Aug. 30	618	Notes Payable	211	800			808
		Interest Expense	912	8			

All of the examples considered thus far have involved notes issued to a creditor on account. A business may also issue notes in borrowing money from a bank. For example, on April 10 C. K. Ramers borrowed $5,000 from the First National Bank, the loan being evidenced by a note payable in 90 days, with interest at the rate of 6%. The entries made by Ramers in his cash receipts and cash payments journals to record the loan and its payment were as follows:

CASH RECEIPTS JOURNAL PAGE 7

DATE	ACCOUNT CREDITED	POST. REF.	GENERAL CR.	SALES CR.	ACCTS. REC. CR.	SALES DISC. DR.	CASH DR.
1953 April 10	Notes Payable	211	5,000				5,000

CASH PAYMENTS JOURNAL   PAGE 13

DATE		CHECK NO.	ACCOUNT DEBITED	POST. REF.	GENERAL DR.	ACCTS. PAYABLE DR.	PUR. DISC. CR.	CASH CR.
1953 July	9	591	Notes Payable	211	5,000			5,075
			Interest Expense	912	75			

NOTES RECEIVABLE   The typical retail business makes most of its sales for cash or on account. If the account of a customer becomes past due, the business may insist that the account be converted into a note. In this way the debtor may be given an extension of time and the creditor may transfer the note to his bank for cash if additional funds are needed in the business. Notes may also be received by retail firms that sell merchandise on long-term credit. For example, a dealer in household appliances may require a down payment at the time of sale and accept a note for the remainder. Such notes frequently provide for payment in monthly installments. Wholesale firms and manufacturers are likely to receive notes more frequently than retailers, although here, too, much depends upon the nature of the product and the length of the credit period.

When a note is received from a customer to apply on his account, the asset Notes Receivable is increased and the asset Accounts Receivable is decreased. These facts are recorded by debiting the notes receivable account and by crediting the accounts receivable account and the account of the customer from whom the note is received.

For example, assume that the account of Robert Stone on the books of George Peck has a debit balance of $400. The account is past due. On May 19 Peck received Stone's note for $400, dated May 18 and due 30 days after the date of issue, bearing interest at the rate of 6%. The receipt of the note was recorded in Peck's general journal as follows:

May	19	Notes Receivable..............	113	400		
		Accounts Rec.—Robert Stone..	115/ √		400	
		Received a 30-day, 6% note dated May 18.				

The debit entry would be posted to the notes receivable account in the general ledger. The credit entry would be posted to the accounts receivable controlling account in the general ledger and to the account of Robert Stone in the subsidiary ledger.

If notes are received quite frequently, the time consumed in recording and posting such transactions could be reduced by the addition of a Notes Receivable Dr. column and an Accounts Receivable Cr. column to the general journal. It is not necessary to maintain a subsidiary ledger for notes receivable because the notes themselves provide adequate information. The amount due from each customer on a note can be ascertained by examining the notes on hand. The due date, the interest terms, and other details can be determined in the same manner. If numerous notes are received, it may be desirable to summarize the details of all notes in a supplementary record. Such a record is described in a later chapter.

RECORDING INTEREST INCOME   Interest income is compensation for credit granted to others. Like other forms of income it represents an addition to proprietorship. It is recorded as a credit in an account entitled Interest Income.

To illustrate the recording of the collection of the principal and interest on a note receivable, assume that George Peck received payment from Robert Stone for the $400, 30-day, 6% note dated May 18. The transaction was recorded in Peck's cash receipts journal as follows:

CASH RECEIPTS JOURNAL   PAGE 11

DATE		ACCOUNT CREDITED	POST. REF.	GENERAL CR.	SALES CR.	ACCTS. REC. CR.	SALES DISC. DR.	CASH DR.
1953 June	17	Notes Receivable	113	400				402
		Interest Income	812	2				

DISCOUNTING NOTES   A note that makes no provision for the payment of interest for the period from the date of issuance to the date of maturity is called a non-interest-bearing note. It does not necessarily follow that there can be no interest charge involved in issuing or transferring such a note. In making loans to customers, banks frequently accept non-interest-bearing notes, deducting the interest charge from the face of the note and paying cash for the remainder. This procedure is referred to as *discounting a note*. The percentage used in computing the interest is sometimes called the *discount rate*, the deduction made for interest is referred to as the *discount*, and the cash paid is called the *proceeds*.

Discount on a note is computed in the same manner as interest is computed on an interest-bearing note except that the discount rate is always applied to the maturity value of the note. For a non-interest-bearing note, the maturity value is the same as the face value.

Notes Payable. To illustrate the discounting of a note payable, assume that on September 10 Charles Parker issued a $2,000, 60-day, non-interest-bearing note to the First National Bank. The bank charged a discount rate of 6%, making the discount $20 and the proceeds $1,980. Parker's transaction with the bank was recorded in his cash receipts journal and his general journal as follows:

CASH RECEIPTS JOURNAL   PAGE 17

DATE		ACCOUNT CREDITED	POST. REF.	GENERAL CR.	SALES CR.	ACCTS. REC. CR.	SALES DISC. DR.	CASH DR.
1953 Sept.	10	Notes Payable	√	1,980				1,980

			POST. REF.		
Sept.	10	Cash............................	√	1,980	
		Interest Expense...............	912	20	
		Notes Payable................	211		2,000
		Discounted a 60-day note payable at 6%.			

Only part of the transaction could be recorded in the cash receipts journal; therefore, the complete entry, including the debit to Cash, was recorded in the general journal. In order to avoid duplication in posting, a check mark was placed in the posting reference column of the cash receipts journal for the credit to Notes Payable and another check mark was placed in the posting reference column of the general journal for the debit to Cash. In posting from the two journals, the checked items would be ignored and the remaining items would be posted as follows:

Cash receipts journal: $1,980 debit posted to Cash (included in column total at end of month)

General journal: $20 debit posted to Interest Expense
$2,000 credit posted to Notes Payable

On November 9 Parker paid the bank $2,000, the maturity value of the note. The transaction was recorded by Parker as follows:

CASH PAYMENTS JOURNAL   PAGE 19

DATE		CHECK NO.	ACCOUNT DEBITED	POST. REF.	GENERAL DR.	ACCTS. PAYABLE DR.	PUR. DISC. CR.	CASH CR.
1953 Nov.	9	761	Notes Payable	211	2,000			2,000

Notes Receivable. A business that owns notes receivable may discount them at the bank rather than hold them until maturity. The bank deducts from the maturity value of the note the discount from the date of discount to the date of maturity, giving the owner the proceeds.

For example, on July 21 Charles Parker received from a customer, F. J. Starr, the latter's 90-day, non-interest-bearing note for $1,150 to apply on his account. This transaction was recorded by Parker as follows:

July	21	Notes Receivable...............	113	1,150	
		Accounts Rec.—F. J. Starr.....	115/ √		1,150
		Received a 90-day, non-interest-bearing note.			

Thirty days later, on August 20, Parker needed additional cash and therefore discounted this note at his bank. From the bank's standpoint, the note was not worth $1,150, inasmuch as that amount could not be collected from Starr, the maker of the note, until 60 days later; consequently it deducted discount, or interest, on $1,150 for 60 days. The bank rate of discount was 6% and the amount of the discount was $11.50. Parker therefore received proceeds of $1,138.50 ($1,150 − $11.50). The transaction with the bank was recorded in Parker's cash receipts journal and general journal as follows:

CASH RECEIPTS JOURNAL   PAGE 16

DATE		ACCOUNT CREDITED	POST. REF.	GENERAL CR.	SALES CR.	ACCTS. REC. CR.	SALES DISC. DR.	CASH DR.
1953 Aug.	20	Notes Receivable	√	1,138.50				1,138.50

Aug.	20	Cash........................	√	1,138 50		
		Interest Expense............	912	11 50		
		Notes Receivable..........	113		1,150 00	
		Discounted Starr's note dated July 21.				

In the illustration above the note did not bear interest and therefore its maturity value was the same as its face value. When an interest-bearing note is discounted, its maturity value must be computed before the amount of the discount and the proceeds can be determined. To illustrate, assume that on June 10 Parker received from Harvey Dixon a 90-day note for $1,200 bearing interest at 5%. The transaction was recorded in Parker's general journal as follows:

June	10	Notes Receivable...............	113	1,200	
		Accounts Rec.—Harvey Dixon.	115/ √		1,200
		Received a 90-day, 5% note.			

Ten days later, on June 20, Parker discounted this note at his bank at a discount rate of 6%. The amount that the maker of the note promised to pay in 90 days was the face amount, $1,200, plus interest of $15, or a total of $1,215. The bank therefore used $1,215 as the basis for computing the discount. Since the bank must wait for 80 days to collect the note, the maturity value of $1,215 was discounted for 80 days at the bank discount rate of 6%, yielding a discount of $16.20. This amount, $16.20, was subtracted from the maturity value, $1,215.00, to determine the proceeds of $1,198.80 received by Parker. These computations may be tabulated as follows:

Face value of note..................	$1,200.00
Interest on note — 90 days at 5%.....	15.00
Maturity value of note.............	$1,215.00
Discount on note — 80 days at 6%....	16.20
Proceeds of note..................	$1,198.80

The same data are presented graphically below:

```
Face Value                                         Maturity Value
$1,200                      + $15                        $1,215
 |———————————————————————————————————————————————————————>|
June 10                    90 days                       Sept. 8


                  Proceeds                        Maturity Value
                  $1,198.80      − $16.20               $1,215
                   |<—————————————————————————————————————|
                  June 20       80 days                  Sept. 8
```

The note that Parker discounted had been recorded on his books at $1,200, its face value. The proceeds of the note amounted to $1,198.80. The difference between these two amounts, $1.20, was interest expense. Parker's transaction with the bank was recorded in his cash receipts journal and his general journal as follows:

CASH RECEIPTS JOURNAL   PAGE 12

DATE		ACCOUNT CREDITED	POST. REF	GENERAL CR.	SALES CR.	ACCTS. REC. CR.	SALES DISC. DR.	CASH DR.
1953 June	20	Notes Receivable	√	1,198 80				1,198 80

June	20	Cash......................	√	1,198 80		
		Interest Expense.............	912	1 20		
		Notes Receivable...........	113			1,200 00
		Discounted Dixon's note dated June 10.				

The proceeds obtained from discounting a customer's interest-bearing note are not always less than the face value of the note. For example, if a note receivable bearing interest at the rate of 7% was discounted at the rate of 6%, the proceeds would be greater than the face value. This would be true even though the note was discounted on the same day that it was issued. Another determining factor is the time elapsed between the issuance date and the discount date as compared to the time between the discount date and the maturity date.

For example, if Parker had discounted Harvey Dixon's note (at the same discount rate) on August 24, 15 days before the note became due, the discount would have amounted to $3.04 and he would have received proceeds of $1,211.96. The $11.96 excess of the proceeds over the face of the note would have been interest income and the entry in the cash receipts journal would have been as follows:

CASH RECEIPTS JOURNAL   PAGE 16

DATE	ACCOUNT CREDITED	POST. REF.	GENERAL CR.	SALES CR.	ACCTS. REC. CR.	SALES DISC. DR.	CASH DR.
1953 Aug. 24	Notes Receivable	113	1,200 00				1,211 96
	Interest Income	812	11 96				

Contingent Liability. When a note receivable is discounted, it is necessary for the owner to endorse the note.[1] By endorsing the note, the endorser becomes responsible to the bank or other endorsee for its payment if the note is not paid by the maker at maturity. Discounting a note therefore results in the creation of a possible future obligation that is known as a *contingent liability*. The liability is contingent rather than real. If the maker pays the note at maturity, which is probable, the contingent liability is discharged without any action on the part of the endorser. If, on the other hand, the note is not paid by the maker at maturity and the endorser is notified of the fact, the liability becomes a real one.

In preparing a balance sheet the total amount of discounted notes receivable that are not yet due at the balance sheet date should be disclosed. This may be done by means of a footnote at the bottom of the balance sheet or by a parenthetical notation in the liability section.

DISHONORED NOTES   A note that is not paid when it becomes due is said to be *dishonored*. When a note receivable held by a business is dishonored, the note is no longer negotiable. For this reason the amount due should ordinarily be transferred to the accounts receivable account. For example, if the $400, 30-day, 6% note dated May 18 and received from Robert Stone on May 19

---

[1]The various kinds of endorsements are described in Appendix A.

(page 193) had been dishonored at maturity, the entry to charge the note back to his account would have been as follows:

June	17	Accounts Rec.—Robert Stone.....	115/ √	402	
		Notes Receivable.............	113		400
		Interest Income.............	812		2
		Dishonored note and interest			
		thereon charged back to Stone.			

If there had been some assurance that Stone would pay the note within a few days after maturity, the foregoing entry could have been omitted. In extending credit to the customer in the future, however, it is desirable that his account disclose the fact that the note was dishonored.

In the event that a customer's note that has been discounted is dishonored, the bank will notify the endorser. The latter will then have to pay the note and any interest accrued. For example, if the Harvey Dixon note that was discounted on June 20 (page 196) is dishonored, Parker, the endorser, will have to pay the bank the face of the note, $1,200, plus interest of $15. The entire amount of the payment would be charged to Dixon's account, as shown in the following entry:

CASH PAYMENTS JOURNAL   PAGE 15

DATE	CHECK NO.	ACCOUNT DEBITED	POST. REF.	GENERAL DR.	ACCTS. PAYABLE DR.	PUR. DISC. CR.	CASH CR.
1953 Sept. 8	895	Accts. Rec. — Harvey Dixon	115/ √	1,215			1,215

In some cases the bank submits to the endorser a notarized statement of the facts of the dishonor. The fee paid by the bank for obtaining this statement, known as a *protest fee*, is charged to the endorser, who in turn charges it to the maker of the note. For example, if there had been a protest fee of $2 in connection with the dishonor of Dixon's note, the debit to his account and the credit to Cash would have been $1,217.

REPORTING INTEREST ON THE PROFIT AND LOSS STATEMENT   Interest income is usually reported on the profit and loss statement as *other income*; interest expense, as *other expense*.

Items listed on the statement under the headings "Other Income" and "Other Expenses" affect the net profit or the net loss of the enterprise. They are considered apart from items representing the ordinary operations of the business and are therefore commonly placed at the end of the statement. A common method of reporting interest on the profit and loss statement is illustrated below:

Net Profit from Operations..........................		$4,087.85
Other Income:		
Purchases Discount................ $570.10		
Interest Income................... 30.40		
Total Other Income......................	$600.50	
Other Expenses:		
Sales Discount..................... $194.70		
Interest Expense.................. 93.65		
Total Other Expenses......................	288.35	
Net Addition..		312.15
Net Profit...		$4,400.00

Partial Profit and Loss Statement Showing Treatment of Interest Items

If the total other expenses are greater than the total other income, the difference may be labeled "Net Deduction." It would be deducted from the net profit from operations to obtain the net profit.

THE CREDIT CYCLE   Credit may be received on purchases or may be extended on sales. In either case business operations are facilitated and the accounting is extended and complicated. The illustrations below show various transactions involved in making a sale and collecting the cash.

(1) Sale for cash.

CASH	SALES
(a) 500	(a) 500

(2) (a) Sale on account; (b) cash collected at the end of the credit period.

CASH	ACCOUNTS RECEIVABLE	SALES
(b) 500	(a) 500 | (b) 500	(a) 500

Transaction (b) occurred at the end of the credit period and represents a delayed receipt of cash for the sale.

(3) (a) Sale on account; (b) non-interest-bearing note accepted at the end of the credit period; (c) note collected at maturity.

CASH	NOTES RECEIVABLE	ACCOUNTS RECEIVABLE	SALES
(c) 500	(b) 500 | (c) 500	(a) 500 | (b) 500	(a) 500

Transaction (b) extended the time for payment beyond the normal credit period and cash was received in transaction (c). Note that the net result of the three transactions was a debit to Cash and a credit to Sales.

(4) (a) Sale on account; terms 2/10, n/30; (b) cash collected within discount period.

CASH	ACCOUNTS RECEIVABLE		SALES	SALES DISCOUNT
(b) 490	(a) 500	(b) 500	(a) 500	(b) 10

In the accounts shown above, Accounts Receivable was debited and Sales was credited at the time of the sale. The customer paid the invoice within the discount period and was therefore entitled to a $10 discount. The net effect of the two transactions was a debit to Cash, a debit to Sales Discount, and a credit to Sales.

(5) (a) Sale on account; (b) interest-bearing note accepted at the end of the credit period; (c) note collected with interest.

CASH	NOTES RECEIVABLE		ACCOUNTS RECEIVABLE	
(c) 505	(b) 500	(c) 500	(a) 500	(b) 500

SALES	INTEREST INCOME
(a) 500	(c) 5

In the case above the customer was permitted to extend the normal credit period by giving his 60-day, 6% note. The note, together with interest, was collected at maturity. The net effect of the three transactions was a debit to Cash, a credit to Sales, and a credit to Interest Income.

(6) (a) Sale on account; (b) note received; (c) note discounted.

CASH	NOTES RECEIVABLE		ACCOUNTS RECEIVABLE	
(c) 499.70	(b) 500	(c) 500	(a) 500	(b) 500

SALES	INTEREST EXPENSE
(a) 500	(c) .30

In this case the 60-day, $5\frac{1}{2}\%$ note accepted from the customer was discounted at the bank at the rate of 6% two days after the date of issuance. From the maturity value of $504.58 the bank deducted discount for 58 days at 6%, which amounted to $4.88. The maturity value ($504.58) less the discount ($4.88) yielded proceeds of $499.70.

After the three transactions were completed, the seller's books showed debits to Cash and Interest Expense and a credit to Sales. If a balance sheet is prepared before the due date of the note, the contingent liability of $500 should be disclosed.

CREDIT TRANSACTIONS INVOLVE A SERIES As has been pointed out, credit transactions permit delayed payments and involve additional transactions before the deal is closed by final payment. These additional transactions are based on the credit period established at the time of the initial transaction. Any departure from this basic credit period may result in financial advantage or disadvantage to the parties. For example, early payment benefits the debtor by the amount of the agreed-upon cash discount, whereas late payment may involve interest expense to the debtor and interest income to the creditor. The relation of cash discounts and interest to the basic credit period may be illustrated as follows:

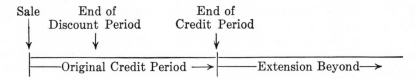

The difference in computing cash discount and interest should be noted. The amount of cash discount is the same on the first and the last day of a particular cash discount period. For example, the discount of $60 on an invoice for $6,000, dated June 1, terms 1/10, n/30, can be deducted either on June 2 or June 11 or any date between. In the case of interest, the amount to be added becomes greater day by day. Assuming that the credit period is extended by issuance of a $6,000, 6% note dated July 1, the interest would accumulate at the rate of $1 each day. To pay the note on July 2 would require a total of $6,001; on July 11, $6,010; on July 31, $6,030; and so on.

QUESTIONS

1. In negotiating a 90-day loan, Warren Green has the option of either (1) issuing a $10,000, non-interest-bearing note that will be discounted at the rate of 6%, or (2) issuing a $10,000 note bearing interest at the rate of 6% that will be accepted at face value. (a) What would be the amount of his interest expense in each case? (b) What would be the amount of the proceeds in each case? (c) Which of the two alternatives is more favorable to Green? (d) Assuming that he adopts the first alternative, give the entry, in general journal form, at the time the note is issued and at the time the note is paid.

2. James Steel issued the following note to Kenneth Johnson on account:

```
$ 500.00                    Minneapolis, Minnesota, August 10,              19 53

---------------Ninety days---------------AFTER DATE____I____  PROMISE TO PAY TO

THE ORDER OF Kenneth Johnson

Five Hundred 00/100------------------------------------------------- DOLLARS

PAYABLE AT City Bank and Trust Company

VALUE RECEIVED WITH INTEREST AT --6--- %

No. 93                                          James Steel
```

(a) Name the payee. (b) Name the maker. (c) Give Steel's general journal entry to record the issuance of the note. (d) Give Johnson's general journal entry to record receipt of the note. (e) What is the due date of the note? (f) What is the amount of interest to be paid at maturity? (g) Give Steel's entry, in general journal form, to record the payment of the note and the interest at maturity. (h) Give Johnson's entry, in general journal form, to record receipt of payment at maturity.

3. W. B. Davis holds a 60-day, non-interest-bearing note for $600, dated March 9, that he had received from a customer on account. On April 23 he discounts the note at his bank at the rate of 6%. (a) What is the maturity value of the note? (b) How many days are there in the discount period? (c) What is the amount of the discount? (d) What is the amount of the proceeds? (e) Give the entry, in general journal form, to record the transaction on April 23.

4. Ralph Morris holds a 90-day, 5% note for $800, dated May 18, that he has received from a customer on account. On June 17 he discounts the note at his bank at the rate of 6%. (a) What is the maturity value of the note? (b) How many days are there in the discount period? (c) What is the amount of the discount? (d) What is the amount of the proceeds? (e) Give the entry, in general journal form, to record the transaction on June 17.

5. On December 31, the end of the fiscal year, Gordon Burns is contingently liable for $20,000 of customer's notes that he has discounted. Why should this fact be disclosed on his balance sheet as of December 31?

6. John Folsom receives a 2-month, non-interest-bearing note for $450, dated February 20, from Homer Beckett on account. The note is dishonored on April 20 and Folsom charges the note to Beckett's account. Give the general journal entries for Folsom on February 20 and April 20.

7. Assume the same facts as in Question 6, except that the note bears interest at the rate of 6%. Give the general journal entries for Folsom on February 20 and April 20.

8. On November 10 Mark Hollis receives notification from his bank that a 90-day, 6% note for $1,000, on which he is contingently liable, has been dishonored. The note had been received by Hollis from Ralph Bailey on account. (a) Give the entry, in general journal form, to record the payment to the bank on November 10. (b) If the bank had charged a protest fee of $2, what effect would it have had on the entry in (a)?

9. The series of five transactions recorded in the following "T" accounts were incident to a sale to a customer. Describe each transaction briefly.

CASH		NOTES RECEIVABLE		ACCOUNTS RECEIVABLE	
(c) 603.24	(d) 606	(b) 600	(c) 600	(a) 600	(b) 600
(e) 611.70				(d) 606	(e) 606

SALES		INTEREST INCOME	
	(a) 600		(c) 3.24
			(e) 5.70

PROBLEMS

11-1. The Riverside Equipment Co. received the notes described below:

DATE	TERM	INTEREST RATE	FACE AMOUNT
(a) Feb. 1	2 months	$5\frac{1}{2}\%$	$1,000
(b) Mar. 10	90 days	—	1,200
(c) Mar. 18	30 days	6%	960
(d) Apr. 23	60 days	5%	625
(e) Apr. 30	6 months	6%	2,000

Instructions: (1) Determine the due date and the amount of interest due on each note at maturity. In your solution identify each note by letter.

(2) Assuming that note (b) was discounted on March 28 at the rate of 6% and that note (d) was discounted on May 13 at the rate of 6%, determine for each the maturity value, the discount period, the amount of discount, and the proceeds. Identify the notes by letter.

11-2. A. F. Davis completed the transactions listed below, among others, during a three-month period:

April 1. Sold merchandise on account to M. White, Sale No. 163, $500.

7. Purchased merchandise on account from Best Garment Co., $900; invoice dated April 5.

11. Received cash from M. White for the invoice of April 1 less 1% discount.

15. Issued a 60-day, non-interest-bearing note payable for $2,000 to the First National Bank, receiving proceeds of $1,980.

17. Sold merchandise on account to G. Wheeler, Sale No. 182, $800.

26. Sold merchandise on account to R. Adams, Sale No. 206, $1,400.

May 2. Purchased merchandise on account from Harris & Co., $1,000; invoice dated May 1.

7. Gave Best Garment Co. a 30-day, 5% note for $900 on account.

12. Issued Check No. 628 to Harris & Co. for the amount due on the invoice of May 1 less 2% discount.

17. Received from G. Wheeler on account a 30-day, 6% note for $800, dated May 17.

26. Received from R. Adams on account a 1-month, 5% note for $1,400, dated May 26.

June 1. Discounted G. Wheeler's $800 note, dated May 17, at the First National Bank, receiving proceeds of $801.99.

June 6. Issued Check No. 687 to Best Garment Co. for the amount owed on the note dated May 7: principal, $900; interest, $3.75.

14. Issued Check No. 709 to the First National Bank for the amount owed on the note payable dated April 15, $2,000.

26. Received payment from R. Adams for the note dated May 26: principal, $1,400; interest, $5.83.

Instructions: Record the transactions using a sales journal (one money column), a purchases journal (one money column), a cash receipts journal and a cash payments journal like those illustrated in this chapter, and a two-column general journal.

11-3. Donald Boone completed the transactions listed below, among others, during the current fiscal year:

Jan. 4. Gave Richard Peterson, a creditor, a 3-month, 6% note for $4,000, dated January 4, on account.

Mar. 12. Received from John North, a customer, a 90-day, non-interest-bearing note for $3,000, dated March 10, on account.

Apr. 1. Purchased store equipment from Apex Co. for $5,000, issuing Check No. 72 for $1,000 and a 6% note dated April 1 for the balance. The note provides for payments of $500 of principal plus accrued interest every six months. (Record the entire transaction in the general journal and the payment in the cash payments journal. Insert check marks where necessary to avoid duplicate posting.)

4. Issued Check No. 79 to Richard Peterson in payment of the note dated January 4.

9. Discounted at the Security Bank at 6% the note received from John North, dated March 10.

May 3. Received from L. B. Harrison, a customer, a 60-day, 5% note for $600, dated May 2, on account.

25. Discounted a 90-day, non-interest-bearing note payable for $2,000, dated May 25, at the Security Bank; discount rate, 6%.

June 15. Discounted at the Security Bank at 6% the note received from L. B. Harrison, dated May 2.

July 1. Notified by Security Bank of the dishonor of the note of May 2 signed by L. B. Harrison. Issued Check No. 111 to the bank for the principal and the interest due plus a protest fee of $4. Charged principal, interest, and protest fee to Harrison's account.

Aug. 1. Received payment in full from L. B. Harrison for the note of May 2, including interest at 5% from the date of maturity to July 31 on the face value of the note.

23. Issued Check No. 178 to the Security Bank for the amount due on the note payable dated May 25.

Sept. 30. Received from Philip Walker, a customer, a 90-day, 6% note for $400, dated September 29, on account.

Oct. 1. Issued Check No. 203 to Apex Co. for installment due on note, together with interest on $4,000 for six months.

Dec. 28. Philip Walker dishonored his note dated September 29. Charged the amount due, including interest, to his account.

Instructions: Record the transactions using a cash receipts journal, a cash payments journal, and a general journal like those illustrated in this chapter.

Chapter | 12

Prepaid, Unearned, and Accrued Items

NEED FOR CONSIDERATION Business enterprises determine their financial condition and the results of operations at regular intervals. The data on financial condition are presented in the balance sheet, and the summary of operations is presented in the profit and loss statement. The maximum interval of time between these periodic summaries is one year.

True statements of the financial condition of the business and of the income and the expenses ordinarily cannot be prepared from the ledger accounts that include only current transactions, since there are some income and expense items that are not recorded currently. For example, insurance expense takes place day by day but it is not until a balance sheet and a profit and loss statement are being prepared that insurance expense is made a matter of record. At that time the insurance expense applicable to the fiscal period is recorded in one entry covering the period. In a similar way provision must be made to see that all income and expense items of the period, but no others, are included in the profit and loss statement. Any part belonging to future periods should appear, not on the profit and loss statement, but on the balance sheet.

CLASSIFICATION AND TERMINOLOGY There are various kinds of prepaid, unearned, and accrued items and there is also some variation in the terms used to describe them. The remainder of this chapter is devoted to a discussion of the following four classes:

(1) Prepaid expenses; also called deferred charges to expense.
   Items in this category are assets, usually current assets.
(2) Unearned income; also called deferred credits to income.
   Items in this category are liabilities, usually current liabilities.
(3) Accrued liabilities.
   Items in this category are liabilities, usually current liabilities.
(4) Accrued assets.
   Items in this category are assets, usually current assets.

PREPAID EXPENSES *Prepaid expenses* are commodities and services purchased for consumption that are unconsumed at the end of the accounting period. The portion of the asset that has been used during the period has become an expense; the remainder will become an expense in the future. It is because of this deferment of benefits to the future that prepaid expenses are frequently termed *deferred charges to expense*. Prepaid expenses include such items as prepaid insurance, prepaid rent, prepaid advertising, prepaid interest, office supplies, and store supplies.

Two methods of accounting for prepaid expenses will be explained. Prepaid insurance will be used to illustrate the first method and prepaid interest will be used to illustrate the second method. It should be understood that either of the alternative methods may be employed in any particular case.

Prepaid Expenses Recorded as Assets. When prepaid insurance or other consumable services or supplies are purchased, they may be charged to an asset account. Although it is known at the time of purchase that part of the services or supplies will be consumed during the accounting period, the determination of the amount is postponed until the statements are prepared.

When premiums on property and casualty insurance are paid, Prepaid Insurance is debited and Cash is credited. At the end of the accounting period the amount of the premiums expired during the period is ascertained. The policies may be referred to in determining the effective date, the period of time covered, the premium paid, and other details. It is the usual practice, however, to maintain an insurance register with a column for each accounting period to which the premiums will be charged. As a policy is purchased, the amount of premium allocable to each period is entered in the appropriate column. At the end of a period, the amount of insurance expired is obtained by adding the amounts in the columns assigned to that period.

The expired insurance may be analyzed according to the various types of property insured, so that the amount allocable to selling expense and the amount allocable to general expense can be determined. For example, expired insurance on merchandise and store equipment is considered a selling expense; that on office equipment and building, a general expense.

To illustrate, assume that the prepaid insurance account has a balance of $695 at the close of the year. This amount represents the unexpired insurance at the beginning of the year plus the total of premiums paid during the year. From the insurance register it is ascertained that $310 of insurance has expired during the year, of which $270 represents selling expense and $40 represents general expense. The adjusting entry to record the expired insurance appears as follows:

Dec.	31	Insurance Expense — Selling.....	615	270	
		Insurance Expense — General....	716	40	
		Prepaid Insurance...........	118		310

After this entry has been posted, the three accounts affected appear as follows:

PREPAID INSURANCE   Acct. No. 118

1953					1953				
Jan.	1	Balance	√	422	Dec.	31	Adjusting	J25	310
Mar.	18		CP6	93					
Aug.	25		CP16	65					
Nov.	10		CP21	115					
				695					

INSURANCE EXPENSE — SELLING   Acct. No. 615

| 1953 | | | | |
| Dec. | 31 | Adjusting | J25 | 270 |

INSURANCE EXPENSE — GENERAL   Acct. No. 716

| 1953 | | | | |
| Dec. | 31 | Adjusting | J25 | 40 |

After $310 of expired insurance is transferred to the expense accounts, the balance of $385 remaining in Prepaid Insurance represents the premiums on various policies that apply to future periods. It is an asset and is shown on the balance sheet. The amounts transferred to the two expense accounts appear on the profit and loss statement.

Prepaid Expenses Recorded as Expenses. In the foregoing illustration the prepaid expenses were originally charged to the asset accounts. An alternative is to charge them directly to the appropriate expense account as they are acquired. This method was used in the previous chapter, when prepaid interest on notes payable was charged directly to the account Interest Expense. To illustrate this alternative method, assume that the interest expense account has a balance of $380 at the end of the year. Included in this amount is a debit of $150 for discount on a 90-day, $10,000 note discounted at the bank on December 1. The complete entry for this particular transaction, in general journal form, was as follows:

Dec.	1	Cash........................	√	9,850	
		Interest Expense.............	912	150	
		Notes Payable..............	121		10,000
		Discounted a 90-day note at			
		6%.			

As of December 31, the last day of the fiscal year, 30 days of the original 90-day term of the note have passed and the note has another 60 days to run. Therefore, only one third of the $150 is an expense of the current year. The remaining two thirds ($100) is a prepaid expense that will benefit the following year. The adjusting entry to transfer to the asset account the prepaid portion of the interest (⅔ of $150) appears below:

Dec.	31	Prepaid Interest................	117	100	
		Interest Expense.............	912		100

After this entry has been posted, the prepaid interest account and the interest expense account appear as follows:

PREPAID INTEREST   Acct. No. 117

1953									
Dec.	31	Adjusting	J25	100					

INTEREST EXPENSE   Acct. No. 912

1953						1953					
Feb.	4		CP3	30		Dec.	31	Adjusting	J25	100	
Apr.	10		J9	110							
Sept.	21		CP18	90							
Dec.	1		J23	150							
				380							

After the prepaid interest of $100 is transferred from the expense account to the asset account, the balance of $280 remaining in Interest Expense represents the actual expense for the period. The balance sheet shows Prepaid Interest of $100, and the profit and loss statement shows Interest Expense of $280.

In the process of closing the books at the end of the period, the debit balance in Interest Expense is closed to Profit and Loss Summary. After all the closing entries have been posted, the balance in Prepaid Interest is transferred to Interest Expense. This is consistent with the policy of charging prepaid interest directly to the expense account as it is incurred. The entry that effects this transfer is the exact reverse of the adjusting entry made at the end of the period and is called a *reversing entry* or *readjusting entry*. Continuing the illustration, the reversing entry is as follows:

Jan.	1	Interest Expense................	912	100	
		Prepaid Interest.............	117		100

After this entry has been posted, the prepaid interest account and the interest expense account appear as follows:

PREPAID INTEREST   Acct. No. 117

1953					1954				
Dec.	31	Adjusting	J25	100	Jan.	1	Reversing	J26	100

INTEREST EXPENSE   Acct. No. 912

1953					1953				
Feb.	4		CP3	30	Dec.	31	Adjusting	J25	100
Apr.	10		J9	110		31	Closing	J25	280
Sept.	21		CP18	90					
Dec.	1		J23	150					
				380					
				380					380
1954									
Jan.	1	Reversing	J26	100					

The prepaid interest of $100 is now in Interest Expense. As additional interest expense is incurred during the year, it will be debited directly to Interest Expense. Whenever it is the policy to debit prepayments of a particular expense directly to the expense account as they are paid, it is necessary to make a reversing entry after the books are closed.

Comparison of the Two Methods. The two methods of recording prepaid expenses and the related entries at the end of an accounting period may be summarized as follows:

(1) Prepaid expense recorded as an *asset.*

    (a) Adjusting entry: Transfer amount *used* to the appropriate *expense* account.

    (b) Closing entry: Transfer balance of expense account to the profit and loss summary account.

    (c) Reversing entry: None required.

    (d) Balance of prepaid expense at beginning of new period: In the *asset* account.

(2) Prepaid expense recorded as an *expense.*

    (a) Adjusting entry: Transfer amount *unused* to the appropriate *asset* account.

    (b) Closing entry: Transfer balance of expense account to the profit and loss summary account.

    (c) Reversing entry: Transfer amount *unused* back to the *expense* account.

    (d) Balance of prepaid expense at beginning of new period: In the *expense* account.

When prepaid expenses are charged to the asset account as they are incurred (first method), the balance of the prepayment is in the asset account after the work of the periodic summary is completed. When prepaid expenses are charged to the expense account as they are incurred (second method), the balance of the prepayment is in the expense account after the work of the periodic summary is completed.

The amount of expense that will be reported on the profit and loss statement will be the same regardless of which method is used. Similarly, the amount of the prepayment that will be listed as an asset on the balance sheet will be the same regardless of which method is used. Some accountants prefer the first method, others prefer the second method, and still others prefer the first method for some types of prepayments and the second for other types. The method adopted in any particular case should be consistently followed from year to year.

UNEARNED INCOME   Income that is received during the period may not have been entirely earned by the end of the period. Such items of income that are received in advance represent a liability that may be termed *unearned income*. That portion of the liability that is discharged during the period through delivery of commodities or services has been earned; the remainder will be earned in the future. It is because of this deferment of income to the future that unearned incomes are frequently called *deferred credits to income*. For example, magazine publishers ordinarily receive advance payment for subscriptions extending for periods ranging from a few months to a number of years. At the end of an accounting period, the portion of the receipts applicable to future periods has not been earned and should appear on the balance sheet as a liability.

Other examples of unearned income are rent received in advance on property owned, interest deducted in advance on notes receivable, premiums received in advance by an insurance company, tuition received in advance by a school, an annual retainer fee received in advance by an attorney, amounts received in advance by an advertising firm for advertising services to be rendered in the future, and amounts received in advance by a restaurant for meal tickets.

By accepting payment for the commodity or the service in advance, a business renders itself liable to furnish the commodity or the service at some future time. At the end of the period, if some portion of the commodity or the service has been furnished, part of the income has been earned. The earned income appears on the profit and loss statement. The unearned portion of the income represents a liability of the business to furnish the commodity or the service in a future period and is reported on the balance sheet as a liability. Since these facts appear on the reports, they should also be recorded in the accounts.

As in the case of prepaid expenses, two methods of accounting for items of unearned income will be described. Unearned rent will be used in illustrating both methods.

Unearned Income Recorded as a Liability. When income is received in advance, it may be credited to a liability account. For example, assume that on July 1 a business rents a portion of its building for a period of two years, receiving $4,800 in payment for the entire term of the lease. The transaction is recorded by a debit to Cash and a credit to Unearned Rent. On December 31, the end of the fiscal year, one fourth of the amount has been earned and three fourths of the amount remains a liability. The adjusting entry to record the income appears as follows:

Dec.	31	Unearned Rent...............	218	1,200	
		Rent Income...............	813		1,200

After this entry has been posted, the unearned rent account and the rent income account appear as follows:

UNEARNED RENT   Acct. No. 218

1953					1953					
Dec.	31	Adjusting	J25	1,200	July	1			CR13	4,800

RENT INCOME   Acct. No. 813

					1953					
					Dec.	31	Adjusting	J25	1,200

After the amount of the earned rent, $1,200, is transferred to the income account, the balance of $3,600 remaining in Unearned Rent is a liability to render a service in the future and it would therefore appear as a current liability on the balance sheet. Rent Income would appear in the "Other Income" section of the profit and loss statement, and this income account would be closed along with other income and expense accounts.

Unearned Income Recorded as an Income. Instead of being credited to a liability account, unearned income may be credited to an income account. For example, assume the same facts as in the preceding illustration, except that the transaction was recorded on July 1 by a debit to Cash and a credit to Rent Income. On December 31, the end of the fiscal year, three fourths of the balance in Rent Income is still unearned and the remaining one fourth has been earned. The adjusting entry to record the transfer to the liability account appears as follows:

Dec.	31	Rent Income..................	813	3,600	
		Unearned Rent..............	218		3,600

After this entry has been posted, the unearned rent account and the rent income account appear as follows:

UNEARNED RENT Acct. No. 218

					1953				
					Dec.	31	Adjusting	J25	3,600

RENT INCOME Acct. No. 813

1953					1953				
Dec.	31	Adjusting	J25	3,600	July	1		CR13	4,800

The unearned rent of $3,600 is listed as a current liability on the balance sheet, and the rent income of $1,200 is listed as "Other Income" on the profit and loss statement. In the process of closing the books, the balance of the rent income account is closed to the profit and loss summary account.

After the closing entries are posted and the accounts are ruled, the balance in Unearned Rent is transferred back to Rent Income by the following reversing entry:

Jan.	1	Unearned Rent..............	218	3,600	
		Rent Income..............	813		3,600

After this entry has been posted, the unearned rent account and the rent income account appear as follows:

UNEARNED RENT Acct. No. 218

1954					1953				
Jan.	1	Reversing	J27	3,600	Dec.	31	Adjusting	J25	3,600

RENT INCOME Acct. No. 813

1953					1953				
Dec.	31	Adjusting	J25	3,600	July	1		CR13	4,800
	31	Closing	J26	1,200					
				4,800					4,800
					1954				
					Jan.	1	Reversing	J27	3,600

The unearned rent of $3,600 is now in the rent income account. This is consistent with the policy of crediting the receipt of unearned income directly to the income account. When this method of recording the receipt of the unearned income is employed, it is necessary to make a reversing entry after the books have been closed.

Comparison of the Two Methods. The two methods of recording unearned income and the related entries at the end of the accounting period may be summarized as follows:

(1) Unearned income recorded as a *liability.*
  (a) Adjusting entry: Transfer amount *earned* to the appropriate *income* account.
  (b) Closing entry: Transfer balance of income account to the profit and loss summary account.
  (c) Reversing entry: None required.
  (d) Balance of unearned income at beginning of new period: In the *liability* account.

(2) Unearned income recorded as an *income.*
  (a) Adjusting entry: Transfer amount *unearned* to the appropriate *liability* account.
  (b) Closing entry: Transfer balance of income account to the profit and loss summary account.
  (c) Reversing entry: Transfer amount *unearned* back to the *income* account.
  (d) Balance of unearned income at beginning of new period: In the *income* account.

When unearned income is credited to a liability account as it is received (first method), the amount unearned is in the liability account after the work of the periodic summary is completed. When unearned income is credited to the income account as it is received (second method), the amount unearned is in the income account after the work of the periodic summary is completed.

As was explained in connection with prepaid expenses, the results obtained are the same under both methods. The method adopted for each particular kind of unearned income should be consistently followed from year to year.

ACCRUED LIABILITIES At the end of an accounting period the ledger should show all of the expenses applicable to that period and the liabilities owed on the last day of the period. In addition to the expenses recorded in the accounts during the period, there may be expenses that have been incurred but not recorded. In such cases it is necessary to record the amount of the accrual by debiting the expense account and crediting the appropriate liability account.

It is for this reason that the amount of the accrual may be referred to as either an *accrued liability* or an *accrued expense*.

To illustrate the adjusting entry for an accrued liability, assume that on December 31, the end of the fiscal year, the salary expense account has a debit balance of $24,620. During the year salaries have been paid each Saturday for the week then ended. For this particular fiscal year December 31 falls on Thursday. Reference to the records of the business reveals that the salary accrued for these last four days of the year amounts to $320. The adjusting entry to record the additional expense and the liability is as follows:

Dec.	31	Salary Expense.................	611	320	
		Salaries Payable.............	214		320

After this entry has been posted, the salaries payable account and the salary expense account appear as follows:

SALARIES PAYABLE   Acct. No. 214

					1953					
					Dec.	31	Adjusting	J33	320	

SALARY EXPENSE   Acct. No. 611

1953										
Dec.	31	Balance	√	24,620						
	31	Adjusting	J33	320						

The accrued salaries of $320 recorded in Salaries Payable will appear on the balance sheet of December 31 as a current liability. The salary expense of $24,940 now recorded in Salary Expense will appear on the profit and loss statement for the year ended December 31. The salary expense account will be closed to the profit and loss summary account in the usual manner.

When the weekly salaries are paid on January 2 of the following year, part of the payment will discharge the liability of $320 and the remainder will represent salary expense of January. In order to avoid the necessity of analyzing the payment, a reversing entry is made at the beginning of the new year. The effect of the entry is to transfer the credit balance in the salaries payable account to the credit side of the salary expense account. This entry appears as follows:

Jan.	1	Salaries Payable................	214	320	
		Salary Expense..............	611		320

After this entry has been posted, the salaries payable account and the salary expense account appear as follows:

SALARIES PAYABLE   Acct. No. 214

1954					1953				
Jan.	1	Reversing	J34	320	Dec.	31	Adjusting	J33	320

SALARY EXPENSE   Acct. No. 611

1953					1953				
Dec.	31	Balance	√	24,620	Dec.	31	Closing	J34	24,940
	31	Adjusting	J33	320					
				24,940					24,940
					1954				
					Jan.	1	Reversing	J34	320

The liability for salaries on December 31 now appears as a credit in Salary Expense. Assuming that the salaries paid on Saturday, January 2, amount to $480, the debit to Salary Expense will automatically record the discharge of the liability of $320 and the expense of $160 ($480 – $320).

The discussion of the treatment of accrued salary expense is illustrative of the method of handling accrued liabilities in general. If, in addition to accrued salaries, there are other accrued liabilities at the end of a fiscal period, separate liability accounts may be set up for each type. When these liability items are numerous, however, one liability account, termed Accrued Payables, may be used. All accrued liabilities may be recorded as credits to this account instead of to separate accounts.

ACCRUED ASSETS   All assets belonging to the business at the end of an accounting period and all income earned during the period should be recorded in the ledger. But, during a fiscal period, it is the customary practice to record some types of income only as the cash is received; consequently, at the end of the period there may be items of income that have not been recorded. In such cases it is necessary to record the amount of the accrued income by debiting an asset account and crediting an income account. Because of the dual nature of such accruals, they are referred to as either *accrued assets* or *accrued incomes*.

To illustrate the adjusting entry for an accrued asset, assume that on December 31, the end of the fiscal year, the interest income account has a credit balance of $425. Assume further that on the same date the business owns three short-term, interest-bearing notes accepted from customers. The three notes are for varying amounts and have varying due dates in January and February of the succeeding year. The interest accrued on each note from its date of issuance to December 31 is determined, and the three amounts total $43. The adjusting entry to record this asset and the additional income earned is as follows:

Dec.	31	Interest Receivable............	114	43	
		Interest Income.............	812		43

After this entry has been posted, the interest receivable account and the interest income account appear as follows:

INTEREST RECEIVABLE　　　　　Acct. No. 114

1953									
Dec.	31	Adjusting	J25	43					

INTEREST INCOME　　　　　Acct. No. 812

					1953				
					Dec.	31	Balance	✓	425
						31	Adjusting	J25	43

The accrued interest of $43 recorded in Interest Receivable will appear on the balance sheet of December 31 as a current asset. The interest income of $468 now recorded in Interest Income will appear in the "Other Income" section of the profit and loss statement for the year ended December 31. The interest income account will be closed to the profit and loss summary account in the usual manner.

When the amount due on each of the three notes is collected in the succeeding year, part of the interest received will be applied to reduction of the interest receivable and the remainder will represent income for the new year. To avoid the inconvenience of analyzing each receipt of interest, a reversing entry is made after the books are closed. The effect of the entry is to transfer the debit balance in the interest receivable account to the debit side of the interest income account. This entry is shown below:

Jan.	1	Interest Income...............	812	43	
		Interest Receivable..........	114		43

After this entry has been posted, the interest receivable account and the interest income account appear as follows:

INTEREST RECEIVABLE   Acct. No. 114

1953					1954					
Dec.	31	Adjusting	J25	43	Jan.	1	Reversing	J26	43

INTEREST INCOME   Acct. No. 812

1953					1953					
Dec.	31	Closing	J26	468	Dec.	31	Balance	✓	425
						31	Adjusting		43
				468					468
1954									
Jan.	1	Reversing	J26	43					

The interest receivable on December 31 now appears as a debit in Interest Income. When cash is received for the principal and the interest on each note, the transaction will be recorded in the usual manner; that is, the entire amount of the interest will be credited to Interest Income. The excess of the total credits over the debit balance of $43 will be the amount of interest earned on these notes in the new year.

The treatment of interest accrued on notes receivable illustrates the method of handling accrued assets in general. If, in addition to accrued interest, there are other accrued assets at the end of a fiscal period, separate accounts may be set up. Each of these accounts will be of the same nature as the account with interest receivable. When such items are numerous, one asset account, termed Accrued Receivables, may be opened. All accrued assets may be recorded as debits to this account instead of to separate accounts.

QUESTIONS

1. Classify the following items as prepaid expense or unearned income:

(a) Subscriptions collected in advance by a publisher.

(b) Property taxes paid in advance.

(c) Advertising literature on hand.

(d) Receipts from sale of season tickets for a series of concerts.

(e) Life insurance premiums received by an insurance company.

(f) Rent received in advance on property owned.

(g) Interest received in advance by a bank for discounting a note.

(h) Interest paid in advance at the time a note was discounted at the bank.

(i) A fire insurance premium prepaid by a business.

(j) Receipts from sale of $10 meal tickets by a restaurant.

2. In their first year of operations the Midwest Publishing Company collected $125,000 from advertising contracts and $90,000 from magazine subscriptions, crediting the two amounts to Advertising Income and Subscription Income respectively. At the end of the year $20,000 of the receipts from advertising and $50,000 of the receipts from subscriptions were applicable to succeeding periods. (a) If no adjustments are made at the end of the year, will income be overstated or understated, and by what amount? (b) Present the adjusting entries that should be made at the end of the first year. (c) Present the necessary reversing entries.

3. Needing additional storage facilities, Atlas Mercantile Co. rented part of a warehouse for one year, beginning with October 1. The year's rent of $2,400 was paid in advance and was debited to Prepaid Rent. (a) Present the necessary adjusting entry at December 31, the end of the fiscal year. (b) Should a reversing entry be made at the beginning of the following year?

4. Assume the same facts as in Question 3, except that the $2,400 was debited to Rent Expense instead of to Prepaid Rent. (a) Present the necessary adjusting entry at December 31, the end of the fiscal year. (b) Should a reversing entry be made at the beginning of the following year?

5. In adjusting and closing the books of Paul Ryan at the end of the fiscal year, no provision was made for accrued sales salary expense of $650. (a) What effect did this omission have on the amount of net profit reported on the profit and loss statement? (b) What was the effect on the amounts reported on the balance sheet for total assets, total liabilities, and proprietorship? (c) Assuming that the error is discovered in March of the following year, present the correcting entry.

6. Classify the following as (1) prepaid expense, (2) unearned income, (3) accrued liability, or (4) accrued asset:

    (a) Salaries Payable
    (b) Prepaid Interest
    (c) Office Supplies
    (d) Interest Receivable
    (e) Unearned Rent
    (f) Taxes Payable

7. Give entries in general journal form for the following (the accounting period is the calendar year):

    Oct. 19. Received from Ralph Forbes in provisional settlement of his account a $2,400, 90-day note dated October 17 and bearing interest at 6%.

    Dec. 31. Made an adjusting entry for accrued interest on the note of October 17.

    Dec. 31. Closed the interest income account. The only entry in this account originated from the above adjustment.

    Jan. 1. Made a reversing entry for accrued interest.

    Jan. 9. Discounted the note at a discount rate of 6%.

8. The entries in the following account that are identified by letters are related to the work of the periodic summary. Describe each of these entries and give the name of the account to which the offsetting debit or credit was posted.

INTEREST EXPENSE

19 --				19 --			
Jan.	1	(a)	25.00	Jan.	1	(b)	40.00
Jan.	1	⎰Transactions		Dec.	31	(c)	130.00
to		⎱during the	496.00		31	(e)	396.00
Dec.	31	⎰year					
Dec.	31	(d)	45.00				
			566.00				566.00
19 --				19 --			
Jan.	1	(f)	130.00	Jan.	1	(g)	45.00

9. The accountant for Owens Stores adopted the following uniform procedures in recording certain transactions:

(a) Insurance premiums are debited to Prepaid Insurance when purchased.

(b) Office supplies are debited to Office Supplies Expense when purchased.

(c) Rent received in advance is credited to Unearned Rent when received.

(d) Discount on non-interest-bearing notes accepted from customers is credited to Interest Income at the time the note is received.

At the end of the fiscal year each of the four accounts is adjusted by an adjusting entry. Should any of the adjusting entries be reversed at the beginning of the following year, and if so, which ones?

PROBLEMS

12-1. The following are some of the accounts, together with their unadjusted balances, that appear in the ledger of Walter Grant on December 31, the end of the current fiscal year:

113	Interest Receivable.....	$ —	612	Advertising Expense....	$ 1,600
115	Store Supplies........	800	613	Store Supplies Expense.	—
116	Office Supplies........	300	614	Insurance Expense —	
117	Prepaid Insurance.....	1,600		Selling.............	—
118	Prepaid Advertising....	—	711	Office Salary Expense...	6,700
119	Prepaid Interest.......	—	713	Insurance Expense —	
213	Interest Payable.......	—		General.............	—
214	Salaries Payable.......	—	714	Office Supplies Expense.	—
215	Unearned Rent........	—	811	Interest Income.......	250
313	Profit and Loss Summary	—	812	Rent Income..........	1,800
611	Sales Salary Expense...	19,500	911	Interest Expense.......	400

The following information relating to adjustments at December 31 was obtained from physical inventories, the insurance register, and other sources:

(a) The inventory of store supplies totals $125.

(b) The inventory of office supplies totals $160.

(c) The insurance register indicates that $650 of insurance has expired during the year, of which $450 is allocable to selling expense and $200 is allocable to general expense.

(d) Included in the balance of the advertising expense account is a debit of $600 in October for space in a weekly publication. The agreement provides that the space be used in uniform amounts in 52 consecutive issues. As of December 31, advertisements had appeared in 13 issues.

(e) Included in the interest expense account is a debit of $150 for the discount on a 90-day, non-interest-bearing note payable for $10,000, dated November 1.

(f) In addition to the non-interest-bearing note described in (e), there is a 60-day, 6% note payable for $3,000 outstanding, dated November 11.

(g) Salaries accrued are as follows: sales salaries, $400; office salaries, $150.

(h) The following interest-bearing notes receivable from customers are on hand:
   30-day, 6%, $1,200, dated December 6.
   60-day, 6%, $1,600, dated November 16.

(i) The rent income of $1,800 was received for a 12-month lease that began on May 1.

Instructions: (1) Open the accounts listed, using the account numbers given. Record the balances in the accounts as of December 31, writing "Balance" in the items column.

(2) Prepare adjusting journal entries and post to the appropriate accounts after each entry. Write "Adjusting" in the items column of the accounts.

(3) Prepare a compound journal entry to close the income accounts and another compound entry to close the expense accounts.

(4) Post the closing entries, writing "Closing" in the items column of the income and expense accounts.

(5) Total and rule the income and expense accounts. (Since not all income and expense accounts are given in the problem, do not rule the profit and loss summary account.)

(6) Prepare the reversing journal entries that should be made on January 1 and post to the appropriate accounts after each entry. Write "Reversing" in the items columns of the accounts.

(7) Rule the additional accounts that are now in balance.

12-2. The following information is obtained from a review of the accounts and other records of James Harris for the current fiscal year ended December 31:

(a) Prepaid Advertising has a debit balance of $1,000 on December 31. Of this amount, $600 has been used during the year and $400 applies to the following year.

(b) Prepaid Insurance has a debit balance of $1,760 composed of the following:

Policies in force at the beginning of the year:

POLICY NO.	PREPAID PREMIUM AT JAN. 1	TERM FROM JAN. 1
4785	$120	6 mo.
9647A	440	22 mo.
1-3476	480	16 mo.

Policy purchased during the year:

POLICY NO.	PREMIUM PAID	EFFECTIVE DATE	TERM
5324	$720	July 1	36 mo.

Insurance expired is to be recorded in one account, no allocation being made between selling expense and general expense.

(c) Included in Interest Expense is a debit of $160 for discount on Harris' 120-day, non-interest-bearing note for $8,000 dated December 1, discounted at the Merchants Bank at the rate of 6%.

(d) Salaries accrued for the period December 27–31 are as follows: sales salaries, $720; office salaries, $105.

(e) The unearned rent account had a credit balance of $450 on January 1, representing rent for the first three months of the year. On April 1, the rental agreement was renewed for one year at a monthly rental of $160, and a year's rent of $1,920, collected at that time, was credited to unearned rent.

(f) Store Supplies has a debit balance of $690. The inventory of store supplies on December 31 is $210.

(g) Of the notes received from customers during the year, the following three are on hand at December 31. All were accepted at face value.

DATE	FACE	TERM	INTEREST RATE
Nov. 1	$2,200	90 days	6%
Nov. 21	1,200	60 days	6%
Dec. 16	1,000	30 days	none

(h) Rent Expense has a debit balance of $5,200. Included in this amount is rent of $400 paid on December 31 that is applicable to the succeeding January.

(i) Tax expense of $310 has accrued but is not due until the succeeding February.

Instructions: (1) Prepare adjusting entries as of December 31 of the current fiscal year.

(2) Prepare the reversing entries that should be made as of January 1 of the succeeding fiscal year.

12-3. The account balances in the ledger of Quality Hardware Company on June 30, the end of the current fiscal year, are as follows:

Cash	$13,065	Robert Boyer, Drawing (dr.)	$ 3,600
Notes Receivable	8,500	Sales	103,000
Accounts Receivable	10,430	Purchases	44,500
Merchandise Inventory	46,500	Freight In	1,100
Store Supplies	770	Sales Salary Expense	10,400
Office Supplies	500	Advertising Expense	5,260
Prepaid Insurance	1,800	Misc. Selling Expense	415
Prepaid Rent	3,000	Office Salary Expense	7,800
Store Equipment	2,800	Misc. General Expense	330
Office Equipment	1,250	Interest Income	820
Notes Payable	7,800	Purchases Discount	305
Accounts Payable	5,720	Interest Expense	480
Robert Boyer, Capital	45,700	Sales Discount	845

The data for adjustments are:

(a) Merchandise inventory, June 30, $39,700.

(b) Supplies inventories:
    Store supplies, $230
    Office supplies, $120

(c) Expired insurance, $600.

(d) Rent expense for the year, $2,400.

(e) Additional salaries:
    Sales salaries, $80
    Office salaries, $60

(f) Accrued interest on notes payable, $120.

(g) Accrued interest on notes receivable, $85.

(h) Prepaid interest on notes payable, $65.

(i) Unearned interest on notes receivable, $45.

Instructions: (1) Prepare an eight-column work sheet for the year ended June 30 of the current year.

(2) Prepare a profit and loss statement.

(3) Prepare a classified balance sheet in report form.

(4) Record the adjusting, closing, and reversing entries in a general journal.

Chapter 13

Valuation of Receivables and Merchandise Inventory

NEED FOR CONSIDERATION In the previous chapter accruals and deferments of expense and income were discussed, together with the related adjusting entries required at the end of the fiscal period. The amounts of the adjustments could be determined accurately because they were based on known facts. For example, adjustments for interest are computed on the basis of principal amount, interest rate, and period of time, all of which may be definitely determined. There can be only one correct answer because all of the elements entering into the calculation are known. In this and the following chapter consideration will be given to certain adjustments that are less susceptible of exact determination.

A business enterprise that sells goods or services on account inevitably finds it impossible to collect some of its receivables. In adjusting the accounts at the end of a fiscal period, it is customary to give recognition to this fact. The portion of the accounts receivable that will be uncollectible cannot be determined with exactitude because there are too many factors involved. It is therefore necessary to employ estimates in arriving at the amount of the adjustment.

The procedures employed in valuing merchandise inventory are different from those used in valuing receivables. However, there is more than one acceptable method of determining the value of the merchandise on hand at the end of a fiscal period. In most cases the inventory value determined by the use of one method will not be the same as that obtained by employing another equally acceptable method.

PROVISION FOR BAD DEBTS When goods or services are sold on a credit basis, a portion of the accounts receivable usually proves to be uncollectible. This is true regardless of the care used in granting credit. At the end of the fiscal period it is not possible to determine the particular accounts that will not be collected in full. It would obviously be improper to credit any of the individual customers' accounts on the basis of an estimate. If the accounts receivable controlling account were credited for the estimated bad debts, the balance of the account would not agree with the sum of the balances in the subsidiary ledger. The customary practice, therefore, is to credit the amount estimated to be uncollectible to an account entitled *Allowance for Bad Debts*. This account is sometimes entitled *Reserve for Bad Debts*.[1]

The account Allowance for Bad Debts is usually referred to as a *valuation* account. It may also be described as a *negative asset* account. To illustrate its relationship to Accounts Receivable, assume that at the end of the first year of operation Robert Alden has accounts receivable of $15,000. Assume further that he estimates that $800 of this amount will be uncollectible. This information is shown in the following accounts:

ACCOUNTS RECEIVABLE   Acct. No. 114

1953											
Dec.	31	Balance	√	15,000							

ALLOWANCE FOR BAD DEBTS   Acct. No. 114.1

					1953					
					Dec.	31		J12	800	

The debit in Accounts Receivable represents the amount of the total claims against customers. The credit in Allowance for Bad Debts represents the estimated amount that will be uncollectible. The debit balance in the asset account minus the credit balance in the valuation account yields a net amount of $14,200 ($15,000 − $800), which is the estimated value of the claims against customers on December 31.

In making adjustments for accrued and deferred items, it was observed that each adjusting entry affects a balance sheet account and a profit and loss statement account. The same is true in making the adjustment for uncollectible accounts. In the illustration, the credit of $800 to Allowance for Bad Debts decreased the asset Accounts Receivable. This reduction in value is also an expense of operations and the adjustment is completed by debiting *Bad Debts Expense*. The adjusting entry, in its entirety, is therefore as follows:

Dec.	31	Bad Debts Expense................	717	800		
		Allowance for Bad Debts.........	114.1		800	

----

[1]The Committee on Terminology of the American Institute of Accountants recommends the discontinuance of the use of *reserve* (as in *Reserve for Bad Debts*) in describing deductions from assets. *Accounting Research Bulletin No. 34,* "Recommendation of Committee on Terminology," October, 1948 (New York: American Institute of Accountants), p. 274.

The bad debts expense account is closed into Profit and Loss Summary in exactly the same manner as the other expense accounts are closed. After the adjusting and closing entries have been posted, the asset account, the valuation account, and the expense account appear as follows:

ACCOUNTS RECEIVABLE   Acct. No. 114

1953									
Dec.	31	Balance	√	15,000					

ALLOWANCE FOR BAD DEBTS   Acct. No. 114.1

				1953				
				Dec.	31	Adjusting	J12	800

BAD DEBTS EXPENSE   Acct. No. 717

1953					1953				
Dec.	31	Adjusting	J12	800	Dec.	31	Closing	J13	800

BAD DEBTS ON THE FINANCIAL STATEMENTS The net amount expected to be collected on accounts receivable is an asset and is shown on the balance sheet. The estimated loss from uncollectibility is an expense and is shown on the profit and loss statement.

Although it would not be wholly incorrect to show the accounts receivable at their net figure without disclosing the amount of the allowance for bad debts, the following presentation on the balance sheet is preferable:

ROBERT ALDEN
BALANCE SHEET
DECEMBER 31, 1953

ASSETS		
Current Assets:		
Cash....................................		$ 9,500
Accounts Receivable..................	$15,000	
Less Allowance for Bad Debts........	800	14,200
Merchandise Inventory...............		61,400

The listing of both the gross amount of the accounts receivable and the allowance for bad debts informs the reader (1) of the fact that provision has been made for estimated uncollectibles and (2) of the amount of the provision.

There is a difference of opinion among accountants concerning the classification of bad debts expense. Since the granting of credit and the determination of collection policies are usually the responsibility of the credit department rather than of the sales department, it is treated as a general expense in this text.

WRITING OFF AN UNCOLLECTIBLE ACCOUNT   When it is determined that a claim against a customer cannot be collected, the balance of the customer's account should be written off, that is, reduced to zero. This is accomplished by crediting the accounts receivable controlling account in the general ledger and the customer's account in the subsidiary ledger, and by debiting the allowance for bad debts account.

Thus, if a claim of $120 against John Briggs, which appears in the accounts receivable ledger of Robert Alden on December 31, is definitely ascertained to be uncollectible on February 13, the following general journal entry would be made:

Feb.	13	Allowance for Bad Debts........... 114.1	120	
		Accounts Receivable — John Briggs 114/√		120
		To write off the account.		

It will be noted that the debit is to the valuation account Allowance for Bad Debts rather than to the expense account Bad Debts Expense. The reason is that the loss was previously debited to Bad Debts Expense by means of the adjusting entry. After the entry writing off the account has been posted, the allowance for bad debts account will appear as follows:

ALLOWANCE FOR BAD DEBTS   Acct. No. 114.1

1954				1953			
Feb.	13		120	Dec.	31	Adjusting	800

As additional accounts are determined to be worthless during the year, the amounts are written off against Allowance for Bad Debts. If a portion of an account is collected and the balance is uncollectible because of bankruptcy or other reasons, the amount collected is recorded in the cash receipts journal in the usual manner and the remainder is written off by a general journal entry similar to the one presented above.

The amount of the claims against customers determined to be worthless during the year are rarely, if ever, exactly equal to the amount set up in the allowance account; consequently, the account usually has a balance at the end of the period. If the write-offs were less than the estimate, the allowance account will have a credit balance; if the write-offs exceeded the estimate, the allowance account will have a debit balance. In either case, the adjusting entry at the end of each fiscal period is a debit to Bad Debts Expense and a credit to Allowance for Bad Debts.

COLLECTION OF ACCOUNTS PRE-VIOUSLY WRITTEN OFF   Sometimes a customer's account that has been charged against the allowance for bad debts account is subsequently collected. In such a case the account should be reinstated so that it will contain all the information needed for credit purposes. The entry to reinstate the account is the exact reverse of the entry writing it off.

For example, if John Briggs, whose account of $120 was written off on February 13, pays in full on July 25, the following entry is made in the general journal:

July	25	Accounts Receivable — John Briggs..	114/√	120	
		Allowance for Bad Debts..........	114.1		120
		To reinstate account previously written off.			

The receipt of $120 from John Briggs would be recorded in the cash receipts journal in the usual manner, as a debit to Cash and a credit to Accounts Receivable for $120.

ESTIMATING BAD DEBTS EXPENSE   The estimate of bad debts expense at the end of the fiscal period is based on past experience modified by forecasts of future business activity. When the trend of general sales volume is upward and there is relatively full employment, there is less likelihood of losses from uncollectible accounts than when the trend is in the opposite direction. Some types of businesses tend to incur greater losses than other types; the nature of the product or the service sold, differences in the clientele, length of the credit period, and other factors have a bearing upon the losses incurred. The usual practice is to estimate the amount of the bad debts expense on the basis of sales for the past fiscal period or on the amount and the age of accounts receivable at the end of the fiscal period.

Estimate Based on Sales. Accounts receivable are acquired during a period as a result of sales. The volume of sales during the period may therefore be used as an indication of the probable amount of the accounts that will be uncollectible. For example, if it is known from past experience that about $\frac{1}{2}$ of 1% of net sales will be uncollectible and the total of the net sales for a particular year is $200,000, the amount to be debited to Bad Debts Expense and credited to Allowance for Bad Debts would be $1,000.

Unless the ratio of sales on account to cash sales remains fairly constant, it may be preferable to use net sales *on account* as the base. Thus, if a business has generally experienced bad debt write-offs of 3% of net sales on account and the total of the net sales on account in a particular year amounts to $40,000, the estimate of bad debts expense would be $1,200.

A newly established business enterprise, having no record of credit experience, may obtain data on probable bad debts expense from trade association journals and other publications containing information on credit and collections. If it becomes apparent over a period of time that past estimates are materially at variance with actual experience, the percentage applied against sales should be revised accordingly.

Estimate Based on Analysis of Accounts Receivable. Instead of using sales as a basis for determining the bad debts provision for the period, some businesses analyze their accounts receivable at the end of the period to determine probable uncollectibility.

The balance of each account is classified according to the age of the claim. For example, the age intervals used might be as follows: not due; 0–30 days past due; 31–60 days past due; 61 days–6 months past due; and over 6 months past due. After the amounts in each age group are totaled, a sliding scale of percentages is applied to obtain the estimated uncollectibles in each group, and the group estimates are totaled. The allowance for bad debts account is then credited for the amount needed to bring the balance of this account up to the estimate, and Bad Debts Expense is debited for the same amount.

To illustrate, assume that the allowance for bad debts account at the end of the year before adjustment has a credit balance of $300. A study of the individual balances in the customers' ledger indicates that of the total of $26,000, $1,200 will probably be uncollectible. The amount of the adjustment required is $900 and the entry is as follows:

Dec.	31	Bad Debts Expense................	717	900	
		Allowance for Bad Debts.........	114.1		900

Observe that in this instance the provision for bad debts is based upon an analysis of the accounts receivable at the *end* of the period rather than on sales *during* the period. The estimated amount of uncollectible accounts included in Accounts Receivable at the end of the period is $1,200. Since Allowance for Bad Debts already has a credit balance of $300, it is now credited for $900 to bring it up to the desired amount. When the provision for bad accounts is based on a percentage of sales, the balance in the allowance account is not taken into consideration, except as it may indicate the advisability of increasing or decreasing the percentage to be applied to sales.

NOTES RECEIVABLE AND ALLOWANCE FOR BAD DEBTS   Notes receivable, like accounts receivable, may prove to be uncollectible. In fact, notes are sometimes accepted in settlement of accounts that are past due and hence of doubtful collectibility. The allowance for bad debts may include provision for both uncollectible accounts and notes. When this is the case, the balance sheet presentation is as follows:

Notes Receivable.	$ 6,000	
Accounts Receivable.	32,500	
Total.	$38,500	
Less Allowance for Bad Debts.	1,900	36,600

DIRECT WRITE-OFF METHOD   As an alternative to recording probable bad debts on the basis of estimates, some businesses charge accounts directly to Bad Debts Expense when they are determined to be worthless. When this alternative method is used, the entry to write off an uncollectible account is as follows:

Nov.	15	Bad Debts Expense.	717	22	
		Accounts Receivable — Carl Foster	114/√		22
		To write off the account.			

There would be no adjustment for estimated bad debts at the end of the fiscal period, and accounts receivable would be shown on the balance sheet at their gross amount without a deduction for estimated bad debts. It should be noted that, when this method is used, the expense is recorded in the period in which worthlessness is determined rather than in the earlier period in which the sale was made or worthlessness became a probability.

An account receivable that is written off to Bad Debts Expense in one fiscal period may be collected in a later fiscal period. When this occurs, the amount collected is treated as an income of the later period.

For example, if Carl Foster, whose account was written off in November, pays the amount owed on April 10 of the following fiscal year, the following general journal entry would be made:

April	10	Accounts Receivable — Carl Foster..	114/√	22	
		Bad Debts Collected.............	813		22
		To reinstate account previously written off.			

The receipt of $22 from Carl Foster would be recorded in the cash receipts journal in the usual manner, as a debit to Cash and a credit to Accounts Receivable. The account Bad Debts Collected is reported as "Other Income" on the profit and loss statement and is closed to the profit and loss summary account.

Both the allowance method and the direct write-off method are acceptable in determining net profit for purposes of federal income tax. The method adopted, however, must be consistently followed from year to year.

IMPORTANCE OF INVENTORY VALUATION   The valuation of the merchandise inventory is of particular importance because of its size in comparison with other assets owned by a mercantile business. An error of 10% in determining the value of office supplies on hand at the end of the period is unlikely to have a serious effect on either the balance sheet or the profit and loss statement. On the other hand, a comparable percentage variation in the valuation of the merchandise inventory might result in a material misstatement of net profit, of assets, and of proprietorship. The merchandise inventory adjustment is usually the most important adjustment made at the end of the accounting period. The effect of a small error in this one asset item may be greater than the effect of the omission of an entire adjustment affecting other balance sheet and profit and loss statement accounts.

TAKING THE INVENTORY   Counting the items that comprise the inventory is a laborious task that ordinarily must be done when business operations have ceased. For this reason, physical inventories are commonly taken after the close of business at the end of the month or at the end of the year. Although there are many variations in procedure, one in common use employs two-man teams. One inventory taker counts the units and a second puts down the count on an inventory sheet. After the inventory taking is completed, the items on the sheets are priced and the valuations are determined. This arithmetical process can be done while business is going on, but the counting is usually done during inactivity.

All of the merchandise that the business owns on the inventory date, and only such merchandise, should be included in the inventory. Sales contracts during the last few days of the period may have progressed to the point where title to the goods has passed and the sale has been recorded in the sales journal but the merchandise has not yet been shipped. Such items belong to the customer and should not be included in the inventory. On the other hand, the business may have acquired title to goods purchased but not yet received. The invoices for such purchases should be entered in the purchases journal and the merchandise should be included in the inventory.

INVENTORY VALUATION   The two methods of inventory valuation commonly used are: (1) cost and (2) cost or market, whichever is lower. "Cost" means the price paid for the goods, including transportation. "Market" is the price at which the goods could be replaced. For example, if an item in the inventory that was purchased for $100 could be bought at the inventory date for $97.50, the market price would be $97.50.

Valuing the inventory at the lower of cost or market usually results in a lower and hence more conservative inventory value. If items in the inventory that have declined in value because of deterioration, changes in price levels, or other causes are priced at the market value, the loss is recognized in the current period.

Assume that the cost of goods available for sale during a fiscal period totals $40,000 and that exactly three fourths of the goods are sold during the same period. At the end of the period, the inventory at cost would total $10,000 and the cost of goods sold would be stated at $30,000. Assume further, however, that the market price of each item in the inventory has declined and that the goods could be replaced at the inventory date for $8,000. If the inventory is valued at $8,000, the cost of goods sold would appear as $32,000 ($40,000 − $8,000) and gross profit and net profit would be correspondingly *less* by $2,000.

When the rule of cost or market, whichever is lower, is followed, it should be applied to each item in the inventory. For example, if a particular commodity on hand cost $40 and has a market value of $45 at the inventory date, it should be priced at $40. Another item having a cost of $60 and a market value of $50 should be priced at $50. As shown in the following tabulation, the total cost of the two items is $100 and the total market price is $95. Application of the lower of cost or market to each item, however, yields a value of $90.

	COST PRICE	MARKET PRICE	INVENTORY PRICE
Item A	$ 40	$45	$40
Item B	60	50	50
Total	$100	$95	$90

CHOOSING THE COST FIGURE FOR INVENTORIES In a changing market when prices are fluctuating, several lots of a particular commodity may have been purchased during the year at different unit prices. If some of these articles are on hand at the end of the year, a policy must be adopted and must be consistently followed in determining their cost. The traditional practice is to use the *first-in, first-out* method (*fifo* method), which assumes that the goods are sold in the order in which they are acquired; hence the goods on hand are taken to be those most recently purchased.

To illustrate the first-in, first-out method, assume that of a total of 1,000 units of a particular commodity purchased during the year the inventory count at the end of the year reveals that 300 are still on hand. Details of the purchases are as follows:

PURCHASES

DATE PURCHASED	UNITS	PRICE	TOTAL COST
Mar. 10	300	$10.00	$ 3,000
June 26	500	12.00	6,000
Nov. 30	200	13.50	2,700
Total	1,000		$11,700

It is assumed that the 700 units sold were those first acquired, and therefore the 300 units remaining in the inventory are composed of the 200 purchased on November 30 plus 100 of those purchased on June 26. The cost of inventory is computed as follows:

INVENTORY

DATE PURCHASED	UNITS	PRICE	TOTAL COST
June 26	100	$12.00	$1,200
Nov. 30	200	13.50	2,700
Total	300		$3,900

An alternative method of identifying goods on hand with particular purchases is known as the *last-in, first-out* method (*lifo* method). As the term indicates, the goods sold are identified with the most recent purchases and the inventory, therefore, is composed of the items acquired earliest. Thus, in the illustration above, the 700 units sold would be presumed to be composed of the 200 purchased on November 30 and the 500 units purchased on June 26. The cost of the inventory of 300 units would be the price paid for the earliest lot purchased, or $10 per unit, yielding an inventory cost of $3,000.

In the foregoing illustration the cost of the inventory determined by the last-in, first-out (lifo) method is $900 less than the inventory determined by the first-in, first-out (fifo) method. There is a corresponding difference of $900 in the amount of gross profit and net profit determined under the two methods.

If the prices paid for the three lots had been successively lower instead of higher, the effect of the two methods would be the reverse: that is, during a period of declining prices the first-in, first-out method gives a lower amount for the inventory and a correspondingly lower profit. This may be demonstrated by assuming a reverse order of unit prices in the foregoing illustration. The record of purchases then becomes as follows:

DATE PURCHASED	UNITS	PRICE	TOTAL COST
Mar. 10	300	$13.50	$ 4,050
June 26	500	12.00	6,000
Nov. 30	200	10.00	2,000
	1,000		$12,050

Continuing the assumption that 300 units are on hand at the end of the period, the cost of the inventory determined by the fifo method is $3,200; application of the lifo method results in an inventory of $4,050. Details of the inventory computations under both methods are as follows:

FIFO		LIFO	
100 units at $12.00	$1,200	300 units at $13.50	$4,050
200 units at 10.00	2,000		
Total	$3,200		

The fifo inventory is $850 less than the lifo inventory, and the amount of the profit for the period would differ correspondingly. When price levels are declining, the fifo method reports a lower profit.

Both methods of determining inventory cost are acceptable in determining income for purposes of federal income tax. The method adopted must, of course, be used consistently from year to year.

PERPETUAL INVENTORIES   Because of the substantial amount of work involved and the short time available, complete physical inventories are seldom taken more than once a year. The inventory amount for use in preparing monthly statements may be estimated in various ways or a current record of the number of units of each commodity purchased and sold may be maintained. Such a record is called a *perpetual inventory*. A separate account or inventory card must be kept for each item bought for sale. When goods are purchased, the number of units received must be recorded in the appropriate inventory account. When goods are sold, the number of units disposed of must be recorded in the appropriate inventory account. The balance of each inventory account at any time is the number of units of that commodity that should be on hand.

The expense of maintaining perpetual inventory records is likely to be excessive for businesses handling a great number of different items of low unit selling price. For example, perpetual inventory records might be practicable for a business selling office equipment, but they probably would not be used by a grocery store.

ESTIMATED INVENTORIES   When it is not feasible to take physical inventories at the end of each month and perpetual inventory records are not kept, the inventory may be estimated for use in preparing monthly financial statements. Estimates of inventories are usually based on the prevailing gross profit margin in the business. The simplest of these methods, known as the *gross profit* method, utilizes an estimate of the rate of gross profit realized on sales during the period.

To illustrate, assume that the inventory on January 1, the beginning of the current fiscal year, is $14,000, that net purchases during January amount to $8,000, that net sales during January amount to $10,000, and finally that gross profit is *estimated* to be 30% of net sales. The inventory on January 31 is estimated as shown at the top of the opposite page.

It should be noted that the accuracy of the inventory figure depends entirely on the accuracy of the estimated rate of gross profit. In addition to being used for monthly statement purposes, the gross profit method is sometimes employed in arriving at the estimate of inventory losses resulting from fires.

Known Data:

Merchandise Inventory, January 1...............	$14,000
Net Purchases during January..................	8,000
Merchandise Available for Sale.................	$22,000
Net Sales during January...................... $10,000	

Estimated Data:

Less Gross Profit (30% of net sales)............ 3,000	
Cost of Goods Sold...........................	7,000
Merchandise Inventory, January 31..............	$15,000

The *retail* method of inventory determination employs the same principle as the gross profit method. Instead of being based on past experience, however, the estimate of the rate of gross profit is based on records of the current period. In addition to recording merchandise in the purchases account in the usual manner, a supplementary record of the selling price of the merchandise is maintained. The selling price of the inventory can then be determined by subtracting the amount of sales from the selling price of the merchandise available for sale. The selling price of the inventory is then converted to cost on the basis of the gross profit rate experienced during the period.

Determination of the inventory by the retail method may be illustrated as follows:

	COST PRICE	SELLING PRICE
Merchandise Inventory, January 1...........	$16,000	$23,500
Net Purchases during January..............	8,000	12,500
Merchandise Available for Sale.............	$24,000	$36,000
Less Net Sales during January.............		15,000
Merchandise Inventory, January 31, at Selling Price.....................................		$21,000
Percentage of Cost to Selling Price of Merchandise Available for Sale: ($24,000 ÷ $36,000).		66⅔%
Merchandise Inventory, January 31, at Estimated Cost: (66⅔% of $21,000)..........	$14,000	

In the foregoing example it was assumed that no changes were made during the period in the selling price of the merchandise. Department stores and other businesses using this method must give effect to numerous adjustments for price markdowns and price markups.

QUESTIONS

1. Identify the following accounts as asset, liability, proprietorship, income, or expense: (a) Bad Debts Expense, (b) Allowance for Bad Debts, (c) Bad Debts Collected.

2. The Palace Hardware Store estimates its provision for uncollectible accounts at 2% of net sales on account. On December 31, the end of the current fiscal year, the sales account has a balance of $270,000 and the sales returns and allowances account has a balance of $20,000. Analysis of the two accounts reveals that sales on account and related returns and allowances totaled $185,000 and $15,000, respectively. Give the adjusting entry to record the provision for bad debts.

3. George Madden receives $60 as complete payment of the $150 account of T. L. Brown, a bankrupt. Madden has provided for estimated uncollectibles in his accounts. Give the necessary entries, in general journal form, to record receipt of the cash and to write off the balance of the account. In what journal should each entry be recorded?

4. George Madden (see Question 3 above) subsequently receives $90 from T. L. Brown in payment of the account written off. Give the necessary entries, in general journal form, to record the transaction. In what journal should each entry be recorded?

5. During the three years of operation of his business, Roger Parks has uniformly made provision for bad debts on the basis of 6% of net charge sales. The balances of Accounts Receivable and Allowance for Bad Debts after adjustment at the end of each year were as follows:

END OF YEAR	BALANCE OF ACCOUNTS RECEIVABLE	BALANCE OF ALLOWANCE FOR BAD DEBTS
1	$10,000	$ 700 (cr.)
2	18,000	1,300 (cr.)
3	14,000	2,100 (cr.)

(a) Assuming that accounts have been written off as they became uncollectible, what is the most likely explanation of the increase in the allowance account? (b) Assuming that the allowance for bad debts is excessive, what should have been done about the estimate at the end of the second and third years?

6. Thomas Rollins determines his provision for bad debts on the basis of an analysis of accounts receivable at the end of each fiscal year. Before adjustment at the end of the current fiscal year, the allowance for bad debts account has a credit balance of $460. It is estimated that of the $25,000 of accounts receivable, $1,100 will prove to be uncollectible. Give the adjusting entry to record the provision for bad debts.

7. In determining the inventory at the end of the fiscal year, an inventory sheet listing merchandise totaling $3,000 was omitted. (a) Did the error cause an overstatement or an understatement of the net profit for the year? (b) What items on the balance sheet at the end of the year were affected by this error (indicate whether overstated or understated)?

8. The following values apply to a particular item of merchandise: cost, $50; replacement price, $45; retail price, $60. At what figure should the item be included in the inventory according to the lower of cost or market rule?

PROBLEMS

13-1. During a two-year period of operations, Allen Monroe completed several transactions in connection with bad debts.

Instructions: (1) Open the following accounts in the ledger of Allen Monroe, using the account numbers indicated: Allowance for Bad Debts, 114.1; Profit and Loss Summary, 313; Bad Debts Expense, 718.

(2) Enter a credit balance of $900 in Account No. 114.1 as of January 1, 1953.

(3) Record in general journal form the following transactions and adjusting and closing entries completed during 1953:

Apr. 4. Wrote off the account of Wilbur Staley, $280, as uncollectible.
Sept. 20. Received 20% of the $500 balance owed by Henry London, bankrupt, and wrote off the remainder as uncollectible.
Nov. 15. Wrote off the account of A. R. Morgan, $325, as uncollectible.
Dec. 31. Recorded the provision for bad debts expense at 1% of net charge sales of $120,000.
Dec. 31. Recorded the entry to close Bad Debts Expense.

Instructions: (4) Post the foregoing journal entries to the three accounts in the ledger.

(5) Balance and rule the allowance for bad debts account and rule the bad debts expense account.

(6) Record in general journal form the following transactions and adjusting and closing entries completed during 1954:

Mar. 5. Wrote off the account of Walter Stubbs, $180, as uncollectible.
May 11. Received $100 from A. R. Morgan in partial payment of his account written off on November 15, 1953.
July 28. Wrote off the account of Charles Norwood, $620, as uncollectible.
Oct. 13. Received $9 from the receiver in bankruptcy for Walter Stubbs, in payment of his account written off on March 5, 1954.
Dec. 30. Wrote off the account of Eugene Day, $210, as uncollectible.
Dec. 31. Recorded the provision for bad debts expense at 1% of net charge sales of $112,000.
Dec. 31. Recorded the entry to close Bad Debts Expense.

Instructions: (7) Post the foregoing journal entries to the three accounts in the ledger.

(8) Balance and rule the allowance for bad debts account and rule the bad debts expense account.

(9) Assuming that the accounts receivable account on December 31, 1954, has a debit balance of $23,500, what is the net value of the accounts receivable?

13-2. Ralph Sprague is the Ohio distributor of Nu-Way (tank type) and Sturdy (upright type) vacuum cleaners. His trial balance on December 31, the end of the current fiscal year, is as follows:

Cash	111	$ 10,400	
Accounts Receivable	112	40,000	
Allowance for Bad Debts	112.1		$ 600
Merchandise Inventory	113	12,400	
Notes Payable	211		13,500
Accounts Payable	213		5,000
Ralph Sprague, Capital	311		29,385
Ralph Sprague, Drawing	312	10,000	
Sales	411		145,000
Purchases	511	85,000	
Operating Expenses (Control Account)	611	35,000	
Interest Expense	811	685	
		$193,485	$193,485

Adjustment data:

(a) The merchandise inventory on December 31 is composed of the following items (use cost or market, whichever is lower):

200 Nu-Way cleaners; cost $30 each; replacement price on December 31, $32 each.

156 Sturdy cleaners; cost $26 each, replacement price on December 31, $25 each.

Miscellaneous repair parts; cost, $1,200; replacement price on December 31, $1,100.

(b) Upon the basis of an analysis of accounts receivable it is estimated that $2,000 will be uncollectible. (Debit Operating Expenses for the bad debts expense.)

(c) Prepaid interest on notes payable, $125.

(d) Interest accrued on notes payable, $35.

Instructions: (1) Prepare an eight-column work sheet for the year.

(2) Prepare a profit and loss statement and a balance sheet.

(3) Record adjusting, closing, and reversing entries.

13-3. James Roth established an electric appliance store early in the current year. The items purchased during the first year, together with unit prices paid, are listed below in chronological order. The inventory count on December 31 is shown in the column at the right.

DESCRIPTION	FIRST PURCHASE	SECOND PURCHASE	THIRD PURCHASE	INVENTORY COUNT DEC. 31
#18A Laundry Machine	3 @ $160	4 @ $170	4 @ $170	2
#19A Laundry Machine	2 @ 220	3 @ 230	3 @ 235	3
#43 Refrigerator	4 @ 140	2 @ 145	2 @ 150	3
#71 Refrigerator	10 @ 250	5 @ 265	3 @ 270	3
#72 Refrigerator	1 @ 290	5 @ 300		2
#1 Automatic Mixer	12 @ 32	6 @ 30		6

DESCRIPTION	FIRST PURCHASE	SECOND PURCHASE	THIRD PURCHASE	INVENTORY COUNT DEC. 31
#326 Range	2 @ 135	6 @ 140		2
#432 Range	4 @ 175	5 @ 175	5 @ 185	5
#618 Range	2 @ 197	2 @ 205	2 @ 210	2
#60X Dishwasher	1 @ 170	5 @ 180	5 @ 185	2
#31A Dishwasher	4 @ 200	2 @ 200	1 @ 190	2
#20 Water Heater	4 @ 95	3 @ 100		2
#28 Water Heater	1 @ 125	3 @ 125	3 @ 132	2

Instructions: (1) Determine the cost of the inventory on December 31 by the first-in, first-out method. Present data in columnar form, using th columnar headings indicated below. If some units of a commodity are priced at one figure and others at another figure, use a separate line for each.

DESCRIPTION	QUANTITY	UNIT COST	TOTAL COST

(2) Determine the cost of the inventory on December 31 by the last-in, first-out method, following the same procedures prescribed in instruction (1).

13-4. Charles Smith takes a physical inventory at the end of each fiscal year. In order to prepare a balance sheet and a profit and loss statement at the end of each month, he estimates his inventory. The following information is available on January 31 of the current fiscal year:

	COST PRICE	SELLING PRICE
Merchandise Inventory, January 1..............	$64,000	$96,500
Purchases during January....................	25,000	38,200
Freight In during January................,.....	800	
Purchases Returns and Allowances during January.	1,000	1,500
Sales during January.........................		30,000
Sales Returns and Allowances during January......		1,200

Instructions: (1) Determine the estimated inventory on January 31 using the gross profit method. On the basis of past experience Mr. Smith estimates that his rate of gross profit for the current year will be 34.5% of net sales. Present the data in a form similar to the illustration at the top of page 235.

(2) Determine the estimated inventory on January 31 using the retail method. Present the data in a form similar to the illustration on the lower part of page 235.

13-5. Before Frank Porter's books are closed for the fiscal year ended June 30, an accountant finds the following:

(a) Merchandise inventory is valued at the lower of cost or market. Examination of the inventory sheets reveals that: (1) 800 units of Commodity A, with a unit cost of $5 and a market value of $7, were included in the inventory at $7 per unit; (2) 400 units of Commodity B, with a unit cost of $4 and a market value of $3, were included in the inventory at $4 per unit.

(b) An order of merchandise shipped to a customer on account on June 30 had not been recorded as a sale ($3,500) and was not included in inventory ($2,400). Title passed prior to shipment.

(c) An order of merchandise ready for shipment to a customer on account on June 29 was included in the inventory at a cost of $800. The sale ($1,200) had not been recorded. Title passed on June 29.

(d) An order of merchandise ready for shipment to a customer on account on June 30 had been recorded as a sale ($2,600) and was also included in the inventory ($1,700).

(e) A purchase invoice for $300 had been recorded as a purchase on account; but inasmuch as the goods had not arrived, they were not included in the inventory.

(f) Merchandise with a cost of $2,800 was received on June 30. It was included in the inventory, but the invoice had not been received and hence had not been recorded as a purchase on account.

Before the foregoing errors were discovered, Frank Porter's bookkeeper prepared the following profit and loss statement for the year ended June 30:

Sales...		$190,000
Cost of Goods Sold:		
Merchandise Inventory, July 1..............	$ 45,420	
Purchases	130,000	
Merchandise Available for Sale.............	$175,420	
Less Merchandise Inventory, June 30........	53,300	
Cost of Goods Sold...............................		122,120
Gross Profit on Sales...............................		$ 67,880
Operating Expenses................................		48,200
Net Profit.......................................		$ 19,680

Instructions: (1) Determine the effect of each of the required corrections on Sales and Purchases for the year and on Merchandise Inventory on June 30. Accumulate the corrections in "T" accounts as illustrated below, identifying each by letter.

SALES		PURCHASES		MERCHANDISE INVENTORY	
Decrease	Increase	Increase	Decrease	Increase	Decrease
(a)					
(b)					
(c)					
etc.					

(2) Prepare a corrected profit and loss statement based on the corrections determined in (1).

Chapter | **14**

Valuation of Fixed Assets— Depreciation

COST OF FIXED ASSETS Items of plant and equipment are usually acquired by a mercantile business by purchase or by exchanging an old asset plus cash for a new one. The cost of a fixed asset includes all expenditures necessary to get it in place and in operation. Therefore, in addition to the price paid to the seller, expenditures incurred for sales taxes, transportation, and installation are debited to the fixed asset account. Similarly the cost of constructing a building includes the fees paid to architects for plans and supervision, the cost of temporary sheds to house tools and materials, and other necessary expenditures. When a secondhand asset is purchased, the initial costs of getting it ready for use, such as expenditures for new parts, repairs, and painting, are properly chargeable to the fixed asset account. The determination of the cost of a fixed asset acquired in exchange for another asset is discussed later in this chapter.

DEPRECIATION AND FIXED ASSETS All fixed assets, except land, decline in usefulness as a result of wear, the action of the elements, and the passing of time. This decline in usefulness is called *depreciation*. Land is excepted because as a site for buildings or for other business uses it is permanent, barring such unforeseeable and unusual occurrences as flood or earthquake.

Depreciation of fixed assets must be recognized in the accounts and on the financial statements. It would obviously be incorrect to consider a fixed asset as wholly an expense at the time of acquisition. It is equally obvious that the recognition of depreciation should not be postponed until the period in which the fixed asset is finally traded in, sold, or discarded. It is necessary that depreciation expense be distributed over the fiscal periods that are expected to benefit from the use of the fixed asset.

The most commonly used method of determining depreciation expense is to distribute the cost of the fixed asset equally over all of the periods in the estimated life of the asset. This method is known as the *straight-line method*. To illustrate the straight-line method, assume that a fixed asset that cost $1,000 has an estimated useful life of 10 years. Ignoring any trade-in or scrap value that the asset might be expected to have at the end of 10 years, the depreciation expense would be determined by dividing $1,000 by 10, yielding annual depreciation of $100. The annual depreciation is sometimes expressed as a per cent of the cost of the asset. In this case the rate is 10% ($100 ÷ $1,000).

When the estimated trade-in or scrap value of the asset is taken into consideration, it is subtracted from the cost of the asset and the remainder is divided by the estimated life. For example, if the asset in the foregoing illustration had an estimated trade-in value of $100, the annual depreciation would have been $90 ($900 ÷ 10). Expressed as a per cent of cost, the depreciation rate would have been 9% ($90 ÷ $1,000). In general, there is more reason for considering trade-in or scrap value of assets that are normally traded in after a few years, such as automobiles or typewriters, than for more permanent assets, such as buildings. But in any case, the amount of annual depreciation finally determined is based on estimates.

Since depreciation is based on estimates, it is desirable to allow the cost of the asset to remain in the fixed asset account undisturbed and to record the reduction in value in a separate account. In this way both the original cost and the amount of depreciation accumulated over the years can more readily be determined from the ledger. The customary practice, therefore, is to credit the reduction in value to an account entitled *Allowance for Depreciation*. This account is sometimes entitled *Reserve for Depreciation*.

The account Allowance for Depreciation is a valuation or negative asset account. To illustrate its relationship to the related asset account, assume that a building is acquired at a cost of $40,000 on January 1, the first day of the fiscal year, and that it is to be depreciated at the rate of $1,000 a year. After the adjustment for depreciation has been recorded at the end of the first year, the asset account and the valuation account will appear as follows:

Building   No. 124

Jan.	1		J10	40,000.00						

Allowance for Depreciation—Building   No. 124.1

					Dec.	31		J15	1,000.00

The debit in Building represents the cost of the building. The credit in Allowance for Depreciation—Building represents the reduction in value for the year because of depreciation. The difference between the $40,000 debit balance in the building account and the $1,000 credit balance in the allowance account is the remaining undepreciated cost, or $39,000. This is the value of the building according to the books, usually referred to as the *book value*. Book value does not necessarily have any relationship to assessed value for property tax purposes or to resale value. Because of fluctuations in the real estate market, changes in general price levels, and other business factors, the building might bring more or less than $39,000 if sold after one year of use. Fluctuations in selling prices of fixed assets are not recognized in the accounts.

RECORDING DEPRECIA- It has been observed that each adjustment
TION for store supplies and other prepaid assets affects a balance sheet account and a profit and loss statement account. The same is true of an adjustment for depreciation. In the preceding illustration the credit of $1,000 to Allowance for Depreciation — Building represented a decrease in the value of the asset Building. This reduction in the asset is an expense of operations, and the adjustment is completed by debiting Depreciation Expense — Building. The adjusting entry, in its entirety, is therefore as follows:

| Dec. | 31 | Depreciation Expense — Building........... | 715 | 1,000 | |
| | | Allowance for Depreciation—Building...... | 124.1 | | 1,000 |

The depreciation account is closed into Profit and Loss Summary in exactly the same manner as the other expense accounts are closed. After adjusting and closing entries have been posted, the asset account, the valuation account, and the expense account appear as follows:

				Building					No. 124		
Jan.	1		J10	40,000							

				Allowance for Depreciation—Building					No. 124.1		
					Dec.	31	Adjusting	J15	1,000		

				Depreciation Expense — Building					No. 715		
Dec.	31	Adjusting	J15	1,000	Dec.	31	Closing	J16	1,000		

At the end of each year a similar adjusting entry is made. The debit amount in the expense account is then closed to the profit and loss summary account. The credit balance in the allowance account continues to increase from year to year.

The method of recording the provision for depreciation is the same for all fixed assets. A separate expense account and a separate allowance account are usually maintained for each fixed asset or group of fixed assets, except land. For example, a business owning delivery trucks may have the following related accounts in its ledger: Delivery Equipment (asset), Allowance for Depreciation — Delivery Equipment (valuation), and Depreciation Expense — Delivery Equipment (expense).

In the illustration the fixed asset was purchased on the first day of the fiscal year and the depreciation was computed for the entire year. Depreciation on assets acquired during the year is ordinarily computed on the basis of the time from the date of acquisition to the end of the year. For example, if store equipment is purchased on October 1 and the fiscal year ends on December 31, only one fourth of a full year's depreciation would be charged to expense for the year of acquisition.

The adjusting entry to record depreciation may be made monthly instead of annually. When financial statements are prepared at the end of each month, it is necessary to record the depreciation adjustment on the interim work sheet regardless of whether it is entered on the books on a monthly basis or on an annual basis.

When a fixed asset is purchased during a month instead of at the beginning, depreciation is charged for the nearest month. For example, if the purchase is made before the middle of the month, a whole month's depreciation is charged; if the purchase is made after the middle of the month, no depreciation is charged for that month. Since depreciation expense is, at best, an estimate subject to error, it seems unnecessary to account for a unit of time shorter than a month. To illustrate, for a typewriter purchased on May 12, an entire month's depreciation is charged for May; for a typewriter purchased on May 20, no depreciation is charged for May.

DEPRECIATION ON THE FINANCIAL STATEMENTS   The undepreciated cost of plant and equipment is an asset and is shown on the balance sheet. The periodic charge for depreciation is an expense and is shown on the profit and loss statement.

Although it would not be entirely incorrect to list on the balance sheet the fixed assets at their net amounts without disclosing the original cost and the allowance for depreciation, the following presentation is preferable since it constitutes a more complete disclosure of the facts:

Fixed Assets:			
Store Equipment...............	$ 8,000		
Less Allowance for Depreciation	2,400	$ 5,600	
Office Equipment..............	$ 3,600		
Less Allowance for Depreciation	1,100	2,500	
Building.....................	$40,000		
Less Allowance for Depreciation	1,000	39,000	
Land........................		4,000	
Total Fixed Assets.............			51,100

The depreciation expense accounts are classified according to the use of the assets. If the asset is used in the sales department, the depreciation of the asset is classified as a selling expense. Depreciation of store equipment is classified as a selling expense; depreciation of office equipment and depreciation of buildings are classified as general expenses.

DISCARDING FIXED ASSETS   When a fixed asset is disposed of, it is necessary to relieve the asset account of its cost and to relieve the related valuation account of the accumulated depreciation. For example, if office equipment purchased 10 years ago at a cost of $1,000 is now fully depreciated and is discarded as worthless, the following entry would be made:

Dec.	31	Allowance for Depreciation—Office Equipment......................................	123.1	1,000	
		Office Equipment......................	123		1,000
		To write off fully depreciated asset discarded.			

In actual practice it is not possible to estimate depreciation so accurately. A business may use one asset long beyond the time originally estimated, but it may find that it must discard another asset much earlier than it originally expected to.

After an asset is fully depreciated, no further depreciation on it is recorded even though its use is continued. Therefore, if an asset that has been used longer than was originally estimated is discarded, the entry is still similar to the one shown above. If, on the other hand, an asset that has been used for a shorter time than was anticipated is discarded, a loss results amounting to the difference between the cost of the asset and its allowance for depreciation. This loss is debited to a special account entitled *Loss or Gain on Disposal of Fixed Assets*. This account is debited for any losses and is credited for any gains resulting from the disposal of fixed assets. A debit balance in this account at the end of the accounting period represents a net loss and is shown as "Other Expense" on the profit and loss statement; a credit balance represents a net gain and is shown as "Other Income" on the profit and loss statement.

SALE OF FIXED ASSETS When a fixed asset is sold, the fixed asset account and the related allowance account must be reduced by the appropriate amount, the account receivable or cash must be recorded, and any gain or loss resulting from the sale must be recognized. To illustrate the various possibilities, it will be assumed that office equipment acquired at a cost of $1,000 and depreciated at the rate of $100 per year is sold for cash at the end of the eighth year. Three different assumptions as to the selling price, and the general journal entry required in each case, are given below. The cash received would also be recorded in the cash receipts journal in each case.

(a) Selling price $200, which is the book value of the asset.

Dec.	31	Cash....................................	√	200	
		Allowance for Depreciation—Office Equipment....................................	123.1	800	
		Office Equipment.......................	123		1,000
		Sold office equipment.			

(b) Selling price $450, which is $250 greater than the book value of the asset.

Dec.	31	Cash....................................	√	450	
		Allowance for Depreciation—Office Equipment....................................	123.1	800	
		Office Equipment.......................	123		1,000
		Loss or Gain on Disposal of Fixed Assets...	813		250
		Sold office equipment.			

(c) Selling price $150, which is $50 less than the book value of the asset.

Dec.	31	Cash....................................	√	150	
		Allowance for Depreciation—Office Equipment....................................	123.1	800	
		Loss or Gain on Disposal of Fixed Assets.....	813	50	
		Office Equipment.......................	123		1,000
		Sold office equipment.			

It will be observed that under each of the three assumptions the allowance account was debited for the accumulated depreciation ($800) and the fixed asset account was credited for the cost of the asset

($1,000). If the selling price is greater than the book value, the gain is credited to the loss or gain account; if the selling price is less than the book value, the loss is debited to the loss or gain account.

In the foregoing illustration the fixed asset was sold on the last day of the fiscal year after the depreciation for the year had been recorded. When the asset is disposed of during the period, it is necessary to record the depreciation accrued from the date of the preceding adjustment to the date of the sale before recording the details of the sale. For example, assume that in illustration (b) above the equipment was sold on April 10 of the ninth year rather than on the last day of the eighth year. The depreciation from January 1 to April 10 of the ninth year would be 3/12 of $100 or $25 (the 10 days in April are ignored) and the necessary entries would be as follows:

April	10	Depreciation Expense — Office Equipment..	714	25	
		Allowance for Depreciation—Office Equipment.......................	123.1		25
		To record 3 months' depreciation on equipment sold.			
	10	Cash......................................	√	450	
		Allowance for Depreciation—Office Equipment.....................................	123.1	825	
		Office Equipment.......................	123		1,000
		Loss or Gain on Disposal of Fixed Assets...	813		275
		Sold office equipment.			

EXCHANGE OF FIXED ASSETS   When a fixed asset is given in part payment for the purchase of a new fixed asset with a similar purpose, the exchange and the payment of cash may be recorded in one compound entry. The various elements in the transaction are outlined as follows:

(a) A debit to the allowance account for the accumulated depreciation and a credit to the fixed asset for its cost.

(b) A debit to the fixed asset account for the purchase price of the new asset.

(c) A credit to Cash or to the appropriate liability account for the amount to be paid for the new asset. This amount is the purchase price of the new asset minus the *trade-in allowance* on the old asset.

(d) A debit or a credit to Loss or Gain on Disposal of Fixed Assets. The amount of the loss or the gain is the difference between the book value of the old asset and the trade-in allowance.

To illustrate, assume that a delivery truck with an original cost of $3,000 and an accumulated depreciation of $2,400 is traded in for a new truck with a list price of $3,500; and further, that the old truck is accepted at $900, the balance of $2,600 being paid in cash. The several parts of the transaction are analyzed as follows:

(a) To remove the old asset from the accounts:
Debit Allowance for Depreciation—Delivery Equipment for...................................... $2,400
Credit Delivery Equipment for................... 3,000

(b) To record the new asset at its purchase price:
Debit Delivery Equipment for.................... $3,500

(c) To record the payment of cash ($3,500 − $900 trade-in allowance):
Credit Cash for............................... $2,600

(d) To record the gain on the exchange ($900 − $600 book value):
Credit Loss or Gain on Disposal of Fixed Assets for. . . $ 300

The compound general journal entry to record the transaction is shown below. The cash payment would also be recorded in the cash payments journal.

July	1	Allowance for Depreciation—Delivery Equipment	121.1	2,400	
		Delivery Equipment	121	3,500	
		Delivery Equipment	121		3,000
		Cash	✓		2,600
		Loss or Gain on Disposal of Fixed Assets	813		300
		Purchased new truck.			

To illustrate the entry involved when the trade-in allowance granted is less than the book value of the asset, assume the same transaction except that the old truck is accepted at $400 instead of $900. In this case the loss is $200 (book value of $600 minus allowance of $400) and the cash paid is $3,100 (purchase price of $3,500 minus allowance of $400). The compound general journal entry to record the exchange is given below:

July	1	Allowance for Depreciation—Delivery Equipment	121.1	2,400	
		Delivery Equipment	121	3,500	
		Loss or Gain on Disposal of Fixed Assets	813	200	
		Delivery Equipment	121		3,000
		Cash	✓		3,100
		Purchased new truck.			

When cash and a fixed asset used in the business are given in exchange for another fixed asset of a similar nature, any gain or loss resulting from the transaction is not recognized for federal income tax purposes. The cost of the new asset acquired, for purposes of computing depreciation and gain or loss on its eventual sale, is the sum of: (1) the book value of the old asset given in exchange and (2) the cash paid or to be paid. Assuming the facts of the first of the two illustrations above, the cost of the new asset would be determined as follows:

```
Book value of old truck traded in........$  600
Cash paid................................  2,600
Cost basis of new truck..................$3,200
```

The effect of the nonrecognition of the $300 gain from the exchange on the cost basis of the new truck may also be shown as follows:

```
Purchase price of new truck.............              $3,500
Trade-in allowance on old truck.........    $900
Book value of old truck.................     600
Gain (not recognized)...................                 300
Cost basis of new truck.................              $3,200
```

Many accountants prefer to record such exchanges in conformity with the income tax regulations, thus avoiding the necessity of reconciling the accounts with the income tax returns. When this policy is followed, the entry to record the exchange would be as follows:

July	1	Allowance for Depreciation—Delivery Equipment.............................	121.1	2,400	
		Delivery Equipment......................	121	3,200	
		Delivery Equipment....................	121		3,000
		Cash................................	✓		2,600
		Purchased new truck.			

For the second of the two exchanges illustrated, the cost basis of the new truck for income tax purposes would be determined in the following manner:

```
Book value of old truck traded in.........  $  600
Cash paid.................................     3,100
Cost basis of new truck...................   $3,700
```

As shown in the summary below, the unrecognized loss of $200 on the exchange is added to the purchase price of the new truck:

```
Purchase price of new truck.............              $3,500
Book value of old truck.................    $600
Trade-in allowance on old truck.........     400
Loss (not recognized)...................                 200
Cost basis of new truck.................              $3,700
```

If the exchange is to be recorded in accordance with income tax regulations, the general journal entry would be:

July	1	Allowance for Depreciation—Delivery Equipment	121.1	2,400	
		Delivery Equipment	121	3,700	
		Delivery Equipment	121		3,000
		Cash	✓		3,100
		Purchased new truck.			

It is apparent from the examples that, when the income tax method is employed, the value at which the new asset is recorded will differ from the purchase price except when the trade-in allowance on the old asset is exactly the same as the book value. The cost basis of the new asset will be its purchase price minus the amount of the unrecognized gain or plus the amount of the unrecognized loss. This variation between the purchase price and the value at which the new asset is recorded is gradually eliminated during the life of the asset through the periodic depreciation adjustments.

In the preceding discussion it has been assumed that the transactions occurred at the beginning of an accounting period. When a fixed asset is sold or traded in during an accounting period, the depreciation for the part of the period that has passed must first be recorded; the entries required to record the sale or the exchange are then made.

SUBSIDIARY LEDGERS FOR EQUIPMENT   The general ledger account for equipment usually includes all of the equipment that is used for one function of the business. Typical accounts are Office Equipment, Store Equipment, and Delivery Equipment.

For example, the office equipment account includes such equipment as desks, chairs, filing cabinets, typewriters, and many other items used in the office. Records of cost, date of acquisition, and accumulated depreciation may be maintained for each of these items through the medium of a subsidiary ledger. The account Office Equipment and the related account Allowance for Depreciation—Office Equipment become controlling accounts for the subsidiary ledger. The balance in the office equipment account equals the total cost of the items in the office equipment ledger; the balance of the allowance for depreciation account agrees with the sum of the depreciation allowances in the office equipment ledger.

Although there are no standard account rulings for the equipment ledger, the form should provide space for recording the asset, the allowance for depreciation, and miscellaneous descriptive data. For purposes of illustration, an office equipment ledger of four accounts will be assumed. The controlling accounts in the general ledger and the four accounts in the subsidiary ledger are shown on this and the following page.

General Ledger

Office Equipment   No. 123

1952										
Jan.	4		CP1	225.00						
Apr.	18		P 4	190.00						
Aug.	13		P 8	88.80						

Allowance for Depreciation—Office Equipment   No. 123.1

				1952					
				Dec.	31		J 4		35.08
				1953					
				Dec.	31		J15		49.40

Office Equipment Ledger

FIXED ASSET RECORD

ITEM__Desk_____ GENERAL LEDGER ACCOUNT__Office Equipment____

SERIAL NO.__- - -_____ DESCRIPTION__Metal_____

FROM WHOM PURCHASED__Office Outfitters, Inc._____

ESTIMATED LIFE__20 yrs.__ ESTIMATED SCRAP OR TRADE-IN VALUE__- - -_____ DEPRECIATION PER YEAR__$9.00__

DATE			EXPLANATION	ASSET			DEPRECIATION ALLOWANCE			BOOK VALUE
MO.	DAY	YR.		DR.	CR.	BAL.	DR.	CR.	BAL.	
1	4	52		180 00		180 00				180 00
12	31	52						9 00	9 00	171 00
12	31	53						9 00	18 00	162 00

FIXED ASSET RECORD

ITEM__Chair_____ GENERAL LEDGER ACCOUNT__Office Equipment____

SERIAL NO.__- - -_____ DESCRIPTION__Metal_____

FROM WHOM PURCHASED__Office Outfitters, Inc._____

ESTIMATED LIFE__15 yrs.__ ESTIMATED SCRAP OR TRADE-IN VALUE__- - -_____ DEPRECIATION PER YEAR__$3.00__

DATE			EXPLANATION	ASSET			DEPRECIATION ALLOWANCE			BOOK VALUE
MO.	DAY	YR.		DR.	CR.	BAL.	DR.	CR.	BAL.	
1	4	52		45 00		45 00				45 00
12	31	52						3 00	3 00	42 00
12	31	53						3 00	6 00	39 00

FIXED ASSET RECORD										

ITEM_ Typewriter _____ GENERAL LEDGER ACCOUNT_ Office Equipment ____

SERIAL NO. 46-5794 _____ DESCRIPTION_ Standard _____

FROM WHOM PURCHASED_ Standard Typewriter Agency _____

ESTIMATED LIFE `5 yrs.` ___ ESTIMATED SCRAP OR TRADE-IN VALUE_ $40.00 ___ DEPRECIATION PER YEAR_ $30.00

DATE			EXPLANATION	ASSET			DEPRECIATION ALLOWANCE			BOOK VALUE
MO.	DAY	YR.		DR.	CR.	BAL.	DR.	CR.	BAL.	
4	18	52		190 00		190 00				190 00
12	31	52						20 00	20 00	170 00
12	31	53						30 00	50 00	140 00

FIXED ASSET RECORD										

ITEM_ Filing Cabinet _____ GENERAL LEDGER ACCOUNT_ Office Equipment ____

SERIAL NO. --- _____ DESCRIPTION_ Four drawer, metal _____

FROM WHOM PURCHASED_ Regent Office Equipment Co. _____

ESTIMATED LIFE 12 yrs. ___ ESTIMATED SCRAP OR TRADE-IN VALUE_ --- ___ DEPRECIATION PER YEAR_ $7.40

DATE			EXPLANATION	ASSET			DEPRECIATION ALLOWANCE			BOOK VALUE
MO.	DAY	YR.		DR.	CR.	BAL.	DR.	CR.	BAL.	
8	13	52		88 80		88 80				88 80
12	31	52						3 08	3 08	85 72
12	31	53						7 40	10 48	78 32

When subsidiary equipment ledgers are used, the amount of the periodic adjustment for depreciation is determined for each item. For example, on December 31, 1952, credits to the allowance for depreciation account were recorded in the four subsidiary accounts as follows:

Desk.	$ 9.00	Typewriter.	$20.00
Chair.	3.00	Filing Cabinet.	3.08

The sum of these credits, $35.08, was then recorded in the general journal as a debit to Depreciation Expense—Office Equipment and a credit to Allowance for Depreciation—Office Equipment.

When an asset is sold, traded in, or junked, the debit to the allowance account and the credit to the asset account are also entered in the appropriate subsidiary account, reducing both balances to zero. The sheet is then removed from the ledger and is filed for possible future reference.

COMPOSITE RATES   Not all businesses maintain a record of each individual asset. In such cases a *composite rate* of depreciation may be applied to all items in a particular account. A composite rate is based on the average life of all of the individual assets. For example, if the average life of all office equipment were assumed to be 10 years, an annual depreciation rate of 10% would be applied to the asset account. When a composite rate is used, depreciation on assets acquired or disposed of during the year is frequently computed at one half of the annual rate.

Applying a 10% rate to the office equipment previously illustrated would yield annual depreciation of $50.38. Assuming that one half of the annual depreciation was charged in the year of acquisition, the two accounts would appear as follows at the end of the second year:

Office Equipment   No. 123

1952								
Jan.	4	CP1	225.00					
Apr.	18	P 4	190.00					
Aug.	13	P 8	88.80					

Allowance for Depreciation—Office Equipment   No. 123.1

				1952				
				Dec.	31		J 4	25.19
				1953				
				Dec.	31		J19	50.38

If the composite annual rate of 10% had been applied on a monthly basis, the total depreciation for the year in which the assets were acquired would have been $38.90 instead of $25.19. It does not follow that computation on a monthly basis always yields a greater amount of depreciation in the year of acquisition. If the bulk of the purchases had occurred in the latter half of the year, computation on a monthly basis would have resulted in an amount less than $25.19.

Although fewer records are required when composite rates are used, the results obtained are not so accurate and are therefore less satisfactory than the more detailed method presented earlier.

METHODS OF COM- Of necessity, depreciation is based on esti-
PUTING DEPRECIATION mates. It is usually possible, however, to make the estimates with reasonable exactness. As a business gains experience with various fixed assets, the rates of depreciation can be adjusted accordingly. When the experience of the business is insufficient to be used as a basis, assistance can be obtained from published tables of depreciation rates.

One of the sources to which reference is frequently made is Bulletin F, issued by the Bureau of Internal Revenue. It contains suggested life estimates for many kinds of fixed assets used by a wide variety of industries. Composite life estimates are given for some functional groups, such as office equipment (15 years), and individual life estimates are given for specific items within the group, such as adding machines (10 years) and safes and vaults (50 years). The life estimates are suggestive as guides, but their use for income tax purposes is not mandatory. For example, in a number of disputes that have reached the courts, a composite rate of 10% for office equipment has been allowed.

As was stated earlier in the chapter, the straight-line method of determining depreciation is the method most frequently used. It is based on the principle that depreciation is a function of time. It assumes that the amount of time that the asset is in actual use is fairly uniform from period to period. When there is a change in the intensity of use that was not originally contemplated, the rate of depreciation may be altered to meet the new circumstances, as when a manufacturing plant changes from an 8-hour-per-day operation to a 16- or 24-hour-per-day operation.

Hourly Rate Method. If the extent to which a fixed asset is used varies greatly from time to time, the *hourly rate* method of depreciation may be adopted. It is closely related to the straight-line method in that it is based on time. It depreciates the cost of equipment on the basis of the hours used, however, rather than on the basis of age. For example, if the estimated hours of use of a machine costing $10,000 is 20,000 hours, the rate per hour would be $.50. If the machine were used a total of 1,400 hours during the first year and 2,300 hours during the second year, the depreciation expense for the two years would be $700 and $1,150, respectively.

Reducing-Fraction Method. When a new fixed asset, such as an automobile, is purchased, the repair expense is likely to be low during the first year, but it will gradually increase as the car becomes older. If the straight-line method of depreciation is used, the sum of the depreciation and the repairs tends to increase from year to year. In order to equalize this expense, a method may be used by which the greatest charge for depreciation is made during the first year of the life of the asset and the charge is gradually decreased for each succeeding year.

One such method is known as the *reducing-fraction method.* To illustrate the use of this method, assume that an automobile is purchased with the expectation that it can be used for 4 years. The cost of the property may be written off 4/10 in the first year, 3/10 in the second year, 2/10 in the third year, and 1/10 in the fourth year. The numerator of the fraction is the number of the year, the numbers being used in reverse order, and the denominator is the sum of the years. If the automobile cost $2,800, the depreciation for each of the four years is determined as follows:

YEAR	FRACTIONAL DEPRECIATION	DEPRECIATION EXPENSE	ACCUMULATED ALLOWANCE FOR DEPRECIATION
1	4/10	$1,120	$1,120
2	3/10	840	1,960
3	2/10	560	2,520
4	1/10	280	2,800

The likelihood that the sum of the depreciation expense and the repair expense will yield approximately the same amount each year is somewhat remote. For example, assuming that expenditures for repairs of the automobile during its first year of use amounted to $100, the combined depreciation ($1,120) and repair ($100) expenses would be $1,220. It is highly unlikely that in the fourth year of use the repair expense would amount to $940 ($1,220 less depreciation of $280).

The hourly rate and the reducing-fraction methods are illustrative of variations from the straight-line method of depreciation. There are others that have been devised to meet particular situations. Because of its simplicity and inherent soundness, however, the straight-line method is used by most businesses.

INADEQUACY AND OBSOLESCENCE   Loss of usefulness of a fixed asset because of wear and deterioration is sometimes referred to as *physical* depreciation. There are two other common causes of loss of usefulness that may be classified as *functional* depreciation. One is *inadequacy* and the other is *obsolescence.*

A fixed asset that is replaced because its capacity is insufficient to meet the demands of the business is said to be inadequate. For example, a printing and publishing company expands the size and the circulation of its weekly newspaper beyond the limits originally anticipated when the newspaper press was purchased. In order to meet the increased demand, it is necessary to replace the original press with another press of larger capacity, regardless of the fact that the original press could still be operated efficiently for a number of years.

A fixed asset that is discarded because there is no longer a demand for the product that it produces or because a newer machine can produce the product at less expense or can produce a product of superior quality, is said to be obsolete. The same printing and publishing company may have a job press that must be fed by hand. A new automatic press that will print twice as fast as the old press becomes available on the market. The greater speed of the new press and the saving in man-hours required in its operation may justify its purchase and the discarding of the old machine at a loss.

Inadequacy and obsolescence can be distinguished from physical depreciation by definition, but in practice it is customary to include provision for them in the depreciation rate. It is impossible to forecast future inadequacy or extraordinary obsolescence.

DEPLETION   The reduction in value of a natural resource resulting from its exhaustion is called *depletion*. As minerals are removed from a mineral deposit or lumber from a timber tract, the original cost is written off by a debit to Depletion Expense and a credit to Allowance for Depletion. The difference between the cost of the asset and the accumulated allowance for depletion is the book value.

For example, if it is estimated that a mineral deposit contains 1,000,000 tons of ore of uniform grade and that the cost of the mineral rights is $200,000, the depletion is 20 cents per ton. Assuming that 60,000 tons were mined during a particular fiscal year, the depletion of $12,000 would be recorded by the following entry:

Dec.	31	Depletion Expense—Mineral Deposit....	618	12,000	
		Allowance for Depletion—Mineral Deposit.............................	128.1		12,000

The depletion account is an expense account and is shown on the profit and loss statement and is closed to the profit and loss summary account in the usual manner. The allowance for depletion account is a valuation account and is shown on the balance sheet as a deduction from the cost of the mineral deposit.

QUESTIONS

1. (a) Is the book value of the fixed assets shown on the balance sheet the same as the estimated price at which the assets could be sold? (b) Should the cost of repairing and painting a newly acquired used truck be charged to repair expense?

2. A building acquired at a cost of $50,000 has an estimated life of 40 years. If salvage value is ignored, determine (a) the rate of depreciation, (b) the amount of annual depreciation, and (c) the amount of monthly depreciation.

3. A delivery truck purchased on June 19 of the current year for $3,300 has an estimated life of 6 years and an estimated trade-in value of $600. Give the entry to record the depreciation at December 31, the end of the current fiscal year.

4. In order to increase the size of its customer parking area, the Quality Supermarket buys an adjoining lot and an old building for $6,000.   The net expense incurred in razing the building and leveling the land, after deducting the amounts received from the sale of salvaged building materials, is $1,600. To what account should the $1,600 be charged?

5. On May 28 of the current fiscal year Robert Gordon sells an old electric calculator for $100 cash. The following information about the calculator is obtained from the account in the office equipment ledger: cost, $550; allowance for depreciation on December 31, the close of the previous fiscal year, $405; monthly depreciation, $3.75.   Present the general journal entries necessary to record depreciation on the old equipment for the current year and its sale on May 28.

6. Plastic Products, Inc. purchased a machine at the beginning of the year at a cost of $12,000. Compute the depreciation for each year of its use according to each of the following plans:

    (a) Estimated life, 5 years; straight-line depreciation.
    (b) Estimated operating hours, 10,000; actual hours used in each year, 2,000, 1,500, 2,600, 3,000, 900; hourly rate method of depreciation.
    (c) Estimated life, 5 years; reducing-fraction method.

7. On August 7 of the current fiscal year Earl Jones traded an old book-keeping machine for a new one with a list price of $1,400. He received a trade-in allowance of $225, paying the balance in cash. The following information about the old equipment is obtained from the account in the office equipment ledger: cost, $900; allowance for depreciation on December 31, the close of the previous fiscal period, $733.32; monthly depreciation, $8.33.   Present the following general journal entries: (a) to record depreciation on the old machine for the current year; (b) to record the transaction on August 7, recognizing the gain or the loss; (c) to record the transaction on August 7, conforming with income tax regulations.

8. The Westfield Mining Corporation purchases for $800,000 a property having an estimated mineral deposit of 1,000,000 tons. During the first year of operations 10,000 tons of ore are removed. Give the entry to record the depletion at the end of the year.

PROBLEMS

14-1. *Instructions:* (1) Open the following accounts in the ledger of Henry Dixon, using the account numbers indicated: Delivery Equipment, 121; Allowance for Depreciation—Delivery Equipment, 121.1; Profit and Loss Summary, 313; Depreciation Expense—Delivery Equipment, 614; Loss or Gain on Disposal of Fixed Assets, 813.

(2) Record in general journal form the following transactions:

Apr. 17, 1952. Purchased a used delivery truck for $825, paying cash.

Apr. 24, 1952. Paid garage $191 for new tires and extensive repairs to delivery truck

Dec. 31, 1952. Made adjusting entry to record depreciation. The estimated life of the truck is 2 years, with a salvage value of $200. The straight-line method is to be used; the minimum unit of time to be considered is a month.

Dec. 31, 1952. Recorded the entry to close Depreciation Expense—Delivery Equipment.

Instructions: (3) Post the foregoing journal entries to the selected accounts in the ledger.

(4) Rule Account No. 614.

(5) Record in general journal form the following transactions:

Oct. 10, 1953. Traded in old truck for new one priced at $3,070. Received a trade-in allowance of $300, paying the balance in cash. (Record depreciation to date in 1953; use income tax method of recording the exchange.)

Dec. 31, 1953. Made adjusting entry to record depreciation. The estimated life of the new truck is 4 years, with a trade-in value of $400.

Dec. 31, 1953. Recorded the entry to close Depreciation Expense—Delivery Equipment.

Instructions: (6) Post the foregoing entries to the selected accounts in the ledger.

(7) Balance and rule Accounts No. 121 and 121.1; rule Account No. 614.

(8) Record in general journal form the following transactions:

Dec. 19, 1954. Dixon decides to use the services of a commercial delivery service in the future. He sells the truck for $2,000, receiving cash. (Record depreciation in 1954.)

Dec. 31, 1954. Recorded the entry to close Depreciation Expense—Delivery Equipment and Loss or Gain on Disposal of Fixed Assets.

Instructions: (9) Post the foregoing journal entries to the selected accounts in the ledger.

(10) Balance and rule Account No. 121.1; rule Accounts No. 121, 614, and 813.

14-2. The general ledger of the Queen City Realty Company includes controlling accounts for Equipment and Allowance for Depreciation—Equipment. The details of each item of equipment are recorded in a subsidiary equipment ledger. The following transactions affecting equipment occurred during the three years ending December 31, 1953:

Apr.   10, 1951.   Purchased the following items of equipment from Superior Equipment Co. for cash:

Executive desk...................	$225
Executive chair..................	60
Filing cabinet....................	90

June 18, 1951.   Purchased a rug from The Carpet House on account, $420.

June 25, 1951.   Purchased a Sparton typewriter from Typewriter Exchange for cash, $180. Serial number 47694.

June 26, 1951.   Purchased a stenographic desk, $120, and chair, $42, from Superior Equipment Co. for cash.

Sept. 17, 1952.   Purchased a Monarch electric typewriter from Typewriter Exchange for cash, $240, Serial number A9376.

Sept. 26, 1952.   Sold the Sparton typewriter for cash, $100.

Mar. 30, 1953.   Traded in stenographer's desk for a new one from Superior Equipment Co. The price of the new desk was $150. The allowance granted on the old desk was $70, the balance being paid in cash. (Use the income tax method.)

Additional details necessary for determining depreciation are as follows:

ITEMS	TRADE-IN VALUE	ESTIMATED LIFE
Desks......................	none	$12\frac{1}{2}$ yrs.
Chairs.....................	none	$12\frac{1}{2}$ yrs.
Filing cabinet..............	none	15 yrs.
Typewriter - Sparton........	$40	5 yrs.
Monarch.............	$60	5 yrs.
Rug.......................	none	10 yrs.

Instructions: (1) Open the following general ledger accounts: Equipment, 121, Allowance for Depreciation—Equipment, 121.1. Open an account in the subsidiary ledger, using the form illustrated on page 251, as each item of equipment is purchased.

(2) Record the transactions in general journal form, posting to the two controlling accounts and to the subsidiary ledger after each entry. Journalize and post annual depreciation entries on December 31 of each of the three years.

(3) Make a list of the balances in the subsidiary ledger accounts and compare the totals with the balances of the two controlling accounts.

14-3. The account balances in the ledger of the Ace Appliance Company on December 31, the end of the current fiscal year, are as follows:

Cash.....................	$14,500	Office Equipment........ $	6,200
Accounts Receivable........	51,700	Allowance for Depreciation—	
Allowance for Bad Debts....	900	Office Equipment......	2,100
Merchandise Inventory.....	47,000	Notes Payable..........	20,000
Store Supplies.............	1,320	Accounts Payable........	15,600
Office Supplies............	650	Howard Forman, Capital..	46,690
Prepaid Insurance..........	1,260	Howard Forman, Drawing.	12,000
Store Equipment...........	14,600	Sales....................	278,000
Allowance for Depreciation—		Purchases...............	176,300
Store Equipment.........	5,000	Freight in...............	3,100

Sales Salaries	$16,150	Office Salaries	$5,000
Advertising Expense	4,700	Misc. General Expense	1,200
Misc. Selling Expense	3,900	Purchases Discount	1,620
Rent Expense	9,600	Interest Expense	730

Data for adjustments on December 31 are as follows:

(a) Merchandise inventory, $34,000.

(b) Bad debts, an additional $\frac{1}{2}$ of 1% of sales.

(c) Store equipment and office equipment are depreciated at composite annual rates of 10% and 8%, respectively. Depreciation is charged for one-half year on equipment purchased during the year. Current year's purchases included in the accounts are as follows: Store Equipment, $1,500; Office Equipment, $600.

(d) Inventories of supplies: Store supplies, $530; Office supplies, $210.

(e) Expired insurance, $490.

(f) Accrued interest on notes payable, $200.

Instructions: (1) Prepare an eight-column work sheet.

(2) Prepare a profit and loss statement and a balance sheet.

(3) Record the adjusting, closing, and reversing entries.

14-4. In each of the following unrelated cases it is assumed that subsidiary equipment ledgers are maintained, that depreciation is recorded annually except for items disposed of during the year, and that the fiscal year ends on December 31.

(a) May 4. A delivery truck is sold for cash, $600. The following details are taken from the subsidiary account: cost, $3,000; accumulated allowance for depreciation on previous December 31, $2,600; monthly depreciation, $37. Give the necessary entries in general journal form.

(b) April 19. Discarded a rug (office equipment), realizing no salvage. The subsidiary account reveals the following: cost, $600; accumulated allowance for depreciation on previous December 31, $510; monthly depreciation, $5. Give the necessary entries in general journal form.

(c) November 10. Traded in an old billing machine (office equipment) for a new one priced at $1,500. Received a trade-in allowance of $200, paying $1,300 cash. The subsidiary account shows the following: cost, $900; accumulated allowance for depreciation on previous December 31, $700; monthly depreciation, $8. Give the necessary entries in general journal form to recognize the gain or the loss on the old machine and to record the new machine at $1,500.

(d) June 24. Discarded a show case (store equipment), realizing no salvage. The following details are taken from the subsidiary account: cost, $200; accumulated allowance for depreciation on previous December 31, $200. Give the necessary general journal entry.

(e) December 18. Traded in an old delivery truck for a new one priced at $3,300. Received a trade-in allowance of $900, paying $2,400 cash. The subsidiary account shows the following: cost, $2,700; accumulated allowance for depreciation on previous December 31, $1,350; monthly depreciation, $50. Give the necessary entries in general journal form, using the income tax method.

Trent Wholesale Shoes
Part 2

Part 2 of Practice Set No. 1 is a continuation of Practice Set No. 1 given after Chapter 10. The same books of original entry and ledgers are to be used.

Narrative of Transactions for June

June 1. Mr. Trent invested an additional $15,000 cash in the business.

June 1. Mr. Trent decided to buy the building and the equipment that he had been renting. He bought the building for $40,000, the land for $6,000, the store equipment for $3,000, and the office equipment for $2,000. He paid $21,000 in cash (Check No. 123) and gave a 5% mortgage for $30,000.

June 1. Issued Check No. 124 for $360 for premium on insurance on building and equipment.

June 2. Purchased merchandise on account from Boston Manufacturing Co., $2,305.90; invoice dated June 1.

June 2. Received a check for $450 for three months' rent of space in the building.

June 3. The auditor called attention to the fact that an allowance for bad debts had not been set up for the preceding months and that an adjustment should be made. Set up an allowance for bad debts of $103.29. (Debit the capital account.)

June 3. Issued Check No. 125 for $44.70 to Freeman Supply Co. in payment of its invoice for $44.70.

June 3. Received checks as follows:
A check for $470.40 from Ralph Stevens in payment of our invoice for $522, less the return of $42, less a 2% discount.
A check for $842.80 from Norton Shoe Store in payment of our invoice for $892.40, less the return of $32.40, less a 2% discount.

June 3. Sold merchandise on account to Decker Department Store, $1,062.30; Sale No. 1093.

June 3. Issued checks as follows:
Check No. 126 for $250 for office supplies.
Check No. 127 for $24.75 for repairs to storeroom. (Charge Miscellaneous Selling Expense.)

June 3. Received $1,321.50 from cash sales for June 1-3.

Post to the accounts in the accounts receivable ledger and the accounts payable ledger.

June 5. Made the following sales on account:

Sale No. 1094, Paul Eastland, $1,296.82.

Sale No. 1095, Lee & Laird, $750.60.

June 6. Mr. Trent borrowed $5,000 from the bank on his 60-day, non-interest-bearing note. The bank charged 6% interest in advance. Received credit for the proceeds, $4,950.

June 6. Issued Check No. 128 for $2,959.60 to Boston Manufacturing Co. in payment of its invoice for $3,068.90, less the return of $48.90, less a 2% discount.

June 7. Issued Check No. 129 for $27.50 for advertising posters.

June 7. Issued Credit Memo No. 205 for $62.30 to Decker Department Store for the return of merchandise on the sale of June 3.

June 8. Issued Check No. 130 for $137.20 to Smart Shoes, Inc. in payment of its invoice for $270, less the return of $130, less a 2% discount.

June 8. Made the following purchases on account:

Lite-Tred Shoe Co., merchandise, $608; invoice dated June 7.

Freeman Supply Co., office supplies, $79.65, store supplies, $89.56; invoice dated June 7.

June 9. Issued Check No. 131 for $17.50 for repairs to desks. (Charge Miscellaneous General Expense.)

June 10. Received a check for $927.28 from Adams Men's Furnishings in payment of our invoice for $946.20 less a 2% discount.

June 10. Issued checks as follows:

Check No. 132 for $2,259.78 to Boston Manufacturing Co. in payment of its invoice for $2,305.90 less a 2% discount.

Check No. 133 for $1,100 for biweekly salaries divided as follows: sales salaries, $850; office salaries, $250.

June 10. Received $1,650.60 from cash sales for June 5–10.

Post to the accounts in the accounts receivable ledger and the accounts payable ledger.

June 12. Issued Check No. 134 for $300 to Frank Trent for personal use.

June 12. Purchased merchandise on account from Turner Shoe Corp., $987.50; invoice dated June 10.

June 13. Made the following sales on account:

Sale No. 1096, Waite's Apparel Shop, $1,030.

Sale No. 1097, Harvey Bootery, $920.52.

June 13. Received a check for $980 from Decker Department Store in payment of our invoice for $1,062.30, less the return of $62.30, less a 2% discount.

June 15. Received checks as follows:

A check for $1,270.88 from Paul Eastland in payment of our invoice for $1,296.82 less a 2% discount.

A check for $735.59 from Lee & Laird in payment of our invoice for $750.60 less a 2% discount.

June 15. Made the following purchases on account:
Horace & Co., store equipment, $200; invoice dated June 14.
Olds, Penny & Gold, Inc., merchandise, $475; invoice dated June 14.

June 16. Made the following sales on account:
Sale No. 1098, Adams Men's Furnishings, $1,252.98.
Sale No. 1099, Greene's Footwear, $2,182.50.

June 17. Received a credit memorandum for $87.50 from Turner Shoe Corp. for the return of merchandise on its invoice of June 10.

June 17. Issued Check No. 135 for $595.84 to Lite-Tred Shoe Co. in payment of its invoice for $608 less a 2% discount.

June 17. Received from Greene's Footwear a 60-day, 6% note for $982.30, dated June 17, in settlement for the sale of May 20.

June 17. Issued Credit Memo No. 206 for $20.52 to Harvey Bootery for the return of merchandise on the sale of June 13.

June 17. Received $1,596.60 from cash sales for June 12–17.

Post to the accounts in the accounts receivable ledger and the accounts payable ledger.

June 19. Issued Check No. 136 for $452.60 for store supplies.

June 19. Received from Waite's Apparel Shop a 60-day, 6% note for $2,076.80, dated June 19, in settlement for the sale of May 20.

June 20. Made the following purchases on account:
Boston Manufacturing Co., merchandise, $3,641.20; invoice dated June 19.
Freeman Supply Co., office supplies, $72.50; store supplies, $55.20; invoice dated June 20.

June 20. Issued Check No. 137 for $882 to Turner Shoe Corp. in payment of its invoice for $987.50, less the return of $87.50, less a 2% discount.

June 21. Made the following sales on account:
Sale No. 1100, Norton Shoe Store, $990.30.
Sale No. 1101, Ralph Stevens, $1,210.65.

June 23. Received checks as follows:
A check for $1,009.40 from Waite's Apparel Shop in payment of our invoice for $1,030 less a 2% discount.
A check for $882 from Harvey Bootery in payment of our invoice for $920.52, less the return of $20.52, less a 2% discount.

June 23. Purchased merchandise on account from Lite-Tred Shoe Co., $1,070; invoice dated June 22.

June 24. Issued Credit Memo No. 207 for $46.55 to Ralph Stevens for the return of merchandise on the sale of June 21.

June 24. Issued checks as follows:

Check No. 138 for $470.25 to Olds, Penny & Gold, Inc. in payment of its invoice for $475 less a 1% discount.

Check No. 139 for $1,100 for biweekly salaries divided as follows: sales salaries, $850; office salaries, $250.

June 24. Received a credit memorandum for $541.20 from Boston Manufacturing Co. for the return of merchandise on its invoice of June 19.

June 24. Received $1,702.10 from cash sales for June 19–24.

Post to the accounts in the accounts receivable ledger and the accounts payable ledger.

June 26. Discounted at the bank at 6% the Greene's Footwear note for $982.30 and received credit for the proceeds, $983.69.

June 26. Issued Check No. 140 for $118.75 to Freeman Supply Co. in payment of its invoice for $118.75.

June 26. Received checks as follows:

A check for $1,227.92 from Adams Men's Furnishings in payment of our invoice for $1,252.98 less a 2% discount.

A check for $2,138.85 from Greene's Footwear in payment of our invoice for $2,182.50 less a 2% discount.

June 27. Made the following sales on account:

Sale No. 1102, Decker Department Store, $1,245.62.

Sale No. 1103, Lee & Laird, $1,794.10.

June 28. Purchased merchandise from Boston Manufacturing Co., $2,076.82; invoice dated June 27.

June 28. Issued Check No. 141 for $85 to Horace & Co. in payment of its invoice for $85.

June 29. Issued Check No. 142 for $3,038 to Boston Manufacturing Co. in payment of its invoice for $3,641.20, less the return of $541.20, less a 2% discount.

June 30. Purchased new office equipment, giving in exchange old office equipment and $404 in cash (Check No. 143). The old office equipment was on the books at a cost value of $240. The depreciation for the month of June on the old equipment traded in was $4.

June 30. Issued checks as follows:

Check No. 144 for $150 for advertising in local newspaper.

Check No. 145 for $278.75 for freight charges on merchandise purchased.

Check No. 146 for $200 to Frank Trent for personal use.

Check No. 147 for $125 for heat, light, and power bills. (Charge Miscellaneous General Expense.)

Check No. 148 for $56.98 for the telephone bill. (Charge Miscellaneous General Expense.)

June 30. Received $1,926.02 from cash sales for June 26–30.

Cash Proof and Posting

Total all columns of the cash receipts journal and the cash payments journal, entering the totals in small pencil figures. On a separate sheet of paper, add the debit totals and the credit totals for each journal to prove that in each journal the total of the debits is equal to the total of the credits.

Find the cash balance according to the books by adding the beginning balance in the ledger account and the total of the cash receipts and subtracting the total of the cash payments. This balance should be $12,470.64, the cash actually on hand and in the bank. If your balance is not this amount, find the error before proceeding with the posting.

Post to the accounts in the accounts receivable ledger and the accounts payable ledger.

Post to the general ledger accounts from the general columns of the purchases journal, the cash receipts journal, and the cash payments journal.

Total and rule the various special journals and post the totals to the appropriate general ledger accounts.

Periodic Summary

As the proprietor, Frank Trent, considers each month to be a separate fiscal period, the periodic summary must now be completed. The additional data required for this summary are:

Interest accrued on notes receivable on June 30 . . . . $	3.81
Allowance for bad debts: an additional $\frac{1}{2}$ of 1% of sales. .	109.67
Merchandise inventory on June 30	18,012.25
Inventories of supplies on June 30:	
Store supplies	575.00
Office supplies	400.00
Insurance expired during the month	80.00
Prepaid interest on notes payable on June 30	30.00
Depreciation for June:	
Store equipment	35.00
Office equipment	20.00
Building	150.00
Interest accrued on mortgage on June 30	125.00
Salaries payable on June 30:	
Sales salaries	354.15
Office salaries	104.15
Unearned rent on June 30	300.00

Complete all the work required by the periodic summary, following the same procedure that you followed at the end of May.

Chapter 15

Accounting Procedures

RECORDING ROUTINE   The minimum of commonly used records was explained in an early chapter where the accounting system consisted of a journal, a ledger, a trial balance, and the financial statements. This threefold sequence of journal, ledger, and statements was at the time stated to be adequate for any business not interested in efficiency and economy in recording. If efficiency and economy are disregarded, this simple routine of recording is sufficiently flexible to take care of any transaction, no matter how complex it may be.

From a single journal record and a single ledger to special journals and special ledgers, recording routine has been elaborated to achieve economy and efficiency. These objectives have been accomplished at the expense of simplicity, and routine has become increasingly complex. Special journals result in less flexible records, but they save much labor in recording and posting. Subsidiary ledgers complicate the posting from journals and require the use of statements with supporting schedules, but they provide useful means of checking the accuracy of summaries. Special columns in books of original entry make these books more complex, but they reduce posting labor in transactions that occur frequently. Business papers prepared in typewriting and bookkeeping machines, with several copies available, provide opportunity for further economies. Standard routine is constantly being modified in the interest of economy and efficiency.

Whatever variations may be made in recording practice, there still remain four well-defined steps. These four steps are:

1. The business paper, evidencing the transaction.
2. The journal record, showing accounts affected.
3. The ledger record, classifying transactions under accounts.
4. The statements, summarizing financial progress.

In this chapter particular attention will be given to the accounting procedures incident to the use of (1) a bank account as a substitute for cash; (2) supplementary records not integral with the accounting system to provide useful information; and (3) the combined cash journal as a substitute for special journals in small businesses. In the following chapter, a more involved and complete procedure, the voucher system, will be described.

BUSINESS PAPERS AND BOOKKEEPING MACHINES — Modern bookkeeping practice makes more and more use of machines to provide the requisite detail at a low cost. Through the use of carbon copies, it is possible to prepare simultaneously (1) the business paper, (2) the journal record, and (3) the posting to the subsidiary ledger. For example, the sales invoice, the entry in the sales journal, and the posting to the customer's account may be provided on a machine by a single recording.

Bookkeeping machines are frequently equipped with accumulating mechanisms, which provide totals of amounts recorded. Columnar totals are thus provided at the same time as the duplicate recording described in the previous paragraph. For example, when checks are drawn for payroll purposes, columnar totals for regular pay, overtime pay, income tax withholdings, and other deductions may be provided, and at the same time carbon copies for the payroll record and the employee's record may be prepared. These two features, (1) *duplicating* and (2) *accumulating*, are distinct advantages of mechanical accounting or machine bookkeeping.

It has been estimated that in modern big business enterprises 90 per cent of bookkeeping records are products of mechanical equipment. The larger the enterprise, the greater the advantage in the use of machines. Machines may be highly specialized, and through their specialization great volumes of work may be accomplished at a relatively low cost. This low cost has made possible the recording of an amount of detail that would otherwise be prohibitively expensive. In addition to this saving in costs, the use of machines has the advantages of greater speed and accuracy, plus a legibility that cannot generally be attained in handwritten records.

CHECK REGISTERS — Control over business transactions may be aided by issuing pads of business papers, serially numbered, to those responsible for the transactions and requiring a record of all the business papers used. For example, checks are often numbered serially in a checkbook. Accompanying the pad of checks there is a book containing a line for the record of each check, the number of the check having been entered on the line. This book contains columns for the essential information appearing on each check. Such a book is called a *register*.

A check register that takes the place of the cash payments journal and also registers serially numbered checks is shown on page 268. The account First National Bank takes the place of the cash account. A separate line is reserved for each serially numbered check, and on that line is entered the information about the check that is considered most useful in a book record. All other details of each payment are available in the file containing carbon copies of the checks or on the checkbook stub. The canceled check will eventually be returned and will form the basic part of the paper record.

CHECK REGISTER   Page 7

DATE		ACCOUNT DEBITED	CHECK NO.	POST. REF.	GENERAL DR.	ACCOUNTS PAYABLE DR.	PURCHASES DISCOUNT CR.	FIRST NATIONAL BANK CR.
1953 Oct.	1	John Edwin	123	✓		600 00	12 00	588 00
	1	Rent Expense	124	713	250 00			250 00
	1	Petty Cash	125	112	50 00			50 00
	2	Voided check	126					
	2	Office Supplies	127	119	70 00			70 00
	2	Sanders, Inc.	128	✓		330 00		330 00
	31	Sales Salaries	203	611	640 00			640 00
	31	Totals		✓	1,640 00	4,725 40	78 20	6,287 20
					(✓)	(213)	(811)	(111)

Check Register

It will be noticed that a check mark (✓) is used to indicate posting to an account in the accounts payable ledger, and a number is used for each item posted to an account in the general ledger. This method illustrates posting to loose-leaf ledgers. When loose-leaf ledgers are used, a new account may be inserted at any time in its proper place. For a creditor's account, the proper place is determined alphabetically; for a general ledger account it is determined by the place of the item on the balance sheet or the profit and loss statement.

On Line 4 of the check register a report is made that Check No. 126 was not used. Every serially numbered check is thus accounted for in the check register.

DOUBLE RECORD OF CASH　　One of the most common accounting procedures is set up to secure effective control over cash. By depositing all cash receipts in a bank, the business has a secondary record of its cash transactions in the shape of a periodic bank statement. This accounting procedure provides what is technically known as a *double record of cash*. The checks, deposit slips, and bank statement provide an outside record of cash transactions.

In order that the bank's record may correspond with the cash record, all cash received must be deposited in the bank. If that is done, it follows that all cash disbursed must be withdrawn from the bank by means of checks. The bank's record of deposits will correspond to the cash receipts record; the bank's record of checks paid will correspond to the cash disbursements record; and the balance on the bank's monthly statement should agree with the cash balance of the business. These balances will agree except for the adjustment items described in the discussion of the reconciliation of the bank statement in Chapter 9.

PETTY CASH   When a business has established a policy of depositing all cash receipts and making all payments by checks, it will probably find that some small payments can be made more conveniently with cash. A fund for such payments is established by drawing a check payable to the order of Petty Cash for the estimated amount of the payments during a certain period of time, frequently one month. Check No. 125, the third entry in the check register on page 268, shows the entry to establish the petty cash fund.

The check is cashed by the petty cashier, and the currency is placed in a special drawer called the *petty cash drawer*. As disbursements are made in currency from this drawer, they are recorded in a supplementary record known as a *petty cash book*. A typical form of petty cash book is shown in the illustration below.

PETTY CASH BOOK   Page 1

| | | | | | DISTRIBUTION OF PAYMENTS | | | |
DATE	EXPLANATION	VCHR. NO.	RECEIPTS	PAYMENTS	MISC. SELLING EXPENSE	MISC. GENERAL EXPENSE	SUNDRIES ACCOUNT	AMOUNT
1953 Oct. 1	Check No. 125		50 00					
2		1		1 30		1 30		
2		2		6 25	6 25			
5		3		1 28			Store Supplies	1 28
8		4		16 90	16 90			
12		5		1 75	1 75			
13		6		85		85		
16		7		3 72			Freight In	3 72
20		8		11 50			Office Supplies	11 50
20	Totals		50 00	43 55	24 90	2 15		16 50
20	Balance			6 45				
			50 00	50 00				
20	Balance		6 45					
20	Check No. 187		43 55					

Petty Cash Book

In this illustration provision is made for a record of serially numbered vouchers or receipts to evidence petty cash disbursements.
These vouchers provide a control over the petty cash fund and may be
used as the basis for the replenishing check. Petty Cash Voucher No. 1
to support the payment of October 2 for a telegram is shown below:

PETTY CASH VOUCHER

No. 1 _____   Date October 1, 1953 _____

                                                                  AMOUNT

Paid to Western Union _____

                                                                  1 | 30

For _____ Telegram _____

PAYMENT RECEIVED   RAMSEY AND KANE

       F. O. Weber _____   Approved by H. E. H. _____

Petty Cash Voucher

The petty cash vouchers may be filed with the page of the petty
cash book shown above. Another method is to file the petty cash
vouchers in an envelope on the back of which is a record similar to the
petty cash book record shown above. This practice is just another
illustration of the tendency to move away from book records.

At the end of each fiscal period and whenever the petty cash fund
needs replenishing, a check is drawn for the amount of the disbursements. The check is cashed, the currency is placed in the petty cash
drawer, and an entry is made in the petty cash book. (See the entry
in the petty cash book for Check No. 187.) The amount of the currency
in the petty cash drawer now agrees with the balance of the petty cash
account.

The check to replenish the petty cash is recorded in the check
register by the entry shown below:

CHECK REGISTER   Page 7

DATE	ACCOUNT DEBITED	CHECK NO.	POST. REF.	GENERAL DR.	ACCOUNTS PAYABLE DR.	PURCHASES DISCOUNT CR.	FIRST NATIONAL BANK CR.
20	Misc. Selling Exp.	187	618	24 90			43 55
	Misc. General Exp.		719	2 15			
	Store Supplies		118	1 28			
	Freight In		412	3 72			
	Office Supplies		119	11 50			

The details of the petty cash payments included in the replenishing check are recorded in the check register by an entry debiting each item for which petty cash payments were made and crediting First National Bank for the total amount.

At the end of each accounting period, before the statements are prepared, it is necessary to draw a check to replenish the petty cash fund. Otherwise, the expenses represented by the disbursements would not appear in the statements for the period. The charges made to the expense accounts when the replenishing check is recorded bring these expense items into the ledger and keep the petty cash fund at the predetermined amount. The debit in the petty cash account will remain at the same amount unless the fund is decreased or increased because it is decided that it is too large or too small.

REGISTERS AS SUPPLE-MENTARY RECORDS In addition to registers that serve as special journals, and in some instances as subsidiary ledgers, there are registers that serve as supplementary records. Such registers are usually classifying and accumulating devices. Examples of such registers are the insurance policy register, the notes receivable register, the notes payable register, and the fixed assets register.

Insurance Policy Register. When there is a possibility that property may be destroyed by fire or by any other accidental cause, the owner should protect himself against such loss by entering into a contract with an insurance company. He agrees to pay to the company a certain amount in return for the protection afforded by the contract. This contract is known as an *insurance policy,* and the compensation paid to the insurance company is known as the *insurance premium.* The insurance policy is made for a definite period of time, and the premium is payable in advance.

A record of each of these policies should be kept in such a form that information pertinent to the insurance contracts can be obtained at any time. This is accomplished by keeping an insurance policy register similar to that shown on pages 272 and 273. In this record the cost of the insurance, or the premium, is divided into the monthly charges representing insurance expense.

In the illustration, the three policies carried over from previous years are shown at the top of the page that records the insurance policy history for 1953. The first two of these had only 2 months to run in 1953 before expiration; the third had 6 months. In each of these cases the monthly charges are the same as they were for the preceding period. The fourth entry records a 1-year policy purchased on January 2, 1953, and charged equally to the 12 months of 1953.

INSURANCE POLICY REGISTER FOR YEAR 1953

DATE OF POLICY		POLICY NO.	NAME OF COMPANY	PROPERTY INSURED	AMOUNT		TERM	EXPIRATION DATE	UN-EXPIRED PREMIUM	
1948 Mar.	1	24983	Alliance Ins. Co.	Furniture and Fix.	3,500	00	5 yrs.	Mar. 1, 1953	2	00
1950 Mar.	1	34702	U. S. Fire Ins. Co.	Building	28,000	00	3 yrs.	Mar. 1, 1953	18	50
1952 July	1	43284	Amer. Auto. Ins. Co.	Delivery Equipment	4,100	00	1 yr.	July 1, 1953	78	00
1953 Jan.	2	41529	U. S. Fire Ins. Co.	Merchandise	15,000	00	1 yr.	Jan. 2, 1954	60	00
Mar.	1	96304	Alliance Ins. Co.	Furniture and Fix.	3,500	00	5 yrs.	Mar. 1, 1958	75	00
Mar.	10	72107	U. S. Fire Ins. Co.	Building	28,000	00	3 yrs.	Mar. 1, 1956	333	00
June	26	49756	Amer. Auto. Ins. Co.	Delivery Equipment	4,100	00	1 yr.	June 26, 1954	144	00
									710	50

Insurance Policy Register, Left Page

The fifth entry records a 5-year policy purchased on March 1 for $75. Since it has 60 months to run, the monthly cost is $1.25. The policy runs for 10 months in 1953; this leaves a balance for this policy of $62.50 of prepaid insurance on December 31, 1953. The policies taken out on March 10 and June 26 also continue beyond the end of the year and have unexpired balances at the end of the year.

If the policy is effective during the first half of the month, the full month expiration is usually charged. If, however, the policy is not effective until the second half of the month, no charge is made for that month.

At the end of each month the insurance expired is determined by adding the column for that month. The amount thus obtained is used in the adjusting entry to record the insurance expired. At the end of the year the amount of the expired premiums and the amount of the unexpired premiums are recorded in the columns at the extreme

NOTES RECEIVABLE REGISTER

DATE RECEIVED		OUR NO.	BY WHOM PAYABLE	WHERE PAYABLE (BANK OR FIRM AND ADDRESS)	DATE OF PAPER		
					YEAR	MONTH	DAY
1953 Jan.	5	111	Henry Jameson	First National Bank of Canton	1953	Jan.	3
	9	112	C. L. Collins	Our office	1953	Jan.	7
	13	113	Lyle & Glosser	Central Trust Co., City	1953	Jan.	12
	24	114	K. M. Jones	Second National Bank, Marion	1953	Jan.	23
Feb.	3	115	John F. Freeman	Merchants Bank, City	1953	Feb.	2
	10	116	H. H. Wheeler	Union Bank, Akron	1953	Feb.	9

Notes Receivable Register, Left Page

INSURANCE POLICY REGISTER FOR YEAR 1953

JAN.	FEB.	MAR.	APR.	MAY	JUNE	JULY	AUG.	SEPT.	OCT.	NOV.	DEC.	EXPIRED PREMIUM	UNEXPIRED PREMIUM 12/31/53
1.00	1.00											2.00	
9.25	9.25											18.50	
13.00	13.00	13.00	13.00	13.00	13.00							78.00	
5.00	5.00	5.00	5.00	5.00	5.00	5.00	5.00	5.00	5.00	5.00	5.00	60.00	
		1.25	1.25	1.25	1.25	1.25	1.25	1.25	1.25	1.25	1.25	12.50	62.50
		9.25	9.25	9.25	9.25	9.25	9.25	9.25	9.25	9.25	9.25	92.50	240.50
						12.00	12.00	12.00	12.00	12.00	12.00	72.00	72.00
28.25	28.25	28.50	28.50	28.50	28.50	27.50	27.50	27.50	27.50	27.50	27.50	335.50	375.00

Insurance Policy Register, Right Page

right. The unexpired policies are then recorded at the top of the page for the following year.

Notes Receivable and Notes Payable Registers. If the notes received by a business are not too numerous, they may be recorded in the general journal. There is, however, important detailed information with reference to the notes that cannot be shown conveniently in the book of original entry or in the notes receivable account. This information may include the name of the maker, where the note is payable, the date, the time, the amount, and the rate of interest. All of these facts, together with others that may be useful, may be recorded conveniently in a notes receivable register that provides a special column for each type of information. A common form of a notes receivable register is shown below.

A similar register may be maintained for notes payable whenever such notes are numerous. The arrangement of the notes payable

NOTES RECEIVABLE REGISTER

TIME	WHEN DUE													FACE	INTEREST RATE	DATE PAID	REMARKS
	YEAR	J	F	M	A	M	J	J	A	S	O	N	D				
60 days	1953			4										280.75	6%	Mar. 4, 1953	
30 days	1953		6											250.00	—	Feb. 6, 1953	
90 days	1953				12									500.00	6%		Discounted 2/4
60 days	1953			24										118.50	—	Dishonored 3/24	Charged to maker's account
60 days	1953				3									687.50	5%	Apr. 3, 1953	
60 days	1953				10									200.00	6%	Apr. 10, 1953	Sent to bank for collection 4/8

Notes Receivable Register, Right Page

NOTES PAYABLE REGISTER

DATE GIVEN		OUR NO.	TO WHOM PAYABLE	WHERE PAYABLE (BANK OR FIRM AND ADDRESS)	DATE OF PAPER		
					YEAR	MONTH	DAY
1953							
Jan.	10	28	Central Trust Co.	Central Trust Co., City	1953	Jan.	10
Jan.	31	29	Banner Mfg. Co.	Chase Bank, Cleveland	1953	Jan.	31
Feb.	9	30	First National Bank	First National Bank, City	1953	Feb.	9

Notes Payable Register, Left Page

register is quite similar to that of the notes receivable register. A common form is illustrated at the top of pages 274 and 275.

Fixed Assets Register. When a business has a large number of fixed assets, a record is needed to show the cost of each asset, the estimated trade-in or scrap value, the estimated life, the annual rate of depreciation, the number of years during which the asset has been owned, the total amount of depreciation charged in previous years, and the monthly charges for depreciation during the current year. Maintaining such a record of fixed assets insures that the proper amount of depreciation will be calculated on each item and also calls attention to errors in estimates, which might otherwise be overlooked.

Since this register is used to accumulate depreciation charges, a separate page should be set up for each class of fixed assets. For example, the illustration below and on page 275 contains only office equipment and provides for a monthly charge for depreciation of office equipment. Another page would contain only store equipment and would provide a monthly charge for depreciation of store equipment. Each page in such a fixed asset register would provide detail supporting the balance of each fixed asset account in the ledger.

FIXED ASSETS REGISTER (OFFICE EQUIPMENT) FOR YEAR 1953

DATE OF PURCHASE		NO.	DESCRIPTION	COST		TRADE-IN OR SCRAP VALUE	LIFE OF ASSET IN YEARS	ANNUAL RATE OF DEPR.	ACCRUED DEPRECIATION	
									NO. OF YEARS	AMOUNT
1945										
Jan.	2	1	Office Safe	1,200	00		20	5%	8 yrs.	480	00
1947										
Jan.	2	2	Office Files	1,000	00		10	10%	6 yrs.	600	00

Fixed Assets Register, Left Page

NOTES PAYABLE REGISTER

TIME	WHEN DUE													FACE	INTEREST RATE	DATE PAID	REMARKS
	YEAR	J	F	M	A	M	J	J	A	S	O	N	D				
60 days	1953		11											500 00	—	Mar. 10, 1953	
30 days	1953		2											260 83	—	Mar. 2, 1953	
90 days	1953				10									1000 00	6%	May 9, 1953	

Notes Payable Register, Right Page

In some cases a card is set up for each fixed asset. If this is done, the card record amounts to a subsidiary ledger record of fixed assets. Such a record was illustrated in Chapter 14.

THE COMBINED CASH JOURNAL   In previous chapters dealing with special journals, attention was called to the fact that the transactions of one day may be recorded in several journals. For example, the sales transactions may be recorded in the sales journal and the cash receipts transactions of the same date, in the cash receipts journal. In order to have a complete record of the transactions of one day, reference would have to be made to each of the special journals.

In a small business it is possible to arrange transactions in chronological order and to have the labor-saving benefits of the special journal by the use of special columns in a single journal. Since most transactions affect cash, this journal is commonly called the *combined cash journal*. Whenever transactions affect an account sufficiently often, a special column is set up for that account. Transactions affecting accounts without special columns are entered in a pair of

FIXED ASSETS REGISTER (OFFICE EQUIPMENT) FOR YEAR 1953

JAN.	FEB.	MAR.	APR.	MAY	JUNE	JULY	AUG.	SEPT.	OCT.	NOV.	DEC.	CARRIED FORWARD	DISPOSITION
5 00	5 00	5 00	5 00	5 00	5 00	5 00	5 00	5 00	5 00	5 00	5 00	540 00	
8 33	8 33	8 34	8 33	8 33	8 34	8 33	8 33	8 34	8 33	8 33	8 34	700 00	

Fixed Assets Register, Right Page

	CASH		CHECK NO.	DATE	DESCRIPTION	POST. REF.	GENERAL		
	DR.	CR.					DR.	CR.	
				1953					
1		200 00	121	Dec. 1	Rent Expense	712	200 00		1
2	235 20			2	Hanson and Holmes				2
3				2	Silas Company				3
4				3	J. B. Macey				4
5				3	Dalton Bros. — Notes Payable	211		500 00	5
6		7 50	122	4	Miscellaneous General Expense				6
7		294 00	123	4	J. L. Samson				7
39	315 07			29	Dane and Tyson				39
40				29	John C. Fulton				40
41	743 80			29	Cash sales				41
42		62 95	142	30	Freight In	512	62 95		42
43		425 00	143	31	Sales Salaries	611	260 00		43
44					Office Salaries	711	175 00		44
45		41 35	144	31	Store Supplies	118	14 55		45
46					Freight In	512	3 75		46
47					Miscellaneous Selling Expense	618	8 10		47
48	2,790 15	2,076 75		31	Totals		805 33	610 00	48
49	(111)	(111)					(✓)	(✓)	49

Combined Cash Journal, Left Page

columns headed "General." This treatment is similar to that described in Chapter 5 for the four-column journal.

If a business follows the practice of depositing all cash in the bank, as was described earlier in this chapter, the cash columns may be headed "Cash" or they may be considered to be the record with the bank and may be headed with the name of the bank.

A combined cash journal is shown above and on page 277. It should be noted that the columns set up with special headings have already been illustrated before in this and previous chapters.

This type of single-journal record is frequently found in ready-made bookkeeping systems for small businesses and professional men. The column headings are printed in to meet the requirements of the business for which the system is designed. In some cases, the accountant is called upon to determine the column headings and to write them in himself on a blank form obtained from a commercial stationery store.

GENERAL LEDGER FORMS The ruling of general ledger accounts does not vary so much as does the ruling of books of original entry, but nevertheless there are many possible variations.

		ACCOUNTS RECEIVABLE			ACCOUNTS PAYABLE		SALES DISCOUNT DR.	PURCHASES DISCOUNT CR.	SALES CR.	PURCHASES DR.	MISC. GENERAL EXPENSE DR.	
		DR.	CR.		DR.	CR.						
1												1
2	✓		240 00				4 80					2
3				✓		498 50				498 50		3
4	✓	174 00							174 00			4
5				✓	500 00							5
6											7 50	6
7				✓	300 00			6 00				7
39	✓		321 50				6 43					39
40	✓	119 45							119 45			40
41									743 80			41
42												42
43												43
44												44
45											14 95	45
46												46
47												47
48		1,075 60	832 50		1,550 72	1,695 30	16 70	18 80	2,737 95	1,695 30	37 50	48
49		(115)	(115)		(213)	(213)	(911)	(811)	(411)	(511)	(719)	49

Combined Cash Journal, Right Page

The three-column (debit, credit, balance) form used in this text for subsidiary accounts receivable and accounts payable ledgers may also be used for general ledger accounts instead of the traditional two-column form. When the three-column form is used for general ledger accounts, a narrow column is ordinarily placed directly to the left of the balance column. In this narrow column the bookkeeper may indicate whether the balance is a debit or a credit.

A widely used form for general ledger accounts provides two columns for the balance, one for the debit balance and one for the credit balance. The accounts at the top of the following page use this ruling.

When general ledger accounts are kept on a posting machine, the balance is automatically recorded after each entry. When the posting is done by hand, the balance may be obtained only at the end of the month as was done in the cash account illustrated on page 278, or it may be obtained after each entry as was done in the accounts payable account. Either method may be used, but usually the balance is obtained only at the end of the month. The balance is needed only at that time, and recording the balance after each transaction does require some extra time.

CASH   ACCT. NO. 111

DATE	ITEMS	POST. REF.	DEBIT	CREDIT	DEBIT BALANCE	CREDIT BALANCE
1953 Jan. 1	Balance	√	5,364 35			
31		CR4	9,863 21			
31		CP3		9,033 68	6,193 88	

ACCOUNTS PAYABLE   ACCT. NO. 213

DATE	ITEMS	POST. REF.	DEBIT	CREDIT	DEBIT BALANCE	CREDIT BALANCE
1953 Jan. 1	Balance	√		3,560 75		3,560 75
31		P3		7,134 20		10,694 95
31		PR1	98 50			10,596 45
31		CP3	6,951 25			3,645 20

SUMMARIZING IN BUSINESS RECORDS   When a single journal and a single ledger were used in Chapter 5, transactions affecting each account were summarized in the ledgers. For example, all sales transactions were found individually in the sales account and the total of sales was obtained by adding these items in the sales account. Later, when the sales journal was set up to save time and labor, this summarizing was done in the special journal; the ledger account Sales no longer showed the detail but only the total for the month. These conditions are illustrated below:

SALES JOURNAL

Oct.	1		200
	1		100
	2		300
	2		200
	2		350
	3		400
	3		150
	31		400
	Sales Cr.		16,450

SALES

Oct. 31		16,450

(The journal record takes over the *summarizing* formerly found in the sales account.)

(The detail of sales for October has been removed from the ledger account. A single posting saves posting labor.)

The accounting periods summarized in the special journals need not correspond to the periods summarized in the ledger or covered by the statements. For instance, the cash receipts and cash payments journals, or the combined cash journal, could be posted at the end of each week; the sales and the purchases journals could be posted twice a month; the trial balance could be taken once a month; and the balance sheet and the profit and loss statement could be prepared only annually. The accounts affected by many transactions could be summarized often; those affected by a small number of transactions, less often.

When business papers become an integral part of the accounting system, they can sometimes be used as summarizing devices. When they are so used, a journal may contain a record of only the total for the day. The amounts of cash sales for a day may be listed on an adding machine from the sales tickets; the tickets may be filed as supporting records; and only one entry need be made in the cash receipts journal. In this case summarizing has been moved forward another step, to the business papers; individual transactions no longer appear in the journal.

THE FUNCTION OF RECORDS　　　Business records must be so constructed that at any time in the future it will be possible to trace a transaction from the record of its occurrence to its effect on some item in one of the two principal statements. Or, reversing the procedure, it should be possible to account for any amount on either statement by tracing backward to the first record of the transactions affecting this amount. This may be illustrated graphically as follows:

Trace forward————————————————————————————————————→

Transaction — Paper — Journal — Ledger — Work Sheet — Statement

←———————————————————————————————— Trace backward

If a sale of $250 is made on account, it should be possible to trace that sale until it appears on the profit and loss statement as part of the total sales. Or, if the profit and loss statement shows rent expense of $1,500, it should be possible to trace back from the statement, through the work sheet, ledger, journal, and business papers to rent transactions totaling $1,500.

The record of transactions may be considered as a stream of information that flows from the business papers to the periodic accounting statements. This flow must be uninterrupted and rapid so that the accounting statements will be complete and timely. Any procedure or any mechanism that will insure the continuous and speedy flow of this information merits the attention of the bookkeeper or the accountant.

**INTERNAL CHECK
OF OPERATIONS**   When accounting procedures and systems are designed for a business, they should be so constructed that no section of the system is under the sole control of one person. The work of each employee should be related to the duties of another. When such a system is used, the accounting is said to possess "internal check" and control. The purpose of such a control is to prevent error and fraud.

Of the many accounting functions of a business, the most elaborate controls are generally provided for the handling of cash. This chapter has described methods that secure internal control of cash by depositing all receipts and by making payments only by check except for properly vouchered petty cash items. Control of cash is further achieved by separating the duties of those employees charged with receipts and payments of cash from the duties of those who keep the journal and ledger records and who prepare statements of account for customers.

If cash receipts are received in the mail, it is necessary to have separate employees open the mail and make a list of all receipts in duplicate. One copy accompanies the receipts to the cashier; the other serves as the underlying document for the accounting entry.

Similar controls are usually provided for customers' accounts, inventories, plant assets, and other groups of accounts.

QUESTIONS

1. Does the use of business papers, journals, and ledgers mean that recording is thereby tripled in volume? Explain your answer.

2. (a) Is there any principle that can be followed in determining how often summaries of transactions should be made? (b) Must summaries be made only at the end of the accounting period?

3. What is meant by the expression "take the books out of bookkeeping"?

4. "The trial balance is the only reliable proof of posting." Do you agree with this statement?

5. The term *double record of cash* refers to the record in the cashbook and the record in the ledger. Is this statement correct?

6. It is necessary for Tate and Loren to pay out a large number of small amounts varying from 25 cents to $5. Those receiving the payments prefer cash rather than checks. An accountant recommends that the petty cash system be used. (a) Describe how such a record and fund should be operated. (b) How is this record correlated with a "double record of cash"? (c) What advantages do you see in its use?

7. Give journal entries for the following: (a) A petty cash fund of $100 is established. (b) The fund is replenished for expenditures of $98.62, chargeable $44.32 to Miscellaneous Selling Expense and $54.30 to Miscellaneous General Expense. (c) The fund is increased to $150.

8. In designing a combined cash journal for a doctor, what columns would you omit that are shown in the combined cash journal on pages 276 and 277? What columns would you add?

9. If an amount was entered in the wrong column in a combined cash journal, would it throw the trial balance out of balance? Explain.

10. What are the advantages of the use of bookkeeping machines?

11. (a) Under what conditions would you recommend that a business use notes receivable and notes payable registers? (b) What types of businesses would be more likely to use a notes receivable register than a notes payable register? (c) What types of businesses would be more likely to use a notes payable register than a notes receivable register? (d) What information should each of these registers provide?

PROBLEMS

15-1. The following transactions involving petty cash were completed by the Carlson Garment Co. during the month of March:

(a) Mar. 1. Drew Check No. 189 for $100 to establish a petty cash fund.
(b) The following amounts were paid from petty cash on the dates indicated:

Mar.   5. Water bill, $2 (Miscellaneous General Expense).
      6. To Speedy Service Co. to deliver garments, $6. 25(Miscellaneous Selling Expense).
      7. Gas bill, $5.95 (Miscellaneous General Expense).
      9. Postage, $10 (Office Supplies).
   24. Store Supplies, $15.
   27. To Speedy Service Co., $5.15.
   31. Electric bill, $7.50 (Miscellaneous General Expense).
(c) Mar. 31. Drew Check No. 267 to replenish the petty cash fund.

Instructions: (1) Record in a check register the check to establish the petty cash fund. Enter the amount of the fund in a petty cash book having the same form and columns as the book illustrated on page 269 of the text.

(2) Record the payments in the petty cash book.

(3) Total and rule the columns of the petty cash book and bring down the balance.

(4) Record the replenishing check in the check register and the petty cash book.

15-2. The store equipment of the Xano Mercantile Co. was acquired as follows:

DATE PURCHASED	DESCRIPTION	COST	ESTIMATED LIFE
Jan. 2, 1951	Carpeting	$ 540	3 yrs.
Oct. 1, 1951	Counters	$2,400	10 yrs.
Apr. 1, 1952	Cash register	$960	8 yrs.

Instructions: (1) Prepare a fixed assets register for store equipment for the year 1953. Use the same form and columns as illustrated in the fixed assets register on pages 274 and 275.

(2) Prepare a journal entry for the depreciation for January, 1953.

15-3. Harvey Benson decides to maintain a notes receivable register. On July 1 of the current year he has the following notes receivable on hand:

OUR NO.	BY WHOM PAYABLE	WHERE PAYABLE	DATE OF PAPER	TIME	FACE	INT. RATE
41	Henry Potter	Our office	Apr. 27	90 days	$400.00	——
42	C. M. Barnes	First National Bank, Toledo	May 8	60 days	$198.50	6%
43	A. J. Clifford	Merchants Bank, City	May 14	90 days	$200.00	4%
44	L. D. Burke	Our office	June 2	30 days	$450.00	6%
45	James Finley	Ajax Bank, Ajax	June 22	60 days	$368.40	5%

During the month of July, Mr. Benson completed the following transactions with notes receivable:

July 2. Received a check from L. D. Burke in payment of his note and interest due today.

5. Sent C. M. Barnes's note to the First National Bank, Toledo, for collection. (Make a memorandum notation only in the Remarks column of the notes receivable register.)

7. Received a check from the First National Bank, Toledo, for the face of C. M. Barnes's note plus interest, minus a collection charge of 75 cents. (Record the collection charge as a debit to Miscellaneous General Expense.)

12. Received a 60-day, 6% note for $300 from L. P. Taylor in settlement of his account. The note is dated July 11 and is payable at our office.

19. Discounted A. J. Clifford's note at 6% at our bank and received credit for the proceeds.

29. Henry Potter did not pay his note when it was due. Charged the dishonored note to the maker's account.

Instructions: (1) Record in a notes receivable register like the one in this chapter, under date of July 1 of the current year, the notes receivable on hand on that date.

(2) Record the transactions with notes receivable in a combined cash journal like the one in this chapter and make the necessary entries in the notes receivable register.

15-4. Ralph Lipman began business on April 1, 1953, as the Lipman Products Co. The following transactions were completed during the month of April. Begin checks with No. 1.

Apr. 1. Invested cash, $16,000.

    1. Paid rent for the month, $700.

    2. Issued check to establish petty cash fund, $50.

    2. Sold merchandise on account to Frank Greer, $1,000.

    3. Purchased merchandise on account from Wilson and Kline Co., $3,200.

    4. Paid $10 for miscellaneous general expenses.

    6. Received $980 from Frank Greer for invoice of April 2 less 2% discount.

    7. Purchased merchandise on account from Matchless Products, Inc., $4,700.

    8. Sold merchandise on account to Keith Monroe, $800.

   10. Paid $12.50 for minor repairs to the office, which were charged to Miscellaneous General Expense.

   11. Paid $3,168 to Wilson and Kline Co. for invoice of April 3 less 1% discount.

   13. Sold merchandise on account to Payton Borden, $550.

   14. Check No. 6 was spoiled and voided.

   15. Purchased merchandise on account from Wilson and Kline Co., $2,600.

   16. Paid $4,653 to Matchless Products, Inc., for invoice of April 7 less 1% discount.

   18. Received note from Keith Monroe for $800 covering invoice of April 8.

   18. Sold merchandise on account to Frank Greer, $600.

   23. Purchased merchandise on account from Matchless Products, Inc., $1,600.

   24. Gave Wilson and Kline Co. a note for $2,600 covering April 15 purchase.

   27. Reimbursed petty cash: Freight In, $25; Miscellaneous General Expense, $15.

   28. Received $588 from Frank Greer for invoice of April 18 less 2% discount.

   30. Paid salaries for the month, $400.

   30. Cash sales for month, $1,500.

Instructions: (1) Record the transactions in a combined cash journal similar to the one illustrated on pages 276 and 277.

(2) Open the ledger accounts listed below and post to them.

General Ledger Accounts: Cash, 111; Petty Cash, 112; Notes Receivable, 113; Accounts Receivable, 115; Notes Payable, 211; Accounts Payable, 213; Ralph Lipman, Capital, 311; Sales, 411; Purchases, 511; Freight In, 512; Salary Expense, 611; Rent Expense, 612; Miscellaneous General Expense, 619; Purchases Discount, 711; Sales Discount, 811.

Accounts Receivable Ledger: Payton Borden; Frank Greer; Keith Monroe.

Accounts Payable Ledger: Matchless Products, Inc.; Wilson and Kline Co.

(3) Prepare a trial balance.

15-5. Edward Lyle's accounting records include a check register, a petty cash book, and an insurance policy register similar to those illustrated in this chapter, and a two-column general journal.

The following transactions were among those completed in October, 1953:

Oct. 1. Issued Check No. 527 to establish a petty cash fund, $70.

1. Issued Check No. 528 to C. Irwin for October rent, $400.

3. Issued Check No. 529 to Holden Insurance Agency for two insurance policies. One policy, No. M43692, is with the Aetna Fire Insurance Company, covers merchandise for $40,000, has a premium of $360 and is effective for 3 years from October 1, 1953. The second policy, No. F9801, is with the same company, covers equipment for $30,000, has a premium of $480, and is effective for 5 years from October 1, 1953.

6. Paid $15 from petty cash for stamps. (Office Supplies)

8. Issued Check No. 530 for $2,000 in payment of a note payable to the First National Bank.

10. Paid $10 from petty cash for express charges on a shipment of merchandise received. (Freight In)

14. Spoiled Check No. 531.

14. Issued Check No. 532 to Olson Products, Inc. for invoice for $5,000 less 2% discount.

26. Paid $10 from petty cash for: repairs to cash register, $6 (Miscellaneous Selling Expense); repairs to office equipment, $4 (Miscellaneous General Expense).

31. Issued Check No. 533 for salaries, $1,500.

31. Issued Check No. 534 to replenish the petty cash fund.

31. Issued Check No. 535 to Edward Lyle for personal use, $400.

Instructions: (1) Record the foregoing transactions. When petty cash is replenished, rule and balance the petty cash book.

(2) Enter and distribute insurance policy premiums for the balance of the year. Prepare a journal entry to adjust prepaid insurance on October 31.

(3) Rule and foot the check register.

(4) The bank statement for October shows an October 31 bank balance of $6,435. With the exception of Nos. 534 and 535, all checks were returned with the statement. The cash account has an October 31 balance of $6,000. Prepare a bank reconciliation.

Chapter 16

The Voucher System

ACCOUNTING SYSTEMS The accounting papers, journals, ledgers, and reports, and the routines and procedures employed in using these records, constitute the accounting system of a business. When accounting principles and practices are applied to any given enterprise or to any set of conditions in a going business, the result is an accounting system. For any such system there is a selection of the useful elements from the entire field of accounting practice and the arrangement of these elements into an organized whole.

One of the most complete accounting systems is that concerned with the payment of obligations. This system not only adjusts the accounting records to a practice of account payment, but also affects the accounting from the first record of the transaction. The *voucher system* consists of an organized group of accounting practices that begin with the first recording of purchases of merchandise, other assets, and services, and end with the payment of obligations to suppliers. This chapter will be devoted to a complete discussion of the voucher system. This system should be considered as concrete evidence of a more general principle of organizing accounting practices.

THE VOUCHER SYSTEM In the operation of either a mercantile or a manufacturing business, it is necessary to purchase the following:

1. *Goods or Materials.* In a mercantile business goods are purchased and resold without modification. In a manufacturing business materials are purchased and used in the production of the commodity or the service that the business sells.

2. *Assets for Use in the Business.* Both mercantile and manufacturing businesses purchase assets such as land, buildings, machinery, equipment, and supplies with which to carry on their operations.

3. *Services.* In order to operate, all businesses must purchase services such as labor, heat, light, and power. Such services, which are ordinarily termed expenses, may be used in the production of the commodity or the service that the business sells, or they may be used in selling the product after it has been purchased or produced.

In a large business, expenditures for these purposes amount to large sums and cannot be closely supervised by the chief executive. It is therefore necessary to delegate the responsibility for incurring obligations and making expenditures and yet to retain a proper control.

THE VOUCHER   One method of obtaining control over expenditures is to require for each expenditure a written authorization. This authorization is usually in the form of a *voucher*. The voucher is prepared from the invoice or from other data that serve as evidence of the expenditure to be made. The outside of the voucher provides space for (1) a brief summary of the invoice data, (2) the details of the actual payment, (3) a list of the accounts to be charged, (4) the signature of the one who approves the payment, and (5) the signature of the one who enters the voucher in the voucher register. The inside of the voucher provides space for the details of the transaction and for the signature of the one who approves the voucher. When the business paper from which a voucher is prepared contains all of the necessary details about the transaction, the business paper may be attached to the inside of the voucher and no further items need be entered on the inside of the voucher. The outside and the inside of a voucher are illustrated at the right and on page 287.

When the voucher system is in use, every invoice or bill received must be *vouchered*. This procedure necessitates that the invoice or bill be approved as to:

(1) Quantities, prices, grades, sizes, and quality by the purchasing agent.

(2) Actual receipt by the receiving clerk.

VCHR. NO. 376 DATE 6/1/53		DUE DATE 6/8/53
TO J. C. Foam Co.		
ADDRESS 4193 Erie Ave.		
Cleveland STREET 5		Ohio
CITY	ZONE	STATE

DATE June 8, 1953
PAID CHECK NO. 423   AMOUNT : 240.69
APPROVED BY James Wade

ACCOUNTS DEBITED	AMOUNT	
Purchases	245	60
Freight In		
Store Supplies		
Office Supplies		
Sales Salaries		
Advertising Expense		
Miscellaneous Selling Expense		
Delivery Salaries		
Miscellaneous Delivery Expense		
Office Salaries		
Miscellaneous Office Expense		
TOTAL ACCOUNTS PAYABLE CR.	245	60

APPROVED FOR PAYMENT BY H. E. Sloan

RECORDED IN VOUCHER REGISTER PAGE 8   BY L. R. N.

Outside of a Voucher

Voucher

SUPERIOR TRADING COMPANY

No. 376   Date June 1   1953 Terms 2/10, n/30   Due June 8   19 53

To _____ J. C. Foam Co.

Address 4193 Erie Ave.

City _____ Cleveland _____ Zone 5 _____ State Ohio

For the following: (Attach all invoices or other papers permanently to voucher)

DATE	VOUCHER DETAILS	AMOUNT
June 1	Invoice dated 5/29/53	245.60

Approved by *H. E. Sloan*
CONTROLLER

Inside of a Voucher

(3) Mathematical accuracy of extensions by the checking clerk in the accounting department.

(4) Terms of payment by the purchasing agent.

(5) Distribution (accounts to be charged) by the bookkeeper or the auditor.

These approvals are usually indicated on the invoice before the voucher is prepared. In order to prevent mistakes, the bookkeeper or the auditor designates the distribution on the invoice before it is copied on the voucher. If the accounts in the ledger are numbered, the bookkeeper indicates the charges by means of these numbers. After the voucher has been prepared, the invoice is fastened on the inside and the voucher is folded so that the distribution, as shown on the outside, will be visible. The voucher is then recorded in the appropriate record, which is explained in later paragraphs, and is filed in the unpaid vouchers file.

FILING VOUCHERS Unpaid vouchers are most frequently filed under the date of payment, for this method automatically brings to the attention of the disbursing officer the vouchers that are to be paid on each day and provides a convenient means by which those who are interested can determine the amount that must be paid at any time.

Occasionally unpaid vouchers are filed alphabetically under the name of the vendor. While this makes the finding of the vendors' accounts easier, it usually requires a supplementary record, known as a *tickler*, that shows the accounts to be paid each day. The tickler record shows the vouchers to be paid day by day.

Another alternative is to prepare two copies of each voucher, an original and a carbon. The original copies are then filed by due dates, and the carbon copies are filed alphabetically.

When the due date arrives, the voucher is taken from the file and a check is issued in payment. If this check shows the invoice or invoices for which it is issued in payment, it is known as a *voucher check*. After payment, the voucher is filed in the paid vouchers file.

THE VOUCHER
REGISTER
It has been explained in the preceding paragraphs that, when the voucher system of authorizing payments is used, a voucher is prepared for each expenditure, whether the expenditure is for goods or materials, assets for use in the business, or services. In fact, under the voucher system a check is never issued except in payment of a properly authorized voucher.

Each voucher is recorded in a book known as a *voucher register*. The form of the voucher register may vary widely, depending largely

VOUCHER REGISTER

	DATE	VCHR. NO.	CREDITOR	PAID DATE	PAID CHK. NO.	ACCOUNTS PAYABLE CR.	PURCHASES DR.	STORE SUPPLIES DR.	
	1953								
1	June 1	376	J. C. Foam Co.	6/ 8	423	245 60	245 60		1
2	1	377	E. S. Crane	6/ 1	419	300 00			2
3	1	378	Petty Cash	6/ 1	420	50 00			3
4	2	379	Carter Supply Co.	6/ 2	421	51 50		35 10	4
5	2	380	Daily Register	6/12	433	65 60			5
6	3	381	Oliver & Bent	6/ 3	422	455 00	455 00		6
7	4	382	B. A. Boon	6/13	435	515 00	515 00		7
8	4	383	B. L. Moore, Inc.			160 00			8
						*25 00**	*25 00**		
36	27	411	R. E. Stone Co.	6/30	451	366 10	366 10		36
37	27	412	C. C. Shaw	6/27	448	150 00	150 00		37
38	29	413	Dower & Pike	6/29	450	505 00			38
39									39
40	30	414	Pacific Electric Co.			36 60			40
41	30	415	Petty Cash	6/30	452	41 80	12 00	5 50	41
						*25 00**	*25 00**		
42	30		Totals			13,562 14	8,614 10	205 12	42
43						(213/213)	(511/512)	(117)	43

*The amounts printed in italics are written in red ink or are written in black ink and circled.

Voucher Register, Left Page

on the size of the business and the number of accounts maintained with purchases and expenses. The illustration on pages 288 and 289 shows a typical form.

The voucher register is usually ruled to provide columns for the date of entry, the voucher number, the name of the creditor, the date of payment, and the number of the check issued in payment. In addition, it contains one amount column for credits to the accounts payable account and as many columns for debits as are necessary to show the distribution and classification of all purchases and expenses. A space to record charges to accounts for which there are no special columns is provided at the extreme right.

Every amount entered in the voucher register appears as a credit to the accounts payable account and as a debit to the account or accounts charged for the commodities or the services represented by the invoice or the bill.

At the time the voucher is prepared and approved, it is entered in numerical order in the voucher register. When it is paid, the date of payment and the number of the check issued in payment are entered in the appropriate columns of the register. The total of the unpaid vouchers as shown by the voucher register must at all times agree with the total of the vouchers in the unpaid vouchers file.

VOUCHER REGISTER

	ADVER-TISING EXPENSE DR.	MISC. SELLING EXPENSE DR.	MISC. DELIVERY EXPENSE DR.	OFFICE SUPPLIES DR.	MISC. GENERAL EXPENSE DR.	GENERAL DR. ACCOUNT	P. R.	AMOUNT	
1									1
2						Rent Expense	712	300 00	2
3						Petty Cash	112	50 00	3
4				16 40					4
5	65 60								5
6									6
7									7
8						Office Fur. & Fix.	123	160 00	8
36									36
37									37
38						Notes Payable	211	500 00	38
39						Interest Expense	911	5 00	39
40		10 50			26 10				40
41		7 20	3 90	5 10	8 10				41
42	360 10	80 26	85 18	66 15	79 92			4,071 31	42
43	(614)	(617)	(616)	(118)	(719)			(√)	43

Voucher Register, Right Page

The entries in the voucher register are not posted until the end of the month. At that time all the columns are totaled and the voucher register is proved by comparing the sum of the totals of all the debit columns with the total of the Accounts Payable Cr. column. Unless these totals agree, an error has been made either in entering amounts in the columns or in obtaining the various totals. This error must be corrected before the posting is begun.

After the voucher register is proved, the total of each column is posted to the account stated at the head of the column. The total of the Accounts Payable Cr. column is posted to the credit of the payable account, and the totals of all the other amount columns, except the General Dr. Amount column, are posted to the debit of the respective accounts. The items in the General Dr. Amount column are posted individually to the debit of the accounts stated in the Account column.

THE CHECK REGISTER　　Postings from the voucher register result in debits to various asset, trading, and expense accounts and credits to the liability account Accounts Payable. This latter account shows the total amount owed to creditors.

When a voucher is paid, an entry debiting Accounts Payable and crediting the bank account is made in the check register. If the terms of the invoice provide for discount, the amount of the voucher is entered in the Accounts Payable Dr. column; the discount, in the Purchases Discount Cr. column; and the amount of the check, in the column providing for credits to the bank account. If a form similar to that illustrated on page 291 is used, the amount of the check issued in payment of each voucher is entered in the column provided for the bank on which the check is drawn. The date of payment and the number of the check must also be entered in the Paid columns of the voucher register.

The check register is not posted until the end of the month. At that time the totals of the columns are posted to the accounts indicated in the columnar headings. For example, the total of the first amount column in the check register shown on page 291 is posted to the debit of the accounts payable account; the totals of the other columns are posted to the credit of the purchases discount and bank accounts. The individual items in this check register are not posted.

**RELATION OF THE
VOUCHER SYSTEM
TO ACCOUNTING
PROCEDURES**　　The use of the voucher system as described in the previous pages makes unnecessary the use of the accounts payable ledger. The vouchers in the unpaid vouchers file serve as a record of the amounts

CHECK REGISTER

DATE		NAME OF PAYEE	CHECK NO.	VCHR. NO.	ACCOUNTS PAYABLE DR.		PURCHASES DISCOUNT CR.		MERCHANTS NATIONAL BANK CR.	
1953										
June	1	E. S. Crane	419	377	300	00			300	00
	1	Petty Cash	420	378	50	00			50	00
	2	Carter Supply Co.	421	379	51	50			51	50
	3	Oliver & Bent	422	381	455	00			455	00
	8	J. C. Foam Co.	423	376	245	60	4	91	240	69
	26	P. F. Mills	449	391	142	12	1	42	140	70
	29	Dower & Pike	450	413	505	00			505	00
	30	R. E. Stone	451	411	341	10	6	82	334	28
	30	Petty Cash	452	415	41	80			41	80
	30	Totals			9,619	04	101	16	9,517	88
					(213)		(811)		(111)	

Check Register

owed. Emphasis is placed on the date when a bill should be paid rather than to whom it is to be paid.

The voucher system modifies the accounting procedures described in the preceding chapter under the heading "Double Record of Cash." Under the voucher system, each payment not only must be represented by a check (which later appears on the depositor's bank statement) but also must be authorized in advance by a voucher. The voucher thus serves as authorization for the check that is to be written. It would be uneconomical and inadvisable to prepare a voucher for each disbursement to be made from petty cash. Petty cash disbursements are therefore given special treatment under the voucher system.

When a petty cash fund is to be established, a voucher authorizes the drawing of a check payable to Petty Cash. Accounts Payable is credited in the voucher register and Petty Cash is debited. The check is then drawn; an entry debiting Accounts Payable and crediting Cash or the bank account is made in the check register; the check is cashed; and the money is turned over to the person in charge of the fund. Whenever a disbursement is made from the petty cash fund, a receipt is obtained from the one to whom payment is made. The entries required in establishing a petty cash fund are shown in the illustrations of the voucher register and the check register (Voucher No. 378) on pages 288, 289, and 291.

When the fund is to be replenished, a voucher authorizes a check to be drawn for the total amount of the disbursements that have been made. The various accounts to be debited are determined from the petty cash book or a summary of the petty cash vouchers and are indicated on the voucher. The entry to record the voucher in the register consists of a credit to Accounts Payable and debits to the accounts indicated on the voucher. The check is recorded in the check register by debiting Accounts Payable and crediting Cash or the bank account. The money obtained by cashing the check is placed in the petty cash fund, which should then equal the original amount. The entries required in replenishing a petty cash fund are shown in the illustrations of the voucher register and the check register (Voucher No. 415) on pages 288, 289, and 291.

VOUCHER SYSTEM ADJUSTMENTS   Adjustments are not easily made in the voucher system. The steps involved in the voucher system are designed to eliminate as far as possible the need for adjustments. Some adjustments are necessary, however, to provide for (a) purchases returns or allowances, (b) payments by the issuance of a note, and (c) partial payments.

Purchases Returns and Allowances. When credit is received for a return or an allowance on a purchase, the amount of the unpaid voucher is thereby reduced. In order that the voucher register will show the correct amount payable, an entry may be interlined in red ink immediately above the entry for the voucher. The debit to Accounts Payable is entered in the Accounts Payable Cr. column, and the amount of the asset or the expense on which the return or the allowance was made is adjusted by indicating the deduction in the corresponding debit amount column. When the columns are totaled, the figures in red should be added separately and written immediately above the columnar totals of the figures in black. The totals indicated in black ink are posted in the usual manner. The total in red ink in the Accounts Payable Cr. column is posted as a debit to the accounts payable account, and the corresponding red totals in the debit amount columns are posted as credits to the appropriate accounts. In practice, accountants often show a "red ink" entry in black, encircling the amount to show that it represents a deduction. The method of recording credit received for a return or an allowance is shown in the voucher register illustration (Voucher No. 411), page 288. At the end of the month, after the columns were totaled, Accounts Payable was debited for $25 and Purchases Returns and Allowances was credited for the same amount. The credit memorandum from the creditor or a note showing the amount of credit received should be filed with the adjusted voucher.

When credit is received for a return or an allowance to apply on a purchase recorded in an earlier month, the method just outlined cannot be followed. In this case a new voucher for the adjusted amount payable must be prepared, and the original voucher should be marked "Canceled" with a reference to the new voucher. The amount of the original voucher has, however, already been posted in the columnar total for the previous month. An adjusting entry must therefore be made in the general journal.

Assume, for example, that on May 29 merchandise was purchased for $180 from C. C. Shaw. An entry debiting Purchases and crediting Accounts Payable for $180 was made in the voucher register at that time. In June, however, a portion of the order was returned and a credit memorandum for $30 was received on June 27. The following entry was then made in the general journal:

June 27	Accounts Payable	180	
	Purchases Returns and Allowances		30
	Purchases		150
	To record the return of merchandise purchased in May and to cancel Voucher No. 373.		

A reference to this journal entry was placed in the Paid columns for the old voucher. A new voucher for $150 was then prepared and recorded in the voucher register. This new voucher is Voucher No. 412 in the voucher register on page 288. The net effect of the two entries on June 27 is a debit to Accounts Payable of $30 and a credit to Purchases Returns and Allowances of $30.

The posting of the totals for the month of June to Accounts Payable and Purchases from the voucher register and the check register is shown below. In addition to the totals, the entries to record the two purchases returns and allowances discussed in the foregoing paragraphs are posted.

Accounts Payable				Purchases			Purchases Returns and Allowances		
1953		1953		1953		1953		1953	
June 27	180.00	June 1 Bal.	3,281.90	June 30 8,614.10		June 27 150.00		June 27	30.00
30	9,619.04	30	13,562.14					30	25.00
30	25.00								

Notes Payable. If a voucher is paid by the issuance of a note or by the acceptance of a draft or a trade acceptance, an entry debiting Accounts Payable and crediting Notes Payable should be made in the general journal or the notes payable journal. An explanation indicating the method of payment is written on the voucher; and a similar explanation, with reference to the page of the journal in which the entry was made, is entered in the Paid columns of the voucher register. The voucher is then filed in the paid vouchers file.

At the time the note or the acceptance is to be paid, a new voucher will be issued. The entry in the voucher register will consist of a credit to Accounts Payable and a debit to Notes Payable. The payment of this voucher will then be recorded in the usual manner. The entries required in the payment of a note are shown in the illustrations of the voucher register and the check register (Voucher No. 413) on pages 288, 289, and 291.

Partial Payments. The plan of the voucher register assumes that each voucher is a unit and will be paid as a unit. No provision is made in the register for partial payments. If, then, a business customarily makes partial payments on its invoices, it should not plan to use a voucher register but should use some other method that is more adaptable to the recording of partial payments.

If, at the time an invoice is received, the management knows that it will be paid in installments, several vouchers may be prepared, one for each installment. If the decision to pay a voucher in installments is made after the voucher is recorded, the method used varies according to whether the new entry is to be made in the same month in which the voucher was recorded or in a later month. If the change is to be made in the same month in which the voucher was recorded, the voucher and the entry in the voucher register may be canceled and two or more new vouchers may be issued. If the change is to be made after the amount of the voucher has been posted, an entry may be made in the general journal reversing the first entry in the voucher register. Two or more new vouchers may then be issued and recorded in the voucher register.

VOUCHER SYSTEM CORRECTIONS   The careful checking of the records used in the voucher system will not eliminate errors entirely, but it should reduce them to a minimum. If an error is discovered in the same month in which a voucher was recorded, the voucher and the entry in the register may be canceled and a new voucher may be issued. If the error is discovered after the voucher register has been posted, the correction may be made by a general journal entry reversing the entry to be corrected and the issuing of a new voucher for the correct amount.

THE VOUCHER REGISTER AS A BOOK OF ORIGINAL ENTRY AND SUBSIDIARY LEDGER   The use of the voucher register proves very convenient. Liabilities are recorded as soon as they are incurred, an accounts payable ledger is not needed, and a great saving of labor in posting is effected through the use of the columns in the register.

Each line of the voucher register may be considered as a separate account with a voucher. This account is credited when the voucher is recorded; it is debited when the voucher is indicated as paid. At any time, then, the voucher register will give the detail regarding the balance of the accounts payable account. In this respect the voucher register is comparable to the accounts payable ledger, and it may be considered as a subsidiary ledger. The entry of the date of payment in the voucher register from the paid voucher is in the nature of a posting to a subsidiary ledger.

The voucher itself is a business paper coordinating the activities of a number of specialized employees in a business organization. The vouchers, which are numbered serially, constitute a journal record of the obligations incurred and of the accounts to be charged. When the vouchers are filed in an unpaid vouchers file, they provide a subsidiary ledger showing the amounts due at various times. When vouchers are placed in the file, they represent credits; when they are removed from the file, they represent debits. Hence, vouchers themselves serve as business papers, a journal record, and a ledger record.

The voucher register is a record that facilitates the accumulation of summaries to be posted to the general ledger. As indicated in a preceding paragraph, the voucher register may be considered as a subsidiary ledger of authorized obligations, supporting the controlling account Accounts Payable.

THE VOUCHER SYSTEM AND FINANCIAL MANAGEMENT The voucher system illustrates the adaptability of accounting procedure to new conditions in business practice. As a well-defined system it proves of great use to financial management. Its adoption has resulted in the following advantages:

1. *Information regarding invoices to be paid is furnished promptly.* When the prevailing practice of a business provides for the payment of creditors from funds received through the collection of accounts receivable, the purchases journal and the accounts payable ledger provide the needed information. When emphasis is placed on meeting the terms of payment on all invoices and bills, the voucher system serves the needs of the financial officer more effectively than do the purchases journal and the accounts payable ledger. The disbursing officer is more interested in knowing when payments should be made than in knowing to whom the amounts are payable. The voucher system provides a flexible record in furnishing prompt information regarding invoices and bills authorized for payment.

2. *Misunderstandings are avoided by having payments cover specific invoices.* In the interest of both the debtor and the creditor, the voucher system provides that each check issued shall cover a specific invoice or a specific group of invoices. This practice provides for the easy identification of amounts charged and amounts paid so that there can be agreement regarding the balance owed. The payment of round amounts to apply on account is unsatisfactory from the point of view of both the creditor and the debtor. Discrimination among creditors by debtors is equally unsatisfactory from both points of view. The voucher system represents a modification of accounting practice to fit improved financial practices.

3. *The practice of taking cash discounts is facilitated.* The voucher system is particularly useful in providing the necessary information for those concerns that follow the practice of taking cash discounts. As a matter of financial policy it is always less costly to borrow funds at a local bank in order to take advantage of cash discounts than to permit such discounts to be neglected. Under the voucher system each invoice can be approved promptly and filed in the unpaid vouchers file under the last date when the discount can be taken. The unpaid vouchers file provides an orderly list of all future obligations arranged according to the dates of payment. By taking the discounts, the business gets the maximum use of its cash balance and at the same time provides a maximum return from available cash discounts.

4. *Authorization of future disbursements is given at the proper time.* The voucher system provides for the approval of expense items at the time when such approval can be given most intelligently. The adequacy of a service purchased should be determined at the time the service is rendered rather than at a later date when payment is to be made. If the service is satisfactory, future payment should be authorized at once. Hence, no further investigation is necessary when the check is to be drawn.

Such advantages are, however, accompanied by a lack of flexibility in the use of the register. Whenever records with special columns are used, the procedure is necessarily rigid. It has already been shown that a special journal does not allow so complete an explanation as the general journal. In the use of the voucher register the procedure is even more formal. This fact has been shown in the difficulties encountered in making corrections and in handling purchases returns and allowances, notes payable, and partial payments.

QUESTIONS

1. (a) From the point of view of the chief disbursing officer, which is usually of greater significance: the time when an amount payable will be due, or the person or business to which payment is to be made? (b) Which of these two factors does the voucher system stress?

2. (a) Which is the more flexible record: the general journal or the voucher register? (b) Which is more closely fitted to a recognized business practice? (c) Are your answers consistent? Explain.

3. The special journals to be used in any given business are determined by the frequency of occurrence of similar transactions. Does the same principle determine the special columns to be used in the voucher register? Explain.

4. (a) Is the voucher register a book of original entry? (b) a summarizing device? (c) a ledger? Explain.

5. Would the number of unrecorded transactions tend to be more or less under the voucher system? Explain your answer.

6. (a) Which is the better time to authorize a cash disbursement: at the time the disbursement is to be made or at the time the goods or the services are received? (b) When is such authorization made under the voucher system?

7. "The voucher system is useful in assuring the taking of all purchases discounts." Is this statement true?

8. Does the introduction of the voucher system prevent the use of a petty cash fund? Explain.

9. (a) What characteristics does the voucher register have that the sales and the cash receipts journals do not have? (b) Is this true of the check register?

10. What advantages of the voucher system would you explain to the treasurer of a corporation who is considering the use of this system?

PROBLEMS

16-1. Edward Nolan, whose accounts payable on August 31 were as follows, installed the voucher system.

Aug.	28	Thomas Simpson	Merchandise	$600
	30	James Horan	Repairs	500
	31	Blare Co.	Merchandise	400
				$1,500

During the first week in September he completed the following transactions:

Sept. 3. Purchased merchandise from Thomas Simpson, $750.

        5. Received an invoice from James Horan for repairs, $80.

        6. Purchased machinery from the Blare Co., $2,000.

Sept. 6. Issued Check No. 414 for $588 to Thomas Simpson in payment of Voucher No. 1.

   7. Issued Check No. 415 for $500 to James Horan in payment of Voucher No. 2.

Instructions: (1) Use a voucher register with the following amount column headings: Accounts Payable Cr., Purchases Dr., Repairs Dr., and General Dr. Use a check register with the following amount column headings: Accounts Payable Dr., Purchases Discount Cr., and Second National Bank Cr.

(2) Under the date of the original purchase, enter the unpaid invoices in the voucher register beginning with Voucher No. 1. Then rule double lines across all the amount columns of the voucher register so that the amounts just recorded will not be included in the columnar totals posted at the end of September.

(3) Enter the transactions for September 3-7 inclusive.

16-2. The Clayton Company uses a voucher system. Vouchers issued during July and August that were unpaid on August 31 were:

VOUCHER No.	COMPANY	FOR	DATE OF INVOICE	AMOUNT
364	Jule Company	Merchandise	July 6	$ 6,000
401	Fall & Gains	Merchandise	August 27	7,500
				$13,500

The following transactions were completed during September:

Sept. 1. Issued Voucher No. 410 to Steady Realty Co. for September rent, $600, and utilities, $50 (charge expense for utilities to Miscellaneous General Expense); then issued Check No. 853 in payment of this voucher.

   2. Issued Voucher No. 411 for $200 to establish a petty cash fund; then issued Check No. 854 in payment of this voucher.

   3. Issued Voucher No. 412 to The Nevada Products Company for the purchase of merchandise, $8,200.

   4. Issued Voucher No. 413 to the Midwest Oil Company for gas, oil, and repairs. The tickets attached to the invoice indicate that delivery trucks used $170 (charge to Miscellaneous Delivery Expense) and salesmen's cars used $80 (charge to Miscellaneous Selling Expense). Issued Check No. 855 in payment of this voucher.

   6. Issued Voucher No. 414 to the L & Y Railroad Company for freight on merchandise purchases, $68; then issued Check No. 856 in payment of this voucher.

   7. Gave Jule Company a 15-day, 6% note in payment of Voucher No. 364.

   9. Received a credit memorandum for $500 from Fall & Gains for merchandise returned to them. Canceled Voucher No. 401 and issued Voucher No. 415 for the adjusted amount.

Sept. 13. Issued Voucher No. 416 to The Pico Company for the purchase of merchandise and supplies as follows: merchandise, $3,500; store supplies, $100; office supplies, $150; advertising circulars, $175.

15. Purchased a new cash register from National, Inc. for $1,250. Issued Voucher No. 417 for $250 for the down payment and Voucher No. 418 for the balance of $1,000 that is to be paid in 30 days if the machine is satisfactory. (Charge Store Equipment.) Issued Check No. 857 in payment of Voucher No. 417.

18. Issued Voucher No. 419 to Fulsom Laboratory for the purchase of merchandise, $900.

22. Issued Voucher No. 420 to Jule Company for the note of September 7 plus interest; then issued Check No. 858 in payment of this voucher.

23. Issued Check No. 859 in payment of Voucher No. 416 less a 2% discount.

24. Received a credit memorandum for $200 from The Nevada Products Company for merchandise returned to it that was included in Voucher No. 412. Made a "red ink" entry to record the return.

25. Issued Check No. 860 in payment of Voucher No. 415 less a 1% discount.

30. Issued Voucher No. 421 to replenish the petty cash fund. The charges were distributed as follows: Store Supplies, $35; Advertising Expense, $10; Miscellaneous Selling Expense, $40; Miscellaneous Delivery Expense, $15; Office Supplies, $25; Miscellaneous General Expense, $8. Issued Check No. 861 in payment of this voucher.

30. Received a credit memorandum for $100 from Fulsom Laboratory as an allowance on damaged merchandise that was included in Voucher No. 419. Made a "red ink" entry to record the allowance.

Instructions: (1) Under date of the original purchase, enter the unpaid vouchers on August 31 in a voucher register like the one illustrated on pages 288 and 289; then rule double lines across all the amount columns of the voucher register so that the amounts just recorded will not be included in the columnar totals posted at the end of September.

(2) Record the September transactions in the voucher register, in a check register like the one illustrated on page 291, and in a two-column general journal.

(3) Total and rule the voucher register and the check register.

(4) Open the following general ledger accounts: Account No. 213, Accounts Payable; Account No. 512, Purchases Returns and Allowances.

(5) Enter in the accounts payable account the August 31 balance of $13,500. Post the general journal entries to the accounts payable account and to the purchases returns and allowances account. Post the debit and the credit totals of the accounts payable column in the voucher register and the total of the accounts payable column in the check register. Post to the purchases returns and allowances account the total of the returns and allowances shown in the purchases column of the voucher register.

(6) Prove the September 30 balance of the accounts payable account by preparing a schedule of unpaid vouchers as shown by the voucher register.

Chapter 17

Accounting for Payrolls —
Payroll Taxes

NEED FOR PAYROLL RECORDS   Detailed and accurate information about the compensation of employees must be maintained by employers. In all businesses the amounts due employees are paid at regular intervals: weekly, biweekly, semimonthly, monthly, or in accordance with some other fixed plan. Most employers are required by federal laws to collect certain taxes levied against the earnings of their employees. They are also subject to federal taxes based upon the amount of compensation paid. Many employers are required to pay state payroll taxes, and in some states and cities they are required to collect other taxes levied upon the earnings of their employees. All of these federal, state, and city payroll taxes must be paid and detailed reports must be submitted at prescribed intervals.

Employers frequently obligate themselves to withhold specified sums from employees' earnings for the payment of union dues, insurance premiums, or charitable contributions. They may also, at the request of the employee, make payroll deductions for the purchase of federal bonds. Most employers protect their workers against complete loss of income resulting from accidents while on the job. The premiums on this insurance, called workmen's compensation insurance, are based in part on payroll information. This brief recital of some of the legal requirements and customary practices is evidence of the need for accurate and complete payroll records.

FORMS OF COMPENSATION   The term *salary* is usually applied to compensation for managerial, administrative, or similar services. The rate of salary is ordinarily expressed in terms of a month or a year. Compensation paid for manual labor, both skilled and unskilled, is commonly referred to as *wages* and is stated on an hourly, weekly, or piecework basis. In practice, the terms are used interchangeably. Other designations commonly employed are commissions, bonuses, profit sharing, and cost-of-living adjustments. Although compensation is usually paid in money, payment may be in other media such as meals, lodging, or securities.

EMPLOYER-EMPLOYEE RELATIONSHIP   Not all persons who perform services for a business are classified as employees. The relationship of employer and employee generally exists when the person for whom the services are performed has the right to control and direct the individual in the performance of his services. A lawyer who performs services for a client on a fee basis is an independent contractor rather than an employee. He chooses his own means of accomplishing the tasks for which he is engaged without the control or the direction of his client. Similarly, a public accountant engaged to audit the accounting records is an independent contractor. Other examples are plumbers, carpenters, electricians, painters, and others who may be engaged for a specific job.

Payments to independent contractors are not wages and should not be included in the payroll.

COMPUTATION OF EARNINGS   The earnings of each employee for each pay period are usually calculated by multiplying the time worked during the period by the agreed rate per hour, week, month, or other unit of time. In some cases, earnings are the product of the units of work completed times the rate per unit or piece. The earnings of salespeople are sometimes calculated by multiplying their sales for the period by an agreed percentage.

Timekeeping. When compensation is based upon time, a record of the time worked by each employee is needed. Maintaining such records is called *timekeeping*. The records that are compiled may be very simple or quite elaborate, depending upon the nature of the business and the number of employees. Sometimes such records are merely notations in a small memorandum book. In other cases the employees may be required to record the times of their arrivals and departures each day. Many businesses use mechanical or electric time clocks to compile this information. Although a record of the exact work done by each employee may not be needed in order to calculate earnings, other considerations sometimes make it desirable to keep this information.

Wage Rates, Overtime. Wages and salaries must be paid at the rate agreed upon in each case. For businesses engaged in interstate commerce, the rates must also conform to the requirements of the Federal Fair Labor Standards Act. This Act, commonly known as the Wages and Hours Law, requires employers who are covered by the statute to pay a minimum rate of $1\frac{1}{2}$ times the regular rate for all hours worked in excess of 40 per week. Persons holding executive, administrative, and certain supervisory positions are not covered by this provision of the law.

In many industries the practice of paying premium rates for overtime hours has been considerably extended. Certain overtime hours may be paid for at twice the base rate. Work on Sundays and holidays may be paid for at overtime rates regardless of the total number of hours worked during the week. It is a common practice for companies that work night shifts to pay premium rates to those who work during these generally less desirable hours.

Illustration. To illustrate the calculation of the gross earnings of an employee, the following facts are assumed: Employee Richard Burke is paid at the rate of $1.80 per hour for the first 40 hours each week and $2.70 ($1.80 + .90) per hour for all hours in excess of 40. His time card for the week ended October 31 shows that he worked 8 hours each day, Monday through Thursday, 9 hours on Friday, and 5 hours on Saturday. His earnings would be calculated as follows:

DAY	HOURS WORKED	REGULAR HOURS	OVERTIME HOURS
Monday..................	8	8	
Tuesday.................	8	8	
Wednesday..............	8	8	
Thursday...............	8	8	
Friday.................	9	8	1
Saturday...............	5		5
	46	40	6

Total hours worked at regular rate: 40 × $1.80 = $72.00
Total hours worked at overtime rate: 6 × 2.70 =   16.20

                                        $88.20

DEDUCTIONS FROM EARNINGS   In most instances the amount paid to the worker is less than the amount of his earnings. The difference is due primarily to the taxes assessed against the employee that the employer is required to withhold. In addition to these, the employee may authorize various other deductions.

F.I.C.A. Tax. Most employers are required by the Federal Insurance Contributions Act to withhold a portion of the earnings of each of their employees. The amount withheld is the employees' contribution to the federal program of old age and survivors' insurance. It is frequently referred to as the *F.I.C.A.* tax or the *F.O.A.B.* tax, the latter term emphasizing the benefits rather than the contributions feature of the law. Certain types of employment, such as agricultural labor, are exempt from the tax. Unless specifically exempted, every employer is required to withhold the tax. At the present time the rate is $1\frac{1}{2}\%$ of the first \$3,600 paid to each employee in any calendar year. Although Congress may change the tax rate and the maximum amount subject to the tax, such changes will not affect the accounting principles or the method of recording the transactions.

Federal Income Tax. Except for certain types of employment, all employers are required to deduct a portion of the earnings of their employees for federal income tax purposes. As a part of the pay-as-you-go system of paying income taxes, it is frequently referred to as the *withholding tax.* The amount to be withheld varies with the amount of earnings and the number of exemptions to which the employee is entitled. An exemption is allowed for the worker, for each person that qualifies as a dependent, and for the worker's wife, provided she is not also employed and claiming her own exemption. Additional exemptions are allowed to the worker and his wife for old age (65 or older) and for blindness. Every employee is required to inform his employer of his status in this respect by submitting a withholding exemption certificate, a copy of which is reproduced below:

Form W-4 (Rev. July 1952) U. S. Treasury Department Internal Revenue Service	**EMPLOYEE'S WITHHOLDING EXEMPTION CERTIFICATE**

Print full name ......Richard..Alan..Burke.. Social Security No. 259-08-8114......

Print home address .20830 Stratford Ave., Rocky River 16, Ohio..........................,.........

EMPLOYEE:
File this form with your employer. Otherwise, he must withhold U. S. Income tax from your wages without exemption.
 	
EMPLOYER:
Keep this certificate with your records. If the employee is believed to have claimed too many exemptions, the Director should be so advised.
	HOW TO CLAIM YOUR WITHHOLDING EXEMPTIONS
	1. If SINGLE, and you claim an exemption, write the figure "1"..................................... ‒‒‒‒‒‒
	2. If MARRIED, one exemption each for husband and wife if not claimed on another certificate.
	   (a) If you claim **both** of these exemptions, write the figure "2" ⎫
	   (b) If you claim **one** of these exemptions, write the figure "1" ⎬ 2
	   (c) If you claim **neither** of these exemptions, write "0" ⎭
	3. If you claim exemptions for one or more dependents, write the number of such exemptions. (Do not claim 1
	   exemption for a dependent unless you are qualified under instruction 3 on other side.)................
	4. Exemptions for age and blindness (applicable only to you and your wife but **not** to dependents):
	   (a) If you **or** your wife will be 65 years of age or older at the end of the year, and you claim this exemption,
	   write the figure "1"; if **both** will be 65 or older, and you claim both of these exemptions, write the
	   figure "2".. ‒‒‒‒‒‒
	   (b) If you **or** your wife are blind, and you claim this exemption, write the figure "1"; if **both** are blind,
	   and you claim both of these exemptions, write the figure "2".....................
	5. Add the number of exemptions which you have claimed above and write the total.................. ⬚3⬚

I CERTIFY that the number of withholding exemptions claimed on this certificate does not exceed the number to which I am entitled.

(Date) ....January 10,........, 19 53   16—54717-4   (Signed) *Richard A. Burke*..........

Withholding Exemption Certificate

The amount of the tax to be withheld from the earnings of each employee is calculated by taking into account the amount of his earnings, the length of the pay period, the number of exemptions claimed, and the tax rates currently in force. Many employers find it expedient to consult withholding tables prepared by the government. From a table for the appropriate pay period (daily, weekly, biweekly, semi-monthly, monthly, etc.) the amount of tax to be withheld can be found for any amount of earnings and any number of exemptions.

Other Taxes. All states have a program of unemployment compensation insurance that is financed, in part, by a tax on employers. A few states also require contributions from employees, in which case the employer is compelled to withhold the amount of the contribution from the employees' earnings and to remit this amount to the state bureau or agency that administers the program.

A number of states and a few cities levy a tax based on income. The state or the city statutes may require the employer to withhold the tax from his employees' earnings.

Other Deductions. The deductions from earnings discussed above are compulsory; neither the employer nor the employee has any choice in the matter. In addition to these deductions, however, there may be other deductions authorized by employees either individually or as a group. For example, the deduction of union dues or group insurance premiums may be provided for in the contract between the employer and the union representing the workers. A partial list of reasons for other deductions from earnings of employees follows:

(1) Deductions to accumulate funds to be used to purchase United States Savings Bonds for the employees.

(2) Deductions to pay the premiums on life, health, hospital, or accident insurance for the employees.

(3) Deductions authorized by the employees for some sort of supplementary retirement annuity or pension.

(4) Deductions authorized to be paid to some charitable organization (Red Cross, Community Chest, etc.)

(5) Deductions authorized to repay a loan or an advance from the company or a loan from the company credit union.

(6) Deductions authorized to pay for purchases of a product or a service of the company.

Whatever the nature of the deduction, the accounting problem is essentially the same. If the employer makes these deductions, he must keep an accurate record of their amount and must dispose of the funds as authorized. Most of the deductions made from employees' earnings are current liabilities of the employer.

CALCULATION OF NET PAY ILLUSTRATED According to the computations of Richard Burke's earnings presented earlier, his total compensation for the week ended October 31 was $88.20. Assuming that his earnings thus far during the year, exclusive of the current week, amount to $3,560, the portion of the $88.20 subject to the F.I.C.A. tax is $40 ($3,600 maximum minus $3,560). The tax on $40 at the rate of $1\frac{1}{2}\%$ is $.60. (When the computation yields a fractional part of a cent, the fraction is disregarded unless it amounts to one-half cent or more, in which case the product is increased to the next cent.)

It will be assumed that Burke is employed in a state that does not require employee contributions to its unemployment insurance program; hence there is no deduction for this purpose.

The withholding exemption certificate illustrated earlier shows that Burke claims three exemptions for income tax purposes. Reference to the income tax withholding table for a weekly payroll period discloses that for earnings of $88.20, with three exemptions claimed, the amount to be withheld is $10.10.

The employer has a group insurance arrangement whereby part of the premium is borne by the employer and the remainder is deducted from the employees' earnings. The amount deducted from Burke's pay is 50 cents per week. Burke has also authorized the employer to withhold $3.75 each week for the purchase of United States Savings Bonds. At the end of each five-week period, a bond is purchased in his name and is delivered to him. He has also authorized a deduction of $1 each week for a period of five weeks for his contribution to the local Community Chest.

The various deductions and the amount to be paid to Burke for the week ended October 31 are summarized as follows:

Earnings (as calculated).........................		$88.20
Deductions:		
F.I.C.A. Tax.................................	$ .60	
Federal Income Tax..........................	10.10	
Group Insurance.............................	.50	
U. S. Savings Bond..........................	3.75	
Community Chest............................	1.00	
Total Deductions.............................		15.95
Amount of paycheck (take-home pay)............		$72.25

It is customary for the employer to furnish a statement of withholdings to the employee with each paycheck or pay envelope. Paychecks with detachable stubs are widely used. The pay period, the earnings, and the various deductions are shown on the stub. The employee removes the stub before cashing the check. An illustration of this form of paycheck is shown on the following page.

THE PAYROLL   A *payroll* is a list of employees showing their earnings for a stated period together with other relevant information. The columnar headings and the arrange-

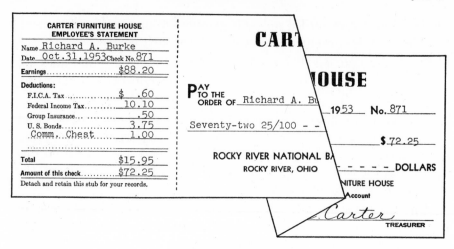

Payroll Check

ment of data on payroll forms varies considerably, though all payrolls provide for essentially the same information. A typical weekly payroll form is illustrated below and on page 307.

There are a number of points that should be noted in this illustration. The exact period covered by the payroll should be clearly indicated; in this case it is the week ended October 31, 1953. This particular payroll covers all employees of the business, both sales personnel and office personnel. If there were a large number of employees divided into several departments or categories, a separate payroll sheet could be prepared for each department or category. In the illustration the employees are listed in alphabetic order. They could be listed by order of employee number.

PAYROLL FOR WEEK ENDED

| | | DAILY TIME | | | | | | | REGU-LAR HOURS | OVER-TIME HOURS | REGU-LAR RATE | EARNINGS | | |
NAME	EM-PLOYEE NO.	S	M	T	W	TH	F	S				AT REGU-LAR RATE	AT OVER-TIME RATE	TOTAL
Allen, Thomas..	6		8	8	8	8	8	0	40		1.50	60.00		60.00
Burke, Richard.	10		8	8	8	8	9	5	40	6	1.80	72.00	16.20	88.20
Clark, Alice....	4		8	8	8	8	8	4	40	4	1.20	48.00	7.20	55.20
Davis, Howard.	7		8	8	8	8	8	0	40		1.50	60.00		60.00
Fisher, Joseph..	1											120.00		120.00
Janes, Sue.....	9		8	8	8	8	8	0	40		1.30	52.00		52.00
Loomis, Roy...	3		8	8	8	8	9	2	40	3	1.60	64.00	7.20	71.20
Morrison, John.	5		8	8	8	8	4	0	36		1.30	46.80		46.80
Tucker, Ralph..	2		8	8	8	8	8	5	40	5	1.80	72.00	13.50	85.50
Vance, Cynthia.	8		8	8	0	8	8	0	32		1.00	32.00		32.00
Total												626.80	44.10	670.90

Weekly Payroll Record, Left Page

The Daily Time columns are self-explanatory. The information as to hours worked is secured from a time-clock record or a similar record of the arrivals and departures of employees. The regular hours worked are multiplied by the regular rate to yield the regular earnings; the overtime hours are multiplied by the overtime rate to yield the overtime earnings; the two amounts are then added to determine the total earnings. It will be noted that there is no record of hours worked by Joseph Fisher. He is employed in an administrative capacity and is paid at the rate of $120 per week, regardless of the number of hours spent on the job.

The two columns under the heading Taxable Earnings are for memorandum purposes only. Employers are subject to unemployment compensation taxes based upon the first $3,000 of compensation paid to each employee during the calendar year. They are also required to pay federal insurance contribution (F.I.C.A.) taxes based upon the first $3,600 of compensation paid to each employee during the calendar year. Information regarding each employee's year-to-date earnings is obtained from the *employees' earnings record,* which is discussed later in the chapter. As stated earlier, Richard Burke's cumulative earnings, exclusive of the current week, were $3,560; therefore none of the current week's earnings are subject to the unemployment compensation taxes and only $40 is subject to the F.I.C.A. tax. Joseph Fisher has exceeded the $3,600 level prior to the current week; hence none of his compensation for the current week is included in the Taxable Earnings columns. The same is apparently true of Ralph Tucker. The earnings of Roy Loomis have previously exceeded the $3,000 level but have not

OCTOBER 31, 1953

TAXABLE EARNINGS		DEDUCTIONS						PAID		ACCOUNTS DEBITED	
UNEM-PLOYMENT COMP.	F.I.C.A.	F.I.C.A. TAX	FEDERAL INCOME TAX	GROUP INSUR-ANCE	U.S. BONDS	OTHER	TOTAL	NET AMOUNT	CHECK NO.	SALES SALARY EXPENSE	OFFICE SALARY EXPENSE
60.00	60.00	.90	4.50	.20	1.25	CC 1.00	7.85	52.15	870	60.00	
	40.00	.60	10.10	.50	3.75	CC 1.00	15.95	72.25	871	88.20	
55.20	55.20	.83	8.50	.10	1.25	CC 1.00	11.68	43.52	872		55.20
60.00	60.00	.90	9.60	.20			10.70	49.30	873	60.00	
			19.40	1.00	7.50	CC 3.00	30.90	89.10	874		120.00
52.00	52.00	.78	5.40	.20		AR 4.00	10.38	41.62	875	52.00	
	71.20	1.07	3.90	.40	1.25	CC 1.00	7.62	63.58	876	71.20	
46.80	46.80	.70	6.70	.20			7.60	39.20	877	46.80	
			9.30	.60	2.50	CC 1.50	13.90	71.60	878	85.50	
32.00	32.00	.48	3.90	.10			4.48	27.52	879		32.00
306.00	417.20	6.26	81.30	3.50	17.50	CC 8.50 AR 4.00	121.06	549.84		463.70	207.20

Weekly Payroll Record, Right Page

yet reached $3,600; therefore his weekly earnings of $71.20 are excluded from the Unemployment Compensation column but are included in the F.I.C.A. column.

The Deductions columns are self-explanatory, with the exception of the "Other" column. This column is used to list withholdings for which no special column is provided. In the illustration, the column records withholdings for Community Chest donations (marked "CC") and a deduction of $4 from the pay of Sue Janes to apply on an account receivable (marked "AR"). The individual items are sorted and classified and a separate total is shown for each class.

The difference between the total earnings and the total deductions is the net amount to be paid, which is entered in the Paid column. The check number is recorded as the checks are written.

The last two columns of the payroll illustrated are used to accumulate the total wages or salaries to be charged to the expense accounts. This process is usually termed *payroll distribution*. If there is an extensive account classification of labor expense, the charges may be analyzed on a separate payroll distribution sheet instead of adding more columns to the payroll sheet.

The columns in the payroll sheet should be added and the totals should be proved before the payroll is entered in the books of account or checks are issued to employees. The following tabulation indicates the method of verification:

Earnings:

At Regular Rate..........................	$626.80	
At Overtime Rate.........................	44.10	
Total...................................		$670.90

Deductions:

F.I.C.A. Tax............................	$ 6.26	
Income Tax Withheld......................	81.30	
Group Insurance.........................	3.50	
U. S. Bonds.............................	17.50	
Community Chest.........................	8.50	
Accounts Receivable......................	4.00	
Total...................................		121.06

Paid — Net Amount........................ $549.84

Accounts Debited:

Sales Salary Expense......................	$463.70	
Office Salary Expense.....................	207.20	
Total (as above).........................		$670.90

There are innumerable variations in the procedures that may be followed in preparing payrolls. As the number of employees becomes greater, it is customary to use specialized machines for accumulating and recording the data. A wide variety of equipment is available. It is possible to obtain the various totals needed, to write the checks, and to accumulate data in the employees' earnings records from a single machine recording of the basic data. Regardless of the mechanical aids employed, however, all payroll procedures and systems have the same purpose: to compile and record the necessary information in an expeditious manner.

ENTERING THE PAY-ROLL IN THE ACCOUNTS   The general journal entry to record the payroll illustrated on the preceding pages is as follows:

Oct.	31	Sales Salary Expense............	611	463 70			
		Office Salary Expense............	711	207 20			
		F.I.C.A. Taxes Payable........	215.1			6 26	
		Employees Income Taxes Payable....................	215.2			81 30	
		Group Insurance Payable......	216.1			3 50	
		Bond Deductions Payable......	216.2			17 50	
		Community Chest Donations Payable...................	216.3			8 50	
		Accounts Receivable—Sue Janes	114/√			4 00	
		Salaries Payable..............	214			549 84	
		Payroll for week ended October 31.					

The two debits in the entry are to expense accounts. The amount and the nature of the deductions from the workers' earnings have no effect on the amount of expense incurred by the business. Of the seven credits in the entry, six represent an increase in a specific liability and one represents a decrease in the asset Accounts Receivable. The liabilities will be paid at various times. For example, payments to the insurance company for group insurance may be made annually or quarterly, bonds are purchased as the accumulation for each particular employee reaches the necessary amount, and the Community Chest donations will be paid at the conclusion of the period during which deductions are made. The payment of the liability for F.I.C.A. taxes, employees' income taxes, and salaries will be discussed later in the chapter.

An alternative to recording the payroll information in the general journal is to treat the payroll record as a special journal. If this is done, totals of the various columns are posted directly to the appropriate ledger accounts and the posting references are written below the totals in the payroll record.

While direct posting of the payroll may be expedient, it is often preferable to summarize the payroll in the general journal, as illustrated. Sometimes the data relating to all of the pay periods that ended during the month are combined into one monthly general journal entry. Regardless of the method used, the payroll record should be retained for a minimum period of four years, as required by federal statutes.

PAYING THE PAYROLL The procedures for recording payment of the payroll vary in accordance with the particular system used by the business in making cash payments generally.

Cash Payments Journal. When cash payments are recorded in a cash payments journal, the payment of the payroll may be recorded as follows:

CASH PAYMENTS JOURNAL

DATE	CHECK NO.	ACCOUNT DEBITED	POST. REF.	GENERAL DR.	ACCOUNTS PAYABLE DR.	PURCHASES DISCOUNT CR.	CASH CR.
1953 Oct.	31 870-9	Salaries Payable......	214	549 84			549 84

The foregoing entry assumes that a separate check is drawn for each employee and therefore indicates that checks 870 to 879 have been drawn. If desired, each check could be listed separately in the cash payments journal; but there is little need for recording the details in the cash payments journal because the name of each employee, the amount paid, and the check number are available in the payroll record.

If employees are paid in currency, one check payable to Payroll may be drawn for the total amount to be paid to employees, and this check may be taken to the bank and cashed. The money may then be inserted in individual payroll envelopes by the employer, or the bank may render this service for a fee.

If a business prefers to use special payroll checks instead of its regular checks in paying employees, it may draw one check payable to Payroll Bank Account for the total amount to be paid to employees. This check is deposited in a special account and individual payroll checks are then drawn against this account.

A special payroll bank account is ordinarily used for large payrolls. The executives who sign all regular checks are relieved of the task of signing hundreds or thousands of payroll checks each week. That duty will probably fall to the paymaster. Sometimes mechanical means of signing the checks are employed. The task of reconciling the regular bank statement is simplified, as the payroll checks are returned separately with an accompanying statement of the payroll bank account.

Voucher System. When the voucher system is used to control cash disbursements, a voucher must be prepared before the payroll can be paid. The use of the voucher system, then, requires two entries to replace the one entry in the cash payments journal.

(1) A voucher is prepared for the amount to be paid to the employees and is recorded in the voucher register. The effect of this entry is a debit to Salaries Payable and a credit to Accounts Payable. The voucher register after this voucher is recorded may appear as follows:

VOUCHER REGISTER

DATE		VCHR. NO.	CREDITOR	PAID		ACCOUNTS PAYABLE CR.	GENERAL DR.		
				DATE	CK. NO.		ACCOUNT	POST. REF.	AMOUNT
1953 Oct.	31	650	Payroll........	10–31	624	549 84	Salaries Payable.	214	549 84

(2) The employees are paid and the payment is recorded in the check register. The entry shown below is made when only one check is drawn. This check may be in favor of Payroll and may be cashed so that employees can be paid in cash, or it may be in favor of Payroll Bank Account and the employees may be paid with special payroll checks. If one of the regular checks is written for each employee, the same entry is made in the check register, but the check numbers are shown as they were in the cash payments journal on page 310.

CHECK REGISTER

DATE		CHECK NO.	PAYEE	VCHR. NO.	ACCOUNTS PAYABLE DR.	PURCHASES DISCOUNT CR.	BANK CR.
1953 Oct.	31	624	Payroll....................	650	549 84		549 84

The credits to the various liability accounts for amounts withheld accumulate until the time for payment, at which time a voucher is prepared in the usual manner and a check is drawn on the general bank account.

EMPLOYEE'S EARNINGS RECORD   In order to determine the amount of F.I.C.A. tax to be withheld from the earnings of each employee, it is necessary to know the cumulative earnings for the year to date. The amounts to be entered in the Taxable Earnings columns of the payroll record are also determined by reference to the cumulative earnings of each employee. In addition, quarterly and annual amounts of earnings and of certain deductions of each employee must be reported by the employer on various federal and state tax forms. For these reasons, if no other, an individual record of earnings and deductions for each employee is essential.

The form of the employee's earnings record varies, but all types show essentially the same information. A portion of the earnings record of Richard Burke is presented below and on page 313. The upper portion of the form is used to record miscellaneous personal data about the employee, including such information as the employee's address,

EMPLOYEE'S

NAME _____ Burke, Richard Alan _____

ADDRESS _____ 20830 Stratford Avenue. _____   PHONE ____ ED 1-1149

_____ Rocky River 16, Ohio _____

MALE √   MARRIED √   NUMBER OF   PAY   PER DAY ____

FEMALE __   SINGLE ____   EXEMPTIONS 3   RATE $ 72.00   WEEK √

_____ MONTH ____

OCCUPATION _____ Salesman _____   EQUIVALENT HOURLY RATE $ 1.80

LINE NO.	PERIOD ENDED	TIME WORKED DAYS	TIME WORKED HOURS	RATE	EARNINGS AT REGULAR RATE	EARNINGS AT OVERTIME RATE	TOTAL	CUMULATIVE TOTAL
39	Sept.26		42	1.80	72.00	5.40	77.40	3,253.10
THIRD QUARTER					936.00	86.40	1,022.40	
40	Oct. 3		40	1.80	72.00		72.00	3,325.10
41	Oct. 10		45	1.80	72.00	13.50	85.50	3,410.60
42	Oct. 17		42	1.80	72.00	5.40	77.40	3,488.00
43	Oct. 24		40	1.80	72.00		72.00	3,560.00
44	Oct. 31		46	1.80	72.00	16.20	88.20	3,648.20
45	Nov. 7		40	1.80	72.00		72.00	3,720.20
51	Dec. 19		48	1.80	72.00	21.60	93.60	4,217.00
52	Dec. 26		43	1.80	72.00	8.10	80.10	4,297.10
FOURTH QUARTER					936.00	108.00	1,044.00	
YEARLY TOTAL					3,744.00	553.10	4,297.10	

Employee's Earnings Record, Left Page

employee number, social security number, and number of withholding exemptions.

The record should provide a line for each payroll period in the year, a line for each of the quarterly totals, and a line for the yearly totals. Columnar headings are similar to those on the payroll record. The entries to Burke's record for the week ended October 31 should be compared with the entries opposite Burke's name in the payroll record for the same week (pages 306 and 307). Note that the amount in the Cumulative Total column for the week ended October 24 is $3,560.00. It was on the basis of this information that the amount of F.I.C.A. tax to be withheld on October 31 was based on earnings of $40 ($3,600 — $3,560).

EARNINGS RECORD

SOC. SEC. NO. _259 -08 -8114_   EMPLOYEE NO. __10__   YEAR _1953_

DATE EMPLOYED ___April 10, 1950___

DATE OF BIRTH ___March 24, 1926___

DATE EMPLOYMENT TERMINATED _____

		DEDUCTIONS				PAID		
F.I.C.A. TAX	FEDERAL INCOME TAX	GROUP INSURANCE	U. S. BONDS	OTHER	TOTAL	NET AMOUNT	CHECK NO.	LINE NO.
1.16	7.70	.50	.75		13.11	64.29	819	39
15.34	106.40	6.50	48.75	AR 32.00	208.99	813.41		
1.08	6.90	.50	3.75		12.23	59.77	829	40
1.28	9.30	.50	3.75		14.83	70.67	840	41
1.16	7.70	.50	3.75		13.11	64.29	850	42
1.08	6.90	.50	3.75		12.23	59.77	861	43
.60	10.10	.50	3.75	CC 1.00	15.95	72.25	871	44
	6.90	.50	3.75	CC 1.00	12.15	59.85	881	45
	10.90	.50	3.75		15.15	78.45	935	51
	8.50	.50	3.75		12.75	67.35	946	52
5.20	110.10	6.50	48.75	CC 5.00	175.55	868.45		
54.00	460.70	26.00	195.00	CC 5.00 AR 32.00	772.70	3,524.40		

Employee's Earnings Record, Right Page

WITHHOLDING   On or before January 31 of each year most
STATEMENT   employers must furnish to each employee a
statement of the total compensation paid (before payroll deductions)
and the total amount of F.I.C.A. tax and income tax withheld during
the preceding calendar year. The report is made on Form W-2; the
original and the duplicate are given to the employee and a triplicate
copy is sent to the Director of Internal Revenue for the district. The
employee is required to submit the original Form W-2 with his income
tax return. The withholding statement for Richard Burke is reproduced below:

Form W-2 U. S. Treasury Department Internal Revenue Service	**WITHHOLDING STATEMENT—1953** Federal Taxes Withheld From Wages		EMPLOYEE'S COPY (DUPLICATE)
FEDERAL INSURANCE CONTRIBUTIONS ACT (FEDERAL OLD-AGE AND SURVIVORS INSURANCE)		**U. S. INCOME TAX WITHHOLDING INFORMATION** (TO BE REPORTED ON EMPLOYEE'S INCOME TAX RETURN)	
Total F.I.C.A. wages (before payroll deductions) paid in 1953*	F.I.C.A. employee tax withheld, if any	Total wages (before payroll deductions) paid in 1953	Federal income tax withheld, if any
$3,600.00	$ 54.00	$4,297.10	$ 460.70
EMPLOYEE (Print employee's social security account number, name, and full address below)		**EMPLOYER** (Print employer's identification number, name, and address below)	
259-08-8114 Richard Alan Burke 20830 Stratford Ave. Rocky River 16, Ohio		27-0118342 Carter Furniture House 21763 Lake Road Rocky River 16, Ohio	
*If your wages were subject to F.I.C.A. taxes, but are not shown above, your F.I.C.A. wages are the same as wages shown under "U. S. INCOME TAX WITHHOLDING INFORMATION," but not more than $3,600.		**EMPLOYEE:** Detach this copy and keep it as part of your tax records. Do NOT send it to the Director of Internal Revenue with your income tax return.	
			16—67819-1

Withholding Statement

The information for the withholding statement was obtained from
Burke's earnings record. This is just one example of the usefulness of
employees' earnings records in preparing tax forms. They may also be
useful in such matters as determination of rights of employees to
bonuses, vacation leave, questions in connection with the Wages and
Hours Law, etc.

EMPLOYER'S PAYROLL The payroll taxes discussed thus far were
TAXES   those imposed upon employees. The employer is concerned with these because he is obliged by law to withhold
the proper amounts from the workers' pay and to remit these amounts
to the appropriate governmental agency. The taxes to be discussed in
the following sections are borne by the employer, that is, they are
business *expenses.*

F.I.C.A. Tax. Employers, as well as employees, are required to
contribute to the Federal Insurance Contributions Act tax. This con-

tribution is the same as that required of employees, namely $1\frac{1}{2}\%$ of the first \$3,600 of earnings paid (before payroll deductions) to each employee during the calendar year.[1]

Federal Unemployment Compensation Tax.   Unemployment insurance is a major feature of the national social security program. It provides some relief to those who become unemployed as a result of economic forces outside of their control and it also tends to encourage full employment. To finance the administration of the program, all employers covered by the law are nominally subject to a federal tax of 3% on the first \$3,000 paid to every covered employee during a calendar year. Since credits are given for payments to the various states for the state unemployment compensation tax, the effective federal rate is actually only $.3\%$. No part of the federal unemployment compensation tax is levied on the employees.

The number of employers covered by this federal law is not so large as under the F.I.C.A. tax. Only employers of eight or more persons are subject to the federal unemployment compensation tax. The types of employment excluded are substantially the same for both taxes.

State Unemployment Compensation Tax.   The amounts collected by the federal government from the tax discussed in the preceding section are paid to the various states for use in administering their unemployment compensation programs.   Money paid to unemployed persons who qualify for benefits comes from the state tax levied upon the employers, based upon the earnings of employees. A very few states require employee contributions. The various state laws differ with respect to the types of covered employment and the number of workers an employer must have before the tax is applicable. In no case is the required number of workers greater than eight; in a number of states it is one.

The state taxes all have the same base: the first \$3,000 of earnings paid to each covered employee during the calendar year. The tax rates are not uniform among the states. In general, however, the maximum rate is 2.7%, although in a number of states the upper limit is higher. Almost every state has a merit-rating plan under which employers who provide steady employment for their workers earn a rating that reduces the tax rate below the maximum charged in that state.

RECORDING EMPLOYER'S PAYROLL TAXES   The employer's payroll taxes may be determined and recorded at the end of each payroll period or at the end of each month. In either case the basic data

---

[1]The rate of the F.I.C.A. tax on employers, like the rate on employees, may be changed by the Congress at any time.

needed to compute the taxes are obtained from the payroll records. According to the payroll record of the Carter Furniture House for the week ended October 31 (pages 306 and 307), the amount of earnings subject to the F.I.C.A. tax is $417.20, that subject to the unemployment compensation taxes is $306, and the F.I.C.A. tax withheld is $6.26. Assuming that the Carter Furniture House is in this year subject to a state unemployment tax rate of 1.9%, the taxes accrued for the week are as follows:

F.I.C.A. — 1½% of $417.20............................	$ 6.26
State Unemployment Compensation — 1.9% of $306.......	5.81
Federal Unemployment Compensation — .3% of $306......	.92
Total...	$12.99

The general journal entry to record the expense for the week and the liability for the taxes accrued is as follows:

Oct.	31	Payroll Tax Expense...................	719	12|99			
		F.I.C.A. Taxes Payable..............	215.1			6	26
		State Unemployment Taxes Payable..	215.3			5	81
		Federal Unemployment Taxes Payable	215.4				92
		Payroll taxes accrued for the week ended October 31.				

If the employer's taxes are recorded monthly instead of weekly, the procedure is exactly the same as illustrated above except that the data for the four or five payroll periods ending within the month are combined before the several taxes are computed.

Practice differs as to the disposition of the debit for the amount of the payroll tax expense. Since the taxes have a direct relationship to compensation paid, some accountants charge them directly to the appropriate wage and salary accounts. Others charge them to Payroll Tax Expense, as was done above, and classify the account as a general expense on the profit and loss statement.

PAYMENT OF   The requirements for paying the employer's
PAYROLL TAXES   payroll taxes and the amounts withheld from employees vary. The regulations governing the filing of returns and the payment of the liabilities are summarized in the sections that follow.

Income Taxes Withheld and F.I.C.A. Taxes. The income taxes and the F.I.C.A. taxes withheld from employees, together with the employer's share of the F.I.C.A. taxes, are required to be paid quarterly. Both taxes are reported on a single tax form, which must be filed during the month following the close of the quarter. For example, the taxes for January, February, and March must be reported and paid by April 30.

If the sum of the income taxes withheld from employees and the total F.I.C.A. taxes (on employer and employee) exceeds $100 for the first or the second month of any quarter, the employer is required to deposit the amount due for that month in the Federal Reserve Bank in his district. The deposit, which may be accepted by authorized commercial banks, should be made by the fifteenth of the following month. For example, if during the month of January an employer withholds $87.50 of income taxes and the F.I.C.A. taxes (both employer's and employees' share) are $18, the total of $105.50 must be deposited by February 15. The employer receives as evidence of the deposit a "Federal Depositary Receipt." These receipts are then submitted with the quarterly tax report.

The amount due for the third month of the quarter, regardless of the amount, may accompany the quarterly return or may be deposited by the employer. When the amounts due for each month in the quarter are deposited by the fifteenth of the following month, the employer is allowed an additional ten days in which to file the quarterly report. For example, if the taxes for January, February, and March are deposited by February 15, March 15, and April 15 respectively, the quarterly return need not be filed until May 10; otherwise it is due on April 30.

State Unemployment Compensation Tax. The state laws vary with respect to the type and the number of tax forms or returns that employers must file. In general, employers are required to file a tax return and to pay the tax during the month following each calendar quarter.

Federal Unemployment Compensation Tax. The federal unemployment compensation tax is payable annually. The tax return for the calendar year, accompanied by the remittance, must be filed by January 31 of the following year.

Recording Payment. Payment of the various taxes is recorded in the same manner as the payment of other liabilities, that is, by a debit to the particular liability account—Employees Income Taxes Payable, F.I.C.A. Taxes Payable, State Unemployment Taxes Payable, or Federal Unemployment Taxes Payable—and a credit to Cash or Bank. Monthly payments to a Federal Reserve Bank for federal income taxes withheld and for F.I.C.A. taxes are considered as payments of the respective liabilities.

When the voucher system is used, it is necessary to prepare a voucher immediately prior to the payment of each tax due. To illustrate, assume that Carter Furniture House, whose fiscal year ends on December 31, follows the procedures previously outlined in recording its liability for taxes. After the books have been adjusted and closed for December 31, 1953, the balances in the various tax liability accounts as of January 1, 1954, are as follows:

F.I.C.A. Taxes Payable (December).....................	$ 45.28
Employees Income Taxes Payable (December)...........	331.90
State Unemployment Taxes Payable (October-December)...	53.46
Federal Unemployment Taxes Payable (January-December)	114.52

The vouchers for the payment of these liabilities will be recorded in the voucher register as follows, assuming arbitrarily that each liability is to be paid on January 30:

VOUCHER REGISTER

DATE	VCHR. NO.	CREDITOR	PAID DATE	PAID CK. NO.	ACCOUNTS PAYABLE CR.	GENERAL DR. ACCOUNT	GENERAL DR. POST. REF.	GENERAL DR. AMOUNT
1954 Jan. 30	778	Director of Internal Revenue	1-30	899	377 18	F.I.C.A.TaxesPay.	215.1	45 28
						Employees Income Taxes Pay..........	215.2	331 90
30	779	State Treasurer.	1-30	900	53 46	State Unemployment Taxes Pay...........	215.3	53 46
30	780	Director of Internal Revenue	1-30	901	114 52	Federal Unemployment Taxes Pay..........	215.4	114 52

ADJUSTMENTS AT THE END OF THE FISCAL PERIOD   If the end of a fiscal period does not coincide with the end of a payroll period, it is necessary to record the accrued salaries for the incomplete payroll period; otherwise the expenses for the period will be understated and, as of the last day of the period, proprietorship will be overstated and liabilities will be understated. An adjustment may be made not only for the accrued payroll but also for the employer's accrued payroll taxes. It is unnecessary to consider the withholding of income tax and the employees' share of the F.I.C.A. tax on the accrued payroll because (1) there is no withholding until the payroll is paid and (2) in any case the *total* liabilities and expenses of the employer are not affected by withholdings.

For example, suppose the Carter Furniture House has accrued salaries for the incomplete pay period December 28-31, 1953, (Monday through Thursday) as follows: sales salaries, $290.50; office salaries, $134.10.   Using a rate of 1½% for the F.I.C.A. tax, 1.9% for the state unemployment tax, and .3% for the federal unemployment tax, the adjusting entry is as follows:

Dec.	31	Sales Salary Expense.............	611		290 50		
		Office Salary Expense.............	711		134 10		
		Payroll Tax Expense..............	719		15 71		
		F.I.C.A. Taxes Payable.........	215.1			6 37	
		State Unemployment Taxes Payable....................	215.3			8 07	
		Federal Unemployment Taxes Payable....................	215.4			1 27	
		Salaries Payable...............	214			424 60	

After the books have been closed, the foregoing adjusting entry is reversed so as to avoid disrupting the usual payroll procedures.   The entry to record the first payroll in January would be made in the usual manner, as would the entry to record the employer's payroll taxes. The foregoing adjustment for the incomplete payroll period will in no way affect the tax payment procedures discussed in the previous section.   The payroll taxes are based on compensation *paid* rather than on compensation *earned*.   The compensation for the incomplete period has been earned but not paid.

In this connection it should be pointed out that in many businesses there is a lag of a variable number of days between the end of the payroll period and the payment of the payroll.   Such a delay may be necessitated by the time required to complete the necessary records and to prepare the checks.   In the illustrations presented in this chapter, payment was assumed to be made on the last day of the payroll period. This was merely to simplify the explanation and to avoid confusion over dates.   The accounting procedures are not affected by a time lag between the end of the payroll period and the date of payment.   The usual entries are made for *completed* payroll periods and an adjusting entry is required only for the current *incomplete* payroll period.

Accrued taxes on accrued payroll are not deductible as an expense for income tax purposes, because for income tax purposes there is no expense until wages are actually paid.   As the amount of accrued taxes on accrued payroll is usually small, many businesses do not record these accrued taxes.   Since the effect upon final net profit is not material, they consider it preferable to follow income tax procedures.

PAYROLL PROCEDURE FOR FEW EMPLOYEES   It is unnecessary for a business with a few employees to have a formal payroll record or a special payroll bank account. If the volume of cash payments is small and under the control of the proprietor, it is unlikely that the voucher system will be used.

As a basis for illustrating a simplified payroll procedure, the following situation is assumed: the enterprise has three employees, who are paid semimonthly on the last day of the payroll period. Payment is made by regular checks drawn on the regular bank account and all compensation is charged to Salary Expense. The voucher system is not used.

In such a situation it is not likely that a formal payroll would be prepared. At the end of each month, reference to previous records or informal notations will provide the information for the calculation of the earnings of each person. Similar sources will provide all necessary data for the determination of the amount of income tax to be withheld in each case. It is almost a certainty that some form of earnings record will be kept for each employee, as even the smallest business needs such a record to provide the information necessary for the preparation of the various tax returns and statements. Reference to this record will indicate when the earnings of each employee reaches the $3,000 or $3,600 level. Other notations will provide information about any other deductions.

A payroll check on the regular check form is given to each employee on the last day of the semimonthly period, accompanied by a memorandum showing the date, the earnings, the deductions, and the net amount paid. Each check is recorded individually as shown in the cash payments journal below. The amount of the salaries is recorded in the Salary Expense Dr. column; the liabilities for income tax and F.I.C.A. tax withholdings are recorded in the credit columns provided for this purpose; and the amount of each check is recorded in the Bank Cr. column.

CASH PAYMENTS JOURNAL

DATE		CHECK NO.	DESCRIPTION	POST. REF.	SALARY EXPENSE DR.		EMPLOYEES INCOME TAXES PAYABLE CR.		F.I.C.A. TAXES PAYABLE CR.		PURCHASE DISCOUNT CR.	BANK CR.	
1953													
Apr.	15	623	D. M. Evans........	√	220	00	22	80	3	30		193	90
	15	624	Ruth Gordon.......	√	150	00	24	40	2	25		123	35
	15	625	J. B. Smith........	√	175	00	18	10	2	63		154	27

As indicated earlier in the chapter, the employer's payroll tax may be recorded on each payday or may be deferred until the end of the month. In this illustration it will be assumed that the salaries for the second half of April are the same as for the first half and that the payroll taxes are recorded on a monthly basis. Since the employer has less than eight employees, he is not subject to the federal unemployment tax.

The laws vary as to the number of employees required to subject the employer to the state unemployment tax. Approximately half of the states exempt employers of less than eight persons. Among the others the minimum ranges from one to six; in a few cases the amount of the quarterly or annual payroll is the determining factor rather than the number of employees. Assuming that the employer is not subject to the state unemployment tax, the entry to record the F.I.C.A. tax for April is as follows:

April	30	Payroll Tax Expense....................	717	16 35	
		F.I.C.A. Taxes Payable...............	215		16 35
		Payroll tax accrued for April.			

Inasmuch as the salaries are paid on the last day of each semimonthly pay period, there is no salary accrual to record. When tax returns are prepared and checks are drawn in payment of the taxes, a record of each payment is made in the cash payments journal as a debit to the appropriate tax liability account.

This simplified procedure can be used in many situations that may be a little more complicated than the one illustrated. For example, weekly payrolls can be similarly handled, though this may give rise to end-of-fiscal-period general journal entries to record salary and tax accruals. Such entries would be reversed as of the first of the next period. Sometimes formal payrolls are prepared, but *only* for the purpose of facilitating the preparation of the paychecks themselves. The first journal record is made in the cash payments journal as illustrated.

QUESTIONS

1. Most employers are required to withhold two amounts from the earnings of their employees. (a) What are the two deductions called? (b) In what section of the employer's balance sheet will they be shown?

2. If the weekly payroll record illustrated on pages 306 and 307 was to be treated as a special journal, which of the money column totals would *not* be posted? Why?

3. What are the advantages of using a special payroll bank account?

4. The Perfection Baking Co. pays its employees semimonthly by checks drawn on a payroll bank account. (a) At what times should deposits be made in the account? (b) How is the amount of the deposit determined? (c) Will an account for the special payroll bank account be set up in the ledger? Explain.

5. Total wage and salary expense of Miami Valley Drycleaners for the year was $100,000, of which $6,000 was exempt from the F.I.C.A. tax and $15,000 was exempt from state and federal unemployment taxes. Determine the employer's payroll tax expense for the year, using the following rates: F.I.C.A., 1½%; state unemployment, 2.7%; federal unemployment, .3%.

6. When an employer who uses the voucher system pays his employees every week, a voucher is prepared for each payroll. Should a voucher also be prepared for each tax liability at the same time? Explain.

7. Apex Machinery Co. pays its employees on Friday for the week ended on Wednesday. Assuming that December 31, the last day of the fiscal year, falls on Saturday, what days must be considered in determining the year-end adjustments for wages and payroll taxes?

8. Assume the same facts as in Question 7 except that December 31 falls on Thursday. (a) What days must be considered in determining the year-end adjustment for wages and payroll taxes? (b) After the year-end adjustment has been posted to Salaries Payable, the balance of the account will represent the accrual for what period of time?

9. Why should the entry that is made at the end of the fiscal period to adjust for earnings during the current incomplete pay period be reversed at the start of the new fiscal period?

PROBLEMS

17-1. The Perfect Products Co. has nine employees. They are paid on an hourly basis, receiving time-and-one-half pay for all hours worked in excess of 40 a week. The record of time worked for the week ended Saturday, September 26, of the current year, together with other relevant information, is summarized at the top of the opposite page.

Cumulative earnings paid (before deductions) prior to the current week were as follows: A, $2,150; B, $3,120; C, $3,900; D, $2,340; E, $3,520; F, $1,050; G, $2,960; H, $2,808; I, $3,620.

E and F are office employees, the others are salesmen. A group insurance deduction of $.20 per week is made from each employee's earnings. The following tax rates apply: F.I.C.A., 1½%; state unemployment (employer only), 2.2%; federal unemployment, .3%.

| NAME | No. | M | Hours Worked | | | | | RATE PER HOUR | BOND DEDUCTION | INCOME TAX WITHHELD |
			T	W	TH	F	S			
A	41	8	8	8	8	8	4	$1.20		$ 8.50
B	36	8	8	8	4	8	4	2.00	$1.25	11.10
C	18	8	8	8	8	8	5	2.20	3.75	11.20
D	46	8	8	0	8	8	8	1.50		7.10
E	35	6	8	6	8	8	4	2.20	3.75	12.70
F	38	4	4	4	4	4	0	1.10		1.90
G	42	8	8	8	8	8	0	1.90		7.70
H	39	8	4	8	4	8	8	1.80		9.50
I	19	8	8	8	8	8	4	2.20	1.25	10.20

Instructions: (1) Prepare a payroll record similar to that illustrated on pages 306 and 307.

(2) Journalize the entry to record the payroll for the week.

(3) The company uses a voucher system and a payroll bank account. Give the entries in *general journal form* to record the payroll voucher and the payment of the payroll. The payroll checks are issued in the order of the names on the payroll, beginning with Check No. 345.

(4) Journalize the entry to record the employer's payroll taxes for the week.

17-2. The following accounts, with the balances indicated, appear in the ledger of True Value Sales Co. on December 1 of the current year:

214	Salaries Payable...............................	——
215.1	F.I.C.A. Taxes Payable.......................	$ 62.23
215.2	Employees Income Taxes Payable.............	725.30
215.3	State Unemployment Taxes Payable...........	104.60
215.4	Federal Unemployment Taxes Payable.........	190.80
216.1	Bond Deductions Payable.....................	202.25
216.2	Hospital Deductions Payable..................	52.00
611	Sales Salary Expense.........................	55,320.50
711	Officers Salary Expense.......................	22,000.00
712	Office Salary Expense.........................	6,610.30
719	Payroll Tax Expense..........................	2,622.42

The following transactions relating to payroll, payroll deductions, and payroll taxes occur during December:

Dec. 1. Prepared Voucher No. 942, payable to State Bank, for $112.50 to purchase U. S. Savings Bonds (1 at $37.50 and 4 at $18.75) for employees.

2. Issued Check No. 925 in payment of Voucher No. 942.

13. Prepared Voucher No. 968, payable to State Bank, for the amount of employees' income tax and F.I.C.A. tax due on December 15. (Pay balance of Accounts Nos. 215.1 and 215.2.)

13. Issued Check No. 950 in payment of Voucher No. 968.

Dec. 14. Prepared a general journal entry to record the biweekly payroll for the period ending today. A summary of the payroll record follows:

Deductions: F.I.C.A. tax, $27.20;   income taxes withheld, $365.20; bond deductions, $67.50; hospital deductions, $52.

Salary Distribution: officers salaries, $1,000; sales salaries, $2,515; office salaries, $310.

Cash Paid: $3,313.10.

14. Prepared Voucher No. 971, payable to Payroll Bank Account, for the net amount of the biweekly payroll.

14. Issued Check No. 953 in payment of Voucher No. 971.

15. Prepared Voucher No. 975, payable to State Bank, for $93.75 to purchase U. S. Savings Bonds (5 at $18.75) for employees.

15. Prepared Voucher No. 976, payable to Mercy Hospital, for $104 for contributions withheld from employees' earnings during the past two pay periods.

16. Issued Check No. 969 in payment of Voucher No. 975.

16. Issued Check No. 970 in payment of Voucher No. 976.

28. Prepared a general journal entry to record the biweekly payroll for the period ending today. A summary of the payroll record follows:

Deductions: F.I.C.A. tax, $24.10; income taxes withheld, $384.20; bond deductions, $67.50.

Salary Distribution: officers salaries, $1,000; sales salaries, $2,670; office salaries, $310.

Cash Paid: $3,504.20.

28. Prepared Voucher No. 998, payable to Payroll Bank Account, for the net amount of the biweekly payroll.

28. Issued Check No. 986 in payment of Voucher No. 998.

29. Prepared Voucher No. 1000, payable to State Bank, for $56.25 to purchase U. S. Savings Bonds (3 at $18.75) for employees.

29. Issued Check No. 989 in payment of Voucher No. 1000.

29. Prepared a general journal entry to record the employer's payroll taxes on earnings paid in December. Taxable earnings for the two payrolls, according to the payroll records, are as follows: subject to F.I.C.A. tax, $3,420; subject to unemployment compensation tax, $2,205. The following rates apply: F.I.C.A., $1\frac{1}{2}\%$; state unemployment, 2.1%; federal unemployment, .3%.

Instructions: (1) Open the accounts listed, and enter the balances shown under date of December 1.

(2) Record the transactions, using a voucher register like the one on page 311, a check register like the one on page 311, and a general journal. After each entry, post all items affecting the accounts opened in the ledger.

(3) Journalize the adjusting entry on December 31 to record salaries and related payroll taxes for the incomplete payroll period. Salaries accrued are as follows: officers salaries, $200; sales salaries, $534; office salaries, $62. Compute the accrued taxes at the rates given above, applying them to the full amount of the salaries. Post to the accounts.

(4) Journalize the entry to close the salary expense and payroll tax expense accounts to Profit and Loss Summary. Post to the accounts.

(5) Extend the account balances to the appropriate balance columns.

(6) Journalize the entry on January 1 to reverse the adjustment of December 31. Post to the accounts.

(7) Assume that three vouchers are prepared on January 29 for the payment of the liabilities for payroll taxes shown on December 31. Identify the taxes, the period of time to which they apply, and the amount due. Arrange your answer as follows:

VOUCHER	NAME OF TAX	PERIOD	AMOUNT
1			
2			
3			

17-3. Carl Rush, who owns the Rush Hardware Store, employs twelve people. Three office employees and four salesmen are paid straight weekly salaries; three salesmen and two deliverymen are employed on an hourly basis with time-and-a-half for hours in excess of 40 a week. The data necessary for the preparation of the payroll for the week ended September 5 of the current year are presented in the tabulation and notations below:

NAME	EMPLOYEE NO.	HOURS WORKED M T W Th F S	HOURLY OR WEEKLY RATE	INCOME TAX WITHHELD	SALARY CLASSIFICATION
Adkins, Thomas...	17	8 8 8 8 4 8	$ 1.20	$ 6.00	Sales
Barker, George....	8	8 6 8 8 8 4	1.10	4.40	Delivery
Davis, Robert.....	9		90.00	10.50	Sales
Decker, Elizabeth..	6		75.00	7.30	Office
Hatch, Fred......	2		150.00	25.90	Office
Kelley, Donald....	13		82.00	14.00	Sales
Little, Chester.....	14	8 6 8 8 8 4	1.00	3.60	Delivery
Parker, Carolyn...	12		60.00	9.60	Office
Rogers, David.....	18	8 8 8 8 8 8	1.40	6.90	Sales
Runkle, Lester....	16	8 8 6 6 8 8	1.50	5.70	Sales
Stone, Walter.....	10		85.00	6.70	Sales
Williams, Edward..	15		72.00	12.00	Sales

Prior to the present week the compensation paid (before considering deductions) to Robert Davis, Fred Hatch, and Walter Stone totaled $3,150, $5,250, and $2,975, respectively. No other employee will exceed $3,000 during the current week. The following tax rates apply: F.I.C.A., 1½%; state unemployment, 1.8%; federal unemployment, .3%.

Instructions: (1) Prepare a payroll record similar in form to the one on pages 306 and 307, deleting the deductions columns not needed and adding another column for payroll distribution.

(2) Journalize the entry to record the payroll for the week.

(3) Assuming the use of a voucher system and payment by regular check, give the entries, in *general journal form*, to record the payroll voucher and its payment. Record the check numbers on the payroll record, beginning at the top with No. 549.

The following transactions are selected from those completed by Rush Hardware Store during the remainder of September:

Sept. 14. Prepared a voucher, payable to First National Bank, for employees' income taxes, $456.40, and F.I.C.A. taxes, $92.36, on salaries paid in August. Total amount of voucher, $548.76.

   14. Issued a check to First National Bank in payment of the above voucher.

   28. Prepared a general journal entry to record the employer's payroll taxes for the payroll periods ending September 5, 12, 19, and 26. A summary of relevant information taken from the four payroll sheets follows: taxable earnings subject to F.I.C.A. tax, $3,094.30; taxable earnings subject to unemployment compensation tax, $2,419.30.

Instructions: (4) Give the entries, in *general journal form*, to record the transactions of September 14 and 28.

(5) Journalize the adjusting entry on September 30 to record the salaries and the payroll taxes for the incomplete payroll period, September 28 to 30 (Monday, Tuesday, and Wednesday). Accrue one half of the weekly salary for employees on a weekly basis. All employees on an hourly basis worked 8 hours on each of the three days. There have been no changes in weekly or hourly salary rates. The tax rates given above are to be used in accruing the payroll taxes; the salaries of Robert Davis, Fred Hatch, and Walter Stone are above the $3,000 level and are exempt from unemployment compensation taxes; the salary of Fred Hatch is above the $3,600 level and is exempt from the F.I.C.A. tax. Assemble the accrued payroll information on a form employing the following columnar headings:

				TAXABLE EARNINGS				
TOTAL						SALES	OFFICE	DELIVERY
EMPLOYEE	TIME	RATE	EARNINGS	F.I.C.A.	UNEMPLOY.	SALARY	SALARY	SALARY

18

Accounting for Taxes

NATURE OF TAXES   The operations of most governmental units are supported by required contributions called *taxes*. Taxes are levied on various segments of the population, such as property owners, consumers, business units, wage earners, and employers. There are many taxing agencies, including the federal and state governments and various local units, such as the county, city, township, and school district.

Taxes are frequently classified according to the relationship of the tax rate to the base against which the rate is applied. A tax rate that remains constant regardless of the size of the tax base is said to be a *proportional* tax. For example, when a real estate tax is levied at a single fixed rate per dollar of valuation, it is proportional. If the tax rate increases as the base against which it is levied increases, it is termed a *progressive* tax. As an example, income tax systems usually provide for successively higher rates against additional segments of income. The opposite of a progressive tax is a *regressive* tax, which is levied at lower rates as the tax base increases. For example, the fee for obtaining a corporation charter is frequently based upon the number of shares authorized, with a successively lower rate per share as the number of shares increases.

Expansion of the scope of governmental activities has been accompanied by increases in the revenue requirements. As a result, tax rates have increased and new taxes have been imposed. The particular taxes with which each business enterprise is directly concerned depend, in part, upon the location of the business, the form of its organization, the nature of its operations, and the types of property it uses.

RELATIONSHIP TO ACCOUNTING   Accounting and taxes are closely interrelated. The taxes incurred by a business enterprise usually amount to a substantial portion of the sales dollar, and it is necessary that these taxes be properly recorded in the accounts and reported in the financial statements. Some taxes are payable in advance; others accrue and are payable after the close of the period to which they relate. A knowledge of the various tax laws is essential in the determination of the period to which the tax applies and the amount of the prepayment or the accrued liability at the time a balance sheet is prepared.

The amount of the liability for many taxes is determined from information supplied by the accounting records. Outstanding examples of this type are payroll taxes, sales taxes, and income taxes. Failure on the part of the taxpayer to maintain accurate records may result in the assessment of penalties or the payment of a greater amount of tax than is required. The responsibility for preparing tax reports for a business usually rests with the accounting department.

There are four types of taxes that affect almost every business: (1) payroll taxes, (2) property taxes, (3) sales taxes, and (4) income taxes. Payroll taxes were discussed in the preceding chapter. This chapter will be devoted to a brief discussion of the remaining three. A detailed explanation of the accounting procedures applicable to each type of tax assessed against business units is obviously beyond the scope of this discussion.

NATURE OF PROPERTY TAXES   Property taxes are a principal source of revenue for local governmental units. Counties, cities, and school districts, for example, secure most, and in some cases all, of their funds by imposing taxes upon the owners of property. In some states, the state government imposes taxes on property.

Types of Property. In law, all property is either real property or personal property. *Real property*, also called *realty* or *real estate*, includes land and anything permanently attached to the land. Buildings, trees, fences, sewers, sidewalks, and other improvements to land come within the definition of real property. *Personal property*, also termed *personalty*, includes all property that is not real property.

In some states only *tangible* personalty, such as equipment and merchandise, are subject to tax. In others, a tax is also levied on *intangible* personalty, such as investments in stocks and bonds, accounts and notes receivable, and bank deposits.

It is not always a simple matter to distinguish between realty and personalty. A steam heating system permanently installed in a building is obviously a part of the building and hence real property. A portable machine used in the building is just as obviously personal property. In the case of heavy machines requiring special foundations, however, it may be necessary to consult regulations issued by the taxing authority to determine their classification for tax purposes.

Value of Property. Real estate taxes are usually based upon values determined by the tax assessor without reference to any accounting records that the owner may have. The assessed value is generally lower than the fair market value of the property. Personal property may also be appraised by an assessor, or the property owner may be required to declare his property and state its value. In the latter case the cost as recorded in the accounts is usually the starting point in determining tax value. The balance in the depreciation allowance account may be deducted from cost or the taxing authority may prescribe the rates of depreciation to be applied in arriving at the value for tax purposes.

Tax Rates. A governmental unit determines its tax rate each year by dividing the total revenue to be raised from the tax by the total assessed value of the property within its jurisdiction. For example, if the budgeted revenue requirements of a county for the year amount to $2,000,000 and the value of all taxable property in the county is $100,000,000, the county tax rate will be set at 20 mills (2 cents) per $1 of assessed value ($2,000,000 ÷ $100,000,000). A person whose property is assessed at $30,000 will be required to pay a tax of $600 for the year (.02 x $30,000). In some cases the tax rate on personal property is lower than the tax rate on real property. The tax on personal property may be determined from a separate schedule of rates, or the law may provide that personal property be listed for taxation at a specified per cent of its value, such as 50% or 70% of actual value.

Payment of Taxes. The time specified for payment of property taxes varies greatly among governmental units. Real estate and personal property taxes may be billed together or they may be billed separately and at different times. Frequently the law provides for payment in two installments. If taxes are not paid on time, they become *delinquent* and the property owner may be charged with an additional sum as a penalty. If the taxes and the penalties are not paid within a specified number of months or years, the property may be seized by the government and sold. Property taxes become a *lien* against the property, usually from the date of assessment until they are paid. A purchaser of property on which the taxes have not been paid acquires it subject to the lien, or prior claim, of the government.

In many cases property is subject to property taxes levied by more than one jurisdiction. For example, all the property located in a certain school district may also be within the boundaries of a town or city, and the latter, in turn, within a county. In such cases, it is not unusual for the county to bill and collect the taxes for all of the jurisdictions. The money collected is then distributed among the units in the proper proportion. This procedure avoids a duplication of effort and expense and is more convenient for the taxpayers.

ACCOUNTING FOR   Taxes levied on property used in a business
PROPERTY TAXES   are an operating expense.   Such property
taxes do not accrue day by day in the same way as interest or depreciation expense. The tax relates to the ownership of property at a specific
moment of time rather than to its ownership or use over a period of
time. Because the tax expense recurs each year, however, the expense
should be spread over the various months in the year. If financial
statements are prepared only once a year and a property tax billing of
$918 is received, the general journal entry would be as follows:

Mar. 25 Property Tax Expense................   918.00
          Property Taxes Payable..............   918.00
          Property tax for the year.

Payment of the tax, whether in a lump sum or in installments,
would be recorded in the usual manner, by a debit to Property Taxes
Payable and a credit to Cash. If the voucher system were employed,
an intermediate entry would be made in the voucher register to transfer
the amount to be paid from Property Taxes Payable to Accounts
Payable.

If monthly financial statements are prepared, it is necessary to
charge each month with one twelfth of the actual or estimated tax
expense for the year. In the example above, the tax statement was
received in March, the third month of the taxpayer's fiscal year. If
monthly statements are prepared, it would be necessary at the end of
January to record the estimated tax for the current month. The
estimate is based on the amount of tax paid for the preceding year,
adjusted perhaps to reflect known changes in the tax rate or assessed
value. Assuming that the estimate of property tax expense for the
current year is $900, the amount allocable to January is one twelfth of
this amount, or $75. The adjusting entry to record the accrual is as
follows:

Jan. 31 Property Tax Expense..................   75.00
          Property Taxes Payable...............   75.00

After the same entry is made at the end of February, the property
taxes payable account will have a credit balance of $150. When the tax
statement, showing a total tax of $918, is received on March 25, it is
necessary to record the additional liability of $768 ($918 minus $150).
The fact that the actual monthly expense of $76.50 ($918 ÷ 12) is
$1.50 greater than the amount estimated for January and February
may be ignored and the additional $3 may be prorated over the remain-
ing months of the year. When the difference between the actual expense
and the estimate is inconsequential, as is usually the case, there is no

need to make corrections for the months that have passed. The liability account must be credited for $768 to bring it up to $918; since the remaining $768 is to be prorated over the remaining months of the year, it is debited to Prepaid Property Taxes. The entry is as follows:

Mar. 25 Prepaid Property Taxes................ 768.00
        Property Taxes Payable..............   768.00
          Balance of liability for property taxes.

When payments of the tax are made, the liability account is debited in the usual manner.

The balance in the prepaid property taxes account is transferred to the property tax expense account on a prorata basis during the remainder of the year. The adjusting entry at the end of March is:

Mar. 31 Property Tax Expense.................   76.80
        Prepaid Property Taxes..............   76.80

The same entry is made at the end of each month. After the December 31 entry is posted, the prepaid property taxes account will be in balance.

DELINQUENT TAXES ON PROPERTY PURCHASED It is not unusual to purchase property that is subject to a lien for delinquent property taxes and penalty charges. These amounts constitute an additional cost of the property rather than expenses, since they are taken into account in arriving at the price the purchaser is willing to pay the vendor. To illustrate, assume that on February 16 Ralph Harris purchased a building site for which he agreed to pay the vendor $6,000. Delinquent taxes, penalties, and interest accumulated on the property amounted to $575. The total cost of the property is $6,575 and this amount should be debited to Land. Credits totaling the same amount will be made to Cash and the appropriate liability accounts in accordance with the terms agreed upon.

SPECIAL ASSESSMENTS The owners of land are sometimes subject to a special tax to reimburse the local government for the cost of improvements on or adjacent to their property. Such taxes are called *special assessments*. Improvements commonly financed in this way include the installation of sewers, water mains, and street lights; the paving of streets; and the laying of curbs and sidewalks. Because the benefits received for special assessment taxes continue over a long period of time, these taxes are properly chargeable to the land account rather than to an expense account. Any subsequent expenditures for repairs to the improvements, whether by way of additional assessments or through general tax levies, constitute expense.

NATURE OF SALES TAXES   Sales taxes are an important source of revenue for many states and cities. These taxes are usually imposed upon *retail* sales only, there being no tax when merchandise is purchased by a dealer for resale. In some cases certain types of rentals and the sale of services are taxable. The sale of food is sometimes exempt, as are gasoline, cigarettes, and other commodities upon which a special tax is assessed.

The tax is levied as a per cent of all sales except those specifically exempted. The tax imposed by each jurisdiction applies only to sales within its boundaries. In some cases the tax is levied directly upon the seller. It is more usual, however, to find that the law imposes the tax upon the purchaser but makes it the duty of the seller to collect the tax. Some states have a companion *use* tax on goods purchased outside the state. When use taxes are collected directly from the consumer, they are understandably difficult to administer.

Sales tax returns, accompanied by a remittance for the amount due, are required to be filed monthly, quarterly, or semiannually, depending upon the law of the state or the city. In some states merchants are required to pay in advance by purchasing sales tax stamps. When sales are made, the merchant charges the customer for the tax and gives him canceled tax stamps as a receipt. When this system is used, the merchant reports on his tax return the monetary amount of stamps canceled and also the amount of taxable sales for the period. If the application of the tax rate to the total taxable sales yields an amount larger than the sum of the stamps canceled, the merchant is required to pay the deficiency.

ACCOUNTING FOR SALES TAXES   If the law imposes a sales tax on the purchaser and requires that the merchant collect and remit to the taxing authority, the proper amount of tax must be added to each taxable sale. The tax usually attaches at the time of sale, regardless of the terms of the sale. Hence, for every taxable sale there is a debit to Cash or Accounts Receivable for the selling price plus tax, a credit to Sales for the selling price, and a credit to Sales Taxes Payable for the amount of the sales tax.

In the case of sales for cash, it is desirable, though not always feasible, to keep a record of the tax collected on each sale. If a sales ticket or invoice is prepared for each cash sale, the tax will be shown separately. If invoices are not prepared for each sale, any of several procedures may be followed. The amount of the sale and the amount of the tax may be separately recorded in the cash register if the machine has the capacity to accumulate the totals of both these elements separately. If this is not possible, the amount of the sale only may be recorded and placed in the register, and cash for the amount of the tax may be placed in a separate box or container. Any of these procedures makes it possible to know the exact amount of sales taxes collected each day on cash sales. This amount can be recorded in a special sales taxes payable column in the cash receipts journal as illustrated below:

CASH RECEIPTS JOURNAL

DATE		ACCOUNT CREDITED	POST. REF.	SALES CR.	SALES TAXES PAYABLE CR.	CASH DR.
1953						
June	1	Cash sales	✓	634.10	12.68	646.78
	2	G. L. Breen	✓			135.46
	2	Cash sales	✓	848.20	16.96	865.16

The liability for sales taxes arising from sales on account may be recorded in a special column in the sales journal as illustrated below:

SALES JOURNAL

DATE		SALE NO.	ACCOUNT DEBITED	POST. REF.	ACCOUNTS RECEIVABLE DR.	SALES TAXES PAYABLE CR.	SALES CR.
1953							
June	2	708	D. M. Madison	✓	15.30	.30	15.00
	2	709	F. J. Dolan	✓	87.72	1.72	86.00
	2	710	R. S. Andrews	✓	168.81	3.31	165.50

The total of the Sales Taxes Payable Cr. column in both journals is posted at the end of each month. It may be necessary to make similar provisions for recording reductions in Sales Taxes Payable resulting from sales returns and allowances.

Some business organizations do not find it expedient to maintain a separate record of the sales tax on each sale. In such cases the combined amount of the sale and the sales tax is recorded as a credit to Sales. At the end of the month the tax liability is computed and a general journal entry is made debiting Sales and crediting Sales Taxes Payable. To illustrate, assume credits to sales for the month, including sales taxes, of $16,520.12, and a sales tax rate of 2%. It is also assumed that all sales were subject to tax. The total of $16,520.12 is therefore assumed to be 102% of sales and the amount of sales is $16,520.12 ÷ 1.02, or $16,196.20. The sales taxes are 2% of $16,196.20, or $323.92. The entry to transfer the sales taxes from the sales account to the liability account would be as follows:

```
May 31 Sales...............................    323.92
          Sales Taxes Payable..................            323.92
             To transfer sales taxes to liability
             account.
```

An additional problem arises if not all of the sales of the business are subject to sales tax. This may be the case because certain items are exempted by law or because some of the sales are made to out-of-state or out-of-city customers. Under such circumstances it is necessary to keep a record that will show both taxable and nontaxable sales. If there is a large number of each kind of transaction, it may be necessary to use memorandum columns in the sales and cash receipts journals to accumulate the information.

Payment of the tax liability is recorded in the same manner as the payment of other liabilities. Any balance in the sales taxes payable account on a balance sheet date is reported as a current liability.

SALES TAXES IMPOSED UPON THE SELLER If the law imposes a sales tax upon the seller, the accounting problem is somewhat simplified, since there are no tax collections, as such, to be recorded. However, the records must show the amount of sales that are subject to tax in case some sales are tax-exempt. When this is known, the taxes can be computed at the end of each month and an entry made to record the expense and the liability. For example, suppose that the sales taxes for the month of April were determined to be $291.34. The following general journal entry would be necessary:

```
April 30 Sales Tax Expense.....................    291.34
            Sales Taxes Payable.................            291.34
              Sales taxes for the month.
```

Any balance in the sales taxes payable account on a balance sheet date is reported as a current liability. The sales tax expense account is closed to Profit and Loss Summary at the end of the fiscal period. There is not complete agreement as to where Sales Tax Expense should be shown on the profit and loss statement. Some accountants classify it as an operating expense, often under the heading of "Selling Expenses." Many accountants show the item as a deduction from gross sales. This latter treatment is preferable, as it shows the amount of revenue actually provided *to the business* by the sales of the period.

FEDERAL INCOME TAX The federal income tax system, which is codified in the Internal Revenue Code, dates from the ratification of the 16th Amendment to the Constitution in 1913. It is the largest single source of revenue for the federal government. For a recent year some fifty-three million income tax returns were filed by individuals; approximately three fourths of these returns required the payment of tax.

The income tax is based upon the *net income* of individuals, estates, trusts, and corporations. It is important to note that the tax is not imposed upon business units, as such, but upon taxable entities. A corporation is a legal entity that has an existence entirely apart from its stockholder owners. All business corporations are required to file an annual income tax return and to pay the amount of tax due. Even though a corporation operates several distinct and unrelated businesses, the operating results of all units are combined in a single tax return.

An unincorporated business is usually treated as a distinct entity for accounting purposes, but the business and its owners are not separable under the income tax law. The proprietor must report the net profit or the net loss of his business enterprise (or enterprises) in his personal income tax return, together with any other items of taxable income and allowable deductions of a personal nature. Partnerships are not taxable units, but they are required to file an informational return showing the results of operations and each partner's share of the profit or the loss. The individual partners then report their respective shares of the profit or the loss in their personal returns.

It is the *distributive* share of the income rather than the amount actually withdrawn that must be reported in the personal tax return of the proprietor or the partner. To illustrate, assume that John Barth is the sole proprietor of a grocery business that earned $20,000 during the current taxable year. Assume further that he is entitled to one half of the profits of Fulton and Barth, a partnership that earned $30,000 during the current taxable year. On his personal income tax return he would report the details of the operation of the grocery business, resulting in a net income of $20,000, and his distributive share of the partnership income, or $15,000. The fact that during the year he may have withdrawn only $8,000 from the sole proprietorship and $5,000 from the partnership is immaterial.

ACCOUNTING METHODS   Although there are governmental regulations prescribing the method of determining income for particular transactions and situations, the law recognizes that no uniform method of accounting can be prescribed for all taxpayers. Since each taxpayer is required to make a return of his true income, he must necessarily maintain such records as will enable him to do so. In general, taxpayers have the option of using either the *accrual basis* or the *cash basis* of determining income.

Accrual Basis. Under the accrual basis or method of accounting, income is recorded when earned, even though it is not received during the same period, and expenses are recorded when incurred, even though they are not paid during the same period. This is the method of accounting that has been developed throughout the preceding chapters of this book. The effect of the various adjusting entries for property taxes illustrated earlier in this chapter was to assign the expense to the appropriate period regardless of when the taxes were paid. Inventory adjustments at the end of the accounting period represent another of the many examples of procedures that are necessary to conform to the accrual method of accounting.

Income tax regulations require that taxpayers use inventories at the beginning and the end of the year when production, purchase, or sale of merchandise is an income-producing factor. In addition, the accrual basis must be used in accounting for purchases and sales of merchandise. Thus, a sale must be recorded as such in the year in which the goods are sold regardless of when the cash is received in payment. Similarly, the recording of purchases of merchandise may not be postponed until some later period in which payment is made. Entirely apart from income tax considerations, the accrual basis yields a fair determination of the annual income of business enterprises.

Cash Basis. In contrast to the accrual basis, the cash basis or method of accounting recognizes income in the period in which it is actually received and recognizes expenses only as they are paid. Business and professional enterprises that sell services rather than commodities frequently use the cash basis of accounting. Under this system, for example, a doctor would maintain a memorandum record of fees charged to patients, recording the fees as income only as cash is received. No provision would need to be made in the books for estimated uncollectible accounts. Accounts that eventually proved to be uncollectible would not be recorded as bad debts expense because the amounts had not previously been recorded as income. Bills for rent, electricity, and other expenses would not be recorded until they were paid. It is readily apparent that the cash basis of accounting requires fewer entries and records and is less complex than is the accrual basis.

For income tax purposes it is necessary to recognize income when it has been *constructively* received even though it has not been reduced to possession. Income is said to be constructively received when it is available to the taxpayer without any limitations. For example, if on December 31 a taxpayer receives a check or money order in payment of services, the income should be reported as earned in December, even though the instrument is not "cashed" until the following January. Other examples are interest credited to a savings account and maturing interest coupons on bonds. They are constructively received on the date the money becomes available, regardless of when the taxpayer may actually receive the cash.

A taxpayer using the cash basis may not treat the entire cost of long-lived business assets as an expense in the year of purchase. As under the accrual basis, he may deduct depreciation each year. Similarly, when property or casualty insurance premiums are paid in advance for more than one year, only the prorata amount is deductible each year.

The cash basis is used almost exclusively by individuals not engaged in business. When a taxpayer's income is composed exclusively of salary, dividends, interest, and perhaps rentals, this basis is simpler and in general yields satisfactory results. Taxpayers who do not maintain books of account are *required* to report income on the cash basis. The basis adopted must be followed consistently from year to year and may be changed only with official permission.

GROSS INCOME   An income tax return must be filed by every *individual* whose *gross income* for the taxable year equals or exceeds the minimum amount stated in the law.[1] The following excerpts from the general definition of gross income is indicative of the breadth of the term: "... includes gains, profits, and income derived from ... compensation for personal service, ... or from professions, vocations, trades, businesses, commerce, or sales, or dealings in property ... ; also from interest, rent, dividends, ... or profits and income derived from any source whatever ..."[2]

In spite of the inclusiveness of this general definition of gross income, a number of items are excluded either because they do not constitute income under the 16th Amendment or because they are specifically exempted by the Internal Revenue Code. A tabulation of the principal items included in gross income and the principal items excluded from gross income is given at the top of the following page.

The lists are illustrative only and are not meant to be complete. In practice it is often necessary to refer to the law and to interpretations of the law in order to determine whether a particular item of income is taxable or exempt from tax.

---

[1]The minimum has been $600 for a number of years. It may be changed by Congress at any time.
[2]Internal Revenue Code, Sec. 22 (a).

INCLUDED IN GROSS INCOME (Must be Reported)	EXCLUDED FROM GROSS INCOME (Not Reported)
Wages, salaries, bonuses, and commissions.	Pensions and disability compensation to war veterans and their families.
Tips and gratuities for services rendered.	Federal and state social security benefits.
Dividends and interest.	Gifts, inheritances, and bequests.
Industrial, civil service, and other pensions, and endowments (annuities may be partially exempt).	Workmen's compensation insurance, damages, etc., for bodily injury or sickness.
Rents and royalties.	Life insurance proceeds received because of death of insured.
Profits from a business or a profession.	
Taxable gains from the sale of real estate, securities, and other property.	Interest on state and municipal bonds.
	Interest on certain federal bonds issued before March 1, 1941.
The taxpayer's share of partnership profits.	Certain military pay while in a combat zone.
The taxpayer's share of estate or trust income.	
Contest prizes.	G. I. benefits and military bonuses received from federal or state governments.
Gambling winnings.	

THE TAX BASE　　The amount of the tax each individual is required to pay depends upon the amount of his gross income, the amount of the deductions that he may subtract from gross income to arrive at net income, the number of exemptions to which he is entitled, and the tax rates currently in effect. The deductions allowed by the law are of two types: (1) deductions from *gross income* to arrive at what is termed *adjusted gross income* and (2) deductions from *adjusted gross income* to arrive at *net income.* Individuals may use a so-called *standard deduction* in place of their actual deductions in the second category.

The foregoing may be presented in outline fashion as follows:

Gross Income	$9,600
Less Deductions (generally of a business nature)	2,700
Adjusted Gross Income	$6,900
Less Deductions (generally of a personal nature) or the Standard Deduction	750
Net Income	$6,150
Less Exemptions	600
Balance subject to tax (tax rates are applied to this base)	$5,550

**DEDUCTIONS FROM
GROSS INCOME**
As indicated in the outline on page 338, the deductions allowable in determining adjusted gross income are generally of a business nature. The five categories of such deductions that are of general applicability are discussed in the following paragraphs.

Business Expenses. Ordinary and necessary expenses incurred by the taxpayer in the operation of a trade, business, or profession (other than as an employee) are deductible from gross income of the business or profession. Salaries and wages, payroll taxes, property taxes, depreciation, utility expenses, insurance, advertising, travel, sales discounts, and interest on business indebtedness are examples of deductible business expenses. The tax forms provide spaces for reporting sales, cost of goods sold, gross income from sales, business expenses, and finally, net profit. This final net profit figure is the *adjusted gross income* derived from the business.

Travel Expenses of Employee. Travel expenses incurred by an employee while *away from home* in connection with his employment are deductible from gross income. Any reimbursement of such expenses received from the employer constitutes income. To illustrate, assume that during the taxable year Thomas Arnold received a salary of $6,000 and $200 as reimbursement for travel expenses. The amount spent for transportation, meals, and lodging while traveling totaled $300. Arnold's *adjusted gross income* from salary is $5,900 ($6,000 + $200 − $300).

Reimbursed Expenses of Employee. Expenses, other than travel, incurred for the benefit of the employer, are deductible from gross income by the employee to the extent of any reimbursement received from the employer. For example, Roger Trent received a salary of $8,000 and an entertainment allowance of $150 during the taxable year. During the same period he spent $200 in entertaining customers and prospective customers of his employer. Trent's adjusted gross income from salary is $8,000 ($8,000 + $150 − $150). (The $50 of expense for which he was not reimbursed is allowable as a deduction *from* adjusted gross income.)

Expenses Attributable to Rents and Royalties. Expenses incurred by a taxpayer that are directly connected with earning rent or royalty income are allowable as deductions from gross income. Expenses commonly incurred in connection with rental properties include depreciation, taxes, repairs, utilities expense, wages of custodian, and interest on indebtedness related to the property. It is apparent that the net profit derived from rental of an apartment building or other property is a part of *adjusted gross income.*

Losses from Sale or Exchange of Property. Deductible losses from the sale or the exchange of property are deductible from gross income in arriving at adjusted gross income. In order for the loss to be deductible, the property must have been acquired or held for the production of income. For example, losses from the sale of stocks and bonds are deductible; a loss from the sale of the taxpayer's residence is not deductible.

It is entirely possible for the deductible expenses in one of the above five categories to exceed the gross income to which they are related, in which case the net loss is deductible from adjusted gross income in the other categories. This may be illustrated by the following summary of adjusted gross income for Wallace Field for the current taxable year:

SOURCE OF INCOME	GROSS INCOME	TOTAL DEDUCTIONS	ADJUSTED GROSS INCOME
Salary	$5,600	$ 300	$5,300
Dividends	320		320
Interest	150		150
Rentals	1,600	1,950	(350)
Adjusted Gross Income			$5,420

DEDUCTIONS FROM ADJUSTED GROSS INCOME Allowable deductions from adjusted gross income may be classified as (1) personal expenses and (2) expenses relating to investments held for the production of income that are not a part of the taxpayer's business or profession. Items in the second category are frequently referred to as *nonbusiness* expenses. Both categories are frequently treated as one class under the term *personal* expenses. The more usual items in these two categories are discussed in the paragraphs that follow.

Contributions. Contributions by an individual to religious, charitable, educational, scientific, or literary organizations, provided they are nonprofit and are not organized for the purpose of influencing legislation. The deduction is limited to 20% of adjusted gross income.

Interest. Interest may be personal, such as on indebtedness on the taxpayer's home, or nonbusiness, as on indebtedness incurred to buy securities. (Interest attributable to a business or to rents and royalties are deductible from *gross income.*)

Taxes. Most nonfederal taxes are deductible from adjusted gross income. Examples of taxes that are deductible and that are not deductible follow:

DEDUCTIBLE	NOT DEDUCTIBLE
Real estate taxes.	State inheritance taxes.
Personal property taxes.	Hunting and fishing licenses.
State income taxes.	Auto inspection fees.
Retail sales taxes assessed against the consumer.	Federal estate and gift taxes.
Auto license fees.	Federal income taxes.
State gasoline taxes.	F.I.C.A. taxes (employee's share).
Poll taxes.	Federal excise taxes on *personal* expenditures, such as taxes on furs, jewelry, cosmetics, admissions, transportation, and telephone.

Losses. Losses of nonbusiness property resulting from fire, storm, automobile accident, or other casualty, or from theft, are deductible to the extent not compensated for by insurance. It should be noted that only loss or damage to the taxpayer's own property is deductible; there is no deduction for personal injuries or for damages to another's property caused by the taxpayer. The basis for determining the amount of any casualty loss of nonbusiness property is the cost less depreciation or the fair market value of the property, whichever is lower.

Medical Expenses. Medical and dental expenses paid are deductible to the extent that they exceed 5% of adjusted gross income. For example, if the taxpayer has adjusted gross income of $6,000 and medical expenses of $350, only $50 of the medical expenses can be deducted ($350 − 5% of $6,000). Medical expenses include such items as the cost of eyeglasses, hearing aids, artificial teeth, medicines, and hospital expenses. If the taxpayer or his spouse are 65 years of age or older, they are not subject to the 5% restriction on medical expenses incurred for either one. There are also maximum limits on the total amount of medical expenses that can be deducted, based on marital status and the number of exemptions claimed.

Miscellaneous. Certain expenses incurred in the production of income are deductible. Examples are union dues, rental of safe deposit box used for safekeeping of securities, and fees paid to an investments counselor.

If the total of the foregoing deductions of the taxpayer is less than the amount of the standard deduction, the taxpayer should use the latter. The standard deduction is equal to 10% of the adjusted gross income or $1,000, whichever is the lesser amount. For example, if the taxpayer's adjusted gross income is $7,000 and the itemized deductions total $450, he may claim the standard deduction of $700 (10% of $7,000), reporting net income of $6,300. If adjusted gross income is

$12,000 and the itemized deductions total $1,400, the taxpayer should itemize his deductions (the standard deduction may not exceed $1,000), reporting net income of $10,600. The standard deduction was claimed on about 80% of all individual tax returns filed in a recent year.

EXEMPTIONS   As a means of adjusting the burden of taxation to the economic responsibilities of the taxpayers, the law permits a credit against net income for certain exemptions. In recent years the amount of each exemption has been $600, though it may be changed at any time by Congress. Each taxpayer is entitled to one exemption for himself.

If husband and wife file a joint return (combining the income and the deductions of both) they may claim two exemptions. An additional exemption may be taken for each dependent. A dependent is a person who meets all of the following requirements: (1) received over one half of his support from the taxpayer during the year, (2) had less than $600 of gross income during the year, and (3) is closely related to the taxpayer.

A taxpayer and his spouse may each claim an extra exemption for blindness, and another exemption if he or she is 65 years of age or older. Thus, if both a taxpayer and his wife are over 65 and both are blind, they may take a total of six personal exemptions. The extra exemptions for blindness and old age do not apply to dependents.

The amount of income to which the tax rates apply is net income less the sum of the exemption credits.

For the convenience of taxpayers who have adjusted gross incomes of less than $5,000 and who do not wish to itemize their personal deductions, the government has prepared tax tables that provide for the standard deduction. The table shows the tax for any amount of adjusted gross income (up to $5,000) for various numbers of exemptions.

CAPITAL GAINS AND LOSSES   Gains and losses resulting from the sale or the exchange of certain kinds of assets are accorded special treatment for income tax purposes. Such properties are termed *capital assets*, and the gains and losses incurred upon their sale or exchange are called *capital gains* and *capital losses*. Capital assets most commonly held by taxpayers include shares of stock, bonds, personal residence, and land. Under certain conditions equipment and buildings used in business are also treated as capital assets. Details of capital gains and losses must be reported on a special schedule provided for the purpose and attached to the income tax return. The statutes and regulations regarding this subject are too voluminous and complex for inclusion in this brief discussion of the federal income tax.

INCOME TAX RATES   The taxable net income of each individual is subject to both a *normal tax* and a *surtax.* At one time these rates applied to different bases in almost every case. Certain types of income were subject to the surtax only. This is still true, but to a very limited extent. At the present time all of the net income of most taxpayers is subject to both taxes. For that reason the government provides combined normal tax and surtax rate schedules to meet the needs of the majority of taxpayers.

A characteristic of the income tax rates is their progressive nature. The rates are established on a bracketed basis; successive segments of income are subject to increasing percentages of tax. Following is a short table of hypothetical rates, presented in a form that illustrates the progressive feature:

First $2,000 of taxable income subject to a rate of 20%.
Next $2,000 of taxable income subject to a rate of 22%.
Next $2,000 of taxable income subject to a rate of 26%.
Next $2,000 of taxable income subject to a rate of 30%.
Next $2,000 of taxable income subject to a rate of 34%.
Next $2,000 of taxable income subject to a rate of 38%.
Etc.

At these assumed rates, the tax on an income of $5,000 (net after all deductions and exemption credits) would be as follows:

$2,000 at 20% = $ 400
 2,000 at 22% =   440
 1,000 at 26% =   260
                 ———————
    Total $1,100

The schedule of rates is frequently changed by Congress, but the progressive characteristic is a permanent feature of the income tax system.

Husband and Wife. Husbands and wives may file separate returns or they may combine their income, deductions, and exemptions in a single *joint* return. In recent years a husband and wife filing a joint return have been permitted to calculate their tax as twice the amount of the tax on one half of their combined net taxable income. For example, assume that on a joint return of a married couple the final balance subject to tax amounts to $10,000. The tax on $5,000 (½ of $10,000), computed at the hypothetical rates above, is $1,100. Multiplication by two yields a total tax of $2,200. If the tax had been computed on the $10,000 without regard to the split-income provision, the tax, using the same schedule, would have amounted to $2,640. The split-income provision was enacted to give all married taxpayers the tax advantage previously enjoyed only by married residents of states having community property laws.

Head of Household. Beginning with 1952, unmarried persons qualifying as a head of a household have been taxed at lower rates than those applicable to other unmarried persons. The reduced rates were enacted to extend part of the benefits of the split-income provision to unmarried persons who maintain a household in which they and their children or other dependents live. To qualify as the head of a household an individual must be unmarried at the close of the taxable year and must maintain as his home a household in which one or more of the following described persons live: (a) an unmarried son or daughter or one of their descendants, or (b) any other person who qualifies as a dependent.

TAX RETURNS; Every individual who has a gross income for
PAYMENT the year in excess of the minimum stated in
the law must file a tax return. This is true even though he may not have to pay any tax. A taxpayer who maintains books of account may choose for his fiscal year any twelve-month period ending on the last day of a month. Most individual taxpayers choose the calendar year. The period chosen cannot be changed without permission from the government. A taxpayer who does not keep books must file on a calendar year basis.

An annual tax return must be filed within two and one-half months after the end of the taxpayer's taxable year, accompanied by any balance due. A taxpayer whose income has been subject to tax withholding or who has been making payments on his estimated tax may find he has no more to pay, but he must nevertheless file a final return. If his tax has been overpaid, he may either ask for a refund or apply the credit against his tax liability for the next year.

The manner in which employers withhold income tax from wages paid to their employees was discussed in the preceding chapter. An individual whose income is not subject to withholding, or only partially so, or an individual whose income is fairly large must estimate his income tax in advance and file a tax form known as a *Declaration of Estimated Income Tax*. The estimated tax for the year, after deducting the estimated amount to be withheld and any credit for overpayment from previous years, must be paid during the year. There is provision for installment payments in most cases. In general, owners of businesses, professional people, taxpayers whose estimated income from salary exceeds certain minimum amounts, and persons with anticipated income from investments are required to follow this procedure. They must, of course, also file a final return at the proper time and pay any balance due or indicate the disposition of any overpayment.

INDIVIDUAL INCOME TAX PROBLEM ILLUSTRATED John B. Walsh owns and operates a grocery store; he also owns an apartment house. He is married and has three children, whom he supports. The oldest child received income of $650 during the year; the second child earned $70; the third child and Mrs. Walsh had no income. Both Mr. and Mrs. Walsh are under 65 years of age and are not blind.

According to Mr. Walsh's books of account and other records, his gross income for the year and his various deductions were as follows:

Net profit from business owned..........................	$20,000
(Sales, $110,000; cost of goods sold, $64,000; total business expenses, $26,000.)	
Net income from rent of apartment building..............	2,200
(Rent income, $4,000; taxes, $450; insurance, $150; repairs, $400; depreciation, $800.)	
Dividends on corporation stocks........................	400
Interest on corporation bonds..........................	300
Life insurance proceeds received.......................	10,000
(Policy on life of taxpayer's mother, who died during year.)	
Contributions to church, Community Chest, Red Cross, etc...	600
Interest payments on personal loans....................	200
Property taxes on residence............................	250
State sales tax paid on items bought for family use........	150
Fire loss at home.....................................	500
(Damage, $3,000; received from insurance company, $2,500.)	
Family medical expenses...............................	450
Payments during year on Declaration of Estimated Income Tax...	4,500

On the basis of the foregoing facts and the schedule of tax rates appearing on page 343, the tax liability of Mr. and Mrs. Walsh on a joint return will be computed as shown on the following page. It will be realized that in actual practice the official tax form would be used and that additional supporting information would be given.

There are several points in the illustration that should be noted. The allowable deductions from gross income are subtracted from the particular gross income to which they relate, yielding the adjusted gross income for that particular activity. In the tax form special schedules are provided for reporting details of business operations,

MR. AND MRS. JOHN B. WALSH
COMPUTATION OF FEDERAL INCOME TAX

Income:

Business:

Sales		$110,000	
Cost of goods sold		64,000	
Gross profit		$ 46,000	
Expenses		26,000	
Net income from business			$20,000

Apartment building:

Rent income		$ 4,000	
Taxes	$450		
Insurance	150		
Repairs	400		
Depreciation	800	1,800	
Net income from apartment building			2,200
Dividends on corporation stocks			400
Interest on corporation bonds			300
Adjusted gross income			$22,900

Personal Deductions:

Contributions	$ 600	
Interest	200	
Property taxes	250	
State sales tax	150	
Fire loss	500	
Total	1,700	
Net income		$21,200
Less: 4 exemptions at $600 each		2,400
Balance subject to tax		$18,800
One half of balance subject to tax		$ 9,400

Tax on $9,400:

$2,000 at 20%	$ 400	
2,000 at 22%	440	
2,000 at 26%	520	
2,000 at 30%	600	
1,400 at 34%	476	$ 2,436
Total tax (2 x $2,436)		$ 4,872
Tax payments during year		4,500
Balance due (to accompany tax return)		$ 372

rent income, dividends, and interest. The net gain or loss from each schedule is then carried to one page, where all items of adjusted gross income are totaled.

The insurance proceeds of $10,000 are not taxable. The income earned by the two children is not taxable to the parents. Since the earnings of the oldest child exceeded $599.99, the parents may not claim an exemption for him. He would be required to file a tax return.

Contributions were well below the 20% limitation and were fully deductible. The total medical expenses were less than 5% of adjusted gross income; hence none of the amount was deductible. The standard deduction allowable in this case was $1,000; since the actual deductions exceeded this amount, it was advantageous to claim the actual deductions.

INCOME TAX   Most individuals do not find it necessary to
RECORDS   keep formal journals and ledgers relating to
their personal financial affairs. It is apparent, however, that each taxpayer should keep records that are sufficient to enable him to prepare his tax returns. It is wise to keep a copy of all returns submitted. A record of all tax withholdings and payments should also be retained. The burden of proof as to the accuracy of income tax calculations and the payments that have been made rests upon the taxpayer.

Since the income of an unincorporated business, as such, is not taxed, it is not necessary to have an account for income tax in the ledger. If the proprietor pays his tax by checks drawn on the business bank account, the transactions are recorded as personal withdrawals.

QUESTIONS

1. Identify the following as realty or personalty: (a) building, (b) sidewalk, (c) shares of stock, (d) copyright, (e) steam pipes installed in building, (f) notes receivable, (g) portable electric fan.

2. The total assessed value of all real estate in a school district is $10,000,000. The district needs $100,000 to operate the schools for the year. (a) What will the tax rate be? (b) A resident of the district whose real estate is assessed at $12,000 will be required to pay what amount for support of the schools?

3. The current real estate tax rate for Wayne City is $22.41 per thousand dollars of valuation. Equipment and furniture used in business are subject to tax at the same rate, based on 50% of the book value of such personalty. On tax listing day the accounts of Robert Mann show the cost of all equipment and furniture to be $14,400 and total related allowances for depreciation to be $3,200. What is the amount of Mann's tax on equipment and furniture?

4. Edward Jones purchased for $4,000 vacant land on which there are delinquent taxes and penalties amounting to $950. Present the entries, in general journal form, to record (a) payment of $1,000 in cash and the issuance of a mortgage note for $3,000, and (b) payment of the total penalties and interest.

5. All sales of a store are subject to a state sales tax of 3% levied upon consumers but collectible by the seller. As sales are made, the amount of the sale and the tax are credited to the sales account. The total credits to the sales account for a particular day were $982.31. How much of this amount is presumed to be sales and how much is presumed to be tax?

6. Arthur Greene is required to pay a special assessment of $250 for permanent improvements to the street adjoining his business property. Give the entry, in general journal form, to record the payment of the assessment.

7. In each of the following cases state the amount of income that the taxpayer should include in his personal income tax return:
  (a) The taxpayer is the sole proprietor of a business that earned a net profit of $30,000 during the year. The taxpayer withdrew $12,000 from the business during the year.
  (b) The taxpayer is a partner in a business that earned a net profit of $52,000 during the year. The taxpayer's distributive share is $21,000; he withdrew $18,000 from the business during the year.
  (c) The taxpayer owns 50% of the stock of the Mayfield Corporation which earned a net profit of $120,000 during the year before federal income taxes. The corporation federal income tax amounted to $55,000. During the year the taxpayer received cash dividends on his stock in the amount of $20,000.

8. J. M. Gard uses the cash basis in determining income for income tax purposes. State whether the following items should be reported as income in December or in January:
  (a) Bond interest coupons payable on December 31; deposited in the bank on January 20.
  (b) Weekly salary check dated and received on January 2, deposited in the bank on January 4. The salary was in payment of services rendered for the week ended December 30. The three-day interval between the end of the payroll period and the payday is usual for this employer.
  (c) Dividend check dated December 31; received January 3; deposited in the bank on January 7.

9. Which of the items stated below should George Spencer report on his income tax return:
  (a) Salary as salesman for the City Tire Company.
  (b) Dividends on General Motors stock.
  (c) Interest on notes receivable.
  (d) Proceeds from life insurance policy received upon death of a relative.
  (e) Profit on sale of corporation bonds.
  (f) Corporation stocks received as a legacy from a deceased friend.
  (g) Cash gift from an uncle.
  (h) Dividends on stock received as a legacy in (f) above.

10. Identify the following items as (1) deductible from gross income in determining adjusted gross income, (2) deductible from adjusted gross income in determining net income, or (3) not deductible:

    (a) Salaries paid to employees in the taxpayer's business.

    (b) Contributions to a political party.

    (c) Automobile license fee (car not used in business).

    (d) Interest on mortgage on taxpayer's residence.

    (e) Federal excise tax on purchase of jewelry.

    (f) Travel expenses incurred by employee while away from home on employer's business.

    (g) Insurance on taxpayer's residence.

    (h) State sales taxes on goods purchased for personal use.

    (i) Union dues.

    (j) Medical expenses amounting to 2% of the adjusted gross income.

    (k) Loss, not covered by insurance, as a result of an accident to the taxpayer's personal automobile.

11. A taxpayer and his wife file a joint return. Both are over 65 years of age and the wife is blind. State the number of exemptions to which they are entitled.

PROBLEMS

18-1. The Ross Mercantile Company prepares interim statements at the end of each month and closes its books annually on December 31. On January 31 of the current year Mr. Ross estimates that the property taxes assessed against the business for the current year will be $840. The statement for property taxes, showing a liability of $880, is received on March 20. Half of this amount is paid on April 15 and half is paid on October 15.

Instructions: (1) Give all of the entries in chronological order, in general journal form, to record monthly adjusting entries for the first six months of the year, the tax liability upon receipt of the tax bill on March 20, and the payment of half of the tax on April 15.

(2) What items relative to property taxes should appear on the balance sheet of February 28? of March 31? of April 30? of June 30? of November 30? (Give account titles and amounts.)

18-2. The balances in certain accounts of Hart Sales Company on March 31, the end of the first quarter of the current fiscal year, are as follows:

Sales Taxes Payable	Cr.	$ 2,315.22
Sales	Cr.	90,420.00
Sales Returns and Allowances	Dr.	3,160.00

An analysis of supplementary records for the same three-month period reveals the following:

Sales:

Taxable	$80,340
Nontaxable	10,080

Sales Returns and Allowances:

Taxable..	2,850
Nontaxable......................................	310

The state law requires that the dealer collect a sales tax of 3% on all sales to consumers other than those specifically exempted; and further, that the dealer remit the amount collected or 3% of taxable sales, whichever is larger.

Instructions: (1) Give the entry on March 31 to record the additional liability for sales taxes for the first quarter of the year. (Debit Sales Tax Expense.)

(2) Give the entry on April 15, in general journal form, to record payment of the sales tax liability for the first quarter.

18-3. Paul Harris is a physician. He is unmarried, under 65 years of age, and has good vision. During the current calendar year he contributed more than half of the cost of supporting his mother, whose own income during the year amounted to $200. His mother is over 65 years of age and lives with her daughter.

Dr. Harris has maintained a detailed record of his cash receipts and disbursements, including those of a personal nature as well as those connected with his profession. A summary of all receipts and disbursements of cash during the current year, which is his first full year of professional practice, follows:

Receipts:

Professional fees...................................	$19,643
Inheritance from grandfather's estate.................	1,000
Borrowed from bank (professional purposes)...........	2,500
Dividends on corporation stocks......................	120
State bonus to men having served in the armed forces....	100

Disbursements:

Cost of new automobile (purchased January 4)..........	3,000
Medical equipment (purchased July 10)................	800
Salary of receptionist...............................	3,600
Payroll taxes.......................................	45
Rent of office......................................	2,400
Telephone expense (office)...........................	125
Electricity (office).................................	168
Insurance on office and medical equipment (1 year policy)..	32
Payment on loan from bank (see above)...............	1,500
Medical supplies expense............................	112
Interest on bank loan...............................	120
Automobile operating expenses (gasoline, oil, etc.).......	520
Purchase of Ajax Corporation stock..................	926
Life insurance premium..............................	375
Contribution to church, Community Chest, and Red Cross.	350
Personal and living expenses (self and mother)..........	4,865
Payment on Declaration of Estimated Income Tax.......	2,500

The automobile was used 50% of the time for professional purposes. It is to be depreciated on the basis of 4 years of life and a trade-in value of $800. Allocate half of the depreciation and other automobile expenses to professional purposes.

Medical and office equipment was acquired in the previous year at a cost of $4,100. Use a composite depreciation rate of 10%, taking depreciation for one-half year on the medical equipment purchased on July 10 of the current year.

Instructions: Compute Dr. Harris's income tax, patterning your solution after the illustration on page 346. Use the table of tax rates appearing on page 343.

18-4. George L. Hood is married and has three dependent children. One of the children earned $680 during the current year, another earned $100, and the third had no income. Both Mr. and Mrs. Hood are under 65 years of age and have good vision. Details of their receipts and expenditures, exclusive of nondeductible personal expenses, for the current year ended December 31 are as follows:

Receipts — Mr. Hood:

Salary as manager of Monarch Department Store............	$12,726.00
(Earnings, $15,000; income tax withheld, $2,220; F.I.C.A. tax withheld, $54)	
Reimbursement for travel expenses (travel for Monarch).....	628.50
Rent from rental property owned........................	2,400.00
Dividends on corporation stocks........................	350.75

Receipts — Mrs. Hood:

Withdrawals from Johnson Enterprises, a partnership in which she is a partner (distributive share of the net profit for the year, $4,200)..	3,000.00
Dividends on corporation stocks........................	315.00
Interest on corporation bonds..........................	150.00
Interest on bonds of City of Richmond...................	70.00

Expenditures — Mr. Hood:

Travel expenses on trips for Monarch Department Store......	652.00
Rental property:	
Property taxes......................................	165.00
Insurance (one year policies).........................	75.00
Painting and repairs.................................	393.50
Interest on mortgage................................	200.00
Building was acquired several years ago at a cost of $16,000 and is being depreciated at the rate of 5%	
Charitable contributions...............................	650.00
Interest on mortgage on residence.......................	180.00
Automobile license fee on family car....................	15.00
Real estate tax on residence............................	172.51
Sales taxes on items purchased for personal or family use.......	40.00
Damages to family car resulting from an accident (no insurance)...	520.00
Payments during year on Declaration of Estimated Income Tax...	1,600.00

Expenditures — Mrs. Hood

Charitable contributions...............................	200.00

Instructions: Compute Mr. and Mrs. Hood's income tax (joint return), patterning your solution after the illustration on page 346. Use the table of tax rates appearing on page 343.

Chapter 19

Partnership Formation and Operation

THE PARTNERSHIP
DEFINED
If a sole proprietor deems it advisable, he may ask one or more associates to join him in the development of his business. The new party ordinarily contributes cash or other property. The members of the new association are co-owners of the business and share its profits and losses. In this way a partnership is established. A partnership may also be formed when two or more persons decide to start a new business in which they are co-owners and share in profits and losses.

The Uniform Partnership Act, adopted by a large number of the states, calls the partnership "an association of two or more persons to carry on as co-owners a business for profit." This definition states clearly the nature of a partnership from the legal point of view. The partnership may be better understood from the business point of view by considering the characteristics that distinguish it from other forms of business organization.

CHARACTERISTICS OF
THE PARTNERSHIP
The fundamental characteristic of a partnership is expressed in the definition given above, in that it is an association of persons. It is distinctly a personal organization, and from that personal aspect the following essential characteristics are derived:

1. *Mutual Agency.* Each partner is the agent of the partnership. For example, one partner can make an agreement to purchase goods or services for the firm, and the other partners will be bound by his act if the goods or the services are such as the business uses or might use in the course of its affairs.

2. *Limited Life.* A partnership, because of its personal nature, is short lived. It may be dissolved as the result of any one of a variety of causes. The death, incapacity, or withdrawal of one of the partners causes a dissolution of the partnership; if a partner sells his interest, the partnership terminates; if the members admit another partner, the old partnership ends but a new partnership is brought into existence. Partnership reorganization and dissolution are discussed in Chapter 20.

3. *Unlimited Liability.* Each member of a partnership is jointly and individually liable for the debts of the partnership. Therefore a partner may not only lose what he has invested in the partnership, but also be required to use his private property to pay the debts of the partnership if the business becomes insolvent. For example, if Dixon and Regan each invest $10,000 in a partnership and through ill luck or poor management the partnership later has liabilities of $15,000 and assets of only $13,000, the creditors may recover the $2,000 excess of the liabilities over the assets from either Dixon or Regan individually.

4. *Co-ownership of Partnership Property.* The property invested by a partner in a partnership is no longer his own personal property but is jointly owned by all partners. For this reason it is essential that the valuation placed on the contributed property be a fair and just one. For example, if Jackson contributes a building that cost him $15,000 but is now worth $30,000, the value of the building to the partnership is $30,000. After he has made his contribution, the partner has only a dollar and cents claim against all the assets of the partnership.

5. *Participation in Partnership Profits.* Another feature essential to a partnership is the co-ownership of the profits. If the profits are shared on any basis other than co-ownership, a partnership does not exist. For example, an employee who is given a percentage of profits as remuneration for his services is not thereby a partner. There must be an intention of the partners regarding co-ownership of profits and losses.

ACCOUNTING FOR PARTNERSHIPS   Much of the accounting for a partnership is the same as that for a business with any other form of ownership. The current transactions completed in the general operation of the business are similar; and the accounting process, as well as the papers, the records, and the reports employed, is essentially the same. The relationships existing between the members of a partnership give rise to transactions that are not common to the sole proprietorship. These transactions have to do with the formation, the operation, and the dissolution of the partnership. The operation phase is principally that of participation in partnership profits, which will be discussed in this chapter.

FORMATION OF A PARTNERSHIP   A partnership is founded upon a voluntary contract having all the essential elements of any other contract. Since the interest in the partnership here is primarily from the point of view of accounting, the various legal questions arising from the relationship of the partners will not be discussed at any length.

Disputes, misunderstandings, and difficult situations are liable to arise in a partnership because of the peculiar relationship existing between the partners. To prevent these, or at least to reduce them to a minimum, a written contract should be drawn up. This contract is known as the *articles of copartnership*. In addition to the date and the signatures of the partners, it should contain the following data, as well as any other provisions that may be considered desirable:

1. Name and location of the business.
2. Nature and life of the undertaking.
3. Names of the partners and the amount of the investment of each.
4. Provision for sharing in profits and losses.
5. Rights and duties of each partner.
6. Provision for accounting records.
7. Provision for dissolution.
8. Special provisions and stipulations.

After the partners have reached an agreement and have signed the articles of copartnership, the assets may be acquired and the opening entries may be made in the partnership books. The problems of partnership formation may be classified under two headings:

(1) Original formation of partnership by:
    (a) Adding a new member or new members to a sole proprietorship.
    (b) Cash or property contributions by members to set up a new business.
(2) Modification in personnel of a going partnership by:
    (a) Selling an interest to a new partner or new partners.
    (b) Accepting an investment from a new partner or new partners.

The accounting procedures for the first group are treated in this chapter; for the second group, in Chapter 20.

OPENING ENTRIES FOR A PARTNERSHIP — INVESTMENT OF CASH A brief reference to the articles of copartnership may be given in the general journal before the entries to record the investments of the partners are made. For example, when J. R. Morgan and L. C. Evans form a partnership by the investment of cash, the following memorandum entry may be made in the general journal:

> July 2 J. R. Morgan and L. C. Evans formed a partnership for the purpose of conducting a retail hardware business in accordance with the articles of copartnership signed this day in duplicate.

Since the partners in this case are investing only cash, the record of the cash investment will appear in the cash receipts journal. Such an entry is shown below:

CASH RECEIPTS JOURNAL

DATE			ACCOUNT CREDITED	POST. REF.	GENERAL CR.	SALES CR.	ACCTS. REC. CR.	SALES DISC. DR.	CASH DR.
1953 July	2		J. R. Morgan, Capital		10,000				10,000
	2		L. C. Evans, Capital		10,000				10,000

OPENING ENTRIES FOR A PARTNERSHIP — TRANSFER OF ASSETS AND LIABILITIES If the partners invest assets in addition to cash and transfer liabilities to the partnership, either of two methods may be used in recording the investment: (1) An entry may be made in the cash receipts journal to record the cash investment, and another entry may be made in the general journal to record the other assets and the liabilities; or (2) the entire investment may be recorded in the general journal, and the cash investment may be recorded in the cash receipts journal. In the latter case, the cash debits will be checked in the general journal and the capital credits will be checked in the cash receipts journal so that duplicate posting will be avoided.

To illustrate such entries, it is assumed that on January 2 John Davis and Harold Stone, who have been conducting rival sports equipment stores, enter into a partnership by consolidating their assets and liabilities. The assets and the liabilities of John Davis are as follows: cash, $2,000; accounts receivable, $7,000; merchandise inventory, $7,500; store equipment, $4,750; notes payable, $1,000; accounts payable, $4,250. The assets and the liabilities of Harold Stone are as follows: cash, $3,000; notes receivable, $1,000; accounts receivable, $6,000; merchandise inventory, $8,500; office equipment, $2,500; building, $7,500; land, $4,000; accounts payable, $8,500.

The following entries are made in the partnership general journal:

Jan. 2 Cash...	√ 2,000	
Accounts Receivable.............................	7,000	
Merchandise Inventory..........................	7,500	
Store Equipment................................	4,750	
Notes Payable................................		1,000
Accounts Payable..............................		4,250
John Davis, Capital............................		16,000
To record the investment of John Davis.		

```
 2  Cash.......................................... √ 3,000
       Notes Receivable..............................    1,000
       Accounts Receivable...........................    6,000
       Merchandise Inventory.........................    8,500
       Office Equipment..............................    2,500
       Building......................................    7,500
       Land..........................................    4,000
          Accounts Payable...........................              8,500
          Harold Stone, Capital......................             24,000
             To record the investment of Harold Stone.
```

The entries in the cash receipts journal to record the cash invested by Davis and Stone are as follows:

CASH RECEIPTS

DATE			ACCOUNT CREDITED	POST. REF.	GENERAL CR.	SALES CR.	ACCTS. REC. CR.	SALES DISC. DR.	CASH DR.
1953 Jan.	2		John Davis, Capital	√	2,000				2,000
	2		Harold Stone, Capital	√	3,000				3,000

It should be understood that the amounts shown in the foregoing journal entries were those agreed upon by the two partners at the time they set up the partnership. For example, the $4,750 figure for store equipment and the $2,500 figure for office equipment were estimates of present market value established by mutual consent of the partners. Although the book value of assets contributed to a partnership may influence the values at which they are taken over, the values recorded on the books of the new partnership may be quite different from the values at which the assets were carried on the books of their former owners.

Fixed assets are ordinarily recorded on the books of the new partnership at the values assigned to them in the partnership agreement. Future depreciation on the partnership records is based on these values. For income tax purposes, however, depreciation of partnership assets must be based on the original cost of the assets. Nevertheless, in the discussions and problems in this book, it will be assumed, unless a statement is made to the contrary, that all depreciation of assets acquired at the time of the formation of a partnership is based on the values assigned to those assets at that time.

In the case of partner Stone, the land may have cost him $2,000 when he acquired it several years before. The building may have cost $10,000 and may have been depreciated to a book value of $5,000. Because of increases in land values and building costs, the only fair course was to establish new values of $4,000 for the land and $7,500 for the building, increases of 100% over the original cost of the land and 50% over the present book value of the building.

DRAWING ACCOUNTS OF THE PARTNERS   The articles of copartnership may provide that each partner will be permitted to withdraw cash at intervals during the course of operations. If this is the case, the withdrawals are debited to the partners' drawing accounts. A partner's drawing account is, in nature, the same as the drawing account of a sole proprietor. At the end of the fiscal period the partner's share of the profit or the loss is closed into his drawing account. The debit or the credit balance of the drawing account is permitted to remain in that account or is transferred to the capital account, the procedure depending upon the partners' agreement.

For example, at the end of the first fiscal year, the drawing accounts of Davis and Stone have debit balances of $10,000 and $5,000 respectively. If the profit for the year, $18,000, is to be distributed equally, the entry to close the profit and loss summary account will consist of a debit of $18,000 to Profit and Loss Summary and a credit of $9,000 to each of the partners' drawing accounts.

Davis' drawing account will now have a debit balance of $1,000; Stone's drawing account, a credit balance of $4,000. In accordance with the terms of the partners' agreement, these balances may be permitted to remain in the drawing accounts, or they may be closed into the partners' capital accounts, reducing the capital of Davis and increasing the capital of Stone.

DIVISION OF PROFITS   The distribution of profits or losses frequently presents one of the most difficult problems in partnership accounting. If the partners have no agreement in this respect, the law provides that profits or losses should be divided equally, regardless of the amounts of the investments. The partners may, however, make any agreement they wish in regard to the division of profits or losses. The agreement should be quite specific so that misunderstandings will be avoided.

Partnership profits include a return for partners' services, for partners' capital investments, and for economic or pure profit. Since the partnership is a personal organization, the services of the partners come free of cost to the partnership. In the absence of a specific agreement, the partners receive no salaries. The capital contributions of partners do not bear interest. Profits must therefore be interpreted to include these two factors as well as pure profits.

If the service and capital contributions of partners are equal, an equal sharing in partnership profits is equitable. But if one partner contributes three times as much capital as the other, the distribution of profits should take into account the unequal contribution of capital. Or, if the services of one partner are much more valuable to the partnership than those of the other, provision for unequal service contributions should be made in profit participation.

Arising out of the recognition of these three factors in partnership profits, many methods of distributing profits or losses are employed. Fundamentally, these methods give effect to the three elements found in partnership profits.

PROFITS DISTRIBUTED ON FIXED RATIO The simplest formula for profit sharing is agreement in advance on a fixed ratio that will continue for the life of the partnership. This fixed ratio may provide for an equal sharing on the assumption that partners' contributions of capital, services, and risk entitle them to such a sharing. It may give one partner two thirds and the other partner one third for similar reasons. Or it may provide any fractional participation that seems fair to all the partners.

When profits are distributed on a fixed ratio, the problem is simple. After the profit for a fiscal period has been determined, it is divided according to this fixed ratio, the profit and loss summary account being debited and the partners' drawing accounts being credited. The table below shows the participation of Davis and Stone in a partnership profit of $18,000 using three different fixed ratios:

FIXED RATIO		DAVIS' SHARE	STONE'S SHARE
(1) ½	½	$9,000	$ 9,000
(2) ⅓	⅔	6,000	12,000
(3) ¼	¾	4,500	13,500

The closing entry on December 31 to record the distribution of the profit under the third fixed ratio above would be as follows:

Dec. 31 Profit and Loss Summary...................... 18,000
     John Davis, Drawing......................... 4,500
     Harold Stone, Drawing...................... 13,500

PROFITS DISTRIBUTED WITH EMPHASIS ON INVESTMENTS If the investments of partners are to be given separate consideration in profit sharing, there is a choice between two commonly used methods. In the first method participation of partners in profits is based solely on their capital investments; in the second method an interest return is allowed on capital investments and the balance is distributed according to the fixed-ratio method. Each of these two methods that emphasize capital contributions will be described.

According to Investments — Opening Capital. The profits may be divided according to the beginning investments. For example, if Davis and Stone had agreed to divide profits or losses on the basis of their original investments, their respective shares of the profit for the first year would have been computed in the following manner:

John Davis, Investment of January 2.................... $16,000
Harold Stone, Investment of January 2.................   24,000
                                                        ————————
Total Investment...................................... $40,000

John Davis, Profit, December 31: $\frac{16,000}{40,000} \times \$18,000 = \$\ 7,200$

Harold Stone, Profit, December 31: $\frac{24,000}{40,000} \times \$18,000 = \ 10,800$

Total Profit.. $18,000

The distribution of profit is shown in detail at the bottom of the profit and loss statement. An illustration of this section of the statement is given below:

Net Profit... $18,000

Distribution of Net Profit:
   John Davis $^2/_5$ of Total..................... $ 7,200
   Harold Stone $^3/_5$ of Total...................   10,800

Net Profit... $18,000

According to Investments — Average Capital. When profits are to be divided according to investments, the agreement may specify that they are to be divided according to the investments at the beginning of the partnership or according to the investments at the beginning of each fiscal period. Whenever the capital accounts of partners change materially during a single fiscal period, the partners may agree to determine the *average capital* and to divide the profits accordingly. The calculation of the average capital is based upon the capital accounts of the partners. A simple method of calculation is described in the following paragraph.

The beginning investment is multiplied by the number of months from the time of the investment to the time when there was a change in the investment. The investment on the latter date is then multiplied by the number of months from that date until the time when another change occurred. This procedure is continued for the entire fiscal period. These amounts are totaled. The results then express capital investments in the same unit, that is, month-dollars. This unit takes into account the time factor as well as the amount factor. Each partner's participation in the profits is determined by the ratio obtained by placing his total month-dollars over the total month-dollars of the partnership. This is the share of the profit to be assigned to the partner.

Any unit of time may be used in determining the average capital. Days or weeks, instead of months, can be used if significant capital changes occur at other than month periods. In such cases the units would be day-dollars or week-dollars.

For example, Davis and Stone might have decided to divide their profit of $18,000 according to the average capital as shown by their capital accounts. Their original investments, additions to capital, and withdrawals from capital might have appeared as follows in their capital accounts at the end of the year:

JOHN DAVIS, CAPITAL — Acct. No. 311

1953					1953				
May	1	CP	11	4,000	Jan.	2		J1	16,000

HAROLD STONE, CAPITAL — Acct. No. 313

					1953				
					Jan.	2		J1	24,000
					May	1	CR	11	4,000

The division of the profit for the year ($18,000) would have been determined in the following manner:

JOHN DAVIS

From January 2 to April 30. .$16,000 × 4 months =   64,000 month-dollars
From May 1 to December 31. 12,000 × 8 months =   96,000 month-dollars

Total. . . . . 160,000 month-dollars

HAROLD STONE

From January 2 to April 30. .$24,000 × 4 months =   96,000 month-dollars
From May 1 to December 31. 28,000 × 8 months = 224,000 month-dollars

Total. . . . . 320,000 month-dollars

The total month-dollars during the year was therefore 480,000 (160,000 + 320,000).

DISTRIBUTION OF PROFIT

$$\text{John Davis: } \frac{160,000}{480,000} \times \$18,000 = \$\ 6,000$$

$$\text{Harold Stone: } \frac{320,000}{480,000} \times \$18,000 = \$12,000$$

Profit for the year. $18,000

The following distribution of profit would have been made on the profit and loss statement:

Net Profit.	$18,000

Distribution of Net Profit:	
John Davis ⅓ of Total.	$ 6,000
Harold Stone ⅔ of Total.	12,000
Net Profit.	$18,000

PROFITS DISTRIBUTED CONSIDERING INVESTMENTS AND SERVICES OF PARTNERS   The articles of copartnership often provide that each partner is to receive a salary for his services. Partners' salaries are not an expense of the business, but are a division of the profit. Therefore, when partners' salaries are paid at regular intervals in fixed amounts, in the same manner as salaries of employees, the partners' drawing accounts should be debited.

Assume that Davis and Stone agreed to divide profits equally after salaries of $400 and $600 a month, respectively, had been allowed. When the partners withdrew their salaries in cash each month, their drawing accounts were debited and the cash account was credited.

The total of the salaries, $12,000, was then deducted from the net profit, $18,000, and the remainder, $6,000, was distributed equally.

The following distribution of profit would have been made on the profit and loss statement:

Net Profit.		$18,000

Distribution of Net Profit:		
John Davis:		
Salary ($400 a month).	$4,800	
½ Remaining Balance.	3,000	
Profit of John Davis.		$ 7,800
Harold Stone:		
Salary ($600 a month).	$7,200	
½ Remaining Balance.	3,000	
Profit of Harold Stone.		10,200
Net Profit.		$18,000

In this case, only services of partners to the partnership were given consideration. No effort was made to provide for unequal capital contributions. When provision is to be made for interest return on capital contributions, in addition to salaries for services rendered, the method may be considered as including all the factors normally found in partnership profits. This method is illustrated below.

In addition to salaries, Davis and Stone might have agreed to allow interest on their original investments at 6%, the balance of the net profit to be divided equally. The distribution of the net profit on the profit and loss statement at the end of the year would have been:

Net Profit.....................................		$18,000
Distribution of Net Profit:		
John Davis:		
Salary ($400 a month)..............	$4,800	
Interest at 6% on Original Investment.	960	
½ Remaining Balance...............	1,800	
Profit of John Davis.....................		$ 7,560
Harold Stone:		
Salary ($600 a month)..............	$7,200	
Interest at 6% on Original Investment	1,440	
½ Remaining Balance...............	1,800	
Profit of Harold Stone....................		10,440
Net Profit.................................		$18,000

The distribution of net profit that is itemized on the profit and loss statement should be utilized in preparing the closing entry that transfers the net profit figure from the profit and loss summary account to Davis' and Stone's drawing accounts. The closing entry in the general journal would have been:

Dec. 31 Profit and Loss Summary.............	18,000	
John Davis, Drawing...............		7,560
Harold Stone, Drawing.............		10,440

When the partnership agreement states, without qualification, that salaries and interest are to be allowed, a distribution providing for salaries and interest, similar to that in the last example, must be made regardless of the fact that the profit for the period may be less than the total of the salaries and the interest or that a loss may have resulted from operations.

If the salaries of Davis and Stone had been $675 and $800 a month, respectively, the distribution of net profit could have been reported in the manner shown at the top of the opposite page.

The salaries and the interest on original investments total $20,100 ($9,060 + $11,040). These allowances are greater than the profit ($18,000) by $2,100; therefore, $2,100 must be divided between the partners according to their profit-sharing ratio in order to show the correct distribution of profit.

Net Profit................................. $18,000

Distribution of Net Profit:
John Davis:
    Salary at $675 a Month............ $ 8,100
    Interest at 6% on Original Investment   960

                                                  $ 9,060
    Less ½ Remaining Debit Balance.... 1,050

    Profit of John Davis............... $ 8,010
Harold Stone:
    Salary at $800 a Month............ $ 9,600
    Interest at 6% on Original Investment 1,440

                                                  $11,040
    Less ½ Remaining Debit Balance.... 1,050

    Profit of Harold Stone....................   9,990

Net Profit................................. $18,000

The net effect of this distribution would have been summarized in the following closing entry:

Dec. 31 Profit and Loss Summary.............. 18,000
        John Davis, Drawing................   8,010
        Harold Stone, Drawing..............   9,990

STATEMENTS FOR A PARTNERSHIP   In preparing a profit and loss statement for a partnership, it is desirable to show the distribution of the profit for the fiscal period. This information is added to the report after the net profit has been shown. This section of the profit and loss statement of Davis and Stone has been shown in four illustrations on preceding pages.

The method of reporting the capital of a partnership on the balance sheet depends primarily on the amount of information that it is thought desirable to show. Sometimes the balance sheet shows for each partner the investment at the beginning of the period, any additional investment, the partner's share of the net profit or the net loss for the period, any withdrawal from capital, and the personal withdrawals made during the period. Instead of reporting such detailed information on the balance sheet, it is often more satisfactory to prepare a report that supplements the balance sheet. This report is known as a *statement of partners' capital accounts*. It is of value to the partners because it shows in detail the reasons for the changes in the proprietorship.

If, during the year, Davis withdrew $8,100 and Stone withdrew $9,600, a statement of partners' capital accounts might be prepared in the following form:

DAVIS AND STONE

STATEMENT OF PARTNERS' CAPITAL ACCOUNTS

FOR YEAR ENDED DECEMBER 31, 1953

	JOHN DAVIS		HAROLD STONE	
Capital, January 2, 1953.		16,000		24,000
Share of Profit for Year.	8,010		9,990	
Less Personal Drawings.	8,100		9,600	
Increase or Decrease*in Capital		90*		390
Capital, December 31, 1953. . .		15,910		24,390

Statement of Partners' Capital Accounts

The proprietorship section of the balance sheet would show the net investments of the two partners in the following manner:

PROPRIETORSHIP

John Davis, Capital.	$15,910
Harold Stone, Capital.	24,390
Total Proprietorship.	$40,300

PARTNERS' PROFITS AND FEDERAL INCOME TAX As stated in Chapter 18, partnerships do not pay income tax. The several partners report their shares of the partnership profits on their individual income tax returns and include them in the income total on which they pay tax. For example, in the partnership of Davis and Stone referred to above, Davis would report $8,010 as his share of the partnership profits for 1953 and Stone would report $9,990.

It should be noted that partners report and pay income taxes on their shares of the partnership profits and not on the amount they draw out of the partnership. Even though the entire amount of the partnership profits is left in the partnership, the taxable amounts would be the profit participation figures.

Partnerships are required to make out income tax returns showing the amount of the partnership profits and the share of each partner. These partnership returns provide the detail supporting the partnership profits shown on the individual returns of the partners.

QUESTIONS

1. Which of the following sentences are true? Which are false

(a) The sale of a partnership asset by a junior partner may be revoked by a senior partner.

(b) In a partnership, the eldest son succeeds to the position of his father.

(c) In a 40 – 60 partnership, the obligation of the 40 partner is 40% of the deficiency due creditors.

(d) A profit of $5,000 made on the sale of a building and lot contributed by partner A belongs to partner A.

(e) In a ⅔ – ⅓ partnership, in the absence of a written statement as to how profits will be shared, a $9,000 profit would be distributed $6,000 and $3,000.

2. Sloan and Green have invested $100,000 and $60,000 respectively in a partnership, agreeing that, after 6% is allowed on capital and after salaries of $8,000 to Sloan and $6,000 to Green are allowed, the balance is to be shared equally. Calculate the share of each partner in the following partnership profits for the year: (a) $10,000; (b) $50,000; (c) $2,000.

3. Anson and Jones are partners with investments of $30,000 and $15,000 respectively. Show the participation of each in profits of $18,000: (a) if nothing is said about profit distribution; (b) if profits are distributed according to investments; (c) if interest is allowed at 8% and the balance is distributed equally; (d) if salaries of $7,200 and $9,000 and interest at 8% are allowed and the balance is distributed equally.

4. Allen, Stevens, and Lake invest $30,000, $18,000, and $12,000 respectively in a retail business. They agree that interest is to be allowed at the rate of 6% and that monthly salaries of $300 are to be allowed to each partner. The profit and loss summary account shows a profit of $12,900 at the end of the year. Give the closing general journal entry showing the distribution of the net profit to the partners.

5. Enders and Ford form a partnership, Enders investing $12,000 in cash and Ford $18,000 in cash. They agree that profits and losses will be shared in the ratio of the investments shown by the capital accounts. During the first year Enders withdraws $2,000 and Ford, $4,000. (a) Assuming that the net profit for the year is $7,500, give the general journal entries to close the profit and loss summary account and to close the partners' drawing accounts. (b) Assuming that the net profit for the year is only $5,000, give the general journal entries to close the profit and loss summary account and to close the partners' drawing accounts.

6. Kane, Barker, and Page are partners in an enterprise. At the close of the six-month period ending June 30, 19--, their capital accounts show credit balances of $20,000, $30,000, and $40,000 respectively. Their drawing accounts show debit balances of $4,000, $2,000, and $5,000. No entries have been made for salaries allowed at the rate of $500 a month for Kane, $400 a month for Barker, and $800 a month for Page. The partners are allowed interest at the rate of 8% per year on invested capital. Profits or losses after salaries and interest are divided equally. The profit and loss summary account shows a credit balance of $24,000. Give the general journal entries to close the profit and loss summary account and to close the partners' drawing accounts.

PROBLEMS

19-1. In contemplating the formation of a partnership, J. Stimson and L. Norton discussed the division of profits. Stimson was to invest $60,000; Norton, $30,000. Stimson agreed to devote one half of his time to the business; Norton, full time.

- (a) Stimson proposed that the profits be divided according to the original capital investments.
- (b) Norton felt that the profits should be divided in the ratio of time devoted to the business; namely, one third to Stimson and two thirds to himself.
- (c) Stimson then suggested that profits be divided equally in order to offset his larger capital investment against Norton's devoting his full time to the business.
- (d) Norton finally recommended that annual salaries should be allowed — $8,000 to Norton and $4,000 to Stimson — and that the remaining profit or loss should be divided equally.
- (e) An accountant who was consulted recommended that plan (d) be followed but that, in addition, each partner should be allowed 5% interest on his original capital investment.

Instructions: Assuming a profit of $18,000, prepare a summary comparing the partners' shares in the profit under the five conditions mentioned above.

19-2. The capital accounts of John Faren, Fred Dodge, and James Fulton, partners, show balances of $20,000, $40,000, and $60,000 respectively. The partnership agreement provides that each partner shall be allowed 5% interest on invested capital, that Faren is to be allowed a yearly salary of $10,000, and that the remaining profits are to be distributed equally.

Assume that the results of operations for the year are as follows:

- (a) Profit is $28,000.
- (b) Profit is $10,000.
- (c) Loss is $2,000.

Instructions: (1) Prepare the distribution section of the profit and loss statement under each of the foregoing assumptions.

(2) Prepare the general journal entry required at the end of the year to close the profit and loss summary account to the partners' drawing accounts under each of the foregoing assumptions.

19-3. At the end of the first year of business, the capital accounts of Peter Lawson and William Sidney, partners, appeared as follows:

PETER LAWSON, CAPITAL   Acct. No. 311

1953					1953				
Oct.	1		CP10	2,000	Jan.	1		CR1	20,000

WILLIAM SIDNEY, CAPITAL   Acct. No. 313

					1953				
					Jan.	1		CR1	15,000
					July	1		CR7	1,000

During the first year of operations the partnership made a net profit of $14,000. According to the partnership agreement, profits and losses are shared according to the average balances in the capital accounts. During the year Lawson's drawing account was debited for withdrawals of $6,100 and Sidney's drawing account was debited for withdrawals of $5,800.

Instructions: (1) Prepare the distribution section of the profit and loss statement.

(2) Prepare the general journal entries to close the profit and loss summary account to the partners' drawing accounts and to close the drawing accounts to the capital accounts.

19-4. On January 2, 1953, Keith Mason and Mark Olson formed a partnership (Mason and Olson) in order to open an electrical repair business. The agreement provided that monthly salaries of $600 and $800 be allowed Mason and Olson respectively. Interest at 5% on the original investments was to be allowed, after which the profit or loss was to be distributed equally. The adjusted trial balance on December 31, 1953, at the end of the first year of business was as follows (capital accounts represent the original investments):

Cash..	$ 24,350	
Accounts Receivable.........................	15,000	
Prepaid Insurance............................	650	
Notes Payable................................		$ 6,000
Keith Mason, Capital........................		20,000
Keith Mason, Drawing.......................	12,000	
Mark Olson, Capital.........................		10,000
Mark Olson, Drawing........................	14,000	
Sales..		120,000
Operating Expenses.........................	90,000	
	$156,000	$156,000

Instructions: (1) Prepare a profit and loss statement including distribution of net profit to partners.

(2) Prepare a statement of partners' capital accounts.

(3) Prepare a balance sheet.

(4) What amounts do the partners report on their income tax returns?

19-5. The capital accounts of L. G. Bradley and O. W. Burns, partners, are shown below. The profit and loss summary account for the partnership, to which all income and expense accounts have been closed, is also given; the balance in this account has not been closed into the partners' drawing accounts.

L. G. BRADLEY, CAPITAL   Acct. No. 311

				1953				
				Jan.	1		J1	30,000
				Sept.	1		CR9	2,500

O. W. BURNS, CAPITAL   Acct. No. 313

1953					1953				
Nov.	1		CP11	5,000	Jan.	1		J1	40,000

PROFIT AND LOSS SUMMARY   Acct. No. 315

1953					1953				
Dec.	31		J12	88,500	Dec.	31		J12	96,900

Instructions: (1) Give the general journal entry that would be required to close the profit and loss summary account under each of the following bases of distribution of profits:

(a) Profits are distributed equally.

(b) Profits are distributed 40% to Bradley and 60% to Burns.

(c) Profits are distributed according to the balances in the capital accounts at the beginning of the year.

(d) Profits are distributed according to the average balances in the capital accounts.

(e) Profits are distributed 40% to Bradley and 60% to Burns after salaries of $400 and $500 a month respectively have been allowed.

(f) Profits are distributed equally after monthly salaries of $300 to Bradley and $400 to Burns have been allowed and after 4% interest on the balances in the capital accounts at the beginning of the year has been allowed.

(g) Same as (f) except that the monthly salaries are respectively $275 and $400 and that the interest is 6%.

(2) Using the results obtained in (g), prepare the distribution section of the profit and loss statement and a statement of partners' capital accounts for the year ended December 31, 1953. Assume that the partners withdrew their salary allowances each month, that these withdrawals were charged to their drawing accounts, and that there were no other withdrawals charged to the drawing accounts during the year.

Chapter 20

Partnership Reorganization and Dissolution

PARTNERSHIP FORMATION
In the preceding chapter each partnership began as a new business or by the addition of one or more individuals to a sole proprietorship. In this chapter the problems in forming a new partnership from an old partnership will be discussed. Even though the old business continues after the new partners are admitted, a new partnership exists from the legal point of view. This is due to the personal nature of the partnership form of business organization.

ADMISSION OF A NEW PARTNER
The admission of a new partner to a going partnership must be made with the consent of all the other partners in the business. Furthermore, new articles of copartnership that include the future profit-and-loss ratio for the partners, as well as all other necessary provisions applicable to the undertaking, should be drawn. A new partner may be admitted to a partnership as the result of (a) the purchase of an interest in the partnership or (b) an additional investment in the partnership. When an interest in the partnership is purchased, the proprietorship of the new partner is obtained from one or more of the old partners. When an interest is obtained through an investment, the total assets of the firm are increased by the property invested by the new partner.

ADMISSION OF A PARTNER BY THE PURCHASE OF AN INTEREST
When a share of the proprietorship in a partnership is sold, the assets and the liabilities of the firm remain unchanged. The amount received for the new partner's interest in the proprietorship is not recorded on the partnership books. The chief result of the transaction is a transfer of a part of the proprietorship to the new partner. Whatever interest the new partner acquires must come from the capital of the selling partner or partners. For example, George Green and Frank Ford are partners, each having a proprietorship of $25,000. They sell to John Shaw a one-fifth, or a $10,000, interest in the partnership. The amount of this new interest is to represent equal reductions in the capital accounts of the old partners. Since the two old partners, instead of the partnership, receive the payment made by Shaw, the only entry required in the books of the firm is:

```
Apr. 1  George Green, Capital.....................  5,000
        Frank Ford, Capital......................  5,000
        John Shaw, Capital.....................            10,000
            To record the sale of a one-fifth interest to
            John Shaw.
```

This entry does not record the amount paid by Shaw to the two partners for the one-fifth interest; rather, it records the transfer of ownership equity. If the partnership had been very profitable and Shaw very desirous of obtaining the interest, he might have paid considerably more than $10,000 to the two partners. Or if the two partners had been eager to add Shaw to the partnership, they might have sold him the interest for less than $10,000. The price paid by Shaw to Green and Ford is a private transaction not entered on the partnership records.

ADMISSION OF A PARTNER BY AN INVESTMENT A new partner may be admitted into the partnership by making an investment. In this case the new partner does not buy an interest from the other partners; he makes a new contribution to the business, and the proprietorship is thereby increased. For example, J. A. Doran and C. B. Steele are partners, each having a proprietary interest of $9,000. On May 1, J. C. Enders invests $6,000 in cash in the business. For this investment he is to receive a proprietorship in the business equal to his investment. The entry in general journal form to record this transaction is:

```
May 1  Cash......................................  6,000
            J. C. Enders, Capital.....................          6,000
            To record the investment of J. C. Enders.
```

Enders has a one-fourth interest in the proprietorship, which now totals $24,000. It should be noted, however, that a one-fourth interest in the partnership does not mean that Enders is entitled to one fourth of the profits unless the partnership agreement states that profits are to be divided in the ratio of the original investments. Enders will share profits equally with the other partners in the absence of any agreement regarding the division of profits. For example, if profits amount to $12,000 and the new partnership agreement is silent on profit-sharing, each partner will receive $4,000. But if profits are to be shared according to investments, then Doran and Steele will receive $4,500 each, and Enders will receive $3,000.

If, instead of investing cash in the business of Doran and Steele, Enders transfers the property and the liabilities of a business that he has been operating, an account must be debited for each of the assets taken over; an account must be credited for each of the liabilities assumed by the firm; and Enders' capital account must be credited for the difference, which is his proprietorship in the new business.

For example, if Enders invests a $5,000 building on a $3,000 lot, subject to a $2,000 mortgage, the entry to record his investment is:

```
May 1  Building...................................   5,000
         Land......................................   3,000
             Mortgage Payable.........................        2,000
             J. C. Enders, Capital.....................        6,000
             To record the investment of J. C. Enders.
```

BONUS OR ALLOW-ANCE FOR GOODWILL TO FORMER PARTNERS The value of a going partnership business may exceed the book value of the proprietorship. Under such conditions a new partner would need to invest more than the amount of the partnership interest he is to receive. The excess investment of the new partner may be credited to the old partners, as explained in case (1) below; or it may cause the recording of goodwill as explained in case (2). The method used will depend upon the agreement among the parties.

(1) *Recording a Bonus.* For example, J. R. White and O. L. Ford formed a partnership, each investing $10,000 in cash. After a few years the firm of White and Ford became quite prosperous. A sufficient amount of the profits had been added to the partners' capital accounts to make the credit balance of each $15,000. James Thorn wishes to join the partnership and is willing to invest $16,000 in cash and to accept a one-fourth interest for this amount, although his investment is greater than that of either of the other two partners.

The amount of the credit to the new partner's capital account is calculated in the following manner:

```
Total proprietorship before admission of James Thorn.......   $30,000
Cash invested by James Thorn...........................    16,000
                                                          ─────────
Total proprietorship of new partnership..................   $46,000

James Thorn's share of total proprietorship (¼ of $46,000)...   $11,500
```

After determining the amount of the credit to the new partner's capital account, the amount of the bonus to the former partners is computed as follows:

```
Cash invested by James Thorn...........................   $16,000
Less: James Thorn's share of total proprietorship..........    11,500
                                                          ─────────
Bonus to former partners (White and Ford)...............   $ 4,500
```

Allocation of bonus in profit-and-loss ratio (50% - 50%):
Credit to White's capital account...................... $ 2,250
Credit to Ford's capital account...................... 2,250

The entry in general journal form made upon the admission of Thorn on January 2 is:

```
Jan. 2  Cash.....................................  16,000
            James Thorn, Capital...................          11,500
            J. R. White, Capital...................           2,250
            O. L. Ford, Capital....................           2,250
            To record the admission of James Thorn as
            a partner upon the investment of $16,000
            in cash.
```

The capital accounts of White and Ford are each credited with one half of the bonus, for the partners share equally in profits and losses. If the articles of copartnership of White and Ford had stated a fixed profit-and-loss ratio of 60% for White and 40% for Ford, the excess contribution of Thorn would have been divided as follows: White, $2,700; Ford, $1,800. The bonus received is always divided among the former partners in the profit-and-loss ratio that was used before the admission of the new partner.

(2) *Recording Goodwill.* The preceding entry records the transaction satisfactorily, but Thorn may object to having his capital shown as $11,500 when he has actually invested $16,000. He is, however, satisfied with a one-fourth interest in the firm. An alternate method of recording the investment will avoid this objection.

It can be seen that since Thorn is willing to invest $16,000 for a one-fourth interest, the value placed on the partnership is $64,000, that is, four times his investment. The value of the partnership without the additional investment is therefore $48,000, which is $18,000 in excess of the proprietorship shown by the partnership accounts. If Thorn is willing to invest $16,000 for a one-fourth interest, the firm must possess certain rights, privileges, or advantages that are of great value. Such rights, privileges, or advantages are assets; but they are different from the other assets in that they are not tangible and ordinarily have value to the business only as a going concern. They are therefore called *intangible assets* and are shown on the balance sheet under this heading. The most common asset in this classification is *goodwill.* Goodwill has been defined by the Treasury Department of the United States Government as "the value attached to a business over and above the value of the physical property." Goodwill arises when a business wins the favor of its customers to such an extent that the customers will probably return to trade in the future; but it is not considered desirable to record goodwill as an asset unless it has been purchased or sold.

In the example used previously, Thorn is willing to invest $16,000 for a one-fourth interest in a partnership having a capital of $30,000. The goodwill to former partners is calculated in the following way:

Investment of James Thorn, for which he is to receive full credit in his capital account...........................		$16,000
Portion of total value of business represented by new partner's investment...		¼
Total value of business ($16,000 × 4).....................		$64,000
Value of business exclusive of goodwill:		
Former partners' (White and Ford) total capital..	$30,000	
Investment of James Thorn...................	16,000	46,000
Goodwill of former partners (White and Ford)............		$18,000
Allocation of goodwill in profit-and-loss ratio (50% - 50%):		
Credit to White's capital account......................		$ 9,000
Credit to Ford's capital account......................		9,000

Since White and Ford share profits and losses equally, the entries in general journal form made in the books of the new partnership upon the admission of Thorn are:

Jan. 2 Goodwill..............................	18,000	
J. R. White, Capital.....................		9,000
O. L. Ford, Capital......................		9,000
To record the asset goodwill and thus to increase the capital of White and Ford to three fourths of the total proprietorship after the admission of Thorn.		
2 Cash.......................................	16,000	
James Thorn, Capital		16,000
To record the investment of Thorn, which is to represent one fourth of the total proprietorship.		

DETERMINING THE AMOUNT OF GOOD-WILL   When goodwill exists in a going business and becomes an item in the investment of a new partner, there should be a recognized procedure for determining its amount. Various ways of measuring the amount of goodwill exist. Two methods will be mentioned.

(1) The value of goodwill may be estimated by the capitalization of the excess profits. For instance, if the capital of a business is $40,000, a yearly return of 10%, or $4,000, may be normal. If the average yearly profit, however, is $6,000, $2,000 represents the excess profit. The goodwill may be determined by capitalizing the $2,000 excess

profit, that is, by dividing $2,000 by 10%, the normal rate of profit. The result, $20,000, is the estimated value of the goodwill. In other words, the investment in this business might be $60,000 and still a 10% return would be made on the capital.

(2) The value of goodwill may be estimated to be equal to the excess profit of several years. If an excess yearly profit of $2,000 is expected for at least the next five years, the goodwill may be estimated at $10,000 (5 times $2,000).

BONUS OR ALLOW-
ANCE FOR GOODWILL
TO NEW PARTNER
In some cases the capital account of a new partner may be credited with an amount in excess of his investment. Either of two methods is commonly used when a partner is admitted on such a basis. The method to be used will depend upon the agreement among the parties.

(1) *Recording a Bonus.* Suppose that A. B. Cole and C. D. Pane are partners with proprietary interests of $12,000 and $18,000 respectively. The firm needs additional capital and the services of G. L. Tabor, an expert in its type of business. The two partners therefore offer Tabor a one-third interest in the partnership if he will invest $9,000 in cash.

The amount of the credit to the new partner's capital account is calculated in the following manner:

Proprietorship before admission of new partner............	$30,000
Cash invested by G. L. Tabor.........................	9,000
Total proprietorship after admission of G. L. Tabor........	$39,000
G. L. Tabor's share of total proprietorship (⅓ × $39,000)....	$13,000

After determining the amount of the new partner's capital account, the amount of the bonus to the new partner and its allocation to the former partners is determined as follows:

New partner's share of total proprietorship..............	$13,000
Cash invested by G. L. Tabor.........................	9,000
Bonus to G. L. Tabor................................	$ 4,000
Allocation of bonus in profit-and-loss ratio (50% - 50%):	
Debit to Cole's capital account......................	$ 2,000
Debit to Pane's capital account......................	2,000

The entries in general journal form made upon the admission of the new partner are:

```
Nov. 1  Cash......................................  9,000
            G. L. Tabor, Capital....................          9,000
              To record the cash investment of Tabor.
Nov. 1  A. B. Cole, Capital........................  2,000
        C. D. Pane, Capital........................  2,000
            G. L. Tabor, Capital....................          4,000
              To adjust the capital accounts so that the
              account of Tabor will show his one-third
              interest in the partnership.
```

This method decreases the proprietorship of the two original partners. It is assumed, however, that the investment of Tabor and the service that this partner will render to the firm will, in the long run, more than offset the present disadvantage.

(2) *Recording Goodwill.* The original partners, Cole and Pane, may not wish to have their capital reduced. Since the admission of Tabor is expected to react favorably on the firm, the old partners may prefer to set up goodwill and to credit the capital account of the new partner with an amount that will increase his proprietary interest to one third of the total capital. The goodwill allowed to the new partner is calculated in the following way:

```
Investment of former partners, whose capital balances are not
   to be reduced.......................................  $30,000
Portion of total value of business represented by former
   partners' investment.................................     2/3
Total value of business ($30,000 ÷ 2/3)..................  $45,000
Value of business exclusive of goodwill:
   Former partners' (Cole and Pane) total capital...  $30,000
   Investment of G. L. Tabor....................    9,000   39,000
                                                           --------
Goodwill of G. L. Tabor................................   $ 6,000
                                                           ========
```

The entries in general journal form made in the books of the new partnership upon the admission of Tabor are:

```
Nov. 1  Cash......................................  9,000
            G. L. Tabor, Capital....................          9,000
              To record the cash investment of Tabor.
Nov. 1  Goodwill..................................  6,000
            G. L. Tabor, Capital....................          6,000
              To record the asset goodwill and thus to
              increase the capital of Tabor to one third of
              the total proprietorship.
```

REVALUATION OF ASSETS ON CONSOLIDATION   When two businesses are consolidated, an examination of the assets may show that certain assets are recorded on the books at more or less than their current values. Before any entries are made in

the books of the new organization, the records of each business that is
being consolidated should be made to show the current values of the
assets according to the partnership agreement.

For example, the sole proprietorship conducted by John Setton and
the partnership of Foster and Aimes are to be consolidated. Upon an
examination of the assets of Setton, it is found that an additional
allowance of $400 for bad debts should be established and that the
present value of the merchandise inventory is $500 more than the book
value. Upon an examination of the assets of Foster and Aimes, it is
found that the building has a present market value of $6,000, which is
$2,000 above the book value.

The entry made on the books of Setton to record the revaluation of
his assets is shown below:

July 31	Merchandise Inventory	500	
	Allowance for Bad Debts		400
	John Setton, Capital		100
	To adjust the allowance for bad debts and the merchandise inventory so that their current values will be recorded.		

The entry made on the books of Foster and Aimes to adjust the
value of their building is as follows. (The journal entry is based on the
assumption that profits and losses are shared equally by the partners.)

July 31	Building	2,000	
	Frank Foster, Capital		1,000
	Allen Aimes, Capital		1,000
	To adjust the building amount, which has been too low.		

After these asset adjustments have been recorded, the opening
entries of the partnership, based on the new values, are made in the
usual manner.

EFFECT OF DISSOLUTION UPON A PARTNERSHIP Dissolution terminates the agreement that
gave the partnership existence, but it does
not necessarily mean the discontinuance of the business. The admission of a new partner or the consolidation of the partnership with
another firm is an act of dissolution. The partnership agreement is
void; but new articles of copartnership may be provided to define the
altered relationship between the partners, and the business may
continue without interruption. Frequently, however, a partnership
may wind up its affairs after dissolution and go out of existence. Some
of the problems that may arise upon the dissolution of a partnership
will now be discussed.

RETIREMENT OF A PARTNER   When a member retires from a partnership, his interest may be purchased by one of the other partners. The entry required in such a case is a debit to the proprietorship account of the one who is retiring and a credit to the proprietorship account of the other partner. This entry is made regardless of the amount paid for the interest of the retiring partner, since the payment represents a transaction between two individuals and consequently does not affect the records of the partnership.

If, upon retirement, a partner withdraws assets from the business, the assets may be (1) equal in value to his proprietorship, (2) greater in value than his proprietorship, or (3) less in value than his proprietorship.

If the assets withdrawn by the retiring partner are equal to his proprietorship, it is necessary only to debit his proprietorship account and to credit the asset accounts with the ledger value of the assets withdrawn.

If, because of the unusually prosperous condition of the firm, or for any other reason, the retiring partner is given assets greater in value than the book value of his proprietorship, the total proprietorship of the other partners is decreased. For example, Hodge, Garson, and Fox are equal partners in a business having a total proprietorship of $30,000. Garson wishes to withdraw from the partnership, but the business has been so unusually prosperous that he is not willing to give up his interest for $10,000, its book value. The partners agree to permit him to withdraw $12,000 as his share of the business. The entry in general journal form on May 31 to record the withdrawal of Garson is:

May 31 Albert Garson, Capital..................	10,000	
Ernest Hodge, Capital...................	1,000	
Harold Fox, Capital...................	1,000	
Cash................................		12,000
To record the withdrawal of Garson, who was allowed $12,000 for his interest in the business.		

Under certain circumstances a partner may be willing to withdraw from a partnership and to accept assets of less worth than the book value of his interest. Rane, Warne, and Quinn are equal partners in a business having a net proprietorship of $45,000. Warne is anxious to withdraw; but he realizes that if he forces a sale, the assets will not bring their book value. He is therefore willing to accept $13,000 in cash, which is $2,000 less than the book value of his interest. The entry in general journal form to record the withdrawal of Warne is:

Aug. 31 C. R. Warne, Capital.................... 15,000
   Cash................................   13,000
   H. P. Rane, Capital.................   1,000
   R. F. Quinn, Capital................   1,000
    To record the withdrawal of Warne, who
    was allowed $13,000 for his interest in the
    business.

DEATH OF A PARTNER Since the death of a partner automatically dissolves the partnership, the books should be closed immediately and the profit or the loss since the last closing date should be determined and distributed in accordance with the partnership agreement. The balance of the capital account of the deceased may then be transferred to a liability account of the business. The surviving partners may draw up new articles of copartnership and either continue in the business by themselves or admit a new partner.

LIQUIDATION OF A PARTNERSHIP When a partnership is to cease operation and liquidation is to take place, it is necessary first to ascertain the net profit or the net loss to date and to distribute it to the partners' accounts so that the net proprietorship of each partner will be shown. It is necessary then to convert the assets into cash. When cash has been realized, it is applied in the following manner:

(1) To pay creditors.
(2) To return the capital belonging to the partners.

The process of liquidation is illustrated by the following example. Logan, Keane, and Kendall are partners who divide profits in the ratio of 50%, 30%, and 20% respectively. They decide to dissolve the partnership on June 30. The books are closed preparatory to liquidation, and a balance sheet is prepared. A condensed form of the report is shown below:

LOGAN, KEANE, AND KENDALL
BALANCE SHEET
JUNE 30, 1953

Cash.................	$ 8,000	Liabilities.............	$ 4,000
Other Assets..........	56,000	Proprietorship:	
		R. S. Logan, Capital..	20,000
		O. A. Keane, Capital..	20,000
		P. M. Kendall, Capital	20,000
Total Assets..........	$64,000	Total Liab. and Prop....	$64,000

The assets are sold for $66,000; the profit on the sale of the assets is distributed in the profit-and-loss ratio; the liabilities are paid; and the remainder of the cash is then distributed according to the investments of the partners.

A summary of the liquidation illustrating a pattern for calculating the distribution to the partners is shown below:

| | | OTHER | | PROPRIETORSHIP | | |
	CASH	ASSETS	LIABILITIES	R. S. LOGAN	O. A. KEANE	P. M. KENDALL
Profit-and-Loss Ratio.....				50%	30%	20%
Balance Before Realization	$ 8,000	$56,000	$4,000	$20,000	$20,000	$20,000
Sale of Assets and Distribution of Gain..........	+66,000	−56,000		+5,000	+3,000	+2,000
Balance After Realization.	$74,000		$4,000	$25,000	$23,000	$22,000
Payment of Liabilities....	−4,000		−4,000			
Balances...............	$70,000			$25,000	$23,000	$22,000
Distribution to Partners...	−70,000			−25,000	−23,000	−22,000

The entries in general journal form on June 30 to record these transactions are:

```
June 30  Cash..................................  66,000
             Assets..................................          56,000
             Loss and Gain on Sale of Assets.........          10,000
                To record the sale of the assets.

      30  Loss and Gain on Sale of Assets...........  10,000
             R. S. Logan, Capital...................           5,000
             O. A. Keane, Capital...................           3,000
             P. M. Kendall, Capital.................           2,000
                To distribute the profit from the sale of
                the assets to the partners' capital ac-
                counts in the profit-and-loss ratio.

      30  Liabilities..............................   4,000
             Cash......................................           4,000
                To record the payment of the liabilities.

      30  R. S. Logan, Capital.....................  25,000
          O. A. Keane, Capital.....................  23,000
          P. M. Kendall, Capital..................  22,000
             Cash......................................          70,000
                To distribute the remaining cash accord-
                ing to the balance of the partners' capital
                accounts.
```

If a loss had resulted from the sale of the assets, it would have been divided among the partners in the profit-and-loss ratio before any payment was made to the partners on their investment. For instance, assume that the assets of Logan, Keane, and Kendall were sold for only $36,000. A summary of the liquidation is shown below:

| | | | | PROPRIETORSHIP | | |
	CASH	OTHER ASSETS	LIABILITIES	R. S. LOGAN	O. A. KEANE	P. M. KENDALL
Profit-and-Loss Ratio.....				50%	30%	20%
Balance Before Realization	$ 8,000	$56,000	$4,000	$20,000	$20,000	$20,000
Sale of Assets and Distribution of Loss..........	+36,000	−56,000		−10,000	− 6,000	− 4,000
Balance After Realization.	$44,000		$4,000	$10,000	$14,000	$16,000
Payment of Liabilities....	− 4,000		−4,000			
Balances................	$40,000			$10,000	$14,000	$16,000
Distribution to Partners...	−40,000			−10,000	−14,000	−16,000

The entries in general journal form are shown below:

June 30	Cash..................................	36,000	
	Loss and Gain on Sale of Assets............	20,000	
	Assets..............................		56,000
	To record the sale of the assets.		
30	R. S. Logan, Capital...................	10,000	
	O. A. Keane, Capital..................	6,000	
	P. M. Kendall, Capital.................	4,000	
	Loss and Gain on Sale of Assets........		20,000
	To distribute the loss on the sale of the assets to the partners' capital accounts in the profit-and-loss ratio.		
30	Liabilities.............................	4,000	
	Cash...............................		4,000
	To record the payment of the liabilities.		
30	R. S. Logan, Capital...................	10,000	
	O. A. Keane, Capital..................	14,000	
	P. M. Kendall, Capital.................	16,000	
	Cash...............................		40,000
	To distribute the remaining cash according to the balances of the partners' capital accounts.		

The part of a loss charged to the capital account of a partner may sometimes be greater than the partner's investment. The debit balance of the capital account will therefore represent an amount owed to the other partners. The remaining cash will not be sufficient, however, to pay the other partners until the partner whose account has a debit balance pays the amount that he owes. In this case cash should be distributed in such a manner that, if the partner is unable to pay, the others will bear this additional loss in the profit-and-loss ratio that exists between themselves. To illustrate, assume that the assets of Logan, Keane, and Kendall realized only $6,000. The liquidation summary then appears as follows:

	CASH	OTHER ASSETS	LIABILITIES	PROPRIETORSHIP		
				R. S. LOGAN	O. A. KEANE	P. M. KENDALL
Profit-and-Loss Ratio.....				50%	30%	20%
Balance Before Realization	$8,000	$56,000	$4,000	$20,000	$20,000	$20,000
Sale of Assets and Distribution of Loss..........	+6,000	−56,000		−25,000	−15,000	−10,000
Balance After Realization.	$14,000		$4,000	$5,000 (Dr.)	$5,000	$10,000
Payment of Liabilities.....	−4,000		−4,000			
Balances...............	$10,000			$5,000 (Dr.)	$5,000	$10,000

At this point there is $10,000 in the cash account, but the capital accounts of Keane and Kendall have a total credit balance of $15,000. Logan should pay $5,000 to the partnership; but if he does not, Keane and Kendall will suffer a $5,000 loss. This loss should be shared in proportion to the profit-and-loss ratio; therefore Keane should suffer a loss of 3/5 and Kendall a loss of 2/5, or $3,000 and $2,000 respectively. In order to bring the capital account balances to these amounts, the $10,000 cash balance is distributed as follows: $2,000 to Keane and $8,000 to Kendall. The balance of Keane's capital account is then $3,000 ($5,000 − $2,000) and the balance of Kendall's capital account is $2,000 ($10,000 − $8,000). Continuing the tabulation given above, the problem may be completed as follows:

	CASH	OTHER ASSETS	LIABILITIES	PROPRIETORSHIP		
				R. S. LOGAN	O. A. KEANE	P. M. KENDALL
Balances...............	$10,000			$5,000 (Dr.)	$5,000	$10,000
Distribution to Partners...	−10,000				−2,000	−8,000
Balances (Keane, 3/5; Kendall, 2/5).........				$5,000 (Dr.)	$3,000	$2,000
Logan pays his indebtedness................	+$5,000			5,000		
Balances...............	$5,000				$3,000	$2,000
Distribution to Partners...	−5,000				−3,000	−2,000

The entries in general journal form are as follows:

```
June 30  Cash...................................   6,000
         Loss and Gain on Sale of Assets............  50,000
             Assets.....................................          56,000
                To record the sale of the assets.

      30  R. S. Logan, Capital....................  25,000
          O. A. Keane, Capital....................  15,000
          P. M. Kendall, Capital..................  10,000
             Loss and Gain on Sale of Assets.........          50,000
                To distribute the loss on the sale of the
                assets to the partners' capital accounts
                in the profit-and-loss ratio.
```

30	Liabilities............................	4,000	
	Cash..................................		4,000
	To record the payment of the liabilities.		
30	O. A. Keane, Capital...................	2,000	
	P. M. Kendall, Capital.................	8,000	
	Cash..................................		10,000
	To distribute the remaining cash to Keane and Kendall so that the balances in their capital accounts will be in the profit-and-loss ratio of 3/5 and 2/5.		
July 10	Cash.................................	5,000	
	R. S. Logan, Capital..................		5,000
	To record the cash received from Logan to pay his indebtedness to Keane and Kendall.		
10	O. A. Keane, Capital...................	3,000	
	P. M. Kendall, Capital.................	2,000	
	Cash..................................		5,000
	To distribute the cash received from Logan according to the balances of the other capital accounts.		

SIGNIFICANCE OF THE PARTNERS' CAPITAL ACCOUNTS The partners may agree to distribute profits and losses in any way they wish, irrespective of their capital interest in the partnership, although, as already explained, one basis of distribution is the investments of the partners. Although the partners' investments may not affect the division of profits and losses, they will determine the amounts of the claims that the partners may have upon the assets when the partnership is dissolved for any reason.

QUESTIONS

1. Which of the following sentences are true? Which are false?

   (a) Partners' salaries are shown as general expenses on the profit and loss statement.

   (b) When the partnership agreement states, without qualification, that salaries and interest are to be allowed, the entries for salaries and interest must be made even if a loss has resulted from operations.

   (c) A salary allowance withdrawn by a partner may be recorded by a credit to the partner's drawing account and a debit to cash.

   (d) In the absence of any specific agreement, partnership profits are divided according to the investments of the partners.

   (e) Interest allowances for partners' capital contributions should be shown as interest expense.

2. If Andrews sells to Willard his interest in the partnership of Andrews and Conley, what entry is required in the partnership books? Does it reflect the selling price? Explain.

3. If the partnership of Jansen and Clement takes over a building owned by Clement that cost him $30,000 but that is valued for the partnership at $45,000, should goodwill be debited for $15,000? Explain.

4. Tiemann and Lyons are partners having equal interests in a $20,000 partnership. Rogers invests $16,000 and receives a one-third interest in the partnership. Give journal entries showing two methods of recording the admission of Rogers.

5. Booth and Davis are partners having investments of $60,000 and $30,000 respectively and sharing profits and losses equally. Give the journal entry for the admission of Elder as a partner under each of the following conditions:

(a) Elder pays Booth $40,000 for one half of his interest.
(b) Elder is given a one-third interest for an investment of $60,000 (bonus method).
(c) Elder pays Booth and Davis $20,000 each for a one-third interest in the partnership.
(d) Elder invests $40,000 and receives a one-fourth interest (goodwill method).

6. Harold Spaid and Roy Taylor are partners with capital investments of $15,000 and $10,000 respectively. They share profits and losses in proportion to capital investments. Walter Watts is to be admitted as a partner. Record in journal form the entries necessary to show the admission of Watts under each of the following conditions:

(a) Watts invests $25,000 and receives a one-half interest in the partnership.
(b) Watts invests $20,000 and receives a one-half interest in the partnership. (Do not use goodwill.)
(c) Watts invests $20,000 and receives a one-third interest in the partnership. (Show goodwill.)
(d) Watts buys one half of the interest of each partner, paying Spaid $9,000 and Taylor $6,000 respectively.
(e) Watts buys one third of Spaid's interest for $6,000 and one half of Taylor's interest for $6,000.
(f) Watts invests $25,000 and receives a one-third interest in the partnership. (Use goodwill.)

7. Duncan and Wheeler are partners with investments of $20,000 and $30,000 respectively. Duncan receives $\frac{2}{3}$ of the profits; Wheeler, $\frac{1}{3}$. (a) Carter invests $20,000 and is given a one-fifth interest in the partnership. Give journal entries showing two methods of admitting Carter to the partnership. (b) Assume that Carter invests $16,000 and is given a one-third interest. Give journal entries showing two methods of admitting Carter to the partnership.

8. Jerome, Ray, and George start a partnership on January 2. Jerome invests $12,000; Ray, $8,000; and George, $4,000. On December 31 they decide to dissolve the partnership. After paying their debts, they have $6,000 in cash. How much should be paid to each partner if profits and losses are shared in proportion to investments?

PROBLEMS

20-1. Mason and Frier are partners sharing profits 80% and 20% respectively. On January 2 their interests in the firm are as follows: Mason, $36,000, and Frier, $12,000. Bishop is admitted as a partner upon the investment of $15,000 in cash.

Instructions: Record the investment of Bishop in general journal form under the following conditions:

(1) Bishop is given a one-third interest, goodwill being recorded.
(2) Bishop is given a one-third interest, a bonus being allowed to the new partner.
(3) Bishop is given credit for the actual investment made.
(4) Bishop is given a one-seventh interest, goodwill being recorded.
(5) Bishop is given a one-seventh interest, a bonus being allowed to the old partners.

20-2. On December 31, Jasper is retiring from the partnership of Raith, Freedman, and Jasper, who share profits equally. The balance sheet on that date is given below:

RAITH, FREEDMAN, AND JASPER
BALANCE SHEET
DECEMBER 31, 19 - -

Cash................	$ 40,000	Liabilities............	$ 10,000
Other Assets.........	60,000	Raith, Capital........	40,000
		Freedman, Capital.....	30,000
		Jasper, Capital........	20,000
Total Assets..........	$100,000	Total Liab. and Prop...	$100,000

Instructions: Construct general journal entries for Jasper's withdrawal under the following circumstances:

(1) Jasper sells his interest to Raith; he receives Raith's personal note for $18,000.
(2) Jasper sells his interest to Jarvis, whom Raith and Freedman have agreed to accept as a partner, for $24,000 cash.
(3) Jasper accepts $6,000 less than the book value of his interest and withdraws that amount in cash.
(4) Jasper withdraws $16,000 in cash and accepts a note from Raith and Freedman for the remainder, equal in total to his proprietorship.
(5) Jasper withdraws $16,000 in cash and $8,000 in other assets in exchange for his interest.

20-3. The partnership of Kole and Yale has the following post-closing trial balance on December 31 of the current year:

KOLE AND YALE
POST-CLOSING TRIAL BALANCE
DECEMBER 31, 19 – –

Cash................................	$18,000	
Accounts Receivable..................	25,000	
Merchandise Inventory................	16,000	
Equipment...........................	10,000	
Allow. for Depr. of Equipment.........		$ 2,500
Accounts Payable.....................		6,500
Frank Kole, Capital...................		32,000
Walter Yale, Capital..................		28,000
	$69,000	$69,000

It is agreed that a new partner, Robert Stevens, is to be admitted to the partnership.

Instructions: (1) Prepare general journal entries to correct the books of Kole and Yale before the new partnership was formed. In making the corrections, assume that Kole and Yale share profits equally. The corrections are:

(a) An allowance for bad debts amounting to 4% of receivables is to be set up.

(b) Merchandise in the amount of $3,000 is found to be obsolete and unsalable.

(c) Various unpaid bills amounting to $600 were not included in accounts payable on December 31.

(2) Prepare a new post-closing trial balance for the partnership of Kole and Yale after the foregoing corrections.

(3) Record the admission of Robert Stevens as a partner, using the bonus method. Stevens invests: cash, $6,600; merchandise, $15,000; equipment, $10,000. He is to receive a one-third interest in the partnership and the profits.

(4) Prepare a balance sheet for the new partnership of Kole, Yale & Stevens as of January 1 of the following year.

20-4. The balance sheet of the firm of Myers, Budge, and Walker just prior to liquidation is as follows:

MYERS, BUDGE, AND WALKER
BALANCE SHEET
JUNE 30, 19 – –

Cash................	$ 10,000		Liabilities............	$ 32,000
Other Assets........	90,000		A. Myers, Capital.....	40,000
			B. Budge, Capital.....	20,000
			C. Walker, Capital....	8,000
Total Assets.........	$100,000		Total Liab. and Prop...	$100,000

Myers, Budge, and Walker share profits in the ratio of 2/5, 2/5, and 1/5.

Instructions: Prepare general journal entries to record the liquidation under each of the following circumstances, considered individually. As the basis for the entries you may find it helpful to prepare liquidation summaries similar to those illustrated in this chapter.

(1) All of the other assets are sold for $100,000.

(2) All of the other assets are sold for $70,000.

(3) All of the other assets are sold for $40,000. If, after the partnership cash has been distributed, one partner's capital account has a debit balance, assume that he pays that balance to the partnership and that the amount of this payment is then distributed.

20-5. The balance sheet of the firm of Lawson, Moore, and Pardee just prior to liquidation is as follows:

LAWSON, MOORE, AND PARDEE
BALANCE SHEET
DECEMBER 31, 19--

Cash.	$ 7,000	Accounts Payable.	$ 2,500
Accounts Receivable. . . .	4,000	Notes Payable.	1,000
Merchandise Inventory.	11,000	Lawson, Capital.	10,000
Supplies.	500	Moore, Capital.	10,000
Equipment.	6,000	Pardee, Capital.	5,000
Total Assets.	$28,500	Total Liab. and Prop. . . .	$28,500

Lawson, Moore, and Pardee share profits in the ratio of 3:2:1.

The following liquidation transactions were completed:

(a) Collected $3,800 in cash from customers' accounts; charged the remainder to Loss and Gain on Sale of Assets.

(b) Sold the merchandise for $8,000 cash.

(c) Sold the equipment for $7,000 cash.

(d) Sold the supplies for $300.

(e) Distributed the loss on the sale of the assets to the partners' capital accounts.

(f) Paid accounts payable in full.

(g) Paid notes payable in full.

(h) Distributed the cash balance to the partners.

Instructions: (1) Enter the balances shown on the December 31 balance sheet in T accounts. Also set up an account entitled Loss and Gain on Sale of Assets.

(2) Prepare general journal entries to record the liquidation.

(3) Post the liquidation entries and rule the accounts.

Boynton & Brooks
Part 1

The purpose of this practice set is to provide material that requires the application of the principles discussed in preceding chapters. The set is divided into two parts. Part 1 includes the transactions for April of a partnership that operates a wholesale and retail automobile accessories business. Part 2, which follows Chapter 24, includes the transactions for May of the same business. The business is incorporated on May 1.

Although the transactions are typical of those completed by an automobile accessories business, the purpose of the set is not to illustrate the methods and the records of a particular type of business, but rather the general principles followed by all businesses.

General Ledger

The general ledger accounts to be used are:

BALANCE SHEET ACCOUNTS

ACCT. No.	1. ASSETS	ACCT. No.	2. LIABILITIES
	11. Current Assets		*21. Current Liabilities*
11.1	Cash	21.1	Notes Payable
11.2	Petty Cash	21.2	Interest Payable
11.3	Notes Receivable	21.3	Accounts Payable
11.4	Interest Receivable	21.4	Employees Income Taxes Pay.
11.5	Accounts Receivable	21.5	F.I.C.A. Taxes Payable
11.6	Allowance for Bad Debts	21.6	Federal Unemployment Taxes Payable
11.7	Merchandise Inventory		
11.8	Store Supplies	21.7	State Unemployment Taxes Payable
11.9	Office Supplies		
11.10	Prepaid Insurance	21.8	Sales Taxes Payable
11.11	Prepaid Interest on Notes Pay.	21.9	Salaries Payable
	12. Investments	21.10	Estimated Income Taxes Pay.
12.1	Investment in Murray Corporation 4% Bonds	21.11	Property Taxes Payable
	13. Fixed Assets		*22. Fixed Liabilities*
		22.1	6% Mortgage Payable
13.1	Store Equipment		**3. PROPRIETORSHIP**
13.2	Allowance for Depreciation of Store Equipment	31.1	R. C. Boynton, Capital
13.3	Delivery Equipment	31.2	R. C. Boynton, Drawing
13.4	Allowance for Depreciation of Delivery Equipment	31.3	E. A. Brooks, Capital
		31.4	E. A. Brooks, Drawing
13.5	Office Equipment	31.5	Preferred Stock, 5%
13.6	Allowance for Depreciation of Office Equipment	31.6	Common Stock
		31.7	Premium on Preferred Stock
13.7	Building	31.8	Reserve for Plant Expansion
13.8	Allow. for Depr. of Building	31.9	Earned Surplus
13.9	Land	31.10	Profit and Loss Summary

PROFIT AND LOSS STATEMENT ACCOUNTS

Acct.
No.   4. SALES

41.1   Sales
41.2   Sales Returns and Allowances

5. PURCHASES

51.1   Purchases
51.2   Freight In
51.3   Purchases Returns and Allowances

6. OPERATING EXPENSES

61. Selling Expenses

61.1   Sales Salaries
61.2   Advertising Expense
61.3   Depreciation of Store Equipment
61.4   Store Supplies Expense
61.5   Insurance Expense — Selling
61.6   Miscellaneous Selling Expense

62. Delivery Expenses

62.1   Delivery Salaries
62.2   Depreciation of Delivery Equipment

Acct.
No.

62.3   Insurance Expense — Delivery
62.4   Miscellaneous Delivery Expense

63. General Expenses

63.1   Office Salaries
63.2   Officers Salaries
63.3   Payroll Tax Expense
63.4   Rent Expense
63.5   Office Supplies Expense
63.6   Depreciation of Office Equipment
63.7   Insurance Expense — General
63.8   Bad Debts Expense
63.9   Repairs on Building
63.10   Depreciation of Building
63.11   Property Tax Expense
63.12   Miscellaneous General Expense

7. OTHER INCOME

71.1   Purchases Discount
71.2   Interest Income

8. OTHER EXPENSES

81.1   Sales Discount
81.2   Interest Expense

Instructions: (1) The accounts listed above are given in the general ledger in the books of account that may be obtained for this practice set. If these books are not used, open the foregoing general ledger accounts in the order in which they are given, allowing at least sixteen lines for each account. Not all of these accounts will be used during the first month of this practice set, but all should be opened at this time.

The post-closing trial balance of Boynton & Brooks as of March 31 of the current year is given on the opposite page.

Instructions: (2) The account balances listed in the post-closing trial balance are already recorded in the general ledger in the books of account that may be obtained for this practice set. If these books are not used, record the balances in the appropriate accounts as of April 1.

Accounts Receivable Ledger

The accounts in the accounts receivable ledger and the balances of those accounts that have balances on March 31 are given on pages 389 and 390. All sales on account are wholesale sales made on terms of 2/10, n/30. There is no sales tax on wholesale sales.

BOYNTON & BROOKS
Post-Closing Trial Balance
March 31, 19 - -

Cash	11.1	2,626 95	
Notes Receivable	11.3	800 00	
Interest Receivable	11.4	5 93	
Accounts Receivable	11.5	4,172 08	
Allowance for Bad Debts	11.6		262 92
Merchandise Inventory	11.7	35,698 27	
Store Supplies	11.8	140 00	
Office Supplies	11.9	100 00	
Prepaid Insurance	11.10	80 00	
Store Equipment	13.1	1,600 00	
Allowance for Depreciation of Store Equip.	13.2		400 00
Delivery Equipment	13.3	1,000 00	
Allowance for Depreciation of Delivery Equip.	13.4		375 00
Office Equipment	13.5	500 00	
Allowance for Depreciation of Office Equip.	13.6		75 00
Notes Payable	21.1		1,500 00
Interest Payable	21.2		4 84
Accounts Payable	21.3		2,804 90
Employees Income Taxes Payable	21.4		202 50
F.I.C.A. Taxes Payable	21.5		75 00
Federal Unemployment Taxes Payable	21.6		19 50
State Unemployment Taxes Payable	21.7		175 50
Sales Taxes Payable	21.8		539 85
R. C. Boynton, Capital	31.1		20,144 11
E. A. Brooks, Capital	31.3		20,144 11
		46,723 23	46,723 23

NAME AND ADDRESS	DATE OF SALE	AMOUNT
Acme Garage, 830 End St., City	Mar. 22	$ 204.00
S. R. Brown, Huntington	Mar. 14	186.15
Coswell Auto Repair, 735 Alcott St., City	Mar. 27	315.08
Drake-Elm Co., 1122 Beaford St., City	Mar. 24	251.86
Frank Elkins, 564 Oxford St., City	Feb. 21	133.52
H. B. Fisher, 6411 Palm Ave., City	Mar. 7	357.00
Harris Auto Co., Groverville	Mar. 26	532.54
B. D. Howe, 1298 Clark Drive, City	Mar. 26	219.71
King & Blake, 4221 Arnaz St., City	Mar. 25	190.28
N. V. Lacy, 274 Maywood St., City	Mar. 2	264.61
William Leeds, 916 Harper Ave., City		
L. K. Lewis, 8956 Holloway St., City	Jan. 15	68.58
McClain Corporation, 423 Patterson St., City	Mar. 27	207.87
Miller's Garage, 1028 Cedar Ave., City	Mar. 26	202.53

This list is concluded on page 390

Name and Address	Date of Sale	Amount
Norton, Inc., 1839 Lakeside St., City	Mar. 25	403.10
James Post, Middletown	Mar. 19	100.25
Harold Roberts, 428 W. Ninth St., City		
B. N. Scott, Westridge	Mar. 19	500.00
Lewis Terry, 908 Rodney Dr., City		
George Wallace, 5910 Winter St., City	Jan. 6	35.00
Total Accounts Receivable		$4,172.08

Instructions: (3) The foregoing accounts receivable and the balances are given in the accounts receivable ledger in the books of account that may be obtained for this practice set. If these books are not used, open accounts for the accounts receivable in the order in which they are given, allowing at least seven lines for each account, and record the balances in the appropriate customers' accounts as of the date of the sale.

Accounts Payable

The vouchers in the unpaid vouchers file on March 31 are as follows:

Date	Vchr. No.	Creditor	Amount
Feb. 27	512	Golden & Williams	$ 175.00
Mar. 10	531	Ace Tire Co.	275.50
11	535	Miller, Inc.	265.75
15	546	Davis & Co.	16.75
15	547	ABC Cushions & Covers	18.50
17	551	Star Auto Radios	37.50
17	552	Sampson Supply Co.	148.00
19	555	Jackson & Sons	60.00
22	560	Glendon Bros.	49.90
28	566	Norwalk Products, Inc.	525.00
29	568	Perfection Products	250.00
29	569	Globe Tubing Co.	325.00
29	570	Seymour Supply House	658.00
		Total Accounts Payable	$2,804.90

Instructions: (4) The unpaid vouchers listed above are already recorded in the voucher register in the books of account that may be obtained for this practice set. If these books are not used, proceed as follows:

(a) Enter the foregoing unpaid vouchers in the voucher register in numerical order as of the date of the voucher.

(b) Foot the Accounts Payable Cr. column, check the footing with the balance of the accounts payable account in the general ledger, record the total, and rule with single and double lines.

(c) Place a check mark directly below the total to indicate that this total need not be posted.

Notes Receivable Register

The notes receivable on hand on March 31 are as follows:

Note for $400 signed by Harold Roberts, dated January 15, our No. 19, payable at the First National Bank, time 90 days, interest 5%.

Note for $250 signed by Norton, Inc., dated February 9, our No. 21, payable at the National Bank & Trust Co., time 60 days, interest 5%.

Note for $150 signed by Coswell Auto Repair, dated March 30, our No. 25, payable at the Union Bank, time 60 days, interest 4%.

Instructions: (5) The notes receivable listed above are already recorded in the notes receivable register in the books of account that may be obtained for this practice set. If these books are not used, record the details of the foregoing notes receivable in the notes receivable register.

Notes Payable Register

The notes payable on March 31 are as follows:

Note No. 18, payable to Brands, Inc., dated February 11, payable at the First National Bank, time 60 days, interest 4%, face $600.

Note No. 20, payable to Westside Company, dated March 9, payable at the First National Bank, time 30 days, interest 5%, face $500.

Note No. 23, payable to Sampson Supply Co., dated March 29, payable at the First National Bank, time 60 days, interest 5%, face $400.

Instructions: (6) The notes payable listed above are already recorded in the notes payable register in the books of account that may be obtained for this practice set. If these books are not used, record the details of the foregoing notes payable in the notes payable register.

Books of Original Entry

The books of original entry consist of:

(1) A two-column general journal.

(2) A sales journal similar to the one illustrated on page 112.

(3) A cash receipts journal with columns headed General Cr., Accounts Receivable Cr., Sales Cr., Sales Taxes Payable Cr., Sales Discount Dr., and Cash Dr.

(4) A voucher register similar to the one illustrated on pages 288 and 289.

(5) A check register with amount columns headed Accounts Payable Dr., Purchases Discount Cr., and Cash Cr.

(6) A petty cash book similar to the one illustrated on page 269.

(7) A notes receivable register similar to the one illustrated on pages 272 and 273.

(8) A notes payable register similar to the one illustrated on pages 274 and 275.

Reversing Entries

Instructions: (7) Under date of April 1, record the reversing entries for interest receivable and interest payable.

Narrative of Transactions for April

April 1. Issued Check No. 761 to ABC Cushions & Covers in payment of Voucher No. 547 less a 2% discount.

April 1. Issued Voucher No. 575 for $50 to establish a petty cash fund; then issued Check No. 762 in payment of this voucher. (Small payments of $5 or less are to be made from the petty cash fund; all payments of more than $5 are to be made by check.)

April 1. Issued Voucher No. 576 for $400 to the Blackmer Realty Co. for April rent; then issued Check No. 763 in payment of this voucher.

April 1. Received checks from customers as follows:

Drake-Elm Co., $246.82, in payment of sale of March 24 less 2% discount.

Norton, Inc., $395.04, in payment of sale of March 25 less 2% discount.

April 2. Paid $3.75 from the petty cash fund for repairs to a typewriter. (Number the petty cash vouchers beginning with 1.)

April 2. Issued checks to creditors as follows:

Check No. 764 to Star Auto Radios in payment of Voucher No. 551 less 2% discount.

Check No. 765 to Sampson Supply Co. in payment of Voucher No. 552 less 2% discount.

Check No. 766 to Glendon Bros. in payment of Voucher No. 560 less 2% discount.

April 3. Made the following wholesale sales on account:

Sale No. 961, Acme Garage, $183.60.

Sale No. 962, B. D. Howe, $273.67.

April 3. Received checks from customers as follows:

King & Blake, $186.47, in payment of sale of March 25 less 2% discount.

Harris Auto Co., $521.89, in payment of sale of March 26 less 2% discount.

H. B. Fisher, $357, in payment of sale of March 7.

April 4. Purchased store equipment for $2,475 from Sweeney Equipment Company, paying $1,475 in cash and giving our 60-day, 5% note for the balance of $1,000. The note (our No. 24) is dated April 4 and is payable at the First National Bank.

Proceed as follows in recording this transaction:

(1) Record the complete transaction in the general journal. Credit Accounts Payable for the amount of the cash payment, since a voucher will be issued for this amount, and check this credit to avoid double posting.

(2) Record the details of the note in the notes payable register.

(3) Issue Voucher No. 577 for the amount of the cash payment, $1,475, checking the Store Equipment debit in the voucher register to avoid double posting.

(4) Issue Check No. 767 in payment of Voucher No. 577.

April 5. Issued vouchers for purchases on account as follows:

Voucher No. 578; Perfection Products, merchandise, $876.40.

Voucher No. 579; ABC Cushions & Covers, merchandise, $695.80.

April 5. Issued Check No. 768 to Jackson & Sons in payment of Voucher No. 555 less 2% discount.

April 6. Sold merchandise on account to Drake-Elm Co., $214.79; Sale No. 963.

April 6. Received checks from customers as follows:

McClain Corporation, $203.71, in payment of sale of March 27 less 2% discount.

Coswell Auto Repair, $308.78, in payment of sale of March 27 less 2% discount.

April 6. Paid $4.50 from the petty cash fund for the preparation of sales letters. (Charge Miscellaneous Selling Expense.)

April 6. Cash retail sales for the week were $2,082.90. Sales taxes collected on these sales amounted to $41.66.

April 8. Received a check for $100.25 from James Post in payment of sale of March 19.

April 8. Issued vouchers as follows:

Voucher No. 580, Globe Tubing Co., purchase of merchandise on account, $159.50.

Voucher No. 581, Westside Company, for our Note No. 20 and interest due today.

April 8. Issued checks as follows:

Check No. 769 to Westside Company in payment of Voucher No. 581.

Check No. 770 to Ace Tire Co. in payment of Voucher No. 531 less 1% discount.

Check No. 771 to Perfection Products in payment of Voucher No. 568 less 1% discount.

April 8. Received from B. N. Scott his 30-day, 4% note for $500 in settlement of sale of March 19. This note (our No. 26) was dated April 8 and is payable at the First National Bank.

April 9. Made the following wholesale sales on account:

Sale No. 964, Coswell Auto Repair, $503.98.

Sale No. 965, Harris Auto Co., $872.20.

April 9. Issued vouchers as follows:

Voucher No. 582, First National Bank, for monthly payment of employes income taxes payable, $202.50, and of F.I.C.A. taxes payable, $75; total of voucher, $277.50.

Voucher No. 583, Bureau of Unemployment Compensation, $175.50, for quarterly payment of state unemployment taxes payable.

Voucher No. 584, Department of Taxation, $539.85, for quarterly payment of sales taxes payable.

April 9. Issued checks as follows:

Check No. 772 to First National Bank in payment of Voucher No. 582.

Check No. 773 to Bureau of Unemployment Compensation in payment of Voucher No. 583.

Check No. 774 to Department of Taxation in payment of Voucher No. 584.

April 9. Received from S. R. Brown his 30-day, 4% note for $186.15 in settlement of sale of March 14. This note (our No. 27) was dated April 9 and is payable at the Union Bank.

April 9. Received a credit memorandum for $150 from ABC Cushions & Covers for merchandise returned on Voucher No. 579.

April 10. Received checks from customers as follows:

Norton, Inc., $252.08, in payment of note and interest due today.

Miller's Garage, $202.53, in payment of sale of March 26.

Acme Garage, $204, in payment of sale of March 22.

April 10. Issued vouchers for purchases on account as follows:
Voucher No. 585, Davis & Company, office supplies, $75.50.
Voucher No. 586, Norwalk Products, Inc., merchandise, $209.52.

April 10. Received from Frank Elkins his 60-day, 5% note for $133.52 in settlement of sale of February 21. This note (our No. 28) was dated April 9 and is payable at the First National Bank.

April 10. Issued checks as follows:
Check No. 775 to Miller, Inc. in payment of Voucher No. 535 less 1% discount.
Check No. 776 to Davis & Company in payment of Voucher No. 546.

April 11. Paid $2.50 from the petty cash fund for repairs to the delivery truck. (Charge Miscellaneous Delivery Expense.)

April 11. Sold merchandise on account to King & Blake, $214.20; Sale No. 966.

April 11. Issued vouchers as follows:
Voucher No. 587, Orr Supply Co., store supplies, $35.
Voucher No. 588, Charles Evans, for washing windows and cleaning office, $15. (Charge Miscellaneous General Expense.)

April 11. Issued checks as follows:
Check No. 777 to Orr Supply Co. in payment of Voucher No. 587.
Check No. 778 to Charles Evans in payment of Voucher No. 588.

April 12. Made the following wholesale sales on account:
Sale No. 967, William Leeds, $91.80.
Sale No. 968, Norton, Inc., $719.10.

April 12. Issued vouchers as follows:
Voucher No. 589, Brands, Inc., for our Note No. 18 and interest due today.
Voucher No. 590, Daily News, newspaper advertising, $25.
Voucher No. 591, Wilshire Garage, repairs on delivery truck, $17.50. (Charge Miscellaneous Delivery Expense.)

April 12. Issued checks as follows:
Check No. 779 to Brands, Inc. in payment of Voucher No. 589.
Check No. 780 to Daily News in payment of Voucher No. 590.
Check No. 781 to Wilshire Garage in payment of Voucher No. 591.
Check No. 782 to Perfection Products in payment of Voucher No. 578 less 1% discount.

April 13. Issued Credit Memo No. 44 for $96.90 to Harris Auto Co. for merchandise returned on sale of April 9.

April 13. Recorded the biweekly payroll from the following data provided by the payroll clerk. Issued Voucher No. 592 for the amount payable; then issued Check No. 783, payable to Payroll, in payment of Voucher No. 592.

Payroll:
Sales Salaries............................ $600.00
Delivery Salaries......................... 150.00
Office Salaries........................... 250.00 $1,000.00
Deductions:
Employees' Income Taxes.................. $ 81.00
Employees' Share of F.I.C.A. Taxes........ 15.00 96.00
Amount Payable.......................... $ 904.00

April 13. Recorded the employer's liability for F.I.C.A. taxes and for federal and state unemployment taxes from the following data provided by the payroll clerk:

F.I.C.A. Taxes	$15.00
Federal Unemployment Taxes	3.00
State Unemployment Taxes	27.00
Total Payroll Taxes	$45.00

April 13. Cash retail sales for the week were $2,105.60. Sales taxes collected on these sales amounted to $42.11.

Prove cash. The cash balance is $2,882.02. Cash is proved by comparing this balance with the sum of the cash on hand at the beginning of the month plus the cash receipts minus the cash payments. The totals may be entered in small pencil figures in the cash columns in the cash receipts journal and the check register, and the balance may be entered in small pencil figures in the account credited column of the cash receipts journal so that the amounts entered before this cash proof will not have to be used when cash is proved again.

Post from the sales journal, the general journal, and the cash receipts journal to the customers' accounts in the accounts receivable ledger. In actual practice this posting would be completed daily; but because of the comparatively small number of transactions in this set, the posting will be completed only at the times indicated in the narrative of transactions. When posting is completed at intervals during the month rather than daily, some of the entries in the accounts will not appear in chronological sequence. This is of no consequence, however, because upon the completion of the posting the balance of each account will be correct as of that date.

April 15. Received a check for $405 from Harold Roberts in payment of his note and interest due today.

April 15. Issued vouchers as follows:

Voucher No. 593, W. C. Vincent, to reimburse him for entertaining customers, $13.50. (Charge Miscellaneous Selling Expense.)
Voucher No. 594, Brands, Inc., merchandise, $1,090.20.

April 15. Issued Check No. 784 to W. C. Vincent for Voucher No. 593.

April 16. Sold merchandise on account to Lewis Terry, $867; Sale 969.

April 16. Received a check for $210.49 from Drake-Elm Co. in payment of sale of April 6 less 2% discount.

April 16. Borrowed $3,000 from the First National Bank on our 60-day, non-interest-bearing note (No. 25). Received credit for the proceeds, $2,980.

April 16. Received a memorandum from Mr. Brooks stating that Mr. George Wallace has been declared bankrupt and that it is not likely that his account will ever be collected. Wrote off the account as a bad debt.

April 17. Paid $3.95 from petty cash for parcel wrappings. (Charge Miscellaneous Selling Expense.)

April 17. Purchased a new delivery truck from Hackett Motors, Inc., trading in the old delivery truck, which had cost $1,000, and paying an additional $2,275 in cash. Recorded depreciation of $20 on the old truck for the current month. Issued Voucher No. 595 for the amount of the cash payment; then issued Check No. 785 in payment of this voucher.

The purchase of the new truck is to be recorded according to the income tax method given on page 249.

April 18. Issued Check No. 786 to ABC Cushions & Covers in payment ot Voucher No. 579 less the return and less 2% discount.

April 19. Sold merchandise on account to Miller's Garage, $237.15; Sale No. 970.

April 19. Received checks from customers as follows:
Coswell Auto Repair, $493.90, in payment of sale of April 9 less 2% discount.
Harris Auto Co., $759.79, in payment of sale of April 9 less the return and less 2% discount.
King & Blake, $209.92, in payment of sale of April 11 less 2% discount.

April 20. Paid $4.50 from the petty cash fund for miscellaneous supplies to be used in the office.

April 20. Issued Credit Memo No. 45 for $25.50 to Norton, Inc. for merchandise returned on sale of April 12.

April 20. Cash retail sales for the week were $2,402.10. Sales taxes collected on these sales amounted to $48.04.
Prove cash. The cash balance is $7,567.88.
Post from the various journals to the customers' accounts in the accounts receivable ledger.

April 22. Received a credit memorandum for $225 from Brands, Inc. for merchandise returned on Voucher No. 594.

April 22. Received a check for $679.73 from Norton, Inc. in payment of the sale of April 12 less the return of April 20 and less 2% discount.

April 23. Sold merchandise on account to S. R. Brown, $502.35; Sale No. 971.

April 23. Made the following payments from the petty cash fund:
$3.06 to a cash customer who returned defective merchandise: merchandise, $3; sales tax, 6 cents.
$3 to Richard Engel for washing the windows.

April 24. Issued vouchers for purchases on account as follows:
Voucher No. 596, Glendon Bros., merchandise, $650.20.
Voucher No. 597, Westside Company, merchandise, $270.
Voucher No. 598, Jones Equipment Co., office equipment, $750.

April 24. Issued checks as follows:
Check No. 787 to Golden & Williams in payment of Voucher No. 512.
Check No. 788 to Jones Equipment Co. in payment of Voucher No. 598.

April 25. Issued Voucher No. 599 for $150 to the *Daily News* for advertising; then issued Check No. 789 in payment of this voucher.

April 26. Issued vouchers for purchases on account as follows:
Voucher No. 600, Seymour Supply House, merchandise, $652.
Voucher No. 601, Perfection Products, merchandise, $542.60.

April 26. Issued Credit Memo No. 46 for $46.92 to Lewis Terry for merchandise returned on sale of April 16.

April 27. Made the following wholesale sales on account:
Sale No. 972, Harold Roberts, $361.10.
Sale No. 973, H. B. Fisher, $519.71.

April 27. Issued checks to creditors as follows:
Check No. 790 to Norwalk Products, Inc. in payment of Voucher No. 566 less 1% discount.
Check No. 791 to Globe Tubing Co. in payment of Voucher No. 569 less 1% discount.

Check No. 792 to Seymour Supply House in payment of Voucher No. 570 less 1% discount.

April 27. Paid $4.95 from the petty cash fund to a cash customer who returned defective merchandise: merchandise $4.85; sales tax, 10 cents.

April 27. Recorded the biweekly payroll and issued Voucher No. 602 and Check No. 793 for the payment. Recorded the employer's liability for payroll taxes. Salaries, deductions, and taxes were the same as on April 13.

April 27. Cash retail sales for the week were $2,010.03. Sales taxes collected on these sales amounted to $40.20.

April 29. Received a check for $232.41 from Miller's Garage in payment of sale of April 19 less 2% discount.

April 29. Issued vouchers for purchases on account as follows:
Voucher No. 603, Sampson Supply Co., merchandise, $945.95.
Voucher No. 604, Davis & Company, store supplies, $43.85, and office supplies, $18.20; total invoice, $62.05.

April 30. Paid $4.65 from the petty cash fund for telegrams. (Charge Miscellaneous General Expense.)

April 30. Issued Credit Memo No. 47 for $9.79 to Harold Roberts for merchandise returned on sale of April 27.

April 30. Issued vouchers as follows:
Voucher No. 605, R. C. Boynton, withdrawal of salary allowance in accordance with partnership agreement, $400.
Voucher No. 606, E. A. Brooks, withdrawal of salary allowance in accordance with partnership agreement, $500.
Voucher No. 607, City Gas & Electric Co., gas and electricity, $21.75. (Charge Miscellaneous General Expense.)
Voucher No. 608, Western Telephone Co., telephone service, $18.85. (Charge Miscellaneous General Expense.)
Voucher No. 609, Wilshire Garage, gas, oil, and miscellaneous delivery truck expenses, $39.84.
Voucher No. 610, Clayton Drayage Co., freight in, $125.
Voucher No. 611, Petty Cash, to replenish petty cash fund, $34.86.

April 30. Issued checks as follows:
Check No. 794 to R. C. Boynton in payment of Voucher No. 605.
Check No. 795 to E. A. Brooks in payment of Voucher No. 606.
Check No. 796 to City Gas & Electric Co. in payment of Voucher No. 607.
Check No. 797 to Western Telephone Co. in payment of Voucher No. 608.
Check No. 798 to Wilshire Garage in payment of Voucher No. 609.
Check No. 799 to Clayton Drayage Co. in payment of Voucher No. 610.
Check No. 800 to Petty Cash in payment of Voucher No. 611.

April 30. Cash retail sales for April 29–30 were $903.65. Sales taxes collected on these sales amounted to $18.07.
Prove cash. The cash balance is $6,839.75.
Post to the accounts in the accounts receivable ledger.
Post to the general ledger accounts from the general columns of the general journal, the cash receipts journal, and the voucher register. If the ledger forms used are similar to those illustrated on page 278, the balance of the accounts should be determined only after all posting for the month is completed.

Total and rule the various special journals and post the totals to the appropriate general ledger accounts from the sales journal, the cash receipts journal, the voucher register, and the check register. (Use "CP" to indicate postings from the check register.)

Periodic Summary

As the proprietors, R. C. Boynton and E. A. Brooks, consider each month to be a separate fiscal period, the periodic summary should now be completed according to the outline on page 163. The partners have agreed that Mr. Boynton is to receive a salary allowance of $400 a month and Mr. Brooks a salary allowance of $500 a month and that remaining profits or losses after these salary allowances are to be divided equally. When the books are closed, any balances in the drawing accounts are to be closed to the capital accounts.

The additional data required for the periodic summary are:

Interest accrued on notes receivable.................. $	2.60
Allowance for bad debts: increase allowance by 1% of gross charge sales..............................	55.61
Merchandise inventory, April 30...................	32,674.07
Inventories of supplies, April 30:	
Store supplies.................................	120.00
Office supplies................................	150.00
Insurance expired:	
Selling.......................................	5.50
Delivery......................................	7.00
General.......................................	1.50
Depreciation:	
Store equipment, 10% a year....................	33.96
Office equipment, 10% a year...................	4.17
(Depreciation is not recorded on the delivery equipment purchased on April 17 because it has been the custom of this business to record a full month's depreciation on an asset owned for a half month or more and no depreciation on an asset owned for less than a half month.)	
Interest accrued on notes payable..................	5.33
Prepaid interest on notes payable.................	15.33
Accrued payroll data:	
Sales salaries.................................	100.00
Delivery salaries..............................	25.00
Office salaries................................	41.67
Employer's F.I.C.A. taxes payable..............	2.50
Federal unemployment taxes payable............	.50
State unemployment taxes payable..............	4.50

Part 2 of this practice set, containing the narrative of transactions for May, begins on page 487 immediately after Chapter 24. The books of account for April will be needed at that time.

Chapter 21

Formation of Corporations

CORPORATION DEFINED The corporation has become the dominant form of business organization in American economic society. With the great expansion of industry there has developed a demand for large amounts of capital, which is best obtainable from the pooled savings of many investors. These investors desire income and price appreciation on their investments, but they are unwilling or unable to undertake active management. Because the corporation offers income without management responsibilities, it is an ideal outlet for the savings of a large number of individuals and institutions.

Corporations may be classified into three types: public, quasi-public, and private. A *public corporation* is created for a public purpose, such as a political unit or an educational institution. A *quasi-public corporation* is a private company performing a public service, such as a telephone or a gas company. A *private corporation* is an ordinary business unit organized to carry on operations for the benefit of its owners. The discussion in this text will be limited to the features of a private corporation.

The most popular definition of a corporation is that given by Chief Justice Marshall: "A corporation is an artificial being, invisible, intangible, and existing only in contemplation of the law." The concept underlying this definition has become the foundation for the prevailing legal doctrine that a corporation is an artificial person, created by law and having a distinct existence, separate and apart from the natural persons who are responsible for its creation and operation. Although the doctrine is admittedly a legal fiction, it is disregarded only when a court believes that justice requires such action. The owners of a corporation are called stockholders, but the stockholders do not constitute the corporation. The corporation is a separate entity.

CHARACTERISTICS OF A CORPORATION As a legal entity the corporation has certain characteristics that distinguish it from other types of business organization. The most important of these characteristics will be considered briefly in the following paragraphs.

(1) *Separate Legal Existence.* Being a distinct legal entity, the corporation may act under a corporate name. It may obtain, hold, and

dispose of property in its corporate capacity. It may borrow funds and assume other obligations. It may enter into contracts with outsiders or with its own stockholders.

(2) *Transferable Units of Proprietorship.* The interests in the proprietorship of a corporation are divided into transferable units known as *shares of stock.* Each share has the same rights and privileges as every other share of the same class. The owners of the corporation, known as *stockholders,* may sell their stock without interfering with the activities of the corporation. A sale of stock on a stock exchange is an independent transaction between the seller and the buyer of the stock and does not affect in any way the financial position of the corporation.

(3) *Limited Liability of Stockholders.* Since a corporation is a separate legal entity, it is responsible for its own acts and obligations. Normally the creditors of a corporation may not look beyond the assets of the corporation for satisfaction of their claims. Thus, the loss that a stockholder may suffer is limited to the amount of his investment. This feature is largely responsible for the phenomenal growth of the corporate form of business.

(4) *Continuity of Existence.* The life of a corporation depends upon the terms of its charter; it may be perpetual or it may continue for a specified number of years. When the life of the corporation is limited by a charter, the term of existence is renewed by an application for a new charter. The life term of the corporation is not affected by the death or the incapacity of its owners as in the case of a partnership.

(5) *Double Taxation of Income.* The earnings of a corporation are subject to various income taxes. When the earnings are distributed to stockholders as dividends, they are again subject to income taxes, comprising what is known as double taxation of the same income. For example, assume that a company earns $100,000 and pays income taxes of $46,000. If the remaining $54,000 is distributed to stockholders who are in the 40% income tax bracket, they will in turn pay $21,600 in personal income taxes. Thus original corporate earnings of $100,000 improved the purchasing power of the stockholders by only $32,400.

WORKING ORGANIZATION OF A CORPORATION   In a corporation the proprietorship is vested in the stockholders, acting as a "legal entity." The ownership of the stockholders is evidenced by shares of stock. Although the ultimate control of the corporation is vested in the stockholders, the control is exercised indirectly. They elect at regular intervals, usually annually, a *board of directors,* to whom they delegate the duties of supervising and controlling the operations of the business. The directors usually submit to the stockholders annual reports showing the results of the operations of the past year. Frequently interim reports are provided for stockholders in order to give them some idea of how operations are progressing for a part of a fiscal period, such as a month or a quarter.

The board of directors select the *general executives*, to whom they delegate the responsibility of administering the activities of the corporation. These executives usually consist of a president, one or more vice-presidents, a secretary, a treasurer, and a controller. The *controller* is the chief accounting officer and meets with the other executives in determining operating policies of the corporation. Although all the executives are selected by the board of directors, they act under the authority and the control of the president.

The following chart shows this narrowing down of the responsibility from the numerous stockholders to the president. It then shows the delegation of administrative duties from the president to the various employees of the corporation.

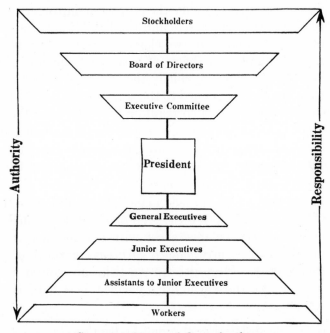

Corporate Form of Organization

An illustration of this delegation of duties is found in a manufacturing firm that has a vice-president in charge of production and under him a superintendent of shops. The latter, in turn, has subordinate to him departmental foremen, who direct and control the activities of the workers.

In many corporations the ownership is so large and widespread that most stockholders are unable to attend the annual meeting. Such stockholders may transfer their voting power to an agent who votes their stock. This delegation is accomplished by signing a paper known as a *proxy*.

STOCKHOLDERS AND PROPRIETORSHIP The proprietorship of a corporation is commonly referred to as *capital, stockholders' interest,* or *net worth*. The stockholders of a corporation have no direct personal ownership in the assets of the enterprise. Neither do they have a direct interest in the earnings of the corporation until the earnings have been distributed in the form of dividends. Instead, they have a contract with the corporation giving them an interest in the corporate assets and the right to participate in the management and the earnings of the enterprise. This right is exercised through the medium of the board of directors.

The capital of a corporation, like the proprietorship of an individual, is the difference between the assets and the liabilities. The corporate capital, however, is composed of two elements: a stated capital, represented by a given number of shares at a specified amount per share, and a residual capital, showing chiefly the results of operations. The stated capital is the value assigned to the stock by the provisions of the charter. When the capital of a corporation is greater than the amount of the stock, the excess is known as *surplus;* when it is smaller than the amount of the stock, the difference is known as *deficit*. Surplus resulting from corporate earnings is known as *earned surplus;* surplus from other sources is referred to as *paid-in surplus*.

There is a tendency in published balance sheets to replace the word "surplus" with more descriptive titles. For example, earned surplus is often reported on the balance sheet with a title such as *retained income, retained earnings, accumulated earnings,* or *earnings retained for use in the business*. More descriptive titles are considered to be desirable, especially for those who use a balance sheet but who are not trained in accounting.[1]

---

[1] In *Accounting Research Bulletin No. 39*, issued by the Committee on Accounting Procedure, American Institute of Accountants, the Subcommittee on Terminology recommended that the term "surplus" be discontinued in the balance sheet presentation of the stockholders' equity. However, in *Accounting Research Bulletin No. 41* on "Presentation of Income and Earned Surplus," the following comment is made:

"In Bulletin No. 39 the committee published as an approved objective a recommendation of the subcommittee on terminology that in balance-sheet

The total capital of a corporation consists of the stock plus the surplus or minus the deficit. These terms are illustrated below:

Stock (par or stated value) .	$50,000	Stock (par or stated value) .	$50,000
Surplus.	10,000	Less Deficit.	5,000
Capital.	$60,000	Capital.	$45,000

To show the difference in the proprietorship accounts of a sole proprietorship and a corporation, assume original investments in each case of $50,000 on January 2, 1953, earnings of $5,000 in 1953, and a loss of $15,000 in 1954, no withdrawal or distribution of profits being made. The proprietorship accounts would appear as follows:

SOLE PROPRIETORSHIP		CORPORATION	
Jan. 2, 1953 Jones, Capital $50,000	Jan. 2, 1953 Stock. $50,000
Dec. 31, 1953 Jones, Capital 55,000	Dec. 31, 1953 Stock. 50,000
	Surplus. 5,000
Dec. 31, 1954 Jones, Capital 40,000	Dec. 31, 1954 Stock. 50,000
	Deficit. 10,000

When surplus is set up as an account, it normally has a credit balance showing the difference between capital and stock. If capital is less than stock, the surplus balance is a debit and is called deficit. This is illustrated below:

SURPLUS

Debit balance is called Deficit	Credit balance is called Surplus

TYPES OF STOCK　　　A corporation may issue several classes of stock, each embodying different terms and carrying different privileges. The most common classification is that of *common stock* and *preferred stock*. Common stock has no preference over any other stock of the company as to dividends or assets, but it carries with it the right to participate in the management of the corporation by voting at stockholders' meetings. Preferred stock usually has no voting rights, but it carries some kind of preference over

---

presentation the use of the term "surplus" be discontinued. The committee believes that further experimentation with substitutes for the term is desirable in financial statements prepared for the general public. However, the committee plans to continue to use the term "surplus" in its bulletins as being a technical term that is well understood among accountants to whom the bulletins are directed."

Similarly, the term "surplus" will be used in the following discussions, but other acceptable and descriptive titles may occasionally be used.

common stock as to the distribution of profits. To understand the effect of this preference, it is necessary to consider briefly the method of distributing the profits of a corporation.

Stockholders invest in a corporation primarily to participate in its earnings. The board of directors determines when the corporation is financially able to distribute to its stockholders a portion of its earnings. Such a distribution of earnings is called *declaring a dividend*. Dividends are usually stated as a certain amount per share, such as $5 per share or $2 per share.

To make its stock more attractive to investors, a corporation may issue a portion of it with preference as to dividends. This means that, whenever profits are distributed, the preferred stockholders will receive their stipulated share first, the common stockholders receiving the balance of the distribution. Preferred stock may also carry preference as to distribution of assets in case of dissolution or liquidation of the corporation. If the net assets are insufficient to repay the total contributions of all stockholders, payment will first be made to the preferred stockholders, and the balance remaining will be distributed to the common stockholders.

If a corporation earns a high rate of return, common stock will be more desirable than preferred stock. For example, assume that the Ames Company has 2,000 shares of common and 1,000 shares of 6% preferred outstanding, each with a par value of $100 per share. In successive years the company earned $20,000 and $36,000 respectively and paid 75% of the earnings in dividends. The distribution of earnings may be tabulated as follows:

	FIRST YEAR	SECOND YEAR
Income...........................	$20,000	$36,000
Per cent of income to be paid as dividends	75%	75%
Dividend distribution................	$15,000	$27,000
Dividends on preferred (6% of $100,000).	6,000	6,000
Balance to common..................	$ 9,000	$21,000
Dividends per share on common........	$ 4.50	$ 10.50

It may be noted that the preferred stock received the same dividend in both years; however, the common stock benefited greatly during the second year because its dividends were not limited by contract.

The participation of holders of preferred stock in the earnings of a corporation is ordinarily limited to the rate specified on the stock. Preferred stock that is limited to the specified rate is known as *non-*

participating. If the holders of preferred stock receive an additional rate when earnings are adequate to pay the holders of common stock more than the specified rate, the preferred stock is known as *participating.* For example, if the preferred stock of the Ames Company were participating, the $27,000 dividend distribution for the second year would have been allocated as follows:

	To PREFERRED	To COMMON	TOTAL
To preferred (6% of $100,000).............	$6,000		$ 6,000
To common (6% of $200,000 to match preferred rate).......................		$12,000	12,000
Balance of $9,000 to all shares ratably, (3% on total capital of $300,000)........	3,000	6,000	9,000
Total dividends........................	$9,000	$18,000	$27,000
Dividends per share....................	$9.00	$9.00	

Since most preferred stock is nonparticipating and has a limited dividend rate, provision is usually made to have any dividends not paid accumulate. Such preferred stock is known as *cumulative* preferred stock. If unpaid dividends do not accumulate, the preferred stock is known as *noncumulative.* The following table illustrates the dividend participation of 6% cumulative, nonparticipating preferred stock and common stock over a six-year period (assuming $100,000 of each kind of stock outstanding) and the effect on surplus.

YEAR	PROFIT OR LOSS*	DIVIDEND TO BE PAID	TO PREFERRED STOCK	TO COMMON STOCK	TO SURPLUS	SURPLUS BALANCE
1949	$15,000	$10,000	$ 6,000	$ 4,000	$ 5,000	$ 5,000
1950	25,000	15,000	6,000	9,000	10,000	15,000
1951	10,000*	–0–	–0–	–0–	10,000*	5,000
1952	30,000	15,000	12,000	3,000	15,000	20,000
1953	2,000	3,000	3,000	–0–	1,000*	19,000
1954	25,000	20,000	9,000	11,000	5,000	24,000

In 1952 the preferred stock was paid $6,000 for back dividends for 1951 and $6,000 for the current year. In 1954 the preferred stock was paid $3,000 for back dividends for 1953 and $6,000 for the current year.

CORPORATE CAPITAL ON THE BALANCE SHEET   The assets and the liabilities of a corporation are reported on the balance sheet in the same manner as the assets and the liabilities of a sole proprietorship or a partnership. The capital section of the balance sheet, however, is different. It ordinarily shows each class of stock and the surplus or the deficit. For example, the capital section of a balance sheet for a corporation with $100,000 of 6% cumulative preferred stock, $200,000 of common stock, and a surplus of $75,000 is as follows:

CAPITAL

Paid-in Capital:		
Preferred Stock, $100 par, 6% cumulative.............	$100,000	
Common Stock, $100 par.........................	200,000	
Total Paid-in Capital............................	$300,000	
Surplus...	75,000	
Total Capital.....................................		$375,000

If the same corporation had suffered losses from operations and had accumulated a deficit of $50,000, its capital would have been reported on the balance sheet in the manner shown below:

CAPITAL

Paid-in Capital:		
Preferred Stock, $100 par, 6% cumulative...........	$100,000	
Common Stock, $100 par........................	200,000	
Total Paid-in Capital............................	$300,000	
Less Deficit....................................	50,000	
Total Capital.....................................		$250,000

DIFFERENT VALUES OF CORPORATE STOCK The value of corporate stock is spoken of in terms of shares. A share may have six different values: par value, book value, market value, stated value, liquidation value, and redemption value. All stock normally has a book value and a market value; it may or may not have the other values listed above.

Par Value. Par value is the value assigned to each share of stock when the charter is issued. The par value is printed on the face of each certificate and is sometimes referred to as *face value*. When stock is sold, the par value must be credited to the stock account and the difference between par value and the proceeds is entered in a surplus account. No-par-value stock does not have par value; its features are discussed in the following chapter.

Book Value. The par value of the stock does not measure the capital of the corporation. The par value of the stock plus the surplus or minus the deficit equals the actual capital. *Book value* is obtained by dividing the net assets or capital by the number of shares outstanding. Thus if the balance sheet of a corporation shows common stock of $100,000 (1,000 shares having a par value of $100) and a surplus of $35,000, the book value of each share is $135, or ($100,000 + $35,000) ÷ 1,000. If, instead of a surplus of $35,000, there is a deficit of $35,000, the book value of each share is $65, or ($100,000 − $35,000) ÷ 1,000.

If a corporation has both preferred and common stock, the par value of the preferred stock must be subtracted from the total capital in arriving at the book value of the common stock. The par value of the preferred stock on the first partial balance sheet on page 406 is $100; therefore, the book value of one share of common stock is $137.50, or ($375,000 − $100,000) ÷ 2,000. When the deficit is $50,000 as shown on the second partial balance sheet on page 406, the book value of one share of common stock is $75, or ($250,000 − $100,000) ÷ 2,000.

The book value of stock does not carry great importance under generally accepted accounting procedures. Assets are recorded at cost upon acquisition, and subsequent accounting for these assets is in terms of historical costs despite the fact that values may have changed considerably. For example, it is not uncommon to find land with a present market value of $30,000 carried on a company's books at $10,000. The book value of stock in such a case would not be a fair indication of its real worth.

Market Value. The prices quoted on the New York Stock Exchange or on other stock exchanges provide the best evidence of market value. Literally, *market value* means the price the stock will bring as a result of the meeting of supply and demand forces. Earning capacity rather than book or par values affects the market value of stocks. The stock mentioned above with a book value of $135 might have a market value of $175 if its earnings were high or a market value of only $75 if its earnings were low.

Other Values. The other values that a stock may have are stated value, liquidation value, and redemption value. *Stated value* is the minimum value required by law or fixed by the board of directors; it is the value of the share credited to the stock account regardless of the price received for that share. From an accounting point of view, there is no essential difference between par value and stated value stock. *Liquidation value* is the amount in dollars that will be paid on each share if the corporation is liquidated. *Redemption value* usually applies to a preferred stock and is the amount the corporation must pay if it chooses to redeem outstanding preferred stock.

INCORPORATION   A corporation is "authorized by law and created by charter." Since a corporation is created by permission from governmental authority and under the supervision of a governmental unit, legal formalities must be met before a charter will be granted. Although these legal requirements vary in the different states, their general nature can be indicated. The typical method of organization involves two steps: (1) obtaining subscriptions to stock and effecting a tentative organization; (2) obtaining the permission of the state to commence business operations. The law usually stipulates what the application for incorporation must contain. In many cases the state merely approves the application for incorporation. The application then becomes the charter of the corporation.

A corporation must conform to the corporate laws of the state in which it has been organized. If it extends its operations beyond the state, it is subject to the federal laws involving interstate commerce and the laws of all states in which it carries on business. It is also subject to that general control which any state exercises over all business organizations.

ORGANIZATION   Expenditures incurred in the organization of
COSTS   a corporation, such as fees paid to the state, promoters' costs, and attorneys' fees, are charged to an asset account called *Organization Costs*. The items charged to this account should be restricted to those having to do with the formation of the corporation and should not include the installation of accounting systems, advertising campaigns, or professional fees for plant construction and layout.

The organization costs account may be classified as an intangible asset or as a deferred charge and theoretically should be written off over the estimated life of the corporation. Since it is difficult to forecast the life of the corporation and since this asset has practically no exchangeable value, it is common practice to write it off over a period of three to five years. The amounts written off are charged to Earned Surplus, as they are not a deductible expense for income tax purposes. Some accountants hold that, since organization costs must be incurred in starting a corporation, such expenditures are as much an asset as plant and equipment and should be permanently retained on the balance sheet so long as the corporation maintains its status as a going concern. While such a position may be justified from a theoretical standpoint, corporations generally adopt the conservative practice of writing off organization costs during the early years of the corporation's existence.

CERTIFICATE OF INCORPORATION   The charter lists the powers that the corporation possesses and the limitations under which it must operate. The provisions governing the form of the application for incorporation vary in different states, but in general they include all the important features peculiar to a corporation, such as the name, the purpose, the duration, the location, and the capitalization.

To illustrate what is required, the following provisions from the statutes of the state of New York are given:

Three or more persons may become a stock corporation for any lawful purpose or purposes . . . by making, subscribing, acknowledging, and filing a certificate . . . which shall state:

(1) The name of the proposed corporation.

(2) The purpose or purposes for which the corporation is to be formed.

(3) Either the amount of the capital stock and the number and par value of the shares of which it is to consist; or if the corporation is to issue shares without par value, the statements required by Section 12.

(4) If the shares are to be classified, the number of shares to be included in each class and all of the designations, preferences, privileges, and voting powers of the shares of each class, and the restrictions or qualifications thereof.

(5) The city, village, or town and the county in which the office of the corporation is to be located.

(6) The duration of the corporation.

(7) The number of its directors . . . not less than three.

(8) The names and post-office addresses of the directors . . .

(9) The name and post-office address of each subscriber listed on the certificate of incorporation and a statement of the number of shares which he agrees to take . . .

The certificate must be signed by the persons who make application for the charter, and their signatures must be acknowledged by a notary public or some other designated official.

ISSUING STOCK AT PAR FOR CASH OR OTHER ASSETS   When a corporation receives its charter, the books of record may be opened. The incorporators, or organizers, of the corporation have, in most cases, performed some transactions prior to the granting of the charter and should have kept a record of them. These transactions are not, however, transactions performed by the corporation; therefore, no entries should be made in the records of the corporation until the charter has been obtained.

The opening entries of a corporation are similar to those of other types of business organizations in that they record the assets that the corporation has acquired and the liabilities, if any, that the corporation has assumed. The capital of the corporation at the time of formation is recorded as one item; it is not credited to accounts with the individual members of the organization, as would be done in the case of a partnership.

The simplest case that can be taken by way of illustration is that of a corporation, the entire authorized capital stock of which has been sold at par value for cash. The Holmes Manufacturing Company is organized on March 15 with an authorized capital stock of $800,000, consisting of 4,000 shares of 5% preferred stock and 4,000 shares of common stock, each having a par value of $100. If all the stock is sold at par for cash on March 15, the entry in general journal form would be:

```
Mar. 15  Cash......................................  800,000
             5% Preferred Stock.......................           400,000
             Common Stock.............................           400,000
               Sold 4,000 shares of 5% preferred stock and
               4,000 shares of common stock at $100 a share
               par value and issued the stock.
```

In the above example it was assumed that stock was sold for cash and that the cash would subsequently be invested in the assets needed by the corporation. Occasionally stock is exchanged for assets directly; in this case a price must be assigned to the assets acquired. For example, if land is to be acquired as a site for a building, the board of directors must agree to the price of the land in order to determine the number of shares to be exchanged for it. If the price is $10,000 and common stock is being sold at par, $100, on the open market, the number of common shares to be given for the land would be 100. The entry made is shown below:

```
Mar. 20  Land......................................  10,000
             Common Stock.............................            10,000
               Exchanged 100 shares of common stock
               for land.
```

If payment for the stock had been made with several pieces of property, such as machinery, buildings, and land, which were to be retained for use by the corporation, the opening entry would have recorded the various assets as follows:

```
Mar. 15  Machinery.................................  150,000
         Buildings.................................  155,000
         Land.....................................   95,000
             Common Stock.............................           400,000
               Issued 4,000 shares of common stock (par
               value $100) in return for machinery, build-
               ings, and land acquired from C. D. Evans
               in accordance with the contract on file.
```

AUTHORIZED STOCK   It is often desirable to have the charter authorize the issuance of more stock than the quantity to be issued at the time of the formation of the corporation. The company is then relieved of the necessity of applying for a change in the charter at the time when it may wish to increase its capital. For example, if the charter of the Adams Company authorizes an issue of only 4,000 shares of $100 par common stock, the amount already issued, and at a later time $200,000 of additional capital is needed, it would be necessary for the company to have its charter revised before it could issue the additional stock. If the charter, however, authorizes the issuance of 6,000 shares of common stock and only 4,000 shares have been issued, the remaining 2,000 shares can be issued at any time without further authorization from the state.

The authorized capital stock of the Adams Company may be reported parenthetically on the balance sheet in the following manner:

CAPITAL

Common Stock, $100 par (6,000 shares authorized)...... $400,000
Surplus.. 120,000

Total Capital.................................... $520,000

CHANGING FROM A   From a legal point of view, changing from
PARTNERSHIP TO   a partnership to a corporation necessitates
A CORPORATION   (1) the dissolution of the partnership, which
is usually effected by an agreement between the partners, and (2) the fulfillment of all the requirements imposed by the state upon the incorporators, which is evidenced by the charter granted by the state. From an accounting point of view, two steps are necessary: (1) the books of the partnership must be closed according to the partnership agreement and (2) the books of the corporation must be opened in compliance with the provisions of the charter.

To illustrate the change of a partnership to a corporation, it may be assumed that Allen and Baker are partners sharing profits and losses equally. In order to obtain additional capital for the expansion of their enterprise and to take advantage of the corporate form of business, the partners decide to incorporate.

Closing the Books of the Partnership. The balance sheet of the partnership of Allen and Baker on December 31, 1953, is shown on the following page.

The new corporation, to be called the Newton Corporation, is to have an authorized capital stock of $500,000, consisting of 5,000 shares of common stock with a par value of $100. The corporation is to take

ALLEN AND BAKER
BALANCE SHEET
December 31, 1953

ASSETS

Current Assets:

Cash...................................		$ 25,000	
Accounts Receivable..................	$105,000		
Less Allowance for Bad Debts.........	5,000	100,000	
Merchandise Inventory........................		150,000	
Total Current Assets............................			$275,000

Fixed Assets:

Store Equipment.......................	$ 6,000		
Less Allowance for Depreciation........	1,000	$ 5,000	
Buildings............................	$100,000		
Less Allowance for Depreciation........	20,000	80,000	
Land..		50,000	
Total Fixed Assets..............................			135,000
Total Assets......................................			$410,000

LIABILITIES

Accounts Payable.................................	$ 80,000

PROPRIETORSHIP

J. C. Allen, Capital..............................	$200,000	
M. R. Baker, Capital.............................	130,000	330,000
Total Liabilities and Proprietorship..................		$410,000

over the assets and to assume the liabilities of the partnership at revised values and is to issue to J. C. Allen and M. R. Baker, in payment for their business, common stock amounting to their respective interests in the partnership. In addition, a new associate, W. A. Carlson, agrees to invest $100,000 in cash. He is to receive 1,000 shares of stock.

Before turning the partnership assets over to the corporation, it is decided to recognize certain changes in the valuation of the firm's assets. It is estimated that $5,000 should be added to the allowance for bad debts, that the merchandise inventory should be written down to $130,000, and that the land should be written up to $65,000. The entries on the books of the partnership to record these changes are as follows:

Jan. 2	Land..	15,000	
	Loss on Revaluation of Assets...................	10,000	
	Allowance for Bad Debts.....................		5,000
	Merchandise Inventory.......................		20,000
	To record revaluation of assets prior to incorporation.		
2	J. C. Allen, Capital...........................	5,000	
	M. R. Baker, Capital..........................	5,000	
	Loss on Revaluation of Assets.................		10,000
	To distribute loss on revaluation to partners' capital accounts in the profit-and-loss ratio.		

The losses or the gains on revaluation may be debited or credited directly to the capital accounts, but in this instance the loss was first recorded in an account entitled Loss on Revaluation of Assets, which in turn was closed to the capital accounts.

The following entries are made in the partnership books to record the sale of the business and the subsequent dissolution of the partnership:

Jan. 2	Receivable from Newton Corporation............	320,000	
	Allowance for Bad Debts......................	10,000	
	Allowance for Depreciation of Store Equipment...	1,000	
	Allowance for Depreciation of Buildings..........	20,000	
	Accounts Payable.............................	80,000	
	Cash.......................................		25,000
	Accounts Receivable.........................		105,000
	Merchandise Inventory.......................		130,000
	Store Equipment............................		6,000
	Buildings...................................		100,000
	Land.......................................		65,000
	Transferred the assets and the liabilities of the business to the Newton Corporation.		
2	Stock of Newton Corporation...................	320,000	
	Receivable from Newton Corporation..........		320,000
	Received 3,200 shares of common stock of the Newton Corporation in payment of the amount due for the partnership business.		
2	J. C. Allen, Capital...........................	195,000	
	M. R. Baker, Capital.........................	125,000	
	Stock of Newton Corporation.................		320,000
	Distributed the 3,200 shares of stock of the Newton Corporation to the partners according to their respective interests.		

The posting of these entries will close all the partnership accounts and the partnership will then be completely dissolved.

Opening the Books of the Corporation. On the books of the corporation, entries must be made to record the assets received, the liabilities assumed, and the issuance of stock. The fixed assets are recorded at their net cost to the corporation; the original cost and the depreciation taken by the former owner are not shown. For accounts receivable, however, both the gross amount and the allowance are shown, because the uncollectible accounts have not actually been determined and the asset therefore cannot be written down to its estimated realizable value.

The opening entries, in general journal form, for the Newton Corporation are as follows:

Jan. 2 Cash...	25,000	
Accounts Receivable............................	105,000	
Merchandise Inventory.........................	130,000	
Store Equipment...............................	5,000	
Buildings......................................	80,000	
Land..	65,000	
Allowance for Bad Debts.....................		10,000
Accounts Payable...........................		80,000
Payable to Allen and Baker..................		320,000
Purchased the assets and assumed the liabilities of Allen and Baker.		
2 Payable to Allen and Baker.....................	320,000	
Common Stock.............................		320,000
Issued 3,200 shares of common stock to Allen and Baker in payment of liability recognized upon the transfer of their business to the corporation.		
2 Cash..	100,000	
Common Stock.............................		100,000
Issued 1,000 shares of stock to W. A. Carlson.		

After these entries have been posted to the ledger, the balance sheet for the Newton Corporation may be prepared as shown on the following page.

When a partnership is converted into a corporation, the market value of the stock issued to the partners may be more than the value of the assets acquired by the corporation. In such instances a goodwill account would be debited on the books of the corporation for the excess payment on the theory that the partnership has a value greater than the value of its physical properties. If the market value of the stock exchanged is different from the par or stated value of the stock, a discount or a premium on the stock would be recognized on the books of the corporation. Discount and premium on stock will be discussed in the following chapter.

NEWTON CORPORATION
BALANCE SHEET
JANUARY 2, 1954

ASSETS

Current Assets:

Cash		$125,000
Accounts Receivable	$105,000	
Less Allowance for Bad Debts	10,000	95,000
Merchandise Inventory		130,000
Total Current Assets		$350,000

Fixed Assets:

Store Equipment	$ 5,000	
Buildings	80,000	
Land	65,000	
Total Fixed Assets		150,000
Total Assets		$500,000

LIABILITIES

Accounts Payable	$ 80,000

CAPITAL

Common Stock, $100 par (5,000 shares authorized)	420,000
Total Liabilities and Capital	$500,000

Balance Sheet of a Corporation

COMPARISON OF THE CORPORATION AND THE PARTNERSHIP A comparison of the corporation and the partnership reveals more completely the nature of the corporation. The chief differences between the two forms of organization are shown in the following outline. From this comparison it can be seen that a partnership, like a sole proprietorship, is legally identified with the persons who own it and is therefore a personal form of business organization. By contrast, the corporation is an impersonal form, since it exists apart from the lives of its owners or officers.

CORPORATION	PARTNERSHIP
1. Separate legal entity.	1. Identification of organization with the individual partners.
2. Continuity of existence.	2. Automatic dissolution arising from death, withdrawal, or incapacity of a partner.
3. Limited liability of the stockholders.	3. Unlimited personal liability of the partners.
4. Obligations arising only from the acts of agents or officers.	4. Obligations arising from the acts of any partner.
5. Profits do not belong to stockholders unless dividends are declared by board of directors.	5. Profits are personal profits of the partners.
6. Control of stockholders is indirect.	6. Control of partners is direct and personal.
7. Payments to stockholders for personal services are expenses.	7. Payments to partners for personal services are distributions of earnings.

QUESTIONS

1. (a) What are the three types of corporations? (b) Name the chief characteristics of a corporation. (c) Define organization costs.

2. What types of preferred stock may be issued by corporations?

3. The par value of one share of common stock of the Sawyer Oil Co. is $10. The book value of the stock is $45 and the market value is $65. Give reasons that may explain the comparatively high market value.

4. The Amalgamated Steel Co. issues 10 shares of $100 par common stock to a promoter for his services in establishing the corporation. How should the issuance of the stock be recorded? What would the entry be if the stock were issued in payment of an account?

5. C. W. Schmidt and L. A. Davy are partners in the firm of Schmidt & Davy, each having a proprietorship of $30,000. The firm is incorporated with an authorized common stock of $80,000, consisting of 800 shares with a par value of $100. Schmidt and Davy each receive 300 shares of common stock for their interest in the partnership. Two hundred shares of common stock are sold at par to John Reed. How is the capital reported on the balance sheet of the corporation?

6. Harry Black is considering the purchase of stock in the Nash Manufacturing Company. He finds that the stock is quoted on the stock exchange at $65 a share. In examining the reports of the company, he obtains the following information from the latest balance sheet: current assets, $250,000; fixed assets, $400,000; current liabilities, $100,000; common stock, $500,000; surplus, $50,000. There are 10,000 shares of stock outstanding. (a) What is the par value of the stock? (b) What is its book value? (c) What is its market value?

7. Ray Sands owns 2,000 of the 6,000 shares (par value $100) of the General Manufacturing Company. The company earned $100,000 in 1953. The board of directors declared $10 a share in dividends during the year. Was Sands' income for 1953 $20,000 or ⅓ of $100,000? Why?

8. C. R. Hoyt purchased 100 shares of the preferred stock ($100 par value) of the Able Manufacturing Company at $90 a share on March 6, 1953. On July 1, he received a semiannual dividend of $350. On January 2, 1954, he received from the company a check for $10,750, canceling the stock. What are the stock values included in this illustration? What was the dividend rate on the preferred stock?

9. The balance sheet of the Jason Corporation shows assets of $350,000, liabilities of $100,000, and surplus of $50,000. It has outstanding 1,000 shares ($100 par) of preferred stock and 1,000 shares ($100 par) of common stock. What is the book value of the common stock?

10. The Fremont Transportation Company made the following net earnings in six successive years: $20,000; $30,000; $10,000; $5,000; $40,000; $50,000. It had outstanding 1,000 shares of common stock and 1,000 shares of 6% preferred stock, each share having a par value of $100. Two fifths of the profits were paid each year as dividends. How much did each stockholder receive on a share if the preferred stock was cumulative and nonparticipating?

11. Ipsom, Inc. has outstanding $100,000 of 6% cumulative and non-participating preferred stock and $100,000 of common stock, each share having a par value of $100. The amounts distributed as dividends during five years were: first year, $4,000; second year, $30,000; third year, $60,000; fourth year, $40,000; fifth year, $12,000. (a) How much was paid each year on each class of stock? (b) What percentage was paid on common stock each year? (c) Which stock was the better investment if both were purchased at the par value?

12. The Noonan Corporation has outstanding 5,000 shares of $100 par, 5% cumulative and participating preferred stock and 20,000 shares of $50 par value common stock. Dividends are in arrears for one year on the preferred stock on January 1, 1953. Compute the dividends to be distributed to each share of preferred and common stock on December 31, 1953, assuming that the following amounts are to be paid out: (a) $40,000, (b) $90,000, (c) $130,000, (d) $184,000.

13. The board of directors of the newly organized Cable Corporation decides to purchase the factory of C. J. Dare. On Dare's books the assets are recorded as follows: land, $10,000; building cost, $35,000; allowance for depreciation of building, $15,000; machinery cost, $60,000; allowance for depreciation of machinery, $25,000. Present market values are: land, $15,000; building, $25,000; machinery, $50,000. Common stock is issued to Dare at par ($100) in exchange for the property. Give in general journal form the entry on the books of the Cable Corporation to record the acquisition of the assets.

14. The Benson Co. acquires the assets and assumes the liabilities of Marcus and Neal by issuing 2,000 shares of $50 par value stock to them in exchange for their business, excluding cash. The partners share profits 3:2. Each partner is to receive 1,000 shares of stock. Cash is to be withdrawn by Marcus and Neal according to the balances in their capital accounts after revaluation of assets and the distribution of stock. The balance sheet of Marcus and Neal is shown below:

MARCUS AND NEAL

BALANCE SHEET

DECEMBER 31, 1953

ASSETS			LIABILITIES AND PROPRIETORSHIP	
Cash....................		$ 20,000	Notes Payable...............	$ 5,000
Accounts Receivable.......		15,000	Marcus, Capital..........	48,000
Merchandise..............		25,000	Neal, Capital.............	57,000
Fixtures..........	$60,000			
Less Allowance for				
Depreciation	10,000	50,000		
Total Assets..............		$110,000	Total Liab. and Prop......	$110,000

Before the business is transferred, assets are to be adjusted to their current market values as follows: •

Merchandise, $20,000

Fixtures, $70,000

Prepare all journal entries on the books of the partnership.

PROBLEMS

21-1. The Stanton Corporation and the Reed Corporation both received their charters and began business on January 2, 1947. Both corporations have since had the same outstanding stock: 4,000 shares of 5% cumulative preferred, par $100; and 2,000 shares of common, par $100. In each case the board of directors declared dividends on preferred stock whenever, and to the extent that, there was a credit balance in the surplus account at the end of the year and declared dividends on common stock amounting to one half of the difference between the earnings in any year and the preferred dividends paid in that year.

The profits (after income taxes) and the losses for a period of seven years are as follows:

	STANTON CORPORATION	REED CORPORATION
1947	$25,000 loss	$ 6,000 loss
1948	12,000 profit	1,000 loss
1949	14,000 profit	45,000 profit
1950	40,000 profit	92,000 profit
1951	97,000 profit	130,000 profit
1952	32,000 profit	60,000 profit
1953	50,000 profit	84,000 profit

Instructions: (1) Show for each year the distribution of the profit (after income taxes) or the loss for each corporation. Use columns with the following headings: Year; Income; To Preferred Stock; Balance Due on Preferred Stock; To Common Stock; To Surplus; Surplus Balance. Indicate negative or minus items by encircling them.

(2) Total the two columns showing the amounts paid on preferred and common stock. What was the amount received per share on common and preferred stock for the seven-year period?

21-2. Raymond Larson, the owner of a retail dry goods business, and two of his clerks decide to form a corporation issuing $20 par common stock and 6% cumulative, $100 par preferred stock. Each clerk is to invest $2,000 in the Larson Corporation and is to receive 100 shares of common stock. Mr. Larson is to receive preferred stock based upon the tangible net assets of his business. Cash is to be withdrawn by Mr. Larson so that an even multiple of 10 shares will be received. Mr. Larson is to receive in addition 300 shares of common stock in payment for the goodwill of his dry goods business.

The post-closing trial balance on December 31, 1953, at the end of a year's operations and before the revaluation of assets and the organization of the corporation, is as follows:

Cash...	$ 5,600	
Merchandise Inventory..........................	51,000	
Equipment.....................................	19,000	
Allowance for Depreciation of Equipment........		$ 8,000
Accounts Payable..............................		15,000
Raymond Larson, Capital......................		52,600
	$75,600	$75,600

Assets are to be revalued as follows:

Merchandise Inventory, $47,000.
Allowance for Depreciation of Equipment is to be increased to $11,000.
Goodwill is to be recognized on the books as agreed.

Instructions: (1) Prepare general journal entries to:
   (a) Revalue the assets and record the goodwill as agreed.
   (b) Record the withdrawal of cash.
   (c) Record the sale of the business to the corporation.

(2) Prepare journal entries to open the books of the corporation.

(3) Prepare the balance sheet for the corporation.

(4) Assuming a profit for the succeeding year of $11,400 after income taxes, what dividends would each of the three men receive if 50% of the profits are to be distributed? What rate will be paid on common stock?

21-3. Three grocery store owners decide to merge and incorporate their respective stores, A, B, and C, to form the Supermarket Stores, Inc. The corporation is authorized to issue 4,000 shares of 6% preferred stock, par value $100, and 40,000 shares of common stock, par value $10. Preferred stock is to be distributed to the three owners on the basis of one share for every $100 of the net assets of their respective stores. All assets are to be revalued as of the date of the proposed merger, June 30, 1953. Common stock is to be issued at par for goodwill of Store A, $30,000, and Store B, $10,000.

To obtain cash to build a new branch, 30,000 shares of common are sold at par to the public.

Balance sheets of the three stores prior to the incorporation of June 30 are:

Assets	A	B	C
Cash...........................	$ 12,000	$ 13,000	$ 7,000
Merchandise Inventory.............	60,000	28,000	50,000
Equipment	40,000	30,000	45,000
Buildings........................	70,000	—	—
Land............................	35,000	—	—
Total Assets.....................	$217,000	$ 71,000	$102,000
Liabilities and Proprietorship			
Accounts Payable.................	$ 40,000	$ 30,000	$ 35,000
Proprietorship...................	177,000	41,000	67,000
Total Liab. and Proprietorship.......	$217,000	$ 71,000	$102,000
Assets are to be revalued as follows:			
Merchandise Inventory.............	$ 54,000	$ 26,000	$ 42,000
Land............................	25,000	—	—

Instructions: (1) Prepare general journal entries for each of the three stores to record the revaluation of assets and the goodwill.

(2) Prepare revised balance sheets for each of the three firms in the form shown in this problem.

(3) Compute the number of shares of preferred and common stock each of the three former owners will receive for his store.

(4) Prepare a balance sheet for the corporation as it will appear after the merger and the sale of the 30,000 shares of common stock to the public for cash at par.

Chapter | 22

Corporate Accounts and Records

ISSUING STOCK AT A PREMIUM OR A DISCOUNT In the preceding chapter it was assumed that the corporation issued stock at par value. Frequently, however, stock is issued for more or less than its par or stated value. Except for legal technicalities, the terms par value and stated value may be used interchangeably. The discussion in this chapter will use the term par value, but the concepts may be considered to apply to stated value stock as well. When stock is sold for more or less than par value, the stock account is credited for the par value and a descriptive paid-in surplus account is credited or debited for the difference between the selling price and the par value. When stock is issued for more than its par value, it is said to be issued at a *premium;* when it is issued for less than its par value, it is issued at a *discount.* In many states corporations are not permitted to issue stock for less than par in order not to weaken the protection for creditors. In some states the purchasers of stock below par value are contingently liable to the corporation for an amount equal to the original discount in the event that the corporation is insolvent and unable to pay creditors from the corporate assets.

The price at which stock is sold by a company depends largely upon: (1) the financial condition of the company, (2) the company's potential earning power, (3) the availability of money for investment purposes, and (4) general business and economic conditions.

When common stock is sold at a premium, the cash account is debited for the amount received, the stock account is credited for the par value, and a premium on stock account is credited for the excess. The premium is not a profit to the corporation; it constitutes additional invested capital and is added to the stock account on the balance sheet as part of paid-in capital. The premium, however, is not part of the legal capital of the corporation and may in some states be used as a basis for dividend distribution.

If the laws of the state allow the sale of stock at a discount, an excess of par value over the sales price is debited to a discount on stock account. The discount account represents a negative capital item and is subtracted from the stock account on the balance sheet in arriving at the actual paid-in capital of the corporation.

To illustrate the concepts mentioned above, assume that the Butler Corporation sells 10,000 shares of $50 par common stock at $56 per share, and 2,000 shares of $100 par, 5% preferred stock at $98 per share. The entries to record these transactions are as follows:

```
July 31  Cash.......................................  560,000
             Common Stock.............................          500,000
             Premium on Common Stock.................           60,000
             Sold 10,000 shares of $50 par value common
             at $56 per share.

     31  Cash.......................................  196,000
         Discount on Preferred Stock..................    4,000
             Preferred Stock.........................           200,000
             Sold 2,000 shares of $100 par, 5 % preferred
             stock at $98 per share.
```

When stock is issued in exchange for assets other than cash, the fair market value of the assets received must be determined in order to record the exchange properly. Assets should not be recorded at the par value of stock given in exchange, but at their fair market value as of the date received. The difference between the asset value and the par value of the stock should be recorded as a stock premium or discount. For example, if the Butler Corporation receives from Alex, Inc. assets having a current market value of $165,000 in exchange for 3,000 shares of $50 par common stock, the exchange may be recorded as follows:

```
July 31  Merchandise Inventory......................   10,000
         Equipment..................................   45,000
         Buildings..................................   80,000
         Land......................................   30,000
             Common Stock.............................          150,000
             Premium on Common Stock.................           15,000
             Received assets value at $165,000 from Alex,
             Inc. in exchange for 3,000 shares of $50 par
             common stock.
```

A balance sheet prepared for the Butler Corporation on July 31, following the foregoing transactions, is shown at the top of the following page.

ACCOUNTING FOR SUBSCRIPTIONS TO CORPORATE STOCK   In the preceding examples it was assumed that the corporation exchanged its stock directly for cash or other property. Ordinarily before stock is actually issued, a corporation accepts subscriptions for its stock. Those who expect to become stockholders subscribe for stock, thereby agreeing to pay cash at a later date or dates for the shares for which they subscribe. This amount represents a receivable

BUTLER CORPORATION
Balance Sheet
July 31, 1953

Assets

Current Assets:

Cash...	$756,000	
Merchandise Inventory.........................	10,000	
Total Current Assets..........................		$766,000

Fixed Assets:

Equipment....................................	$ 45,000	
Buildings....................................	80,000	
Land..	30,000	
Total Fixed Assets...........................		155,000
Total Assets.................................		$921,000

Capital

Paid-in Capital:

5% Preferred Stock, $100 par (2,000 shares authorized and issued)................	$200,000	
Less Discount on Preferred Stock..........	4,000	$196,000
Common Stock, $50 par (20,000 shares authorized, 13,000 shares issued)........	$650,000	
Premium on Common Stock..............	75,000	725,000
Total Capital.................................		$921,000

to the corporation and is debited to a subscriptions receivable account; at the same time the capital of the corporation is increased, and therefore a stock subscribed account is credited. Each of these accounts represents a situation that will involve subsequent transactions: the subscriber must pay his subscription; the corporation must issue the stock certificate. Since stock certificates are freely transferable, it is not advisable for the corporation to issue stock until the subscription is fully paid. Dividends are normally paid on stock subscribed but unissued, unless a contrary agreement is made between the corporation and the subscriber.

Separate receivable and subscribed accounts should be set up for subscriptions to preferred and common stocks. Subscriptions to preferred stock require the use of the accounts Preferred Stock Subscriptions Receivable and Preferred Stock Subscribed; subscriptions to common stock, the accounts Common Stock Subscriptions Receivable and Common Stock Subscribed. When stock is subscribed for at more or less than the par value, a premium or a discount account should be set up at the time the subscriptions are received. As collections are made, Cash is debited and the subscriptions receivable account is credited. When stockholders pay the entire subscription price, the stock is issued and an entry is made debiting the stock subscribed account and crediting Common Stock or Preferred Stock, depending upon which type is involved.

SUBSCRIPTIONS TRANSACTIONS ILLUSTRATED   To illustrate the use of accounts for stock subscriptions, assume that on April 1, 1953, the Evans Corporation receives subscriptions for 500 shares of $100 par value common stock at $108 per share. One half of the subscription price is payable on April 1 and the balance in two equal installments on May 1 and June 1. The entries to record the data relative to the subscriptions are tabulated below:

Transaction	Entry	

(a) April 1, 1953:
Received subscriptions to 500 shares of $100 par value common stock at $108 per share and collected 50% of the subscription price as a down payment.
	Common Stock Subscriptions Receivable.. 54,000
	    Common Stock Subscribed............
	    Premium on Common Stock.........
	
	Cash................ 27,000
	    Common Stock Subscriptions Receivable
		
		50,000
		
		4,000
		
		27,000

(b) May 1, 1953: Collected first installment of 25% on the subscription.	Cash................ 13,500 Common Stock Subscriptions Receivable	 13,500

(c) June 1, 1953:
Collected second installment of 25% on the subscriptions and issued the stock.
	Cash................ 13,500
	    Common Stock Subscriptions Receivable
	
	Common Stock Subscribed............. 50,000
	    Common Stock......
		
		13,500
		
		50,000

The nature of the subscriptions receivable account and the stock subscribed account is shown by the use of "T" accounts in the chart below. They are temporary accounts and cease to function after full payment has been received from the stockholders.

TEMPORARY ACCOUNTS

CASH	COMMON STOCK SUBSCRIPTIONS RECEIVABLE		COMMON STOCK
(a) 27,000 (b) 13,500 (c) 13,500	(a) 54,000	(a) 27,000 (b) 13,500 (c) 13,500	(c) 50,000

	COMMON STOCK SUBSCRIBED		PREMIUM ON COMMON STOCK
	(c) 50,000	(a) 50,000	(a) 4,000

The transactions (a) to (c) illustrated are the same as those shown in the journal entries. It should be noted that the temporary accounts are in balance after full payment has been received and the stock has been issued.

If a corporation receives subscriptions to its preferred stock and later collects cash on these subscriptions, the accounting entries would be similar to those shown above except that the accounts Preferred Stock Subscriptions Receivable and Preferred Stock Subscribed would be used.

If a balance sheet of the corporation is prepared before subscriptions are fully collected, the balance in the subscriptions receivable account would appear as a current asset if it is collectible within one year, and the balance in the stock subscribed account would appear in the capital section.

A balance sheet prepared for the Evans Corporation on May 31, before the June 1 transactions, would appear as follows:

EVANS CORPORATION

BALANCE SHEET

MAY 31, 1953

ASSETS		CAPITAL	
Cash	$40,500	Paid-in Capital:	
Common Stock Subscriptions		Common Stock Subscribed	$50,000
Receivable	13,500	Premium on Common	
		Stock	4,000
Total Assets	$54,000	Total Capital	$54,000

Both of the assets are current assets, since Common Stock Subscriptions Receivable are due on June 1. Premium on Common Stock is shown on the balance sheet as part of the paid-in capital.

On June 1, after the last payment on subscriptions has been collected and the common stock has been issued, the balance sheet would appear as follows:

EVANS CORPORATION

BALANCE SHEET

JUNE 1, 1953

ASSETS		CAPITAL	
Cash	$54,000	Paid-in Capital:	
		Common Stock	$50,000
		Premium on Common	
		Stock	4,000
Total Assets	$54,000	Total Capital	$54,000

DEFAULTS ON STOCK SUBSCRIPTIONS   If a corporation is unable to collect a stock subscription installment, special accounting procedures must be followed. The action that is taken by the corporation depends upon the laws of the state in which the stock was sold. Some states require that whatever has been received by the corporation be returned to the subscriber, less expenses and losses resulting from the resale of the stock. Many states require that the entire amount paid in be returned to the subscriber. Other states permit the forfeiture of the entire sum paid by the subscriber.

The accounting entries are similar for all three procedures. In all cases, the accounts applicable to the forfeited portion of the stock must be eliminated from the books of the corporation. When the corporation plans to remit to the subscriber the difference between what he paid in and any loss upon resale, an account with the subscriber is opened pending the resale. If the resale is made at a price below the original subscription price, the defaulting subscriber is charged for the loss to the company. If the resale is for a higher value than the original subscription price, the entire amount paid in by the defaulting subscriber is returned to him. When the company returns to the defaulting subscriber the entire amount paid in by him, all accounts pertaining to the subscription are closed and Cash is credited for the returned amount. The subsequent resale is recorded in the regular manner.

To illustrate these concepts, assume that a subscriber to 50 shares of Evans Corporation stock in the previous example was unable to meet his first installment on May 1. The stock was subscribed for at $108 per share and one half of the subscription price was collected as a down payment, the balance being payable in equal installments on May 1 and June 1. The stock was resold for cash at $106 per share on May 10. The entries to record the default would be made as follows:

Assuming Subscriber Is to Be Charged with Loss on Resale	Assuming Entire Amount Paid by Subscriber Is to Be Returned
MAY 1:	MAY 1:
Common Stock Subscribed............5,000	Common Stock Subscribed............5,000
Premium on Common Stock............... 400	Premium on Common Stock............... 400
Common Stock Subscriptions Receivable 2,700	Common Stock Subscriptions Receivable 2,700
Payable to Subscriber 2,700	Cash.............. 2,700
To record default and payment to subscriber pending resale of stock.	To record default and return to subscriber of amount paid in.

Assuming Subscriber Is to Be Charged with Loss on Resale	Assuming Entire Amount Paid by Subscriber Is to Be Returned

MAY 10:
Cash............... 5,300
Payable to Subscriber..   100
  Common Stock.....   5,000
  Premium on Com-
  mon Stock........   400
    To record resale of
    stock at $106 per
    share.
	MAY 10:
	Cash............... 5,300
	  Common Stock..... 5,000
	  Premium on Common
	  Stock............. 300
	    To record resale of
	    stock at $106 per
	    share.

MAY 10:
Payable to Subscriber.. 2,600
  Cash.............   2,600
    To record return
    to subscriber of
    amount paid in less
    loss on resale.
	(no entry)

In the first illustration, when the stock is resold for less than the original subscription price, the premium is credited for the original amount upon resale, the defaulting subscriber absorbing the loss. If the entire amount paid in were forfeited, a paid-in surplus account would have been credited for $2,700 on May 1 and the subsequent resale would have been recorded as in the second method above.

METHOD OF HANDLING NO-PAR-VALUE STOCK   Corporations may issue stock without any par or stated value in order to avoid the legal restrictions attaching to stock issued at a discount. Regardless of its issue price, each share of no-par-value stock is equal to every other share of the same class and is deemed fully paid and nonassessable. When the stock has a par value, an inexperienced investor may be misled concerning the true value of the stock. If the stock has no par value, the investor is forced to seek the real value of the stock before he invests.

When no-par-value common stock is sold, the entire amount received is credited to the common stock account. Since the stock does not have a par value, neither a premium nor a discount on the stock needs to be recognized. For example, if the R. F. Monroe Corporation, which is authorized to issue 4,000 shares of no-par-value common stock, sells 2,000 shares at $27 per share, the opening entry is:

Oct. 1 Cash.. 54,000
       Common Stock................................   54,000
           Sold and issued 2,000 shares of no-par-value com-
           mon stock at $27 per share.

The number of shares of no-par-value stock outstanding must be shown on the balance sheet because, in the absence of par value, it would be impossible to know how many shares were in the hands of stockholders. If a balance sheet were prepared after the above entry had been posted, the capital section would be exhibited as follows:

CAPITAL

Common Stock, no-par-value (4,000 shares authorized, 2,000 shares outstanding)............................. $54,000

When subscriptions to stock of no-par value are entered in the books, they are recorded at the selling price of the stock by debits to the subscription account and credits to the stock subscribed account.

Under the laws of some states, the directors of a corporation may specify that a nominal portion of the payment for stock of no-par-value is to be credited to the stock account and the remainder to a premium on stock account. The portion to be credited to the stock account is known as *stated value*. In the previous illustration the stated value might have been $5 per share. The entry would then have been made as follows:

```
Oct. 1  Cash.........................................  54,000
            Common Stock...............................           10,000
            Premium on Common Stock...................           44,000
            Sold 2,000 shares of no-par-value common stock
            at $27 per share. The stated value of the stock is
            $5 per share.
```

ACCOUNTING FOR DONATED TREASURY STOCK   When a corporation reacquires some of its own stock from stockholders either by gift or by purchase, such stock is known as *treasury stock*. Since treasury stock has previously been issued for value by the corporation, it can be sold at any price without the usual limitations on stock sold at a discount. Treasury stock should be distinguished from unissued stock, since the latter has never been issued by the corporation.

Outstanding stock may be donated to the corporation by existing stockholders in order that working capital can be obtained through its resale. This practice is occasionally used by corporations that have issued all of their stock in payment for fixed assets. The donated stock may then be resold for whatever it will bring, and the purchasers are not liable to creditors for the difference between par and sales price even in those states where the initial subscribers may have such a liability.

When the fair market value of the stock is available, the donated treasury stock should be recorded at its current market value with a corresponding credit to Donated Surplus. In the absence of market value, the donated treasury stock may be recorded at par; or in the absence of par value, simply by a memorandum entry. Assuming that the Blair Co. receives 1,000 shares of its own common stock from its stockholders, and that the stock had a quoted market value of $37 per share at this time, the following entry would be made to record the receipt:

Aug. 12 Treasury Stock................................ 37,000
             Donated Surplus.............................   37,000
                 Received 1,000 shares of treasury stock having
                 a current market value of $37 per share.

The treasury stock account cannot be considered as an asset, since a corporation cannot logically own a part of itself; it is a capital valuation account and is to be deducted from the total capital in the preparation of the balance sheet. This treatment is consistent with the nature of treasury stock — that of being temporarily retired stock. The donated surplus account is a form of paid-in surplus and is so reported on the balance sheet.

A stock donation has the effect of increasing the book value of the stock outstanding. For example, the Lamping Corporation has 5,000 shares of stock outstanding with net assets of $500,000, or a book value of $100 per share. A stockholder donates 1,000 shares to the company, thus leaving only 4,000 shares outstanding. The net assets remain at $500,000, but the book value of each remaining share is increased from $100 to $125.

If the 1,000 shares of treasury stock donated to the Blair Co. are resold by the company at $45 per share at some future date, the following entry may be made:

Nov. 10 Cash.. 45,000
             Treasury Stock.............................   37,000
             Treasury Stock Surplus......................   8,000
                 Sold 1,000 shares of treasury stock at $45 per
                 share.

There are strong arguments for recording the increment in the value of the stock from the date received to the date of sale as additional donated surplus. However, the market value of the stock on the date received may be considered to measure the true value of the gift. What took place afterwards was at the risk of the corporation and beyond the control of the original donor. The treasury stock surplus account, then, is a form of paid-in capital. Treasury stock surplus is not a profit to the corporation; a company does not make profits by dealing with its stockholders but rather by dealing with outsiders through the sale of commodities above cost.

PURCHASED TREASURY STOCK   Corporations may purchase shares of their own stock on the open market. Such acquisitions may be made in order to provide shares for resale to employees, to be used as bonuses for officers, or to support the market price of the stock. Purchased treasury stock is recorded at cost and is shown as a deduction from the total capital on the balance sheet. Any gain or loss on the resale of such stock is cleared through the treasury stock surplus account. To illustrate the entries required for purchased treasury stock, assume the following: the Beverly-Bell Co. purchases 800 shares of its common stock at $70 per share. At two later dates it sells 200 shares of the stock at $68 per share and 200 shares at $82 per share. The entries to record the three transactions are shown below:

May 12 Treasury Stock...............................	56,000	
Cash.......................................		56,000
Purchased 800 shares of own stock at $70 per share.		
June 18 Cash.......................................	13,600	
Treasury Stock Surplus........................	400	
Treasury Stock.............................		14,000
Sold 200 shares of treasury stock at $68 per share, cost $70 per share.		
July 6 Cash.......................................	16,400	
Treasury Stock.............................		14,000
Treasury Stock Surplus........................		2,400
Sold 200 shares of treasury stock at $82 per share, cost $70 per share.		

After the above transactions have been posted, the balance sheet for the Beverly-Bell Co. would contain the following capital section:

CAPITAL

Paid-in Capital:			
Common Stock, $50 par (10,000 shares authorized and issued)..	$500,000		
Premium on Common Stock.....	50,000	$550,000	
Treasury Stock Surplus..................		2,000	
Total Paid-in Capital		$552,000	
Earned Surplus..................................		60,000	
Total..		$612,000	
Less Treasury Stock (400 shares at cost)..............		28,000	
Total Capital......................................			$584,000

Treasury stock is considered by some corporations to be an asset and is reported as such on the balance sheet. This is true when the stock has been purchased with the intent to resell it. When companies deal in their own stock as they would in the stock of other companies, the government requires that the company report any gain or loss on such dealings on its tax return. From an accounting point of view, however, treasury stock should always be treated as a reduction in corporate capital. Treasury stock does not have voting power nor does it receive cash dividends.

It is not uncommon to record treasury stock on the books at par. Treasury Stock is debited for the par value of the stock reacquired, Cash is credited for the amount paid, and Treasury Stock Surplus is debited or credited depending upon whether the purchase was made for more or less than the par value. When such a procedure is followed, the treasury stock account is deducted from the stock account on the balance sheet and Treasury Stock Surplus is included in the paid-in surplus section.

RETIREMENT OF TREASURY STOCK   The foregoing discussion assumed that a corporation acquired its own shares with the idea of subsequently reselling them. Often companies purchase their own shares, preferred stock in particular, and permanently retire the reacquired shares. To illustrate the entry that would be made to retire a portion of a stock issue, assume that the Warner Co. acquires 400 shares of its preferred stock at $90 per share and retires the stock permanently. The stock has a par value of $100 per share and was originally issued at a premium for $105 per share. The entry to record the retirement is:

```
Dec. 7  Preferred Stock................................  40,000
        Premium on Preferred Stock....................   2,000
            Paid-in Surplus — from Retirement of Stock.......        6,000
            Cash.......................................               36,000
                Retired 400 shares of $100 par preferred stock at
                $90 per share. Original issue price, $105 per share.
```

It may be noted that the premium applicable to the stock retired is eliminated from the books. The company was able to retire stock for which it had originally received $42,000 at a cost of only $36,000; hence a new paid-in surplus account is established to record the advantageous settlement. Had the company paid more than the original issue price for the stock, the excess would have been debited to the earned surplus account on the theory that the company is paying a bonus out of accumulated earnings to the preferred stockholders.

Most states permit the acquisition of treasury stock only up to the amount of the company's earned surplus. In such cases, a portion of earned surplus represented by the purchase price of treasury stock is restricted and is unavailable for dividend payments. When the stock is resold or properly retired, such restrictions are removed. The restrictions on earned surplus as a result of treasury stock acquisition and other corporate activities will be discussed in the following chapter.

RECORDS REQUIRED BY A CORPORATION The accounts of a corporation are essentially the same as those of any other type of business organization. The additional accounts required can be added in the general ledger. The books of original entry need not be different from those used by a sole proprietorship or a partnership. The only distinctive records required by a corporation are those used to record the activities peculiar to the corporate form. The records most commonly used for this purpose are: (1) the minute book, (2) the subscription book, (3) the subscribers ledger, (4) the stock certificate book, and (5) the stockholders ledger.

Minute Book. The minute book is the legal record of the proceedings of all meetings of the stockholders and of the board of directors. It often includes the charter and the bylaws as well. This record book serves as authority for actions of the officers and furnishes data for important entries to be made by the accountant. In it are found decisions on matters such as the purchase and the sale of property, the investment of excess funds, the declaration of dividends, the obtaining of additional funds through the issue of bonds or additional stock, and the maintaining of reserves and sinking funds.

Subscription Book. In most states the laws governing the creation of corporations provide that a substantial part of the capital stock of a corporation must be subscribed before a charter will be granted. Blanks containing the subscription contract are usually prepared, and the signatures of those who agree to subscribe for stock are obtained. These subscription blanks may later be filed in a binder and referred to as the *subscription book.* The blanks contain the date, the name of subscriber, the number of shares subscribed, the price per share, and the signature of the subscriber.

Subscribers Ledger. The subscribers ledger is a subsidiary ledger containing accounts with the individual subscribers to stock. An account with each subscriber is debited from the subscription book for the amount that the subscriber agreed to pay for the stock and is credited with the amounts received on account. The subscriptions receivable account in the general ledger is also debited with the total of the subscriptions and is credited with the total of the cash received from subscribers.

The accounts Preferred Stock Subscriptions Receivable and Common Stock Subscriptions Receivable control the preferred subscribers ledger and the common subscribers ledger. Summarized postings are made periodically to the controlling accounts; individual or detailed postings are made currently to the subsidiary ledger accounts.

Stock Certificate Book. The stock certificate book consists of blank stock certificates numbered serially and bound in book form with a stub for each certificate. If both preferred stock and common stock are issued, a different kind of certificate is ordinarily used for each class.

As may be seen by reference to the illustration below, each stock certificate contains the name of the corporation, the name of the stockholder, the date of issue, the number of shares authorized, and the number of shares represented by the certificate. When stock is issued, the certificate and the accompanying stub are filled out. The stub serves as a permanent record of the number of shares of stock represented by the certificate, the name of the person to whom the stock has been issued, the date of issue, and the fact that the stock is an original issue or a reissue.

When stock is transferred, the owner must fill out the form that is provided on the back of each certificate.

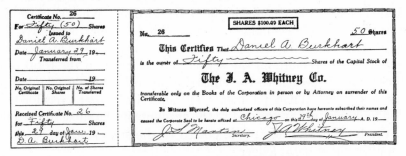

Stock Certificate with Stub

Stockholders Ledger. The stockholders ledger is a subsidiary record of the stock outstanding. It contains a separate account for each stockholder and is controlled by the account or accounts in the general ledger that show the amount of each class of stock outstanding.

The account of each stockholder is credited with the number of shares of stock purchased by him and is debited with the number of shares sold or otherwise transferred by him. The ownership of each stockholder is indicated by the number of shares held. This record is important in determining the number of votes that a stockholder may cast at elections and the amount of dividends to which he is entitled.

REGISTRAR AND
TRANSFER AGENT   Corporations whose stocks are listed on the New York Stock Exchange and other important exchanges are required to engage outside agencies to keep their stock certificate books and stockholders ledgers. This requirement assures proper handling of stock certificates when they change hands. The buyer or his broker turns in the old certificate to the transfer agent, who issues a new certificate and debits the seller and credits the buyer for the number of shares transferred. The new certificate passes through the hands of the *registrar* before it goes to the buyer. Both the transfer agent and the registrar endorse the certificate at either end on the face, showing it has been properly issued. When dividends are declared, an official list of stockholders is prepared to show who are entitled to dividend checks.

CORPORATE RECORDS
AND ACCOUNTING   To summarize: The minute book contains a record of the proceedings of the meetings of the stockholders and of the board of directors. It is not a book of account, but it evidences the authority for important entries made in the books of account.

The subscribers ledger is a subsidiary ledger controlled by the subscriptions receivable account in the general ledger. When subscriptions are received, the blanks may be filed in a binder, which is referred to as the subscription book. The amounts of the subscriptions are posted to the individual accounts in the subscribers ledger, and the total of the subscriptions is posted to the subscriptions receivable account in the general ledger. When payments on subscriptions are received, the individual amounts are posted to the accounts in the subscribers ledger and the total of the receipts is posted to the subscriptions receivable account in the general ledger.

The stockholders ledger is a subsidiary record of the capital stock outstanding. When stock is issued for the first time, the individual accounts in the stockholders ledger are credited for the number of shares issued, and the stock account in the general ledger is credited for the par value of the shares. When stock that has once been issued is transferred from one stockholder to another, an entry in the general ledger is not required since the total number of shares outstanding remains unchanged. The only entry necessary is that which is made from the stock certificate book to the individual accounts in the stock-holders ledger.

A corporation is ready to carry on its operations after a part or all of its stock has been sold and the charter has been obtained. The fact that a business is incorporated does not mean that its activities are distinctly different from those of a sole proprietorship or a partnership. No matter what its legal form of organization may be, an enterprise must buy to sell, or produce to sell; it must incur costs and realize income if it is to continue in business; and it must have these various transactions recorded in books of account in order to be able to show the results of its operations to the various interested parties.

The difference in legal status between the corporation and the other forms of business organization does not materially affect operations. Since the existence of a corporation is made possible by the charter, the corporation is necessarily subject to the regulations and provisions set forth in that document. It is also subject to the federal and the state laws relating to corporations.

QUESTIONS

1. What factors determine the price at which stock is sold?

2. What are the three possible ways of treating the amount already paid in by a defaulting subscriber of stock?

3. (a) What is the nature of treasury stock? (b) Why would a company acquire its own stock on the open market? (c) Where is treasury stock shown on the balance sheet?

4. (a) Why is it desirable to show the premium or the discount on capital stock in a separate account? (b) Is Premium on Common Stock an asset, a liability, or a proprietorship account? Why?

5. (a) The Abner Co. issues 1,000 shares of $100 par common stock for land having a present market value of $120,000. How should the exchange be recorded? (b) Assuming that the land was recorded at $100,000, what correcting entry would be required?

6. The Dilman Manufacturing Company was incorporated with author-ized capital stock of $200,000, consisting of 2,000 shares of common stock with a par value of $100. Seven hundred shares were subscribed for at 96, cash was received, and the stock was issued. What was the capital of the company at that time?

7. The R. C. Bacon Company has an authorized capital stock of $500,000. Subscriptions have been received for 4,500 shares of stock at the par value of $100. Three thousand of these shares have been paid for in full and have been issued. A 50% payment has been made on the remainder. (a) Give the entries, in general journal form, to record these transactions. (b) Prepare a balance sheet to show the results of the transactions to date.

8. The Handel Manufacturing Company has been organized to manufacture shoes. At the end of the first day of its existence a trial balance of its ledger is as follows:

HANDEL MANUFACTURING COMPANY

TRIAL BALANCE

JULY 24, 1953

Cash...	$ 900,000	
Preferred Stock Subscriptions Receivable.........	100,000	
Common Stock Subscriptions Receivable..........	200,000	
Preferred Stock..............................		$ 400,000
Preferred Stock Subscribed.....................		200,000
Common Stock...............................		300,000
Common Stock Subscribed.....................		300,000
	$1,200,000	$1,200,000

(a) Explain the meaning of the balance of each account. (b) How should the proprietorship be reported on a balance sheet prepared at this time? (c) What is the total value of the assets of the corporation?

9. Subscribers to the preferred stock of the Handel Manufacturing Company (Question No. 8) pay $100,000 to apply on their subscriptions. (a) What entry or entries will this payment require? (b) Give the balances of the accounts in the trial balance after these entries have been posted.

10. One thousand shares of Co. A common stock, $100 par value, are subscribed for at $110, 50% of the subscription price being paid as a down payment and the balance to be paid in two equal installments. All subscribers meet their first installment. Subscribers to 900 shares meet the second installment and the stock is issued to them. One subscriber to 100 shares is unable to pay the second installment, and the corporation returns the entire amount paid in. The defaulted shares are then sold for cash at $115. Give all the general journal entries to record the above data.

11. The French Sardine Co. sold and issued 2,000 shares of common stock at $17. Give the entry to record the transaction if: (a) the stock has a par value of $10, (b) the stock is no-par stock without stated value, (c) the stated value of the stock is $5.

12. The Southwest Mining Co. has 20 stockholders, each owning 100 shares of $50 par stock having a market value of $100 per share. The surplus is $40,000. Each stockholder donates to the corporation 20% of his holdings. (a) What is the book value of each share and of the total shares held by each stockholder (1) before the donation and (2) after the donation? (b) What entry would be made when the entire donated stock is subsequently resold at $120 per share?

13. On April 26, 1953, The Brentwood Co. acquired 100 shares of its own stock on the open market for $6,300. On July 9, 1953, it sold 50 of these shares at $80. On January 13, 1954, the remaining 50 shares were issued to a creditor to liquidate an account payable of $2,500. Give the general journal entries to record the foregoing transactions.

14. Bane, Inc. purchases 1,000 shares of its $100 par preferred stock at $105 and immediately retires the stock. (a) What entry would be made to record the retirement, assuming that the stock was originally issued at $110? (b) What entry would be made to record the retirement, assuming that the stock was originally issued at $95?

15. From the following account balances (a) prepare the capital section of the balance sheet and (b) compute the book value per share of common stock.

Preferred Stock, $100 par	$100,000
Common Stock, 10,000 no-par value	550,000
Treasury Stock Common, 1,000 shares	40,000
Premium on Preferred Stock	6,000
Donated Surplus	20,000
Treasury Stock Surplus	5,000
Earned Surplus	70,000

PROBLEMS

22-1. The Armour Supply Company was organized on May 1, 1953, with authorized stock of 1,000 shares of preferred stock, $100 par value, and 50,000 shares of common stock, $10 par value. Subscriptions were taken for common stock on May 1 under the following terms: 25% down payment; balance in three equal installments on May 15, May 30, and June 15. The stock is issued when fully paid for. The amount paid in by a defaulting subscriber, less any loss upon resale, will be returned as soon as the defaulted shares are sold.

The following transactions occurred during May and June:

May 1. Received subscriptions for 30,000 shares of common stock at $12 and collected the down payment.

  1. Paid organization costs of $5,000 in cash.

  3. Exchanged 500 shares of preferred stock for machinery valued at $48,000.

  5. Sold 500 shares of preferred stock at $95 and purchased a building for $50,000 cash.

  15. Collected the first installment on common stock subscriptions from all subscribers except L. Cobb, who had agreed to purchase 5,000 shares.

  17. Sold the 5,000 defaulted shares for cash at $11 and returned the proper amount to L. Cobb.

  30. Collected the second installment on the remaining 25,000 shares.

June 15. Collected the third installment on the remaining 25,000 shares and issued the stock.

  20. Received subscriptions for 10,000 shares of common stock at $12¼. Collected 25% as a down payment.

Instructions: (1) Record the preceding transactions in general journal form and post to the general ledger accounts. The accounts required are:

111 Cash	213 Payable to Subscriber
113 Common Stock Subscriptions	311 Preferred Stock
Receivable	312 Discount on Preferred Stock
122 Machinery	313 Common Stock
125 Buildings	314 Common Stock Subscribed
131 Organization Costs	315 Premium on Common Stock

(2) Prepare a balance sheet in report form as of June 30, 1953.

22-2. The Woodland Hills Corporation received its charter of incorporation on December 31, 1951. Its authorized capitalization was as follows: 1,000 shares of 5% cumulative preferred stock, par value $100, and 11,000 shares of common stock, par value $25. During its first two years of operation the following transactions occurred:

1952
Jan.   4. Received cash for 600 shares of preferred stock at par and for 5,000 shares of common stock at $26. Issued the stock.

    15. Received subscriptions for 250 shares of preferred stock at par and 3,000 shares of common stock at $28, 50% of the sale price being received in cash at the time of subscription.

Feb. 23. Invested $110,000 in other assets.

Mar. 31. Received in cash the balance due on the preferred and common stock subscribed. Issued the stock.

Apr. 30. The attorney who secured the charter and performed other legal services in connection with organization rendered his bill for $4,000. He was paid in cash.

Dec. 31. Net loss for the first year's operations was $13,000. (It will be assumed that the net effect of these operations was a $13,000 decrease in cash and no changes in other assets or in liabilities. Therefore, debit Profit and Loss Summary and credit Cash.)

Dec. 31. Closed Profit and Loss Summary to Earned Surplus. Charged off one fifth of the organization costs to Earned Surplus.

1953
Feb.   3. Exchanged 1,000 shares of common stock for other assets valued at $30,000.

Mar.   2. Acquired 100 shares of its own preferred stock at $95 and permanently retired the stock.

June   6. Purchased 200 shares of its own common stock on the open market at $32.

Nov. 30. Sold 100 shares of treasury stock at $36.

Dec. 31. Net profit after income taxes for 1953 was $35,000 (debit Cash; credit Profit and Loss Summary). Closed Profit and Loss Summary to Earned Surplus. Charged one fifth of the organization costs to Earned Surplus.

Instructions: (1) Record the transactions directly in "T" accounts. The accounts required are: Cash; Preferred Stock Subscriptions Receivable; Common Stock Subscriptions Receivable; Other Assets; Organization Costs; Preferred Stock; Preferred Stock Subscribed; Common Stock; Common Stock

Subscribed; Premium on Common Stock; Treasury Stock — Common; Treasury Stock Surplus; Paid-in Surplus — from Retirement of Stock; Earned Surplus; Profit and Loss Summary.

(2) Prepare a balance sheet as of December 31, 1953.

22-3. The Slauson Corporation was organized on October 1, 1953, with authorized capital stock of 15,000 shares of common, $100 par, and 6,000 shares of 6% preferred, $100 par. The following transactions took place during the month of October:

Oct.   1. Exchanged 3,000 shares of common stock for assets as follows: Merchandise Inventory, $120,000; Buildings, $100,000; Store Equipment, $60,000; and Land, $35,000.

     3. Received subscriptions for 4,000 shares of common stock at $110, with 50% cash received at the time of subscription.

     4. Received cash for 3,000 shares of preferred stock at par.

     7. Purchased machinery for $390,000 cash.

   11. Stockholders donated 600 shares of common stock to the corporation. The stock had a fair market value of $112 on this date.

   15. Sold 400 shares of treasury stock at $116.

   18. Accepted the assets of a going company in payment for 1,000 shares of common stock. The assets received were valued as follows: Buildings $50,000; Land, $30,000; and Goodwill, $30,000.

   20. Received the balance due on the common stock subscribed. Issued the stock.

   21. Purchased 500 shares of own common stock at $112.

   26. Sold 400 shares of treasury stock at $110.

   28. Paid cash for merchandise, $50,000 (debit Merchandise Inventory), and machinery, $100,000.

Instructions: (1) Record the foregoing transactions in "T" accounts. The accounts required are: Cash; Common Stock Subscriptions Receivable; Merchandise Inventory; Store Equipment; Machinery; Buildings; Land; Goodwill; Preferred Stock; Common Stock; Common Stock Subscribed; Premium on Common Stock; Treasury Stock — Common; Treasury Stock Surplus; Donated Surplus.

(2) Prepare a balance sheet in report form as of October 31, 1953.

22-4. The following accounts and their balances appeared in the ledger of Ferndale Corporation on September 1 of the current year:

11.7	Common Stock Subscriptions Receivable..........	———
31.1	6% Preferred Stock (Par $50; 10,000 shares authorized; 8,000 shares issued)......................	$ 400,000
31.2	Premium on Preferred Stock......................	40,000
31.3	Common Stock (No par; 200,000 shares authorized; 100,000 shares issued)........................	1,200,000
31.4	Common Stock Subscribed......................	———
31.8	Retained Earnings.............................	900,000

The corporation, acting upon a plan for changes in capital structure approved by the holders of common stock, entered into the following transactions during the remainder of the year:

Sept. 1. Holders of no-par common stock were given the right to subscribe to additional shares at $18 per share, at the rate of ¼ share for each share held. (No entry)

Oct. 1. Subscriptions were received for 24,000 shares of no-par common stock at $18 per share, together with a down payment of 50% of the subscription price.

Nov. 1. In accordance with the contract provisions of the preferred stock, the 8,000 shares were redeemed at $62 per share and retired.

Dec. 1. Collected the remainder due from all subscribers to the common stock and issued the stock certificates.

15. Issued 1,000 shares of no-par common stock at $20 per share, receiving cash.

31. The net profit for the year, after estimated taxes, is $189,000. (Debit Cash; credit Profit and Loss Summary.) Closed Profit and Loss Summary to Retained Earnings.

Instructions: (1) Open the accounts listed on page 439 and record the balances.

(2) Record the foregoing transactions in general journal form and post to the selected accounts in the ledger.

(3) Prepare the capital section of the balance sheet as of December 31.

(4) What is the book value per share of the common stock as of December 31?

Chapter | **23**

Corporate Surplus and Dividends

CORPORATE SURPLUS Corporate surplus may be defined as that part of the proprietorship of the corporation not represented by capital stock. Surplus should be classified so as to indicate its source. It is essential to know whether surplus has arisen from the activities of the corporation, from contributions by stockholders, or from other sources. The three main classifications of corporate surplus are:

(1) *Paid-in surplus*. Paid-in surplus is that portion of contributed capital in excess of the par or stated value of stock. Paid-in surplus also arises out of donations or gifts of property to the corporation and out of the corporation's dealings in its own stock.

(2) *Appraisal surplus*. Appraisal surplus represents the unrealized appreciation in the value of the company's assets that has been recorded on the books. The creation of such surplus is discouraged by sound accounting principles and is rarely found on corporate balance sheets.

(3) *Earned surplus*. Earned surplus is the accumulated total of the company's undistributed net income since incorporation. It usually represents the largest surplus item on a corporate balance sheet.

Many companies use the term "capital surplus" on their published reports to embrace a variety of meanings. It may be used to include only paid-in surplus or both paid-in and appraisal surplus. Because of the ambiguity attached to its meaning, the use of the term should be avoided.

Because of the difference in nature of the three types of surplus, they should be accounted for separately and should not be combined on the balance sheet. The practice of showing a single surplus item on the balance sheet is still being followed by some companies. Even when this is done, it usually represents the total of the balances of several different accounts in the ledger. These accounts usually indicate the source of the surplus items, such as Premium on Common Stock or Treasury Stock Surplus.

PAID-IN SURPLUS Paid-in surplus is a permanent part of capital, for it arises from dealings with stockholders and not from the earnings of the enterprise. Legally, paid-in surplus

441

is available for dividend distribution in many states. The stockholder in such a case should be informed that he is receiving a part of the invested capital rather than a part of the company's earnings. When a nominal stated value is assigned to common stock, paid-in surplus may be much larger than the amount reflected in the common stock account.

The chief sources of paid-in surplus are: (1) premium on sale of stock, (2) surplus from transactions in treasury stock, (3) donations or gifts of assets to the corporation, and (4) other transactions with stockholders, such as retirements of stock below issuance price. As transactions giving rise to these surplus items are completed, proper entries should be made on the company books. An account whose title describes the nature of the paid-in surplus item is used to record the surplus portion of each entry. For example, assume that the Wells Co. receives a gift of land valued at $40,000 from the county with the understanding that the company is to construct a large factory on the property. The entry would be:

```
May 1  Land...................................................  40,000
             Donated Surplus...............................          40,000
                  To record value of land received as a gift from
                  Ventura County.
```

Transactions such as this are comparatively rare. In most cases the largest item of paid-in surplus will result from the sale of common or preferred stock at a premium.

APPRAISAL SURPLUS   Appraisal or revaluation surplus arises from writing up a fixed asset item to a value higher than its original cost to the company. Accounting is predicated on the "cost principle," under which the accounting value of an asset is determined solely by what the company paid for it. Occasionally, the board of directors will decide that the values of assets as reflected in the accounts is substantially below the current market price. This is frequently true in periods of rising price levels as experienced during and after World War II. The board of directors, then, may authorize the company accountant to write up the value of the corporate assets as determined by professional appraisers. Assuming that the Wells Co. desires to increase the value of its land by $10,000 and the value of its buildings by $20,000, the following entry would be made:

```
July 10  Land — Increase per Appraisal...................  10,000
              Buildings — Increase per Appraisal..............  20,000
                  Appraisal Surplus...........................          30,000
                  To record increase in value of land and buildings
                  as determined by appraisal.
```

EARNED SURPLUS   Earned surplus or retained earnings consists of the corporate income that has not been distributed to stockholders. Assuming no change in the capital structure since incorporation, the earned surplus will exactly equal the difference between total earnings and total dividends paid to date. Operating and nonoperating income of a corporation are transferred to the earned surplus account. Gifts, donations, or dealings with stockholders do not constitute income and should not be closed to the earned surplus account. Assets in an amount equal to earned surplus may be used for dividend distributions since they represent the profits made on the stockholders' investment.

The net operating profit is transferred to Earned Surplus from Profit and Loss Summary. The method of transferring nonoperating items, such as gains on sale of equipment or corrections applicable to prior periods, varies among different companies. Some companies follow the "clean surplus" theory and close all nominal accounts into Profit and Loss Summary; others close nonoperating items directly into Earned Surplus to avoid reporting a distorted "normal profit" on the income statement. Regardless of the method used, the resulting balance in the earned surplus account is the same after the books have been closed.

The chief changes in the earned surplus balance take place as a result of profits or losses and dividend declarations. If the board of directors wishes to make the accumulated earnings a permanent part of capital, or if dividend payments are to be temporarily restricted for some reason, a portion of earned surplus may be transferred into a special account. When such action is taken, the earned surplus of a corporation is divided into two parts. One part is reflected in the earned surplus account and the other part in appropriated balances called *surplus reserves*. This division may be illustrated as follows:

COMPANY'S RETAINED EARNINGS

Reserve for Bond Sinking Fund		Earned Surplus	
	10,000	10,000	100,000
		16,000	
Reserve for Treasury Stock		20,000	
	16,000	15,000	
		Bal. 39,000	
Reserve for Plant Expansion			
	20,000	100,000	100,000
			Bal. 39,000
Reserve for Contingencies			
	15,000		

The accounts on the left represent "earmarked" or appropriated earned surplus, sometimes called surplus reserves. The account on the right represents the unappropriated earned surplus, against which dividend declarations may be charged. In this case the account shows $39,000 to be unappropriated and therefore available for distribution to stockholders. It is important to keep clearly in mind the fact that all of the above accounts are a part of the total earned surplus of the company.

APPROPRIATED EARNED SURPLUS   As pointed out earlier, a portion of earned surplus may be permanently or temporarily restricted or withheld from dividend distribution. This restriction is accomplished by transferring a portion of earned surplus into special accounts as illustrated in the preceding diagram. These transfers of earned surplus may be required by law or contract or they may be made at the discretion of the board of directors. Reserves of the first type are called *contractual reserves;* the latter type are called *discretionary reserves.* Reserve for Bond Sinking Fund and Reserve for Treasury Stock are examples of contractual reserves. Reserve for Plant Expansion and Reserve for Contingencies are examples of discretionary reserves.

Surplus reserves are created in order to limit dividends so that the assets of a company may be preserved for some definite future need. But the existence of the reserve does not imply that some specific fund is available to supply cash for future needs; it merely assures that net assets will be available for the intended purpose. The net assets may be in any form, such as cash or machinery. In certain instances a specific fund may be established to accumulate assets for some future expenditure, such as a bond sinking fund to pay off maturing bonds. A reserve for bond sinking fund may accompany the physical fund as required by the bond contract to provide additional protection to the bondholders.

The surplus reserves are set up by a debit to Earned Surplus and a credit to the reserve account. When the reserve has accomplished its purpose and is no longer required, it is transferred back to Earned Surplus. For example, assume that a company acquires 100 shares of treasury stock for $11,000 in a state where treasury stock purchases are limited to the amount of the earned surplus. In order to make certain that earned surplus equal to this purchase is maintained, a part of the earned surplus may be transferred to a special reserve account by the following entry:

Feb. 18 Earned Surplus.............................. 11,000
         Reserve for Treasury Stock....................   11,000
             To appropriate earned surplus for acquisition of
             treasury stock as required by statute.

When half of the treasury stock is sold, the following entry is made in addition to the entry to record the actual sale:

Apr. 15 Reserve for Treasury Stock.................... 5,500
         Earned Surplus..............................   5,500
             To eliminate portion of reserve no longer required
             by statute.

Discretionary reserves are made at the option of the corporation. The company may plan to expand its plant facilities and may want to preserve the assets accumulated by earnings to provide means of financing the expansion. To accomplish this, a debit may be made to Earned Surplus and a credit to Reserve for Plant Expansion. A company may also desire to protect its ability to meet certain contingent events, such as floods, fires, price declines on inventories, and lawsuits. A Reserve for Contingencies may be set up to guarantee that assets will be on hand to meet these possible losses. When it is determined that the contingency is unlikely to occur, or when it does occur, the reserve is returned to Earned Surplus.

CORPORATION EARNINGS The determination of the profit or the loss for a corporation is similar to that for any other form of business enterprise, except for certain special features. The profit and loss summary account on the corporation books contains income and expense items similar to those for a sole proprietorship or a partnership. However, after the net profit of a corporation has been determined, provision must be made for the income taxes imposed upon the corporation. Taxes on the corporation income may be levied by federal, state, and other governmental units. The only uniform tax for all corporations is the federal tax. The term *income taxes* in the ensuing discussion refers to all the income taxes that the corporation must pay. It must be emphasized that, at the time financial statements are prepared for the corporation, the tax liability may represent an estimate. This is true because the final tax return may not be completed by the time statements are prepared.

Another distinctive feature of corporate earnings is the fact that salaries paid to stockholders and officers are treated as expenses of the business rather than as a distribution of profits as is true in a sole proprietorship or a partnership. Also, the net profit of a corporation is not income of the stockholders except as the board of directors declares dividends. The net profit from the profit and loss summary account is transferred to Earned Surplus, which is in turn debited for any dividend declarations.

INCOME TAXES AND CORPORATE STATEMENTS Of the three main forms of business organizations, only the corporation needs accounts to record income tax liability. Since the payment of the income tax liability is usually made in the year following that for which the tax is assessed, the balance sheet of a corporation shows a current liability for this tax until payment has been made. Several different terms are used to describe the income tax liability on the balance sheet. Such terms as Provision for Income Taxes, Reserve for Income Taxes, or Estimated Income Taxes Payable may be found in practice.

An income tax differs from other taxes in that technically it is not an expense of the business. The law is worded in such a way that income tax represents a participation by the taxing authority in the profits of the corporation. For example, if the earnings of a corporation for one year are $100,000 and the income tax rate on corporations is 40%, the amount of income tax payable during the following year is $40,000. The entries to record the income tax liability and to close the profit and loss summary account in this case are:

```
Dec. 31  Profit and Loss Summary......................  40,000
             Estimated Income Taxes Payable..............          40,000
                 To record the income tax liability for the year.

      31  Profit and Loss Summary......................  60,000
             Earned Surplus..............................          60,000
                 To transfer the net profit after income taxes to
                 earned surplus.
```

Since income taxes are not treated as expenses but are considered to be participations in the profits by the government, they are not included in the expenses on the work sheet or on the profit and loss statement. On the work sheet the estimated income taxes are treated as a distribution of the net profit. On the profit and loss statement, the estimated income taxes are frequently reported as a deduction from the net profit. Parts of the work sheet and the profit and loss statement, showing the treatment of the income tax item, are given on the opposite page.

SURPLUS ON THE BALANCE SHEET The presentation of surplus on the balance sheet should follow a logical sequence to emphasize the nature of the various balances. Paid-in surplus may be shown immediately under the stock accounts as a part of the corporate paid-in capital. Appraisal surplus may be shown following paid-in

ACCOUNT TITLES	PROFIT AND LOSS STATEMENT		BALANCE SHEET	
	DR.	CR.	DR.	CR.
	268,575	368,575	537,290	437,290
Income Taxes.............	40,000			40,000
Net Profit After Income Taxes	60,000			60,000
	368,575	368,575	537,290	537,290

GLENACRE CORPORATION
PROFIT AND LOSS STATEMENT
FOR YEAR ENDED DECEMBER 31, 1953

Sales..	$310,550
Net Profit Before Income Taxes.......................	$100,000
Income Taxes.......................................	40,000
Net Profit After Income Taxes........................	$ 60,000

capital. Earned surplus may be classified as appropriated and un-appropriated. The capital section of the balance sheet of a corporation having various types of surplus items may be illustrated as follows:

CAPITAL

Paid-in Capital:			
Common Stock, $20 par (20,000 shares authorized, 10,000 shares issued)...		$200,000	
Paid-in Surplus:			
Premium on Common Stock....	$20,000		
Treasury Stock Surplus........	15,000	35,000	
Total Paid-in Capital...........................			$235,000
Appraisal Surplus................................			50,000
Earned Surplus:			
Appropriated:			
Reserve for Plant Expansion...	$10,000		
Reserve for Contingencies......	5,000	$ 15,000	
Unappropriated........................		25,000	
Total Earned Surplus...................			40,000
Total Capital............................			$325,000

NATURE OF DIVIDENDS Dividends represent the prime incentive for the investment in corporation stocks. A dividend may be defined as a prorata distribution by a corporation to its shareholders. Dividends may be paid in cash, in stock of the paying company, in scrip, or in other property. All of the above distributions must be made from the accumulated earnings of the company. A *liquidating dividend* is said to be paid when a part of the invested capital is returned to the stockholders upon termination of the business or partial liquidation. The discussion in this chapter will be mainly concerned with the two prevalent types of dividends — *cash dividends* and *stock dividends*.

Normally three conditions are necessary before a cash dividend may be paid: (1) sufficient earned surplus, (2) available assets to be used in the payment, and (3) action by the board of directors. A large earned surplus balance is not conclusive evidence that the company is able to pay dividends; availability of earned surplus must be accompanied by a sufficient balance in the cash account. Earned surplus and cash are not synonymous: earned surplus represents profits of past periods not distributed to stockholders, but the cash provided by these profits may have been used for other purposes such as purchases of fixed assets or reduction of liabilities. The board of directors is not compelled by law to declare dividends even when both earned surplus and cash are available. The board uses its own discretion as to dividend action; but once a dividend is declared, the obligation to pay the dividend becomes a current liability of the corporation.

Financially strong companies attempt to build up a stable dividend record by paying out only a portion of earnings during successful years and by accumulating surplus that may be used for dividend payments during lean years. Typically, approximately 60% of the earnings of good years is distributed as dividends, but the policies vary among different industries and individual companies. Dividends may be paid once a year or several times during the year, although the present tendency is toward quarterly dividends on both common and preferred stock. "Extra" year-end dividends may be paid on common stock when earnings permit.

Three dates are involved in the formal dividend declaration: (1) declaration date, (2) record date, and (3) payment date. The law requires that the date of record follow the date of declaration, in order that the parties to stock transfers may know the dividend situation. Public notice in newspapers is usually made by large companies concerning dividend declaration. The corporation becomes liable for the payment of the dividend as a result of the action by the board of directors. On the declaration date, the earned surplus account is debited and the dividends payable account is credited. No entry is required by the passage of the record date; the record date merely determines the identity of the stockholders who will be entitled to the dividend. Purchasers of the company's stock following the record date will not receive the dividend. On the payment date, the dividends payable account is debited and cash is credited to record the issuance of dividend checks.

Dividends on cumulative preferred stock do not become a liability to the corporation until they are declared. Any dividends in arrears should be shown parenthetically or by footnote on the balance sheet.

CASH DIVIDENDS   By far the largest number of dividends are paid in the form of cash. Only cash dividends are paid on preferred stock, and cash represents the normal medium of payment on common stock as well. Dividends are usually given in terms of dollars and cents per share rather than as a percentage of par value.

Directors may declare each dividend separately or they may declare several quarterly dividends by a single resolution. The amount of cash dividends to be declared, assuming there is earned surplus available, is determined by the board of directors after giving due consideration to the following factors:

(1) The company's working capital position.
(2) Resources required for expansion or replacement of assets.
(3) Maturity dates of large liabilities.
(4) Future business and economic outlook.

These factors must be considered in view of cash requirements for other than dividend purposes and the company's prospects of conducting operations successfully.

To illustrate the entries required in the declaration and the payment of cash dividends, assume the following facts: on December 15, 1953, the Carson Co. declares the regular quarterly dividend of $1.50 per share on $200,000 of its $100 par, 6% preferred stock and a quarterly dividend of $1 per share on the 10,000 shares of $50 par common stock. Both dividends are payable on January 25, 1954, to stockholders of record on January 10, 1954. Entries to record the declaration and the payment of the dividends are:

1953
Dec. 15 Earned Surplus..........................   13,000
     Preferred Dividends Payable...........   3,000
     Common Dividends Payable............   10,000
     Declaration of quarterly dividend on
     preferred and common stock, payable
     January 25, 1954.

1954
Jan. 25 Preferred Dividends Payable.............   3,000
     Common Dividends Payable.............   10,000
     Cash.................................   13,000
     Payment of dividends declared on De-
     cember 15, 1953.

On the balance sheet as of December 31, 1953, the dividend payable items would be shown among the current liabilities.

STOCK DIVIDENDS   A prorata distribution by a corporation of additional shares of its own stock, without the receipt of any consideration therefor, is referred to as a *stock dividend*. Stock dividends are frequently paid when the company has a large earned surplus balance but is unwilling to pay cash dividends because cash has been permanently reinvested by the company in fixed assets. Stock dividends may also be declared to reduce the market price per share of the company's stock so that more prospective buyers will be attracted to it. The market price reduction is accomplished by the fact that a stock dividend does not change the total of a company's capital but simply divides the existing capital among a greater number of shares; hence the value of each share is proportionately reduced.

A stock dividend does not constitute taxable income to the stockholder because, in reality, he has not received anything, his ownership interest simply being represented by a greater number of shares. For example, a holder of 10 shares with a book value of $150 per share will have 15 shares with a book value of $100 per share after a 50% stock dividend. The holder's total equity before and after the dividend is exactly the same, $1,500. It may be seen, therefore, that a stock dividend is actually not a dividend at all. From the point of view of the corporation, a stock dividend is a mere transfer of earned surplus to the common stock account, thus resulting in a permanent appropriation of surplus. Once the additional stock has been issued, it becomes a part of the capital investment of the stockholders and that part of the surplus is no longer available for dividend declaration.

To illustrate the entries involved in a stock dividend, assume that a company with $200,000 of $100 par common stock and $150,000 of earned surplus declares a 50% stock dividend. The entries would be:

Feb. 10 Earned Surplus............................ 100,000
        Stock Dividend Payable....................   100,000
           To record a 50% stock dividend on $200,000
           of $100 par common stock.

Mar. 10 Stock Dividend Payable................... 100,000
        Common Stock............................   100,000
           To record issuance of stock in payment of
           stock dividend.

The capital section of the corporation before and after the 50% stock dividend is shown below:

Before issuance of stock dividend:

CAPITAL

Paid-in Capital:
  Common Stock, par $100 (4,000 shares authorized,
    2,000 shares issued)........................... $200,000
Earned Surplus.................................... 150,000

Total Capital..................................... $350,000

After issuance of 50% stock dividend:

CAPITAL

Paid-in Capital:
  Common Stock, par $100 (4,000 shares authorized,
    3,000 shares issued)........................... $300,000
Earned Surplus.................................... 50,000

Total Capital..................................... $350,000

If a balance sheet had been prepared after the declaration but before the issuance of the stock dividend, Stock Dividend Payable would be shown as a part of the paid-in capital. Stock Dividend Payable is not a liability to be liquidated in cash; it is simply earned surplus on its journey to the common stock account.

STOCK SPLIT-UP   Another method of issuing additional shares of stock to the stockholders without any further contribution being made to the corporation is a *stock split-up*. A stock split-up is a procedure whereby more shares are issued by reducing the par or stated value of the stock in proportion to the additional shares issued. A corporation may, for example, have 10,000 shares of $50 stated value stock outstanding; by a stock split-up it may exchange those shares for 20,000 shares of $25 stated value stock, or 50,000 shares of $10 stated value stock, or any number of shares of no-par stock. Only a memorandum entry is required to record a stock split-up, since there is no change in any account balance.

The primary purpose of a stock split-up is to reduce the selling price of stock when the shares are selling at exceedingly high levels. Such an action will permit more investors to enter the market for this particular security. A stock split-up is seldom employed by small corporations or by corporations whose stock is not listed on the organized stock exchanges.

CORRECTIONS FOR PREVIOUS PERIODS   In spite of every effort to measure accurately the profit or the loss of each period, there frequently arises the necessity for corrections at a later time. A correction applicable to the current period may be recorded by a correcting entry that eliminates the error and records the transaction properly. For example, office equipment was purchased for $900 on April 1, 1953, and was recorded in the purchases account. If the error was discovered on December 20 before the books were closed for 1953, the following correcting entry would be made:

```
Dec. 20  Office Equipment.....................................  900
             Purchases.........................................         900
                To correct accounts for acquisition of office equipment
                recorded in Purchases.
```

The earned surplus account is used in making corrections that are required by the discovery of errors affecting the profits of previous periods. The amount of the profit or the loss that should be recorded in order to correct the error is not normally shown in a profit or loss account of the period in which the error has been discovered but is credited or debited to Earned Surplus. When the errors are of relatively minor amount and will not distort the current income figure, the corrections may be included in a current profit or loss account instead of being cleared through Earned Surplus. Some companies have a fixed policy whereby errors below a given amount, such as $50, are included on the current profit and loss statement. Other firms adopt the "clean surplus" theory and include all errors on the profit and loss statement regardless of the amount involved. In all cases where a correction of an error of a past period is to be made, a careful analysis of the error's effect upon the present account balances is necessary.

For example, on March 1, 1954, the auditor inspecting the books of the Toscano Corporation for 1953 discovers that a purchase of land and buildings on January 5, 1953, was recorded by a debit to Property and a credit to Cash for $20,000. It is determined that the land was worth $5,000 and the buildings $15,000, with a remaining estimated life of 15 years. No depreciation was recorded for 1953 and the books have been closed. The correcting entry to be recorded on March 1, 1954, may be determined as follows:

Entry Made	Entries That Should Have Been Made		Correcting Entry	
Property 20,000 　Cash........20,000	Buildings........... 15,000 Land.............. 5,000 　Cash............ Depreciation Expense 1,000 　Allowance for De- 　preciation of Build- 　ings.............	 20,000 1,000	Buildings........... 15,000 Land.............. 5,000 Earned Surplus...... 1,000 　Property......... 　Allowance for De- 　preciation of Build- 　ings.............	 20,000 1,000

The above tabulation provides an orderly method of determining what correcting entry is required. The correcting entry is determined by comparing what was done with what should have been done. Since the books have been closed for 1953, any nominal account involved must be corrected through Earned Surplus. It is essential to note that, no matter when the error is discovered, the correction adjusts the accounts as of the date that the books were last closed, but the entry itself is currently dated.

ARBITRARY ADJUSTMENTS IN CORPORATE ACCOUNTS Frequently the resolutions of the board of directors call for certain data to be recorded on the books of the company without evidence of a closed transaction. Such entries may be termed *arbitrary adjustments* since they do not involve outsiders and no assets change hands. Several of the more important adjustments are briefly described in the paragraphs that follow.

Organization Costs. It was pointed out in Chapter 21 that organization costs may be retained on the corporate books as long as the corporation maintains its status as a going concern. As a conservative move, however, it is common practice to write off the entire organization costs against earned surplus during the early years of a company's existence. Assuming that a company incurred organization costs of $7,500 and that the costs will be amortized over a period of 5 years, the following entry would be made at the end of each of the first five years:

Dec. 31 Earned Surplus..................................... 1,500
　　　　Organization Costs.............................   1,500
　　　　To write off one fifth of the organization costs.

Goodwill. Goodwill should not be recorded on the books of a company unless it has been acquired by a business transaction. When goodwill is considered to benefit operations and has a limited life, it may be systematically amortized by charges to periodic revenue. Normally it is difficult to associate goodwill directly with periodic operations and hence goodwill may be permanently retained on the books. However, it may be determined at some future date that the value of goodwill has diminished and, as a conservative move, the board of directors may authorize an arbitrary reduction or complete elimination of goodwill by the following entry:

June 30 Earned Surplus.............................. 10,000
             Goodwill......................................   10,000
                  To write off goodwill as authorized by board of
                  directors.

Patents and Formulas. Corporations sometimes pay large sums of money for the development or the purchase of patents and secret formulas. Such assets should be amortized over their estimated useful life. Frequently, patents and formulas become worthless because of new inventions and must be eliminated from the books of the corporation by a debit to Earned Surplus and a credit to the asset account.

Asset Appraisals. During periods of rising price levels, some companies may desire to reflect the increased value of properties on its books. The propriety of such adjustments was discussed earlier in this chapter in relation to appraisal surplus. It is usually an accepted procedure to write up the value of land when oil or other valuable resources have been discovered on it. In periods of falling price levels, companies may write down the value of high-cost assets in order to relieve operations of exceedingly high depreciation charges. Such a reduction in asset value would be accomplished by a debit to Earned Surplus and a credit to the asset account.

EARNED SURPLUS   The earned surplus statement provides a sum-
STATEMENT   mary of all debits and credits made to the
earned surplus accounts during a given period. Corrections applicable to previous fiscal periods and current transactions as authorized by the board of directors are all included. The earned surplus statement also serves to tie together the profit and loss statement and the balance sheet.

The earned surplus statement is divided into two major sections: (1) items affecting unappropriated earned surplus and (2) items affecting surplus reserves. The first section includes: correcting entries; dividend declarations, both preferred and common; write-offs of any assets chargeable to earned surplus; and contractual and discretionary surplus appropriations. The second section shows the changes in the earned surplus appropriated accounts. The final figure gives the total of all earned surplus accounts as of the balance sheet date.

The earned surplus account and the surplus reserve accounts in the ledger of the General Trading Corporation for the fiscal year ended December 31, 1953, appear as follows:

EARNED SURPLUS　　　　　　　　　　　　Acct. No. 314

1953				1953			
Mar.	10	Depreciation	7,600	Jan.	1	Balance	105,500
	20	Dividends	12,250	Mar.	10	Inventory	15,000
June	19	Dividends	11,250	Dec.	31	Net Profit after In-	
Sept.	18	Dividends	11,250			come Taxes	102,400
Dec.	18	Dividends	20,250				
	31	Goodwill	11,000				
	31	Reserve for Bond					
		Sinking Fund	10,000				
	31	Reserve for Plant					
		Expansion	20,000				
	31	Balance	119,300				
			222,900				222,900
				1954			
				Jan.	1	Balance	119,300

RESERVE FOR BOND SINKING FUND　　　　Acct. No. 315

1953				1953			
Dec.	31	Balance	30,000	Jan.	1	Balance	20,000
				Dec.	31		10,000
			30,000				30,000
				1954			
				Jan.	1	Balance	30,000

RESERVE FOR PLANT EXPANSION　　　　　Acct. No. 316

1953				1953			
Dec.	31	Balance	40,000	Jan.	1	Balance	20,000
				Dec.	31		20,000
			40,000				40,000
				1954			
				Jan.	1	Balance	40,000

The earned surplus statement for the year, prepared from the data in the foregoing accounts, is as follows:

GENERAL TRADING CORPORATION
Earned Surplus Statement
For Year Ended December 31, 1953

Earned Surplus Unappropriated:			
Balance, January 1, 1953......................			$105,500
Corrections Applicable to Past Periods:			
Add — Understatement of Inventory, Dec. 31, 1952.	$ 15,000		
Deduct — Understatement of Depreciation in Past			
Years.....................................	7,600		7,400
Balance, January 1, 1953, as corrected..............			$112,900
Current Operations:			
Add — Net Profit for Year after Income Taxes.....		$102,400	
Deduct — Dividends Declared...........	$55,000		
Goodwill Written Off.........	11,000		
Appropriation for Bond Sinking Fund (see below)...........	10,000		
Appropriation for Plant Expansion (see below)...........	20,000	96,000	6,400
Earned Surplus Unappropriated, Dec. 31, 1953......			$119,300
Earned Surplus Reserves:			
Reserve for Bond Sinking Fund, Balance, Jan. 1...............................	$20,000		
Add — Appropriation in 1953 (see above)...	10,000	$ 30,000	
Reserve for Plant Expansion, Balance, Jan. 1.	$20,000		
Add — Appropriation in 1953 (see above)....	20,000	40,000	
Earned Surplus Reserves, December 31, 1953........			70,000
Total Earned Surplus, December 31, 1953.............			$189,300

Earned Surplus Statement

The amounts shown on the earned surplus statement as the final balances of the earned surplus account and of the reserve accounts will, of course, also appear on the year-end balance sheet. The balance sheet of the General Trading Corporation is presented on page 475.

Earned surplus statements are frequently less involved than the one illustrated above. For a corporation that has no surplus reserve accounts and that has made no corrections of profits reported in past periods, the only changes to be reported in the earned surplus statement might well be net profit after income taxes and dividend declarations.

QUESTIONS

1. Describe the three classifications of surplus and mention the main sources of each type.

2. (a) What is the purpose of surplus reserves? (b) Where are surplus reserves reported on the balance sheet?

3. (a) What three conditions are necessary before dividends may be declared? (b) What factors are considered by the board of directors before cash dividends are declared? (c) Discuss the differences between a stock dividend and a stock split-up.

4. The Chesterfield Corporation, with 1,000 shares of cumulative 5% preferred stock outstanding, passed (did not declare) the regular dividend in December. The accountant set up a liability for the amount of the unpaid dividends. Do you approve? Explain.

5. The Standard Corporation (a) issues 1,000 shares of common stock, $100 par, at $105 a share; (b) revalues its buildings, which were recorded at $600,000, at $800,000; (c) accepts from the Glenview Chamber of Commerce a gift of a plot of ground that is appraised at $60,000 and on which a branch plant is to be erected. Give the entry to record each of the transactions. What is the effect of each transaction on the capital of the corporation?

6. The board of directors of The Lyon Manufacturing Co. declares a 20% stock dividend on $400,000 par value of common stock. (a) Give the entry required by this transaction. (b) If A holds 50 shares of the stock of this company, how many shares will he receive as a dividend? How much income has he received?

7. What effect do the following transactions have on the capital of a corporation? on the working capital?

    (a) Declaration of a cash dividend.   (d) Payment of a stock dividend.
    (b) Payment of a cash dividend.   (e) A stock split-up.
    (c) Declaration of a stock dividend.

8. The earnings before income taxes of the Standard Corporation for the current year are $280,000. The income taxes are $112,000. The board of directors (a) appropriates $10,000 in accordance with an agreement with bondholders; (b) appropriates $30,000 for the expansion of the plant; and (c) declares a quarterly dividend of $3 per share on outstanding common stock of 10,000 shares. Give the entries necessary to record these transactions.

9. Give the correcting entry on December 31, 1953, for each of the following errors made during 1953, assuming that books have not been closed:

    (a) In recording a sale of $400 on account, Notes Receivable was inadvertently debited instead of Accounts Receivable.
    (b) A purchase of supplies, $200, was recorded in Purchases.
    (c) A machine that cost $6,000 and that had accumulated depreciation of $4,000 was sold for $1,000. The entry was recorded by a debit to Cash and a credit to Sales for $1,000.

10. Give the correcting entry on January 10, 1954, for each of the following errors made in 1953, assuming that the books have been closed for 1953 (carry corrections through Earned Surplus):

(a) Merchandise inventory on December 31, 1953, was understated by $5,000.

(b) Accrued salaries of $3,000 were not recognized on December 31, 1953.

(c) A one-year insurance policy was acquired on September 1, 1953, for $360 and was recorded in Insurance Expense. No adjusting entry was made on December 31, 1953.

(d) A machine with a 3-year life and no scrap value was purchased on January 2, 1953, and was recorded in Purchases at a cost of $6,000. No depreciation was recorded for 1953.

11. The capital of the Brown Corporation is shown as follows:

Common Stock ($100 par).............................	$50,000
Premium on Common Stock...........................	4,000
Earned Surplus.......................................	30,000

A 20% stock dividend is declared. (a) Give the entries to record the declaration and the payment of the dividend. (b) What was the book value per share before the declaration of the stock dividend? after the issue of the stock dividend? (c) What was the effect of the issue of the stock dividend on the ownership equity of each stockholder in the corporation?

12. Give entries to record the following:

(a) Wrote off organization costs of $2,000.

(b) Wrote off goodwill of $10,000.

(c) Increased the value of land by $15,000 as determined by appraisal.

(d) Effected a stock split-up by reducing the par value of the 10,000 shares outstanding from $100 to $25.

(e) Set up a reserve for contingencies of $10,000.

13. The Uclan Corporation published the following balance sheet on December 31, 1953:

UCLAN CORPORATION

BALANCE SHEET

DECEMBER 31, 1953

Assets:		Liabilities............. $	50,000
Cash................ $ 250,000		Capital:	
Other Assets......... 800,000		Preferred Stock, 6%	
		cumulative, $100 par..	100,000
		Common Stock, $25 par	750,000
		Paid-in Surplus.........	50,000
		Retained Earnings......	100,000
		Total Liabilities and	
Total Assets........... $1,050,000		Capital................	$1,050,000

On January 2, 1954, the board of directors decide to declare dividends. The preferred dividend, payable semiannually, was last paid up to July 1,

1950. The dividends to be distributed are to be of such an amount that the accumulated earnings will be reduced to $25,000. (a) How much will be paid on each share of common stock? (b) What entry should be made on the books of the Uclan Corporation on January 2, 1954, to record the dividend declaration?

14. The following balance sheet is a condensed form of that prepared for the Lakeside Manufacturing Co. at the end of a fiscal year:

LAKESIDE MANUFACTURING CO.
BALANCE SHEET
MAY 31, 1953

ASSETS		LIABILITIES AND CAPITAL	
Current Assets............	$200,000	Current Liabilities........	$100,000
Treasury Stock..........	40,000	Common Stock..........	200,000
Fixed Assets.............	160,000	Donated Surplus.........	40,000
Goodwill................	60,000	Paid-in Surplus..........	60,000
		Earned Surplus..........	60,000
		Total Liabilities and	
Total Assets.............	$460,000	Capital.................	$460,000

(a) Explain the nature and the possible origin of each item. (b) How much is available for distribution of dividends?

PROBLEMS

23-1. The balance sheet of the Apex Corporation on June 30, 1953, consisted of: Cash, $85,000; Merchandise Inventory, $80,000; Common Stock ($25 par value), $150,000; Earned Surplus, $15,000. The following transactions occurred during the fiscal year ended June 30, 1954:

(a) Sold 800 shares 6% preferred stock, par value $100, for cash, $84,000.

(b) It was determined that the inventory on June 30, 1953, was understated by $8,000.

(c) The operations for the year resulted in a profit of $80,000. (It will be assumed that as the result of the operations there was also an increase in Cash of $50,000 and an increase in Merchandise Inventory of $30,000; therefore, debit Cash and Merchandise Inventory and credit Profit and Loss Summary.)

(d) Made provision for income tax liability of $32,000 and closed the balance of Profit and Loss Summary to Earned Surplus.

(e) Declared a preferred dividend of $6 a share and a common dividend of $5 a share.

(f) Paid the dividends.

(g) Appropriated $5,000 of earned surplus for possible inventory losses.

Instructions: (1) Record the June 30, 1953, balances in "T" accounts. Record the transactions directly in these accounts, identifying each debit and each credit with the letter given for that transaction. The accounts required are: Cash; Merchandise Inventory; Estimated Income Taxes Payable; Preferred Dividend Payable; Common Dividend Payable; Preferred Stock; Premium on Preferred Stock; Common Stock; Reserve for Inventory Losses; Earned Surplus; Profit and Loss Summary.

(2) Prepare a balance sheet in report form as of June 30, 1954.

23-2. Following are the transactions of Lipman, Inc. during 1953, its first year of operations:

  (a) Received $94,500 cash for 900 shares of $100 par value common stock.

  (b) Acquired the going business of the Hanson Corporation. Issued 650 shares of $100 par value common stock in exchange for the following: Machinery, $30,000; Buildings, $20,000; Land, $12,000; Goodwill, $3,000.

  (c) Made an operating profit of $35,000 for the year (debit Cash, $38,800; credit Allowance for Depreciation of Machinery, $3,000; credit Allowance for Depreciation of Buildings, $800; and credit Profit and Loss Summary, $35,000).

  (d) Made provision for income tax liability of $14,000 and closed the balance of Profit and Loss Summary to Earned Surplus.

  (e) Declared dividends of $5.50 per share on common stock.

The following transactions occurred in 1954:

  (f) Paid the income tax for 1953.

  (g) Paid the dividends declared in (e).

  (h) Purchased the going business of the Wedel Company for $50,000 in cash. Its assets were valued as follows: Machinery, $20,000; Buildings, $12,000; Land, $10,000; Goodwill, $8,000.

  (i) Made an operating profit of $60,000 for 1954 (debit Cash $67,000; credit Allowance for Depreciation of Machinery, $5,000; credit Allowance for Depreciation of Buildings, $2,000; and credit Profit and Loss Summary, $60,000).

  (j) Made provision for income tax liability of $24,000 and closed the balance of Profit and Loss Summary to Earned Surplus.

  (k) Declared dividends of $7 per share on common stock.

  (l) The depreciation of machinery for 1953 was understated by $1,000.

  (m) Wrote off goodwill of $5,000 against Earned Surplus.

Instructions: (1) Record the above transactions directly in "T" accounts. Identify each debit and each credit with the letter given for that transaction in the list of transactions. The accounts required are: Cash; Machinery; Allowance for Depreciation of Machinery; Buildings; Allowance for Depreciation of Buildings; Land; Goodwill; Estimated Income Taxes Payable; Common Dividend Payable; Common Stock; Premium on Common Stock; Earned Surplus; Profit and Loss Summary.

(2) Take a trial balance as of December 31, 1954.

(3) Prepare a balance sheet as of December 31, 1954.

23-3. The earned surplus account and the surplus reserve accounts of the O'Hearn Corporation for the fiscal year ended December 31, 1953, are given on the following page.

EARNED SURPLUS

1953				1953			
Jan.	20	Organization costs		Jan.	1	Balance	166,000
		written off	2,000	Mar.	13	Understatement of	
	20	Goodwill written off	5,000			inventory on Dec.	
Mar.	13	Correction in depre-				31, 1952	6,000
		ciation for 1951	8,000	Dec.	31	Net profit after in-	
Oct.	1	Cash dividend de-				come taxes	75,000
		clared	40,000				
	1	Stock dividend de-					
		clared	50,000				
Dec.	31	Reserve for plant					
		expansion	18,000				
	31	Reserve for con-					
		tingencies	10,000				
	31	Balance	114,000				
			247,000				247,000
				1954			
				Jan.	1	Balance	114,000

RESERVE FOR PLANT EXPANSION		RESERVE FOR CONTINGENCIES	
	1953		1953
	Jan. 1 Bal. 37,000		Jan. 1 Bal. 15,000
	Dec. 31 18,000		Dec. 31 10,000

Instructions: From the foregoing accounts, prepare an earned surplus statement, similar to the one illustrated on page 456, for the O'Hearn Corporation for the fiscal year ended December 31, 1953.

23-4. The capital section of the balance sheet of the Royce-Hall Corporation as of December 31, 1953, is given below:

CAPITAL

Paid-in Capital:
  Common Stock, $100 par (10,000 shares
    authorized)......................... $800,000
  Premium on Common Stock............. 16,000

  Total Paid-in Capital....................... $ 816,000
Earned Surplus:
  Appropriated:
    Reserve for Plant Expansion.. $ 60,000
    Reserve for Treasury Stock... 115,000 $ 175,000
  Unappropriated...................... 124,000

  Total Earned Surplus........................ 299,000

Total.. $1,115,000
Less Treasury Stock (1,000 shares at cost)........... 115,000

Total Capital................................. $1,000,000

The following transactions and information affecting the capital accounts were recorded in 1954:

Jan. 15. Increased the value of land on the books by $50,000.

Feb. 18. Established a reserve for contingencies of $20,000.

Mar. 1. Wrote off goodwill of $15,000.

15. Corrected the following errors for 1953:

(a) On July 1, 1953, 100 shares of common stock were issued in return for land having a market value of $12,000. The transaction was recorded by a debit to Land and a credit to Common Stock for $10,000.

(b) New machinery with an estimated life of 20 years was purchased on January 2, 1953. The cost of installation was $2,000 and the premium on a 2-year insurance policy was $400. These last two items were charged to expense accounts and were closed to Profit and Loss Summary. (Depreciation and expired insurance must be allowed for in the correcting entry.)

(c) Cash sales of $5,000 on December 20, 1953, were credited to Accounts Payable.

May 12. Sold 400 shares of treasury stock to the public at 125 and gave 100 shares of treasury stock to company officers as a bonus. Reduced the restriction on earned surplus proportionately.

Aug. 24. Received from the Westwood Chamber of Commerce as a donation a plot of land valued at $20,000.

Dec. 31. The operating profit for 1954 was $200,000; the estimated income taxes payable were $80,000. Transferred net profit after income taxes to Earned Surplus.

31. Declared a cash dividend of $10 per share on the common stock outstanding on December 31, 1954 (7,500 shares), payable January 30, 1955.

31. Wrote off organization costs of $2,000.

31. Completed the plant expansion and returned the surplus reserve, which was no longer required, to the earned surplus account.

Instructions: (1) Prepare general journal entries to record the foregoing information.

(2) Record the balances shown in the capital section of the December 31, 1953, balance sheet in "T" accounts. Post the entries prepared in (1) to the capital accounts only. The accounts required are: Common Stock; Premium on Common Stock; Treasury Stock; Treasury Stock Surplus; Donated Surplus; Appraisal Surplus; Reserve for Plant Expansion; Reserve for Treasury Stock; Reserve for Contingencies; Earned Surplus.

(3) Prepare the capital section of the balance sheet as of December 31, 1954.

(4) Prepare an earned surplus statement, similar to the one illustrated on page 456, for the year ended December 31, 1954.

Chapter | **24**

Corporate Stocks and Bonds

CORPORATION CAPITAL AND CORPORATION EARNINGS
When money is invested in a corporation, the corporation is expected to earn profits out of which dividends will be paid to the investors. In previous chapters corporation capital was shown to be contributed largely by stockholders, who participated in corporate profits through dividend declarations. Corporations might issue two kinds of stock, preferred and common, the preferred with a prior but limited claim on earnings and the common with a residual but unlimited claim on earnings.

Because of the ease of transferring stock and the availability of earnings through dividends, corporations have generally found investors ready to exchange their money for shares of stock. Some corporations have acquired the property of competitors in exchange for shares of their own stock. The great business of investment banking and the huge volume of trading on the stock exchanges give evidence of the present-day interest in corporate stocks. The corporation has become the great capital accumulating unit of modern business.

Since some investors prefer a more certain income in the form of interest and a promise of the return of the investment at some future date, many corporations have raised capital through the issuance of bonds. Such capital is, for the corporation, borrowed capital and involves periodic interest payments together with ultimate repayment of the principal. Because interest payments are more certain and because creditors have a prior claim on corporation assets, the cost of borrowed capital is less than the cost of capital obtained by selling preferred or common stock. Interest on bonds is an expense of the corporation and must be paid before income taxes and dividends.

To illustrate the effect of obtaining capital by the methods discussed above, assume that Corporations A, B, and C each have a capital of $4,000,000 and that this capital has been obtained as follows:

Corporation A: 40,000 shares of common stock, $100 par.
Corporation B: 20,000 shares of 5% preferred stock, $100 par.
     20,000 shares of common stock, $100 par.
Corporation C: $2,000,000 of 4% bonds.
     10,000 shares of 5% preferred stock, $100 par.
     10,000 shares of common stock, $100 par.

Assume also that each corporation has earnings, before the payment of bond interest, of $500,000 and that 40% of the net profit is paid as income tax. The following table then shows the calculation of the earnings per share available for the common stockholders of each corporation:

	CORPORATION A	CORPORATION B	CORPORATION C
CAPITAL STRUCTURE:			
4% Bonds......................			$2,000,000
5% Preferred Stock, $100 par..........		20,000 shares	10,000 shares
Common Stock, $100 par.............	40,000 shares	20,000 shares	10,000 shares
Earnings.............................	$500,000	$500,000	$500,000
Less Interest on Bonds.................	....	....	80,000
Balance.............................	$500,000	$500,000	$420,000
Less Income Taxes (40% of income after bond interest).......................	200,000	200,000	168,000
Balance.............................	$300,000	$300,000	$252,000
Dividends on Preferred Stock...........	....	100,000	50,000
Available for Dividends on Common Stock..	$300,000	$200,000	$202,000
Earnings per Share of Common Stock......	$7.50	$10	$20.20

In Corporation A, the earnings per share of common stock are $7.50. In Corporation B, half of the capital is obtained from 5% preferred stock; the balance available for the common stockholders is therefore increased to $10 a share. In Corporation C, half of the capital is obtained from 4% bonds and one quarter from 5% preferred stock. Since bond interest expense is deductible for income tax purposes, the earnings per share of common stock are increased to $20.20.

This table shows the advantage to common stockholders of having corporation capital obtained through bonds and preferred stocks whenever the rate of return on all capital is higher than the interest rate on bonds or the dividend rate on preferred stock. But, if the average rate of earnings on all capital is less than the interest rate on bonds or the dividend rate on preferred stock, there is a disadvantage to common stockholders in having corporation capital obtained through bonds and preferred stock. Assume that in the previous examples the annual earnings of each corporation had been only $170,000 before bond interest and that the income tax rate remained at 40%. The earnings available for common stockholders would then have been:

	CORPORATION A	CORPORATION B	CORPORATION C
CAPITAL STRUCTURE:			
4% Bonds.........................			$2,000,000
5% Preferred Stock, $100 par...........		20,000 shares	10,000 shares
Common Stock, $100 par...............	40,000 shares	20,000 shares	10,000 shares
Earnings..............................	$170,000	$170,000	$170,000
Less Interest on Bonds.................	....	....	80,000
Balance...............................	$170,000	$170,000	$ 90,000
Less Income Taxes (40% of income after bond interest)........................	68,000	68,000	36,000
Balance...............................	$102,000	$102,000	$ 54,000
Dividends on Preferred Stock.............	....	100,000	50,000
Available for Dividends on Common Stock..	$102,000	$ 2,000	$ 4,000
Earnings per Share of Common Stock......	$2.55	10¢	40¢

BONDS PAYABLE   A *bond* is a promise under seal to pay a definite sum of money at a stated time and to pay interest at a stipulated rate. It is a result of a contract, called the *bond indenture*, between the corporation and the bondholder. Assets of the corporation may be pledged as security for the payment of both the principal and the interest, or bonds may be issued without such security. Most bonds provide for semiannual interest payments, although other interest paying arrangements may exist.

The purpose of the bonds payable account is to show the face value of the bonds outstanding. This account is credited with the face value of the bonds issued and is debited with the face value of all bonds redeemed or otherwise retired. When a corporation has several issues of bonds outstanding, a separate account for each issue should be maintained.

Bonds payable are reported on the balance sheet as fixed liabilities as long as their maturity is more than one year removed from the balance sheet date. The description should include the type of security, the interest rate, and the due date.

Bonds are classified in various ways. As to the mode of interest payment, they may be *registered* or *coupon bonds*. If registered, the interest check is made out to the registered owner; if coupon, the coupon is clipped by the bondholder and sent in for payment. As to security, bonds may be *secured*, as explained in the next paragraph, or *unsecured*. As to payment of principal, they may call for payment of a definite amount at a definite date in the future, or they may provide for payment at a time determined by lot, or they may be convertible into some other form of security at the option of the bondholders. Most bonds mature at a definite future date and are known as *term bonds*. Those maturing by lot are called *serial bonds*. Bonds that may be exchanged for other securities are referred to as *convertible bonds*.

A secured bond is one that gives the bondholder a preferred claim on some particular asset. This asset may be a building, it may be the entire plant including buildings and machinery, or it may be stocks or bonds of other companies owned by the debtor corporation.

If bonds are sold at par before interest begins to accrue, Cash is debited and Bonds Payable is credited. If the sale occurs between interest dates, the buyer is charged with the accrued interest. For example, assume that $100,000 worth of 4% bonds dated January 1, 1953, were sold at par on April 1, 1953. Three months' interest at 4% would have accrued between January 1 and April 1. The entry on the records of the selling corporation would be:

April 1 Cash..	101,000	
Bonds Payable...........................		100,000
Bond Interest Expense....................		1,000
Sold $100,000 worth of 4% bonds, dated January 1, at par plus accrued interest.		

Bond Interest Expense is credited for the interest collected from the buyer so that the regular semiannual interest payment on June 30, 1953, may be recorded in the regular manner by a debit to Bond Interest Expense and a credit to Cash for $2,000. After this entry, the balance in the bond interest expense account will reflect the actual expense for the three months during which the bonds were in the hands of investors.

BOND PREMIUM AND DISCOUNT Bonds may be sold at more or less than the face value, depending upon the rate of interest offered and the general credit standing of the corporation. If a business has unusually high credit or offers an exceptionally high rate of interest, buyers may be willing to pay more than the face value for the bonds. For example, at the beginning of 1953, Bland & Company sells $100,000 worth of bonds at 105. The bonds are due in 5 years and bear 6% interest payable annually. The transaction is recorded as follows on the books of Bland & Company:

Jan. 1 Cash..	105,000	
Bonds Payable...........................		100,000
Premium on Bonds Payable...............		5,000
Sold $100,000 worth of 5-year, 6% bonds at 105.		

The investors paid this premium because they were willing to lend money to the corporation at less than the contract rate of 6%. In other words, the prevailing interest rate was less than the contract rate for this particular issue of bonds. The premium represents an advance payment by the investor for the privilege of receiving interest in excess of the prevailing rate. Bland & Company has incurred two liabilities: one to pay the face value of the bonds ($100,000) in 5 years, and the other to pay interest at a higher rate than the prevailing rate.

Since the bond premium has been received because the bond interest rate is higher than the market interest rate, it may be considered as a liability. At the time of each interest payment the corporation will pay interest to the bondholders at the contract rate. Not all of this payment, however, will represent actual interest expense to the corporation, as a portion of the premium previously received is considered as an offset against the interest payment.

The nature of bond premium can be illustrated by emphasizing the movement of cash incident to the bond issue. When bonds are issued at a premium, the total cash received is greater by the amount of the premium than the amount of cash that will be paid on the due date of the bonds. The periodic interest payments during the life of the bonds absorb this difference.

In the previous example, Bland & Company received $105,000 in cash at the time the bonds were sold. During the life of the bonds the corporation pays $6,000 a year as interest, or a total of $30,000. When the bonds come due at the end of the fifth year, the corporation pays the bondholders the principal amount of $100,000. The cash account reflecting the bond transactions is shown below:

CASH

Cash received from sale of
  6% bonds.............. 105,000
	Cash paid for interest over
	  five years.............. 30,000
	Cash paid for principal..... 100,000

The result is a net decrease in cash over the life of the bonds amounting to $25,000, which was the cost of borrowing. Distributed over 5 years, this gives an annual cost of $5,000, or 5% on the face value of the bonds.

If the contract rate of interest on an issue of bonds is less than the prevailing interest rate, investors may be unwilling to pay the face value for the bonds. For example, at the beginning of 1953, the Turner Company sells 5-year, 4% bonds with a face value of $100,000 at 95. This transaction is recorded as follows:

Jan. 1 Cash..	95,000	
Discount on Bonds Payable..................	5,000	
Bonds Payable............................		100,000
Sold $100,000 worth of 5-year, 4% bonds at 95.		

The discount on the bonds represents a deferred charge to bond interest expense. The corporation has contracted to repay at maturity an amount greater than it received in cash. In return, however, it will pay interest at a lower rate than the prevailing one. The discount may be considered analogous to interest paid in advance when a note is discounted.

In the transaction above, the Turner Company received $95,000 in cash at the time the bonds were sold. During the life of the bonds the corporation pays $4,000 a year as interest, or a total of $20,000. When the bonds come due at the end of the fifth year, the corporation pays the bondholders the principal amount of $100,000. The cash account reflecting the bond transactions is shown below:

CASH

Cash received from sale of 4% bonds.............	95,000	Cash paid for interest over five years.............	20,000
		Cash paid for principal.....	100,000

The net cash difference here is $25,000, or $5,000 a year, the same as in the case of the Bland & Company bonds sold at a premium. This amounts to 5% on the face value of the bonds issued. It was assumed in the above examples that the going rate of interest was 5% without consideration being given to compound interest computations.

AMORTIZATION OF BOND PREMIUM AND BOND DISCOUNT The bond premium and the bond discount accounts should be written off, or *amortized,* over the actual outstanding life of the bonds. The amount of the annual write-off is an adjustment of the bond interest expense.

In the case of the 5-year, 6% bonds sold at a premium of $5,000, the annual write-off is $1,000. The entry for the payment of the annual interest on December 31 is:

Dec. 31 Premium on Bonds Payable...................	1,000	
Bond Interest Expense.......................	5,000	
Cash.......................................		6,000
To record the payment of interest at 6% and to amortize the premium for one year.		

In the case of the 5-year, 4% bonds sold at a discount of $5,000, the annual write-off of $1,000 increases the charge to Bond Interest Expense. The entry for the payment of the annual interest on December 31 is:

```
Dec. 31 Bond Interest Expense.......................   5,000
          Cash.........................................           4,000
          Discount on Bonds Payable..................           1,000
            To record the payment of interest at 4% and
            to amortize the discount for one year.
```

In the preceding illustrations the bond interest was paid annually and payments were made on the last day of the fiscal period. But bond interest is usually paid semiannually and the final payment in a year is often made on some other date than the end of the fiscal period. Amortization of bond premium or bond discount may be recorded at the time each interest payment is made and at the end of the fiscal period, or it may be recorded at the end of the fiscal period only. The latter method is satisfactory and summarizes the adjustment for bond premium or discount as well as do more frequent entries.

For example, assume that the Nielsen Corporation issues on April 1, 1953, $100,000 of 10-year, 6% bonds dated March 1, 1953. The bonds were sold for $105,950 to an insurance company. Interest is payable semiannually on March 1 and September 1. The corporation amortizes the premium on December 31, the end of its regular fiscal period. The entries during 1953 applicable to the bonds are as follows:

Transaction	Entry		

APRIL 1, 1953:
To record sale of $100,000 par value 6% bonds for $105,950, plus accrued interest for one month of $500.
	Cash............. 106,450
	  Bonds Payable....
	  Premium on Bonds
	  Payable..........
	  Bond Interest Expense...........
			100,000
			
			5,950
			
			500

SEPTEMBER 1, 1953: Payment of semiannual interest: $100,000 at 6% for 6 months, or $3,000.	Bond Interest Expense............. Cash............	3,000	3,000
DECEMBER 31, 1953: (a) To accrue interest from September 1 to December 31: $100,000 at 6% for 4 months, or $2,000.	Bond Interest Expense............. Interest Payable..	2,000	2,000
(b) To record amortization from April 1 to December 31. Bonds will be outstanding for 9 years and 11 months, or 119 months. Amortization for 1953 is $5,950 x $9/119$, or $450.	Premium on Bonds Payable........... Bond Interest Expense...........	450	450

It should be noted that the premium or the discount on bonds payable is written off over the actual number of months that the bonds are in the hands of investors, since that is the period receiving benefit from the use of the bond proceeds.

BOND PREMIUM AND BOND DISCOUNT ON THE BALANCE SHEET The accounts with bond premium and bond discount may be considered as valuation accounts affecting bonds payable. While this procedure has sound theoretical support in its favor, most companies show the premium and the discount as deferred items on the balance sheet. Since the amortization of bond discount will increase the effective interest expense for the period, it is reasonable to consider Discount on Bonds Payable as a deferred charge to expense on the asset side of the balance sheet. Periodic amortization of the premium will decrease the effective interest expense; hence Premium on Bonds Payable may be shown as a deferred credit on the liability side of the balance sheet.

BOND SINKING FUND When bonds are issued, the agreement with bondholders may have a provision that a definite amount is to be set aside each year to provide for the retirement of the bonds at maturity. The amounts set aside form a *sinking fund*. The total amount of this fund should, upon the maturity of the bonds, equal the face value of the bonds. The fund may be in cash, but it is more often invested in income-producing securities. The periodic payments to the fund plus the earnings on the securities, then, must be sufficient to repay the bonds at maturity. The control of this fund may be in the hands of the corporation or of a third party known as a *trustee*.

When cash is transferred to the sinking fund, an account called Sinking Fund Cash is debited and Cash is credited. As securities are purchased, Sinking Fund Securities is debited and Sinking Fund Cash is credited. Cash receipts representing interest or dividends on the investments are charged to Sinking Fund Cash and credited to Sinking Fund Income. To illustrate the accounting entries for a bond sinking fund, assume that the Bell Corporation issues $100,000 of 10-year bonds dated January 1, 1953, with the provision that equal annual payments be made to the bond sinking fund commencing December 31, 1953. It is estimated that the fund securities will be able to earn approximately 3% per year; thus it may be determined from compound interest tables that an annual deposit of approximately $8,725 is sufficient to provide a fund of $100,000 at the end of 10 years. The entries for the fund transactions will be made as follows:

Transaction	Entry		
DECEMBER 31, 1953: Made the first of the 10 equal annual deposits of $8,725 to the bond sinking fund.	Sinking Fund Cash.. Cash...........	8,725	8,725
JANUARY 2, 1954: Purchased stocks and bonds with sinking fund cash.	Sinking Fund Securities............... Sinking Fund Cash	8,700	8,700
DECEMBER 31, 1954: (a) Made second deposit to bond sinking fund.	Sinking Fund Cash.. Cash...........	8,725	8,725
(b) Received interest and dividends approximating 3% on $8,700 invested during the year.	Sinking Fund Cash.. Sinking Fund Income...........	260	260
DECEMBER 31, 1962: (a) Made the last of the 10 annual deposits to the fund.	Sinking Fund Cash.. Cash...........	8,725	8,725
(b) Received interest and dividends amounting to $2,700 on the sinking fund securities.	Sinking Fund Cash.. Sinking Fund Income...........	2,700	2,700
(c) Sold sinking fund securities at cost.	Sinking Fund Cash.. 88,700 Sinking Fund Securities.........	88,700	88,700
(d) Paid off the bonds and transferred excess sinking fund cash to the cash account.	Bonds Payable..... 100,000 Cash.............. 125 Sinking Fund Cash		100,125

It may be noted that the actual earnings of the sinking fund may differ from the expected earnings. In that case, any excess in Sinking Fund Cash is transferred to the regular cash account and a deficiency is made up by an additional transfer of cash at the time of the last deposit. Sinking Fund Income represents earnings of the corporation and is reported under the heading "Other Income" on the profit and loss statement. The cash and the securities comprising the bond sinking fund are reported on the balance sheet as an asset under the heading "Investments." The investments section is ordinarily given immediately after the current assets section on the balance sheet.

BOND SINKING FUND RESERVE   In order to assure the maintenance of working capital during the life of the bonds, the bond indenture may provide that a reserve for the bond sinking fund be established. The effect of the reserve is to reduce the amount of earned surplus available for dividends and thus to provide greater security to the bondholders. An entry is made to transfer from the earned surplus account to a new account, called Reserve for Bond Sinking Fund, a part of the accumulated profits. For example, if, in the case of the Bell Corporation, a reserve for the bond sinking fund is established from earned surplus, the following entry would be made at the end of each of the ten years of the life of the bonds.

Dec. 31 Earned Surplus................................	10,000	
Reserve for Bond Sinking Fund.............		10,000
To transfer a part of the earned surplus to the reserve for bond sinking fund.		

The reserve for bond sinking fund account is an earned surplus appropriated account, as explained in the preceding chapter. During the ten years there will have been transferred to this account $100,000. This means that this amount of earnings has been unavailable for dividends during the life of the bonds.

It will be observed that the reserve for the bond sinking fund has no direct relation to the bond sinking fund itself, but that its use is simply a means of insuring additional security for the bondholders. After the bonds have been paid, the reserve is no longer necessary. It can therefore be returned to Earned Surplus, and this part of the profits may be distributed as dividends or used in any other way that the board of directors may choose. The entry to return the reserve to the earned surplus account is shown below:

Dec. 31 Reserve for Bond Sinking Fund.............	100,000	
Earned Surplus.........................		100,000
To return the reserve to the earned surplus account.		

REDEMPTION AND CONVERSION OF BONDS   Many bond contracts provide that the corporation may redeem the bonds within a stated period of time at a stipulated price, usually at a premium. Such bonds are known as *callable bonds*. When redemption is not provided for, the corporation may simply retire a portion of its outstanding bonds by purchasing them on the open market. Such an action is advisable when the bonds are selling at a discount and the corporation has available cash that may be used to retire a part of the bond issue. When the corporation retires bonds for less than their book value, a gain accrues to the corporation; when bonds are retired for more than their book value, a loss has taken place. The book value of bonds is obtained by adding the premium to, or deducting the discount from, the par value of the bonds.

Assume that the Acme Corporation has a $100,000 bond issue outstanding on January 2, 1953, with an unamortized premium of $4,000 applicable to these bonds. The corporation has the option of calling the bonds at 105 at any time before maturity. If on this date the corporation redeems the bonds, the following entry would be made:

Jan. 2 Bonds Payable..............................	100,000	
Premium on Bonds Payable.................	4,000	
Loss on Redemption of Bonds...............	1,000	
Cash.....................................		105,000
To record redemption of bonds at 105.		

If the bonds were not callable and were selling at 96 on this date, the corporation might purchase a portion of the bonds on the open market. Assuming that bonds having a par value of $25,000 are thus acquired, the following entry would be made:

Jan. 2 Bonds Payable..............................	25,000	
Premium on Bonds Payable.................	1,000	
Cash.....................................		24,000
Gain on Retirement of Bonds.............		2,000
To record acquisition of own bonds at 96.		

It should be noted that only the portion of the premium relating to the bonds retired is written off the books. The difference between the book value of the liability, $26,000, and the cash paid, $24,000, is recognized as a gain. The company is better off by $2,000 because it was able to liquidate a liability for less than the amount payable.

The bond contract may give the bondholder an option to exchange his bonds for some other security of the corporation such as common stock. The bondholder may be expected to exercise such an option whenever it proves advantageous. If, in the above example for the Acme Corporation, the bonds were convertible into common stock having a par value of $100 at a rate of 10 shares for each $1,000 bond and if half of the bondholders exercise their option on January 2, 1953, the following entry would be made:

Jan. 2 Bonds Payable..............................	50,000	
Premium on Bonds Payable...................	2,000	
Common Stock (par value $100).............		50,000
Premium on Common Stock.................		2,000
To record conversion of bonds into stock.		

Since there are 50 bonds turned in and 10 shares of stock are exchanged for each bond, 500 shares of stock are issued to the bondholders. The common stock account is credited for the total par value of the stock; the difference between the par value of the stock and the book value of the bonds, or $2,000, is recorded as a premium on the stock issued. An alternate procedure calls for the recording of the stock issued at its current market value, thus recognizing a gain or a loss from conversion on the corporate books. The arguments pro and con for such procedures are beyond the scope of this discussion.

LONG-TERM NOTES Corporations may issue notes to obtain fixed capital in place of bonds. These notes may run for a period of 2 to 5 years, anticipating a bond issue when the bond market is more favorable. Or they may be for longer periods, up to 25 years, to avoid the expense of a bond issue, when funds are available from financial institutions such as life insurance companies. For example, if funds are obtained from three or four large life insurance companies, the transaction is less involved than dealing with thousands of bondholders.

These corporation notes may have many features similar to bond issues. They may provide for a note sinking fund. They commonly have safeguards to insure payment at maturity. They differ from bond issues in that they are ordinarily placed privately with a few lenders and that they do not commonly involve premiums or discounts.

The account maintained with an issue of long-term notes is similar to that maintained with an issue of bonds. The title of the account should indicate the nature of the issue. The balance is reported as a fixed liability on the balance sheet.

BALANCE SHEET FOR A CORPORATION The balance sheet on page 475 shows the financial condition of the General Trading Corporation at the end of the sixth year of operations. It should be noted: (a) that by 1953 Organization Costs does not appear on the balance sheet since it has been charged to Earned Surplus over the first five years; and (b) that accounts with subscribers are no longer present. The significance of the items reported on the balance sheet should be carefully studied, since they illustrate several of the accounting concepts described in these chapters. Items worthy of special note have been marked by numbers in parentheses. All related items are given the same number. Brief explanations of these items follow:

(1) The agreement with the bondholders provides that an annual deposit be made in order to provide $100,000 by December 31, 1960, when the bonds mature. Because the company expects to earn ap-

GENERAL TRADING CORPORATION
BALANCE SHEET
DECEMBER 31, 1953

ASSETS

Current Assets:

Cash..	$111,379	
Marketable Securities, at cost (market value, $76,000)...	70,000	
Accounts Receivable, net............................	110,000	
Inventories, at lower of cost or market.................	172,880	
Prepaid Expenses....................................	12,000	
Total Current Assets...............................		$ 476,259

Investments:

(1)	Bond Sinking Fund.................................	26,981

Fixed Assets:

Machinery, net (original cost $480,000)................	$392,000	
Buildings, net (original cost $300,000)..................	210,000	
Land..	50,000	
Total Fixed Assets................................		652,000
Total Assets..		$1,155,240

LIABILITIES AND CAPITAL
LIABILITIES

Current Liabilities:

	Accounts Payable....................................	$ 58,710	
(2)	Dividends Payable....................................	20,250	
(3)	Estimated Income Taxes Payable......................	83,780	
	Accrued Liabilities..................................	3,400	
	Total Current Liabilities............................		$ 166,140

Deferred Credits:

(4)	Premium on Bonds Payable.........................		2,800

Long-term Debt:

(4)	Bonds Payable (5%, 10-year, due December 31, 1960)...		100,000
	Total Liabilities......................................		$ 268,940

CAPITAL

Paid-in Capital:

	6% Cumulative Preferred Stock, par $100 (1,500 shares authorized and issued)...............	$150,000	
(5)	Common Stock, stated value $20 (20,000 shares authorized, 10,000 shares issued)... $200,000		
(5)	Premium on Common Stock......... 420,000	620,000	
	Total Paid-In Capital..............................		$770,000

Earned Surplus:

Appropriated:

(1)	Reserve for Bond Sinking Fund...... $30,000		
(6)	Reserve for Plant Expansion........ 40,000		
	Total Appropriated Surplus................. $ 70,000		
(7)	Unappropriated Earned Surplus.............. 119,300		
	Total Earned Surplus..............................	189,300	
	Total Paid-in Capital and Earned Surplus................	$959,300	
(5)	Less Treasury Common Stock, at cost (1,000 shares).....	73,000	
	Total Capital..		886,300
	Total Liabilities and Capital........................		$1,155,240

proximately 3% annually on the balance of the fund, it is sufficient to deposit $8,723 on December 31 of each year. The fund on December 31, 1953, is composed of three such deposits plus earnings of $264 in 1952 and $548 in 1953, a total of $26,981. Each year the board of directors has authorized a transfer of $10,000 from Earned Surplus to Reserve for Bond Sinking Fund, bringing the total to $30,000 on December 31, 1953.

(2) Dividends are payable quarterly on both the preferred stock and the common stock. The balance of $20,250 in Dividends Payable represents dividends declared on December 18, payable on January 11 to stockholders of record as of December 31. The dividend payable on preferred stock is the quarterly dividend of $1\frac{1}{2}$% of $150,000 or $2,250. The dividend payable on common stock is a quarterly dividend of $1 plus an extra dividend of $1. Since dividends are not declared on treasury stock, the total dividend payable to common stockholders is $18,000 (9,000 shares outstanding x $2).

(3) The net profit before income taxes of the General Trading Corporation was $186,180. Income taxes are estimated at $83,780, which is shown as a current liability on December 31, 1953.

(4) Ten-year bonds were issued on January 1, 1951, at 104. The $4,000 premium has been amortized at the rate of $400 per year for 3 years, thus leaving a balance of $2,800 to be amortized over the succeeding 7 years. Interest is payable on the bonds on June 30 and December 31 of each year; hence there is no accrued interest applicable to the bonds as of December 31.

(5) At the time the corporation was organized, 10,000 shares of no-par common stock were sold at $62. Common Stock was credited for the total stated value of the stock, $200,000, and Premium on Common Stock was credited for $420,000, the excess of cash received over the stated value. On April 16, 1953, the company purchased 1,000 shares of its common stock at $73 on the open market. The company plans to resell the stock when it needs working capital and when market conditions are favorable.

(6) Reserve for Plant Expansion was credited during 1952 and again in 1953 for $20,000 in order to conserve funds within the business for a contemplated expenditure of $100,000 on additional factory facilities during 1956. The reserve will be increased to $100,000 in 1956 and may be returned to Earned Surplus when the expansion is completed.

(7) Since the company's organization 6 years ago, it has accumulated earnings of $189,300, $70,000 of which is appropriated for particular purposes, and $119,300 of which is unappropriated.

There are innumerable variations in the order and the arrangement of items in financial statements, as well as many alternatives in the terminology employed.   A selection of statements taken from the annual reports of a number of corporations is presented in Appendix B.

INVESTMENTS IN   The issuance of stocks and bonds, the declara-
STOCKS AND BONDS   tion and the payment of dividends, and other related transactions have been discussed from the standpoint of the issuing corporation.   Whenever a corporation records a transaction between itself and the owners of its stock or bonds, there is a reciprocal entry on the books of the investor.   Investments in corporate securities may be made by individuals, partnerships, industrial corporations, financial corporations such as banks and life insurance companies, and other types of organizations.   In this and the following sections of the chapter, attention will be given to some of the principles underlying the accounting for investments in stocks and bonds on the books of investors.

Corporate securities may be purchased directly from the issuing corporation or from other investors.   Stocks and bonds may be *listed* with an organized exchange, such as the New York Stock Exchange, and purchased through that exchange; or they may be *unlisted*, in which case they are said to be bought and sold *over the counter*.   The services of a broker are usually employed in buying and selling both listed and unlisted securities.   The record of transactions on stock exchanges is reported daily in the financial pages of newspapers.   This record shows the volume of sales as well as the high, low, and closing prices for each security traded during the day.   Prices for stocks are quoted in terms of fractional dollars, $1/8$ of a dollar being the usual minimum fraction.   Some low-priced stocks are sold in lower fractions of a dollar, such as $1/16$ or $1/32$. A price of $40^3/8$ per share means \$40.375; a price of $40^1/2$ means \$40.50; and so on.   Prices for bonds are quoted as a percentage of par value; thus the price of a \$1,000 bond quoted at $104^1/2$ would be \$1,045.

The cost of securities purchased includes not only the price paid but also other costs incident to the purchase, such as broker's commission and postage charges for delivery.   When bonds are purchased between interest dates, the purchaser pays the seller the interest accrued from the last interest payment date to the date of purchase.   The amount of the interest paid should be debited to Interest Income, as it is an offset against the amount that will be received at the next interest date.   To illustrate, assume that a \$1,000 bond is purchased at

102 plus brokerage fees of $5.30 and accrued interest of $10.20. The entry to record the transaction, in general journal form, is as follows:

April 2 Investment in Taylor Co. 4% Bonds.........	1,025.30	
Interest Income.........................	10.20	
Cash...................................		1,035.50

When stocks are purchased between dividend dates, there is no separate charge for the prorata amount of the dividend. Dividends do not accrue from day to day, since they become an obligation of the issuing corporation only as they are declared by the directors. The price of stocks may be affected by the anticipated dividend as the usual declaration approaches, but this anticipated dividend is only one of many factors that influence stock prices. Commissions and delivery charges paid to brokers are, of course, added to the price paid in arriving at the total cost of stocks purchased.

TEMPORARY INVESTMENTS   A corporation may have on hand an amount of cash considerably in excess of its immediate requirements, but it may believe that this cash will be needed in operating the business, possibly within the coming year. Rather than allow this excess cash to lie idle until it is actually needed, the corporation may invest all or a portion of it in income-yielding securities. Such securities are known as *temporary investments*. These investments may actually be held by the corporation for several years, but they are still considered to be temporary if they can be turned into cash readily at any time that the business needs additional cash in its normal operations. Because of their ready marketability and comparative price stability, United States Government bonds and notes are particularly suitable for this purpose.

Securities representing a temporary investment are classified on the balance sheet as current assets and are shown immediately below cash. As in the case of other current assets, they may be valued at cost or at the lower of cost or market. Valuation at cost with a parenthetical statement of current market value has the advantage of simplicity and also provides complete disclosure. The method may be illustrated as follows:

MEADOWS CORPORATION
BALANCE SHEET
DECEMBER 31, 1953

ASSETS

Current Assets:

Cash..	$150,000
Marketable Securities, at cost (market value $29,400)...	31,000

LONG-TERM INVESTMENTS   Investments that are not a ready source of cash in the normal operations of the business are known as *long-term investments*. A business may make long-term investments simply because it has cash that it cannot use in its normal operations; but a corporation is more likely to make long-term investments for other reasons.

It is not unusual for a corporation to purchase stocks or bonds as a means of establishing or maintaining business relations with the issuing company. Such investments are ordinarily held for an indefinitely long period and are not sold so long as the relationship remains satisfactory. Corporations may also acquire all or a substantial portion of the voting stock of another corporation in order to control its activities. Similarly, a corporation may organize a new corporation for the purpose of marketing a new product, or for some other business reason, receiving stock in exchange for the assets transferred to the new corporation. Cash and securities in bond sinking funds are also considered long-term investments, as they are accumulated for the purpose of paying the bond liability.

Investments in long-term securities are recorded in the accounts at cost and are so shown on the balance sheet. Fluctuations in price subsequent to acquisition are ordinarily ignored except when there has been a material decline, in which case the value may be reduced or the facts may be disclosed by a parenthetical notation on the balance sheet. Long-term investments are listed on the balance sheet under the caption "Investments," which follows current assets.

INCOME FROM INVESTMENTS IN STOCKS   Cash dividends on stock owned either as temporary investments or as long-term investments should be reported in the accounting period in which they are declared. The entry to record a dividend declared but not yet received is a debit to Dividends Receivable and a credit to Dividend Income. The receivable account is then credited when the cash is received. If accounts are kept on the cash basis, as is the case with most individuals, no entry is made for the dividend until it is received as cash.

A dividend on common stock in the form of additional shares of common stock is not income and hence no entry is necessary beyond a notation as to the additional number of shares now owned. The receipt of such a stock dividend does, however, affect the cost basis of each share of stock. For example, if a 50-share common stock dividend is received on 100 shares of common stock originally purchased for $4,500

($45 per share), the unit cost of the 150 shares becomes $4,500 ÷ 150, or $30 per share.

INCOME FROM INVESTMENTS IN BONDS
Interest on bonds held as temporary investments is recorded in the same manner as interest on notes receivable. Interest received during a fiscal period is recorded as a debit to Cash and a credit to Interest Income. At the end of a fiscal period an adjusting entry debiting Interest Receivable and crediting Interest Income is made for interest accrued at the end of the period. After the books are closed, the entry is reversed in order that all receipts of bond interest during the year may be credited to the income account.

When interest is recorded on temporary bond investments, the fact that these investments may have been purchased for more or less than their face value is ignored. But when the cost of bonds purchased for long-term investments is greater or less than the par value, the amount of the premium or the discount may be written off over the remaining life of the bonds in much the same manner in which the debtor corporation accounts for a premium or a discount on the original issuance of the bonds. To illustrate, assume that twenty $1,000, 5% bonds of the Standard Corporation are purchased on July 1, 1953, at 105½ plus a brokerage fee of $55. Interest on the bonds is payable semiannually on April 1 and October 1 and the bonds are due 8¾ years from the date of purchase. Entries on the books of the purchaser at the time of purchase and for the remainder of the year would be as follows:

Transaction	Entry		
JULY 1, 1953: Purchase of bonds: $20,000 par value at 105½... $21,100 Brokerage.............. 55 Total cost................ $21,155 Accrued interest, $20,000 at 5% for 3 months, or $250.	Investment in Standard Corp. Bonds.... Interest Income..... Cash..................	21,155 250	21,405
OCTOBER 1, 1953: Receipt of semiannual interest; $20,000 at 5% for 6 months.	Cash.............. Interest Income...	500	500
DECEMBER 31, 1953: (a) Interest accrued: $20,000 at 5% for 3 months. (b) Amortization of premium: $1,155 for 8¾ years, or $66 for 6 months.	Interest Receivable.. Interest Income... Interest Income..... Investment in Standard Corp. Bonds..........	250 66	250 66

The net effect of the four entries in the interest income account is a credit of $434, which represents interest at 5% for 6 months ($500) less amortization of premium for 6 months ($66). By following the foregoing procedures, the premium of $1,155 will be amortized against interest income over the life of the bonds, and the investment account will be reduced to $20,000 at the maturity date.

A similar procedure may be applied to bonds purchased at a price below par value. The amount of the discount is accumulated by periodic entries debiting the investment account and crediting Interest Income. It may be noted that when speculative bonds are purchased at a substantial discount, it would be imprudent to accumulate the discount because of the uncertainty of payment at maturity.

The federal income tax regulations governing amortization of premiums are quite detailed and should be consulted in particular cases. In general, taxpayers may elect to amortize premium on bonds in determining income but are not required to do so.

SALE OF INVESTMENTS When shares of stock that have been held as either temporary or long-term investments are sold, the cash account is debited for the proceeds (selling price less commission and other costs) and the investment account is credited for the cost of the shares sold. If there is a gain, it is credited to an account entitled Gain on Sale of Stocks; if there is a loss, it is debited to an account entitled Loss on Sale of Stocks.

A sale of bonds held as temporary investments is recorded in the same manner as a sale of stocks. A sale of bonds held as a long-term investment is also recorded in the same manner except when a premium or a discount has been amortized. If a premium or a discount has been amortized, the investment account is credited for the book value of the investment and not its original cost value. The gain or the loss is then the difference between the book value and the amount received. For example, assume that the bonds of the Standard Corporation in the previous example are sold at 98 on December 31, 1955. At that time the following entries are made:

Dec. 31	Interest Receivable..............................	250	
	Interest Income...............................		250
	Accrued interest for three months, Oct. 1 to Dec. 31.		
31	Interest Income.................................	132	
	Investment in Standard Corp. Bonds...........		132
	Amortization of premium for entire year.		

```
31  Cash.........................................  19,850
      Loss on Sale of Bonds.........................   1,225
        Interest Receivable...........................              250
        Investment in Standard Corp. Bonds...........           20,825
          Sold bonds with a book value of $20,825 for
          $19,600 plus accrued interest of $250.
```

The balance in the investment account used in the foregoing transaction is composed of the original cost of $21,155 reduced by premium amortization to date. The balance is determined as follows:

```
Original cost............................................  $21,155

Less premium amortization:
  1953...........................................  $ 66
  1954...........................................   132
  1955...........................................   132      330

Balance, December 31, 1955..............................  $20,825
```

QUESTIONS

1. (a) Why does a corporation normally issue bonds? (b) Describe briefly the various types of corporate bonds.

2. Two corporations with about equal credit ratings issue bonds amounting to $100,000. The A Corporation offers bonds with 6% interest and sells them above face value. The B Corporation offers bonds with 4% interest and sells them below face value. (a) Does the A Corporation gain by selling its bonds above par? (b) Does the B Corporation lose by selling its bonds below par? (c) How will each of the corporations determine the annual interest cost on the bonds?

3. Assume that the bonds in the previous question were 10-year bonds and that the 6% bonds were sold at 110 and the 4% bonds at 90. Set up a "T" account for cash in each case, showing by summary debits and credits the total cash received and disbursed for the life of the bonds. What do these accounts show regarding the total interest expense for the 10-year period in each case?

4. The earned surplus account for the Baker Co. on December 31, 1953, shows a balance of $18,000. During 1953, profits of $15,000 were earned and dividends of $9,000 were declared. (a) What was the earned surplus balance on January 1, 1953? (b) The Baker Co. on December 31, 1953, has outstanding 20-year bonds of $100,000 and a discount on bonds payable of $3,150. What entry was made to record the sale of the bonds on January 1, 1948?

5. The Graham Corporation borrows $10,000,000 by issuing bonds at face value payable in 20 years. The agreement with the bondholders provides that the corporation set aside 20 equal periodic amounts in a bond sinking fund starting one year after the bonds are issued. Since the fund is expected to earn approximately 4% annually, the annual deposit amounts to $336,000. Determine the balance of the fund at the end of the third year (after the third deposit), assuming that the fund earned 4% annually. Show computations.

6. The Biltmore Co. transfers $24,000 cash to a bond sinking fund without appropriating any earned surplus. Securities of $23,800 are purchased by the fund trustee. During the year, the trustee receives $950 cash in interest and dividends on the sinking fund securities. (a) Give general journal entries to record the foregoing transactions. (b) What is the composition of the bond sinking fund after these transactions?

7. The Allen Corporation issued $500,000 of 10-year, 4% bonds dated April 1, 1953. Interest is payable semiannually on April 1 and October 1. (a) Give all journal entries for 1953 relating to the bonds, assuming that the bonds were sold on July 1, 1953, for $476,600 plus accrued interest. Amortization is recorded on December 31 for the entire year. (b) What reversing entry should be made on January 1, 1954?

8. What entry would be made on April 1, 1955, if $100,000 of the bonds in Question 7 are purchased by the corporation on the open market at 93 and retired?

9. Assuming that the bonds in Question 7 are convertible into $100 par common stock at a rate of 9 shares for each $1,000 bond, what entry would be made on April 1, 1955, if $50,000 of the bonds are converted?

10. John Griffith purchased 100 shares of Amalgamated Copper Co. common stock several years ago at $63 plus brokerage fees of $30. During the current year he received a common stock dividend of 50 shares. What was Griffith's cost basis per share after he received the stock dividend?

11. (a) Differentiate between short-term and long-term investments. (b) Where is each class listed on the balance sheet?

12. From the data presented below, compute the earnings per share on common stock for 1953 and 1954:

	1953	1954
Bonds Payable, 5%.	$100,000	$100,000
Preferred Stock, 6%, $100 par.	200,000	300,000
Common Stock, no par, 60,000 shares.	670,000	670,000
Earnings before deductions for bond interest and income taxes of 40%.	405,000	515,000

PROBLEMS

24-1. The following transactions were completed by the General Machinery Corporation during 1953 and 1954:

1953

Oct. 1. Issued $500,000 of 10-year, 5% bonds, receiving $542,000 in cash. Interest is payable semiannually on April 1 and October 1.

Dec. 31. Recorded the adjusting entry for interest payable.

31. Recorded amortization of premium on bonds.

1954

Jan. 1. Reversed the adjusting entry for interest payable.

Apr. 1. Paid the semiannual interest on the bonds.

Oct. 1. Paid the semiannual interest on the bonds.

Dec. 31. Recorded the adjusting entry for interest payable.

31. Recorded amortization of premium on bonds.

Instructions: (1) Record the foregoing transactions in general journal form. (Entries for amortization of bond premium are to be made on December 31, the end of the fiscal year.)

(2) State the amount of the bond interest expense in (a) 1953 and (b) 1954.

24-2. The following transactions were completed by the Stockert Corporation during the first two years of its operations, 1953 and 1954:

1953

(a) Exchanged 1,000 shares of common stock, par $100, for machinery, $108,000.

(b) Received $210,000 for 2,000 shares of 5% cumulative preferred stock (par value $100).

(c) Net loss for the year, $18,000. (Debit Profit and Loss Summary and credit Cash.)

(d) Closed Profit and Loss Summary to Earned Surplus.

1954

(e) Sold $100,000 worth of 10-year, 4% bonds for $94,000 (January 2).

(f) Paid $75,000 for new machinery.

(g) Paid annual interest on bonds and recorded amortization of discount for year.

(h) Made a net operating profit of $124,600. (Debit Cash and credit Profit and Loss Summary.) Closed Bond Interest Expense to Profit and Loss Summary.

(i) Recorded income taxes of $49,840. Closed Profit and Loss Summary to Earned Surplus.

(j) Declared preferred dividends on the cumulative preferred stock for the first two years.

(k) Declared and issued a 15% stock dividend on common stock outstanding.

(l) Appropriated earned surplus for bond sinking fund, $10,000.

Instructions: (1) Record the transactions directly in "T" accounts. The accounts required are: Cash; Machinery; Income Taxes Payable; Preferred

Dividends Payable; Bonds Payable; Discount on Bonds Payable; Preferred Stock; Premium on Preferred Stock; Common Stock; Premium on Common Stock; Reserve for Bond Sinking Fund; Earned Surplus; Profit and Loss Summary; Bond Interest Expense.

(2) Prepare a balance sheet in report form as of December 31, 1954.

24-3. The Monarch Equipment Co. completed the following transactions relating to the issuance of $1,000,000 of 10-year, 3% bonds, dated January 1, 1953. Interest is payable annually on December 31.

1953
Feb. 1. Sold the entire bond issue, receiving $958,350 cash plus accrued interest for 1/12 of a year.

Dec. 31. Paid the annual interest on the bonds.

31. Recorded the amortization of the discount on the bonds.

31. Deposited $100,000 cash in a bond sinking fund. (Debit Sinking Fund Cash.)

1954
Jan. 10. Purchased various securities with sinking fund cash at a cost of $99,600.

Dec. 31. Received $2,920 in interest and dividends on sinking fund securities. (The cash is not deposited in the sinking fund.)

31. Sold sinking fund securities that cost $10,000 for $9,000.

31. Paid the annual interest on the bonds.

31. Recorded the amortization of the discount on the bonds.

31. Deposited $100,000 cash in the bond sinking fund.

31. Purchased and retired $100,000 of own bonds outstanding at 95. (These bonds were paid for with regular cash and not sinking fund cash.)

1955
Jan. 7. Purchased various securities with sinking fund cash at a cost of $100,210.

Dec. 31. Received $6,150 in interest and dividends on sinking fund securities. (The cash is not deposited in the sinking fund.)

31. Paid the annual interest on the bonds.

31. Recorded the amortization of the discount on the bonds.

31. Deposited $87,500 cash in the bond sinking fund.

Instructions: (1) Record the foregoing transactions in general journal form.

(2) State the amount of the bond interest expense in (a) 1953, (b) 1954, and (c) 1955.

(3) Show how the foregoing items would appear on the balance sheet prepared on December 31, 1955.

24-4. The Ferndale Corporation has substantial investments in stocks and bonds of various corporations. The following transactions in 1953 and 1954 are selected from a number that relate to certain investments:

1953

Feb. 10. Purchased as a long-term investment 100 shares of Acme Corp. common stock at 62½ plus brokerage and other costs of $38.

Mar. 1. Purchased $60,000 of Bernard Co. 10-year, 5% coupon bonds, dated January 1, 1953, directly from the issuing company for $64,720 plus accrued interest for 1/6 of a year. Bernard Co. is a valuable customer and Ferndale Corporation expects to hold the bonds until maturity.

June 20. Received a semiannual dividend of $2 per share on the Acme Corp. stock.

     30. Received the semiannual interest on the Bernard Co. bonds.

Dec. 20. Received a semiannual dividend of $2 per share and a 20% stock dividend on the Acme Corp. stock.

     31. Received the semiannual interest on the Bernard Co. bonds.

     31. Recorded the amortization of the premium on the Bernard Co. bonds.

1954

Apr. 15. Sold $40,000 of Carlton, Inc. bonds at 96¼ plus accrued interest of $400. The broker deducted a commission of $100 and a transfer tax of $20, remitting $38,780. The bonds were carried on the books at $40,100. (Debit Loss on Sale of Investments for any loss involved.)

June 20. Received a semiannual dividend of $2 per share on the Acme Corp. stock.

     26. Sold 50 shares of the Acme Corp. stock at 63. The broker deducted a commission and other costs of $15 from his remittance. (Credit Gain on Sale of Investments for any gain involved.)

Instructions: Record the foregoing transactions in general journal form.

Boynton & Brooks, Inc.
Part 2

Part 2 of Practice Set No. 2 is a continuation of Practice Set No. 2 given after Chapter 20. The same books of original entry and ledgers are to be used.

Narrative of Transactions for May

May 1. R. C. Boynton and E. A. Brooks incorporated their wholesale and retail automobile accessories business under the name of Boynton & Brooks, Inc. The charter authorized the issuance of 300 shares of 5% preferred stock, par value $100, and 1,000 shares of common stock, par value $50.

In payment for their interests in the partnership business, Boynton received 100 shares of preferred stock and 200 shares of common stock and Brooks received 100 shares of preferred stock and 200 shares of common stock. The difference between the capital accounts and the par value of the stock issued was paid to the partners from the cash of the business.

Since the same books of account are to be maintained, the only entries required are those to close the partners' capital accounts, to record the issuing of stock, and to record the cash payments. Proceed as follows:

(1) Record the complete transaction with each partner in the general journal, crediting Accounts Payable for the amounts to be paid in cash.

(2) Issue Voucher No. 612 to R. C. Boynton and Voucher No. 613 to E. A. Brooks for the amount of the cash payment each is to receive.
   In order to avoid double posting, in the general journal place check marks in the posting reference column for the two credits to Accounts Payable. Also, in the voucher register place check marks in the posting reference column for the two debits to the capital accounts.

(3) Issue Check No. 801 in payment of Voucher No. 612 and Check No. 802 in payment of Voucher No. 613.

You are not required to record the stock issued in the stockholders ledger, as the stock certificate book and the stockholders ledger are maintained by the secretary of the corporation.

May 1. Sold 50 shares of preferred stock at $115. Received cash, $5,750, and issued the stock.

May 1. Sold 120 shares of common stock at par. Received cash, $6,000, and issued the stock.

May 1. Purchased for $15,000 from the Blackmer Realty Co. the land and the building in which the business is located, paying $5,000 in cash and giving a 6% mortgage for the balance. The amount of the mortgage is to be paid at the rate of $1,000 a year, and interest at 6% is to be paid semi-annually at the end of April and of October. The value of the building is estimated at $9,000 and the value of the land is estimated at $6,000.

Recorded the complete transaction in the general journal; issued Voucher No. 614 for the amount of the cash payment, $5,000; and issued Check No. 803 in payment of Voucher No. 614.

May 1. Issued vouchers as follows:

Voucher No. 615 to Security Brokerage Co. for the purchase of three $1,000, 4% bonds of the Murray Corporation for $3,086 plus accrued interest for five months of $50.

Voucher No. 616 to Ira Miller, a lawyer, for examining the title to the land that has been purchased, $55. (Charge Land, as expenditures incurred in connection with the purchase of a fixed asset are considered a part of the cost of the asset.)

Voucher No. 617 to Landis Insurance Agency for the premium on a three-year insurance policy on the building, $108.

May 1. Issued checks as follows:

Check No. 804 to Security Brokerage Co. in payment of Voucher No. 615.

Check No. 805 to Ira Miller in payment of Voucher No. 616.

Check No. 806 to Landis Insurance Agency in payment of Voucher No. 617.

May 2. Received a check for $183.60 from Acme Garage in payment of sale of April 3.

May 2. Issued Check No. 807 to Glendon Bros. in payment of Voucher No. 596 less 2% discount.

May 2. Issued Voucher No. 618 to Perfection Products for the purchase of merchandise on account, $703.62.

May 2. Paid $4.95 from the petty cash fund for refinishing a desk.

May 3. Issued checks as follows:

Check No. 808 to Westside Company in payment of Voucher No. 597 less 2% discount.

Check No. 809 to Perfection Products in payment of Voucher No. 601 less 1% discount.

May 3. Made the following wholesale sales on account:

Sale No. 974, Harold Roberts, $342.50.

Sale No. 975, N. V. Lacy, $482.95.

May 4. Recorded the biweekly payroll from the following data provided by the payroll clerk. Issued Voucher No. 619 for the amount payable; then issued Check No. 810 in payment of this voucher.

Payroll:

Sales Salaries	$720.00	
Delivery Salaries	180.00	
Office Salaries	300.00	
Total Payroll		$1,200.00
Deductions:		
Employees' Income Taxes	$122.00	
Employees' Share of F.I.C.A. Taxes	18.00	
Total Deductions		140.00
Amount Payable		$1,060.00

May 4. Recorded the employer's liability for F.I.C.A. taxes and for federal and state unemployment taxes from the following data provided by the payroll clerk:

F.I.C.A. Taxes	$18.00
Federal Unemployment Taxes	3.60
State Unemployment Taxes	32.40
Total Payroll Taxes	$54.00

May 4. Cash retail sales for May 1–4 were $1,592.80. Sales taxes collected on these sales amounted to $31.86.

May 6. Received a check for $264.61 from N. V. Lacy in payment of sale of March 2.

May 6. Issued Voucher No. 620 to Brands, Inc. for the purchase of merchandise on account, $409.10.

May 6. Paid $2.80 from the petty cash fund for store supplies.

May 7. Received from B. D. Howe his 30-day, 4% note for $493.38 in settlement of sales of March 26 and April 3. This note (our No. 29) was dated May 6 and is payable at the First National Bank.

May 7. Issued Check No. 811 to Globe Tubing Co. in payment of Voucher No. 580 less 1% discount.

May 8. Sold merchandise on account to King & Blake, $249.80; Sale No. 976.

May 8. Received a check for $501.67 from B. N. Scott in payment of his note and interest due today.

May 8. Issued checks as follows:

Check No. 812 to Davis & Company in payment of Voucher No. 585.

Check No. 813 to Norwalk Products, Inc. in payment of Voucher No. 586 less 1% discount.

May 9. Received a check for $186.77 from S. R. Brown in payment of his note and interest due today.

May 9. Received a credit memorandum for $75 from Brands, Inc. for merchandise returned on Voucher No. 620.

May 10. Made the following wholesale sales on account:

Sale No. 977, Acme Garage, $354.98.

Sale No. 978, James Post, $780.40.

May 10. Issued Voucher No. 621 to First National Bank for monthly payment of employees income taxes payable, $162, and of F.I.C.A. taxes payable, $60; total of voucher, $222. Issued Check No. 814 in payment of this voucher.

May 11. Issued checks as follows:

Check No. 815 to Sampson Supply Co. in payment of Voucher No. 603 less 2% discount.

Check No. 816 to Perfection Products in payment of Voucher No. 618 less 1% discount.

May 11. Cash retail sales for the week were $1,963.40. Sales taxes collected on these sales amounted to $39.27.

Prove cash. The cash balance is $8,181.59.

Post from the various journals to the customers' accounts in the accounts receivable ledger.

May 13. Issued Check No. 817 to Brands, Inc. in payment of Voucher No. 594 less the return and less 1% discount.

May 13. Received checks from customers as follows:

William Leeds, $91.80, in payment of sale of April 12.

L. K. Lewis, $35, to apply on account. A memorandum from Mr. Brooks directed that the remaining balance of $33.58 in the L. K. Lewis account be written off as a bad debt.

May 13. Paid $4.75 from the petty cash fund to Mr. Boynton to reimburse him for entertaining a customer at lunch. (Miscellaneous Selling Expense)

May 13. Received from S. R. Brown his 60-day, 5% note for $502.35 in settlement of sale of April 23. This note (our No. 30) was dated May 11 and is payable at the Union Bank.

May 14. Issued vouchers for purchases on account as follows:

Voucher No. 622, Westside Company, merchandise, $395.80.

Voucher No. 623, Sampson Supply Co., merchandise, $298.60.

Voucher No. 624, Orr Supply Co., store supplies, $77.30, and office supplies, $10.20; total invoice, $87.50.

May 14. Issued Check No. 818 to Orr Supply Co. in payment of Voucher No. 624.

May 15. Paid $4.08 from the petty cash fund to a cash customer who returned merchandise: merchandise, $4; sales tax, 8 cents.

May 15. Sold merchandise on account to H. B. Fisher, $610.03; Sale No. 979.

May 15. Issued Voucher No. 625 to *Tower News*, the local school paper, for an advertisement, $10; then issued Check No. 819 in payment of this voucher.

May 16. Issued vouchers as follows:

Voucher No. 626, Star Auto Radios, merchandise, $385.

Voucher No. 627, Davis & Company, store supplies, $45.15, and office supplies, $20.80; total invoice, $65.95.

Voucher No. 628, Morris Miller Co., repairs to the building, $48.50. (Expenditures of this type, which are incurred in maintaining a fixed asset in good condition, are considered as expenses of the period in which they are incurred.)

May 16. Issued Check No. 820 to Morris Miller Co. in payment of Voucher No. 628.

May 17. Made payments from the petty cash fund as follows:
97 cents for registry of letter.
$4.68 for deliveries.

May 17. Received a check for $244.80 from King & Blake in payment of sale of May 8 less 2% discount.

May 18. Made the following wholesale sales on account:

Sale No. 980, Miller's Garage, $400.45.

Sale No. 981, Norton, Inc., $199.

May 18. Recorded the biweekly payroll and issued Voucher No. 629 and Check No. 821 for the payment. Recorded the employer's liability for payroll taxes. Salaries, deductions, and taxes were the same as on May 4.

May 18. Cash retail sales for the week were $2,096.52. Sales taxes collected on these sales amounted to $41.93.

May 20. Made the following wholesale sales on account:

Sale No. 982, McClain Corporation, $407.70.

Sale No. 983, Harris Auto Co., $455.60.

May 20. Issued vouchers for purchases on account as follows:

Voucher No. 630, Globe Tubing Co., merchandise, $592.50.

Voucher No. 631, Jackson & Sons, merchandise, $693.58.

May 20. Issued Credit Memo No. 48 for $37.56 to Miller's Garage for merchandise returned on sale of May 18.

May 21. Issued vouchers as follows:

Voucher No. 632, ABC Cushions & Covers, merchandise, $300.92.

Voucher No. 633, Perfection Products, merchandise, $742.96.

Voucher No. 634, C. W. Gardner, repairs in storeroom, $25.50. (Charge Miscellaneous Selling Expense.)

May 21. Issued Check No. 822 to C. W. Gardner in payment of Voucher No. 634.

May 21. Issued Credit Memo No. 49 for $56.61 to N. V. Lacy for merchandise returned on sale of May 3.

May 22. Paid $4.50 from the petty cash fund for extra help in wrapping merchandise sold. (Charge Miscellaneous Selling Expense.)

May 23. Issued vouchers as follows:

Voucher No. 635, Brands, Inc., merchandise, $802.

Voucher No. 636, Norwalk Products, Inc., merchandise, $527.80.

Voucher No. 637, C. W. Gardner, minor repairs on building, $35.60.

May 23. Issued checks as follows:

Check No. 823 to C. W. Gardner in payment of Voucher No. 637.

Check No. 824 to Westside Company in payment of Voucher No. 622 less 2% discount.

May 24. Paid $1.75 from the petty cash fund for repairs to a typewriter. (Charge Miscellaneous General Expense.)

May 24. Issued Check No. 825 to Seymour Supply House in payment of Voucher No. 600 less 1% discount.

May 25. Cash retail sales for the week were $2,495.32. Sales taxes collected on these sales amounted to $49.91.

Prove cash. The cash balance is $10,079.86.

Post from the various journals to the customers' accounts in the accounts receivable ledger.

May 27. Made the following wholesale sales on account:

Sale No. 984, Drake-Elm Co., $305.80.

Sale No. 985, Coswell Auto Repair, $767.65.

May 27. Received from H. B. Fisher his 30-day, 4% note for $519.71 in settlement of sale of April 27. This note (our No. 31) was dated May 25 and is payable at the National Bank & Trust Co.

May 27. Made payments from the petty cash fund as follows:
$2.50 for paint to be used on the store counters. (Charge Miscellaneous Selling Expense.)
$3.90 for telegram charges.

May 27. Received checks from customers as follows:

Norton, Inc., $195.02, in payment of sale of May 18 less 2% discount.

Miller's Garage, $355.63, in payment of sale of May 18 less the return and less 2% discount.

Harold Roberts, $351.31, in payment of sale of April 27 less the return.

May 28. Issued vouchers as follows:

Voucher No. 638, Seymour Supply House, merchandise, $302.95.

Voucher No. 639, Golden & Williams, merchandise, $406.85.

Voucher No. 640, Sampson Supply Co., for our note No. 23 and interest due today.

Voucher No. 641, Globe Tubing Co., merchandise, $696.89.

May 28. Issued Check No. 826 to Sampson Supply Co. in payment of Voucher No. 640.

May 29. Received a check for $151 from Coswell Auto Repair in payment of its note and interest due today.

May 29. Issued checks as follows:

Check No. 827 to Davis & Company in payment of Voucher No. 604.

Check No. 828 to Sampson Supply Co. in payment of Voucher No. 623 less 2% discount.

Check No. 829 to Star Auto Radios in payment of Voucher No. 626 less 2% discount.

Check No. 830 to Perfection Products in payment of Voucher No. 633 less 1% discount.

May 30. Received a credit memorandum for $49.95 from Seymour Supply House for merchandise returned on Voucher No. 638.

May 31. Sold merchandise on account to S. R. Brown, $986.20; Sale No. 986.

May 31. Paid $1.50 from the petty cash fund for having the delivery truck washed.

May 31. Received checks from customers as follows:

McClain Corporation, $399.55, in payment of sale of May 20 less 2% discount.

Harris Auto Co., $446.49, in payment of sale of May 20 less 2% discount.

May 31. Recorded the monthly officers' payroll and recorded the employer's liability for payroll taxes from the following data provided by the payroll clerk:

Officers Salaries...............................		$900.00
Deductions:		
Employees' Income Taxes......................	$86.40	
Employees' Share of F.I.C.A. Taxes............	13.50	
Total Deductions...........................		99.90
Amount Payable...............................		$800.10
Company's Payroll Taxes on Officers Salaries:		
F.I.C.A. Taxes...............................		$ 13.50
Federal Unemployment Taxes..................		2.70
State Unemployment Taxes...................		24.30
Total Payroll Taxes.........................		$ 40.50

May 31. Issued vouchers as follows:

Voucher No. 642, Payroll, officers salaries, $800.10.

Voucher No. 643, *Daily News*, newspaper advertising, $225.

Voucher No. 644, Western Telephone Co., telephone service, $28.62.

Voucher No. 645, City Gas & Electric Co., gas and electricity, $21.60.

Voucher No. 646, Wilshire Garage, gas, oil, and miscellaneous truck expense, $40.20.

Voucher No. 647, Clayton Drayage Co., freight in, $210.05.

Voucher No. 648, Petty Cash, to replenish petty cash fund, $36.38.

May 31. Issued checks as follows:

Check No. 831 to Payroll in payment of Voucher No. 642.

Check No. 832 to *Daily News* in payment of Voucher No. 643.

Check No. 833 to Western Telephone Co. in payment of Voucher No. 644.

Check No. 834 to City Gas & Electric Co. in payment of Voucher No. 645.

Check No. 835 to Wilshire Garage in payment of Voucher No. 646.

Check No. 836 to Clayton Drayage Co. in payment of Voucher No. 647.

Check No. 837 to Petty Cash in payment of Voucher No. 648.

May 31. Received semiannual interest on Murray Corporation bonds, $60. Recorded amortization of premium, $2.

May 31. Cash retail sales for May 27–31 were $1,965.43. Sales taxes collected on these sales amounted to $39.31.

Prove cash. The cash balance is $10,810.81.

Post from the various journals to the customers' accounts in the accounts receivable ledger.

Post to the general ledger accounts from the general columns of the general journal, the cash receipts journal, and the voucher register.

Total and rule the various special journals and post the totals to the appropriate general ledger accounts.

Periodic Summary

The periodic summary must now be completed according to the outline on page 163. In addition to the profit and loss statement and the balance sheet, prepare a statement of earned surplus. The additional data required for the periodic summary are:

Interest accrued on notes receivable....................$	4.08
Allowance for bad debts: increase allowance by 1% of	
gross charge sales..................................	63.43
Merchandise inventory, May 31......................	31,683.52

Inventories of supplies, May 31:

Store supplies.....................................	140.00
Office supplies....................................	130.00

Insurance expired:

Selling...$	5.50
Delivery..	7.00
General...	4.50

Depreciation:

Store equipment, 10% a year.......................	33.96
Delivery equipment, 25% a year....................	60.00
Office equipment, 10% a year......................	10.42
Building, 4% a year...............................	30.00

Interest accrued:

On notes payable.................................	7.92
On mortgage......................................	50.00
Prepaid interest on notes payable....................	5.00

Accrued payroll data:

Sales salaries.....................................	660.00
Delivery salaries..................................	165.00
Office salaries....................................	275.00
Employer's F.I.C.A. taxes payable..................	16.50
Federal unemployment taxes payable................	3.30
State unemployment taxes payable..................	29.70
Accrued property taxes.............................	20.00
Estimated income taxes payable.....................	825.00
Appropriation of earned surplus as a reserve for plant expansion..	1,000.00

Chapter 25

Departmental Accounting

DEPARTMENTAL INCOME When a business sells several classes of commodities or services, the income from each class may be accounted for separately. It is then possible to know which classes are most profitable and which classes are least profitable. When management is so informed, it can develop policies much more intelligently. Accounting that classifies income and expenses according to departments is known as *departmental accounting*.

All the sales of a given enterprise may be classified according to the types of commodities or services sold. To determine the net profit for each sales classification, it is necessary to break down on the profit and loss statement each item that enters into net profit. The result is a departmentalization of business operations and the accounting for the business as if the business were a group of departments instead of a single unit.

In a small business the owner is concerned primarily with the net profit obtained as a result of trading operations in all classes of merchandise carried by the business. In a large business, however, it is often desirable to classify the commodities bought and sold into two or more groups and to determine the profit made from each group. To illustrate: If a business deals in both hardware and furniture, it may be advisable to maintain accounts so that the profit made from each class of merchandise can be determined readily. The owner of the business can then judge the profitableness of the department handling each class of merchandise and can better plan for the future. If each department has a separate manager, the efficiency of the manager can also be better judged from the profit made by his department.

INCOME AND EXPENSES BY DEPARTMENTS The organization of business enterprises into departments to facilitate operations is a common practice in modern business. The delegation of operating responsibility to department heads has increased the effectiveness of the whole enterprise. If income and expense accounts are set up by departments, the top management can learn how successful each department head has been.

This increase in income and expense accounts multiplies the number of accounts to be included in the ledger and the trial balance. If there are only two or three departments, the new accounts can be added in the general ledger. If there are many departments, it is advisable to make use of the controlling account device described in previous chapters. In this chapter the departmental income and expense accounts will be included in the general ledger.

DEPARTMENTAL ANALYSIS IN ACCOUNTS AND BOOKS OF ORIGINAL ENTRY The records of a departmentalized business should be so planned that they will supply all the information desired about each department. In a small business, such as a retail store in which the various classes of merchandise are handled together and are sold by the same sales force, the departmental records for each department will show only the gross profit on sales. The expenses will not be divided according to departments but will be grouped together.

If gross profit on sales is to be determined by departments, the accounts should furnish information about sales, sales returns and allowances, purchases, purchases returns and allowances, freight in, and inventories of each department.

If the accounts are to show this departmental analysis of trading operations, the books of original entry must be designed to provide the same analysis. This provision can best be made by the introduction of additional columns into the books of original entry. In order that the use of these special columns may be shown, the books of original entry for a business operating hardware and furniture departments will be illustrated.

THE PURCHASES JOURNAL In the purchases journal shown on page 497, the purchases of the firm of Stone & Stone have been recorded. The amount of each purchase has been entered first in the Accounts Payable Cr. column and then in the Hardware Purchases Dr. or the Furniture Purchases Dr. column according to whether the purchase was for the hardware department or the furniture department. Additional columns might also have been added for the recording of the purchase of items other than merchandise. If that had been done, the purchases journal of Stone & Stone might have been the same as the one illustrated on pages 126 and 127, except for the use of separate columns for Hardware Purchases Dr. and Furniture Purchases Dr. instead of one column for Purchases Dr.

The credits to the accounts of the vendors were posted currently. At the end of the month the three amount columns were totaled and the journal was ruled. The totals were posted to the accounts indicated in the columnar headings.

PURCHASES JOURNAL   PAGE 5

DATE OF ENTRY		DATE OF INVOICE		ACCOUNT CREDITED	POST. REF.	ACCOUNTS PAYABLE CR.		HARDWARE PURCHASES DR.		FURNITURE PURCHASES DR.	
1953 May	1	1953 Apr.	28	Jason Furniture Co.	√	950	00			950	00
	8	May	6	Stillwell Hardware Co.	√	800	00	800	00		
	19		15	Olsen Hardware Co.	√	450	00	450	00		
	27		25	J. R. Fox & Co.	√	1,250	00			1,250	00
	31			Totals	√	3,450	00	1,250	00	2,200	00
						(213)		(511)		(514)	

Purchases Journal Showing Departmental Analysis

THE PURCHASES RETURNS AND ALLOWANCES JOURNAL   Purchases returns and allowances require the same analysis as purchases if the returns and allowances for each department are to be deducted from the purchases for that department. The purchases returns and allowances journal of Stone & Stone is shown below. The amount of each purchase return or allowance has been entered in two columns: the Accounts Payable Dr. column and the returns and allowances column that corresponds to the department for which the return or the allowance was made. At the end of the month the amount columns were totaled and the journal was ruled. The accounts payable account was debited and the hardware purchases returns and allowances account and the furniture purchases returns and allowances account were credited for the totals of the respective columns.

PURCHASES RETURNS AND ALLOWANCES JOURNAL   PAGE 5

DATE		ACCOUNT DEBITED	POST. REF.	ACCOUNTS PAYABLE DR.		HARDWARE PUR. RET. & ALLOW. CR.		FURNITURE PUR. RET. & ALLOW. CR.	
1953 May	19	Stillwell Hardware Co.	√	130	00	130	00		
	29	J. R. Fox & Co.	√	280	00			280	00
	31	Totals	√	410	00	130	00	280	00
				(213)		(512)		(515)	

Purchases Returns and Allowances Journal Showing Departmental Analysis

THE SALES JOURNAL   In a departmentalized wholesale business in which virtually all sales are made on account, a sales journal similar to that of Stone & Stone (illustration on page 498) may be used. The total of each sale made by Stone & Stone was recorded in the Accounts Receivable Dr. column, and the total of this column was posted at the end of the month to the debit of Accounts Receivable. The hardware sales and the furniture sales were recorded in separate columns, and the totals of these columns were

SALES JOURNAL   PAGE 5

DATE	SALE NO.	ACCOUNT DEBITED	POST. REF.	ACCOUNTS RECEIVABLE DR.	HARDWARE SALES CR.	FURNITURE SALES CR.
1953						
May 4	68	Munn Furniture Co.	√	1,200 00		1,200 00
8	69	Ford Mercantile Co.	√	350 00	350 00	
15	70	Jobe Furniture Co.	√	550 00		550 00
18	71	Mapes & Co.	√	750 00		750 00
22	72	Hook & Son	√	800 00	800 00	
27	73	Lyon & Reed	√	700 00	700 00	
31		Totals	√	4,350 00	1,850 00	2,500 00
				(113)	(411)	(413)

Sales Journal Showing Departmental Analysis

posted at the end of the month to the credit of the hardware sales account and the furniture sales account. The debits to the customers' accounts were posted currently.

In a retail business there are many cash sales. These are usually recorded as daily totals. If a departmental analysis of sales is made, separate columns for the cash sales of the various departments may be provided in the cash receipts record, and the total of each column may be posted at the end of the fiscal period to the credit of the departmental sales account. If a business sells largely on account, however, and makes relatively few cash sales, it may not wish to have in its cash receipts record a separate column for the cash sales of each department. In this case the need for these special columns in the cash receipts record may be avoided by providing a debit column for cash in the sales journal.

For example, the credit and cash sales of a wholesale firm dealing in hardware and furniture are recorded in a sales journal having a special column entitled "Cash Dr." The journal illustrated on the opposite page shows the sales that were made during April by this firm. The cash sales were recorded as totals in the Cash Dr. column and in the column corresponding to the department in which these sales were made. The totals of the cash sales were also recorded in the cash receipts journal in the manner shown in the second illustration on page 499.

Since the entries for cash sales in the sales journal were not to be posted to a separate account, they were checked in the Posting Reference column. The total of the Cash Dr. column was also checked in order to prevent double posting from the sales journal and the cash receipts journal. As a result the amounts of cash sales were posted from the sales journal only as a part of the totals of the Hardware Sales Cr. and the Furniture Sales Cr. columns.

SALES JOURNAL   PAGE 31

DATE	SALE NO.	ACCOUNT DEBITED	POST. REF.	ACCOUNTS RECEIVABLE DR.	CASH DR.	HARDWARE SALES CR.	FURNITURE SALES CR.
1953 Apr.	7 88	Jones Hardware Co.	√	300 00		300 00	
	11 89	C. A. Adams	√	250 00			250 00
	16	Cash Sales	√		850 00		850 00
	20 96	Stevens Hdwe. Co.	√	440 00		440 00	
	25	Cash Sales	√		960 00	960 00	
	30 104	Denver Furn. Co.	√	120 00			120 00
	30	Totals	√	1,110 00	1,810 00	1,700 00	1,220 00
				(114)	(√)	(411)	(413)

Sales Journal with a Column for Cash Sales

CASH RECEIPTS JOURNAL   PAGE 56

DATE	ACCOUNT CREDITED	POST. REF.	GENERAL CR.	ACCOUNTS RECEIVABLE CR.	SALES DISCOUNT DR.	CASH DR.
1953 Apr.	1 L. C. Andrew	√		400 00	8 00	392 00
	6 Notes Receivable	113	600 00			600 00
	10 Store Supplies	118	4 00			4 00
	16 Sales	√	850 00			850 00
	17 Jones Hardware Co.	√		300 00	6 00	294 00
	21 C. A. Adams	√		250 00	5 00	245 00
	25 Sales	√	960 00			960 00

Cash Receipts Journal Showing Entries for Cash Sales That Were Also Recorded in the Sales Journal

In the cash receipts journal a check mark was placed in the Posting Reference column opposite each entry for cash sales to indicate that the entry was not to be posted. As a result, the amounts of cash sales were posted from this book only as a part of the total of the Cash Dr. column. The equality of the debits and the credits was maintained in posting the columnar totals from both books because the credits to Hardware Sales and to Furniture Sales were equal to the debit to Accounts Receivable posted from the sales journal plus the amount of cash sales posted from the cash receipts journal as a part of the total of the Cash Dr. column.

THE SALES RETURNS AND ALLOWANCES JOURNAL   If sales returns and allowances are numerous and are to be analyzed by departments, they may be recorded in a columnar journal similar to that illustrated on page 500. This journal is used by Stone & Stone and provides special columns for the analysis of the sales returns and allowances of each department.

SALES RETURNS AND ALLOWANCES JOURNAL   PAGE 5

DATE		CR. MEMO. NO.	ACCOUNT CREDITED	POST. REF.	ACCOUNTS RECEIVABLE CR.	HARDWARE SALES RET. & ALLOW. DR.	FURNITURE SALES RET. & ALLOW. DR.
1953 May	7	13	Munn Furniture Co.	√	15 00		15 00
	21	14	Mapes & Co.	√	75 00		75 00
	29	15	Lyon & Reed	√	30 00	30 00	
	31		Totals		120 00	30 00	90 00
					(113)	(412)	(414)

Sales Returns and Allowances Journal Showing Departmental Analysis

FREIGHT IN
All transportation charges on incoming shipments of merchandise represent a part of the cost of the merchandise purchased and are therefore added to the cost price. Transportation charges on outgoing shipments of merchandise represent the cost of delivering goods to customers and are usually treated as a selling expense.

If a business is departmentalized, the freight in should be departmentalized in order to obtain an accurate departmental cost of sales. If the freight in can be charged directly to the various departments, more accurate figures result. If it is not possible to charge the freight in directly to the departments, it should be assigned on some satisfactory basis. If commodities in the several departments are of similar bulk, the cost of purchases would be acceptable for such an assignment. If the bulk varies, then weight might be used. A discussion of what basis should be used to distribute various expense items, including freight, will be found in a following section.

Since freight outward is usually classified as a selling expense, it will not be necessary to departmentalize it, unless net profit by departments is to be obtained. If so, the basis for charging it to the several departments may follow that used for charging freight in to departments.

THE WORK SHEET —
GROSS PROFIT SHOWN
BY DEPARTMENTS
In preparing a work sheet for a departmentalized business at the close of the accounting period, it is customary to set up, under the heading "Profit and Loss Statement," a pair of columns in which will be entered the income and the costs of each department. An additional pair of columns is included for expenses and nondepartmental items. A business with two departments would therefore need six columns under "Profit and Loss Statement." The sales, purchases, inventories, and other departmental items would be segregated by departments in

two pairs of columns, and all expenses and items not applicable to any department would be entered in the additional pair of columns. The work sheet for an enterprise with two departments might have the following columns:

Account Titles	Trial Balance		Adjustments		Profit and Loss Statement						Balance Sheet	
					Hardware		Furniture		Nondept.			
	Dr.	Cr.	Dr.	Cr.	Dr.	Cr.	Dr.	Cr.	Dr.	Cr.	Dr.	Cr.

The columns under the heading "Profit and Loss Statement" would provide the data for the profit and loss statements of the business.

Since only gross profit is to be departmentalized, the trial balance accounts entering into the determination of gross profit would appear in the appropriate departmental columns. The operating expenses in this case would all appear in the last pair of profit and loss statement columns, headed "Nondepartment."

THE PROFIT AND LOSS STATEMENT — GROSS PROFIT SHOWN BY DEPARTMENTS   If the departmental analysis is carried to the gross trading profit earned by the departments, only the trading section of the profit and loss statement is affected. A separate report may be prepared to show the gross trading profit earned by each department, or a single statement may be presented in a comparative form. If the business has only two departments, the comparative form can be used to advantage. The first illustration on page 502 shows the trading section of such a statement for a business having two departments. The remainder of this statement would be the same in form as that part of the statement for a nondepartmentalized business that shows the determination of the net profit.

If the business has more than two or three departments, the use of additional columns at the right of the statement would make such a form awkward in appearance and use. In such cases it is advisable to prepare a separate trading report for each department. Each of these reports would show as a final item the gross profit on sales for one department. The second illustration on page 502 shows such a report for one of the departments of the business operated by Donald Cox.

After the trading reports for the various departments have been completed, another report is prepared to show the net profit of the business as a whole. The various amounts of gross profit are added on this profit and loss statement to show the total gross profit. The state-

STONE & STONE
PROFIT AND LOSS STATEMENT
FOR MONTH ENDED MAY 31, 1953

TRADING SECTION	HARDWARE		FURNITURE	
Income from Sales:				
Sales..............................		$1,850		$2,500
Less Sales Returns and Allowances.......		30		90
Net Sales.............................		$1,820		$2,410
Cost of Goods Sold:				
Purchases...........................	$1,250		$2,200	
Add Freight In......................	90		160	
Delivered Cost of Purchases............	$1,340		$2,360	
Less Purchases Returns and Allowances...	130		280	
Net Purchases.......................	$1,210		$2,080	
Add Inventory, May 1, 1953...........	3,150		5,300	
Goods Available for Sale...............	$4,360		$7,380	
Less Inventory, May 31, 1953..........	2,910		5,850	
Cost of Goods Sold....................		$1,450		$1,530
Gross Trading Profit...................		$ 370		$ 880
Total Gross Trading Profit...............				$1,250

Partial Profit and Loss Statement Showing an Analysis of Trading Items for Two Departments

DONALD COX
DRAPERY DEPARTMENT, GROSS PROFIT ON SALES
FOR YEAR ENDED DECEMBER 31, 1953

Income from Sales:			
Sales..		$15,500	
Less Sales Returns and Allowances..................		45	
Net Sales.......................................			$15,455
Cost of Merchandise Sold:			
Merchandise Inventory, January 1, 1953..............		$ 2,550	
Purchases.................................	$10,200		
Add Freight In...........................	120		
Delivered Cost of Purchases.................	$10,320		
Less Purchases Returns and Allowances.......	55		
Net Purchases.................................		10,265	
Merchandise Available for Sale.....................		$12,815	
Less Merchandise Inventory, Dec. 31, 1953...........		1,560	
Cost of Merchandise Sold.........................			$11,255
Gross Profit on Sales.................................			$4,200

Trading Report Showing the Gross Profit of a Department

ment is then completed in the usual manner. The illustration on page 504 is the profit and loss statement of Donald Cox, with which the trading report in the preceding illustration correlates.

OPERATING EXPENSES DEPARTMENTALIZED A small departmentalized business may use only the departmental trading accounts that have been discussed in the preceding paragraphs. From these accounts the gross profit on the sales of each department can be determined. A large business, however, will probably wish to have the expenses analyzed according to departments so that the net profit for each department can be determined.

Whenever possible, the expenses of a department may be charged to the departmental expense accounts as the payments are made. For example, if a business having two departments pays salaries each week, the salaries may be charged to separate departmental accounts, such as Sales Salaries — Furniture Department and Sales Salaries — Hardware Department.

Many expenses can be divided more conveniently at the end of the fiscal period than at the time they are paid or recorded. For example, the management may decide that rent is to be distributed to the various departments according to a fixed ratio. To establish the ratio, both the amount and the desirability of the space used by each department are taken into consideration. Space in a prominent position on the first floor may be considered as being worth more than space on upper floors or in less prominent positions on the same floor.

If the rent is paid monthly, it may be distributed to the departments at the time each payment is made and the departmental rent accounts may be charged directly. If the books are closed only once a quarter or once a year, however, it probably would be more convenient to charge all rent payments to a rent account and then to distribute the rent to the various departments at the close of the fiscal period.

APPORTIONMENT OF OPERATING EXPENSES TO DEPARTMENTS Departments naturally fall into two main divisions: (1) those departments that make sales or sell services and (2) those departments that assist or serve the selling departments. The departments in the second class are called service departments. Their expenses should be charged against the selling departments in accordance with the cost of the service rendered these departments. For example, a departmentalized retail store may maintain a central office, with files, desks, and office employees, which serves the various selling depart-

DONALD COX
PROFIT AND LOSS STATEMENT
FOR YEAR ENDED DECEMBER 31, 1953

Gross Profit:			
Drapery Department.............................		$ 4,200	
Rug Department....................................		3,300	
Furniture Department.............................		12,150	
Household Utilities Department.....................		1,850	
Total Gross Profit.................................			$21,500
Operating Expenses:			
Selling Expenses:			
Sales Salaries.............................	$5,960		
Advertising Expense.......................	2,100		
Depreciation of Store Fixtures..............	140		
Store Supplies Expense....................	200		
Insurance Expense — Merchandise..........	30		
Insurance Expense — Store Fixtures........	20		
Miscellaneous Selling Expense..............	70		
Total Selling Expenses............................		$ 8,520	
Delivery Expenses:			
Delivery Salaries..........................	$1,570		
Depreciation of Delivery Equipment........	215		
Delivery Supplies Expense.................	110		
Insurance Expense — Delivery Equipment...	65		
Miscellaneous Delivery Expense............	80		
Total Delivery Expenses.......................		2,040	
General Expenses:			
Office Salaries............................	$2,880		
Rent Expense.............................	2,500		
Depreciation of Office Equipment...........	35		
Office Supplies Expense....................	85		
Insurance Expense — Office Equipment......	5		
Bad Debts Expense........................	200		
Miscellaneous General Expense.............	550		
Total General Expenses........................		6,255	
Total Operating Expenses...........................			16,815
Net Profit from Operations.........................			$ 4,685
Other Income:			
Purchases Discount.........................	$ 615		
Interest Income...........................	55		
Total Other Income.........................		$ 670	
Other Expenses:			
Sales Discount.............................	$ 195		
Interest Expense...........................	60		
Total Other Expenses............................		255	
Net Addition......................................			415
Net Profit...			$ 5,100

Profit and Loss Statement of a Departmentalized Business

ments. If the service rendered by this central office is proportionate to sales made, then its costs should be apportioned among the several selling departments according to sales. Or, a parking lot for the convenience of customers may be maintained at considerable cost. Customers make purchases in the various departments of the store. The cost of operating the parking lot should be apportioned to the various selling departments on some equitable basis.

If there are a number of selling departments and a number of service departments, a columnar distribution sheet provides an effective accounting device for this apportionment. Such an expense distribution sheet is shown below:

OPERATING EXPENSES	BASIS OF DISTRIBUTION	TOTAL	DISTRIBUTION				
			PUR-CHASING	GENERAL OFFICE	LINGERIE	SUITS – COATS	DRESSES
Salaries	Direct	6,000	800	1,400	600	1,200	2,000
Supplies	Direct	2,100	130	590	180	500	700
Insurance	Value of equipment	500	25	50	100	125	200
Rent	Space occupied	1,400	70	140	210	350	630
Depreciation	Value and life of equipment	1,200	95	180	200	305	420
Heating	Space occupied	240	12	24	36	60	108
Lighting	No. of lights	110	8	16	20	20	46
Advertising	Volume of sales	1,600			200	600	800
Total Expenses		13,150					
Purchasing	Volume of purchases		1,140		190	380	570
General Office	Volume of sales			2,400	300	900	1,200
					2,036	4,440	6,674
Reconciliation:							
Lingerie Dept.		2,036					
Suits & Coats Dept.		4,440					
Dresses Dept.		6,674					
		13,150					

This distribution sheet provides for the collection and the distribution of the expenses of two service departments, (1) Purchasing and (2) General Office, to three selling departments designated Lingerie, Suits and Coats, and Dresses. It also indicates in the second column the basis of distribution or apportionment. The sum of the Total column should agree with the sum of the selling department columns since all costs are eventually charged against the selling departments.

On the distribution sheet, each operating expense is distributed first to all the departments on some equitable basis. The operating expenses for the two service departments, Purchasing and General Office, are then totaled and in turn are distributed to the selling departments. The operating expenses of the purchasing department are distributed on the basis of volume of purchases by each of the selling departments. For example, assume that the purchases of the Lingerie,

Suits and Coats, and Dresses Departments were $20,000, $40,000, and $60,000 respectively. Of the total purchases, Lingerie would have ⅙; Suits and Coats, ⅓; and Dresses, ½. These fractions are used in the distribution of the total purchasing expenses, $1,140, to the three selling departments. In a similar manner the operating expenses of the General Office Department are distributed on the basis of departmental sales volume. Assume that the sales of the three departments were $25,000, $75,000, and $100,000 respectively. Of the total sales, Lingerie would have ⅛; Suits and Coats, ⅜; and Dresses, ½.

The operating expenses have been identified with the departments to which they belong on a distribution sheet. This reclassification of items could be transferred to ledger accounts, but the foregoing distribution is illustrated as a supplement for the work sheet to be used in the preparation of the departmental profit and loss statements.

**THE WORK SHEET —
NET PROFIT SHOWN
BY DEPARTMENTS**   In preparing a work sheet that will itemize departmental net profits at the end of the accounting period, the work sheet illustrated below may be used. The major change in the completion of the work sheet will be the addition of expenses to the income and cost figures in the department columns under the heading "Profit and Loss Statement." By departmentalizing the operating expenses, the net profit for each department may be found in the same manner in which the net profit is determined for a nondepartmental business. The Nondepartment columns would be reserved for other income and other expense items, such as Interest Income and Sales Discount.

The distribution of operating expense items not set up in separate departmental accounts in the ledger is illustrated below. The proper portions belonging to each department are entered in the departmental columns on the work sheet.

ACCOUNT TITLES	TRIAL BALANCE		ADJUSTMENTS		PROFIT AND LOSS STATEMENT						BALANCE SHEET	
					HARDWARE		FURNITURE		NONDEPT.			
	DR.	CR.	DR.	CR.	DR.	CR.	DR.	CR.	DR.	CR.	DR.	CR.
Advertising	1,200				300		900					
Rent	1,500				300		1,200					
Supplies Expense			1,800		200		1,600					
Insurance Expense			900		450		450					

The advertising amount of $1,200 is distributed on the basis of volume of sales: Hardware Department, $20,000; Furniture Department, $60,000. The rent amount of $1,500 is distributed on the basis of area occupied: Hardware Department, 500 square feet; Furniture Department, 2,000 square feet. The supplies expense amount of $1,800 is distributed on the basis of direct usage of supplies by the departments. The insurance expense of $900 is distributed on the basis of insurance carried applicable to the two departments, which in this example calls for an equal distribution.

THE PROFIT AND LOSS STATEMENT — NET PROFIT SHOWN BY DEPARTMENTS　　If the net profit for each department is determined separately, a separate profit and loss statement showing net profit is made for each department. The departmental profit and loss statements are much the same in form as the statement of a nondepartmentalized business. Each statement closes with the net profit from the operations of a particular department. On a separate report the net profits from the operations of the various departments are added to show the total net profit for the period. To this amount the other income is added and the other expenses are subtracted, in the same manner in which these items are treated in the profit and loss statement of a nondepartmentalized business. The following illustration is a statement showing the method of reporting the net profits earned by various departments and of handling the other income and expense of the business.

CLINTON ELLIOT

PROFIT AND LOSS STATEMENT

FOR YEAR ENDED DECEMBER 31, 1953

Net Profit from Operations:		
Office Fixtures Department........................	$ 1,750	
Office Machines Department.......................	12,830	
Office Furniture Department.......................	13,680	
Total Net Profit from Operations..................		$28,260
Other Income:		
Purchases Discount...........................	$560	
Interest Income..............................	38	
Total Other Income...........................	598	
Other Expenses:		
Sales Discount..............................	$186	
Interest Expense............................	72	
Total Other Expenses........................	258	
Net Addition.......................................		340
Net Profit...		$28,600

Profit and Loss Statement of a Departmentalized Business

**EFFECT OF
ELIMINATION OF
A DEPARTMENT**
The use of departmental accounting to aid management in policy development and in evaluation of the degree to which the various departments are profitable has been discussed earlier in this chapter. The following discussion will illustrate a portion of the analysis that is possible when a business utilizes a departmental accounting process.

In the illustration on page 507, the profit and loss statement of Clinton Elliot shows net profits from operations for three departments: Office Fixtures, $1,750; Office Machines, $12,830; and Office Furniture, $13,680. A study of these figures might result in a decision to eliminate the Office Fixtures Department and to attempt to expand the volume of business in the other two departments.

Before this decision can be justified, however, a careful analysis must be made of the various factors that determine the profitableness of the Office Fixtures Department. It may be found that the department has had to carry too large a portion of the indirect expenses distributed among the departments, thereby understating its net profit. A detailed analysis of the basis of allocation of expenses to the three departments may prove beneficial.

A study of the effect, if any, that the elimination of the department will have on individual expenses must be made. Selling expenses may not be appreciably diminished, since salesmen will still cover the same territories; in fact, they may need to increase their activities in order to increase sales of furniture and machines to balance the loss of income caused by the elimination of the fixtures department. The rental of the building will not be decreased. Insurance premiums, lighting, heating, and repairing and maintaining the building may not be appreciably reduced by the elimination of one of the departments.

The profitableness of an individual department may have values that cannot be determined solely by a study of the accounting statements. Therefore, after all the expenses have been analyzed, the interrelation or the interdependence of the departments must also be considered. In this example, Mr. Elliot may find that the Office Fixtures Department has actually been responsible for sales in other departments. The service of supplying desk accessories and light fixtures may have enabled Mr. Elliot to keep in touch with his customers throughout the year. This frequency of contact may have resulted in an increased volume of sales of furniture and machines. If this is the case, the Office Fixtures Department should not be eliminated despite the fact that its net profit is much less than the net profits of the other two departments.

ADJUSTING AND CLOSING ACCOUNTS OF A DEPARTMEN- TALIZED BUSINESS The departmentalization of a business results in no essentially new problems in adjusting and closing the ledger. For each department, separate inventory, sales, sales returns and allowances, purchases, freight in, and purchases returns and allowances accounts are required. If the reports show only the gross profit of each department, the trading accounts for each department are closed into a trading summary account for that department. The balances of these departmental trading summary accounts are then closed into a profit and loss summary account for the enterprise as a whole. The expense accounts are closed into the latter account just as they are when a business is not departmentalized. The other income and the other expense accounts are also closed in the usual manner. If the net profit or the net loss of each department is determined, departmental profit and loss summary accounts are used, and only the net profits or the net losses of the various departments are closed into a general profit and loss summary account.

QUESTIONS

1. (a) When a business is divided into five departments and the gross profit is to be determined by departments, what accounts must be departmentalized? (b) In this case which item will be the most difficult to departmentalize?

2. Does the establishment of three departments result in three times as much posting from the purchases journal? Explain.

3. When sales are classified by departments, how may cash sales be recorded in order to show departmentalization?

4. John Avery operates a mercantile store in which three kinds of merchandise are sold. He believes one kind is resulting in a loss. What accounts could be set up to help him determine whether he should continue to carry this particular kind of merchandise?

5. David Miller owns and operates the Miller Drug Store. He has installed a soda fountain and a lunch counter and wishes to be able to determine the profit of the soda fountain separately. (a) What new accounts should he set up? (b) What changes will be made in his books of original entry?

6. Walter Kline, a retail shoe dealer, maintains three departments, for ladies', men's, and children's shoes respectively. It is not practicable to separate the freight in costs at the time payments are made. How would you apportion the total freight in costs to the three departments at the end of the year?

7. The Clark Service Station provides various services for automobile drivers. It is located in a high-class residential suburb of a large city on a main traffic artery. It is owned by William Clark and it regularly employs six men besides the proprietor. (a) What departmentalization would you advise? Name the departments in order, if there were to be three, four, five, or six departments. (b) Would you determine gross profit or net profit departmentally?

8. In departmental accounting, what basis of distribution to departments should be used for the following expense items: (a) freight in, (b) advertising expense, (c) depreciation of fixed assets, (d) general manager's salary, (e) property taxes, and (f) delivery expenses?

9. The Lawson Department Store has five departments. In the past, separate gross profit figures have been obtained for each department. The general manager decides that in the future he should know the net profit of each department instead of the gross profit. What changes in the accounting procedure will be necessary?

PROBLEMS

25-1. The Uptown Super Market has four sales departments: (1) Grocery, (2) Bakery, (3) Meats, and (4) Vegetables; and three service departments: (1) Purchasing, (2) Advertising, and (3) General Office. The following pertinent information was taken from the books:

	GROCERY	BAKERY	MEATS	VEGETABLES
Sales for the Year 1953	$600,000	$100,000	$200,000	$300,000
Purchases for the Year 1953	400,000	50,000	150,000	200,000
Inventory, January 1, 1953	125,000	1,500	20,000	15,000
Inventory, December 31, 1953	120,000	3,000	30,000	20,000

Operating expenses for the year were:

	ADVERTISING	SALARIES, SUPPLIES, AND INSURANCE
Purchases		$ 31,950
Advertising		25,800
General Office		78,500
Grocery	$16,000	33,400
Bakery	4,000	15,575
Meats	8,000	29,600
Vegetables	12,000	45,175
	$40,000	$260,000

The annual depreciation charges were $15,000. They are to be distributed as follows:

Purchasing.......	15%	Grocery..........	30%
Advertising.......	5%	Bakery...........	10%
General Office....	10%	Meats............	15%
		Vegetables........	15%

The annual lighting charges were $4,000. These should be distributed according to the number of kilowatt-hours used. The number used was:

Purchasing.......	200	Grocery..........	1,500
Advertising......	200	Bakery...........	800
General Office.....	400	Meats...........	500
		Vegetables........	400

The purchasing expenses are to be distributed on the basis of purchases; the advertising expenses, on the basis of direct advertising charges; and the general office expenses, on the basis of sales.

Instructions: (1) Prepare an expense distribution sheet.

(2) Prepare one departmentalized profit and loss statement for all departments.

25-2. The trial balance of the C. B. Rader Company at the end of the fiscal year on June 30, 1953, is given below:

C. B. RADER COMPANY
Trial Balance
June 30, 1953

Cash.......................................	$ 37,500	
Accounts Receivable........................	110,400	
Allowance for Bad Debts.....................		$ 2,200
Merchandise Inventory, Department A.........	60,000	
Merchandise Inventory, Department B.........	45,000	
Store Supplies.............................	26,000	
Store Equipment............................	75,000	
Allowance for Depreciation of Store Equipment.		22,500
Capital Stock..............................		200,000
Surplus....................................		80,000
Sales, Department A.........................		220,000
Sales, Department B.........................		110,000
Purchases, Department A.....................	150,000	
Purchases, Department B.....................	70,000	
Selling Expenses (control)...................	37,200	
General Expenses (control)..................	22,500	
Interest Income.............................		1,600
Interest Expense...........................	2,700	
	$636,300	$636,300

The following adjustments are to be made on June 30:

Merchandise inventory, Department A	$70,000
Merchandise inventory, Department B	40,000
Store supplies inventory	10,100

Depreciation of store equipment, 10%.
Allowance for bad debts, an additional 1% of sales.
Estimated income taxes payable, 40%.

All selling and general expenses are to be distributed to the two departments, A and B, in proportion to their sales.

Instructions: (1) Prepare a twelve-column work sheet with columns similar to those in the illustration on page 506 of the textbook. The work sheet is to show the net profit or loss earned by each department of the business and the net profit of the entire business.

(2) Prepare a profit and loss statement for each department.

(3) Prepare a profit and loss statement showing the net profit of the business. This statement should begin with the net profits or losses earned by the two departments.

25-3. The departmental analysis on the profit and loss statement of the Clinton Hope Corporation for the year ended December 31, 1953, is shown on the following page.

The Paint Department shows a large loss. You are to determine the advisability of eliminating the Paint Department.

The elimination of the Paint Department would bring the following savings:

(1) Selling Expenses:
   (a) Salaries and advertising expense of the paint department would be completely saved.
   (b) An estimated saving of 10% of the total store supplies expense, insurance expense on merchandise, and miscellaneous selling expense would result.
   (c) The remaining selling expenses would be unchanged.

(2) General Expenses:
   (a) An estimated saving of 20% of the total of office supplies expense, allowance for bad debts, and miscellaneous general expense would result.
   (b) The remaining general expenses would be unchanged.

(3) Other Income and Other Expenses:
   (a) The total purchases discount would decrease 20%.
   (b) The total sales discount would decrease 20%.
   (c) Other items would remain unchanged.

Instructions: Prepare a profit and loss statement showing the changes that would result by eliminating the Paint Department in order to determine the advisability of this proposal.

	PAINT DEPT.	HARDWARE DEPT.	TOTAL
Gross Profit on Sales..................	$15,300	$64,800	$80,100

Operating Expenses:
Selling Expenses:

	PAINT DEPT.	HARDWARE DEPT.	TOTAL
Sales Salaries....................	$ 8,000	$17,000	$25,000
Advertising Expense..............	5,000	12,000	17,000
Depr. of Store Fixtures...........	500	1,500	2,000
Store Supplies Expense...........	750	2,200	2,950
Insurance Expense — Mdse........	320	960	1,280
Insurance Expense — Store Equip..	100	300	400
Misc. Selling Expense............	80	460	540

General Expenses:

	PAINT DEPT.	HARDWARE DEPT.	TOTAL
Office Salaries..................	2,000	4,000	6,000
Rent...........................	3,000	9,000	12,000
Depr. of Office Equip............	90	150	240
Office Supplies Expense..........	200	400	600
Insurance Expense — Office Equip..	20	80	100
Bad Debts Expense...............	400	700	1,100
Misc. General Expense...........	90	260	350
Total Operating Expenses	$20,550	$49,010	$69,560
Net Profit or Loss* from Operations....	$ 5,250*	$15,790	$10,540

Other Income:

	PAINT DEPT.	HARDWARE DEPT.	TOTAL
Purchases Discount...............	$ 600	$ 1,370	$ 1,970
Interest Income..................	30	80	110
Total Other Income..............	$ 630	$ 1,450	$ 2,080

Other Expenses:

	PAINT DEPT.	HARDWARE DEPT.	TOTAL
Sales Discount...................	$ 120	$ 350	$ 470
Interest Expense.................	70	130	200
Total Other Expense..............	$ 190	$ 480	$ 670
Net Addition	$ 440	$ 970	$ 1,410
Net Profit and Loss*..............	$ 4,810*	$16,760	$11,950

Chapter 26

Branch Accounting

BRANCH OPERATIONS AND BRANCH ACCOUNTING In the attempt to increase volume of sales, many business concerns have established branches. Through operation at various points, the needs of consumers are more effectively met and sales are built up. Whenever sales occur at different locations, there is need for branch accounting for income and expense. Whenever assets and liabilities are connected with branch operations, there is need for branch accounting for balance sheet items. Branch accounting goes beyond departmental accounting in that it requires the maintenance of records at each branch location.

The development of branch activity by large business corporations has been one of the outstanding movements in modern business. The corporation that sells merchandise in a hundred or a thousand stores over a state or over the entire country is a well-known feature of present-day merchandising. The chain store, operating under a central management, but each store with a branch manager in charge locally, has become an accepted characteristic of the business of today.

For efficient management, it is necessary to know the profitableness of each branch. The earning capacity of various locations under the several managers is an important part of branch administration. It is also necessary to know the investment in each branch and all factors entering into the financial conditions. Branch accounting should provide a balance sheet of assets and liabilities at each branch, as well as a profit and loss statement showing the effect of branch operations.

In this chapter it will be possible to deal only with a central office and one or two branches. The fundamental considerations, however, are not materially changed when there are many branches. An understanding of the transactions of a home office and its branches should contribute to a better understanding of this current economic phenomenon.

METHODS OF BRANCH ACCOUNTING Several methods of branch accounting are found in actual practice. Although there are many variations of these methods, they may in general be classified as follows:

514

First Method. No accounting records except those of a memorandum nature are kept at the branch. The books of original entry and the ledger records of the branch transactions are maintained at the home office. While this method centralizes the bookkeeping at the home office, it fails to provide branch managers with current, up-to-date information regarding their own activities. Branch managers must rely on such periodic reports as may be furnished by the home office.

In nearly all cases a branch is given a *working fund,* which is sufficient to meet its needs for a limited period of time. The branch reports its disbursements to the home office when it needs additional funds, and the home office sends it a check for the amount of the disbursements. The accounting for such a working fund is similar to that used for petty cash, described in Chapter 15.

Second Method. The branch maintains books of original entry but does not post the entries to a general ledger. Instead, summaries of the entries are forwarded to the home office each month. For example, the branch records all sales made by it, and at the end of the month it sends to the home office a report showing the total to be debited to Accounts Receivable and credited to Sales. Similar reports are made for purchases, cash receipts, and cash disbursements. The general journal entries for the month are reported individually. The branch makes the periodic summaries on journal vouchers. The home office files the vouchers in loose-leaf binders and uses them as mediums of posting either to an individual ledger maintained for the branch or directly to the general ledger.

Third Method. The branch maintains books of original entry and also a ledger. In short, it has a complete accounting system. In the branch ledger is an account with the home office, which takes the place of the customary proprietorship accounts. In the ledger of the home office is an account with the branch. A periodic report, usually prepared monthly, is made by the branch to the home office; and from this report an entry is made in the records of the home office to record the profit or the loss of the branch. This method of branch accounting will be illustrated in the remaining pages of the chapter.

RECIPROCAL ACCOUNTS IN BRANCH ACCOUNTING   The home office records its investment in the branch in an account entitled *Branch Office,* which is debited for cash or other assets that the home office sends to the branch. Whenever a profit is reported by the branch, the home office records this profit in its books by a debit to Branch Office and a credit to a suitable income account. Conversely, cash or other assets received from the branch or a loss reported by the branch are recorded as credits to Branch Office, for the reduction in the net assets of the branch represents a decrease in the ownership interest in the branch.

The branch keeps a corresponding account known as *Home Office*. This account represents the ownership interest of the home office in the branch. The receipt of cash or other assets from the home office is recorded as a credit to Home Office. When a profit is made by the branch, Home Office is credited, for a profit increases the ownership interest of the home office. Whenever the branch sends cash or other assets to the home office or incurs a loss, Home Office is debited, since the ownership interest of the home office in the branch is decreased.

The two accounts, Branch Office and Home Office, are called *reciprocal accounts*. When the branch office account is debited by the home office, the home office account is credited by the branch office. When the branch office account is credited by the home office, the home office account is debited by the branch office. The debit items in the branch office account correspond to the credit items in the home office account; the credit items in the branch office account correspond to the debit items in the home office account. The reciprocal nature of the two accounts is shown in the following diagram:

| IN THE HOME OFFICE LEDGER | | IN THE BRANCH LEDGER | |
BRANCH OFFICE		HOME OFFICE	
Cash sent to branch.	Cash received from branch.	Cash sent to home office.	Cash received from home office.
Other assets sent to branch.	Loss reported by branch.	Loss suffered by branch.	Other assets received from home office.
Profit reported by branch.			Profit earned by branch.

When $1,000 cash is sent to the branch by the home office, the entry on the home office books in general journal form is:

```
Branch Office...................................  1,000
    Cash........................................         1,000
```

and the entry on the branch books in general journal form is:

```
Cash...........................................  1,000
    Home Office................................         1,000
```

In a similar manner, all transactions indicated on the two reciprocal accounts might be set up in journal form.

When merchandise is shipped from the home office to the branch, the home office debits Branch Office and credits Shipments to Branch. The branch debits Shipments from Home Office and credits Home Office. The two accounts, Shipments to Branch and Shipments from Home Office, are also reciprocal accounts. They differ from the first pair of reciprocal accounts described above in that each account has entries on one side only. Shipments to Branch has credit entries only; Shipments from Home Office has debit entries only. It is obvious that the debit total of the latter account must, of necessity, equal the credit total of the former.

In the previous discussion it was assumed that shipments to the branch were made at cost. If such shipments were made at selling price or at a price higher than cost, the charge to the branch would include an element of profit that will not be realized until the merchandise is sold by the branch. Whenever shipments to the branch are made at prices higher than cost, it is necessary to adjust the reciprocal accounts in order to know the true equity of the home office in the branch and to know the true profit or loss. In this chapter all shipments will be at cost, thus making such adjustments unnecessary.

ILLUSTRATION OF ACCOUNTING FOR A BRANCH The accounting procedure of a home office and a branch does not differ from the usual accounting procedure except for the introduction of the reciprocal accounts described above. The new home office ledger accounts, Branch Office and Shipments to Branch, and their reciprocal accounts in the branch ledger, Home Office and Shipments from Home Office, constitute the chief distinguishing characteristics of branch accounting. To illustrate branch accounting, a summary of transactions performed by a home office and a branch and the journal entries completed from these transactions are given below:

(1) A home office opened a branch and sent it $10,000 in cash and $30,000 worth of merchandise, with which to start operations.

HOME OFFICE BOOKS			BRANCH BOOKS		
Branch Office 40,000			Cash 10,000		
Cash		10,000	Shipments from Home		
Shipments to Branch		30,000	Office 30,000		
			Home Office		40,000

(2) The branch purchased on account merchandise costing $10,000.

HOME OFFICE BOOKS		BRANCH BOOKS	
No entry		Purchases 10,000	
		Accounts Payable . . .	10,000

(3) The branch sold merchandise for $16,000 in cash and for $8,000 on account.

HOME OFFICE BOOKS | BRANCH BOOKS
No entry

Cash............... 16,000
Accounts Receivable... 8,000
Sales.............   24,000

(4) The branch paid operating expenses amounting to $3,500.

HOME OFFICE BOOKS | BRANCH BOOKS
No entry

Operating Expenses... 3,500
Cash.............   3,500

(5) The branch collected $6,000 on accounts receivable.

HOME OFFICE BOOKS | BRANCH BOOKS
No entry

Cash............... 6,000
Accounts Receivable   6,000

(6) The branch paid $1,000 on accounts payable.

HOME OFFICE BOOKS | BRANCH BOOKS
No entry

Accounts Payable..... 1,000
Cash.............   1,000

(7) The branch sent $20,000 in cash to the home office.

HOME OFFICE BOOKS | BRANCH BOOKS

Cash............... 20,000
Branch Office.......   20,000

Home Office.......... 20,000
Cash.............   20,000

The entries to adjust and close the books of the branch, together with the entries on the books of the home office to record the net profit of the branch, are as follows:

(a) To record the ending merchandise inventory of the branch, $22,000.

HOME OFFICE BOOKS | BRANCH BOOKS
No entry

Merchandise Inventory 22,000
Profit and Loss Summary.............   22,000

(b) To close the sales account of the branch.

HOME OFFICE BOOKS | BRANCH BOOKS
No entry

Sales............... 24,000
Profit and Loss Summary.............   24,000

(c) To close the cost and expense accounts of the branch.

HOME OFFICE BOOKS | BRANCH BOOKS
No entry

Profit and Loss Summary............... 43,500
Shipments from
Home Office........   30,000
Purchases.........   10,000
Operating Expenses.   3,500

(d) To close the profit and loss summary account on the books of the branch and to record the net profit of the branch on the books of the home office.

HOME OFFICE BOOKS			BRANCH BOOKS		
Branch Office.........	2,500		Profit and Loss Sum-		
Profit of Branch....		2,500	mary...............	2,500	
			Home Office.......		2,500

Entry (d), shown in both the branch journal and the general office journal, records the profit of the branch and the taking up of the profit by the general office. Whenever profits or losses are recorded by a branch, the general office must record the increase or the decrease in the branch investment.

The transactions illustrated on the foregoing pages include two sets of reciprocal accounts: (1) Branch Office and Home Office and (2) Shipments to Branch and Shipments from Home Office. The first set are balance sheet accounts; the second set are profit and loss statement accounts. There will be as many groups of these four accounts as there are branches.

After the foregoing entries have been posted, the accounts in the ledger of the home office that are affected by these transactions and the branch ledger appear as follows:

HOME OFFICE LEDGER

CASH

(7)	20,000	(1)	10,000

Other cash transactions of the home office would also be recorded in this account.

BRANCH LEDGER

CASH

(1)	10,000	(4)	3,500
(3)	16,000	(6)	1,000
(5)	6,000	(7)	20,000
		Bal.	7,500
	32,000		32,000
Balance	7,500		

ACCOUNTS RECEIVABLE

(3)	8,000	(5)	6,000
		Balance	2,000
	8,000		8,000
Balance	2,000		

MERCHANDISE INVENTORY

(a)	22,000		

HOME OFFICE LEDGER   BRANCH LEDGER

ACCOUNTS PAYABLE

(6)	1,000	(2)	10,000
Balance	9,000		
	10,000		10,000
		Balance	9,000

BRANCH OFFICE   HOME OFFICE

(1)	40,000	(7)	20,000	(7)	20,000	(1)	40,000
(d)	2,500	Balance	22,500	Balance	22,500	(d)	2,500
	42,500		42,500		42,500		42,500
Balance	22,500					Balance	22,500

PROFIT OF BRANCH   PROFIT AND LOSS SUMMARY

		(d)	2,500	(c)	43,500	(a)	22,000
				(d)	2,500	(b)	24,000
					46,000		46,000

Profit of Branch will be closed to the home office profit and loss summary account.

SALES

(b)	24,000	(3)	24,000

SHIPMENTS TO BRANCH   SHIPMENTS FROM HOME OFFICE

		(1)	30,000	(1)	30,000	(c)	30,000

Shipments to Branch is a deduction from purchases. It will be closed to the home office profit and loss summary account.

PURCHASES

(2)	10,000	(c)	10,000

OPERATING EXPENSES

(4)	3,500	(c)	3,500

The profit and loss statement and the balance sheet that the branch prepared for the home office were as follows:

BRANCH
PROFIT AND LOSS STATEMENT
FOR MONTH ENDED JANUARY 31, 1954

Sales......................................		$24,000
Cost of Goods Sold:		
Purchases.................................	$10,000	
Shipments from Home Office.................	30,000	
Merchandise Available for Sale during Month....	$40,000	
Less Merchandise Inventory, January 31, 1954...	22,000	
Cost of Goods Sold.........................		18,000
Gross Profit on Sales.......................		$ 6,000
Operating Expenses..........................		3,500
Net Profit from Operations...................		$ 2,500

Profit and Loss Statement of a Branch

BRANCH
BALANCE SHEET
JANUARY 31, 1954

ASSETS		LIABILITIES AND CAPITAL	
Cash.....................	$ 7,500	Accounts Payable.........	$ 9,000
Accounts Receivable.......	2,000	Home Office..............	22,500
Merchandise Inventory.....	22,000		
Total Assets..............	$31,500	Total Liab. and Capital.....	$31,500

Balance Sheet of a Branch

CONSOLIDATED STATEMENTS   It is desirable to have consolidated statements showing the combined results of the home office and the branch activities for each period. A consolidated profit and loss statement is prepared by the use of a work sheet. For example, the work sheet used by the home office mentioned in the preceding discussion is shown at the top of the following page.

On the work sheet the accounts Shipments to Branch and Shipments from Home Office were eliminated since they did not represent transactions with outsiders. The elimination of these items made possible the preparation of a consolidated statement that showed the results of the operations of the home office and the branch as one organization. The consolidated report that was prepared from the Consolidated Profit and Loss Statement column of the work sheet is shown at the bottom of the following page.

HOME OFFICE AND BRANCH

Work Sheet for Consolidated Profit and Loss Statement
For Month Ended January 31, 1954

	Home Office	Branch Office	Eliminations		Cons. Profit and Loss Statement
			Dr.	Cr.	
Sales.................	47,000	24,000			71,000
Cost of Goods Sold:					
Mdse. Inv., January 1..	41,000				41,000
Purchases............	52,000	10,000			62,000
Shipments from Home Office.............		30,000		30,000	
	93,000				
Less Shipments to Branch............	30,000		30,000		
Mdse. Available for Sale	63,000	40,000			103,000
Less Mdse. Inv., Jan. 31	35,000	22,000			57,000
Cost of Goods Sold.....	28,000	18,000			46,000
Gross Profit on Sales.....	19,000	6,000			25,000
Operating Expenses......	6,500	3,500			10,000
Net Profit from Operations................	12,500	2,500	30,000	30,000	15,000

Work Sheet for a Consolidated Profit and Loss Statement

HOME OFFICE AND BRANCH

Consolidated Profit and Loss Statement
For Month Ended January 31, 1954

Sales.......................................		$71,000
Cost of Goods Sold:		
Merchandise Inventory, January 1, 1954......	$ 41,000	
Purchases...............................	62,000	
Merchandise Available for Sale..............	$103,000	
Less Mdse. Inventory, January 31, 1954.......	57,000	
Cost of Goods Sold.......................		46,000
Gross Profit on Sales.........................		$25,000
Operating Expenses..........................		10,000
Net Profit from Operations...................		$15,000

Consolidated Profit and Loss Statement

In a similar manner a consolidated balance sheet may be prepared at the end of the period from a work sheet. For instance, the home office mentioned in the preceding discussion used the following work sheet in the preparation of its consolidated balance sheet:

HOME OFFICE AND BRANCH
WORK SHEET FOR CONSOLIDATED BALANCE SHEET
JANUARY 31, 1954

	HOME OFFICE	BRANCH OFFICE	ELIMINATIONS		CONSOLIDATED BALANCE SHEET
			DR.	CR.	
ASSETS:					
Cash..............	53,000	7,500			60,500
Accounts Receivable...	46,000	2,000			48,000
Merchandise Inventory	35,000	22,000			57,000
Branch Office........	22,500			22,500	
Total Assets...........	156,500	31,500			165,500
LIABILITIES & CAPITAL:					
Accounts Payable.....	28,000	9,000			37,000
Home Office..........		22,500	22,500		
Capital Stock........	100,000				100,000
Surplus.............	28,500				28,500
Total Liab. and Capital...	156,500	31,500	22,500	22,500	165,500

Work Sheet for a Consolidated Balance Sheet

On the work sheet the accounts Branch Office and Home Office were eliminated so that a consolidated report showing the assets, the liabilities, and the capital of the home office and the branch as one organization could be prepared. The consolidated report that was prepared from the Consolidated Balance Sheet column of the work sheet is illustrated below:

HOME OFFICE AND BRANCH
CONSOLIDATED BALANCE SHEET
JANUARY 31, 1954

ASSETS		LIABILITIES AND CAPITAL	
Cash....................	$ 60,500	Accounts Payable........	$ 37,000
Accounts Receivable.......	48,000	Capital Stock............	100,000
Merchandise Inventory....	57,000	Surplus.................	28,500
Total Assets.............	$165,500	Total Liab. and Capital...	$165,500

Consolidated Balance Sheet

The consolidation of the statements of several branches with that of the home office would be accomplished in a manner similar to that illustrated with a single branch. The only difference would be a lateral expansion of the work sheet. Instead of one column for Branch Office, there would be as many columns as there were branches.

ACCOUNTING FOR MANY BRANCHES The preceding illustrations concern the relations of one branch to the home office. The principles would not differ if there were hundreds of branches, as there are today in many chain-store organizations. While there are unity of ownership and a central management, there must exist at the various branches separate managements having autonomy and directing operations within certain prescribed limits. The operating accounts must, if they are to be most useful, represent the operations of each of the branches. Sales and the expenses incident to sales must be identified with the several branches in which activities are carried on.

At the end of each period the several branch statements need to be combined into consolidated statements for the enterprise as a whole. The consolidation of many statements follows the same general plan that is illustrated in this chapter, though each additional branch adds just that much to the detail to be incorporated in the consolidated statement.

Departmental and branch accounting are only two illustrations of the use of analytical accounts to provide detailed reviews of activities that are later to be consolidated into a single statement covering the enterprise as a unit. As the size of the business unit increases, the need for reporting currently the income, the costs, and the expenses of the parts of which the whole is composed increases to the same extent. From the point of view of the administrative control of operations through accounts, such departmental and branch analyses are extremely helpful.

ANALYSES OF INTERNAL OPERATIONS With the ever-increasing size of business units, the need for internal accounting is likewise growing. It is necessary to account separately for the various parts of which these large units are made up. This accounting involves first a breakdown of the accounts, departmentally or by branches, followed by a consolidation to show the unit as a whole.

In the large five-and-ten-cent store chains, for example, there is first a breakdown by commodities sold and second a breakdown by branches selling these commodities. For efficient administration of these large mercantile establishments, it is necessary to have the departmental analysis and the branch analysis. More and more attention is being directed to accounting for small units under a central administration.

QUESTIONS

1. Distinguish between controlling accounts and reciprocal accounts. Give an illustration of reciprocal accounts. Give four illustrations of controlling accounts.

2. What amount on the branch balance sheet appears also on the home office balance sheet?

3. How does closing the accounts of a branch differ from closing the accounts of the home office?

4. The ledger of a branch office may contain two accounts with incoming merchandise. (a) What are these accounts called? (b) Why are both kept?

5. Why are the accounts Shipments to Branch and Shipments from Home Office needed in addition to Sales and Purchases in preparing the profit and loss statements for the branch and the home office?

6. The following branch office account was taken from the ledger kept in the home office of L. C. Ryan Company. Give the corresponding entries that were made in the records of the San Francisco Branch.

SAN FRANCISCO BRANCH OFFICE

1954				1954			
April	6	Cash	5,000	May	31	Loss	900
	30	Profit	2,100	June	20	Cash	2,000
May	13	Display Equip.	3,000				
June	30	Profit	4,000				

7. The following home office account was taken from the branch office ledger of Cole & Porter, Inc. Give the journal entries that were made on the books of the home office.

HOME OFFICE

1954				1954			
June	30	Loss	800	Feb.	6	Cash	4,000
Aug.	14	Cash	2,400	Mar.	2	Furn. & Fix.	5,000
				Dec.	31	Profit	3,000

8. Does the ledger account in Question 7 contain all the entries during the period? If not, what entries are omitted?

9. Give the journal entries to record the following transactions on the books of the branch. (This is not a complete list of transactions for the period.)

Oct. 1. The branch receives from the home office: cash, $1,500; furniture and fixtures, $450; merchandise at cost, $2,700.
    4. The branch purchases merchandise on account from an outside firm, $1,200.
    8. The branch sells merchandise on account for $2,400; for cash, $1,200.
  15. The branch pays general operating expenses of $400.
  21. The branch sends the home office $500 in cash.
  24. The branch receives merchandise at cost, $1,100, from the home office.
  30. The branch reports a net profit of $750.

10. The Glenway Co. maintains accounts entitled Evanston Branch Office and Berwyn Branch Office. Each branch maintains an account entitled Home Office. The Berwyn branch received instructions from the home office to ship to the Evanston branch merchandise costing $750 that had been received from the home office. Give the journal entry to record the transfer of the merchandise on the books of (a) the home office, (b) the Berwyn branch, and (c) the Evanston branch.

11. Modern Fashions opened a branch store on July 1. Between that date and the end of the year, the shipments of merchandise to the branch, billed at selling price, totaled $120,000. Net sales of the branch for the period totaled $105,000, and the inventory, taken at billed (selling) prices, totaled $15,000. The goods shipped to the branch were uniformly marked up 50% on cost in order to give a gross profit rate of $33\frac{1}{3}\%$. Determine (a) the gross profit on sales of the branch and (b) the cost price of the inventory at the branch.

PROBLEMS

26-1. Stanton, Inc., of Chicago, opened a branch office in Denver on January 1, 1954. Transactions and adjustments reflecting branch operations for the year ended December 31, 1954, were as follows:

(a) Cash advanced by the home office, $60,000.
(b) Shipments of merchandise from the home office to the branch, $387,000.
(c) Sales for cash by the branch, $400,000.
(d) Remittances to home office, $250,000.
(e) Operating expenses paid in cash by the branch, $50,000. (Charge Operating Expenses Control.)
(f) Merchandise inventory, December 31, 1954, $57,000.

Instructions: (1) Set up "T" accounts for the branch office as follows: Cash, Merchandise Inventory, Home Office, Profit and Loss Summary, Sales, Shipments from Home Office, and Operating Expenses Control. Record the foregoing transactions and adjustments in these accounts.

(2) Set up "T" accounts for the home office as follows: Cash, Branch Office, Profit of Branch, and Shipments to Branch. Record the effect of the transactions on these accounts.

(3) Close the branch office income and expense accounts to Profit and Loss Summary and the balance of Profit and Loss Summary to Home Office. Record the branch profit in the home office "T" accounts.

(4) Prepare a profit and loss statement and a balance sheet for the branch.

26-2. The trial balance of the home office and that of the branch of the Juel Corporation on July 31, 1954, the close of a monthly fiscal period, are given below:

| | HOME OFFICE | | BRANCH | |
	DR.	CR.	DR.	CR.
Cash........................	$150,000		$ 30,000	
Merchandise Inventory.........	160,000		80,000	
Branch Office..................	90,000			
Accounts Payable..............		$ 60,000		$ 15,000
Home Office...................				90,000
Capital Stock..................		200,000		
Surplus.......................		70,000		
Sales.........................		190,000		110,000
Shipments to Branch...........		75,000		
Purchases.....................	130,000		20,000	
Shipments from Home Office....			75,000	
Operating Expenses Control.....	65,000		10,000	
	$595,000	$595,000	$215,000	$215,000

Merchandise Inventory, July 31: home office, $140,000; branch, $85,000.

Instructions: (1) Prepare a profit and loss statement and a balance sheet for the branch.

(2) Prepare a profit and loss statement and a balance sheet for the home office.

(3) Prepare a work sheet for a consolidated profit and loss statement and a work sheet for a consolidated balance sheet.

(4) Prepare a consolidated profit and loss statement and a consolidated balance sheet.

26-3. Lardner, Inc., of Columbus, Ohio, operates a branch in Toledo. On April 30, 1954, the post-closing trial balance of the home office and that of the branch were as follows:

| | HOME OFFICE | | BRANCH | |
	DR.	CR.	DR.	CR.
Cash........................	$45,000		$ 3,000	
Merchandise Inventory.......	36,000		15,000	
Branch Office...............	18,000			
Home Office.................				$18,000
Capital Stock...............		$75,000		
Surplus.....................		24,000		
	$99,000	$99,000	$18,000	$18,000

The transactions and adjustments for May were as follows:

(a) Merchandise shipped from the home office to the branch, $30,000.

(b) All sales were for cash: home office, $60,000; branch office, $30,000.

(c) The following cash expenditures were made:

	HOME OFFICE	BRANCH
Merchandise purchases........	$70,200	
Operating expenses..........	4,000	$2,200
	$74,200	$2,200

(d) Inventories:

	HOME OFFICE	BRANCH
Merchandise................	$30,000	$18,000

Instructions: (1) Open "T" accounts as follows for the home office: Cash; Merchandise Inventory; Branch Office; Capital Stock; Surplus; Profit and Loss Summary; Sales; Shipments to Branch; Purchases; Operating Expenses Control; and Profit or Loss of Branch. Open the following "T" accounts for the branch: Cash; Merchandise Inventory; Home Office; Profit and Loss Summary; Sales; Shipments from Home Office; and Operating Expenses Control.

(2) Record the beginning balances and the transactions and adjustments for May directly in the "T" accounts (no journal entries required).

(3) Close the branch office ledger.

(4) Record branch profit or loss in the home office ledger. Close the home office ledger.

Chapter 27

Accounting for Manufacturing

DESCRIPTION OF MANUFACTURING OPERATIONS — Thus far, consideration has been given to the accounting procedures used by service and mercantile enterprises. Mercantile enterprises obtain from manufacturing concerns the merchandise that they sell. Manufacturers employ labor and use machinery in converting raw materials into finished goods. In thus changing the form of the commodities, their activities differ from those of merchandisers.

The commodities purchased by a manufacturer are his raw materials, but they were finished goods to the manufacturer from whom he bought them. Flour is raw material to the baker but finished goods to the miller. Steel plate is raw material to the automobile manufacturer but finished goods to the steel producer. The designation *raw materials* or *finished goods* has significance only in connection with a specific manufacturer and his relation to the commodity.

The extent of business activity in manufacturing is apparent to anyone who contemplates the vast variety of changes in form that take place in producing the commodities and the services used by society. Manufacturing provides work for a large percentage of the employed, uses a large share of the capital equipment of the country, and makes possible a substantial portion of the profit shown on profit and loss statements.

Manufacturing activities require separate treatment in the accounts. Statements showing manufacturing operations are needed by business management. On manufacturing statements, payrolls for factory labor and expenses incident to the use of machinery are important items. Other expenses found in manufacturing include power to run the machinery, maintenance to keep it in condition, and supervision to plan and direct production.

Manufacturing adds many new items to the balance sheet and the profit and loss statement. New assets and liabilities are valued in new balance sheet accounts, and new operating activities are measured in new expense accounts. The general ledger is expanded to take care of the additional accounts, and new subsidiary ledgers account for much of the manufacturing detail. The treatment of these accounts, together with the recording and the summarizing of transactions

529

affecting the accounts, constitutes the subject matter of this chapter and the two following chapters.

BALANCE SHEET ACCOUNTS Each of the asset classifications on the balance sheet contains additional accounts as a result of the manufacturing function. Under "Current Assets" inventory accounts, factory supplies, and additional types of prepaid insurance are added; under "Fixed Assets" new accounts for various kinds of machinery and equipment are shown; under "Intangible Assets" accounts with such assets as patents and copyrights may be reported; and under "Deferred Charges to Expense" accounts of a long-term nature with prepaid expenses that are characteristic of the factory are shown. The liability accounts of a manufacturing enterprise are similar to those of other businesses, but even in this classification there is greater likelihood of bonds payable secured by mortgages on the manufacturing plant.

Current Assets. The single inventory of merchandise found on the balance sheet of a merchandising business is displaced by three inventories representing (1) goods in the state in which they were acquired, (2) goods in the process of manufacture, and (3) goods in the state in which they are to be sold. These inventories are called respectively *raw materials, work in process,* and *finished goods.* The costs of operating the factory, including labor and the various manufacturing expenses, are added to the cost of the raw materials in determining the cost of work in process and finished goods. These inventories are illustrated below:

MERCHANDISING		MANUFACTURING		
Merchandise Inventory	$15,000	Inventories:		
		Finished Goods	$20,000	
		Work in Process	15,000	
		Raw Materials	30,000	$65,000

Other current assets added are factory supplies on hand that were purchased to maintain and service machinery, prepaid insurance of various kinds, largely due to the use of machinery, and unused services that assist in manufacturing. The accounts entail additional adjusting entries to be made at the end of each accounting period.

Fixed Assets. Because of the extensive use of machinery in manufacturing, the percentage of capital invested in fixed assets tends to be larger than that of the trading concern. The building or buildings housing this machinery must be adapted to that purpose and are therefore usually owned by the manufacturer. The number of accounts with machinery and equipment is often sufficient to warrant the use of a machinery and equipment subsidiary ledger.

The subsidiary ledger carrying an account with each individual piece of machinery is called the *plant ledger*. Space is provided in the heading of each account for recording the model, size, and serial number of the machine, the name of the vendor from whom it was purchased, and other useful information. Columns are also provided for accumulating the periodic increase in the allowance for depreciation applicable to the machine and for recording the ever-diminishing book value of the machine. Such a record of each machine is thought to give better control over the machinery used and to provide a more accurate determination of the periodic depreciation charges. Fixed asset ledger accounts have been illustrated in Chapter 14.

Intangible Assets. The manufacturer may have exclusive rights to manufacture particular products. Such rights, called *patents*, are issued by the federal government. On the balance sheet patents are reported at cost less amortization. The life of a patent is 17 years, but its useful life may often be less because of the subsequent invention of new and improved devices. The estimated annual decrease in the value of the patent becomes a yearly manufacturing expense. Thus a patent acquired at a cost of $50,000 and having an estimated useful life of 10 years would be annually reduced in value $5,000. The amount of this reduction would be charged to the manufacturing cost of each year.

Exclusive rights, known as *copyrights*, to publish written material are granted for a period of 28 years; but they often have a useful life of a much shorter period. Because of the uncertainty regarding their useful life, these intangible assets are often written off the books over a short period of time by charges to operations.

Deferred Charges to Expense. Manufacturing activities add a number of new items to the deferred charges to expense. Prepayments that are chargeable to operations of a number of years, such as bonus payments to secure a long-term lease, should be exhibited in the balance sheet under the heading "Deferred Charges to Expense."

CAPITAL CHARGES AND REVENUE CHARGES   Quite often, especially in accounting for manufacturing enterprises, it becomes difficult to distinguish between expenditures that add to the value of fixed assets and those that are chargeable as current expenses. All expenditures incurred up to the time at which a fixed asset is ready for use should be considered a part of the cost of the asset; they should therefore be debited to the asset account. For example, the following items should be considered as the original cost of a machine purchased for use in a factory: (1) the purchase price as indicated by the purchase invoice, (2) the cost of transporting the machine from the place of business of the seller to the factory of the purchaser, (3) the cost of unpacking and setting up the machine, (4) the cost of installation (including the cost of constructing a metal or a concrete base), (5) the cost of testing to determine the usefulness of the machine, and (6) the cost of any changes or alterations necessary before the machine is in proper condition for operation.

After the fixed asset is put into service, only those expenditures that increase its life or efficiency may be added to its value. A machine with an estimated life of 4 years may be overhauled, or worn parts may be replaced, with the result that the life of the machine may be increased to 5 years. The cost of the overhauling or the replacement, to the extent of the value added through the increased life of the machine, may be added to the book value by charging the asset account or the related allowance for depreciation account. Such expenditures are said to be *charges to capital*. For example, assume that the replacement of certain moving parts, at a cost of $600, increases the output of a certain machine from 200 to 300 units per day. The entry for such an expenditure may be made as shown below:

Machinery and Equipment............................. 600
    Cash..   600

As an asset continues in use, some expenditures are necessary to maintain it in an efficient operating condition. A building requires repairs and paint, and taxes and insurance premiums must be paid. Machinery requires repairs from time to time, as well as supplies necessary for its operation, such as oil; taxes and insurance premiums must also be paid. Expenditures of this type, representing a part of the necessary cost of using the asset during the current period, should be charged as part of the current operating expenses of the business. These expenditures are said to be *charges to revenue* since they are deductible from the revenue of the period. For example, assume that the factory building was painted at a cost of $1,300. The entry for such an expenditure is shown below:

Painting Expense.................................. 1,300
    Cash..   1,300

Unless care is used, capital expenditures and revenue expenditures may be confused. For example, an expenditure which, if its effects were carefully analyzed, would be found to be necessary in the maintenance of a particular asset may be considered an addition to the value of the asset. On the other hand, a real addition to capital may be mistaken for an operating expense. The distinction between capital expenditures and revenue expenditures is an important one, since the reporting of manufacturing costs, the determination of the profit for each period, and the presentation of the proprietorship from time to time depend on the accuracy with which this distinction is made.

PROFIT AND LOSS STATEMENT ACCOUNTS   The profit and loss statement of a manufacturing enterprise contains groups of items representing selling expenses and general and administrative expenses similar to those of a trading enterprise. In addition, it contains an entirely new group of items representing purely manufacturing activities. This group includes the cost of raw materials put into production; the cost of labor used directly in converting the raw materials into finished goods; and the expenses that arise from labor not used directly and from all the facilities employed in the process. For convenience in analysis, these threefold groups are known as *materials*, *direct labor*, and *overhead*. Materials represent the delivered cost of raw materials that are used in producing the finished article. Direct labor represents the wages of the workmen who devote their time to converting the raw materials into work in process and finished goods. Overhead represents all the other expenses of operating the factory that are not included in the first two items.

The overhead items represent perhaps the most important group in present-day manufacturing. With increasing use of machinery, much of the factory payroll is related to the care and upkeep of the machinery rather than being applied directly to raw materials. Overhead includes not only taxes, insurance, depreciation, and maintenance incident to the use of machinery, but also all expenses of housing the machinery and furnishing satisfactory working conditions for employees. In fact, the overhead group includes all manufacturing expenses other than direct materials and direct labor.

THE COST OF GOODS MANUFACTURED SCHEDULE   Since manufacturing functions differ from trading functions, it is customary to separate the profit and loss statement accounts having to do with manufacturing from those having to do with trading. The manufacturing group is frequently placed in a separate schedule to avoid the presentation of an extended profit and loss statement. This schedule gives the cost of goods manufactured during the latest period. It is therefore comparable to that section of the profit and loss statement of a merchandising enterprise that shows the cost of goods purchased. When the schedule is used, the profit and loss statement of the manufacturing concern is similar to that of a trading company except for a reference to the supporting schedule showing the cost of goods manufactured.

Other schedules may be used to simplify the principal accounting statements by removing detail from them. In large enterprises having many accounts, it is customary to have a number of schedules supporting items on the balance sheet and the profit and loss statement. For example, the cash balance may be supported by a schedule giving the balances on deposit in several banks; the accounts receivable, by a schedule showing the names of the customers and the balances owed; the sales, by a schedule showing sales by territories or by commodities; and the selling expenses and general expenses, by schedules showing the individual items.

The schedule showing the cost of goods manufactured provides all of the information incident to the manufacturing activities of the period. In addition to beginning and ending inventories of raw materials and work in process, it contains purchases of new materials, labor items, and all manufacturing expenses.

THE PERIOD COVERED BY THE PROFIT AND LOSS STATEMENT Manufacturing operations frequently make advisable the choice of a fiscal year that differs from the calendar year. It is not uncommon for manufacturing concerns to choose as their fiscal year any period of twelve months that best fits in with the recurring cycle of their manufacturing activities. An attempt is usually made to make the close of the fiscal year come at a relatively inactive period.

Such a choice of fiscal year is called the *natural business year*. The use of the natural business year tends to make the interpretation of statements less complicated and more informative.

For control of manufacturing operations, it is advisable to have a much shorter reporting period than a year. It is customary therefore to have monthly interim reports for the use of management.

ADJUSTING AND CLOSING MANUFACTURING ACCOUNTS The adjusting of manufacturing accounts is similar to the adjusting of trading accounts. When inventories of supplies, such as factory supplies, exist, and when expenses, such as insurance, have been prepaid, only the amounts actually consumed are charged to manufacturing. When unrecorded liabilities, such as accrued wages of factory workers and accrued taxes, exist, the liabilities and the related expenses should be provided for by adjusting entries.

When the accounts of a manufacturing enterprise are to be closed, all the accounts pertaining to the manufacturing process, which are ordinarily presented in the schedule of the cost of goods manufactured, are closed first. It is advisable to close these accounts into an account called *Manufacturing Summary*. The balance of this account is the cost of goods manufactured during the period. The balance of the manufacturing summary account is closed to the profit and loss summary account. The items appearing on the profit and loss statement are then closed to the profit and loss summary account.

The relation of the manufacturing summary account to the profit and loss summary account is shown below:

MANUFACTURING SUMMARY

1954			1954		
June 30	Work in Process Inventory (beginning)	20,000	June 30	Work in Process Inventory (ending)	26,000
30	Raw Materials Inventory (beginning)	42,000	30	Raw Materials Inventory (ending)	48,725
30	Raw Materials Purchases	120,000	30	Raw Materials Returns and Allowances	2,600
30	Freight In	3,400	30	To Profit and Loss Summary	285,825
30	Direct Labor	98,750			
30	Manufacturing Expenses (total)	79,000			
		363,150			363,150

PROFIT AND LOSS SUMMARY

1954		
June 30	From Manufacturing Summary	285,825

The items closed to Manufacturing Summary are reported on the schedule of cost of goods manufactured, which is illustrated later in the chapter. The amount transferred from Manufacturing Summary to Profit and Loss Summary, $285,825, is the cost of goods manufactured during the period.

THE WORK SHEET OF A MANUFACTURING ENTERPRISE   An additional pair of columns is added to the work sheet of a manufacturing enterprise in order to segregate the accounts used in determining the cost of goods manufactured. All items that enter into the

THE PARKER MANUFACTURING COMPANY
WORK SHEET
FOR YEAR ENDED JUNE 30, 1954

Account Titles	Trial Balance Dr.	Trial Balance Cr.	Adjustments Dr.	Adjustments Cr.	Manufacturing Schedule Dr.	Manufacturing Schedule Cr.	Profit and Loss Statement Dr.	Profit and Loss Statement Cr.	Balance Sheet Dr.	Balance Sheet Cr.
Cash	10,390								10,390	
Accounts Receivable	48,000								48,000	
Allowance for Bad Debts		450		(a) 2,050						2,500
Finished Goods Inventory	25,000		(c) 41,000	(b) 25,000					41,000	
Work in Process Inventory	20,000		(e) 26,000	(d) 20,000					26,000	
Raw Materials Inventory	42,000		(g) 48,725	(f) 42,000					48,725	
Factory Supplies	10,000			(h) 6,000					4,000	
Shipping Department Supplies	7,000			(i) 3,800					3,200	
Office Supplies	6,500			(j) 5,000					1,500	
Prepaid Insurance	4,000			(k) 2,600					1,400	
Office Equipment	18,000								18,000	
Allow. for Depr. of Office Equipment		6,000		(l) 1,800						7,800
Shipping Department Equipment	16,000								16,000	
Allow. for Depr. of Shipping Dept. Equip.		2,200		(m) 1,600						3,800
Machinery and Equipment	160,000								160,000	
Allow. for Depr. of Machinery and Equip.		44,000		(n) 16,000						60,000
Buildings	105,000								105,000	
Allow. for Depr. of Buildings		17,000		(o) 5,250						22,250
Land	55,000								55,000	
Patents	25,000			(p) 3,000					22,000	
Accounts Payable		60,000								60,000
First-Mortgage 5% Bonds Payable		95,000								95,000
Common Stock		140,000								140,000
Surplus		129,000								129,000
Sales		413,000						413,000		
Sales Returns and Allowances	3,000						3,000			
Raw Materials Purchases	120,000				120,000					
Freight In	3,400				3,400					
Purchases Returns and Allowances		2,600				2,600				
Direct Labor	97,860		(r) 890		98,750					
Indirect Labor	9,000		(r) 300		9,300					
Superintendence	10,000				10,000					
Maintenance and Repairs	8,000				8,000					
Heat, Light, and Power	11,800				11,800					
Property Taxes	5,000				5,000					
Totals Carried Forward	819,950	909,250	116,915	134,100	266,250	2,600	3,000	413,000	560,215	520,350

Account	Trial Balance Dr.	Trial Balance Cr.	Adjustments Dr.	Adjustments Cr.	Cost of Goods Manufactured Dr.	Cost of Goods Manufactured Cr.	Income Statement Dr.	Income Statement Cr.	Balance Sheet Dr.	Balance Sheet Cr.
Totals Brought Forward	819,950	909,250	116,915	134,100	266,250	2,600	3,000	413,000	560,215	520,350
Sundry Factory Expense	2,050				2,050					
Sales Salaries and Commissions	21,000		(r) 700				21,700			
Traveling Expense	6,800						6,800			
Advertising Expense	19,300						19,300			
Shipping Department Salaries	4,500		(r) 110				4,610			
Sundry Shipping Department Expense	660						660			
Officers Salaries	20,400						20,400			
Office Salaries	8,300						8,300			
Sundry Office Expense	2,790						2,790			
Purchases Discount		2,100						2,100		
Bond Interest Expense	5,600		(q) 1,700				7,300			
	911,350	911,350								
Bad Debts Expense			(a) 2,050				2,050			
Manufacturing Summary			(d) 20,000 / (f) 42,000	(e) 26,000 / (g) 48,725	20,000 / 42,000	26,000 / 48,725				
Profit and Loss Summary				(c) 41,000				41,000		
Depreciation of Office Equipment			(g) 25,000				25,000			
Depreciation of Shipping Dept. Equipment			(i) 1,800				1,800			
Depreciation of Machinery and Equipment			(n) 16,000		16,000					
Depreciation of Buildings			(o) 5,250		5,250					
Patents Expense			(m) 1,600 / (p) 3,000		3,000		1,600			
Factory Supplies Expense			(h) 6,000		6,000					
Shipping Department Supplies Expense			(l) 3,800				3,800			
Office Supplies Expense			(j) 5,000				5,000			
Insurance Expense			(k) 2,600		2,600					
Interest Payable				(q) 1,700						1,700
Wages Payable				(r) 2,000						2,000
			253,525	253,525						
Cost of Goods Manufactured						285,825	285,825			
					363,150	363,150	419,935		560,215	524,050
Estimated Income Taxes							13,300			13,300
Net Profit after Estimated Income Taxes							22,865			22,865
							456,100	456,100	560,215	560,215

Work Sheet of a Manufacturing Enterprise

cost of goods manufactured, or that are deductions from the cost of goods manufactured, are entered in the Manufacturing Schedule columns. The difference between the totals of the Manufacturing Schedule columns is the cost of goods manufactured. This amount is transferred to the Profit and Loss Statement columns.

The use of the Adjustments columns is similar to the use of those in the work sheet illustrated in Chapter 10. The chief difference is the addition of new items having to do with manufacturing operations.

PREPARING THE PERIODIC SUMMARY The preparation of the periodic summary may be illustrated from the records of The Parker Manufacturing Company. At the end of the fiscal year, June 30, 1954, a trial balance is taken. This trial balance is entered in the first pair of amount columns on the work sheet in the manner shown in the illustration on pages 536 and 537. The accounts are then examined, and the additional data that will be needed in adjusting the accounts to make them show present facts are obtained. The data for the adjustments are:

(1) Allowance for bad debts, ½ of 1 % of net sales.

(2) Inventories:

Finished goods	$41,000
Work in process	26,000
Raw materials	48,725
Factory supplies	4,000
Shipping department supplies	3,200
Office supplies	1,500

(3) Prepaid insurance 1,400

(4) Depreciation and amortization:

Office equipment	10%
Shipping department equipment	10%
Machinery and equipment	10%
Buildings	5%
Patents	3,000

(5) Accrued expenses:

Interest accrued on bonds payable	1,700
Payroll:	
Direct labor	890
Indirect labor	300
Sales salaries	700
Shipping department salaries	110

(6) Property taxes, insurance expense, and building expenses are chargeable to manufacturing.

The treatment of these adjustments on the work sheet, except those for the work in process, the raw materials, and the finished goods inventories, is similar to that explained and illustrated in earlier chapters. The work in process inventory account and the raw materials inventory account are adjusted through the manufacturing summary account because all manufacturing expenses are summarized in this account.

The raw materials inventory at the beginning of the fiscal period has become a part of the cost of goods manufactured. Raw Materials Inventory is therefore credited for the value of the beginning inventory, $42,000, and Manufacturing Summary is debited for the same amount. The raw materials inventory at the end of the period must be recorded as an asset and must be shown as a deduction from the cost of goods manufactured. Raw Materials Inventory is therefore debited for $48,725, and Manufacturing Summary is credited for the same amount.

In a like manner, the inventory of work in process at the beginning of the period must be transferred to the manufacturing summary account, and the work in process at the end of the period must be deducted from the cost of work in process and must be shown as an asset. The first transfer is accomplished by crediting Work in Process Inventory and by debiting Manufacturing Summary for $20,000. The second transfer is accomplished by debiting Work in Process Inventory and by crediting Manufacturing Summary for $26,000.

The finished goods inventory account is adjusted through the profit and loss summary account in the same manner as the merchandise inventory of a mercantile business. The finished goods inventory at the beginning of the period is transferred to the profit and loss summary account by crediting Finished Goods Inventory for $25,000 and by debiting Profit and Loss Summary for the same amount. The finished goods inventory at the end of the period is recorded by debiting Finished Goods Inventory for $41,000 and by crediting Profit and Loss Summary for the same amount.

After the Adjustments columns have been totaled to prove the equality of debits and credits, all items representing the cost of goods manufactured are extended into the columns headed "Manufacturing Schedule." These items include the raw materials purchases, the freight in, the purchases returns and allowances, the direct labor, all manufacturing expenses, and the costs and deductions from costs arising from the inventories of raw materials and work in process at the beginning and the end of the fiscal period. The balance of each item, except the items written on a line with "Manufacturing Summary," is extended into the proper column. The items appearing opposite "Manufacturing Summary" represent the inventories of raw materials and work in process at the beginning and the end of the fiscal period.

As will be seen later, these inventories are used in the manufacturing schedule and are therefore entered individually in the Manufacturing Schedule columns. The difference between the totals of the Manufacturing Schedule columns represents the cost of goods manufactured. This amount is carried forward into the Profit and Loss Statement Dr. column.

The balances of the income accounts are extended into the Profit and Loss Statement Cr. column, and the balances of all expense accounts that do not represent manufacturing expenses are extended into the Profit and Loss Statement Dr. column. The amounts of the assets, the liabilities, and the proprietorship are carried forward into the proper Balance Sheet columns in the same manner as they are in the preparation of a work sheet for a trading concern. The amount of estimated income taxes payable is then calculated. The estimated income taxes and the net profit after income taxes are then entered in the Profit and Loss Statement Dr. column and the Balance Sheet Cr. column, and the columns are totaled and ruled.

The profit and loss statement of The Parker Manufacturing Company is shown in the illustration on page 541. All the data required for this statement, including the cost of goods manufactured, have been obtained from the Profit and Loss Statement columns of the work sheet. The cost of goods manufactured is reported as a single amount, and reference is made to the schedule that shows how the amount was determined.

The cost of goods manufactured schedule is shown on page 542. This schedule contains the same amounts as those shown in the Manufacturing Schedule columns of the work sheet. The amounts are arranged, however, so that the desired information can be obtained readily. The right-hand amount column contains the beginning work in process inventory. To this amount is added the total of the elements of manufacturing cost for the period, and from this sum the ending work in process inventory is subtracted to obtain the cost of the goods completed during the year. The amount column second from the right contains the three elements of cost: the materials used, the direct labor, and the total of the manufacturing expenses.

The cost of raw materials consumed is made up of the beginning inventory of raw materials, the purchases made during the period, and the freight in on the purchases, less the purchases returns and allowances and the ending inventory. The manufacturing expenses, totaling $79,000, consist of all expenses incident to operating the factory except labor applied directly to the conversion of raw materials into finished goods.

THE PARKER MANUFACTURING COMPANY
PROFIT AND LOSS STATEMENT
FOR YEAR ENDED JUNE 30, 1954

Income from Sales:		
Gross Sales....................................	$413,000	
Less Sales Returns and Allowances.................	3,000	
Net Sales.....................................		$410,000
Cost of Goods Sold:		
Finished Goods Inventory, July 1, 1953.............	$ 25,000	
Cost of Goods Manufactured (Schedule 1)............	285,825	
Total Cost of Finished Goods Available for Sale..	$310,825	
Less Finished Goods Inventory, June 30, 1954........	41,000	
Cost of Goods Sold..............................		269,825
Gross Profit on Sales..............................		$140,175
Operating Expenses:		
Selling Expenses:		
Sales Salaries and Commissions.......... $21,700		
Traveling Expense..................... 6,800		
Advertising Expense................... 19,300		
Total Selling Expenses........................	$ 47,800	
Shipping Department Expenses:		
Shipping Department Salaries........... $ 4,610		
Depr. of Shipping Dept. Equip........... 1,600		
Shipping Dept. Supplies Expense........ 3,800		
Sundry Shipping Dept. Expense......... 660		
Total Shipping Department Expenses............	**10,670**	
General Expenses:		
Officers Salaries...................... $20,400		
Office Salaries......................... 8,300		
Depreciation of Office Equipment........ 1,800		
Office Supplies Expense................. 5,000		
Bad Debts Expense.................... 2,050		
Sundry Office Expense.................. 2,790		
Total General Expenses.......................	40,340	
Total Operating Expenses........................		98,810
Net Profit from Operations........................		$ 41,365
Other Income:		
Purchases Discount..............................	$ 2,100	
Other Expense:		
Bond Interest Expense...........................	7,300	
Net Deduction...................................		5,200
Net Profit Before Estimated Income Taxes............		$ 36,165
Less Estimated Income Taxes......................		13,300
Net Profit After Estimated Income Taxes.............		$ 22,865

Profit and Loss Statement of a Manufacturing Enterprise

THE PARKER MANUFACTURING COMPANY
Cost of Goods Manufactured — Schedule 1
For Year Ended June 30, 1954

Work in Process Inventory, July 1, 1953.....			$ 20,000
Raw Materials:			
Inventory, July 1, 1953................		$ 42,000	
Purchases............................	$120,000		
Freight In...........................	3,400		
Delivered Cost of Purchases.............	$123,400		
Less Purchases Returns and Allowances....	2,600		
Net Purchases........................		120,800	
Total Cost of Materials Available for Use...		$162,800	
Less Inventory, June 30, 1954.............		48,725	
Cost of Materials Consumed.............		$114,075	
Direct Labor...........................		98,750	
Manufacturing Expenses:			
Indirect Labor.........................	$ 9,300		
Superintendence.......................	10,000		
Maintenance and Repairs...............	8,000		
Heat, Light, and Power.................	11,800		
Property Taxes........................	5,000		
Depreciation of Machinery and Equipment.	16,000		
Depreciation of Buildings...............	5,250		
Patents Expense......................	3,000		
Factory Supplies Expense...............	6,000		
Insurance Expense.....................	2,600		
Sundry Factory Expense.................	2,050		
Total Manufacturing Expenses...........		79,000	
Total Manufacturing Costs..............			291,825
Total Work in Process during Period.......			$311,825
Less Work in Process Inventory, June 30, 1954			26,000
Cost of Goods Manufactured.................................			$285,825

Cost of Goods Manufactured Schedule

The order in which the items are listed on the schedule follows the sequence of operations in the factory. At the beginning of a period there are unfinished goods, represented by the beginning work in process inventory. During the period materials, labor, and manufacturing expenses are added to this inventory. At the end of the period the work in process is inventoried. This amount is subtracted from the sum of the beginning work in process inventory and the materials, labor, and manufacturing expenses. The result is the cost of the goods manufactured.

THE PARKER MANUFACTURING COMPANY
BALANCE SHEET
JUNE 30, 1954

ASSETS

Current Assets:

Cash		$ 10,390
Accounts Receivable	$ 48,000	
Less Allowance for Bad Debts	2,500	45,500
Inventories:		
Finished Goods	$ 41,000	
Work in Process	26,000	
Raw Materials (lower of cost or market)	48,725	115,725
Factory Supplies		4,000
Shipping Department Supplies		3,200
Office Supplies		1,500
Prepaid Insurance		1,400
Total Current Assets		$181,715

Fixed Assets:

Office Equipment	$ 18,000		
Less Allowance for Depreciation	7,800	$ 10,200	
Shipping Department Equipment	$ 16,000		
Less Allowance for Depreciation	3,800	12,200	
Machinery and Equipment	$160,000		
Less Allowance for Depreciation	60,000	100,000	
Buildings	$105,000		
Less Allowance for Depreciation	22,250	82,750	
Land		55,000	
Total Fixed Assets			260,150

Intangible Assets:

Patents	22,000
Total Assets	$463,865

LIABILITIES

Current Liabilities:

Accounts Payable	$ 60,000	
Wages Payable	2,000	
Interest Payable	1,700	
Estimated Income Taxes Payable	13,300	
Total Current Liabilities		$ 77,000

Fixed Liabilities:

First-Mortgage 5% Bonds Payable (due 1959)	95,000
Total Liabilities	$172,000

CAPITAL

Common Stock ($100 par)	$140,000	
Retained Earnings	151,865	
Total Capital		291,865
Total Liabilities and Capital		$463,865

Balance Sheet of a Manufacturing Enterprise

The distinction between manufacturing costs and cost of goods manufactured is shown in the schedule on page 542. Manufacturing costs consist of materials used, $114,075, direct labor, $98,750, and manufacturing expenses, $79,000, a total of $291,825. Cost of goods manufactured takes into account the two work in process inventories and amounts to $285,825.

The balance sheet of The Parker Manufacturing Company is shown on page 543. Three inventories, instead of one, are reported on this balance sheet; the current assets include Factory Supplies; the fixed assets include Machinery and Equipment; and an intangible asset, Patents, appears on the report. The liabilities include a current liability, Wages Payable, and a fixed liability, First-Mortgage 5% Bonds Payable.

After the financial reports have been prepared, the adjusting and closing entries are recorded in the general journal. The Adjustments columns of the work sheet are used as the basis for these entries. Since all manufacturing costs are to be summarized in an account called Manufacturing Summary, the adjustments for the raw materials inventory and the work in process inventory are posted to this account. The adjustments for the finished goods inventory are posted to the profit and loss summary account.

After the adjustments have been recorded, the closing entries are made. All manufacturing items are transferred to the manufacturing summary account. The balance of the manufacturing summary account is then a debit that represents the cost of goods manufactured. The balance is transferred to the profit and loss summary account, and all remaining income and expense items are closed into the same account. The balance of the profit and loss summary account then represents the profit or the loss for the period and, after provision for any income taxes, is transferred to Surplus. The manufacturing summary account of The Parker Manufacturing Company is shown on page 545.

VALUATION OF THE INVENTORIES OF A MANUFACTURING ENTERPRISE The valuation of the inventory of raw materials at the end of a fiscal period does not differ from the practice followed in trading concerns. Cost or market prices are available and are used. The inventory value of finished goods and of work in process must be built up from raw materials by adding direct labor and overhead items. This computation involves the use of estimates based on information derived largely from the accounting records.

In estimating the cost of finished goods and work in process, it has become customary to consider the cost as being composed of three

MANUFACTURING SUMMARY Acct. No. 31.5

1954					1954				
June	30	Work in Process Inv. 7/1/53	J21	20,000	June	30	Work in Process Inv. 6/30/54	J21	26,000
	30	Raw Mat. Inv. 7/1/53	J21	42,000		30	Raw Mat. Inv. 6/30/54	J21	48,725
	30	Raw Mat. Purchases	J22	120,000		30	Pur. Ret. and Allow.	J22	2,600
	30	Freight In	J22	3,400		30	Cost of Goods Mfd. (To		
	30	Direct Labor	J22	98,750			Profit and Loss Sum-		
	30	Indirect Labor	J22	9,300			mary)	J23	285,825
	30	Superintendence	J22	10,000					
	30	Maintenance and Re-pairs	J22	8,000					
	30	Heat, Light, and Power	J22	11,800					
	30	Property Taxes	J22	5,000					
	30	Depr. of Mach. and Equip.	J22	16,000					
	30	Depr. of Buildings	J22	5,250					
	30	Patents Expense	J22	3,000					
	30	Factory Supplies Exp.	J22	6,000					
	30	Insurance Exp.	J22	2,600					
	30	Sundry Factory Exp.	J22	2,050					
				363,150					363,150

Manufacturing Summary Account

elements: raw materials, direct labor, and overhead. The raw materials and the direct labor are embodied in the goods being produced and represent direct costs. All other costs, which are not directly identifiable with goods being produced and which apply to the factory as a whole, are called indirect costs and are reported under the heading "Manufacturing Expenses" on the cost of goods manufactured schedule. Included with manufacturing expenses are the cost of indirect labor and that of factory supplies used. Factory supplies may be considered indirect materials since they represent materials used to facilitate production within the factory. The total of the manufacturing expenses, including indirect materials and indirect labor, comprises the item overhead. Factory overhead is commonly expressed as a percentage of the direct labor cost. By referring to the figures on the cost of goods manufactured schedule on page 542, the following percentage of overhead to direct labor is obtained:

$$\text{Ratio of Overhead to Direct Labor Cost } \frac{\$79,000}{\$98,750} = 80\%$$

The valuation of the work in process and the finished goods requires information regarding the cost of direct materials, the cost of direct labor, and the overhead rate. In estimating the value of finished goods at $41,000 and that of work in process at $26,000, The Parker Manufacturing Company prepared the following summaries:

FINISHED WORK
COST PER UNIT

	DIRECT MA-TERIALS	DIRECT LABOR	OVERHEAD (80% OF DIRECT LABOR)	TOTAL COST PER UNIT	No. OF UNITS	TOTAL COST OF COMMODITY INVENTORY
Commodity A . .	$5.50	$2.50	$2.00	$10.00	2,500	$25,000.00
Commodity B . .	2.20	1.00	.80	4.00	4,000	16,000.00

Total Value of Finished Work $41,000.00

WORK IN PROCESS
COST PER UNIT

	DIRECT MA-TERIALS	DIRECT LABOR	OVERHEAD (80% OF DIRECT LABOR)	TOTAL COST PER UNIT	No. OF UNITS	TOTAL COST OF COMMODITY INVENTORY
Commodity A . .	$3.10	$ .50	$ .40	$ 4.00	1,000	$ 4,000.00
Commodity A . .	2.85	1.50	1.20	5.55	2,000	11,100.00
Commodity B . .	1.10	.50	.40	2.00	3,500	7,000.00
Commodity B . .	1.47	.85	.68	3.00	1,300	3,900.00

Total Value of Work in Process $26,000.00

The cost of any item in the finished goods or the work in process inventory is thus seen to be made up of the three elements mentioned previously. For example, the cost per unit of Commodity A in the finished goods inventory results from the following combination:

Direct Materials	$ 5.50
Direct Labor	2.50
Overhead (80% of Direct Labor)	2.00
Total Estimated Cost Per Unit	$10.00

PERPETUAL OR BOOK INVENTORIES The accounting procedures described in this chapter require the taking of physical inventories of raw materials, work in process, and finished goods whenever a balance sheet and a profit and loss statement are prepared. To take these inventories monthly would require a great deal of time and labor and would interfere with manufacturing operations. As a substitute for physical inventories, perpetual or book inventories are being increasingly used.

When book inventories are kept in a manufacturing plant, accounts are set up with raw materials, work in process, and finished goods;

and entries debiting and crediting these accounts are made currently. For example, the raw materials account is debited for each receipt of raw materials and is credited for each withdrawal of raw materials for manufacturing. The balance of the account gives the amount of raw materials that should be on hand. It is therefore not necessary to take a physical inventory of raw materials to determine the balance for statement purposes. It is necessary only to check occasionally the balance of the account with the quantity on hand.

When book inventories of all three manufacturing inventory items are kept, the system of accounting is known as cost accounting. A description of cost accounting as it is found in manufacturing or trading concerns is presented in the following two chapters. Under a cost accounting system, it is possible to prepare monthly balance sheets and profit and loss statements with accompanying schedules of cost of goods manufactured, without the cessation of operations that is necessary when physical inventories have to be taken.

QUESTIONS

1. List three current assets and three other assets that are commonly found in the records of a manufacturing business but not in those of a trading business.

2. Indicate the types of manufacturing enterprises to which the following commodities are raw materials and those to which the same commodities are finished goods: (The first item is given as an example.)

COMMODITY	FINISHED GOODS TO	RAW MATERIALS TO
flour	flour-milling business	bakery
suit fabrics		
storage batteries		
lumber		
lacquer		
sugar		
leather		
Yale locks		

3. (a) Are the items designated as manufacturing expenses more closely related to direct materials or direct labor? (b) As a group should they be applied as a percentage of the direct materials cost or the direct labor cost?

4. In a given factory the materials used amount to $160,000, of which $30,000 represents indirect materials. The payroll amounts to $140,000, of which $20,000 represents indirect labor. The other manufacturing expenses amount to $40,000. If overhead is applied as a percentage of the direct labor cost, what is the inventory value of a finished article having a direct materials cost of $60 and a direct labor cost of $50?

5. Howard Elder, C.P.A., finds real estate valued at $25,000 on the balance sheet of Ferson and Lee, Inc. The account in the ledger shows that the land was purchased for $8,000 ten years ago and was held for six years before a building was erected at a cost of $17,000. Taxes and assessments during the ten years amounted to $2,500, of which amount $1,200 occurred prior to the erection of the building. The estimated life of the building is twenty years with a salvage value of $1,000. What correcting entry or entries should be made?

6. Which of the following sentences are true? Which are false?

(a) The percentage of capital invested in fixed assets is larger in manufacturing than it is in merchandising.

(b) The decrease in patent values should be shown in an allowance for depreciation account.

(c) Copyrights should be charged off evenly over 28 years.

(d) Revenue charges are deductible from the revenue of the current period.

(e) The manufacturing schedule includes the finished goods inventories.

(f) Market prices are used for valuing finished goods inventories.

7. From the following items, select those needed and construct a cost of goods manufactured schedule for the Blair Manufacturing Company for March.

Raw Materials Purchased	$90,000
Direct Labor	95,000
Finished Goods Inventory, March 1	55,000
Raw Materials Inventory, March 1	30,000
Freight In	2,500
Work in Process Inventory, March 1	15,000
Sales Commissions	20,000
Manufacturing Expense	60,000
Finished Goods Inventory, March 31	90,000
Purchases Returns	6,000
Work in Process Inventory, March 31	20,000
Raw Materials Inventory, March 31	36,700

8. The cost of goods manufactured schedule of the Steele Manufacturing Company for the year ended on October 31, 1954, shows raw materials consumed, $15,000; direct labor, $40,000; overhead, $30,000; ending work in process inventory, $12,000. (a) What is the relation between the overhead and the direct labor? (b) If the direct labor cost of the goods in process inventory is $4,000, what is the direct materials cost?

PROBLEMS

27-1. A cost of goods manufactured schedule is shown on the following page:

THE TILDEN CORPORATION
Cost of Goods Manufactured Schedule
For Year Ended December 31, 1954

Work in Process Inventory, January 1, 1954		$ 70,000
Raw Materials:		
Inventory, January 1, 1954............	$200,000	
Purchases.........................	320,000	
Total Cost of Materials Available for Use.	$520,000	
Less Inventory, December 31, 1954......	225,000	
Cost of Materials Consumed.............	$295,000	
Direct Labor........................	150,000	
Manufacturing Expenses:		
Indirect Labor............. $65,000		
Depreciation Expense............. 27,500		
Sundry Manufacturing Expense......... 47,250		
Total Manufacturing Expenses........	139,750	
Total Manufacturing Costs.............		584,750
Total Work in Process During Period......		$654,750
Less Work in Process Inventory, December 31, 1954...........................		54,750
Cost of Goods Manufactured............		$600,000

Instructions: (1) Prepare journal entries to adjust the raw materials inventory account and the work in process inventory account on December 31, 1954, the end of the fiscal year.

(2) Prepare the journal entry to close the purchases, the direct labor, and the manufacturing expense accounts to the manufacturing summary account.

(3) Prepare the journal entry to close the manufacturing summary account.

(4) Set up a manufacturing summary account and post the foregoing entries affecting it.

27-2. The work sheet for the Miller Manufacturing Company, without the Adjustment columns, for the year ended December 31, 1954, is given on page 550.

Instructions: (1) Based on the work sheet on page 550, prepare the following journal entries:

(a) To record inventory adjustments, depreciation, patent write off, factory supplies used, and bond interest and discount.

(b) To close the manufacturing accounts into the manufacturing summary account.

(c) To close the manufacturing summary account and the profit and loss accounts to the profit and loss summary account.

MILLER MANUFACTURING COMPANY
Work Sheet
For Year Ended December 31, 1954

Name of Account	Trial Balance Dr.	Trial Balance Cr.	Manufacturing Schedule Dr.	Manufacturing Schedule Cr.	Profit and Loss Statement Dr.	Profit and Loss Statement Cr.	Balance Sheet Dr.	Balance Sheet Cr.
Cash in Bank	70,000						70,000	
Finished Goods Inventory	35,000						25,000	
Work in Process Inventory	52,000						50,000	
Raw Materials Inventory	10,000						12,000	
Factory Supplies	14,000						7,000	
Machinery and Equipment	200,000						200,000	
Allow. for Depr. of Mach. and Equipment		120,000						140,000
Buildings	160,000						160,000	
Allow. for Depr. of Buildings		48,000						56,000
Land	90,000						90,000	
Patents	16,000						15,000	
4% First-Mortgage Bonds		100,000						100,000
Discount on Bonds	4,000						3,000	
Common Stock		150,000						150,000
Unappropriated Earned Surplus		72,000						62,000
Reserve for Bond Sinking Fund		60,000						70,000
Sales		700,000				700,000		
Raw Material Purchases	125,000		125,000					
Direct Labor	180,000		180,000					
Indirect Labor	85,000		85,000					
Miscellaneous Factory Expense	64,000		64,000					
Operating Expense (control)	145,000				145,000			
	1,250,000	1,250,000						
Profit and Loss Summary					35,000	25,000		
Mfg. Summary — Work in Process			52,000	50,000				
Mfg. Summary — Raw Materials			10,000	12,000				
Depr. of Machinery and Equipment			20,000					
Depr. of Buildings			8,000					
Patents Expense			1,000					
Factory Supplies Expense			7,000					
Bond Interest Expense					5,000			
Bond Interest Payable								4,000
Cost of Goods Manufactured				490,000	490,000			
			552,000	552,000				
Estimated Income Taxes					20,000			20,000
Net Profit after Estimated Income Taxes					30,000			30,000
					725,000	725,000	632,000	632,000

(d) To record the liability for estimated income taxes.

(e) To close the profit and loss summary account to Earned Surplus Unappropriated.

(f) To increase the bond sinking fund reserve.

(2) Post to the manufacturing summary and profit and loss summary accounts and rule the accounts.

(3) Prepare a profit and loss statement supported by a cost of goods manufactured schedule.

27-3. The Bloom Manufacturing Company was incorporated on December 28, 1953, and began operations on January 2, 1954. The trial balance on December 31, 1954, was as follows:

Cash....................................	$ 161,000	
Factory Supplies..........................	18,000	
Machinery and Equipment.................	600,000	
Common Stock...........................		$ 600,000
Sales....................................		1,050,000
Raw Materials Purchases..................	375,000	
Direct Labor............................	296,250	
Indirect Labor...........................	19,750	
Rent of Factory Building.................	37,500	
Sundry Factory Expense..................	22,500	
Selling Expenses (control)................	90,000	
General Expenses (control)...............	30,000	
	$1,650,000	$1,650,000

Data for adjustments are:

(1) Inventories (overhead rate is 50% of direct labor):

(a) Finished goods: 2,700 units — material, $1.00; direct labor, $6.00.

(b) Work in process: 3,750 units — material, $0.80; direct labor, $4.80.

(c) Raw materials: Material X, 6,000 units at $1.00; Material Y, 18,000 units at $0.50.

(2) Estimated depreciation of:
Machinery and equipment   10%

(3) Factory supplies inventory $10,000

(4) Accrued payroll:
Direct labor $3,750
Indirect labor $2,250

Income taxes are estimated at 40% of net profit.

Instructions: (1) Prepare a work sheet with manufacturing schedule columns.

(2) Prepare a profit and loss statement with a supporting cost of goods manufactured schedule.

(3) Prepare a balance sheet.

Chapter 28

Job Order Cost Accounting

COST ACCOUNTING SYSTEMS The application of accounting procedures to manufacturing processes is not a simple operation. The activities of American industry are so intricate and involved that great care and intelligent understanding must be used to have an effective accounting. Over the years there has been an evolutionary growth of cost accounting systems. Today there are three principal types: *job order cost accounting, process cost accounting,* and *standard cost accounting.*

Although the last of these three, standard cost accounting, is perhaps most favored in modern manufacturing, it is most readily understood by one who has an understanding of the first two. In this chapter the whole emphasis will be on the cost of jobs being manufactured. In the succeeding chapter attention will be focused on process cost accounting and standard costs.

COST ACCOUNTING AND GENERAL ACCOUNTING General accounting contains references to costs. For example, in the beginning chapters of this book, accounts were assembled on the profit and loss statement to determine *cost of goods sold.* In dividing the life of a mercantile enterprise into periods of a year or a month, only *costs* applicable to such periods were reported on the profit and loss statement. In Chapter 27, the balances of certain accounts were assembled in a periodic schedule to determine *cost of goods manufactured.*

The difference between general accounting and cost accounting is primarily a matter of emphasis. When costs incurred in a manufacturing enterprise are related to the products manufactured in such a way as to determine respective *unit costs*, the accounting system employed is commonly referred to as cost accounting.

In job order cost accounting, records are provided for accumulating the various manufacturing costs incurred in producing the units called for on each order. All manufacturing costs may be classified as direct materials, direct labor, and manufacturing expense or factory overhead. Accounts are provided for recording the direct material and direct labor costs on each job. To these direct costs there must be added a portion of the factory overhead. When a job is completed, the total cost as shown in the appropriate account is divided by the number of units finished, yielding the cost of each unit of the finished goods. This procedure requires a careful determination of the items of cost entering into each job.

The elements of cost incurred in completing a job are shown in the following tabulation:

JOB ORDER NO. 147 — 1,000 UNITS OF PRODUCT A

Direct Materials Used......................................	$146
Direct Labor Used...	246
Factory Overhead Applied..................................	128
Total Cost...	$520

Unit Cost, 52¢ ($520 ÷ 1,000)

FLOW OF COSTS IN PERPETUAL INVENTORY ACCOUNTS   When a manufacturing plant is operated under a cost system, perpetual inventory accounts are maintained for Raw Materials, Work in Process, and Finished Goods. These accounts are debited currently for all additions and are credited for all subtractions. As a result, the three inventory accounts show the goods on hand at the beginning of the period, the debits and the credits during the period, and the remaining inventory at the end of the period.

All expenditures incident to manufacturing move through the work in process account and into the finished goods account. The flow of costs through the perpetual inventory accounts is shown in the following diagram:

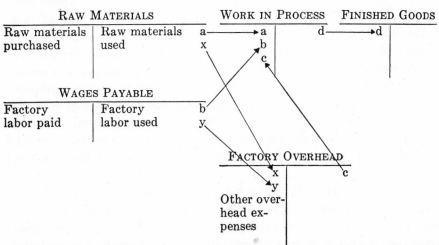

Raw materials used and factory labor used are classified as either direct or indirect. In the diagram the direct costs are transferred to

Work in Process (a and b) and the indirect costs are transferred to Factory Overhead (x and y). The factory overhead costs, which include indirect materials and indirect labor as well as depreciation, insurance, and other indirect manufacturing expenses, are also transferred to Work in Process (c). As a job is completed, the costs are transferred from Work in Process to Finished Goods (d).

RAW MATERIALS ACCOUNT   Raw materials are recorded in an asset account, which is treated in much the same way as the cash account; that is, it is debited for additions and credited for withdrawals. When materials are purchased, they are charged at invoice price plus transportation cost to the raw materials account. When they are withdrawn from the storeroom for use in the process of manufacture, their value is credited to Raw Materials. Direct raw materials that will become a part of finished goods are charged to the work in process account, and indirect raw materials that will be used to assist in some process of manufacture are charged to the factory overhead account. These entries record internal transactions and necessitate the determination of the cost price of the materials entering into production. This price is ordinarily the actual price paid for the materials plus the transportation cost. The following journal entry accounts for the use of materials:

Work in Process.................................	6,500	
Factory Overhead...............................	350	
Raw Materials.................................		6,850

Since the raw materials account represents many kinds of units rather than one, it is set up as a controlling account. The related subsidiary ledger is called the *raw materials ledger* or *stores ledger;* it contains an account with each kind of material in the storeroom. Postings are made currently to the raw materials accounts in the subsidiary ledger, and the balances of these accounts are compared at intervals with the actual amounts of the various kinds of materials on hand. This continuing comparison eliminates, in most companies, an annual shutdown for the purpose of taking at one time complete physical inventories.

Entries are made in the subsidiary raw materials ledger by the *stores clerk* from materials received reports and from materials requisitions. The debit to the controlling account Raw Materials is made from the voucher register or other book of original entry. The materials requisitions are summarized for the month and the total is credited to Raw Materials.

The raw materials controlling account may be compared with the accounts receivable controlling account described in Chapter 7. Posting to the subsidiary raw materials ledger is similar to posting to the customers' ledger, the postings being made from business papers rather than from journals. At the end of the month the balance of the controlling account Raw Materials should agree with the sum of the balances in the raw materials ledger.

FACTORY LABOR　　　　Factory labor, unlike raw materials, cannot be obtained in advance of its use; hence there is no perpetual inventory account for Direct Labor. Payment for the services of workers is not made until after the services have been performed. In order to charge each job order with the cost of the direct labor incurred on the job and to charge factory overhead with the indirect labor cost, it is necessary to keep detailed records on time tickets. Each time ticket provides space for recording the time that the particular employee began work on a job, the time he ceased work on that job, the total time worked, the rate of pay, and the total cost. If a particular employee works on three different job orders during a day, the data will be recorded on three different time tickets. A similar report must be made for employees whose services are classified as indirect labor.

At the end of the month or other accounting period, the total labor costs incurred are summarized from the time tickets or other memorandums. This summary serves as the basis for the debit to Work in Process and to Factory Overhead and the credit to Wages Payable or Accrued Payroll. The entry is illustrated as follows:

Work in Process..................................	5,000	
Factory Overhead...............................	1,100	
Wages Payable................................		6,100

At the time the payroll is paid, which may be weekly, biweekly, or at some other regular interval, the wages payable account is debited and the cash account is credited.[1] The credit balance of the wages payable account at the end of an accounting period is the amount of the liability for labor costs incurred but not paid.

PREDETERMINED FACTORY OVERHEAD RATE　　In order that the work in process account will show all manufacturing costs, those costs not identifiable with particular production orders must be grouped and applied to Work in Process as a percentage of

---

[1]The provisions to be made for income taxes and F.I.C.A. taxes withheld, and for other withholdings, were outlined in Chapter 17. They are ignored in this discussion in order to concentrate attention on cost accounting techniques.

one or more of the known items. In the previous chapter the factory overhead, consisting of indirect materials, indirect labor, and other manufacturing expenses, was ascertained and expressed as a percentage of the direct labor cost. This percentage was determined at the end of the accounting period by summarizing all indirect manufacturing expenses and expressing the total as a percentage of direct labor costs. In order that the cost of a job order may be known as soon as the job is completed, a *predetermined factory overhead rate* is used.

This rate may be based on estimates of the total amount of factory overhead and of the total amount of direct labor for the year ahead. For example, if it is estimated that the total factory overhead expenses for the year will be $40,000 and that the total direct labor cost will be $50,000, an overhead rate of 80% ($40,000 ÷ $50,000) may be applied to the direct labor cost of the job orders of the year.

The actual overhead costs incurred are debited to the factory overhead account and the amount applied to Work in Process through the use of the predetermined rate is credited to the factory overhead account. Assuming that the actual cost of direct labor during a month is $5,000 and that the predetermined overhead rate is 80%, the entry to apply factory overhead to production would be as follows:

Work in Process..................................	4,000	
Factory Overhead............................		4,000

Since there is bound to be a variance between the estimated and the actual figures, the factory overhead account will have a balance at the end of the period. If this is a credit balance, overhead is said to be *overabsorbed;* if it is a debit balance, overhead is said to be *underabsorbed.* The factory overhead account below illustrates both conditions:

Factory Overhead

Actual costs incurred during month...................	4,510	Balance (beginning)..........	300
		Applied to Work in Process during month.............	4,000
		Balance (ending).............	210
	4,510		4,510
Balance (ending).............	210		

The $300 credit balance at the beginning of the month is an overabsorbed balance. During the month actual costs incurred amounted to $4,510 and overhead applied amounted to $4,000. The final balance at the end of the month is a debit or underabsorbed balance of $210.

The balance of the factory overhead account is carried forward from month to month until the end of the year. If the balance fluctuates from debit to credit or is relatively small in amount, there is evidence that the predetermined rate is satisfactory. If a debit balance accumulates month after month until a considerable amount is involved, it indicates that the rate is too low. If a credit balance accumulates, the rate is too high. In either case the rate should be raised or lowered to prevent the accumulation of a large balance.

WORK IN PROCESS ACCOUNT Raw Materials is credited and Work in Process is debited for direct materials withdrawn from the storeroom and put into production. Wages Payable is credited and Work in Process is debited for direct labor costs incurred. Factory Overhead is credited and Work in Process is debited for overhead costs applied to production on the basis of a predetermined overhead rate.

Since there are usually a number of different jobs in process at the same time, the work in process account represents many kinds of units rather than one. It is a controlling account. The related subsidiary ledger is known as the *cost ledger*. In the cost ledger an account is established for each factory job order and to it are charged all materials and labor costs identifiable with that order, as well as a portion of the indirect expenses that represent factory overhead. Postings to the accounts in the subsidiary ledger, called *cost sheets,* may be made currently from the materials requisitions and time tickets. Each of these accounts (cost sheets) is closed and removed from the cost ledger when the order to which it relates is completed. A summary of the completed job orders provides the information for the entry at the end of the month, in which the work in process account is credited and the finished goods account is debited.

The relation of the controlling account Work in Process to the subsidiary cost ledger is shown in the following accounts:

CONTROLLING ACCOUNT

WORK IN PROCESS

Balance...................	1,500	Job Nos. 71, 72, 73..........	15,960
Direct Materials...........	6,500	Balance...................	1,040
Direct Labor..............	5,000		
Factory Overhead..........	4,000		
	17,000		17,000
Balance...................	1,040		

SUBSIDIARY COST LEDGER

JOB No. 71		JOB No. 72	
Balance...................	1,500	Direct Materials...........	2,000
Direct Materials...........	1,000	Direct Labor...............	1,500
Direct Labor...............	1,200	Factory Overhead..........	1,200
Factory Overhead..........	960		
			4,700
	4,660		

JOB No. 73		JOB No. 74	
Direct Materials...........	3,000	Direct Materials...........	500
Direct Labor...............	2,000	Direct Labor...............	300
Factory Overhead..........	1,600	Factory Overhead..........	240
	6,600		

The following relationships between the controlling account and the subsidiary ledger may be noted:

CONTROLLING ACCOUNT		SUBSIDIARY COST LEDGER	
WORK IN PROCESS		COST SHEETS	
Balance (beginning).....	$1,500	= Job No. 71...	$1,500
Debits:			Direct Materials
		Job No. 71...	$1,000
		Job No. 72...	2,000
Direct Materials......	$6,500	= Job No. 73...	3,000
		Job No. 74...	500
		Total........	$6,500
			Direct Labor
		Job No. 71...	$1,200
		Job No. 72...	1,500
Direct Labor.........	$5,000	= Job No. 73...	2,000
		Job No. 74...	300
		Total........	$5,000
			Factory Overhead
		Job No. 71...	$ 960
		Job No. 72...	1,200
Factory Overhead.....	$4,000	= Job No. 73...	1,600
		Job No. 74...	240
		Total........	$4,000

Total Cost

Credit:

Jobs Nos. 71, 72, 73...	$15,960	=	Job No. 71...	$ 4,660
			Job No. 72...	4,700
			Job No. 73...	6,600
				$15,960

Balance (ending)........   1,040   =   Job No. 74 ($500 +
                                             $300 + $240) $ 1,040

The cost ledger is composed of a cost sheet for each job in process. A cost sheet, providing for the current accumulation of cost elements entering into a job order and for a summary at the time the production order has been completed, is shown below for Job No. 72.

When Job No. 72 is completed, the direct materials costs and the direct labor costs are totaled and entered in the summary column at the right of the cost sheet. Factory overhead is added at the predetermined

Job. No. __72__   Date____ January 7, 1954 ____

For__ 5,000 Type C Containers __   to be completed on__January 23, 1954__

                                    For__ Stock __

DIRECT MATERIALS		DIRECT LABOR				SUMMARY	
Req. No.	Amount	Time Sum- mary No.	Amount	Time Sum- mary No.	Amount	Items	Amount
434	400.00	2202	83.60	Bt. fwd.	1,158.00		
438	500.00	204	108.40	2234	45.20	Materials	2,000.00
441	700.00	205	67.00	237	70.00	Labor	1,500.00
464	400.00	210	129.00	242	61.60	Overhead	
		211	98.30	248	22.50	(80%)	1,200.00
	2,000.00	213	107.20	250	87.30		
		216	110.00	253	55.40	Total Cost	4,700.00
		222	77.60				
		224	217.40	Total	1,500.00		
		225	106.30			No. of units	
		231	53.20			finished	5,000
		Fwd.	1,158.00			Cost per unit	.94

Job Cost Sheet

rate of 80% of the direct labor cost, and the total cost of the job is determined. The total cost of the job, $4,700, divided by the number of units produced, 5,000, yields a unit cost of 94 cents for the Type C Containers produced.

At the time each job is completed, the related cost sheet is removed from the subsidiary cost ledger. At the end of the accounting period the completed job cost sheets are summarized and the total is recorded as a debit to Finished Goods and a credit to Work in Process. The remaining balance in the work in process account then represents the total costs charged to the uncompleted job cost sheets.

Continuing the illustration, the entry to transfer the cost of the three completed jobs to the finished goods account is as follows:

Finished Goods................................... 15,960
    Work in Process............................. 15,960

After the entry is posted, the work in process account has a debit balance of $1,040. This corresponds to the total costs incurred on uncompleted Job Order No. 74.

FINISHED GOODS ACCOUNT Finished Goods is debited for the cost of all goods transferred from the factory to the stockroom and is credited for the cost of all goods shipped.

The finished goods account is also a controlling account. The related subsidiary ledger, which has an account for each kind of commodity produced, is called the *finished goods ledger* or *stock ledger*. On the debit side of each account in the subsidiary finished goods ledger there are columns for the quantity manufactured by and received from the factory, the unit cost, and the total cost of the lot. On the credit side there are columns for the number of units shipped, the unit cost, and the total cost of the units shipped. The relation between the finished goods account and the subsidiary ledger is illustrated below and on the following page.

CONTROLLING ACCOUNT
FINISHED GOODS

Balance	7,190	Shipping Order Nos. 641–646.	15,084
Job Nos. 71, 72, 73..........	15,960	Balance..................	8,066
	23,150		23,150
Balance....................	8,066		

FINISHED GOODS LEDGER

TYPE A CONTAINERS

Received				Sold				Balance	
Job Order No.	Quantity	Unit Cost	Amount	Ship. Order No.	Quantity	Unit Cost	Amount	Quantity	Amount
Bal.	1,000	1.48	1,480					1,000	1,480
71	3,282	1.42	4,660					4,282	6,140
				641	1,000	1.48	1,480	3,282	4,660
				644	1,700	1.42	2,414	1,582	2,246

TYPE B CONTAINERS

Received				Sold				Balance	
Job Order No.	Quantity	Unit Cost	Amount	Ship. Order No.	Quantity	Unit Cost	Amount	Quantity	Amount
Bal.	3,000	1.25	3,750					3,000	3,750
				642	2,000	1.25	2,500	1,000	1,250
73	5,500	1.20	6,600					6,500	7,850
				645	1,000	1.25	4,850	2,500	3,000
					3,000	1.20			

TYPE C CONTAINERS

Received				Sold				Balance	
Job Order No.	Quantity	Unit Cost	Amount	Ship. Order No.	Quantity	Unit Cost	Amount	Quantity	Amount
Bal.	2,000	.98	1,960					2,000	1,960
				643	2,000	.98	1,960	—	—
72	5,000	.94	4,700					5,000	4,700
				646	2,000	.94	1,880	3,000	2,820

Often a finished goods ledger account will show several lots on hand that were produced at different times at different unit costs. In such cases the unit cost that is listed first may be applied to the first shipment of the commodity. When the number of units shipped exceeds the number manufactured at the first unit cost, the second unit cost is used until that lot of the commodity has been exhausted. This pricing procedure, known as the *first-in, first-out* method, is perhaps the one most widely used in crediting accounts in the finished goods ledger. The same method is also widely used in crediting accounts in the raw materials ledger. The application of this method in connection with finished goods is illustrated by the accounts for Type A Containers and Type B Containers in the preceding illustration.

The credits to the finished goods ledger for the quantities sold are posted from the shipping order or similar memorandum. The finished goods ledger clerk then records the total cost of the commodity sold on the shipping order. A summary of the cost data on the shipping orders becomes the basis for the following entry:

Cost of Goods Sold............................... 15,084
    Finished Goods.................................   15,084

As its title indicates, the balance of the cost of goods sold account is the total cost price of the finished goods that have been sold during the accounting period. If goods are returned by a buyer and put back in stock, it is necessary, of course, to debit Finished Goods and credit Cost of Goods Sold for the cost. On the profit and loss statement the balance of the cost of goods sold account is deducted from net sales to yield gross profit on sales.

SALES   Sales of finished goods are recorded on the books of a manufacturer employing cost accounting in the same manner in which they are recorded on the books of a mercantile establishment. The sales invoices are entered in a sales journal, or the invoices themselves are used as a sales journal. Assuming that the sales for the month, all of which were on account, totaled $24,930, the summary entry is as follows:

Accounts Receivable............................ 24,930
    Sales...   24,930

It should be noted that for each sale of finished goods it is necessary to maintain a record of both the cost price and the selling price of the goods sold. As indicated above, the cost data may be recorded on the shipping orders. The sales journal may be expanded by the addition of a column for recording the total cost of the goods billed, the total of the column being posted at the end of the month as a debit to Cost of Goods Sold and a credit to Finished Goods.

ILLUSTRATION OF JOB ORDER COST ACCOUNTING To illustrate further the procedures described, the following facts are assumed: The Logan Manufacturing Co. operates a factory and has a job order cost accounting system as an integral part of its accounting. The post-closing trial balance of the general ledger appears as follows on January 1, 1954, the first day of the fiscal year:

LOGAN MANUFACTURING CO.

POST-CLOSING TRIAL BALANCE

JANUARY 1, 1954

Cash...	$ 85,000	
Accounts Receivable................................	73,000	
Finished Goods.....................................	40,000	
Work in Process....................................	20,000	
Raw Materials......................................	30,000	
Prepaid Expenses...................................	2,000	
Plant and Equipment................................	850,000	
Allowance for Depreciation of Plant and Equipment...		$ 473,000
Accounts Payable...................................		70,000
Wages Payable......................................		15,000
Common Stock......................................		500,000
Surplus..		42,000
	$1,100,000	$1,100,000

In order to shorten the illustrative entries to a manageable number, all transactions for the month of January and adjustments at the end of January are summarized as follows:

(a) Raw materials purchased on account, $62,000.

(b) Prepaid expenses incurred on account, $1,000.

(c) Expenses incurred on account: Factory Overhead, $56,000; Selling Expenses, $25,000; General Expenses, $10,000.

(d) Materials used: Direct Materials, $60,000; Indirect Materials, $3,000.

(e) Factory labor used: Direct Labor, $100,000; Indirect Labor, $20,000.

(f) Factory overhead applied to jobs at the rate of 90% of direct labor cost, $90,000.

(g) Jobs completed, $229,000.

(h) Sales on account, $290,000; cost of goods sold, $220,000.

(i) Received cash on accounts receivable, $300,000.

(j) Cash paid on accounts payable, $190,000.

(k) Factory payrolls paid, $125,000.

(l) Depreciation expense: Factory Overhead, $7,000; Selling Expenses, $200; General Expenses, $100.

(m) Expiration of prepaid expenses: Factory Overhead, $1,000; Selling Expenses, $100; General Expenses, $100.

In actual practice the transactions would be recorded from day to day in the various journals employed by the Logan Manufacturing Co. The net effect of the entries is shown below in summary general journal form:

(a)

Raw Materials..................................	62,000	
Accounts Payable.............................		62,000
Raw materials purchased on account.		

(b)

Prepaid Expenses................................	1,000	
Accounts Payable.............................		1,000
Miscellaneous prepayments.		

(c)

Factory Overhead...............................	56,000	
Selling Expenses.................................	25,000	
General Expenses................................	10,000	
Accounts Payable.............................		91,000
Expenses incurred on account.		

(d)

Work In Process.................................	60,000	
Factory Overhead...............................	3,000	
Raw Materials................................		63,000

Summary of materials requisitions:

By Use

Job No. 1001..............	$12,000	
Job No. 1002.............	26,000	
Job No. 1003.............	22,000	$ 60,000
Factory Overhead........		3,000
Total.................		$ 63,000

By Materials

Material A......................	$ 16,000
Material B......................	18,000
Material C......................	15,000
Material D......................	14,000
Total........................	$ 63,000

(e)

Work in Process	100,000	
Factory Overhead	20,000	
Wages Payable		120,000

Summary of time tickets:

Job No. 1001	$60,000	
Job No. 1002	30,000	
Job No. 1003	10,000	$100,000
Factory Overhead		20,000
Total		$120,000

(f)

Work in Process	90,000	
Factory Overhead		90,000

Summary of factory overhead applied:

Job No. 1001 (90% of $60,000)	$ 54,000
Job No. 1002 (90% of $30,000)	27,000
Job No. 1003 (90% of $10,000)	9,000
Total	$ 90,000

(g)

Finished Goods	229,000	
Work in Process		229,000

Summary of completed cost sheets:

Job No. 1001	$146,000
Job No. 1002	83,000
Total	$229,000

(h)

Accounts Receivable	290,000	
Sales		290,000

Sales on account.

Cost of Goods Sold	220,000	
Finished Goods		220,000

Summary of shipping orders:

Product X	$ 15,000
Product Y	125,000
Product Z	80,000
Total	$220,000

(i)

Cash	300,000	
Accounts Receivable		300,000

Cash received on account.

(j)

Accounts Payable..	190,000	
Cash..		190,000
Cash paid on account.		

(k)

Wages Payable....................................	125,000	
Cash..		125,000
Payrolls paid.		

(l)

Factory Overhead...............................	7,000	
Selling Expenses................................	200	
General Expenses................................	100	
Allowance for Depreciation of Plant and Equipment		7,300
Adjustment for depreciation.		

(m)

Factory Overhead...............................	1,000	
Selling Expenses................................	100	
General Expenses................................	100	
Prepaid Expenses...............................		1,200
Adjustment for prepaid expenses.		

The flow of costs through the manufacturing accounts, together with summary details of the subsidiary ledgers, are illustrated on page 567. Entries in the accounts are identified by letters to facilitate comparisons with the summary journal entries presented above.

The trial balance taken from the general ledger of the Logan Manufacturing Co. on January 31 is as follows:

LOGAN MANUFACTURING CO.
TRIAL BALANCE
JANUARY 31, 1954

Cash...	$ 70,000	
Accounts Receivable............................	63,000	
Finished Goods.................................	49,000	
Work in Process................................	41,000	
Raw Materials..................................	29,000	
Prepaid Expenses...............................	1,800	
Plant and Equipment...........................	850,000	
Allowance for Depreciation of Plant and Equipment...		$ 480,300
Accounts Payable...............................		34,000
Wages Payable..................................		10,000
Common Stock..................................		500,000
Surplus..		42,000
Sales..		290,000
Cost of Goods Sold. ⚫...........................	220,000	
Factory Overhead...............................		3,000
Selling Expenses................................	25,300	
General Expenses...............................	10,200	
	$1,359,300	$1,359,300

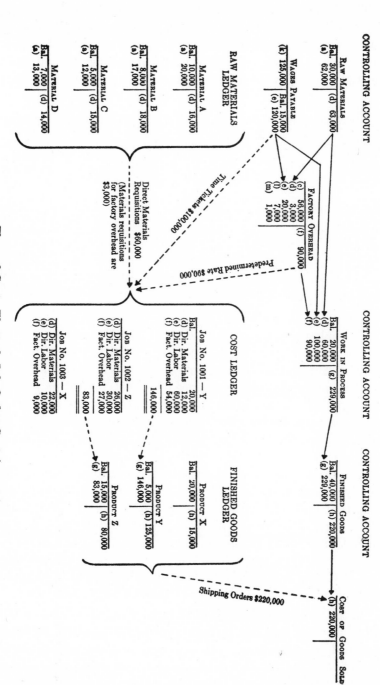

Flow of Costs Through Job Order Cost Accounts

The balances of the three inventory accounts, Raw Materials, Work in Process, and Finished Goods, represent the respective inventories on January 31. Each account controls a subsidiary ledger. A comparison of the balance of each controlling account, taken from the trial balance, with its subsidiary ledger, reveals the following:

CONTROLLING ACCOUNT	SUBSIDIARY LEDGER		
Raw Materials........... $29,000	Material A......... $14,000		
	Material B......... 7,000		
	Material C......... 2,000		
	Material D......... 6,000	$29,000
Work in Process.......... $41,000			
Finished Goods........... $49,000	Job No. 1003............. $41,000		
	Product X......... $ 5,000		
	Product Y......... 26,000		
	Product Z......... 18,000	$49,000

The balance in the account Cost of Goods Sold represents the cost price of the goods sold during the period. It is deducted from net sales on the profit and loss statement. Factory Overhead appears on the trial balance with a credit balance of $3,000, indicating that the overhead applied has exceeded the overhead incurred by that amount; hence the term *overabsorbed* or *overapplied* overhead. The balance of the factory overhead account is shown on interim balance sheets during the year as a deferred charge (underabsorbed) or a deferred credit (overabsorbed). Any balance in the account at the end of the year is usually closed into the cost of goods sold account, the justification being that most of the goods manufactured during the year have been sold. If the balance of the factory overhead account is material in amount or if many of the goods manufactured are still on hand, the balance may be allocated to Work in Process, Finished Goods, and Cost of Goods Sold on the basis of the total amounts of applied overhead included in those balances at the end of the year.

In the foregoing illustration all factory overhead costs were charged to one account and one predetermined rate was used in applying the overhead to production. In practice, it is customary to set up a separate account for each department or *cost center* in the factory. It is also usual to maintain a subsidiary ledger for each factory overhead account in order that the amounts of each type of expense (depreciation, repairs, indirect labor, etc.) may be known.

QUESTIONS

1. How does the cost section of an accounting department identify raw materials costs and labor costs with a particular order?

2. The Kellogg Manufacturing Co. purchases 1,000 units of A at $1 and later purchases 500 units at $1.20. When the balance on hand is 700 units, a materials requisition is made out for 400 units chargeable to Job Order No. 62. What amount is charged to Work in Process for materials if the first-in first-out method is used?

3. The work is process account has a debit balance of $5,464. The accounts with the two jobs that are uncompleted have respectively charges of $688 and $1,104 for direct materials and charges of $872 and $1,168 for direct labor. What is the rate of factory overhead?

4. (a) State the types of information that are shown on a cost sheet. (b) Explain how this information is obtained.

5. (a) Name three controlling accounts found in cost accounting and the subsidiary ledgers controlled by each. (b) Give the sources of posting for each of these accounts and its subsidiary ledger.

6. The general ledger of T. L. Brown contains the following account:

WORK IN PROCESS

Direct Materials............	24,000	Finished Goods............	66,000
Direct Labor...............	30,000		
Factory Overhead..........	20,000		

If the direct materials charged to the uncompleted job amount to $3,000, what are the direct labor and the factory overhead charges?

7. (a) Explain the use of the cost ledger. (b) How are indirect costs shown in the cost ledger? (c) How is the cost ledger related to manuacturing operations?

8. What is the term applied to (a) a debit balance in Factory Overhead and (b) a credit balance in Factory Overhead?

9. Give in general journal form the entries required to record the following sale of finished goods on account: sales price, $14,000; cost price, $10,000.

10. The following accounts appear on the trial balance of Atlas Manufacturing Co. at the end of the fiscal year:

Work in Process......................	$	200,000
Finished Goods.......................		500,000
Cost of Goods Sold...................		25,000,000
Factory Overhead....................		9,000 (cr.)

Give the journal entry to close the factory overhead account.

PROBLEMS

28-1. The transactions completed by the Dover Manufacturing Company during the month of April are summarized as follows:

(a)	Raw materials purchased on account	$220,000
(b)	Materials requisitioned for production orders	148,000
(c)	Materials requisitioned for general factory use	28,000
(d)	Labor used on production orders	160,000
(e)	Indirect labor used	56,000
(f)	Factory overhead is applied at the rate of 100% of direct labor cost.	
(g)	Repairs and maintenance to factory incurred on account	54,000
(h)	Factory building rental paid	18,000
(i)	Products finished and transferred to stock	360,000
(j)	Goods sold on account: cost, $220,000; selling price	300,000
(k)	Factory wages paid	208,000

Instructions: Prepare entries in general journal form to record the summarized transactions given above.

28-2. On June 1, the beginning of the sixth month of the current fiscal year, the following balances appeared in the accounts in the Greene Manufacturing Company's general ledger and subsidiary ledgers:

Cash	$ 76,000	
Accounts Receivable	60,000	
Finished Goods — Commodity N, 1,000 units	20,000	
Work in Process — Job No. 601	6,000	
Raw Materials — Material X	12,000	
Plant and Equipment	1~0,000	
Allowance for Depreciation of Plant and Equipment		$ 66,000
Accounts Payable		36,000
Wages Payable		2,000
Capital Stock		100,000
Surplus		24,000
Sales		300,000
Cost of Goods Sold	210,000	
Factory Overhead		1,000
Selling and General Expenses	25,000	

The transactions completed during June are summarized as follows:

(a) Raw materials were purchased on account as follows:

Material X	$10,000
Material Y	14,000
Material Z	2,000

(b) Raw materials were requisitioned from the stores clerk as follows:

Job No. 601: Mat. X, $3,000; Mat. Y, $2,000	$5,000
Job No. 602: Mat. X, $5,000; Mat. Y, $4,000	9,000
For general factory use: Mat. Z	1,000

(c) Time tickets for the month were chargeable as follows:

Job No. 601	$12,000
Job No. 602	10,000
Indirect labor	3,200

(d) Factory pay checks for $22,000 were issued.

(e) Cash of $40,000 was received on accounts receivable.

(f) Various factory maintenance charges of $4,800 were paid.

(g) Depreciation on factory equipment was recorded, $1,000.

(h) Miscellaneous factory expenses were incurred on account, $4,400.

(i) Factory overhead was applied to jobs at the rate of 60% of direct labor cost.

(j) Selling and general expenses incurred on account, $5,600.

(k) Payments on account, $38,000.

(l) All job orders were completed during the month: Job Order No. 601 produced 1,000 units of Commodity O; Job Order No. 602 produced 1,000 units of Commodity P.

(m) Total sales on account, $58,000. The goods sold were as follows:

850 units of Commodity N
500 units of Commodity O
400 units of Commodity P

Instructions: (1) Prepare "T" accounts for the general ledger, the raw materials ledger, the cost ledger, and the finished goods ledger. Record directly in these accounts the balances as of June 1 and the transactions completed during the month. Identify balances as "Bal." and transactions by letter.

(2) Take a trial balance.

(3) Prove the subsidiary ledgers with the controlling accounts in the general ledger.

(4) Prepare a profit and loss statement for the six months ended June 30.

28-3. The Selby Manufacturing Corporation prepares financial statements at the end of each month but closes its accounts only on December 31. On November 30 of the current year the accounts in the general ledger showed the following balances:

Cash..	$ 58,000	
Finished Goods...............................	12,400	
Work in Process..............................	9,000	
Raw Materials.................................	12,000	
Wages Payable................................		$ 1,000
Common Stock................................		50,000
Surplus...		30,000
Sales..		176,000
Cost of Goods Sold..........................	142,000	
Factory Overhead.............................	1,600	
Operating Expenses...........................	22,000	
	$257,000	$257,000

Operations for the month of December were as follows:

(a) All sales were for cash:

Selling price....................................	$ 24,000
Cost of goods sold.............................	16,000

(b) Cash disbursements:

Wages payable.................................	14,000
Factory overhead expenses.....................	5,000
Operating expenses............................	2,000

(c) Withdrawals of raw materials:

Chargeable to jobs............................	8,000

(d) Factory labor:

Chargeable to jobs............................	12,000
Chargeable to factory overhead.................	3,800

(e) Cost of goods completed......................... 24,000

(f) Overhead rate applied to jobs, 70% of direct labor cost.

Instructions: (1) Set up "T" accounts and record the balances as of December 1. Include an account for Profit and Loss Summary following the surplus account.

(2) Record the transactions directly in the accounts.

(3) Prepare a profit and loss statement and a balance sheet for the year ended December 31. Underabsorbed overhead is to be added to Cost of Goods Sold.

(4) Record closing entries directly in the accounts. Balance and rule the accounts.

Chapter 29

Process Cost Accounting

PROCESS COSTS DESCRIBED
In the preceding chapter, where the job order cost system was described, manufacturing cost elements were identified with the product directly. Material, labor, and overhead were applied directly to the units comprising the job order. In this chapter the same cost elements will be identified first with a manufacturing process and only secondarily with the product. This indirect method of finding the cost of products and services is known as *process cost accounting*.

In many industries it is not possible to identify the raw materials with specific job orders as they are converted into finished goods. In the manufacture of ink, paint, soap, paper, and other similar products, the raw materials processed form a homogeneous mass, which cannot be broken up into job orders. In such cases the cost elements must first be identified with processes and then with the product of those processes. For example, the cost of a gallon of paint is the aggregate cost of the separate processes divided by the number of gallons turned out.

The items charged to the process account are similar to the items charged to the work in process account under the job order system. They include the three elements of cost: direct materials, direct labor, and factory overhead. A simple process account is illustrated below:

PROCESS A

Direct materials	4,000	To Process B, 10,000 units	12,000
Direct labor	5,000	Cost per unit $\dfrac{\$12,000}{10,000} = \$1.20$	
Factory overhead	3,000		
	12,000		12,000

When the manufacturing procedure takes place in a sequence of different processes, the finished goods of Process A become the raw materials of Process B, the finished goods of Process B become the raw materials of Process C, etc.

As manufacturing becomes more and more standardized and the units of output tend to be alike, the importance of job order costs decreases and greater emphasis is placed on the costs of the different processes. Such processes characterize not only manufacturing operations but selling operations as well. Retailing and wholesaling consist of a series of processes that result in sales. The cost of almost any activity may be divided by the units of output, and a process cost per unit may be obtained. Process cost accounting is therefore more universally applicable than job order cost accounting. It is the purpose of this chapter to describe process cost accounting as it applies to manufacturing and other fields.

JOB ORDER AND PROCESS COSTS DISTINGUISHED In job order cost accounting the three elements of cost are charged directly to job orders. All production consists of job orders, and all costs ultimately are identified with some specific job. As illustrated above, in process cost accounting the elements of cost are charged to processes, and the cost of a unit produced in a given period is obtained by dividing the cost of the process by the number of units produced. Since all goods produced by a process are identical units, it is no longer useful to classify production into job orders. Process costs give average costs.

If there were but one process in a factory, the cost accounting procedures would be very simple. The manufacturing cost elements would be charged to the single process account, and the process unit cost would be determined by dividing the total cost by the number of units produced. In the process account illustrated on page 573, the cost of the process, $12,000, is divided by the output, 10,000 units, to obtain a cost per unit of $1.20.

Ordinarily there are several processes in a factory. It therefore becomes necessary to account for each process separately, just as it was necessary in the preceding chapter to account for each job order separately. Since the number of processes is frequently small, the various process cost accounts commonly appear in the general ledger rather than in a subsidiary ledger.

Process costs result in averaging the costs of given operations as they apply to goods manufactured. Job order costs differentiate the costs applicable to goods manufactured. Job order systems involve more detail and give more specific information than process systems. Since process costs provide only one cost figure for each cost period, they require considerably less detailed work.

In a factory where a number of processes exist, it is customary to have additional departments that do not process the raw materials directly but that assist the processing departments. For example, if processing uses power machinery, the power to run the machinery may be furnished by a power department. If the product involves chemical engineering, the formulas used may be controlled by a chemical engineering department. Such departments are known as *service departments*.

SERVICE DEPARTMENTS When service departments exist, the factory
AND PROCESS COSTS is considered not as a unit but as a collection
of departments. The service departments are not directly engaged in production, but they facilitate the processing departments in producing finished goods. They include such departments as the factory office, the building department, the power plant, and the maintenance and repair shop.

The existence of the departments in a factory gives rise to additional internal transactions. The services rendered by a service department result in internal transactions between that department and the processes that receive the benefit of the services. In these internal transactions, as in those discussed in the previous chapter, the basis of the amount involved in the transaction is the cost of the service rendered. For example, if the total charges to the power department for the period of a month are $4,500 and this department provides power service to two processes, the debits to the two processes will be based on the $4,500, the cost of the service rendered. If the power department rendered 150,000 kilowatt-hours of service, then the charge would be made at the rate of 3 cents per kilowatt-hour. If Process 1 used 100,000 kw. hours and Process 2 used 50,000 kw. hours, the service department account and the charges to Process 1 and Process 2 would appear as follows:

POWER DEPARTMENT

Fuel	1,800	To Process 1	3,000
Wages	1,300	To Process 2	1,500
Depreciation	400		
Maintenance	400		
Taxes	400		
Insurance	200		
	4,500		4,500

PROCESS 1	PROCESS 2
Power.....3,000	Power.....1,500

In a departmentalized factory, the service department costs are charged periodically to the process accounts. The period usually chosen is a month. At the end of the month the process accounts will include the total manufacturing expenses for the month. Each account will have been charged on some reasonable basis for all costs applicable to it, both direct and indirect. The account for Process B is shown below:

PROCESS B

10,000 units at $1.20 from Process A............... 12,000	To Process C, 10,000 units.... 20,000	
Direct labor.......... 4,600	Cost per unit $\dfrac{\$20,000}{10,000} = \$2.00$	
Factory overhead...... 2,300		
Service Dept. 1........ 500		
Service Dept. 2........ 600 8,000		
_____		
20,000	20,000	

On the debit side of this account are shown all the cost elements entering into Process B, including the direct materials cost, the direct labor, the factory overhead, and the service department costs chargeable to Process B. The total cost of processing in Process B consists of all charges, except the materials cost of $12,000. This amount, $8,000, is called the *processing cost*. Since 10,000 units have been processed, the cost of a completed unit is $2, of which $1.20 represents the materials cost and 80 cents the processing cost. This cost of $2 per unit, the finished goods cost in Process B, becomes the materials cost in Process C.

INVENTORIES OF PARTIALLY PROCESSED MATERIALS   In the preceding illustration it was assumed that the goods placed in production were completely processed at the end of the accounting period. In such cases the determination of unit costs is a simple problem in division. Frequently, however, work in process exists at the end of the period, and not all of the charges to the process account should be included in the cost of the finished units. A portion of the charges to the process belongs to the partly processed materials. An equitable allocation of the total costs within the process must be made between the finished and the unfinished units if the cost of goods sold during the period and the ending inventories are to be accurately reported.

Materials may be placed in production at different stages of the manufacturing process. The stage at which materials are placed in production depends upon the nature of the product being manufactured. For some products it is necessary to have all the raw materials on hand before any work commences. For other products the materials may be added to production in relatively the same proportion as processing costs are incurred. In still other situations materials enter the process at relatively few points, which may or may not be evenly spaced throughout the process.

In assigning dollar values to the goods that were finished and to the goods still in process at the end of the accounting period, it is necessary to account separately for materials costs and processing costs. This is true because the materials content in the partly finished goods may not be in proportion to the processing costs incurred to date. The assignment of processing costs to goods necessitates the computation of (a) the number of *equivalent units* of production during the period and (b) the *processing cost per equivalent unit* in that period.

The equivalent units of production measure the actual productive efforts for a period. It represents the number of complete units that would have been produced if all the work performed during the current period had been applied to units that were begun and finished during this period. Thus, if a process with no beginning inventory starts work on 1,000 units and at the end of the period all of the units are on the average 75% completed, the equivalent production is 750 units.

The method used to calculate equivalent units is illustrated below:

Units completed and placed in stock during period...........	4,000
Deduct equivalent units in process at beginning of period, 600 units $^1/_3$ completed, or..............................	200
	3,800
Add equivalent units in process at end of period, 1,000 units $^2/_5$ completed, or......................................	400
Equivalent units of work performed.......................	4,200

When materials, labor, and overhead are consumed uniformly throughout the manufacturing process, the total costs of the process would be divided by 4,200 units to obtain the unit cost. If all of the materials are placed in production at the beginning, the full materials cost per unit must be assigned to the partly processed goods. If materials enter production at particular intervals rather than continuously, only that portion of material placed in process to date is to be assigned to the uncompleted units. In the latter two situations, the 4,200 units above would be divided into the processing costs only, excluding the cost of materials. The resulting conversion cost per unit would be added to the materials cost to obtain the total unit cost.

To illustrate the assignment of costs to units finished and unfinished when all materials are present at the beginning, the following process account is taken as an example:

PROCESS H

Work in process May 1, 600 units ⅓ completed........	1,160	Goods finished during May, 4,000 units...............		14,060
Direct materials, 4,400 units @ $1.00.................	4,400	Work in process May 31, 1,000 units ²/₅ completed......		2,000
Direct labor........... 6,000				
Factory overhead 2,500				
Service departments.... 2,000	10,500			
	16,060			16,060

The equivalent units of work are shown by the computation on page 577 to be 4,200 units. The total processing costs of $10,500 divided by 4,200 units gives a processing cost per unit of $2.50. The assignment of values may now be completed as follows:

COST OF GOODS FINISHED DURING MAY:

$$4,000 \text{ units} \begin{cases} 600 \text{ units} \begin{cases} \text{Cost carried forward from April.... } \$1,160 \\ \text{Processing costs in May, } 600 \times {}^2/_3, \\ \quad \text{or } 400 \ @ \ \$2.50............... \quad 1,000 \\ \hline \text{Cost of first 600 units completed} \\ \quad (\$3.60 \text{ per unit})............... \quad\quad\quad \$\ 2,160 \end{cases} \\ \\ 3,400 \text{ units} \begin{cases} \text{Materials cost in May, } \$1.00 \text{ per} \\ \quad \text{unit........................} \$3,400 \\ \text{Processing cost in May, } \$2.50 \text{ per} \\ \quad \text{unit.......................} \quad 8,500 \\ \hline \text{Cost of 3,400 units started and com-} \\ \quad \text{pleted in May (}\$3.50 \text{ per unit)...} \quad\quad 11,900 \end{cases} \end{cases}$$

Cost of 4,000 units transferred to stock during May............... $14,060

COST OF WORK IN PROCESS ON MAY 31:

$$1,000 \text{ units} \begin{cases} \text{Materials cost in May, } \$1.00 \text{ per unit............ } \$1,000 \\ \text{Processing cost in May, } 1,000 \times {}^2/_5, \text{ or } 400 \ @ \ \$2.50 \quad 1,000 \end{cases}$$

Cost of 1,000 units ²/₅ completed on May 31........................ $ 2,000

The process account shown above is for one cost period, May. The beginning work in process inventory contains materials costs and equivalent unit processing costs of the previous period. Since these units are finished first, they will contain the April materials costs and processing costs made up ¹/₃ at the April rate and ²/₃ at the May rate. The ending inventory will contain the May materials cost and processing costs on ²/₅ at the May rate.

The preceding illustration shows the emphasis that is placed on each accounting period's processing. The processing costs for each period are kept distinct from the processing costs of the preceding period. The materials costs of the new period are also kept separate. The production of each period is treated in the accounts as if it were processed separately.

The usual cost period is one month in length, but it is possible to have shorter or longer periods, such as a day, a week, three months, or six months. The length of the period depends upon the situation in each processing department.

BY-PRODUCTS   If one of the products resulting from a process has little value in relation to the principal product, it is known as a *by-product*. In this case, it is assumed that the cost of processing belongs to the main product. Whatever return there may be from the sale of the by-product is treated as a deduction from the total cost of the main product. The amount credited to the process account for the by-product should be the *net* return from its sale. The net return is considered to be the sales value of the by-product reduced by any additional costs to complete or to sell.

For example, if Process T resulted in a principal product X and a by-product M, and the net return from M was only $100, that amount should be credited to the cost of producing Product X. The account for Process T is shown below:

PROCESS T

Direct materials............	1,000	Net return from Product M....	100
Direct labor................	4,000	Cost of Product X...........	6,300
Factory overhead...........	1,000		
Service departments........	400		
	6,400		6,400

JOINT PRODUCTS   The manufacturing activities of a process may result in two or more major products instead of one, as assumed above. In such a case it becomes necessary to apportion among the resulting products the processing costs of the period reduced by any amount assigned to by-products. To accomplish this apportionment, some basis must be chosen.

The most widely used method of allocating costs to joint products is by considering the relative sales values of the different products. Assume, for example, that instead of Product X, Products Y and Z resulted from Process T illustrated above. Product Y is currently selling at $3 per unit and Product Z is selling at $1.20 per unit. In Process T 1,000 units of Product Y and 5,000 units of Product Z were manufactured during the period. The assignment of the total cost of $6,300 may be tabulated as follows:

JOINT PRODUCT COST ALLOCATION

Product	Units Manufactured	Sales Price per Unit	Total Sales Value
Y	1,000	$3.00	$3,000
Z	5,000	1.20	6,000
			$9,000

Cost allocated to Product Y: $\dfrac{3,000}{9,000} \times \$6,300$, or $2,100

Cost allocated to Product Z: $\dfrac{6,000}{9,000} \times \$6,300$, or   4,200

$6,300

Unit cost of Product Y: $\dfrac{\$2,100}{1,000}$, or $2.10

Unit cost of Product Z: $\dfrac{\$4,200}{5,000}$, or $ .84

Since joint products result from the same process, one cannot be manufactured without the other. The assignment of cost, then, cannot be based on actual expenditures because it is impossible to determine how much of the cost effort was directed in the production of each product. By apportioning costs based on relative sales values, it is assumed that the cost of producing an item is proportional to its sales value. This method of cost allocation results in a uniform gross profit on all products. In the example above, the gross profit on Y is 90 cents, or 30% of sales price; the gross profit on Z is 36 cents, or 30% of sales price.

ILLUSTRATION OF PROCESS COST ACCOUNTING   The features of process cost accounting described and explained individually on the previous pages are now combined in a single illustration. This illustration includes the relation of service department accounts to process accounts and the determination of unit costs. The accounts affected are arranged in a flow chart illustration similar to that used in Chapter 28. This illustration is found on page 585 and shows the movement of costs from left to right.

The Allen Processing Company has two processes in the factory. Raw materials enter Process 1 and are worked on, resulting in Product A and Product M. When Product M is further processed in

Process 2, Product B results. Product A is a by-product and is sold as soon as it leaves Process 1 at a price of 60 cents per pound. Since Process 1 is of relatively short duration, it usually has no inventory in process at the end of the month. Process 2 is of longer duration and in-process inventories are normally present at the end of the month. The company uses the first-in, first-out method of inventory valuation for all inventory items.

In addition to the two processing departments, there are two service departments in the factory. These are utilized by the processing departments in the following proportions:

	PROCESS 1	PROCESS 2
Maintenance Shop	25%	75%
Power Department	30%	70%

The condensed post-closing trial balance of the Allen Processing Company as of March 31, 1954, is as follows:

ALLEN PROCESSING COMPANY
POST-CLOSING TRIAL BALANCE
MARCH 31, 1954

Other Assets (Net)............................	$199,895	
Raw Materials, 500 units at $6................	3,000	
Work in Process (Process 2), 400 units $1/2$ completed......................................	3,605	
Product B (200 units at $11)...................	2,200	
Supplies......................................	1,300	
Accounts Payable.............................		$ 10,500
Wages Payable...............................		500
Capital......................................		199,000
	$210,000	$210,000

The following entries summarize the company's operations during April:

Transactions	Entry
(a) Purchased 1,800 units of raw material at $6.20, or $11,160.	Raw Materials....... 11,160 Accounts Payable... 11,160

(b) Raw materials requisitioned for use in Process 1, 2,000 units:
    500 units at $6.00..... $ 3,000
    1,500 units at $6.20.....   9,300
 	
    2,000 units........... $12,300
	Process 1............ 12,300
	    Raw Materials...... 12,300

Transactions	Entry

(c) Supplies purchased, $2,000.

Supplies	2,000	
Accounts Payable		2,000

(d) Factory labor charges, $8,380:

Process 1	$1,530
Process 2	4,850
Maintenance Shop	1,200
Power Department	800
Total	$8,380

Process 1	1,530	
Process 2	4,850	
Maintenance Shop	1,200	
Power Department	800	
Wages Payable		8,380

(e) Depreciation, taxes, insurance, and other expenses allocated to the factory:

Process 1	$ 500
Process 2	650
Maintenance Shop	250
Power Department	100
Total	$1,500

Process 1	500	
Process 2	650	
Maintenance Shop	250	
Power Department	100	
Other Assets		1,500

(f) Supplies requisitioned for use in the factory:

Process 1	$ 120
Process 2	200
Maintenance Shop	150
Power Department	100
Total	$ 570

Process 1	120	
Process 2	200	
Maintenance Shop	150	
Power Department	100	
Supplies		570

(g) Amount of wages paid during April, $8,500.

Wages Payable	8,500	
Other Assets		8,500

(h) Allocation of service department charges:

	Process 1	Process 2
Maintenance Shop (25%, 75%)	$400	$1,200
Power Department (30%, 70%)	300	700
Total	$700	$1,900

Process 1	700	
Process 2	1,900	
Maintenance Shop		1,600
Power Department		1,000

Transactions	Entry

(i) The 2,000 units of materials placed in Process 1 were completed, producing 250 pounds of Product A valued at 60 cents per pound, and 2,000 units of Product M moved to Process 2.

Process 2..... 15,000
Product A.... 150
  Process 1...   15,150

(j) During April, 1,950 units of Product B were completed and transferred to stock. The remaining 450 units are $1/3$ completed on April 30.

Product B.... 22,230
  Process 2...   22,230

Equivalent units:
Goods finished.............. 1,950
Less: Work in process on April 1, 400 units $1/2$ completed.. 200

1,750

Add: Work in process on April 30, 450 units $1/3$ completed. 150

Equivalent units........... 1,900

Unit processing cost,

$\frac{\$7,600}{1,900}$ or $\$4.00$

Ending work in process inventory:
Total charges in Process 2..... $26,205
Less work in process on April 30:
Materials, 450 @ $7.50, or......... $3,375
Processing costs, (450 × $1/3$) @ $4.. 600 3,975

Cost of 1,950 units completed.. $22,230

(k) Sales were made as follows:
Product A, 250 lbs. @ $.60.... $ 150
Product B, 1,800 units @ $20.. 36,000

Total..................... $36,150

Other Assets.. 36,150
  Sales.......   36,150

(l) Cost of goods sold during April:
Product A, 250 lbs. at cost of $.60..................... $ 150
Product B, 200 units at cost of $11......... $2,200
1,600 units at cost of $11.40............. 18,240 20,440

Cost of goods sold............ $20,590

Cost of Goods Sold.........20,590
  Product A..   150
  Product B..   20,440

It should be noted that the cost of goods completed was determined in entry (j) above by simply subtracting the cost allocated to ending work in process from the total charges in the Process B account. This procedure is easier than computing the cost of goods finished by the regular procedure illustrated below:

400 units in process April 1	Costs carried forward from March. $ 3,605 Processing costs in April (400 × ½) @ $4	800	$ 4,405
1,550 units started and completed in April	Materials cost in April, $7.50 . . . . . $11,625 Processing costs in April, $4 6,200		17,825

1,950 units

Cost of goods transferred to stock during April. $22,230

Another point worthy of emphasis is the fact that original expenditures were allocated to the four departments. The service department costs were then distributed to the two processing departments. This distribution resulted in total charges of $15,150 to Process 1. The proceeds of $150 from the sale of the by-product were credited to Process 1, thus reducing the cost of the 2,000 units of Product M to $15,000, or $7.50 per unit. Product M was then transferred to Process 2 and was treated as the raw material of that department.

A trial balance of the accounts shown on the chart on page 585 is as follows:

ALLEN PROCESSING COMPANY

TRIAL BALANCE

APRIL 30, 1954

Other Assets.	$226,045	
Raw Materials, 300 units at $6.20.	1,860	
Work in Process (Process 2) 450 units ⅓ completed.	3,975	
Product B.	3,990	
Supplies.	2,730	
Cost of Goods Sold.	20,590	
Accounts Payable.		$ 23,660
Wages Payable.		380
Sales.		36,150
Capital.		199,000
	$259,190	$259,190

PROCESS COSTS IN SELLING AND OTHER FIELDS   Retailing and wholesaling consist of a series of processes that taken together produce sales. These processes of distribution are sometimes called *functions of distribution*. These may be broadly

GENERAL ACCOUNTS

OTHER ASSETS (NET)

Bal.	199,895	(e)	1,500
(k)	36,150	(g)	8,500
		Bal.	226,045
	236,045		236,045
Bal.	226,045		

SUPPLIES

Bal.	1,300	(f)	570
(c)	2,000	Bal.	2,730
	3,300		3,300
Bal.	2,730		

WAGES PAYABLE

(g)	8,500	Bal.	500
Bal.	380	(d)	8,380
	8,800		8,880
		Bal.	380

RAW MATERIALS

Bal.	3,000	(b)	12,300
(a)	11,160	Bal.	1,860
	14,160		14,160
Bal.	1,860		

ACCOUNTS PAYABLE

Bal.	23,660	Bal.	10,500
		(a)	11,160
		(c)	2,000
	23,660		23,660
		Bal.	23,660

CAPITAL

	Bal.	199,000

SALES

	(k)	36,150

SERVICE DEPARTMENT ACCOUNTS

MAINTENANCE SHOP

(d)	1,200	(h)	1,600
(e)	250		
(f)	150		
	1,600		1,600

POWER DEPARTMENT

(d)	800	(h)	1,000
(e)	100		
(f)	100		
	1,000		1,000

PROCESSING DEPARTMENT ACCOUNTS

PROCESS 1

(b)	12,300	(i)	15,150
(d)	1,530		
(e)	500		
(f)	120		
(h)	700		
	15,150		15,150

PROCESS 2

Bal.	3,605	(j)	22,230
(d)	4,850	Bal.	3,975
(e)	650		
(f)	200		
(h)	1,900		
(i)	15,000		
	26,205		26,205
Bal.	3,975		

FINISHED GOODS ACCOUNTS

PRODUCT A

(i)	150	(l)	150

PRODUCT B

Bal.	2,200	(l)	20,440
(j)	22,230	Bal.	3,990
	24,430		24,430
Bal.	3,990		

COST OF GOODS SOLD

(l)	20,590	

Flow of Costs Through Factory Accounts

classified into four groups: (1) advertising, (2) selling, (3) delivering, and (4) collecting. Whatever the classification may be, each process or function involves expense items, the sum of which gives the total cost of that function.

Assume, for example, that selling is deemed to consist of two processes — advertising and personal selling. If in a given period the advertising costs are $200,000 and the personal selling costs are $1,300,000 for 100,000 units sold, the analysis of selling processes may be expressed as follows:

Advertising	$ 200,000	÷ 100,000 =	$ 2 per unit
Personal selling	1,300,000	÷ 100,000 =	13 per unit
Total	$1,500,000	÷ 100,000 =	$15 per unit

If the advertising is tripled, with a resulting decrease in personal selling of $300,000 and an increase in units sold of 60%, an analysis of unit selling process costs would show:

Advertising	$ 600,000	÷ 160,000 =	$ 3.75 per unit
Personal selling	1,000,000	÷ 160,000 =	6.25 per unit
Total	$1,600,000	÷ 160,000 =	$10.00 per unit

It is important for the management of any mercantile business to know what relative proportions of the various functions result in the optimum profit for the company.

It has been said that it costs more to sell the world's goods than to produce them. Efforts are constantly being made to reduce the price margin between the producer and the consumer. If services are provided to the consumer that he does not need or wish, the margin may be narrowed by the elimination of such service costs. Thus, today, the margin on numerous commodities has been reduced through the elimination of delivery and credit costs and the use of self-service. Careful studies of the costs of mercantile processes should point the way toward a more efficient system of distribution.

The utilization of process cost data is not limited to manufacturing and mercantile operations. In railroad transportation, for example, it is common practice to calculate the cost of freight service per ton-mile or the cost of passenger service per passenger-mile. In motor truck operations, calculations are made to determine the amounts of various costs per mile and the costs per ton-mile. In banks and other financial institutions, costs are assembled and unit cost prices are determined in order to learn the relative profitableness of carrying the various accounts.

PROCESS COSTS AND Some cost is attached to every business opera-
BUSINESS OPERATIONS tion. To know the amount of this cost is to
increase the intelligence applied to business activities by management.

Cost accounting goes beyond the first, or original, expense. The
cost of coal itself may not be so important as the cost of heating or the
cost of each unit of power. The fact that delivery expenses in general
have decreased from $3,000 to $2,500 may not be so significant when
it is also determined that the cost per ton-mile has increased from
10 cents to 12 cents. It is not the original outlay that is so important,
but rather the use made of that original outlay. Such use is adequately
expressed by the cost reports and the data accumulated by cost accounting procedures. Some of the most important managerial decisions
require data that cannot be obtained directly from the accounts. If a
choice must be made between methods of production, product line, or
departments to be dropped or added, special computations employing
cost data are required to insure that the most intelligent decision will
be made by management.

FIXED AND VARIABLE The nature of indirect manufacturing costs
EXPENSES has great significance to the cost accountant
and to management. Many factory expenses tend to be independent
of the volume of output. Depreciation, taxes, foremen's salaries, and
insurance remain relatively constant in total regardless of the level of
output. Such expenses are called *fixed expenses*, since they do not move
in accordance with the increase or the decrease in activity.

Other expenses, such as direct labor and direct materials, vary
directly with the volume of output. These expenses are known as
variable expenses. If output is doubled, then variable expenses will
double; if output is halved, then variable expenses will be cut in two.

Still other expenses are only partially variable; they do not move in
direct ratio, but they tend to increase when output is increased and to
decrease when output is decreased. Such expenses are commonly
referred to as *semifixed* and may sometimes be broken down into
their fixed and variable components. The accountant can assist in the
management estimates if fixed expenses are separated from variable
expenses.

All of the expenses charged to a given process in a particular period
may normally be divided between fixed and variable. Because certain
expenses are present regardless of the level of output, the unit cost
tends to decrease as volume increases. For example, the Jones Co. is
currently producing 1,000 units of product at an average cost of $45,
of which $20 is fixed and $25 is variable. The sales price of the article

is $80. The total fixed expense of $20,000 is incurred regardless of the
level of output. If the company is able to double its production without
increasing its fixed costs, the cost per unit would be $35, or [$20,000 +
(2,000 × $25)] ÷ 2,000.

The relative amounts of fixed and variable costs are important in
making many managerial decisions. For example, the Jones Co. mentioned above may receive from a foreign buyer an offer to buy 1,000
units at $30 per unit. It would appear that the offer should be rejected
since the average cost of producing 2,000 units is $35 per unit. One
should be aware, however, that the $35 unit cost includes a fixed cost
element. Since fixed costs are present regardless of output, only the
variable cost per unit need be considered in arriving at a decision
whether to accept this special offer. The total proceeds from the
foreign offer would be $30,000 as compared to a total *differential cost*
of $25,000; hence the company would gain $5,000 by accepting the
offer. Differential cost may be defined as the increase in the total costs
(manufacturing, selling, and administrative) that occurs as production
is increased or decreased from one level to another. Assuming that the
sale to the foreign customer would not disrupt the domestic market in
any way, a comparison of the present and prospective situation may
be summarized as follows:

		Present Situation		Proposed Situation
Sales (1,000 units at $80).............		$80,000		$ 80,000
Foreign sale (1,000 units at $30).......				30,000
Total sales......................		$80,000		$110,000
Fixed expenses....................	$20,000		$20,000	
Variable expenses applicable to:				
Regular sales (1,000 units at $25)...	25,000		25,000	
Foreign sale (1,000 units at $25)....			25,000	
Total cost of sales...............		45,000		70,000
Gross margin.....................		$35,000		$ 40,000
Net gain if foreign offer is accepted.....				$ 5,000

STANDARD COSTS   The use of predetermined overhead rates involves estimates of expense items entering
into overhead. When actual transactions are debited to the overhead
account, which has been credited for overhead at the predetermined
rate, the balance at the end of any cost period represents an over-

absorbed or underabsorbed item. Sometimes predetermined estimates of all three cost elements — materials, labor, and overhead — are made. Such costs represent what the product should cost if planned scientifically and manufactured efficiently and are therefore called *standard costs*. They represent standards of performance by which the efficiency of manufacturing processes can be measured and controlled.

Since standard costs are estimates, there are differences, called *variances*, between actual costs and standard costs. Variances receive the special attention of factory executives, because management wants to know why the actual costs differ from the standards. For example, if a standard for materials has been set at 10,000 units to cost $1 per unit and 10,400 units were actually consumed at a cost of $1.05, the $920 variance would receive special managerial attention. Part of the variance is due to excess usage of materials and part to higher prices paid for materials. The variance is briefly summarized below:

Actual materials cost, 10,400 @ $1.05....................	$10,920
Standard materials cost, 10,000 @ $1.00.................	10,000
Variance, analyzed as follows:	$ 920

Usage variation loss (10,400 − 10,000) × $1.00, or $400
Price variation loss ($1.05 − $1.00) × 10,400, or   520

Total loss from standard............................... $ 920

If an average cost of 95 cents were paid for the 10,400 units of materials above, then the variance would have been analyzed as follows:

Actual materials cost, 10,400 @ $.95....................	$ 9,880
Standard materials cost, 10,000 @ $1.00.................	10,000
Variance, analyzed as follows:	$ 120

Price variation gain ($1.00 − $.95) × 10,400, or $520
Usage variation loss (10,400 − 10,000) × $1.00, or   400

Total gain from standard.............................. $ 120

It is essential to note that the price variation gain or loss is obtained by multiplying the price differential per unit by the *actual consumption*, while the usage gain or loss is obtained by multiplying the difference in units consumed by the *standard unit cost*. This procedure is employed in order to charge the proper amount of the variance against the individuals responsible for the variance. If the shop foreman, for example, was responsible for the excess usage of 400 units, he should not be relieved of his share of the variance merely because he was fortunate in having the market price of the materials decrease. The above concepts of analyzing materials variances are very similar to those employed in analyzing labor and overhead variances.

QUESTIONS

1. (a) Differentiate between job order and process cost accounting. (b) Would you recommend a job order or a process cost system for (1) a print shop? (2) a flour mill? (3) an oil refinery? (4) an iron foundry?

2. (a) What is meant by the term *equivalent units*? (b) When is it necessary to compute equivalent units of work completed within a process?

3. On March 1, Process 2 has a balance of $2,400. (a) What elements of cost are included in this balance? (b) Will an increase in raw materials prices affect the unit cost of the completed product derived from this balance? Explain.

4. A large department store, occupying four floors in a building with 4,800 square feet of space on each floor, distributes its rent expense on the basis of the floor space. (a) Can you suggest a more equitable basis for distribution? (b) Assuming that a total of $18,000 is paid for rent and that the main floor is considered to be three times as valuable as any one of the other three floors, how much of the rent expense would be allocated to Department R, which occupies 600 square feet on the fourth floor?

5. Distinguish between (a) a physical inventory and a perpetual inventory; (b) direct labor and indirect labor; (c) by-products and joint products; (d) service department and process department; (e) actual costs and standard costs.

6. Process H produces two products. How should the processing cost be allocated (a) if the products are joint products? (b) if one of the products is treated as a by-product?

7. In a certain factory, which produces normally only for the domestic market, the cost of 100,000 units is $5 a unit; of 50,000 units, $7.50 a unit. Assume that the estimated sales volume of the domestic market for the year 1954 is 50,000 units. A large foreign corporation offers $4 a unit for 50,000 units to be delivered in 1954, promising to market all of the 50,000 units abroad. Would you advise the acceptance of this offer? Why?

8. The charges to Process B during March were: direct materials, $4,050; direct labor, $2,600; factory overhead, $1,300. Three products resulted: By-product X, 1,000 units selling at 25 cents a unit; Product A, selling at $1.60 per unit; and Product B, selling at $4 per unit. During the month 4,000 units of A and 900 units of B were produced. Set up the process account showing the cost allocation to the three products. Show computations.

9. The standard and the actual expenditures for materials and labor of the Kite Company are as follows:

	MATERIALS	LABOR
Standard, 20,000 units @ $1.00............	$20,000	
Actual, 21,000 units at $1.10...............	23,100	
Standard, 30,000 hours at $1.50...........		$45,000
Actual, 29,000 hours at $1.55..............		44,950

Determine the variance for materials and labor, segregating the portions due to price and usage gains or losses.

10. Complete the following process account, assuming that all materials are placed in process at the beginning of production.

PROCESS A

1,500 units $^{1}/_{3}$ completed...... 1,200	Units completed
Direct materials 3,000 at $.50.. 1,500	500 units $\frac{1}{2}$ completed
Direct labor................. 900	
Factory overhead........... 1,350	

Determine the cost of completed units and partially completed units.

11. The Blair Co. started business on October 15, 1953. To December 31, the following expenditures were incurred in the Grinding Process, its only productive process:

Direct materials, 10,000 units @ $2.50..................	$25,000
Direct labor..	26,000
Factory overhead....................................	11,200

The company charged the 9,000 units transferred to finished goods with the total manufacturing costs of $62,200. What correcting entry is required on January 3, 1954, assuming that the goods in process are 100% completed as to materials and 30% completed as to processing costs and that none of the completed goods have yet been sold?

12. Complete the following process account, assuming that 10 pounds of material are required to manufacture one finished unit.

PROCESS 1

In process, 1,000 units, 80% completed as to materials and 60% as to processing costs.................... 5,200	Units completed, 8,000 In process, 2,800 units, 100% completed as to materials and 75% as to processing costs
Direct materials, 100,000 lbs.. 50,000	
Direct labor................ 14,000	
Factory overhead.......... 5,000	
74,200	74,200

PROBLEMS

29-1. Plumers, Inc. sells a large line of household appliances. They also service and repair household equipment. The products and the services are classified as three income-producing units: Stove and Refrigerator Department; Repair Shop; Small Appliances Department. The manager wishes to know costs per dollar-income of operating the three units. Operating expenses that can be directly identified with one of the income-producing units are charged to that unit. Other expenses are charged to Buildings and Grounds Expense and to General Expense; they are then redistributed.

	STOVE AND REFRIG. DEPT.	REPAIR SHOP	SMALL APPLI-ANCES DEPT.	BLDGS. AND GROUNDS EXPENSE	GENERAL EXPENSE
Buildings, cost........				$30,000	
Equipment, cost.......	$2,400	$4,000	$3,200		$600
Annual expenses:					
Salaries............	10,200	2,550	1,860		1,500
Insurance and taxes..	40	110	50	100	24
Maintenance........				610	
Parts used.........		900			
Advertising........					600
Utilities and supplies.					256
Depreciation:					
Buildings..........				4%	
Equipment........	10%	10%	10%		10%
Distribution of:					
Electricity, $450......	1/5	1/5		1/5	2/5

Instructions: (1) Set up "T" accounts for the three income-producing units and the two expense accounts shown above. Record the foregoing data. Redistribute the buildings and grounds expense and the general expense to the income-producing units. The buildings and grounds expense is distributed in proportion to the annual sales. The annual sales for the three income-producing departments are: Stove and Refrigerator Department, $60,000; Repair Shop, $24,000; Small Appliances Department, $12,000. The general expense is distributed ¼ to Stove and Refrigerator Department, ¼ to Repair Shop, and ½ to Small Appliances Department.

(2) Compute operating cost per dollar-income for each of the three units.

29-2. The Pacific Co. manufactures a single product in which the raw materials must pass through Processes A, B, and C, in that order, before completion. The first-in, first-out inventory method is used throughout. The degree of completion refers to the processing costs only.

Inventories of Process C and of Finished Goods on April 1 were as follows:
    Process C — 900 units ⅔ completed, $2,781.
    Finished Goods — 300 units @ $3.50 per unit.
During April the following transactions were completed:
    2,200 units with a value of $3,300 were transferred from Process B.
    Direct labor applied to Process C was $3,630; overhead costs applied to Process C were $2,120.

Inventories on April 30 are as follows:
   Process C — 500 units 3/5 completed.
   Finished Goods — 500 units.

Instructions: (1) Reconstruct the Process C account and the finished goods account as they should appear on the books of The Pacific Co. (Show all computations clearly.)

(2) Assuming that the sales price of each unit is $6.50 and that selling, general, and administrative expenses amounted to $4,300, prepare a profit and loss statement for April.

29-3. A condensed trial balance for the Hansen Chemical Co. was as follows on January 1, 1954:

Other Assets...............................	$100,000	
Raw Material — 3,500 lbs....................	10,500	
Preparation 25 — 600 lbs. (finished product)....	7,800	
Preparation 27 — 200 lbs. (finished product)....	4,500	
Factory Supplies...........................	200	
Accounts Payable..........................		$ 20,570
Wages Payable.............................		430
Capital...................................		102,000
	$123,000	$123,000

No preparations were in process on January 31. Preparation 25 is the product of refining raw material in Processes A and B. Preparation 27 is produced when Preparation 25 is further refined in Process C. The company has a selling market for both preparations.

The products are subject to considerable weight loss in all three processes; costs are therefore determined by dividing the accumulated costs by the number of pounds produced in each process.

The operations for January are summarized as follows:

(a) Purchased 4,000 lbs. of raw material at $3.50 per pound, $14,000, on account.

(b) Purchased factory supplies, $1,030, on account.

(c) Paid factory payroll, $14,680.

(d) Paid expenses applicable to the factory, $1,700, apportioned as follows: Service Department, $950; General Factory Expense, $750.

(e) Supplies used: Service Department, $450; General Factory Expense, $350.

(f) Recorded payroll of $14,600, chargeable as follows: Process A, $2,200; Process B, $5,500; Process C, $4,000; Service Department, $1,600; General Factory Expense, $1,300.

(g) Distributed service department expenses to Process A, 50%; Process B, 30%; Process C, 20%.

(h) Distributed general factory expenses equally to the three processes.

(i) Placed 2,500 lbs. of raw material into Process A, where a loss of 500 lbs. took place.

(j) Placed the 2,000 lbs. produced in Process A into Process B, from which 1,600 lbs. of Preparation 25 were produced and placed in stock.

(k) Placed into Process C the 600 lbs. of Preparation 25 on hand January 1 and 400 lbs. of the current month's production, from which 900 lbs. of Preparation 27 were produced.

(l) Shipped finished products to customers on first-in, first-out basis as follows:

Preparation 25 — 1,000 lbs., sales value, $20,000.
Preparation 27 —   600 lbs., sales value, $22,000.

(m) Paid operating expenses, $11,400.

Instructions: (1) Set up "T" accounts for Other Assets, Raw Materials, Process A, Process B, Process C, Preparation 25, Preparation 27, Factory Supplies, Accounts Payable, Wages Payable, Service Department, General Factory Expense, Capital, Sales, Cost of Goods Sold, and Operating Expenses. Enter the balances in the accounts.

(2) Record the foregoing operations for January directly in the accounts, identifying each entry by letter. Keep a memorandum of quantities and prices per pound in the item spaces.

(3) Balance and rule the accounts and take a trial balance as of January 31, 1954.

29-4. The Jeffreys Manufacturing Company produces Product X by a continuous processing procedure. Materials enter production at the start of processing. On March 31, 1954, the process account appeared as follows:

PROCESS A

Direct materials (15,000 at	
$3.00)..................	45,000
Direct labor...............	60,000
Factory overhead..........	37,500
	142,500

During March 12,000 units of Product X were completed. On March 31, 3,000 units remained in process, estimated to be ⅓ completed.

In April the following internal transactions were completed:

(a) 10,000 additional units of raw materials were put into production at $3.20 per unit.

(b) Labor costs for the month were $55,000.

(c) Overhead amounted to $37,000.

(d) The 3,000 units in process on March 31 were completed during the month, as well as 8,000 of the 10,000 that were put in process during the month; the remainder were ¾ completed on April 30, 1954.

Instructions: (1) Complete the process account as of March 31.

(2) Enter the foregoing transactions and complete the process account for April.

Chapter | 30

Budgets

ACCOUNTING FOR ESTIMATED FUTURE TRANSACTIONS
In previous chapters the accountant's role has been primarily that of a historian. The discussion and the illustrations have been devoted to the recording and the summarizing of transactions of a business enterprise. Only minor attention has been given to the use of accounting data in planning the course of future action and to the role of the accountant as an adviser to management.

Business transactions are normally planned by the executives of an enterprise. Before any sales are made, the sales manager estimates their volume. Before any goods are produced, the factory manager schedules their production. Before any funds are raised by bank loan or bond issue, the method of the raising exists in the mind of the treasurer. These estimated future transactions, planned by management, precede the actual transactions that are recorded in the accounting system.

It is advisable to measure in accounting terms the financial effect of these plans of management. Because of his experience in measuring the financial effect of actual transactions, the accountant is best qualified to deal with these estimated future transactions. He assembles these plans for future transactions into an estimated profit and loss statement and an estimated balance sheet. He reports the effect of the coordinated plans before any action takes place. This preliminary report puts the plans down in black and white for permanent reference.

This dealing with estimated future transactions is called *budgeting*. If the plans deal with all the transactions of the ensuing period, they are known as a *master budget*. If they deal only with transactions affecting cash, they are called a *cash budget*. If they involve only income and expense transactions, they are called an *operating budget*. The *master budget*, which includes all of the data found in the cash budget and the operating budget, will form the principal subject matter of this chapter.

THE BUDGET PERIOD
In accounting projected into the future, as well as in accounting dealing with the past, a fiscal period must be set up. The period to be covered by planning

595

ordinarily equals the period covered by reports of the past. Hence it happens that the most commonly used budget period is the year. Just as the accounting year is broken down into quarters or months, so is the budget year divided into shorter intervals. The annual budget with a "breakdown" into months is the type of budget commonly found. The planning of the next year's operations is the prevailing budget procedure.

In some planning the budget period is longer than a year. If the plans involve the purchase of fixed assets that will last several years, and a corresponding permanent increase in output, the budget period for such plans must necessarily be longer. Public utilities, such as the telephone company, budget five or ten years ahead. Automobile companies budget a year at a time because of yearly models offered consumers.

PLANNING AND DOING IN BUSINESS MANAGEMENT In the development of scientific business management the separation of planning and doing has been a marked feature. Complete plans are drawn up before actual operations are begun. The proposed course of action is first put down on paper and approved by all of the executives concerned.

This planning inevitably involves future transactions. The sales manager plans to increase sales. To provide the goods to be sold, the factory superintendent plans to expand the plant and to increase employment. The financial officer plans to extend additional credit and to seek new sources of capital. All of these plans anticipate the actual transactions of the new period.

If these planned transactions are organized in accounts and set up in a balance sheet and a profit and loss statement, a more complete picture is afforded of the combined effect of the plans on the business. The cost of expanded operations may be so large that net profit is reduced. In such a case contraction rather than expansion may be more desirable. The net effect of all the proposed activities should be carefully considered by the management before such plans are put into action.

In budgeting, planned transactions are accounted for by journal entries or by entries made directly in "T" accounts. For example, if new machinery costing $200,000 must be purchased to provide for a proposed expansion in sales, it may be necessary to issue bonds in order to provide the funds. Assuming the issue of $200,000 of 5% bonds in this case, the effect of the proposed transactions is illustrated on the following page in "T" accounts:

CASH			
(a)	200,000	(b)	200,000

MACHINERY	
(b)	200,000

ALLOWANCE FOR DEPR. OF MACHINERY		
	(c)	20,000

INTEREST PAYABLE		
	(d)	10,000

BONDS PAYABLE		
	(a)	200,000

PROFIT AND LOSS SUMMARY

(c) Depr. of Machinery 20,000	
(d) Interest on Bonds 10,000	

The estimated transactions (a) to (d) shown above illustrate the effect of this proposal on assets, liabilities, and expenses. When applied to the beginning account balances, these transactions, combined with all of the other planned transactions, will provide an estimated balance sheet at the end of the year and an estimated profit and loss statement for the year. The portrayal of budgeted transactions on accounting statements is an important part of the budget program.

If the resulting statements appear favorable and desirable, the planned operations should be distributed among the months of the new year. Actual transactions month by month should be compared with the estimated transactions. This comparison of real transactions with estimated transactions period by period is one of the valuable features of budgeting.

ESSENTIALS OF BUDGETARY CONTROL The procedure by which budgetary control is obtained must, of necessity, vary from business to business. Rarely can any two enterprises follow exactly the same procedure. In all cases, however, the essential features of budgetary control include (1) departmental estimates, (2) coordination of estimates, and (3) budget reports.

(1) *Departmental Estimates.* Each department should prepare an estimate of its activities for the budget period. The method of stating these activities depends on the nature of the operations of the department. The sales department should usually show its estimated sales in both volume and value, and it should also show its estimates of the cost of making these sales. The production department should state the volume of production that it plans for the period and the amount of materials, labor, and manufacturing expenses that it estimates will be necessary to carry out this program. The purchasing department, the office manager's department, and similar departments should indicate their estimated expenditures for the period. Finally,

the financial department, using all the other estimates as a basis, should estimate the cash receipts and the cash disbursements for the period.

Accurate estimates of future operations are admittedly difficult to prepare. Nevertheless plans must be made for the future; and the more difficult it is to plan, the more urgent it is that plans be made. Even though the departmental estimates are not entirely accurate, they are better than no estimates at all. There must be some chart for the future even if it is in rough outline.

(2) *Coordination of Estimates.* Because of the interdependence of business departments, some departments will need the estimates of other departments in making their own estimates. The sales, production, and finance departments must work on the same fundamental plan. They must agree on the quantity and kinds of goods to be produced and sold.

The budget committee, consisting of the departmental heads, considers the proposed budget and makes such revisions as it thinks advisable. The members are given an opportunity to defend their original estimates. Finally the completed budget as revised is approved by the committee.

(3) *Budget Reports.* Periodic reports comparing the estimated and the actual performance for the period should be made. These periodic reports are usually for one month's operations. In order to make possible the monthly reports, the budgeted annual figures should be set up by months. These monthly budgeted figures may then be compared with the actual figures as shown in the illustration on the opposite page.

BUDGETARY CONTROL NOT A NEW IDEA All business firms practice budgetary control to some degree, although many of them do not realize the fact. When rates of depreciation are established on fixed assets, a budget on the life of these assets is made; when standard dividend rates are approved by the board of directors, a budget on the earning capacity of the organization is established; when the salaries of employees are agreed upon, a budget on the earning capacity of the employees is made. All these budgets are changed from time to time as experience shows the need for correction in the original estimates.

It may be found that the assets are depreciating more rapidly than was originally estimated; that the earning capacity of the business is greater or less than was originally believed; that the employees are more or less efficient than was originally supposed. In the same

DEANE & HOLLEY, INC.

Budget Report

For Month Ended March 31, 1954

	Actual This Month	Budget This Month	Increase or Decrease*
Sales.....................	$35,000	$30,000	$ 5,000
Cost of Goods Sold:			
Mdse. Inventory, Mar. 1, 1954	$40,000	$38,000	$ 2,000
Purchases................	25,000	26,000	1,000*
Mdse. Available for Sale.....	$65,000	$64,000	$ 1,000
Less Mdse. Inv., Mar. 31, 1954	45,000	48,000	3,000*
Cost of Goods Sold........	$20,000	$16,000	$ 4,000
Gross Profit on Sales.........	$15,000	$14,000	$ 1,000
Operating Expenses:			
Selling Expenses:			
Sales Salaries............	$ 2,100	$ 2,000	$ 100
Advertising Expense......	1,000	800	200
Depr. of Store Equipment..	500	500	. . .
Store Supplies Expense....	800	700	100
Misc. Selling Expense.....	1,200	1,100	100
Total Selling Expenses....	$ 5,600	$ 5,100	$ 500
General Expenses:			
Office Salaries............	$ 1,200	$ 1,200	. . .
Rent Expense............	1,500	1,500	. . .
Depr. of Office Equipment.	400	400	. . .
Bad Debts Expense.......	500	500	. . .
Misc. General Expense....	1,400	1,200	$ 200
Total General Expenses....	$ 5,000	$ 4,800	$ 200
Total Operating Expenses....	$10,600	$ 9,900	$ 700
Net Profit from Operations.....	$ 4,400	$ 4,100	$ 300
Other Income:			
Purchases Discount.........	$ 600	$ 700	$ 100*
Other Expenses:			
Sales Discount.............	$ 400	$ 400	. . .
Interest Expense..........	500	500	. . .
Total Other Expenses.......	$ 900	$ 900	. . .
Net Deduction..............	$ 300	$ 200	$ 100
Net Profit for March.........	$ 4,100	$ 3,900	$ 200

manner estimates of sales, production, finances, and expense should be made in the light of the best information available; and these estimates should be changed whenever more complete or more accurate information so dictates.

PROCEDURE FOR MASTER BUDGET The master budget is usually the product of the budget committee. It coordinates the departmental budgets and organizes them into a single budget for the business as a whole. In the master budget are found all of the estimated transactions for the coming year. When these transactions are accounted for, the estimated financial position at the end of the coming year, together with the estimated financial progress during the year, will be available. It is the function of the accountant to express the effect of the budgeted transactions in these two reports.

In the construction of these reports, the profit and loss statement and the balance sheet of the past year are used. The amounts of proposed activities are expressed as fractional parts or percentages of the amounts for the year just past. Because of his knowledge of these past statements and his ability to account for transactions, the accountant is peculiarly fitted to serve the budget committee in the preparation of the accounting statements in the master budget.

The estimated sales for the new year is the logical beginning point and perhaps the most significant figure in the budget plans aside from net profit. If the business outlook is unfavorable, the sales manager may estimate a 25% decline in sales unless prices are lowered; he may, however, believe that, with a decrease of about 10% in the selling price, he can sell as many units as in the previous year. If sales consist of two or more types, each type must be calculated separately. Assume that sales in 1953 consisted of 10,000 units of A at $30 and 20,000 units of B at $15, with total sales of $600,000. If prices are maintained but the number of units sold declines 25%, the estimated sales will be $450,000. If, however, A units are reduced in price to $27.50 and B units to $12.50, and if the volume of units sold is maintained, the estimated sales will be $525,000.

At the budget meeting it will be necessary to determine whether it is better to maintain prices and lose in number of units sold and sales in dollars ($450,000), or to lower prices and maintain unit sales and thus have a better showing in total sales ($525,000). As explained in the previous chapter, certain expenses are fixed and cannot be reduced even though the number of units sold declines. Other expenses are variable and move up and down with the quantity sold. By listing the operating expenses under each plan, it is possible to determine which plan will produce the greater net profit.

If, in place of contraction, the outlook promises increased volume and the sales manager estimates an increase of 25% at the existing prices, the effect of such an increase in output on production policies and costs must be considered. The estimated increase in the number of units to be sold may make advisable the installation of new machinery that would reduce labor costs. The payment for the new machinery may require that additional stock be sold or that bonds be issued. The increase may require expansion of the sales force and an increased advertising appropriation.

ACCOUNTING FOR THE MASTER BUDGET PLANS The general ledger account balances as of the beginning of the budget period should be set up in "T" accounts. The transactions incident to the proposed budget are then entered in these accounts. Since the master budget ordinarily includes the ending inventories, the estimated depreciation, and the bad debts expense, the trial balance prepared from the "T" accounts is an adjusted trial balance. It therefore provides, without need for adjustment, the amounts for the two estimated statements.

It may seem odd to prepare in January a profit and loss statement for the year ending in the following December and a balance sheet for a date almost a year hence. But to do this sets up a pattern with which actual transactions may be compared. It also coordinates in the financial statements the proposed actions for the coming year.

In order to carry out the comparison month by month, it is necessary, as stated before, to break down the annual budget into twelve monthly budgets. This breakdown makes possible monthly comparisons similar to that illustrated on page 599.

ILLUSTRATION OF ACCOUNTING FOR A MASTER BUDGET The profit and loss statement for the year ended December 31, 1953, and the balance sheet as of December 31, 1953, for the Johnson Mercantile Company are given on pages 602 and 603. In addition there are given the budgeted transactions for the year 1954, as planned at the final meeting of the budget committee. The accountant is asked to show the effect of the budgeted transactions on the financial position of the company, together with a budget of operations. The "T" accounts on pages 605 and 606 record the budgeted transactions and show what the results, as budgeted, would be. In order to save space, all budgeted profit and loss statement items are entered directly in the profit and loss summary account.

Profit and loss statement for the preceding year:

JOHNSON MERCANTILE COMPANY
PROFIT AND LOSS STATEMENT
FOR YEAR ENDED DECEMBER 31, 1953

Sales...............................			$350,000
Cost of Goods Sold:			
Merchandise Inventory, Jan. 1, 1953....		$ 85,000	
Purchases...........................		247,000	
Merchandise Available for Sale.........		$332,000	
Merchandise Inventory, Dec. 31, 1953...		87,000	
Cost of Goods Sold...................			245,000
Gross Profit on Sales..................			$105,000
Operating Expenses:			
Selling Expense:			
Sales Salaries...............	$30,000		
Advertising Expense.........	4,000		
Depreciation of Equipment...	5,000		
Total Selling Expenses...............		$ 39,000	
General Expenses:			
Officers Salaries.............	$15,000		
Office Salaries...............	15,000		
Depreciation of Buildings.....	5,000		
Bad Debts Expense	1,750		
Misc. General Expense.......	5,000		
Total General Expenses............		41,750	
Total Operating Expenses.............			80,750
Net Profit from Operations..............			$ 24,250
Other Income:			
Purchases Discount...................		$ 4,940	
Other Expense:			
Interest Expense.....................		3,000	
Net Addition..........................			1,940
Total Net Profit before Estimated Income			
Taxes.............................			$ 26,190
Less Estimated Income Taxes...........			10,476
Net Profit after Estimated Income Taxes ..			$ 15,714

Balance sheet at the end of the preceding year:

JOHNSON MERCANTILE COMPANY
BALANCE SHEET
DECEMBER 31, 1953

ASSETS		
Current Assets:		
Cash................................	$ 23,000	
Accounts Receivable......... $ 45,000		
Less Allowance for Bad		
Debts................. 2,200	42,800	
Merchandise Inventory...............	87,000	
Total Current Assets................		$152,800
Fixed Assets:		
Equipment................. $ 50,000		
Less Allowance for Depr..... 25,000	$ 25,000	
Buildings.................. $100,000		
Less Allowance for Depr..... 25,000	75,000	
Land..............................	30,000	
Total Fixed Assets..................		130,000
Total Assets.........................		$282,800
LIABILITIES AND CAPITAL		
LIABILITIES		
Current Liabilities:		
Accounts Payable........... $ 62,000		
Estimated Income Taxes Pay-		
able.................... 10,476		
Total Current Liabilities..............	$ 72,476	
Fixed Liabilities:		
Mortgage Payable..................	50,000	
Total Liabilities......................		$122,476
CAPITAL		
Common Stock........................	$120,000	
Retained Earnings....................	40,324	
Total Capital........................		160,324
Total Liabilities and Capital		$282,800

Summary of estimated transactions for the budget year:

(a) It is estimated that sales will increase, but that this increase can be accomplished without any change in the value of the inventory.

(b) Sales, all of which will be made on account, will increase 40% in volume with a 6% reduction in price.

> Computations:
>
> > 1.40 × .94 (sales price plus increase times volume minus volume decrease) = 1.316
> > 1.316 × $350,000 (Sales for 1953) = $460,600

(c) Purchases, all of which will be made on account, will increase 40% in volume with a 10% decrease in unit prices.

> Computations:
>
> > .90 × 1.40 (old price minus decrease times volume plus volume increase) = 1.26
> > 1.26 × $247,000 (Purchases for 1953) = $311,220

(d) Sales salaries must be increased 30% to take care of the increased sales.

> Computations:
>
> > 1.30 × $30,000 = $39,000

(e) The amount to be spent for advertising will be $4,800.

(f) To provide for increased sales, a $40,000 addition to the building must be made. New equipment costing $10,000 will be needed. These improvements are expected to be completed by April 1, 1954.

(g) Estimated income taxes payable of $10,476 will be paid.

(h) Depreciation of equipment, 10% yearly.

> Computations:
>
> > .10 × $50,000 (old equipment)   = $5,000
> > .10 × $10,000 (new equip.) × 9/12 =   750
> >
> > $5,750

(i) Officers salaries will be raised $2,500.

(j) Office salaries are estimated to be $16,500.

(k) Depreciation of building, 5% yearly.

> Computations:
>
> > .05 × $100,000 (old buildings)   = $5,000
> > .05 × $40,000 (new buildings) × 9/12 = 1,500
> >
> > $6,500

(l) Bad debts expense, $\frac{1}{2}$% of sales.

> Computations:
>
> > .005 × $460,600 = $2,303

(m) Miscellaneous general expense is estimated the same as for 1953.

(n) Purchases discount, 2% of purchases (to nearest dollar).

    Computations:

        $.02 \times \$311,220 = \$6,224$ (to nearest dollar)

(o) Interest on mortgage, 6%.

    Computations:

        $.06 \times \$50,000 = \$3,000$

(p) In order to pay for the addition to the building and the new equipment, the company will issue at the beginning of the year 500 ten-year, 5%, $100 bonds.

    Computations:

        $500 \times \$100 = \$50,000$

(q) Collections on account will have been made so that the balance of the accounts receivable account will be $48,000.

(r) Payments on account will have been made so that the balance of the accounts payable account will be $32,700.

(s) Estimated income taxes payable, 40% of net profit for 1954 (to nearest dollar). The balance of the profit and loss summary account is closed into Retained Earnings.

    Computations:

        $.40 \times \$52,751$ (net profit) $= \$21,100$ (to nearest dollar)

The data provided by estimated transactions are entered in "T" accounts as shown below:

CASH				MERCHANDISE INVENTORY		
Balance	23,000	(d)	39,000	Balance	87,000	
(p)	50,000	(e)	4,800			
(q)	457,600	(f)	50,000			
		(g)	10,476			
		(i)	17,500	EQUIPMENT		
		(j)	16,500	Balance	50,000	
		(m)	5,000	(f)	10,000	
		(o)	3,000			
		(p)	2,500			
		(r)	334,296			

ACCOUNTS RECEIVABLE				ALLOWANCE FOR DEPRECIATION OF EQUIPMENT		
Balance	45,000	(q)	457,600		Balance	25,000
(b)	460,600				(h)	5,750

ALLOWANCE FOR BAD DEBTS				BUILDINGS		
		Balance	2,200	Balance	100,000	
		(l)	2,303	(f)	40,000	

ALLOWANCE FOR DEPRECIATION
OF BUILDINGS

| | | Balance | 25,000 |
| | | (k) | 6,500 |

MORTGAGE PAYABLE

| | | Balance | 50,000 |

LAND

| Balance | 30,000 | | |

BONDS PAYABLE

| | | (p) | 50,000 |

ACCOUNTS PAYABLE

| (n) | 6,224 | Balance | 62,000 |
| (r) | 334,296 | (c) | 311,220 |

COMMON STOCK

| | | Balance | 120,000 |

ESTIMATED INCOME TAXES PAYABLE

| (g) | 10,476 | Balance | 10,476 |
| | | (s) | 21,100 |

RETAINED EARNINGS

| | | Balance | 40,324 |
| | | (s) | 31,651 |

PROFIT AND LOSS SUMMARY

(c) Purchases	311,220	(b) Sales	460,600
(d) Sales Salaries	39,000	(n) Purchases Discount	6,224
(e) Advertising Expense	4,800		
(h) Depr. of Equipment	5,750		
(i) Officers Salaries	17,500		
(j) Office Salaries	16,500		
(k) Depr. of Buildings	6,500		
(l) Bad Debts Expense	2,303		
(m) Misc. General Expense	5,000		
(o) Mortgage Interest Exp.	3,000		
(p) Bond Interest Expense	2,500		
(s) Est. Income Taxes Pay.	21,100		
(s) To Retained Earnings	31,651		
	466,824		466,824

The accountant must use his best judgment in determining just what the budgeted plans actually mean. Literal interpretations have been given to the preceding statements of estimated transactions. The purchases discounts are set up at 2% of Purchases rather than 2% of the total debits to Accounts Payable. The amount of goods purchased is taken as 40% above the purchases for 1953 rather than 40% above cost of sales for 1953. The amounts used for depreciation include nine months' depreciation on the new assets put into use on April 1, 1954.

From the "T" accounts are prepared the estimated profit and loss statement and the estimated balance sheet for 1954 shown on pages 607 and 608. These statements show the financial effect of the budgeted

Estimated profit and loss statement for the budget year:

JOHNSON MERCANTILE COMPANY
ESTIMATED PROFIT AND LOSS STATEMENT
FOR YEAR ENDING DECEMBER 31, 1954

Sales..		$460,600
Cost of Goods Sold:		
Merchandise Inv., Jan. 1, 1954.........	$ 87,000	
Purchases............................	311,220	
Merchandise Available for Sale.........	$398,220	
Less Merchandise Inventory, Dec. 31, 1954	87,000	
Cost of Goods Sold....................		311,220
Gross Profit on Sales....................		$149,380
Operating Expenses:		
Selling Expenses:		
Sales Salaries.............. $39,000		
Advertising Expense........ 4,800		
Depreciation of Equipment.. 5,750		
Total Selling Expenses..............	$ 49,550	
General Expenses:		
Officers Salaries............ $17,500		
Office Salaries............. 16,500		
Depreciation of Buildings.... 6,500		
Bad Debts Expense......... 2,303		
Misc. General Expense...... 5,000		
Total General Expenses.............	47,803	
Total Operating Expenses............		97,353
Net Profit from Operations.............		$ 52,027
Other Income:		
Purchases Discount...................	$ 6,224	
Other Expense:		
Mortgage Interest Expense.... $ 3,000		
Bond Interest Expense........ 2,500		
Total Other Expense..................	5,500	
Net Addition........................		724
Total Net Profit before Estimated Income Taxes............................		$ 52,751
Less Estimated Income Taxes...........		21,100
Net Profit after Estimated Income Taxes...		$ 31,651

Estimated balance sheet at the end of the budget year:

JOHNSON MERCANTILE COMPANY
ESTIMATED BALANCE SHEET
DECEMBER 31, 1954

ASSETS			
Current Assets:			
Cash		$ 47,528	
Accounts Receivable	$ 48,000		
Less Allowance for Bad Debts	4,503	43,497	
Merchandise Inventory		87,000	
Total Current Assets			$178,025
Fixed Assets:			
Equipment	$ 60,000		
Less Allowance for Depreciation	30,750	$ 29,250	
Buildings	$140,000		
Less Allowance for Depreciation	31,500	108,500	
Land		30,000	
Total Fixed Assets			167,750
Total Assets			$345,775
LIABILITIES AND CAPITAL			
LIABILITIES			
Current Liabilities:			
Accounts Payable	$ 32,700		
Estimated Income Taxes Payable	21,100		
Total Current Liabilities		$ 53,800	
Fixed Liabilities:			
Mortgage Payable	$ 50,000		
Bonds Payable	50,000		
Total Fixed Liabilities		100,000	
Total Liabilities			$153,800
CAPITAL			
Common Stock		$120,000	
Retained Earnings		71,975	
Total Capital			191,975
Total Liabilities and Capital			$345,775

transactions. They indicate the goal that will be reached if every member in the organization measures up to the plans laid down in the budget.

ADVANTAGES OF BUDGETARY CONTROL The preparation of the budget, the presentation of the periodic comparisons, and the use of these accounting data by executives and their assistants provide a more effective working organization. If budgets are to be prepared intelligently, all those who are responsible for the preparation of budgets must think through their problems thoroughly. Executives are given a chance to discuss with their assistants all the details of plans for the coming year. Disagreements among members of the executive group are less likely to arise when budgeted plans have been agreed upon. The comparative reports presented by the accounting department provide a satisfactory control over the operations.

IMPORTANCE OF BUDGETS TO NONPROFIT ORGANIZATIONS Educational, charitable, and other nonprofit organizations are interested primarily in providing a particular service. Since income must be provided to cover expenses or expenses must be limited to the income received, budgets play a very necessary and important role in the financial management of such organizations. In the case of a university or a college, the activities for the year can not be planned definitely until the income to be received is known. In other cases in which an organization is interested primarily in providing a certain service for its members, the cost of providing this service must be estimated in order that the amount to be collected from the members for the service may likewise be calculated. A budget is the best means of matching estimated income against proposed expenditures.

In the case of political units — federal, state, and local governments — the budget is an important feature of public administration. The chief administrative officer plans in advance the scope of the various activities under his administration and includes in this plan the costs. This constitutes the budget of his administration and is usually submitted for approval to the tax-levying body. The rates and kinds of taxes are an important factor in the preparation of every governmental budget.

Since the nature and amount of governmental and personal income can be estimated more accurately than business income, the budget will be more comparable to actual transactions of the ensuing fiscal period. There is, therefore, a tendency to confuse budgeting with accounting in these cases. The recording of the actual transactions is the historical phase of accounting and should be distinguished from the planned transactions of the future, which is the budget. Estimated tax revenue is a budgeted amount; the actual receipts from tax revenues are accountable transactions and therefore a part of the accounting records.

QUESTIONS

1. Robert Cunningham says that he and the heads of the departments of his business spend considerable time in committee meetings, discussing the outlook for business, and that he cannot see any advantage for them in the preparation of a formal budget. Do you agree with Cunningham? Why?

2. Do you believe that the management of a business having a large number of widely scattered branches would find it advantageous to have budgets presented by each branch manager? Why?

3. "It is not easy to coordinate sales possibilities with productive capacity. In fact, this coordination is one of the most difficult administrative problems." Do you think budgets would be of assistance in overcoming this difficulty?

4. "Fifty-one out of 93 companies reported that the executive in charge of budgets is either the treasurer or controller." This seems to differ from the procedure described in the chapter. Can you explain?

5. What advantages does a small firm derive from a budget to compensate for the labor and the time involved in making the budget?

6. "Budgets should be prepared in terms of units of responsibility." What does this statement mean?

7. The Purdue Company manufactures only on special order, whereas the Zenith Company manufactures for stock. Will the methods of preparing the budgets of these companies differ because of the difference in production policies? Explain.

8. The sales manager estimates a 50% increase in quantity sold with a 20% decrease in price. If the sales for the previous year were $142,860, what is the amount of sales in the estimated profit and loss statement?

9. The sales of the Marrone Manufacturing Company for 1953 consisted of 30,000 units at $25. The cost of manufacturing these units was $20 each. Selling expenses were $75,000; general and administrative expenses, $50,000. The sales manager estimates he can sell 40,000 units in 1954 if the price is reduced $2.50 per unit. If fixed costs in manufacturing in 1953 were $240,000 and will not be increased in 1954, if other manufacturing costs vary directly with the number of units produced, if selling costs remain the same percentage of sales, and if general and administrative expenses do not increase, what change would the reduction in price produce on the net operating profit or loss of this company? Show figures to prove your answer.

PROBLEMS

30-1. Each January, Weber, Incorporated prepares an estimated profit and loss statement for the coming year. In January, 1954, the profit and loss statement below and the following information are available:

WEBER, INCORPORATED
PROFIT AND LOSS STATEMENT
FOR YEAR ENDED DECEMBER 31, 1953

Sales (12,000 units @ $100)			$1,200,000
Cost of Goods Sold:			
Merchandise Inventory, January 1 (1,100 units @ $65)		$ 71,500	
Purchases (11,900 units @ $65)		773,500	
Merchandise Available for Sale		$845,000	
Less Merchandise Inventory, December 31 (1,000 units @ $65)		65,000	
Cost of Goods Sold (12,000 units @ $65)			780,000
Gross Profit on Sales			$ 420,000
Operating Expenses:			
Selling Expenses:			
Sales Commissions ($5 per unit)	$60,000		
Advertising Expense ($3 per unit)	36,000		
Depreciation of Store Equipment	20,000		
Miscellaneous Selling Expense	4,000		
Total Selling Expenses		$120,000	
General Expenses:			
Officers Salaries	$30,000		
Office Salaries	18,000		
Office Supplies Expense	9,000		
Depreciation of Office Equipment	2,000		
Bad Debts Expense	6,000		
Rent Expense	25,000		
Total General Expenses		90,000	
Total Operating Expenses			210,000
Net Profit from Operations			$ 210,000
Other Income:			
Purchases Discount		$ 7,735	
Other Expense:			
Sales Discount	$12,000		
Interest Expense	5,735		
Total Other Expense		17,735	
Net Deduction			10,000
Total Net Profit before Estimated Income Taxes			$ 200,000
Less Estimated Income Taxes			80,000
Net Profit after Estimated Income Taxes			$ 120,000

Sales: The selling price, which has been $100 per unit, is to be decreased to $90. It is anticipated that this price reduction will result in a sales volume increase of 2,000 units.

Cost of Goods Sold: The unit cost has been $65, but it has been reduced to $60 as of January 1, 1954. Purchases will be made of as many units as are expected to be sold so that the ending inventory will be 1,000 units.

Selling Expenses:
    (a) Sales commissions will be computed at $6 per unit.
    (b) The amount to be spent for advertising for the coming year is to be $4 per unit.
    (c) Depreciation of store equipment will be the same as for the preceding year.
    (d) Miscellaneous selling expenses will increase by $1,000.

General Expenses:
    (a) Officers salaries will increase $15,000.
    (b) Office salaries will increase $2,000.
    (c) Office supplies expense will increase $2,750.
    (d) Depreciation of office equipment will be the same as for the preceding year.
    (e) Bad debts expense is estimated at $\frac{1}{2}$ of 1% of sales.
    (f) Annual rental of building increases $5,000 per lease agreement.

Other Income and Expenses: Cash discounts are to be estimated at 1% of sales and purchases respectively. Interest expense is estimated at $5,000.

Income Tax: Income taxes are estimated at 40% of net profit for 1954.

Instructions: Prepare an estimated profit and loss statement for the year ended December 31, 1954.

30-2. The estimated profit and loss statement included in the 1954 annual budget of Jordan-Jones, Inc. is given on page 613. The actual profit and loss statement for the month of January, 1954, is given on page 614.

In order to compare the actual profit and loss statement figures for January, 1954, with the budgeted figures for the same month, it will be necessary to take into account the following variations in the monthly breakdown of the annual budget figures:

    (a) Sales for January were estimated at 10% of annual sales. Expenses that were expected to vary proportionally with sales were: sales commissions, advertising expense, store supplies expense, bad debts expense, and interest income.

    (b) The beginning inventory in the January budget was estimated at $50,000; the ending inventory at $40,000. The cost of goods sold and the gross profit on sales were computed at the same percentage of sales as in the annual budget. (Note: Purchases will not be 10% of annual budget.)

    (c) Fixed expenses that were not expected to vary with sales were: sales and office salaries, rent expense, depreciation of store and office equipment, office supplies expense, and miscellaneous general expense.

JORDAN-JONES, INC.
ESTIMATED PROFIT AND LOSS STATEMENT
FOR YEAR ENDING DECEMBER 31, 1954

Sales..			$800,000
Cost of Goods Sold:			
Merchandise Inventory, January 1, 1954............	$ 50,000		
Purchases......................................	580,000		
Merchandise Available for Sale....................	$630,000		
Less Merchandise Inventory, December 31, 1954.....	70,000		
Cost of Goods Sold..............................			560,000
Gross Profit on Sales..............................			$240,000
Operating Expenses:			
Selling Expenses:			
Sales Salaries.........................	$48,000		
Sales Commissions.....................	20,000		
Advertising Expense...................	16,000		
Depreciation of Store Equipment........	6,000		
Store Supplies Expense.................	5,500		
Total Selling Expenses..........................		$ 95,500	
General Expenses:			
Office Salaries........................	$24,000		
Rent Expense.........................	18,000		
Depreciation of Office Equipment........	3,000		
Office Supplies Expense................	2,400		
Bad Debts Expense....................	8,000		
Miscellaneous General Expense..........	3,600		
Total General Expenses.....................		59,000	
Total Operating Expenses........................			$154,500
Net Profit from Operations........................			$ 85,500
Other Income:			
Purchases Discount.....................	$10,500		
Interest Income.......................	1,000		
Total Other Income.............................		$ 11,500	
Other Expense:			
Sales Discount........................	$16,000		
Interest Expense......................	6,000		
Total Other Expense...........................		22,000	
Net Deduction....................................			10,500
Net Profit..			$ 75,000

JORDAN-JONES, INC.
PROFIT AND LOSS STATEMENT
FOR MONTH ENDED JANUARY 31, 1954

Sales...			$72,000
Cost of Goods Sold:			
Merchandise Inventory, January 1, 1954..............	$55,000		
Purchases......................................	40,400		
Merchandise Available for Sale.....................	$95,400		
Less Merchandise Inventory, January 31, 1954........	45,000		
Cost of Goods Sold................................		50,400	
Gross Profit on Sales..................................			$21,600
Operating Expenses:			
Selling Expenses:			
Sales Salaries............................	$3,750		
Sales Commissions........................	1,800		
Advertising Expense.......................	1,440		
Depreciation of Store Equipment...........	500		
Store Supplies Expense....................	495		
Total Selling Expenses............................	$ 7,985		
General Expenses:			
Office Salaries...........................	$2,000		
Rent Expense.............................	1,800		
Depreciation of Office Equipment..........	250		
Office Supplies Expense...................	200		
Bad Debts Expense........................	720		
Miscellaneous General Expense.............	300		
Total General Expenses.........................	5,270		
Total Operating Expenses...........................		13,255	
Net Profit from Operations.............................			$ 8,345
Other Income:			
Purchases Discount...............................	$ 1,050		
Interest Income..................................	90		
Total Other Income...............................	$ 1,140		
Other Expense:			
Sales Discount..................................	$2,000		
Interest Expense................................	300		
Total Other Expense.............................	2,300		
Net Deduction...		1,160	
Net Profit..			$ 7,185

(d) Because of the increased cash receipts expected during January, the items listed below were estimated as follows:

Purchases Discount, 1/10 of annual figure.

Sales Discount, 1/8 of annual figure.

Interest Expense, 1/20 of annual figure.

Instructions: Prepare a budget report, like the one on page 599, for January, 1954.

30-3. Budget statements for 1954 are to be prepared for Incho, Incorporated, from the following data:

INCHO, INCORPORATED
POST-CLOSING TRIAL BALANCE
DECEMBER 31, 1953

Cash....................................	$ 50,000	
Accounts Receivable......................	30,000	
Allowance for Bad Debts		$ 2,000
Finished Goods...........................	60,000	
Work in Process..........................	70,000	
Raw Materials............................	50,000	
Factory Supplies.........................	16,000	
Machinery and Equipment.................	165,000	
Allowance for Depreciation of Machinery and Equipment		60,000
Accounts Payable.........................		54,000
Dividends Payable........................		18,000
Estimated Income Taxes Payable		14,000
Bonds Payable, 6%.......................		50,000
Common Stock, 2,000 shares, $100 par........		200,000
Surplus..................................		43,000
	$441,000	$441,000

The sales manager estimated during 1954 the sale of 7,500 units of A at $60 and the sale of 6,000 units of B at $50. All sales are made on account.

The general manager has made the following estimates:

(1) Estimated ending inventories of December 31, 1954, are:
    (a) Raw materials, $42,000.
    (b) Work in process, $65,000.
    (c) Finished goods, $50,000.

(2) Purchases to be made on account:

(a) Raw materials.............................	$113,200
(b) Factory supplies...........................	30,000
Total....................................	$143,200

(3) Cash receipts:

(a) Sale of 1,000 shares of common stock at par....	$100,000
(b) Collection of accounts receivable.............	735,000
Total....................................	$835,000

(4) Cash expenditures:

(a)	New machinery and equipment (January 2, 1954)	$100,000
(b)	Direct labor	175,500
(c)	Manufacturing expenses	60,000
(d)	Operating expenses	251,000
(e)	Accounts payable	148,200
(f)	Estimated income taxes payable for 1953	14,000
(g)	Dividends payable on December 31, 1953	18,000
(h)	Annual interest on bonds, 6%	3,000
	Total	$769,700

(5) Manufacturing expenses will include:
- (a) Depreciation of machinery and equipment, 10%.
- (b) Factory supplies expense, $23,800.

(6) Other data:
- (a) Accounts receivable of $3,500 will be charged off against the allowance for bad debts. Bad debts expense for 1954 is estimated at $4,000 (charge Profit and Loss Summary with $4,000).
- (b) Federal income tax liability on 1954 income, 40% of estimated net profit.
- (c) Declaration of a 6% dividend at end of 1954.

Instructions: (1) Set up "T" accounts and record the balances shown on the post-closing trial balance of December 31, 1953. Include accounts for Manufacturing Summary and Profit and Loss Summary.

(2) Record directly in the accounts the estimated transactions for 1954. Record the income and expense transactions directly in the manufacturing and profit and loss summary accounts, with explanations, and close these two accounts.

(3) Prepare an estimated cost of goods manufactured schedule and an estimated profit and loss statement for the year ending December 31, 1954, and an estimated balance sheet as of December 31, 1954.

Chapter 31

Analysis and Interpretation of Financial Statements

NECESSITY FOR ANALYSIS AND INTERPRETATION   After the balance sheet and the profit and loss statement have been prepared to show the financial condition of the business and the results of its operations during the past fiscal period, the significance of the information these statements contain must be interpreted. The accountant who prepares the statements is probably best qualified to explain them; so it is becoming more and more the practice of accountants to analyze and interpret the information that the statements contain. Some of the methods used by accountants to do this will be explained in this chapter.

The accounting statements of corporations are of interest to many groups, chief among these being management, stockholders, and prospective investors. Management is the smaller group with an internal point of view; stockholders and potential investors are the larger group with an external point of view. Management needs continuous information about current transactions in order to know the effects of operations. This understanding of financial condition and operating results is particularly helpful in planning for future fiscal periods. The accountant can give great assistance when the budget of the business is prepared by explaining items found in the accounting statements.

Stockholders, often numbering many thousands of individuals and institutional investors, are more concerned with the broader aspects of the business. Their interpretation is therefore related to the questions of the long-term trend of profits and the comparative position of the business in its industry. They want to know whether to sell their stockholdings, to keep them, or to buy more. With the stockholders may be classed the professional analysts and investment counselors who make an intensive study of companies whose stocks are listed on the organized exchanges and have a large public following.

RESULTS IN BRIEF   Analysis of statement data may be summarized in schedules that show comparisons with previous years at a glance. Many companies include such "highlights" of business activity in publications for their shareholders. The

617

General Motors Corporation schedule shown below presents enough of the statement data to enable the stockholder to analyze his position as an investor in the stock of the corporation. It should be noted that the tabulation provides data for the third quarter of 1952 as well as cumulative results for the first nine months of the year. Comparable 1951 results are included in order to give stockholders some indication of short-term business progress.

RESULTS IN BRIEF

NET SALES In millions

	Civilian	Defense	Total
Third quarter 1952 . . .	$1,348	$ 347	$1,695
Third quarter 1951 . . .	1,513	209	1,722
Nine months 1952	4,538	1,026	5,564
Nine months 1951	5,168	435	5,603

TAXES — **Provision for United States and Foreign Income & Excess Profits Taxes** In millions

	1952	1951
Third quarter	$171	$231
Nine months	729	740

NET INCOME In millions

	1952	1951
Third quarter	$118	$ 93
Nine months	387	373

EARNINGS ON COMMON STOCK Per share

	1952	1951
Third quarter	$1.31	$1.01
Nine months	4.32	4.14

EMPLOYMENT Average

	1952	1951
Third quarter	426,399	453,440
Nine months	446,581	473,620

PAYROLLS In millions

	1952	1951
Third quarter	$ 471	$ 453
Nine months	1,440	1,410

NET WORKING CAPITAL In millions

Sept. 30, 1952	$1,281
Dec. 31, 1951	1,457
Sept. 30, 1951	1,502

INVENTORIES In millions

Sept. 30, 1952	$1,139
Dec. 31, 1951	1,141
Sept. 30, 1951	1,102

Net income, earnings on common stock, and taxes for the third quarter and first nine months of 1951 are as previously reported and include the effect of higher tax rates enacted October 20, 1951 retroactive to the first of that year. The adjustment applicable to the first half reduced earnings in the third quarter of 1951 by 33 cents per share.

Summary Report of a Corporation

Graphic aids are frequently included in published corporate reports in order to make interpretation of the financial statements more meaningful to the layman. An illustration of this type of visual aid in analysis, found in a report of the General Motors Corporation to its stockholders, is shown on page 619.

48½¢ TO SUPPLIERS

TO EMPLOYES 28¢

FOR TAXES 14½¢

FOR WEAR AND TEAR OR OBSOLESCENCE OF 1¾¢ PLANTS AND EQUIPMENT

4¾¢ TO SHAREHOLDERS

2½¢ FOR USE IN THE BUSINESS TO PROVIDE FACILITIES AND WORKING CAPITAL

GM received in 1952   Millions

From sale of its products and other income (net)................... $7,627   **100%**

These receipts went

	Millions	
To suppliers for materials, services, etc............................	3,688	**48½**
To employes for payrolls, etc....................................	2,135	**28**
For Federal, state and local taxes...............................	1,107	**14½**
To provide for depreciation and obsolescence of plants and equipment .	138	**1¾**
To GM shareholders..	362	**4¾**
For use in the business to provide facilities and working capital	197	**2½**

Use of a Visual Aid in a Corporation Report

Reports intended primarily for employees may be prepared in the form of nontechnical statements like the one illustrated on page 620 for the Staley Manufacturing Company.

At December 31, 1952

	Total Amount for the Company	Approximate Amount per Employee

WHAT WE OWN:

Cash on deposit in various banks needed for the prompt payment of payrolls and purchases.	$ 4,513,197	$ 1,563
Due from customers for merchandise delivered to them and from other persons for various charges.	6,016,469	2,084
Invested in corn, soybeans, manufacturing supplies and finished products on hand.	31,666,547	10,969
Plants:		
Total original cost of lands, buildings and equipment.	$60,422,109	$20,929
Less the amount that has been deducted for depreciation and reinvested in various assets.	22,134,943	7,667
Net book value of plants.	$38,287,166	$13,262
Sundry other assets, including railroad and insurance claims.	465,128	161
Insurance, supplies and other expense paid in advance.	2,233,962	774
TOTAL VALUE OF THINGS OWNED	$83,182,469	$28,813

WHAT WE OWE:

To employees for wages and salaries, to manufacturers for material purchased, to local governments for taxes and to bondholders for interest.	$ 3,093,528	$ 1,071
To Federal Government for income taxes.	3,701,000	1,282
Money Borrowed:		
To purchase corn, beans and materials (short-term notes).	14,205,000	4,920
To provide additional working capital (long-term notes).	12,000,000	4,157
Set aside for retirement of employees.	256,000	89
TOTAL WE OWE	$33,255,528	$11,519

SAVINGS OF OWNERS:

The total value owned less the total we owe leaves a balance representing the savings of our 2,517 stockholders invested in our company.	$49,926,941	$17,294

A Simplified Balance Sheet

The data that may be included in the contents of a corporate report are relatively unlimited. The stockholder or the potential investor is provided with various information that may be useful in appraising the financial standing and progress of the company. Frequently, however, certain desirable information may not be available and the interested party must compute the information from the balance sheet or the profit and loss statement included in the report to stockholders. The chief purpose of this chapter is to describe the nature of some of these items and to point out their significance in analyzing the corporate financial position.

COMPARISON OF ITEMS ON A PARTICULAR BALANCE SHEET A simple balance sheet of a merchandising corporation, used to illustrate the comparisons that may be made between items on the same balance sheet, is shown below. To make the comparisons less complicated and easier to follow, amounts have been expressed in even thousands of dollars.

BARTON MERCANTILE COMPANY
BALANCE SHEET
DECEMBER 31, 1954

ASSETS		LIABILITIES	
Current Assets:		Current Liabilities:	
Cash	$ 30,000	Notes Payable	$150,000
Accounts Receivable		Accounts Payable	120,000
(net)	200,000		
Merchandise Inventory	450,000	Total Current Liabilities	$ 270,000
Prepaid Expenses	20,000	Fixed Liabilities:	
		Bonds Payable, 3%	100,000
Total Current Assets	$ 700,000		
Fixed Assets:		Total Liabilities	$ 370,000
Plant (net)	250,000		
Intangible Assets:		CAPITAL	
Goodwill	40,000	5% Preferred Stock, $100	
Deferred Charges:		par	$100,000
Discount on Bonds Payable	10,000	Common Stock, $20 par	400,000
		Total Capital Stock	$500,000
		Retained Earnings	130,000
		Total Capital	630,000
Total Assets	$1,000,000	Total Liabilities and Capital	$1,000,000

Some of the more important comparisons that may be made with reference to this balance sheet are as follows:

(1) *Current Ratio.* Since the funds to be used in paying the current liabilities must be obtained from the liquidation of the current assets, the current ratio is exceedingly important to management and to short-term creditors. The ratio is computed by dividing current assets by current liabilities. Because assets often shrink in value and liabilities

seldom do, it is desirable that the current assets always be materially larger than the current liabilities. Banks for a long time have insisted on a rule-of-thumb ratio of 2 to 1; that is, that the current assets shall be twice as large as the current liabilities. This is not a safe rule to follow arbitrarily, since the ratio that should exist between the current assets and the current liabilities will vary according to the nature of the business, the level of business activity, and other financial conditions. As shown by the balance sheet on page 621, the current assets of the Barton Mercantile Company amount to $700,000 and the current liabilities to $270,000. The current ratio, then, is approximately 2.6 to 1.

The excess of current assets over current liabilities is referred to as *working capital* and represents the margin of protection to short-term creditors. The working capital should be sufficient to absorb any shrinkage that might occur in the value of the current assets and to provide funds to meet current operating expenses. The working capital of the Barton Mercantile Company is $430,000.

The current ratio is a measure of a concern's working capital and an index of its ability to meet maturing obligations. The greater the current ratio, the greater is the relative amount of working capital and the greater is the assurance that the concern will have sufficient funds to meet its current debts as they mature and the costs of carrying on its business operations.

In certain types of businesses, however, concerns may continue to operate even when current liabilities exceed current assets without any financial difficulty being indicated. Such a condition is frequently found in public utility corporations. In businesses that furnish services, that need no inventory of merchandise, and that have a minimum of receivables, a relatively large cash balance is necessary if the current assets are to exceed the current liabilities. Consideration must be given to the nature of the business and the characteristics of its normal financial operations to determine the adequacy of its current ratio.

(2) *Acid-Test Ratio.* This ratio indicates the ability of a business to satisfy immediately the current debts and is also of primary importance to management and to short-term creditors. In the determination of this ratio, consideration is given only to cash and those assets that could readily be converted into cash if the need should arise. Such assets are frequently referred to as *quick assets*. A ratio of 1 to 1, or 100%, is usually deemed satisfactory. The usual formula for the computation of the acid-test ratio is:

$$\frac{\text{CASH} + \text{MARKETABLE SECURITIES} + \text{RECEIVABLES (NET)}}{\text{CURRENT LIABILITIES}}$$

It may be noticed that the formula excludes merchandise inventories and prepaid expenses. These items, although current, may not be readily converted into cash in some cases without a substantial loss. Marketable securities include stocks and bonds of other corporations that have a ready market and that may be liquidated upon short notice at a minimum loss. In order for such securities to be listed as current, it must be the intent of management to consider them as an emergency source of cash. Stocks and bonds purchased for long-term holdings would be classified under "Investments" on the balance sheet. Receivables include claims represented by notes as well as open accounts with trade debtors.

The acid-test ratio of the Barton Mercantile Company is .85 to 1 ($230,000 ÷ $270,000). This ratio appears to be slightly unfavorable. Whether it represents a dangerous situation depends upon whether the notes payable must be paid in the near future or whether they can be renewed or refunded. The nature of the notes payable should be determined before a definite conclusion is made from the acid-test ratio. Again, in the use of this ratio, consideration must be given to the requirements and the operations of the particular business.

(3) *Ratio of Notes Payable to Accounts Payable.* On the balance sheet on page 621 the notes payable are larger than the accounts payable. To determine whether this indicates a desirable condition, it will be necessary to analyze the notes payable according to whether they were issued to (a) merchandise creditors, (b) note brokers and banks, or (c) others. If they were issued to merchandise creditors at the time merchandise was purchased or if they were sold to note brokers or issued to banks in order to obtain funds with which to discount accounts payable, there is no objection to the excess of the notes payable over the accounts payable. If they were issued to merchandise creditors in payment of overdue accounts or were issued to officers or outsiders in order to obtain funds because the bank credit of the company is limited, an unfavorable financial condition is indicated.

The balance sheet should normally indicate whether notes payable are secured or unsecured. If it has been necessary to secure notes by some collateral or mortgage, the effect of their existence may be to limit the additional borrowing capacity of the business and may result in the creation of a strained financial condition.

(4) *Fixed Ratio.* This ratio measures the asset protection of the present mortgageholders or bondholders and is an indication to a prospective long-term creditor whether any additional loans on the fixed assets of the borrower may be safely granted. The ratio is obtained by dividing fixed assets by fixed liabilities. In arriving at this

ratio, current market values of fixed assets rather than book values should be employed if they are available, since the protection to borrowers and the ability to secure additional funds is based on the market values of the assets. Usually the minimum allowable ratio is 2 to 1; that is, the value of the fixed assets should be at least twice the amount of the mortgage or bond debt. The fixed assets of the Barton Mercantile Company amount to $250,000, and the bonds payable amount to $100,000; the ratio is therefore 2.5 to 1.

A concern that has a low current ratio may obtain additional working capital by creating long-term debt and using the funds to pay current liabilities. Such long-term debt may be represented either by a mortgage note or an unsecured debenture bond. The Barton Mercantile Company may be able to obtain funds in this manner since its bonded indebtedness is only 40% of its fixed assets. If additional funds cannot be borrowed, the company may have to resort to equity financing by issuing preferred or common stock.

(5) *Ratio of Owned Capital to Borrowed Capital.* The total assets owned by the Barton Mercantile Company amount to $1,000,000. Of this amount, $630,000, or 63%, has been provided by the stockholders of the company; and $370,000, or 37%, has been provided by the creditors. The ratio of the owned capital to the borrowed capital is 1.7 to 1. This ratio in itself indicates a satisfactory condition, but it should be compared with the same ratio at the end of preceding years to see whether the stockholders are increasing or decreasing their interest in the business. It is a wise and conservative policy for a corporation to use its accumulated earnings to finance expansion, the stockholders thus gradually increasing their equity in the business.

COMPARISON OF CORRESPONDING ITEMS AND RATIOS ON DIFFERENT BALANCE SHEETS   In order that a more complete interpretation of the balance sheet of the Barton Mercantile Company may be made, the balance sheet of the same company as of December 31, 1953, will also be used. Both of these statements are shown in comparative form at the top of the opposite page.

Comparisons may be made of all items on a comparative balance sheet, and some benefit may usually be derived from these comparisons. There are, however, certain comparisons that are of special significance. With reference to the comparative balance sheet on page 625, the more significant comparisons are as follows:

(1) The merchandise inventory of December 31, 1954, is substantially larger than the inventory of December 31, 1953. Any one of several reasons may account for this increase:

BARTON MERCANTILE COMPANY
Comparative Balance Sheet
December 31, 1954, and December 31, 1953

Assets	Dec. 31, 1954	Dec. 31, 1953	Liab. and Capital	Dec. 31, 1954	Dec. 31, 1953
Cash	$ 30,000	$ 40,000	Notes Payable	$ 150,000	$ 50,000
Accounts Receivable (net)	200,000	150,000	Accounts Payable	120,000	105,000
Merchandise Inventory	450,000	290,000	Bonds Payable, 3%	100,000	
Prepaid Expenses	20,000	30,000	5% Pref. Stock, $100 par	100,000	100,000
Plant (net)	250,000	200,000	Common Stock, $20 par	400,000	400,000
Goodwill	40,000	40,000	Retained Earnings	130,000	95,000
Discount on Bonds Payable	10,000				
Total Assets	$1,000,000	$750,000	Total Liab. and Capital	$1,000,000	$750,000

Comparative Balance Sheet

(a) There may have been a large increase in the volume of business that necessitated an increase in the inventory. The comparative profit and loss statement of the company will have to be consulted to ascertain if the volume of business actually increased.

(b) A large amount of merchandise may have been purchased because of an anticipated increase in price or because of an estimated increase in business within the immediate future. Investigation will show whether much merchandise was purchased for either of these reasons.

(c) A large amount of unsalable goods may have been accumulated during the past year; or a large amount of merchandise may have been purchased because increased sales were anticipated during the year, but this merchandise is now on hand because the sales failed to materialize. A calculation of the merchandise turnover from the comparative profit and loss statement will make it possible to determine whether either of these conditions exists.

(2) The balance sheet of December 31, 1954, shows an increase in the net plant over the amount of this item on the balance sheet of December 31, 1953. An increase in the amount of fixed assets may arise from any one of the following sources:

(a) Additional assets may have been purchased or constructed. If the actual or anticipated increase in business warranted such additions, they were properly made.

(b) The cost of repairs on the assets may have been improperly charged to the asset accounts instead of to expense accounts. Or extensive improvements that prolong the life of the assets may have been debited to the allowance for depreciation account, thus increasing the book value of plant.

(c) The assets may have been appraised, and, on the basis of this revaluation, their values may have been increased. In most cases it is contrary to conservative accounting and good management to enter the appreciation of fixed assets in the accounts or to show it on the financial reports. Since fixed assets are not to be sold but are to be used in the conduct of the business, an increase in their market values does not increase their efficiency, and their value to the business is therefore not increased.

A careful inspection should be made to ascertain the cause for the increases in fixed assets shown on the comparative balance sheet of the Barton Mercantile Company. An analysis of the retained earnings account of the company and of the expense accounts for the year will assist in the determination of the cause for these increases.

(3) By turning to the liabilities and capital side of the comparative balance sheet, it will be observed that the notes payable have greatly increased during 1954. The amount outstanding on December 31, 1954, is three times the amount outstanding at the end of the previous year. The accounts payable also have increased, but not in proportion to the increase in the notes payable. An analysis of the notes payable item is desirable in order to determine to whom the notes have been issued. If the notes have been issued to banks in order to obtain funds with which to discount merchandise invoices, good financial management is indicated. An inspection of the comparative profit and loss statement to see whether the purchases discounts for the latest year are larger than those for the previous year will indicate whether notes were issued for that reason. This, however, will not be conclusive evidence, and an analysis of the notes payable account should be made.

(4) A new issue of $100,000 of 3% bonds has been sold during the year at a discount. The funds provided by the bond issue were more than the increase in fixed assets during the year; hence, even if the increase in fixed assets is found to be correct, some additional funds for use as working capital have been obtained by means of the bond issue. If this method of obtaining funds improves the current ratio, it may be considered as good financing. The more conservative method, however, calls for additional working capital to be provided by increasing the stockholders' equity, either by retaining earnings within the business or by issuing more stock.

(5) A comparison of considerable significance is that of the current ratios for the two years. On December 31, 1954, this ratio was 2.6 to 1, whereas a year earlier it was 3.3 to 1. There has therefore been a considerable decrease in this important measure of liquidity. Although the ratio for 1954 does not in itself appear unfavorable, the tendency indicated by the decrease in this ratio during the year may be undesirable. It seems necessary to ascertain whether the plans for the coming year will maintain the present ratio or whether a continued decrease is probable.

(6) The preferred stock and the common stock of the company have remained stationary during the year, but the retained earnings have increased by $35,000. The increase in the retained earnings

looks favorable; but before a final decision on this point can be made, it will be necessary to ascertain:

(a) The origin of the increase in the retained earnings. It is important to know whether this increase has originated from the earnings of the year, whether it is the result of the writing up of fixed assets, or whether it has resulted from other transactions.

(b) The total earnings for the year. These earnings should be determined to see what part of them has been retained as surplus. It will also be desirable to ascertain whether any dividends have been paid during the year.

COMPARISON OF ITEMS ON ONE PROFIT AND LOSS STATEMENT   The profit and loss statement of the Barton Mercantile Company for the year ended December 31, 1954, is shown in the illustration on page 628. The most important comparisons that may be drawn in connection with a single profit and loss statement are illustrated by the percentages entered on this report. Each percentage represents the ratio of the particular item on the statement to net sales. These ratios are of very great importance when taken in connection with the same ratios of previous years but are of little significance when taken by themselves. This is due to the fact that, unless there is some standard by which to judge these ratios, there is no means of knowing whether they are too large or too small.

The percentage ratios on the profit and loss statement also indicate the distribution of the sales dollar over the cost of merchandise, the operating expenses, and the net profit. These ratios show that each dollar of the sales income of the Barton Mercantile Company is distributed as follows:

Cost of Goods Sold	$ .77
Operating Expenses	.15
Net Profit from Operations	.08
Total	$1.00

These figures mean that in each dollar of sales for the year, approximately 77 cents represents the cost of merchandise, 15 cents represents the operating expenses, and 8 cents represents the net profit from operations.

COMPARISON OF ITEMS ON TWO OR MORE PROFIT AND LOSS STATEMENTS   Of more importance, however, in the analysis of corporate profit and loss statements is a comparison of the corresponding items on a series of profit and loss statements. Such a series of statements covering a period of years will provide a normal

BARTON MERCANTILE COMPANY
PROFIT AND LOSS STATEMENT
FOR YEAR ENDED DECEMBER 31, 1954

Income from Sales:			
Sales........................		$1,224,000	102.0%
Less Sales Returns and Allowances		24,000	2.0%
Net Sales.....................		$1,200,000	100.0%
Cost of Goods Sold:			
Merchandise Inventory, Jan. 1, 1954......................	$ 290,000		
Purchases....................	1,080,000		
Merchandise Available for Sale....	$1,370,000		
Less Merchandise Inventory, Dec. 31, 1954....................	450,000		
Cost of Goods Sold.............		920,000	76.7%
Gross Profit on Sales.............		$ 280,000	23.3%
Operating Expenses:			
Selling Expenses................	$ 120,000		
General Expenses...............	60,000		
Total Operating Expenses........		180,000	15.0%
Net Profit from Operations.........		$ 100,000	8.3%
Other Income:			
Purchases Discounts.............	$ 10,000		
Other Expenses:			
Bond Interest Expense.... $3,000			
Interest Expense......... 7,000			
Total Other Expenses....	10,000		
Net Profit before Estimated Income Taxes........................		$ 100,000	8.3%
Less Estimated Income Taxes......		40,000	3.3%
Net Profit after Estimated Income Taxes........................		$ 60,000	5.0%
To Payment of:			
5% Preferred Dividends.........	$ 5,000		
Common Dividends.............	20,000	25,000	2.1%
Increase in Retained Earnings......		$ 35,000	2.9%

Profit and Loss Statement Showing Significant Ratios to Net Sales

standard of profit margin and of expense ratios. It will also indicate the trend of the size and the progress of the business in measuring the efficiency and the resourcefulness of the management.

A comparative profit and loss statement for the Barton Mercantile Company for the years 1954 and 1953 is shown on page 630.

A number of interesting comparisons can be made from this comparative profit and loss statement. The most significant are:

(1) Net sales have increased one third. This increase in itself looks very favorable, but the results of the sales must be considered before a final conclusion may be drawn.

(2) For the year 1953 the sales returns and allowances represented 1.0% of the net sales. For the year 1954 they represent 2.0% of the net sales. This increase probably indicates one of the following two conditions:

    (a) Poorer service is being given to the customers since more goods are being returned and more allowances are being claimed.

    (b) New territories are being entered and, in the process of establishing new relations, more liberal privileges are being accorded to customers.

An analysis should be made of these returns and allowances to ascertain the reason for this increase even though the amount may not appear to be excessive.

(3) In 1953 the gross profit on sales was 30% of net sales, whereas in 1954 it decreased to 23.3% of net sales. This decrease may have been caused by an advance in cost of merchandise or a decrease in sales price. Perhaps both cost and sales price have increased but not in the same proportion. Examination should be made to ascertain if the plans for the coming year contemplate making provisions to improve the gross margin rate.

(4) The merchandise turnover for the year 1953 was 2.6, whereas that for the year 1954 decreased to 2.5. Since there is a slight decrease in the rate of turnover, attention should be given to this matter. Had the decrease been of a more material amount, a careful analysis of the cause would have been in order.

Merchandise turnover is found by dividing the cost of goods sold by the average inventory. It represents the number of times the average inventory (beginning inventory + ending inventory ÷ 2) was exchanged for cash or other assets. It is important, since the greater the merchandise turnover, the greater the profit that can be made from a given investment in merchandise. In order to obtain a more accurate turnover rate, monthly or quarterly inventories may be used in developing the average inventory figure. Since fiscal periods frequently

BARTON MERCANTILE COMPANY
COMPARATIVE PROFIT AND LOSS STATEMENT
FOR YEARS ENDED DECEMBER 31, 1954, AND DECEMBER 31, 1953

	DECEMBER 31, 1954		DECEMBER 31, 1953	
Income from Sales:				
Sales..........................	$1,224,000	102.0%	$909,000	101.0%
Less Sales Returns and Allow......	24,000	2.0%	9,000	1.0%
Net Sales......................	$1,200,000	100.0%	$900,000	100.0%
Cost of Goods Sold:				
Merchandise Inventory, Jan. 1....	$ 290,000		$200,000	
Purchases.....................	1,080,000		720,000	
Merchandise Available for Sale....	$1,370,000		$920,000	
Less Mdse. Inventory, Dec. 31....	450,000		290,000	
Cost of Goods Sold..............	$ 920,000	76.7%	$630,000	70.0%
Gross Profit on Sales..............	$ 280,000	23.3%	$270,000	30.0%
Operating Expenses:				
Selling Expenses.................	$ 120,000	10.0%	$ 81,000	9.0%
General Expenses..............	60,000	5.0%	45,000	5.0%
Total Operating Expenses........	$ 180,000	15.0%	$126,000	14.0%
Net Profit from Operations.........	$ 100,000	8.3%	$144,000	16.0%
Other Income:				
Purchases Discounts.............	10,000		6,000	
Other Expense:				
Bond Interest Expense...........	$ 3,000			
Interest Expense................	7,000		$ 4,200	
Total Other Expenses............	$ 10,000		$ 4,200	
Net Profit before Estimated Income				
Taxes.........................	$ 100,000	8.3%	$145,800	16.2%
Less Estimated Income Taxes	40,000	3.3%	58,500	6.5%
Net Profit after Estimated Income				
Taxes.........................	$ 60,000	5.0%	$ 87,300	9.7%
To Payment of:				
5% Preferred Dividends..........	$ 5,000		$ 5,000	
Common Dividends..............	20,000		31,000	
	$ 25,000	2.1%	$ 36,000	4.0%
Increase in Retained Earnings......	$ 35,000	2.9%	$ 51,300	5.7%

**Comparative Profit and Loss Statement for Two Years
Showing Significant Ratios to Net Sales**

end during a lull in business activity, inventories taken at that time may not be representative of the average amount of goods in stock during the year.

(5) The selling expenses were 9% of net sales for the year 1953 and 10% for 1954. This increase shows that, though the sales are increasing, they are more expensive to obtain. These increased expenses may have been incurred to obtain additional business and to build up goodwill for the company through advertising and other sales efforts. The tendency for such expenses to increase faster than sales is, however, a dangerous one, and care should be taken that it does not continue over an extended period of time.

(6) The net profit from operations for the year 1954 was smaller than that for 1953. This is the most discouraging information shown by the comparative statement. Since the net sales have increased $33\frac{1}{3}\%$, it is unsatisfactory to find that the net profit has decreased. It may be found upon examination that some of the expenses incurred during 1954 are expected to result in increased business during the coming years. Under such circumstances there would be some excuse for the reduced net profits of the current year. A careful examination should be made to ascertain if this is the situation.

RELATION OF COMPAR- When the comparative balance sheet on
ATIVE BALANCE SHEET page 625 is studied in connection with the
AND PROFIT AND comparative profit and loss statement on
LOSS STATEMENT page 630, a number of significant facts are indicated:

(1) The comparative balance sheet shows a large increase in the merchandise inventory, and the comparative profit and loss statement indicates that this increase is much larger proportionately than the increase in sales. Whereas the sales have increased $33\frac{1}{3}\%$, the merchandise inventory has increased 55%. The comparative profit and loss statement also shows that the merchandise turnover has decreased. These comparisons may indicate that an accumulation of unsalable merchandise is the cause of the large increase in the merchandise inventory.

(2) The amount shown on the profit and loss statement for 1954 as an increase in retained earnings agrees with the increase in retained earnings for 1954 shown on the comparative balance sheet. But the increase in 1954 is much less than that in 1953, despite the fact that larger dividends were distributed in 1953. Unless the expansion of business justifies this decline as a temporary item, it is not favorable.

(3) The comparative profit and loss statement shows that the dividends on common stock have been decreased as a result of a decline in net profit and a tightening of the company's working capital position. Dividends of $1.55 per share were paid on the common stock during 1953 and only $1 per share was distributed in 1954.

The earnings per share represent an important computation to the common stockholders, since dividends depend upon the level of income. The earnings on each share of common stock for the two-year period may be tabulated as follows:

	1954	1953
Net profit after estimated income taxes...	$60,000	$87,300
Less preferred dividend requirement.....	5,000	5,000
Earnings available to common stock.....	$55,000	$82,300
Number of shares of common...........	20,000	20,000
Earnings per share of common..........	$2.75	$4.12

The Barton Mercantile Company is following a conservative dividend policy, since only 41% of the total net profit during the two-year period has been distributed to stockholders.

(4) The status of the accounts receivable may be determined by reference to the balance sheet and the profit and loss statement. The *age of receivables* is calculated to determine how many days' sales are tied up in accounts receivable at the end of the year. Assuming 300 business days during 1954, the computation of the average age of receivables for the Barton Mercantile Company is illustrated below:

Accounts receivable on December 31, 1954...............	$200,000
Average daily sales ($1,200,000 ÷ 300).................	4,000
Number of days' sales in receivables..................	50

The significance of this measure depends upon the relative amount of credit sales in comparison to total sales and the credit terms offered by the company. Assuming that 50% of the total sales for the Barton Mercantile Company were made on credit, then the number of days' credit sales included in accounts receivable would be 100, since the average daily credit sales would be $2,000. If the company's credit terms call for payment within 60 days, the above computations suggest that the status of the receivables is unfavorable since many of them are past due. Such a condition indicates laxity in credit granting and the possibility of substantial losses on accounts receivable.

COMPARISONS WITH COMPETING CONCERNS   A comparison of items and ratios shown on the financial statements of the Barton Mercantile Company with similar data taken from the financial statements of competitive concerns is of particular interest both to the management and to the stockholders. To both groups such results are indicative of the company's position in its industry. To the management it shows the degree of success or failure in meeting the problems of the industry. To the investor, it reveals whether his choice of a stock has been wise. As a result of comparisons, the investor may choose to sell this stock and buy that of a more promising competitor.

In comparing the financial statements of two or more corporations, care must be taken to make the comparison on the same accounting basis. Unless uniform procedures have been consistently employed in the accounting records of both companies, misleading conclusions may result.

STATEMENT NOTES AND ANALYSIS   All ratio measurements are subject to certain basic limitations. The significance of the ratios should not be overemphasized. One must be aware that ratios measure financial conditions as of a given date. The relationships obtained among the various items may have been quite different for a major portion of the year; perhaps it changed for better or for worse soon after the preparation of the statement.

In order to provide the reader of the balance sheet and the profit aɪ l loss statement with facts that cannot be presented in the body of th- statements, the practice has developed of appending supplementary notes to accounting reports explaining certain matters affecting financial condition and operations of the enterprise. These notes may be presented in statement footnotes, in special notes accompanying the statements, or in the auditor's report. A few of the many items that should be recognized in presenting the full financial story may be listed as follows:

(a) Valuation methods employed for current and fixed assets.

(b) Maturity dates of large receivables or payables.

(c) Material differences between costs of assets reported on the balance sheet and present estimated values.

(d) Purchase commitments outstanding, pledges of any assets, and the existence of contingent liabilities.

(e) Basis used in preparing consolidated statements or estimating income taxes.

(f) Dividends in arrears on preferred stock and the nature of surplus restrictions.

(g) Accounting methods employed in measuring income and any departures from accepted accounting principles.

(h) Miscellaneous items, such as financing operations, major property transactions, union negotiations, legal suits filed or settled, and action taken on major policies.

Such items are not apparent by simply observing the financial statements, but the information is useful in evaluating the total financial position of a company. Accounting is utilitarian; the useful data provided by accountants need not be limited to dollars and cents.

QUESTIONS

1. (a) Why is it necessary to analyze financial statements? (b) Name several limitations of financial statement analysis. (c) What is meant by "results in brief"?

2. Describe the computation and the significance of (a) inventory turnover and (b) age of receivables.

3. The Ellis Company made a profit of $150,000 in a certain year. What other information is necessary before one can judge the sufficiency of this profit?

4. It has been suggested that some of the ailments of business are: (1) insufficient profits; (2) too large inventory; (3) too large receivables; (4) overinvestment in fixed assets; and (5) insufficient capitalization. What ratios will assist in diagnosing each of these ailments?

5. The sales of the Parker Chain Stores System increased in five years from $3,000,000 to $5,000,000. Does this increase prove the soundness of the managerial policies in force?

6. The current ratio of the Parker Chain Stores System was as follows for each of the five years mentioned in Question 5 above: 3 to 1, 2.5 to 1, 2 to 1, 1.5 to 1, 1.2 to 1. Is a favorable trend indicated?

7. The Charm Store wishes to borrow $140,000 for 3 years from its bank in order to pay accounts payable. What effect will this transaction have (a) on the current ratio and (b) on the acid-test ratio?

8. The ratio of current assets to current liabilities for the Ace Company is 2.3 to 1. The acid-test ratio is 1 to 1. If the inventories and the prepaid expenses amount to $520,000, what is the amount of the current liabilities?

9. The sales of the Simons Department Store increased from $3,500,000 to $5,400,000. The average inventory increased from $500,000 to $600,000. Do these facts indicate sound management?

10. On successive balance sheets of O'Donnell, Inc., accounts receivable are reported at $60,000 and $90,000. The corresponding profit and loss statements show sales of $480,000 and $900,000 respectively. (a) Are these facts related? (b) What executive is responsible for the condition shown?

11. The profit and loss statement of Sweet Candy Co. shows purchases discounts of $4,760 and interest expense of $1,520. The profit and loss statement of Delicious Candies, engaged in the same kind of business, shows purchases discounts of $170. The sales of both are approximately equal. Interpret this situation.

12. The balance sheet of the Donovan Company is as follows:

DONOVAN COMPANY
BALANCE SHEET
DECEMBER 31, 1954

Cash......................	$ 30,000	Notes Payable...........	$ 20,000
Accounts Receivable......	30,000	Accounts Payable.........	40,000
Merchandise Inventory....	80,000	Mortgage Note Payable...	20,000
Fixed Assets..............	180,000	Common Stock, $50 par...	200,000
		Earned Surplus...........	40,000
	$320,000		$320,000

The profit and loss statement shows: net sales, $450,000; net profit after estimated taxes, $18,000; and dividends, $12,000.

(a) Calculate seven significant ratios. (b) Comment on the company's stock as an investment, assuming that the stock is selling at $45 per share on the market.

PROBLEMS

31-1. The Joanne Corporation reported the following comparative balance sheets as of December 31:

ASSETS	1954	1953	LIAB. AND CAPITAL	1954	1953
Cash...............	$ 12,000	$ 1,000	Notes and Accts. Pay.	$ 20,000	$ 22,000
Notes and Accts. Rec.	18,000	17,000	Mortgage Note Pay-		
Mdse. Inventory.....	50,000	48,000	able (due 1958)....	30,000	28,000
Fixed Assets (net)....	70,000	34,000	Common Stock, $10		
			par..............	75,000	40,000
			Earned Surplus	25,000	10,000
Total Assets........	$150,000	$100,000	Total Liab. and Cap.	$150,000	$100,000

Data from the profit and loss statement of December 31, 1954, include:

Sales....................	$269,500	Depreciation............	$ 5,000
Gross profit.............	122,500	Accounts written off di-	
Sales discounts..........	2,000	rectly as bad debts.....	1,000
Sales returns...........	500	Purchases returns........	1,500

Instructions: (1) Compute the current ratio for 1953 and for 1954.

(2) Compute the inventory turnover for 1954.

(3) Compute the ratio of owned capital to borrowed capital for both years.

(4) How much cash was collected from customers on notes and accounts receivable during 1954, assuming all sales were made on credit? (Take into account sales, sales discounts, sales returns, and bad debts written off.)

(5) How much cash was paid out for fixed assets, assuming no assets were sold and acquisitions were for cash?

(6) What were the gross purchases for 1954?

31-2. The following data were taken from the records of the Martinson Corporation:

BALANCE SHEETS, DECEMBER 31

ASSETS	1954	1953	1952
Cash..	$ 60,000	$ 50,000	$ 30,000
Notes and Accounts Receivable (net)........	140,000	100,000	50,000
Inventories...............................	50,000	50,000	40,000
Plant (net)...............................	180,000	100,000	100,000
Total Assets.............................	$430,000	$300,000	$220,000

LIABILITIES AND CAPITAL	1954	1953	1952
Notes and Accounts Payable...............	$100,000	$100,000	$ 80,000
Mortgage Payable (due 1960)...............	100,000	75,000	80,000
Common Stock, $100 par...................	150,000	100,000	50,000
Earned Surplus...........................	80,000	25,000	10,000
Total Liabilities and Capital...............	$430,000	$300,000	$220,000

PROFIT AND LOSS DATA FOR YEAR ENDED DECEMBER 31

	1954	1953
Sales..................................	$900,000	$660,000
Cost of Goods Sold....................	630,000	495,000
Operating Expenses....................	180,000	112,200

Instructions: (1) Compute the following ratios for each year:
- (a) Current ratio.
- (b) Acid-test ratio.
- (c) Fixed ratio.
- (d) Owned capital to borrowed capital.
- (e) Merchandise turnover (2 years only).

(2) Express profit and loss data as a percentage of sales for each year.

(3) Analyze the trends shown in (1) and (2).

31-3. Frank Jones is contemplating the purchase of 2,000 shares of $10 par common stock from Smith, Inc. at $12 per share. He asks you to investigate the financial condition of this corporation. The following are the comparative statements for the years ended December 31, 1954, 1953, and 1952.

SMITH, INC.

Comparative Balance Sheet
December 31, 1954, 1953, and 1952

Assets	1954	1953	1952
Current Assets:			
Cash................................	$ 60,000	$ 30,000	$ 15,000
Accounts Receivable (net)..............	60,000	50,000	45,000
Inventories...........................	90,000	70,000	40,000
Total Current Assets...................	$210,000	$150,000	$100,000
Fixed Assets:			
Equipment (net).......................	$275,000	$235,000	$250,000
Buildings (net)........................	50,000	55,000	50,000
Land.................................	20,000	20,000	35,000
Total Fixed Assets.....................	$345,000	$310,000	$335,000
Deferred Charges.......................	$ 5,000	$ 10,000	$ 15,000
Total Assets...........................	$560,000	$470,000	$450,000

Liabilities			
Current Liabilities:			
Notes Payable.........................	$ 37,500	$ 40,000	$ 25,000
Accounts Payable......................	67,500	50,000	40,000
Accrued Payables......................	20,000	10,000	10,000
Total Current Liabilities................	$125,000	$100,000	$ 75,000
Fixed Liabilities:			
Bonds Payable, 4%....................	$125,000	$150,000	$200,000
Total Liabilities.......................	$250,000	$250,000	$275,000

Capital			
Common Stock, $10 par (40,000 shares authorized)............................	$210,000	$150,000	$125,000
Retained Earnings:			
Appropriated..........................	30,000	25,000	15,000
Unappropriated.......................	70,000	45,000	35,000
Total Capital..........................	$310,000	$220,000	$175,000
Total Liabilities and Capital..............	$560,000	$470,000	$450,000

SMITH, INC.
COMPARATIVE PROFIT AND LOSS STATEMENT
FOR YEARS ENDED DECEMBER 31, 1954 AND 1953

	1954	1953
Sales	$375,000	$300,000
Cost of Sales	250,000	180,000
Gross Profit on Sales	$125,000	$120,000
Expenses	65,000	75,000
Net Profit before Estimated Income Taxes	$ 60,000	$ 45,000
Estimated Income Taxes	23,700	16,000
Net Profit after Estimated Income Taxes	$ 36,300	$ 29,000
Appropriations for Surplus Reserves	5,000	10,000
Balance of Net Profit	$ 31,300	$ 19,000
Dividends	6,300	9,000
Increase in Unappropriated Retained Earnings	$ 25,000	$ 10,000

Instructions: (1) Compute the following ratios for each year:

    (a) Current ratio.

    (b) Acid-test ratio.

    (c) Fixed ratio.

    (d) Ratio of owned capital to borrowed capital.

    (e) Ratio of owned capital to fixed assets.

    (f) Merchandise turnover (2 years only).

(2) Prepare a comparative profit and loss statement, expressing as a percentage of sales each item through net profit before estimated income taxes.

(3) What trends are indicated by an examination of receivables, inventories, current liabilities, fixed liabilities, and capital?

(4) What trends are indicated by (1) and (2)?

(5) Comment on dividends paid. What is the annual dividend per share of common stock?

(6) Assuming that Jones subscribes to the 2,000 shares of stock, paying cash, how will the transaction affect the ratios?

(7) Assuming that Smith, Inc. pays a dividend of 60 cents per share during 1955, what would be the annual rate of return on Jones's investment?

Chapter 32

Supplementary Statements

ADDITIONAL ACCOUNTING STATEMENTS
It has been shown that every business enterprise must prepare at least two financial statements, the balance sheet and the income statement, in order to report its financial position and the results of its operations. But the balance sheet and the income statement are being supplemented to an increasing degree by other statements and reports. Typical examples discussed previously are the earned surplus statement and comparative statements. The reason for the trend toward the use of supplementary statements may be partly explained by the desire of management and owners, as well as potential investors, to have additional information concerning business operations. The balance sheet and the income statement have certain limitations that restrict their usefulness to management, investors, and other interested parties. The balance sheet, for example, reports the financial position of the business as of a given date. Changes in financial position resulting from transactions during the fiscal period are not reflected on the balance sheet. The income statement reports the results of operations for a given period, but the trend of sales and net profit over a period of years may have greater significance. Supplementary statements are prepared in order to provide a more adequate portrayal of financial position and progress. They provide additional data for use in the analysis and the interpretation of company activities.

Supplementary statements should be distinguished from accounting schedules. Schedules are formal summaries prepared from ledger accounts, supporting items appearing on the principal accounting statements. They are, therefore, integral parts of the balance sheet or the income statement. Supplementary statements tend to elaborate upon, rather than to support, the information presented on the formal accounting reports.

STATEMENT OF APPLICATION OF FUNDS
A widely used supplementary statement is known as the statement of application of funds. This statement summarizes changes of all asset, liability, and proprietorship items between two balance sheet dates. It provides information regarding financial activities that are not apparent from the simple comparison of the balance sheets.

Such a statement, also known as the *funds statement,* the *source and application of funds statement,* the *statement of financial changes,* and the *where-got, where-gone statement,* is usually prepared for one year. It may, however, be constructed covering any life span of the company.

As used in this discussion, the term "funds" refers to "working capital" (current assets minus current liabilities) rather than to cash funds or other specific assets. The application of funds statement summarizes the flow of working capital through the business during a particular period of time. Changes in working capital during a period are significant in the analysis of operating results and of the current financial condition.

Net changes in financial condition during a year or other period of time can be determined from comparative balance sheets. Although a study of the net increases and decreases in the various balance sheet accounts yields significant information, it does not disclose the amount of working capital made available to the business and how it has been employed. For example, assume that working capital has been increased during the year as a result of net earnings. This fact will not necessarily be disclosed by the net change in the earned surplus account because that account may also have been affected by dividend declarations, appropriations, write-offs of organization costs, and perhaps corrections of errors of past periods. Or assume that working capital has decreased as a result of purchases of equipment. This fact cannot be determined by a comparison of the balances in the equipment account because other items of equipment may have been discarded, sold, or traded in during the period.

The application of funds statement answers such questions as: "What happened to the company's profit?" "How much was invested in fixed assets during the year?" "What became of the money provided by the sale of additional stock?"

TRANSACTIONS AFFECTING FUNDS   Since the statement of application of funds reports the flow of current assets and current liabilities through the business, a transaction that affects only current accounts neither increases nor decreases funds. For example, the collection of accounts receivable increases cash and decreases accounts receivable but does not change the total amount of the current assets or of the working capital. Similarly, when payments are made on account, there is a decrease in both the cash account and the accounts payable account, but there is no change in the amount of working capital. It follows, therefore, that only changes in noncurrent accounts reveal sources of funds or their application.

PREPARATION OF THE STATEMENT OF APPLICATION OF FUNDS The data needed for the preparation of the statement of application of funds are obtained from two sources: (1) comparative balance sheets and (2) analyses of the noncurrent accounts that changed during the period. In order to illustrate the form of the statement and the manner in which it is prepared, certain facts regarding the Fisher Corporation will be assumed. Since its organization several years ago, the company has carried on operations in a leased plant. In 1953 land for a plant site was acquired and during 1954 a building was constructed and equipment was purchased. The comparative balance sheets of the company on December 31, 1953 and 1954, are as follows:

ASSETS	DEC. 31, 1953	DEC. 31, 1954	LIABILITIES AND CAPITAL	DEC. 31, 1953	DEC. 31, 1954
Cash.............	$ 80,000	$ 50,000	Notes Payable....	$ 10,000	$ 40,000
Accounts Receivable.........	120,000	160,000	Accounts Payable	150,000	130,000
			Bonds Payable...		100,000
Inventories......	190,000	240,000	Common Stock..	200,000	350,000
Equipment......		180,000	Surplus.........	50,000	130,000
Building........		100,000			
Land...........	20,000	20,000			
			Total Liab. and		
Total Assets.....	$410,000	$750,000	Capital.......	$410,000	$750,000

Although it is possible to prepare the statement of application of funds directly from the comparative balance sheets and the details in the noncurrent accounts, it is preferable to prepare working papers. The working papers for the Fisher Corporation are presented on page 642. The account titles and balances shown on the comparative balance sheets are first listed on the working papers. The net change in each account balance is then determined and is entered in the Net Changes Dr. or Cr. column. If an asset account has increased during 1954, the amount of the increase is listed in the Net Changes Dr. column; if a liability or a capital account has increased, the amount of the increase is listed in the Net Changes Cr. column. Conversely, decreases in asset accounts are listed in the Net Changes Cr. column, and decreases in liabilities and capital are listed in the Net Changes Dr. column. After all of the net debits and credits have been listed, the Net Changes columns are totaled. Obviously, the net debits must be equal to the net credits.

Each amount in the Net Changes columns is extended into one of the remaining four columns. Net debit changes in current assets represent increases in those assets and are therefore increases in working

FISHER CORPORATION
WORKING PAPERS FOR STATEMENT OF APPLICATION OF FUNDS
FOR YEAR ENDED DECEMBER 31, 1954

ACCOUNTS	BALANCES DEC. 31, 1953	BALANCES DEC. 31, 1954	NET CHANGES DR.	NET CHANGES CR.	FUNDS APPLIED	FUNDS PROVIDED	WORKING CAPITAL INCREASE	WORKING CAPITAL DECREASE
Cash	80,000	50,000		30,000				30,000
Accounts Receivable	120,000	160,000	40,000				40,000	
Inventories	190,000	240,000	50,000				50,000	
Equipment		180,000	180,000		180,000			
Building		100,000	100,000		100,000			
Land	20,000	20,000						
	410,000	750,000						
Notes Payable	10,000	40,000		30,000				30,000
Accounts Payable	150,000	130,000	20,000				20,000	
Bonds Payable		100,000		100,000		100,000		
Common Stock	200,000	350,000		150,000		150,000		
Surplus	50,000	130,000		80,000		80,000		
	410,000	750,000	390,000	390,000	280,000	330,000	110,000	60,000
Increase in Working Capital					50,000			50,000
			390,000	390,000	330,000	330,000	110,000	110,000

Working Papers for Statement of Application of Funds

capital. Net debit changes in current liabilities represent decreases in liabilities and are therefore also increases in working capital. Similarly, net credit changes in assets and in liabilities are decreases in working capital. In the illustrative working papers, the increases in working capital items are composed of an increase of $40,000 in Accounts Receivable, an increase of $50,000 in Inventories, and a reduction of $20,000 in Accounts Payable, making a total of $110,000. Decreases in working capital items are composed of a reduction of $30,000 in Cash and an increase of $30,000 in Notes Payable, making a total decrease of $60,000.

Net changes in noncurrent accounts are extended into the Funds Applied or Provided columns. Net debit changes in noncurrent asset accounts indicate that funds have been used in acquiring these assets and therefore they represent funds applied. Net debit changes in noncurrent liability accounts indicate that funds have been used in paying these liabilities and therefore they also represent funds applied. Similarly, net credit changes in all noncurrent accounts represent funds provided.

As indicated earlier, it is necessary to analyze the noncurrent accounts to determine whether the changes in the account balances resulted from one or a series of similar transactions or from a number of dissimilar transactions. Reference to the ledger of the Fisher Corporation reveals that the equipment account was debited during the year for various items purchased at a total cost of $180,000; there were no credit entries in the account. The funds applied to the purchase of equipment were therefore $180,000, and this amount is extended into the Funds Applied column. Examination of the building account reveals debits of $100,000 during the year and no credits; hence the $100,000 is also extended into the Funds Applied column. The remaining noncurrent accounts, Bonds Payable, Common Stock, and Surplus, are examined to determine the details of entries during the year. Bonds Payable increased by $100,000, the amount of bonds issued at face value; Common Stock increased by $150,000 as the result of the issuance of stock at par value; and the sole entry in Surplus was a credit transferring net profit of $80,000 from the profit and loss summary account. The effect of each of these items was to increase funds, and the respective amounts are extended into the Funds Provided column.

After each of the net changes has been extended to the appropriate column, each of the four columns is totaled. In the illustration on page 642 the total of funds provided ($330,000) exceeds the total of funds applied ($280,000) by $50,000, and the increases in working capital ($110,000) exceed the decreases in working capital ($60,000) by $50,000. Thus, of the total funds provided, $50,000 has been retained as an increase in working capital. The last four columns are brought into balance by summarizing the net effect of operations on working capital. If the funds applied had exceeded the funds provided, there would have been an accompanying decrease in working capital.

Upon the basis of the foregoing analysis and the working papers, the following statement is prepared:

FISHER CORPORATION

STATEMENT OF APPLICATION OF FUNDS

FOR YEAR ENDED DECEMBER 31, 1954

Funds were provided by:

Profitable operations..........................	$ 80,000	
Issuance of bonds.............................	100,000	
Issuance of common stock......................	150,000	$330,000

Funds were applied to:

Purchase of equipment........................	$180,000	
Purchase of building..........................	100,000	280,000

Increase in working capital......................	$ 50,000

The increase in working capital is accounted for as follows:

	DEC. 31, 1953	DEC. 31, 1954	WORKING CAPITAL INCREASE	DECREASE
Cash..................	$ 80,000	$ 50,000		$ 30,000
Accounts Receivable.....	120,000	160,000	$ 40,000	
Inventories..............	190,000	240,000	50,000	
Notes Payable...........	10,000	40,000		30,000
Accounts Payable........	150,000	130,000	20,000	
			$110,000	$ 60,000
Increase in working capital				50,000
			$110,000	$110,000

Statement of Application of Funds

Although there is considerable variation in the form of the statement of application of funds, it is frequently composed of two distinct sections. The first section summarizes the individual sources and uses of working capital; the second presents the details from which the amount of the net increase or decrease in working capital has been determined.

SOURCES OF FUNDS　　　In the foregoing example funds were provided by profitable operations, the issuance of bonds, and the issuance of common stock. Some of the sources of funds most frequently encountered are briefly discussed in the paragraphs that follow.

Decreases in noncurrent assets. The sale of investments, equipment, buildings, land, and other noncurrent assets provides funds. But the amount provided is not necessarily the same as the amount of reduction in the account. For example, if land carried in the account at $10,000 was sold for $15,000 during the period, the comparative balance sheet would reveal a decrease of $10,000 in land; the gain of $5,000 would be included in the net change in surplus. The funds provided by the sale actually amounted to $15,000. Similarly, if investments carried at $100,000 were sold for $80,000, the net change shown on the working papers would be $100,000, but the funds provided would actually be $80,000.

Increases in noncurrent liabilities. The amount of funds provided by the issuance of bonds or long-term notes is not necessarily measured by the amount of the net increase in the liability account. If bonds with a face value of $100,000 were issued at 90, the bonds payable account would increase by $100,000, but only $90,000 in funds would be provided by the transaction. On the other hand, if bonds were issued at a premium, the amount of the funds actually provided would be greater than the amount of the increase in the bonds payable account.

Increases in capital accounts. Perhaps the most frequently recurring source of funds is net profit. The costs and the expenses that are deducted from gross profit in arriving at net profit usually include depreciation of plant and equipment; but depreciation has not used up any current assets. Although it has been recorded as an expense, it has not decreased working capital. It is necessary, therefore, to add depreciation expense to net profit to obtain the amount of funds provided by normal operations.

If capital stock is issued during the period, the funds so provided will be equal to the total proceeds, which may be either greater or less than the par or stated value of the stock.

APPLICATIONS OF FUNDS　　　Applications of working capital are indicated by net debit changes in noncurrent assets, noncurrent liabilities, and capital accounts. Some of the more usual applications are described in the paragraphs that follow.

Increases in noncurrent assets. Funds may be applied to the purchase of equipment, buildings, land, permanent investments, and patents or other intangibles. But the net increase in the noncurrent asset during the period may not be the measure of the funds applied. For example, if equipment has been purchased at a cost of $50,000 and other equipment with a cost of $10,000 has been discarded, the net increase in the account will be $40,000. These facts can be determined only by an examination of the equipment account.

Decreases in noncurrent liabilities. The liquidation of bonds payable or long-term notes represents an application of funds. In determining the amount of the funds used for such purposes, consideration must be given to bond premium or bond discount accounts and to redemption gains or losses. To illustrate, assume that bonds payable in the principal amount of $20,000, for which there is an unamortized premium of $500, are purchased by the issuing company for $20,500. The amount of working capital used to retire the bonds is $20,500.

Decreases in capital accounts. Probably the most frequent application of funds in reduction of capital results from the declaration of *cash* dividends. The issuance of *stock* dividends requires no funds and hence is not reported on the statement of application of funds. The same is true of increases or decreases in appropriations of earned surplus, as they are also transfers from one capital account to another capital account. Funds may be applied to the purchase of the company's own outstanding stock. Analysis of the accounts will reveal the actual amount of funds expended for such purposes.

EXTENDED ILLUSTRATION   In preparing the working papers for the statement of application of funds, it is advisable to provide some means of giving effect to the various analyses suggested in the foregoing discussion. This may be done by inserting a pair of Adjustment columns between the Net Changes columns and the Funds columns, as shown in the illustration on page 647.

The basic information needed for the illustrative working papers on page 647 was obtained from the comparative balance sheets of the Melville Corporation and from an examination of the noncurrent accounts in the ledger. As in the first illustration, the balance sheet items are listed in the first pair of columns on the working papers. For convenience, the allowance for depreciation account is entered as a credit along with liability and capital accounts. The net increases and decreases in the accounts between balance sheet dates are then determined and extended to the Net Changes columns.

MELVILLE CORPORATION
Working Papers for Statement of Application of Funds
For Year Ended December 31, 1954

Accounts	Balances Dec. 31, 1953	Balances Dec. 31, 1954	Net Changes Dr.	Net Changes Cr.	Adjustments Dr.	Adjustments Cr.	Funds Applied	Funds Provided	Working Capital Increase	Working Capital Decrease
Cash	92,000	98,000	6,000						6,000	
Notes Receivable	20,000	18,000		2,000						2,000
Accounts Receivable (net)	45,000	50,000	5,000						5,000	
Merchandise Inventory	120,000	100,000		20,000						20,000
Prepaid Expenses	3,000	2,000		1,000						1,000
Equipment	158,000	177,000	19,000		(d) 11,000	(e) 30,000				
	438,000	445,000								
Allow. for Depr. of Equip.	60,000	61,000		1,000	(b) 12,000	(d) 11,000				
Accounts Payable	31,000	31,500		500						500
Dividends Payable	2,000	4,500		2,500						2,500
Bonds Payable	100,000	80,000	20,000		(f) 20,000					
Common Stock	200,000	200,000								
Earned Surplus	45,000	68,000		23,000	(a) 32,000	(c) 9,000				
	438,000	445,000	50,000	50,000						
Funds Provided by Net Profit						(a) 32,000 } (b) 12,000 }		44,000		
Add: Depreciation Expense Charged to Operations					(b) 12,000					
Funds Applied to Declaration of Dividends					(c) 9,000		9,000			
Funds Applied to Purchase of Equipment					(e) 30,000		30,000			
Funds Applied to Retirement of Bonds					(f) 20,000		20,000			
					114,000	114,000	59,000	44,000	11,000	26,000
Decrease in Working Capital								15,000	15,000	
							59,000	59,000	26,000	26,000

Explanation of Adjustments:
(a) To record funds provided by net profit, $32,000.
(b) To add depreciation expense to net profit, $12,000.
(c) To record funds applied to declaration of cash dividends, $9,000.
(d) To reverse original entry recording scrapping of fully deprecia-
    ted equipment, $11,000.
(e) To record funds applied to purchase of equipment, $30,000.
(f) To record funds applied to retirement of bonds, $20,000.

Working Papers for Statement of Application of Funds Containing Adjustments Columns

The adjustments, which are next recorded on the working papers, are presented and discussed below:

(a) An examination of the earned surplus account shows that the net profit credited to Earned Surplus at the end of the year was $32,000. The credit to the account is transferred to a line below the balance sheet totals by the following entry:

Earned Surplus............................ 32,000
    Funds Provided by Net Profit..............   32,000

(b) The allowance for depreciation account shows that depreciation charged to operations and credited to the allowance account for the year amounted to $12,000. This expense is a reduction in a fixed asset. Since it did not involve a change in working capital, it is added to net profit as an additional source of funds from operations. The entry is as follows:

Allowance for Depreciation of Equipment....... 12,000
    Depreciation Expense Charged to Operations
    (Funds Provided)........................   12,000

(c) From the earned surplus account it is found that charges to Earned Surplus for cash dividends declared during the year amounted to $9,000. This represents an application of funds because the related credit was to the dividends payable account. It is immaterial whether the dividends are paid in the same year or in the following year, since it is the declaration rather than the payment that affects working capital. The adjustment to transfer the amount of the dividends to the lower portion of the working papers is as follows:

Funds Applied to Declaration of Dividends...... 9,000
    Earned Surplus...........................   9,000

(d) Fully depreciated equipment with an original cost of $11,000 was scrapped during the year, no cash being realized. This action had no effect either on working capital or on net fixed assets. Therefore, in order to dispose of the net changes in the two accounts as shown on the working papers, the following reversing entry is made:

Equipment................................. 11,000
    Allowance for Depreciation of Equipment.....   11,000

(e) Equipment was purchased during the year at a total cost of $30,000. This represents an application of funds, and the following adjusting entry is made to transfer the item to the lower section of the working papers:

Funds Applied to Purchase of Equipment....... 30,000
   Equipment..................................   30,000

(f) Bonds payable in the face amount of $20,000 were purchased and retired during the year, the amount paid being face value. This is also an application of funds and the adjusting entry on the working papers is as follows:

Funds Applied to Retirement of Bonds......... 20,000
   Bonds Payable.............................   20,000

After the foregoing adjustments are recorded on the working papers, all of the net changes in noncurrent accounts are balanced out by amounts in the Adjustments columns. The net changes in current accounts are extended into the Working Capital columns, and the adjustments appearing below the balance sheet accounts are extended into the Funds Applied and Provided columns. After these four columns are totaled, the net increase or decrease in working capital is determined and the four columns are again totaled.

The statement of application of funds for the Melville Corporation prepared from the working papers appears below:

MELVILLE CORPORATION
STATEMENT OF APPLICATION OF FUNDS
FOR YEAR ENDED DECEMBER 31, 1954

Funds were provided by:
  Operations:
    Net profit per income statement................... $32,000
    Add: Depreciation expense charged to operations.... 12,000 $44,000
Funds were applied to:
  Declaration of dividends.......................... $ 9,000
  Purchase of equipment............................ 30,000
  Retirement of bonds.............................. 20,000   59,000
Decrease in working capital.......................... $15,000

The decrease in working capital is accounted for as follows:

	DEC. 31, 1953	DEC. 31, 1954	WORKING CAPITAL	
			INCREASE	DECREASE
Cash....................	$ 92,000	$ 98,000	$ 6,000	
Notes Receivable........	20,000	18,000		$ 2,000
Accounts Receivable (Net)	45,000	50,000	5,000	
Merchandise Inventory...	120,000	100,000		20,000
Prepaid Expenses........	3,000	2,000		1,000
Accounts Payable........	31,000	31,500		500
Dividends Payable.......	2,000	4,500		2,500
			$11,000	$26,000
Decrease in working capital			15,000	
			$26,000	$26,000

COMPLETE STATEMENT A complete statement record of a business
RECORD might be said to consist of a series of three
reports summarizing (1) operating results and (2) financial condition.
These reports would cover (a) the latest fiscal period, (b) the life of the
business, and (c) the historical progress. These may be tabulated as
follows:

1. Operating Reports:
   (a) Income statement (latest fiscal period).
   (b) Cumulative income statement (life of business).
   (c) Tabulation of operating data (historical progress).

2. Reports of Financial Condition:
   (a) Statement of application of funds (latest fiscal period).
   (b) Balance sheet (life of business).
   (c) Tabulation of financial data (historical progress).

The nature of the income statement, the balance sheet, and the
statement of application of funds has already been described. The
cumulative income statement and the tabulation of operating and
financial data will be illustrated in the following sections.

CUMULATIVE INCOME The cumulative income statement covers the
STATEMENT operating activities of a business since it
began operations. It therefore consists of the sum of all the annual
income statements. If there have been ten annual income statements,
the cumulative income statement would cover a ten-year period; the
sales on the cumulative statement would be the sum of the sales items
on the annual statements, and the net profit or loss for the company's
existence would be the net difference between total revenues and total
expenses listed on the ten yearly statements.

The period of time covered by the transactions summarized in the
cumulative income statement for the life of the business is the same as
that covered by the balance sheet. Just as the cash balance in the
balance sheet prepared at the end of the tenth year summarizes all the
cash transactions during the ten-year period, so the purchases item in
the cumulative income statement summarizes all purchases for the
ten-year period. There is, therefore, a closer relationship between
cumulative income statement items and balance sheet items than
there is between annual income statement items and balance sheet
items.

It should be noted that all statements based on time data are in a
sense cumulative statements. The term is ordinarily used, however,
to mean statements including operating data for the current and prior
periods. Cumulative statements summarizing total operations since

the date of organization, or for some other life span of the company's existence, may be of considerable interest. This is true because of the accounting period that breaks up the operating history of the company into arbitrary time segments. It may be more informative to know that the company has earned total profits of $600,000 during the past ten years than to be notified that the profits in 1954 were $30,000. The cumulative income statement may be a desirable supplement to the conventional statements, especially for enterprises subject to fluctuating sales and profits. For most companies, however, the trend of earnings probably has greater significance than either of the two measures suggested above. The cumulative income statement does not disclose trends and hence must be interpreted with the aid of other statements and summaries.

An illustration of a cumulative income statement of the Adams Manufacturing Company for a twelve-year period is illustrated below. The net results of twelve years of operations and the disposition of the earnings are incorporated within the scope of the statement.

ADAMS MANUFACTURING COMPANY
CUMULATIVE INCOME STATEMENT
FOR TWELVE YEARS ENDED DECEMBER 31, 1954

Sales...............................		$10,070,000
Cost of Goods Manufactured..............	$6,505,000	
Inventories, December 31, 1954...........	140,000	
Cost of Goods Sold......................		6,365,000
Gross Profit on Sales.....................		$ 3,705,000
Selling and Administrative Expenses........		2,099,000
Net Profit from Operations...............		$ 1,606,000
Bond Interest Expense...................		56,000
Net Income before Income Taxes...........		$ 1,550,000
Income Taxes...........................		195,000
Net Income after Income Taxes............		$ 1,355,000
Reserve for Bond Sinking Fund............		80,000
Income Available for Dividends............		$ 1,275,000
Dividends Paid in Cash..................	$ 715,000	
Stock Dividends........................	500,000	1,215,000
Earned Surplus, December 31, 1954........		$ 60,000

Cumulative Income Statement

TABULATION OF OPERATING DATA It is sometimes desirable to classify the operations by years. In this case a few of the more significant items on the cumulative income statement are chosen in order to simplify the resulting tabulation. The significant operating items on the cumulative income statement of the Adams Manufacturing Company have been classified by years in the tabulation shown on page 653. The amounts, as in the case of the cumulative income statement, have been obtained from the twelve annual income statements of the company.

Such a supplementary report by years gives significant information regarding the activities of the company during its history. The person who receives such a report gains a much more satisfactory understanding of the operations of the company than one who receives a report of the latest period only. While the analytical detail of the operations of any one fiscal period may be restricted, the useful information provided by such a tabulation more than compensates for this limitation.

Both the cumulative income statement and its supporting tabulation are being used today by large organizations in an attempt to give a better understanding to management and stockholders. It is believed that the lengthening of the period to include the life of the enterprise provides a summary that effectively supplements the balance sheet and the periodic income statement.

TABULATION OF FINANCIAL DATA It is often interesting to know how the principal balance sheet items have changed from year to year. The annual ups and downs in current assets, capital stock, and other items provide significant information. The totals of the main sections of each balance sheet from the beginning to the present time are shown in the tabulation of financial data for the Adams Manufacturing Company on page 654.

By comparing the changes in the various items from year to year, it is possible to visualize many of the financial transactions. For example, in 1947 both current and fixed assets rose sharply. During the same year bonds of $100,000 were issued. The proceeds of the bond issue and the $85,000 of reinvested income as shown by the tabulation of operating data on page 653 provided the funds used in acquiring the new assets. In 1948 the expansion of plant facilities evidently continued because fixed assets again increased, current assets decreased, and current liabilities reflected an increase.

ADAMS MANUFACTURING COMPANY
Tabulation of Operating Data
For Twelve Years Ended December 31, 1954

Year	Net Sales	Net Income After Income Taxes	Cash Dividends Paid	Per Cent of Income Paid as Dividends	Income Reinvested	Annual Dividend Per Share
1943	$ 820,000	$ 115,000	$ 10,000	9%	$105,000	$ 2.00
1944	430,000	55,000	. . . . . .	. . . . .	55,000	. . . . .
1945	100,000	35,000	5,000	14	30,000	1.00
1946	300,000	60,000	10,000	17	50,000	2.00
1947	550,000	105,000	20,000	19	85,000	4.00
1948	800,000	130,000	45,000	35	85,000	9.00
1949	1,050,000	152,000	50,000	33	102,000	10.00
1950	1,300,000	165,000	100,000	61	65,000	10.00*
1951	800,000	75,000	75,000	100	. . . . . .	7.50
1952	1,020,000	130,000	125,000	96	5,000	12.50
1953	1,400,000	160,000	125,000	78	35,000	12.50
1954	1,500,000	173,000	150,000	87	23,000	15.00
Totals	$10,070,000	$1,355,000	$715,000	53%	$640,000	. . . . .

*100% stock dividend December 15, 1950.

Tabulation of Operating Data for a Twelve-Year Period

LIMITATIONS OF FINANCIAL STATEMENTS Published financial statements of large corporations are commonly reported in condensed form so that readers will not be confused by a mass of data. Summaries prepared in this manner are referred to as *simplified* or *condensed statements*. Most investors are not skilled in interpreting accounting reports. For this reason several related balance sheet or income statement items may be combined and described in nontechnical and explanatory terms. This practice tends to reduce the amount of detail reported, thus making the statements more useful to the average individual. Such statements are of limited value to those interested in making comprehensive studies of trends and changes in various company activities.

ADAMS MANUFACTURING COMPANY
TABULATION OF FINANCIAL DATA (in thousands of dollars)
DECEMBER 31, 1943, TO DECEMBER 31, 1954

	1943	1944	1945	1946	1947	1948	1949	1950	1951	1952	1953	1954
Current Assets............	190	215	245	332	403	390	495	582	494	520	436	481
Fixed Assets............	425	470	480	455	569	651	646	643	769	724	795	1,010
Other Assets............	50	60	75	80	91	131	122	130	98	106	90	110
Total Assets............	665	745	800	867	1,063	1,172	1,263	1,355	1,361	1,350	1,321	1,601
Current Liabilities........	60	85	110	127	138	162	151	178	184	168	104	131
Bonds Payable...........					100	100	100	100	100	100	100	100
Capital Stock............	500	500	500	500	500	500	500	1,000	1,000	1,000	1,000	1,200
Premium on Capital Stock.												30
Reserve for Bond Sinking Fund.................					10	20	30	40	50	60	70	80
Earned Surplus..........	105	160	190	240	315	390	482	37	27	22	47	60
Total Liab. and Capital....	665	745	800	867	1,063	1,172	1,263	1,355	1,361	1,350	1,321	1,601

Tabulation of Financial Data for a Twelve-Year Period

Conventional accounting statements also have certain characteristics that limit their usefulness. The balance sheet, for example, reports the financial position as of a certain date. There is no way of knowing what the position was the week preceding or the week following the balance sheet date. The income statement reports results of a small segment of time in the total life of a company. It may be seen, then, that the balance sheet and the income statement are essentially interim reports for a going concern. Periodic income measurements reflect to a considerable degree estimates and individual judgment as to the allocation of costs, such as depreciation, to the various accounting periods.

Accounting is historical in nature. Statements are prepared in terms of original acquisition costs without any consideration being given to present values. Such statements are stated in terms of a fluctuating unit of value. Depreciation on a machine purchased for $10,000 is combined with depreciation on a similar machine purchased for $5,000 at a time of lower price levels. The inconsistencies in both asset reporting and income measurement are readily apparent. Further, there are numerous factors affecting financial condition that do not receive recognition on the balance sheet — efficient management, consumer goodwill, favorable location, and the credit rating of the business. Such items may easily outweigh in importance the figures reported on the balance sheet and the income statement.

The accounting profession has developed certain doctrines of reporting that have been accepted because of their logic and usefulness. The terms *conservatism, full disclosure, materiality,* and *consistency* adequately describe these doctrines. Conservatism refers to the idea that the accountant should provide for all possible losses but anticipate no gains. It does not sanction deliberate understatement of assets or income; it is only a choice between permissible alternatives. Full disclosure calls upon the accountant to report all facts necessary in reaching an intelligent conclusion regarding the financial position of a company. The concept of materiality requires that items of relatively large proportions should receive due recognition or comment on the statements. Consistency refers to the desirability of applying accounting methods in a similar manner, from year to year, in order to assure comparability of accounting statements. The specific meaning attached to each of these doctrines varies with individual accountants. Interpretations of financial statements must be made with due regard to the foregoing limitations.

QUESTIONS

1. (a) Does the statement of application of funds supplement the balance sheet or the income statement? (b) What information is required for the preparation of the statement of application of funds?

2. At the end of the year The Jones Co. declared and issued a 100% stock dividend. During the following year it declared and paid the same total amount in cash dividends as in the preceding year. What effect did the stock dividend have on the rate of the cash dividend?

3. A statement of application of funds shows large increases in notes payable and accounts payable and large increases in accounts receivable and inventories. Is a favorable or an unfavorable condition indicated?

4. What statements may be considered to provide a complete picture of a company's operations and financial standing?

5. (a) List five transactions that do not affect funds. (b) How are such items treated on the working papers? (c) What types of changes in the various accounts represent sources and applications of funds?

6. The Ruth-Loretta Co. reports net income of $55,000 on the income statement. In arriving at this amount, the following items were included:

(a) Depreciation, $20,000.
(b) Uninsured loss of equipment resulting from a fire, $4,000.
(c) Amortization of patents, $2,000.
(d) Accrued interest on bonds payable $1,500.
(e) Amortization of premium on bonds payable, $300.

What were the actual funds provided by operations?

7. Give the adjustments that would be required on the working papers for the statement of application of funds as a result of the following changes in the earned surplus account:

EARNED SURPLUS

Cash dividends	5,000	Balance Jan. 1, 1954	18,000
Stock dividends	10,000	Net income for 1954	12,000
Organization costs written off	1,000		

PROBLEMS

32-1. The balance sheets of the Cramer Corporation for 1953 and 1954 were:

	DECEMBER 31	
	1954	1953
DEBITS		
Cash..	$ 45,000	$ 30,000
Accounts Receivable........................	42,000	50,000
Merchandise Inventory......................	43,000	20,000
Plant and Equipment.......................	150,000	100,000
	$280,000	$200,000

	1954	1953
CREDITS		
Allowance for Depreciation of Plant and Equipment....................................	$ 17,500	$ 10,000
Accounts Payable...........................	19,500	15,000
Bonds Payable.............................	60,000	20,000
Common Stock.............................	120,000	100,000
Earned Surplus............................	63,000	55,000
	$280,000	$200,000

The earned surplus account on December 31, 1954, was as follows:

EARNED SURPLUS

1954		1954		
Dec. 15 Cash dividends	12,000	Jan. 1 Balance		55,000
		Dec. 31 Net profit		20,000

A plant expansion of $50,000 was completed on June 28, 1954. Depreciation is computed at 6% a year to the nearest month.

During the year 200 shares of common stock were issued for cash at par, $100.

Instructions: (1) Prepare working papers for the statement of application of funds.

(2) Prepare a statement of application of funds with a supporting schedule of changes in working capital.

32-2. The balance sheets of Mannix, Inc. for 1953 and 1954 are as follows:

	DECEMBER 31	
	1954	1953
DEBITS		
Cash..	$ 63,000	$ 35,000
Merchandise Inventory.......................	97,000	45,000
Equipment..................................	105,000	100,000
Buildings..................................	150,000	100,000
Land..	45,000	20,000
Goodwill...................................	———	10,000
	$460,000	$310,000
CREDITS		
Allowance for Depreciation of Equipment.......	$ 20,000	$ 10,000
Allowance for Depreciation of Buildings........	7,500	3,000
Bonds Payable.............................	100,000	———
Capital Stock..............................	250,000	200,000
Earned Surplus............................	82,500	97,000
	$460,000	$310,000

The equipment accounts and the earned surplus account on December 31, 1954, were as follows:

EQUIPMENT

1954			1954		
Jan.	1 Balance	100,000	Jan. 10 Sale of equipment	5,000
	3 Additions	10,000		

ALLOWANCE FOR DEPRECIATION OF EQUIPMENT

1954			1954		
Jan. 10 Sale of equipment	500	Jan.	1 Balance	10,000
		Dec. 31 Depreciation for	
			year	10,500

EARNED SURPLUS

1954			1954		
Jan. 10 Loss on sale of equip.	500	Jan.	1 Balance	97,000
Dec. 14 Cash dividends	12,000	Dec. 31 Write-up of land	25,000
14 Stock dividend	50,000	31 Net profit for year	33,000
31 Goodwill written off	10,000		

A $50,000 addition to the buildings was started on January 10 and completed on June 23, 1954.

Instructions: (1) Prepare working papers for the statement of application of funds. (Allow four lines for Earned Surplus.)

(2) Prepare a statement of application of funds with a supporting schedule of changes in working capital.

32-3. The comparative balance sheets of the Joy Corporation for 1953 and 1954 are as follows:

	DECEMBER 31	
	1954	1953
DEBITS		
Cash......................................$	70,000	$ 50,000
Notes Receivable...........................	30,000	40,000
Accounts Receivable........................	75,000	60,000
Merchandise Inventory......................	140,000	100,000
Prepaid Expenses...........................	5,700	5,000
Investment in Stock of Aren Co.............	100,000	80,000
Plant and Equipment.......................	630,000	570,000
Discount on Bonds Payable.................	4,300	5,000
	$1,055,000	$910,000

CREDITS		
Allowance for Depreciation of Plant and Equipment....................................$	150,000	$110,000
Notes Payable.............................	57,000	40,000
Accounts Payable..........................	48,000	60,000
Bonds Payable, 4% due in 1961.............	100,000	100,000
6% Preferred Stock, $100 par..............	70,000	80,000
Common Stock, $20 par....................	480,000	400,000
Premium on Common Stock...............	70,000	50,000
Retained Earnings........................	80,000	70,000
	$1,055,000	$910,000

The retained earnings account for 1954 is reproduced below:

RETAINED EARNINGS

1954			1954		
Feb. 20	Retirement of preferred stock	1,000	Jan. 1	Balance	70,000
Dec. 15	Cash dividends paid	50,000	Dec. 31	Net profit for year	61,000

Equipment costing $70,000 was purchased during 1954. Equipment that cost $10,000 with an accumulated depreciation allowance of $6,000 was sold for $2,000. 4,000 shares of common stock were sold at 25 during 1954 and 100 shares of preferred stock were redeemed at 110, the excess over par being charged to retained earnings. Bonds were sold at 93 in 1951 and the discount is being amortized on a 10-year basis. Additional stock of the Aren Co. was acquired as a permanent holding.

Instructions: (1) Prepare working papers for the statement of application of funds. (Allow two lines for Retained Earnings.)

(2) Prepare a statement of application of funds with a supporting schedule of changes in working capital.

Appendix A

Business Papers

Various business papers are illustrated throughout ACCOUNTING PRINCIPLES as the basis for the record of business transactions. These business papers include the following: purchase order, purchase invoice, credit memorandum, sales invoice, deposit ticket, check and check stub, bank statement, interest-bearing note, non-interest-bearing note, petty cash voucher, voucher jacket, payroll check, stock certificate. Further information about some of these business papers and about additional business papers that are important in connection with the completion of business transactions is given in this appendix.

NEGOTIABLE INSTRUMENTS A negotiable instrument is a written promise or order to pay money, the instrument being transferable from one person to another by indorsement and delivery.

The most common form of written *promise* to pay money is the *promissory note*. There are two original parties to every promissory note: (1) the one who signs the note and makes the promise to pay, called the *maker;* and (2) the one to whom the money is to be paid, called the *payee*.

The most commonly used forms of written *orders* to pay money are checks, bank drafts, commercial drafts, trade acceptances, and money orders. There are three original parties to every written order to pay money: (1) the one who signs the order, called the *drawer;* (2) the one who is ordered to make the payment, called the *drawee;* and (3) the one to whom the money is to be paid, called the *payee*.

Negotiable instruments may be classified according to their use into two general groups, namely, those that are used as substitutes for money and those that are used as evidence of debt. The instruments most commonly used as substitutes for money are checks, cashier's checks, certified checks, bank drafts, and money orders. Those most commonly used as evidences of debt are promissory notes, sight drafts, time drafts, and trade acceptances.

Essential Elements of Negotiable Instruments. In order to be negotiable, an instrument must have the following characteristics:

1. It must be in writing and must be signed by the maker or the drawer.
2. It must contain an unconditional promise or order to pay a certain sum of money.

3. It must be payable on demand or at a time that is either fixed or determinable.

4. It must be payable to bearer or to order.

It may be wholly or partly printed, typewritten, or handwritten, preferably in ink.

Words of Negotiability. To be negotiable (transferable by indorsement and delivery), an instrument must contain words of negotiability, such as "to the order of" or "to bearer." The following are examples of wording that may be used to indicate negotiability: "I promise to pay to the order of Ray Nolton," "I promise to pay Ray Nolton or order," "I promise to pay to the bearer," "Pay to the order of Ray Nolton," and "Pay to bearer."

INDORSEMENT OF NEGOTIABLE INSTRUMENTS   It is frequently necessary to transfer a negotiable instrument from one party to another. The legal transfer of a negotiable instrument is effected by (1) indorsement by the payee or the holder and (2) delivery to the party to whom the instrument is to be transferred. In addition to effecting the transfer of the negotiable instrument, the indorsement serves as a guaranty that the instrument is valid and genuine and that the indorser has a legal title to it. In case the payer fails to pay the instrument on the date of maturity, the holder can usually hold the indorser responsible for payment, provided the holder complies with the legal requirements in reference to presentation and to giving notice to the indorser.

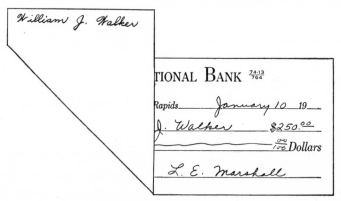

Position of an Indorsement

The indorsement is customarily written or stamped on the back of the negotiable instrument. The first indorsement is, through custom, placed near the left end of the instrument. The position of an indorsement is shown in the illustration above.

A negotiable instrument should be signed by the party or parties responsible for its payment or by an authorized agent. Any partner in a trading partnership may sign a negotiable instrument and thus bind the firm by his action if the instrument is issued in the regular conduct of the business. In a corporation such instruments are signed by some officer or employee authorized by the bylaws to do so. When issued by a partnership or a corporation, negotiable instruments are signed with the name of the business and, in addition, with the name of the officer who is authorized to sign the name of the business.

There are several forms of indorsements, each being used for a different purpose. The most important forms are the following:

1. *Blank.* An indorsement in blank is one that merely shows the name of the payee or the holder across the back of the instrument without any qualifying or limiting words. It has the same effect as making the paper payable to bearer; and the instrument may be transferred by any subsequent holder without further indorsement. But the indorsement of each transferor is usually required so that each can be readily identified as one of the parties responsible for the payment of the instrument in case the one who should make payment does not do so.

> *William Johnson*

2. *Full.* An indorsement in full contains the words "Pay to the order of" and the name of the person or the firm to which the instrument is transferred, in addition to the name of the payee or the holder who transfers the instrument. The person to whom the instrument is transferred must indorse it before any succeeding holder can obtain title to it. All papers sent through the mail or to be held for some time by the person who receives them should be indorsed in full.

> *Pay to the order of*
> *Harold Jackson*
> *William Johnson*

3. *Qualified.* A qualified indorsement is one that passes the title to the instrument without rendering the indorser liable in the event that the maker is unable or refuses to pay. It is accomplished by writing the words "Without recourse" above the signature of the indorser.

> *Pay to the order of*
> *R. E. Duff*
> *Without recourse*
> *M. L. Rose*

4. *Restrictive.* A restrictive indorsement is one that makes the indorsee an agent of the the indorser. For example, a note left at a bank for collection may have the words "For collection" written above the indorsement. This prevents the paper from being used as the property of the bank. Other restricting phrases that are used include the words "For collection and credit" or "For deposit."

> Pay to the order of
> The Hyde Park State Bank
> For collection
> M. L. Rose

A payee or indorsee whose name has been misspelled on a negotiable instrument should indorse the instrument twice, first writing his name exactly as it is spelled on the paper and then writing an indorsement containing his correct signature.

PROMISSORY NOTES   A *promissory note* or a *note* is an unconditional promise in writing, signed by the promisor, to pay a certain sum of money on demand or at a definite time to the order of a designated person or to the bearer. There are two original parties to a note: (1) the *maker*, who signs the note and makes the promise to pay; and (2) the *payee*, who is to receive the payment and in whose favor the promise is made. The purpose of the note is to provide written evidence of the maker's indebtedness to the payee, which may be transferred from one person to another by indorsement.

A note may be interest-bearing or non-interest-bearing. It is non-interest-bearing unless it contains an express statement to the effect that interest is to be paid. If a note contains the words "with interest" but does not specify the rate, it is assumed that interest is to be paid at the legal rate. An interest-bearing promissory note is illustrated on page 187.

Maturity of Notes. Promissory notes may be so drawn as to be payable (1) a stated number of days, months, or years after the date of the note; (2) on a specified date, as "On July 14 I promise to pay"; (3) on demand, as "On demand (or At sight) I promise to pay"; or (4) on or before a specified date, as "On or before March 28 I promise to pay."

Rights and Responsibilities of the Parties to a Note. By signing a promissory note, the maker acknowledges the existence and the amount of the debt for which the note is issued, and agrees to pay the note in accordance with its terms. The payee may hold the note and receive payment from the maker at maturity, or he may indorse it to a third person, who may again transfer it or hold it until maturity and collect from the maker. If the payee transfers the note, he becomes liable as an indorser and is responsible for its payment if the maker fails to pay.

The holder of a note is not required to present it to the maker at maturity in order to hold the maker liable for its payment. The maker's obligation is unconditional; it is his duty to seek the holder and to tender payment when payment is due. For the convenience of both the maker and the holder, most notes are drawn payable at a special place, usually the maker's bank. Either the holder or his agent is expected to go to that place to receive payment, but his failure to do so does not release the maker from his obligation to pay. However, if there are any indorsements on the note, the holder is required by law to present the note promptly at maturity and to demand payment if it is his intention to hold the indorsers liable.

If the maker fails to tender payment or refuses to pay when payment is due, the note is said to be dishonored and is no longer negotiable. The holder has the right to bring legal action at once against the maker to enforce payment; and the maker will be required to pay the costs of such action as well as the amount due on the note, including interest from the date of dishonor to the date of payment.

Accounting for Promissory Notes. Various uses of promissory notes and the methods of accounting for them are discussed and illustrated in Chapter 11, pages 187 to 201 of this textbook. The registers that may be used in recording notes receivable and notes payable are discussed and illustrated in Chapter 15, pages 272 to 275.

COMMERCIAL DRAFTS A draft is a written order by which one party directs another to pay a specified sum of money to the order of the first party or to the order of a third party. A draft is sometimes referred to as a *bill of exchange,* but this term is most frequently applied to drafts used in international transactions.

There are three parties to a draft. The person who makes the request or order and whose signature is written at the lower right on the face of the instrument is called the *drawer;* the person on whom the draft is drawn and who is directed to make the payment is called the *drawee;* and the person in whose favor the draft is drawn and to whom the amount is to be paid is called the *payee.*

Drafts may be used either as evidence of debt or as substitutes for money. Those used as evidence of debt are known as commercial drafts. A *commercial draft* may be defined as a written order drawn by one person on his debtor, directing the latter to pay a certain sum of money to the drawer or to a third person. The drawee named in a commercial draft is always an individual or a firm other than a bank.

The forms of drafts most commonly used as substitutes for money are bank drafts and checks. A *bank draft* is a written order drawn by one bank on another and is evidence that the bank drawing the draft has money on deposit in the bank on which the draft is drawn. A *check* is a written order drawn on a bank by a depositor who is an individual or a firm other than a bank. It should be observed that in both of these forms the drawee, that is, the party on whom the draft is drawn, is a bank. In the case of a bank draft, the drawer is a bank also; whereas in the case of a check, the drawer is a party other than a bank.

Kinds of Commercial Drafts. According to the time of payment commercial drafts may be classified as follows:

1. *Sight drafts.* A sight draft is a draft that is payable at sight; that is, it is payable as soon as it is presented for payment.
2. *Time drafts.* A time draft is a draft that is payable a certain number of days after sight or after date.

According to the number of original parties, commercial drafts may be classified as follows:

1. *Three-party drafts.* A three-party draft is a draft in which the drawer, the drawee, and the payee are different persons.
2. *Two-party drafts.* A two-party draft is a draft in which the drawer and the payee are the same person.

Commercial Sight Drafts. Commercial sight drafts are used for two purposes, namely, to collect accounts that are past due and to collect for C.O.D. freight shipments.

Sight Draft Used for Collecting an Account. Sight drafts are often used by creditors as a means of demanding payment of past-due accounts. The procedure in detail is as follows:

1. The creditor draws a two-party sight draft on the debtor. The creditor indorses it and gives it to his bank for collection.
2. The creditor's bank indorses and forwards the draft to a correspondent bank in the city where the debtor, or drawee, is located.
3. The receiving bank presents the draft to the drawee for payment.
4. If payment is obtained, the draft is marked "Paid" by the receiving bank and is given to the drawee as a receipt for his payment. If the

receiving bank is unable to obtain payment, it returns the draft to the sending bank with a notation giving the reason for the drawee's failure to pay.

5. The receiving bank then remits the amount of the paid draft, less possibly a collection fee, by bank draft to the sending bank or credits it to an account carried with the sending bank.

6. Upon receiving the remittance from the receiving bank, or a notice of the credit, the sending bank credits the proceeds to the account of the drawer.

To illustrate, the draft shown below was drawn by King & Wilson who wished to collect $326.39 from C. R. Ankromm & Son. Since this draft was made payable to the order of "ourselves," that is, to the order of King & Wilson, they were obliged to indorse it in order to make it further negotiable. The draft was then given to King & Wilson's bank in Topeka to be forwarded to a bank in St. Louis. The St. Louis bank received the draft and presented it to C. R. Ankromm & Son for payment. When C. R. Ankromm & Son paid the draft, the bank in St. Louis either remitted the proceeds by bank draft to the Topeka bank or credited the amount to the Topeka bank's account. The Topeka bank then credited the proceeds to the bank account of King & Wilson.

Commercial Sight Draft

Instead of drawing the draft in favor of themselves, King & Wilson could have made it payable to their bank in Topeka. It would then have been a three-party draft. The procedure of collecting the draft would have been the same as before except that King & Wilson would not have been required to indorse the draft before giving it to their bank for collection.

The drawee is not compelled to pay the draft, but his refusal to pay may reflect unfavorably on his credit with the local bank. In order that his credit standing may not be impaired, the drawee is likely to pay the draft when it is presented, unless there is some justifiable reason for refusing payment.

Sight Draft Used to Collect C.O.D. Freight Shipment. Express,freight, and parcel-post shipments may be sent C.O.D., and the agent or postmaster at the point of destination will collect the amount due before he delivers the merchandise to the purchaser. Railroad and steamship companies, however, allow the seller to make shipment in such a manner that a third party, usually a bank, may act as the seller's collection agent at the point of destination and obtain payment from the purchaser before the merchandise is delivered to him. In general, the details of the procedure for making collection through a bank on a C.O.D. freight shipment are as follows:

1. The seller ships the goods on an order bill of lading[1] in which the merchandise is consigned to the order of himself, and he attaches to it a sight draft drawn on the purchaser.

2. The seller indorses the order bill of lading and the sight draft, and sends both papers to his bank for collection.

3. The seller's bank, in turn, indorses both papers and sends them to a bank in the city of the purchaser.

4. Upon receipt of the draft and the bill of lading, the receiving bank notifies the purchaser that these two papers have arrived.

5. The purchaser pays the draft and is given the bill of lading, properly indorsed to him by the receiving bank, with which he can obtain the merchandise from the transportation company. The draft is marked "Paid" by the receiving bank and is given to the purchaser as a receipt for his payment.

6. The receiving bank then remits the amount collected, less possibly a collection fee, by bank draft to the sending bank or credits the amount to the latter's account.

7. The sending bank, in turn, credits the proceeds to the bank account of the seller.

Commercial Time Drafts. A time draft is one that is payable a certain number of days after sight or after date. If the person directed to pay is willing to do so, he indicates this by writing his name across the face of the draft if the draft is payable a certain number of days after date, or by writing his name and the date if the draft is payable a certain number of days after sight. He may also precede his name with the word "Accepted." The drawee who signs in this manner is then known as the *acceptor* of the draft, and the draft is referred to as an *acceptance.*

---

[1]An order bill of lading is illustrated on page 675.

$250.⁰⁰ _____ Cincinnati, Ohio, May 12, 19___
Thirty days after date _____ Pay to the
Order of First National Bank of Cincinnati
Two Hundred Fifty ⁰⁰⁄₁₀₀ _____ Dollars
Value received and charge to account of
To L. J. Reynolds
No. 20   Hamilton, Ohio   J. D. Williams

Accepted Time Draft

If the draft is payable a certain number of days after sight, the date of maturity is the given number of days after the date on which the drawee accepts the draft. If it is payable a certain number of days after date, the date of maturity is the given number of days after the date on which the draft is drawn. The draft shown on this page is payable 30 days after date, that is, 30 days after May 12. If the draft had been payable 30 days after sight, Mr. Reynolds would have written the date of acceptance as well as his signature, and the draft would have been due 30 days after that date.

A time draft is usually drawn for one of the following purposes: (1) to obtain a debtor's formal written acknowledgment of his indebtedness and his agreement to pay at a definite time; (2) to obtain a negotiable instrument that the drawer can discount at his bank; (3) to obtain written evidence of a sale on credit.

Obligations of the Parties to a Commercial Draft. The drawee of a draft is under no obligation to accept it. If he does accept it, he pays a sight draft or he writes his acceptance across the face of a time draft. The acceptance of a time draft makes it the written promise of the acceptor to pay the amount stipulated at the specified time. The instrument thus becomes to all intents and purposes a promissory note and is so treated by the original parties and subsequent holders.

Trade Acceptance. The trade acceptance is a negotiable instrument that is designed to serve as a substitute for the open account. It is a special form of time draft that shows on its face that it has arisen out of a purchase of goods by the acceptor. It is drawn by the seller at the time of the sale and is accepted by the purchaser when he receives the merchandise. It differs from an ordinary time draft or promissory note in the following respects:

1. It is always given at the time of the sale and is drawn to mature at the end of the regular term of credit granted by the seller, whereas a time draft or a note may be given at any time and for any period of time.

2. It arises out of a merchandise transaction and cannot be given for a loan of money or an extension of time on an overdue account.

3. It is self-liquidating in that the resale of the merchandise by the acceptor will provide funds out of which the acceptance may be paid at maturity. Notes and time drafts are not, as a rule, self-liquidating because they are generally given for a loan of money or an extension of the time on an indebtedness that is overdue.

4. It is taken for discount by banks more readily than an ordinary note or time draft because it is self-liquidating in character and likely to be paid at maturity.

5. It is a more liquid asset than is either an ordinary time draft or a promissory note because it is more readily discounted by banks.

The use of the trade acceptance in place of the open account as a means of extending credit has the following advantages for the seller:

1. The seller does not have to wait until the debt matures before getting his money, but can obtain the money immediately by discounting the acceptance. The seller is relieved of the burden of using his own capital to finance the purchases of the buyer.

2. The trade acceptance is presumptive evidence of the acceptor's indebtedness; therefore, the seller may enforce its payment without having to furnish additional evidence of the debt.

3. Losses on bad debts are reduced because the trade acceptance must be paid promptly at maturity.

4. The trade acceptance can be converted into cash with much less expense and inconvenience than can an open account.

The use of the trade acceptance may be explained by an illustration. The Huron Company, of Nashville, sells $314.50 worth of merchandise to G. M. York, of Exeter, terms sixty-day trade acceptance. The Huron Company draws the acceptance, using the form prescribed for a trade acceptance, as shown on page 669. G. M. York accepts the form and returns it to The Huron Company. The latter may keep it for sixty days and then present it for payment, or, if the company desires, it may discount the acceptance at its local bank. In the latter case the bank will give The Huron Company credit for the proceeds of the acceptance at the time it is discounted, and at its maturity will send it to some Nashville bank, which will collect it from G. M. York.

No. 21. Nashville, March 18, 19___

To *S. M. York* Exeter

On *May 17, 19___* Pay to the order of *Ourselves*

Three hundred fourteen and 50/100 Dollars ($314 50/100)

The obligation of the acceptor hereof arises out of the purchase of goods from the drawer. The drawee may accept this bill payable at any bank, banker or trust company in the United States which such drawee may designate.

Accepted at *Exeter* on *Mar. 19 19*
Payable at *Union* Bank
Bank Location *Exeter*
Buyers Signature *S. M. York*
By Agent or Officer _____

The Huron Company

By *R. H. Hall, Treasurer*

Trade Acceptance

Accounting for Drafts and Acceptances. When a draft or a trade acceptance is mailed to a debtor, no entry is made in the books of account because the debtor has not assumed any obligation on the instrument until he has accepted it. It may be convenient, however, for a business to keep a memorandum record of the drafts and acceptances issued and the disposition that is made of them. Such a memorandum record is illustrated below.

DRAFTS AND TRADE ACCEPTANCES ISSUED

DATE OF PAPER	DRAWEE	FACE AMOUNT	WHEN PAYABLE	PRESENTING OR COLLECTING AGENT	DISPOSITION	
					DATE	
19--						
Nov. 5	Butler Co.	250 00	On sight	1st Nat'l Bk.	Nov. 10	Paid
8	A. L. Parks	325 00	30 days after sight	1st Nat'l Bk.	Nov. 12	Accepted
12	S. R. Nash & Co.	500 00	Dec. 12	1st Nat'l Bk.	Nov. 17	Honored
18	L. E. White Co.	295 50	30 days after date	1st Nat'l Bk.	Nov. 21	Accepted
24	Rhodes & Co.	425 00	Dec. 24	1st Nat'l Bk.		
29	C. C. Rolfe & Co.	610 00	On sight	1st Nat'l Bk.		

Memorandum record of drafts and acceptances issued

When a debtor accepts a sight draft, he does so by making payment. He therefore records the transaction in his cash payments journal as a debit to the creditor. When a debtor has accepted a time draft or acceptance, he has assumed the same liability as when he has signed a note. Separate accounts may be maintained for drafts and acceptances receivable and payable, but it is common to record them with the notes receivable and payable. Therefore, when a debtor accepts a time draft or trade acceptance he may make an entry similar to the following:

May 7   Accounts Payable — Farley and Holmes...... 1,250
       Notes Payable.......................   1,250
       Accepted a 30-day trade acceptance, dated
       May 5.

When a creditor receives payment upon the acceptance of a sight draft, he makes an entry in his cash receipts journal, debiting cash and crediting the customer. If the draft was collected through a bank, it is also necessary to record a collection expense. When a creditor receives an accepted time draft or trade acceptance, he makes the following entry:

```
May 9   Notes Receivable........................  1,250
           Accounts Receivable — A. C. Rutledge.....          1,250
              Received 30-day accepted draft, dated
              May 5.
```

Accepted time drafts and trade acceptances may be recorded in a notes payable register by the debtor and in a notes receivable register by the creditor, similar to the registers illustrated in Chapter 15, pages 272–275. If many drafts or acceptances are used, separate registers may be provided for them.

NEGOTIABLE INSTRU- *Checks.* A check is a written order on a bank
MENTS USED AS SUB- directing the bank to pay a certain sum of
STITUTES FOR MONEY money to a designated person. The person
making the demand has money deposited in the bank with the understanding that the bank will deliver it on his order. Since a check is an order to pay money, there are three original parties: (1) the person drawing the order, known as the *drawer;* (2) the bank on which the order is drawn, known as the *drawee;* and (3) the person to whom the draft is payable, known as the *payee.*

Rights and Responsibilities of the Payee. The payee of a check may cash it at the bank on which it is drawn, deposit it in his own bank for collection, or transfer it to another person. Generally the payee deposits it.

When the payee deposits the check or disposes of it in some other manner, he is required to indorse it. By indorsing the check, the payee transfers his title to the instrument, acknowledges receipt of cash or other assets for the amount named, and becomes liable to subsequent holders for the payment of the check.

Rights and Responsibilities of the Drawee. The drawee bank must bear the loss if it pays a check to any person other than the one named, if it pays a check on which the depositor's signature has been forged, if it pays a raised check that bears evidence of alteration, and if it pays a check on which payment has been stopped.

The bank's obligation is to the drawer or depositor, not to the payee or subsequent holders, and the bank may refuse at times to honor a check in order to protect the depositor or itself against possible loss. There are numerous circumstances under which payment of a check is often refused, chief of which are the following:

1. *Insufficient funds.* The bank is under no obligation to honor a check unless the drawer has on deposit sufficient funds to pay it. The bank may, however, pay the check and call upon the drawer for an immediate deposit.

2. *Check drawn in pencil.* It is legal to draw a check in pencil. Many banks will not honor a check drawn in this manner, however, because of the ease with which such a check can be altered and the possibility that it may have been raised or materially altered after leaving the hands of the drawer.

3. *Evidence of erasure or other alteration.* Because of the bank's liability in connection with the payment of an altered check, the bank will not honor a check that bears evidence of erasure or other alteration. The erasure or alteration may have been made by the drawer himself, but the bank has no way of knowing this.

4. *Postdated check.* By dating a check, the drawer indicates the date on or after which the bank may honor the check for payment. The bank will therefore refuse to pay a check that is presented before the date that it bears. To pay it before the date specified would be contrary to the order of the drawer.

5. *Date missing.* Since the bank has authority to pay a check only on or after the date that it bears, the bank may refuse to honor a check on which the date is missing. It may have been the drawer's intention to postdate the check.

6. *Discrepancy between the amount in words and the amount in figures.* When the amount in words differs from the amount in figures, the amount in words is considered the correct amount of the check. If there is a material difference, the bank will probably withhold payment until it obtains from the drawer information as to the correct amount.

7. *Incorrect signature of the drawer.* The bank may refuse to honor a check on which the signature of the drawer is not the same as the one appearing on the drawer's signature card.

8. *Identification of the indorser.* Since the bank must bear the loss if it pays to the wrong person, the bank will refuse payment on a check if the one presenting it cannot identify himself as the payee or indorsee named on the check. In the case of a bearer check — one that is not payable to any specified individual — the person presenting it must be one who is personally known at the bank. Otherwise the bank will refuse to pay it.

9. *Payment stopped.* The bank will refuse to pay a check on which payment has been stopped.

Rights and Responsibilities of the Drawer. The principal rights and responsibilities of the drawer of a check are the following:

1. The drawer may stop payment on a check at any time before it is paid by filing a stop-payment order with the bank on which the check was drawn.
2. The drawer may hold the bank liable for the loss resulting from the payment of a check on which his signature was forged.
3. The drawer must bear the loss on a raised check if the check was drawn carelessly or in such a manner that it could be altered without bearing evidence of the alteration.

Certified Check. A certified check is one the payment of which is guaranteed by the bank on which it is drawn. The procedure of certification is as follows: The drawer or holder of the check presents it at the bank for certification. An officer of the bank examines the drawer's account to see that the balance is sufficient to cover the check. If the drawer's balance is sufficient, the check is stamped "Certified" across the face, this word being followed by the date, the name of the bank, and the signature of the bank's cashier, and is then returned to the person who presented it for certification. The bank immediately debits the amount of the check to the drawer's account and credits the certified checks payable account. Thus the bank assumes responsibility for meeting the check when it is later presented for payment.

The drawer may ask to have his check certified when he has a payment to make to someone who does not know him and who will not accept his personal check. The holder of a personal check, having accepted it but feeling uncertain as to its payment, may request certification at the drawer's bank in order to be assured that payment will be made.

If for any reason the drawer does not make use of a check that he has had certified, he must deposit it in order to get credit for it at his bank.

Cashier's Check. A cashier's check is a check drawn on a bank by its cashier, and is used chiefly in the payment of the obligations of the bank, for remitting collections made for persons who have no accounts with the bank, and as a substitute for certifying the check of a depositor.

Bank Draft. A bank draft is a check drawn by one bank on another bank and is evidence that the bank drawing the draft has money on deposit in the bank on which the draft is drawn. The purpose and use of a bank draft may be explained by means of an illustration.

No. 694

First National Bank 56-906/422

Camden, Ohio_____ JANUARY 17 _____ 19___

PAY TO THE ORDER OF __HARTFORD & SONS__ $500.00

The sum of $500 and 00 cts _____ DOLLARS

TO
FIRST NATIONAL BANK
CINCINNATI, OHIO

Warren S. Compton
CASHIER

Bank Draft

If Hartford & Sons, who live in Camden, Ohio, wish to pay $500 to Arthur Blake, in Cincinnati, Ohio, they may go to their bank in Camden and ask to purchase a draft. Their bank in Camden will probably have money on deposit in some bank in Cincinnati and will draw a draft on this bank, ordering it to pay Hartford & Sons $500. On paying the Camden bank $500, plus a small fee, Hartford & Sons will receive the draft, which they will indorse and send to Arthur Blake. The latter will treat it in the same manner as any incoming check and will either cash it or deposit it in his bank in Camden.

It should be observed that the draft in the foregoing illustration was made payable to Hartford & Sons, the debtor. It was then indorsed by them to the creditor, Arthur Blake. There are two reasons why the draft should be drawn in this manner and should not be drawn payable to the creditor: (1) If in Blake's office the draft should become separated from Hartford & Sons' letter of remittance, Blake can identify the sender by observing the name of the person specified on the draft as the payee. (2) After the draft is indorsed by Blake and is paid by the First National Bank, the draft becomes a receipt in favor of Hartford & Sons. Their indorsement shows that they transferred the draft to Blake, and the latter's indorsement shows that he received the payment. If the draft had been originally drawn with Blake named as the payee, the paid draft would not have constituted a receipt in favor of Hartford & Sons because there would have been no evidence on the draft that it was they who purchased it and gave it to Blake.

Money Orders. A money order is an order for the payment of money. Money orders are of two kinds: postal money orders and express money orders. A postal money order is a government order for the payment of money, which is issued at one post office on the sender's written application, and is payable to the holder upon the latter's proper identification. An express money order is a check that is issued by an express company on the application of the person wishing to make the remittance, who deposits the amount with the express company, and is payable at some specified office to the holder.

BILLS OF LADING   When merchandise is shipped by freight, a *bill of lading* is filled out to include the following information: the name of the carrier receiving the shipment; the place and the date; the name and the address of the shipper and of the consignee; the routing of the shipment, that is, the names of the carriers that are to handle the shipment; and the number, weight, and description of the contents of the packages or cases shipped.

The bill of lading is prepared in triplicate. The first copy, known as the *original*, is signed by both the shipper and the carrier's agent and is issued to the shipper as a receipt for the goods delivered to the carrier. It is both a receipt and a contract. It states that the carrier has received the goods described thereon, and it sets forth the terms and conditions under which the carrier agrees to transport the property. The second copy, called the *shipping order*, is signed by the shipper only and is retained by the carrier as evidence of its authority. The third copy, called the *memorandum*, is a duplicate of the first and is signed by the shipper and the agent. It is issued to the shipper as a duplicate receipt.

There are two forms of the bill of lading, the *straight bill of lading* and the *order bill of lading*. The straight bill of lading is nonnegotiable and is used for shipping an order of merchandise that has been paid for in advance or that has been sold on account. The shipment is consigned to the customer, and the original bill of lading is forwarded to him by mail. When the shipment reaches its destination, the freight agent at that point sends the consignee a freight arrival notice. If the consignee is not personally known to the freight agent, he will be required to present his copy of the bill of lading in order to obtain possession of the goods. He will also be required to present it in case the goods are damaged in transit and he files a claim against the transportation company.

The order bill of lading is negotiable by indorsement, and the shipment for which it is issued is consigned to the order of the shipper or his agent. Possession of the goods at the point of destination can be obtained only upon presentation of the original bill of lading properly indorsed to the person who presents it. This form is used for making C.O.D. freight shipments. It is also used when the goods represented by the bill of lading are to be sold for the shipper by his agent or broker at the point of destination and the shipper does not know who the purchaser will be.

The illustration below shows an order bill of lading. The Selby Mail-Order House shipped to Dayton, Ohio, two cases of electrical supplies and consigned the shipment to their own order. They indorsed the original copy of the bill of lading and mailed it, together with an invoice and a draft for the amount of the invoice, to a bank in Dayton. Upon the payment of the sight draft by the customer, Mr. Worth, the invoice and the bill of lading were given to him. He then presented the bill of lading to the railroad freight office and obtained possession of the merchandise.

Order Bill of Lading

Appendix B

Accounting Statements

Statements of financial condition and operations taken from the annual reports of various corporations are presented on this and the following pages. They are illustrative of the many variations in form of statement, terminology employed, and type of data presented to stockholders. Many notes and references thereto that accompany the complete statements are not shown in this appendix.

Avco Manufacturing Corporation and Consolidated Subsidiaries

STATEMENTS OF CONSOLIDATED INCOME

for the years ended November 30, 1952 and November 30, 1951

	Year ended Nov. 30, 1952	Year ended Nov. 30, 1951
Net Sales	$326,585,641	$286,598,113
Cost of Sales	274,039,561	234,636,584
Gross Profit From Sales	$ 52,546,080	$ 51,961,529
Expenses		
Selling and advertising	$ 20,786,832	$ 21,889,172
General and administrative	7,193,869	7,042,922
	$ 27,980,701	$ 28,932,094
	$ 24,565,379	$ 23,029,435
Other Income		
Interest earned	$ 292,398	$ 341,647
Net profit on sale of securities, less provision for losses	(318,288)	451,125
Miscellaneous	716,322	732,337
	$ 690,432	$ 1,525,109
	$ 25,255,811	$ 24,554,544
Income Deductions		
Interest paid	$ 2,072,481	$ 934,666
Minority interest	—	72,533
Provision for amount payable under extra compensation plan	1,604,403	1,458,131
	$ 3,676,884	$ 2,465,330
	$ 21,578,927	$ 22,089,214
Provision for Federal Income Tax	10,550,000	12,000,000
Net Income for the Year	$ 11,028,927	$ 10,089,214

Provision for depreciation and amortization of property, plant and equipment amounted to $4,235,772 for the year ended November 30, 1952 and $2,580,112 for the year ended November 30, 1951. The increase in the provision for the year ended November 30, 1952 results primarily from amortization of certified emergency facilities (see Note 2) and amortization of patterns, dies, jigs and special tools (see Note 3).

CONSOLIDATED INCOME AND RETAINED EARNINGS
EATON MANUFACTURING COMPANY AND SUBSIDIARIES

INCOME

	1952	1951
Net sales	$181,855,861	$186,771,067
Other income:		
Cash discount and interest earned	590,857	586,304
Other income	112,448	477,737
	$182,559,166	$187,835,108
Less:		
Cost of products sold	$148,179,260	$151,987,891
Selling, advertising, administrative, and general expenses	4,505,999	4,236,389
Other charges	57,130	44,499
Taxes on income—estimated:		
Federal taxes on income:		
Normal tax and surtax	$ 15,100,000	$ 15,700,000
Excess profits tax	4,935,000	5,275,000
Canadian and state taxes on income	345,000	295,000
	$ 20,380,000	$ 21,270,000
	$173,122,389	$177,538,779
NET INCOME	$ 9,436,777	$ 10,296,329

Allowances for depreciation and amortization:
1952—$3,211,716; 1951—$2,476,825.

EARNINGS RETAINED FOR USE IN THE BUSINESS

Balance at beginning of year	$ 34,667,823	$ 29,741,320
Net income for the year	9,436,777	10,296,329
	$ 44,104,600	$ 40,037,649
Cash dividends paid—$3.00 per share	5,369,826	5,369,826
BALANCE AT END OF YEAR	$ 38,734,774	$ 34,667,823

ASSETS

	Dec. 31, 1952	Dec. 31, 1951
CURRENT ASSETS		
Cash	$12,376,666	$12,844,527
Marketable securities—at cost plus accrued interest (quoted market $11,567,275 and $7,552,902, respectively):		
U. S. Government securities	$11,502,908	$ 7,492,214
Dominion of Canada bonds	60,613	60,613
	$11,563,521	$ 7,552,827
Trade accounts receivable	$18,877,916	$15,451,747
Less allowance for doubtful	115,000	115,000
	$18,762,916	$15,336,747
Inventories—at lower of cost (average or standard) or replacement market:		
Finished and in process	$15,974,041	$14,523,881
Raw materials	4,884,110	7,027,042
Manufacturing supplies	1,659,211	1,711,276
	$22,517,362	$23,262,199
Less allowance for shrinkage and obsolescence	1,125,871	1,163,108
	$21,391,491	$22,099,091
TOTAL CURRENT ASSETS	$64,094,594	$57,833,192
OTHER ASSETS	56,497	108,515
PROPERTY, PLANT, AND EQUIPMENT		
Major portion based upon cost, less allowances for depreciation and amortization:		
Land	$ 1,273,036	$ 1,217,208
Buildings and equipment	45,969,957	40,253,152
	$47,242,993	$41,470,360
Less allowances for depreciation and amortization	17,983,753	15,718,136
	$29,259,240	$25,752,224
PATENTS, TRADE-MARKS, LICENSES, ETC.	136,606	89,499
DEFERRED CHARGES	281,987	235,162
	$93,828,924	$84,018,592

BALANCE SHEETS

COMPANY AND SUBSIDIARIES

LIABILITIES AND SHAREHOLDERS' EQUITY

	Dec. 31, 1952	Dec. 31, 1951
CURRENT LIABILITIES		
Notes payable to banks—Dynamatic Corporation, a subsidiary . . .	$ 1,430,000	$ 1,430,000
Accounts payable	9,568,305	7,974,036
Pay rolls and additional compensation	2,810,784	2,540,418
Current portion of Canadian subsidiary long-term debt	—0—	50,000
Taxes (other than taxes on income)	396,858	399,112
Federal, state, and Canadian taxes on income—estimated	$20,765,000	$21,574,000
Less U. S. Treasury Savings Notes	—0—	5,190,000
	$20,765,000	$16,384,000
TOTAL CURRENT LIABILITIES	$34,970,947	$28,777,566
LONG-TERM DEBT		
3½% First Mortgage Bonds of Canadian subsidiary	—0—	450,000
SHAREHOLDERS' EQUITY		
Capital stock, par value $2.00 per share:		
Authorized 2,500,000 shares		
Issued 1,792,520 shares (including shares in treasury)	$ 3,585,040	$ 3,585,040
Capital in excess of par value (no change during year)	$16,563,490	$16,563,490
Earnings retained for use in the business	38,734,774	34,667,823
	$55,298,264	$51,231,313
Less 2,578 shares in treasury—at cost	25,327	25,327
	$55,272,937	$51,205,986
	$58,857,977	$54,791,026
	$93,828,924	$84,018,592

BALANCE SHEET

LIBBEY-OWENS-FORD GLASS COMPANY
December 31, 1952

Assets

CURRENT ASSETS

Cash		$ 15,005,824.56
Trade receivables, less allowance of $500,000.00		12,401,537.08
Inventories—at lower of cost or market:		
Raw materials	$ 3,068,896.62	
In-process products	3,678,051.36	
Finished products	5,626,350.73	
Manufacturing and shipping supplies	8,888,047.87	
Materials and supplies in transit	6,021,126.65	27,282,473.23
TOTAL CURRENT ASSETS		$ 54,689,834.87

PLANT IMPROVEMENT AND REPLACEMENT FUND

Cash on deposit	$ 143,545.70	
U. S. Government securities—at cost and accrued interest		
(quoted market $24,445,506.15)	24,539,278.65	24,682,824.35

INVESTMENTS AND OTHER ASSETS

Sundry deposits and other receivables	$ 393,074.71	
Investments ($100,000.00 in wholly-owned and		
non-operating subsidiary)	217,864.34	
Notes and accounts receivable from employes	101,334.95	712,274.00

MANUFACTURING PROPERTIES, ETC.—at cost

Land, improvements, and buildings	$ 42,737,423.29	
Machinery, equipment, etc.	52,022,502.55	
Employe dwellings, land held for factory extension, etc.	988,351.67	
Construction in progress	6,053,007.09	
	$101,801,284.60	
Less allowances for depreciation and amortization	66,837,883.24	34,963,401.36

GAS PROPERTIES

Equity based on cost after deducting accumulated allowances for depreciation and depletion	1,249,085.76

PATENTS AND LICENSES—nominal value

	1.00

DEFERRED CHARGES

Prepaid expenses and office supplies	525,472.95
	$116,822,894.29

See notes to financial statements.

BALANCE SHEET

LIBBEY·OWENS·FORD GLASS COMPANY

December 31, 1952

Liabilities and Reserves

CURRENT LIABILITIES

Accounts payable and accrued expenses:

Trade accounts, salaries, wages, etc.	$ 14,644,190.77
Federal taxes on income—estimated (less $12,000,000.00	
U. S. Treasury Savings Notes)	11,000,000.00
TOTAL CURRENT LIABILITIES	$ 25,644,190.77

RESERVES

For rebuilding furnaces, etc.	$ 4,356,638.78	
For general contingencies (appropriated surplus)	3,341,360.28	7,697,999.06

CAPITAL

Capital stock:

Common shares—par value $10.00 per share:

Authorized—10,000,000 shares

Issued—5,167,392 shares

(44,460 unissued shares are subject to employe stock options and 20,066 shares are reserved for employes)	$51,673,920.00	
Additional paid in capital	2,904,200.02	
Retained earnings employed in the business	28,902,584.44	83,480,704.46
		$116,822,894.29

Notes to Financial Statements

Note A—Provision for the funding of past service credits and the current year requirements under the Company's pension and retirement plans was paid and charged to earnings of the year 1952.

Note B—A portion of the Company's sales for the year 1952 was subject to the provisions of the Renegotiation Act of 1951, but it is believed that no refund of profits therefrom will be required.

THE BUDD

(A Pennsylvania

RESULTS OF OPERATIONS

	1952	1951
Products sold.	$297,363,844	$317,664,486
Royalties, interest and miscellaneous income	615,784	651,701
	$297,979,628	$318,316,187
Costs allocated to the year:		
Inventories brought forward from previous year . . .	$ 40,563,121	$ 30,393,771
Materials, supplies, services purchased, etc..	165,520,814	192,022,583
Wages, salaries, social security taxes and company con-tributions for pensions, group insurance and management incentive plan	112,684,025	98,845,585
Portion of cost of buildings, machinery and equipment allocated to operations as depreciation.	4,494,428	5,084,667
Property taxes, interest and rents	3,469,735	2,950,089
	$326,732,123	$329,296,695
Deduct—Inventories carried forward to next year . . .	47,843,113	40,563,121
Total costs allocated to the year	$278,889,010	$288,733,574
Profit before taxes on income	$ 19,090,618	$ 29,582,613
Estimated taxes on income:		
State income tax	$ 500,000	$ 600,000
Federal normal and surtax	9,400,000	14,400,000
Federal excess profits tax	—	2,100,000*
	$ 9,900,000	$ 17,100,000
Profit for the year	$ 9,190,618	$ 12,482,613*

ACCUMULATED EARNINGS

Accumulated earnings at December 31, 1951 per 1951 report		$42,008,011
Reduction in excess profits tax for 1951 ($1,600,000) and 1950 ($800,000) by amendment to the Internal Revenue Code in 1952		2,400,000
Accumulated earnings at December 31, 1951 as revised		$44,408,011
Profit for 1952 per statement above		9,190,618
		$53,598,629
Deduct—Dividends to shareholders on:		
Cumulative preferred shares, $5 per share	$ 625,000	
Common shares, $1.00 per share	3,544,040	
		$ 4,169,040
Accumulated earnings invested in the business, December 31, 1952		$49,429,589

*Revised by $1,600,000 reduction in excess profits tax.

COMPANY

Corporation)

STATEMENT OF FINANCIAL POSITION

	December 31, 1952	1951
CURRENT ASSETS:		
Cash	$ 22,589,728	$ 22,195,688
Receivables from customers	29,530,827	24,142,035
Inventories.	47,843,113	40,563,121
Prepaid insurance taxes, etc.	1,417,533	1,477,504
TOTAL CURRENT ASSETS	$101,381,201	$ 88,378,348
LESS: CURRENT LIABILITIES:		
Notes payable to banks	$ 5,000,000	$ —
Payable to material suppliers and others	18,138,793	13,428,684
Accrued wages, salaries, taxes, etc.	10,242,646	7,485,254
Customers' advances on contracts	4,464,355	93,312
Due in following year on long-term debt	—	3,180,000
Estimated taxes on income	11,309,648	18,793,064
TOTAL CURRENT LIABILITIES	$ 49,155,442	$ 42,980,314
NET CURRENT ASSETS	$ 52,225,759	$ 45,398,034
MISCELLANEOUS ASSETS AND DEFERRED CHARGES	881,873	1,000,862
PLANT AND EQUIPMENT LESS DEPRECIATION.	65,358,319	54,950,477
TOTAL ASSETS LESS CURRENT LIABILITIES	$118,465,951	$101,349,373
DERIVED FROM:		
Long-term debt, not due in following year	$ 30,000,000	$ 17,905,000
SHAREHOLDERS' CAPITAL	$ 39,036,362	$ 39,036,362
ACCUMULATED EARNINGS INVESTED IN THE BUSINESS . .	49,429,589	44,408,011
	$ 88,465,951	$ 83,444,373
	$118,465,951	$101,349,373

U.S. STEEL

CONSOLIDATED STATEMENT OF *Income*

	1952	1951
Products and services sold	$3,137,397,336	$3,524,121,226
Costs		
Employment costs		
Wages and salaries	1,176,596,946	1,217,611,480
Pensions, social security taxes, insurance and other employe benefits	145,477,678	156,857,438
	1,322,074,624	1,374,468,918
Products and services bought	1,312,062,864	1,329,670,316
Wear and exhaustion of facilities	176,918,467	162,091,475
War costs included herein provided for in prior years, less associated Federal income tax adjustments	4,480,238	1,750,925
Interest and other costs on long-term debt	1,862,068	1,969,626
State, local and miscellaneous taxes	68,271,805	75,312,029
Estimated Federal taxes on income	117,000,000	398,000,000
Total	2,993,709,590	3,339,761,439
Income	143,687,746	184,359,787
Dividends declared		
On cumulative preferred stock *($7 per share)*	25,219,677	25,219,677
On common stock *($3 per share)*	78,329,268	78,329,268
Income reinvested in business	$ 40,138,801	$ 80,810,842

U.S. STEEL

CONSOLIDATED STATEMENT OF *Financial Position*

	Dec. 31, 1952	Dec. 31, 1951
Current assets		
Cash	$ 215,858,965	$ 233,386,977
United States Government securities, at cost	106,441,431	326,717,100
Receivables, less estimated bad debts	263,654,872	252,784,015
Inventories	424,752,105	399,832,115
Total	1,010,707,373	1,212,720,207
Less		
Current liabilities		
Accounts payable	380,126,199	339,703,119
Accrued taxes	275,040,163	509,773,477
Dividends payable	25,887,237	25,887,237
Long-term debt due within one year	3,098,398	2,438,790
Total	684,151,997	877,802,623
Working capital	326,555,376	334,917,584
Miscellaneous investments, less estimated losses	21,052,134	19,779,076
United States Government securities set aside, at cost		
For property additions and replacements	19,000,000	250,000,000
For expenditures arising out of war	8,000,000	12,000,000
Plant and equipment, less depreciation	1,851,572,655	1,571,334,234
Operating parts and supplies	54,357,497	48,317,344
Costs applicable to future periods	23,745,096	26,528,130
Intangibles	1	1
Total assets less current liabilities	2,304,282,759	2,262,876,369
Deduct		
Long-term debt	61,007,129	54,879,636
Reserves		
For estimated additional costs arising out of war	7,096,110	11,576,348
For insurance, contingencies and miscellaneous expenses	100,061,875	100,441,541
Excess of assets over liabilities and reserves	$2,136,117,645	$2,095,978,844
Ownership evidenced by		
Preferred stock, 7% cumulative, par value $100 (3,602,811 shares)	$ 360,281,100	$ 360,281,100
Common stock (26,109,756 shares)	1,775,836,545	1,735,697,744
Stated capital, $33⅓ per share $870,325,200		
Income reinvested in business *(see page 31 for addition of $40,138,801 in 1952)* 905,511,345		
Total	$2,136,117,645	$2,095,978,844

U. S. STEEL

NOTES TO *Accounts*

Federal Taxes on Income

The Bureau of Internal Revenue has not completed the audit of Federal income and excess profits tax returns for 1942 and subsequent years. It is believed that reasonable provision has been made for any additional taxes which may be levied.

Securities Set Aside for Property Additions and Replacements

Of the $250,000,000 of segregated funds invested in U.S. Government securities at December 31, 1951, $231,000,000 was used in 1952 for property additions and replacements, leaving a balance of $19,000,000.

Plant and Equipment

The amount at which plant and equipment is shown in the consolidated statement of financial position represents acquisition cost less that portion thereof which has been deducted as wear and exhaustion expense. This amount does not purport to be a realizable or replacement value.

Reserve for Estimated Additional Costs Arising out of War

Of the reserve for estimated additional costs arising out of war provided during World War II, $4,480,238 was used in 1952 to cover the higher costs of replacing inventories depleted during the war. This charge and offsetting credit are included in the consolidated statement of income.

Insurance Reserve

U.S. Steel is, for the most part, a self-insurer of its assets against fire, windstorm, marine and related losses. The balance of the insurance reserve is held available for absorbing possible losses of this character, and is considered adequate for this purpose.

Common Stock

The Stock Option Incentive Plan, approved by stockholders May 7, 1951, authorized the option and sale of up to 1,300,000 shares of common stock to key management employes, such shares to be made available from authorized unissued or reacquired common stock. No options to purchase stock were issued or exercised during 1952. At December 31, 1952, 304 employes held options to purchase a total of 373,950 shares at $41 per share.

Products and Services Sold

Products and services sold includes interest, dividends and other income of $5,665,474 in 1952 and $14,421,675 in 1951.

Wages and Salaries

Wages and salaries totaled $1,207,943,140 in 1952. Of this amount, $1,176,596,946 was included in costs of products and services sold and the balance was charged to construction and other accounts.

Products and Services Bought

Products and services bought reflects the changes during the year in inventories and deferred costs. These items increased during 1952 approximately $28,000,000.

Wear and Exhaustion of Facilities

Wear and exhaustion of facilities includes accelerated depreciation as follows:

	1952	1951
Amount presently deductible for Federal income tax purposes (amortization of emergency facilities)	$46,219,552	$12,794,855
Amount not presently deductible for Federal income tax purposes	21,637,772	40,366,211
Total	$67,857,324	$53,161,066

The accelerated depreciation is applicable to the cost of postwar facilities in the first few years of their lives when the economic usefulness is greatest. The amount thereof is related to the excess of current operating rate over U.S. Steel's long-term peacetime average rate of about 70 per cent of capacity. The annual accelerated amount is 10 per cent of the cost of facilities in the year in which the expenditures are made and 10 per cent in the succeeding year, except that the portion of this amount in excess of amortization of emergency facilities is reduced ratably as the operating rate may drop, no acceleration being made at 70 per cent or lower operations. The portion other than amortization is in addition to the normal depreciation on such facilities but the total depreciation over their expected lives will not exceed the cost of the facilities.

Under the Internal Revenue Code that portion of the cost of facilities certified by the Defense Production Administration as essential to the defense effort is covered by a Certificate of Necessity and can be written off for tax purposes at the rate of 20 per cent per year. This more rapid depreciation is generally referred to as amortization of emergency facilities.

Appendix | C

Supplementary Problems

CHAPTER 1

Problem 1-A

This problem may be completed in the workbook in the space provided for Problem 1-2.

Lee Smith is the owner of Lee's Men's Shop, selling men's clothing. Record the following transactions for July in tabular form similar to that used in Question 9 in this chapter. The headings to be used are:

ASSETS	=	LIABILITIES	+	PROPRIETORSHIP
Cash + Mdse. + Store Equip.		Lions, Inc.		Lee Smith

(a) Deposited $15,000 in the bank to be used in the business.
(b) Purchased store equipment for $3,500 cash.
(c) Purchased merchandise on account from Lions, Inc., $15,000.
(d) Sold merchandise costing $9,000 for $12,000 cash.
(e) Paid salesmen's salaries and miscellaneous expenses, $1,500.
(f) Paid Lions, Inc. $10,000 on account.

At the end of July, Mr. Smith decided to enlarge his business to include men's shoes. He rearranged his store to accommodate the new department and hired more salesmen. Record the following transactions for August:

(g) Purchased additional equipment for $2,300 cash.
(h) Purchased complete stock of men's shoes on account from Lions, Inc., $3,750.
(i) Sold merchandise costing $7,500 for $10,000 cash.
(j) Paid Lions, Inc. $5,000 on account.
(k) Paid salesmen's salaries and miscellaneous expenses, $2,200.

Problem 1-B

This problem may be completed in the workbook in the space provided for Problem 1-3.

On June 1, R. A. Chapman opened a dry cleaning agency known as Varsity Cleaners. Record the following transactions for June in tabular form similar to that used in Question 9 in this chapter, using the following headings:

ASSETS	=	LIABILITIES	+	PROPRIETORSHIP
Cash + Century Club + Store Equip. + Truck		Xpert Cleaners, Inc		R. A. Chapman

(a) Invested $2,500 in cash.
(b) Purchased counter and racks, $500, and a used truck, $800, paying cash.

(c) Billed the Century Club $75 for cleaning draperies, allowing them two weeks to pay.

(d) Received $300 from customers during first week.

(e) Received bill from Xpert Cleaners, Inc. for cleaning and pressing during first half of month, $325.

(f) Received $340 from customers during second week.

(g) Received balance due from Century Club.

(h) Purchased a used cash register for cash, $65.

(i) Paid rent for June, $125.

(j) Billed the Century Club for cleaning uniforms, $25.

(k) Received $285 from customers during third week.

(l) Paid balance due Xpert Cleaners, Inc.

(m) Received bill from Xpert Cleaners, Inc. for cleaning and pressing during second half of month, $340.

(n) Received $305 from customers during remainder of month.

(o) Paid $35 for gas, oil, and repairs for delivery truck.

(p) Withdrew $200 for personal use.

Submit answers to the following questions:

(1) What is the total of Chapman's assets after transaction (p)?

(2) What is the net amount of Chapman's increase in capital between transaction (a) through transaction (p)?

(3) Can the increase in capital be identified with any particular asset?

(4) What is the amount of Chapman's net profit for the month?

CHAPTER 2

Problem 2-A

This problem may be completed in the workbook in the space provided for Problem 2-2.

On December 31 the assets and the liabilities of John Williams were as follows:

Accounts Payable.	$ 4,600
Accounts Receivable	8,000
Building	9,000
Cash	7,600
Land	600
Merchandise Inventory	14,400
Mortgage Payable (due April 1, 1963)	6,000
Notes Payable	2,900
Office Equipment	1,300
Prepaid Insurance	1,500
Store Equipment	2,600

On January 1 at the beginning of the year, Mr. Williams' capital account had a balance of $27,200. He made withdrawals of $600 a month. The business showed a net profit for the year of $11,500.

Instructions: (1) Prepare a classified balance sheet in report form as of December 31 of the current year. Include the details of changes in proprietorship as a part of the balance sheet.

(2) Compute the following: (a) working capital and (b) current ratio.

Problem 2-B

This problem may be completed in the workbook in the space provided for Problem 2-3.

On December 31 the assets and the liabilities of R. G. Meyer were as follows:

Accounts Payable....	$ 7,690
Accounts Receivable....	9,700
Building....	15,000
Cash....	2,450
Furniture and Fixtures....	7,650
Land....	4,500
Merchandise Inventory....	10,200
Mortgage Payable (due September 1, 1965)..	10,000
Prepaid Insurance....	970
Salaries Payable....	500
Supplies....	400
Taxes Payable....	1,400

On January 1, at the beginning of the fiscal year, Mr. Meyer's capital was $26,500. On September 1 he invested an additional $1,500 cash in the business, and during the entire year he made weekly withdrawals of $110. As a result of operations for the year, the business earned a net profit of $9,000.

Instructions: (1) Prepare a classified balance sheet in account form as of December 31 of the current year.

(2) Prepare a statement of proprietor's capital for the year ended December 31.

Problem 2-C

This problem may be completed in the workbook in the space provided for Problem 2-4.

On May 31 of the current year the assets and the liabilities of Martin Leonard, owner of Leonard's Department Store, were as follows:

Accounts Payable....	$ 5,025
Accounts Receivable....	4,730
Building....	15,000
Cash....	6,912
Land....	1,500
Merchandise Inventory....	18,433
Mortgage Payable (due April 30, 1962)....	9,000
Notes Payable....	750
Notes Receivable....	1,100
Office Equipment....	1,788
Prepaid Insurance....	180
Prepaid Rent....	450
Store Equipment....	2,697
Supplies....	514
Taxes Payable....	195
Salaries Payable....	125

On May 1, Mr. Leonard's capital had been $37,824. During the month of May he made total withdrawals of $600. As a result of operations for the month of May, the business earned a net profit of $985.

Instructions: (1) Prepare a classified balance sheet in report form as of May 31 of the current year.

(2) Prepare a statement of proprietor's capital for the month ended May 31.

(3) Compute the following: (a) working capital and (b) current ratio.

CHAPTER 3

Problem 3-A

This problem may be completed in the workbook in the space provided for Problem 3-2.

On January 1 of the current fiscal year R. S. McAdam's merchandise inventory amounted to $20,500; on December 31, the end of the current fiscal year, the inventory was $24,000. His accounting records for the current fiscal year show the following additional information:

Advertising Expense	$ 3,050	Purchases	$106,000
Insurance Expense	2,400	Rent Expense	3,450
Misc. General Expense	350	Sales	150,000
Misc. Selling Expense	600	Sales Salary Expense	12,700
Office Salary Expense	4,500	Store Supplies Expense	1,650
Office Supplies Expense	1,300	Transportation on Purchases	2,500

Instructions: (1) Prepare a classified profit and loss statement for the current year.

(2) Compute the percentage of the following items to sales: (a) cost of goods sold, (b) gross profit on sales, (c) total selling expenses, (d) total general expenses, (e) total operating expenses, (f) net profit from operations.

Problem 3-B

This problem may be completed in the workbook in the space provided for Problem 3-3.

Howard Wheland, owner of the Wheland Products Co., had a capital balance of $20,800 on January 1 of the current year. On July 1 he invested an additional $3,000 in cash. The following asset and liability balances are as of December 31 of the current year; the income and expense figures are for the current year ended on that date.

Accounts Payable	$ 7,300	Prepaid Insurance	$ 300
Accounts Receivable	6,500	Purchases	95,000
Advertising Expense	1,850	Rent Expense	3,850
Cash	8,710	Sales	160,000
Commissions Payable	2,300	Sales Commission Expense	18,000
Insurance Expense	3,200	Store Equipment	5,000
Office Equipment	1,800	Store Supplies	740
Office Salary Expense	4,900	Store Supplies Expense	950
Office Supplies	350	Transportation on Purchases	1,400
Office Supplies Expense	850		

The merchandise inventories were: January 1, $34,000; December 31, $26,400. Withdrawals of $6,000 were made by Mr. Wheland during the period.

Instructions: (1) Prepare a classified profit and loss statement for the year.

(2) Prepare (a) a classified balance sheet as of December 31 of the current year in report form and (b) a statement of proprietor's capital for the current year.

(3) Compute the percentage of the following items to sales: (a) cost of goods sold, (b) gross profit on sales, (c) total selling expenses, (d) total general expenses, (e) total operating expenses, (f) net profit from operations.

(4) Compute the following: (a) working capital and (b) current ratio.

CHAPTER 4

Problem 4-A

This problem may be completed in the workbook in the space provided for Problem 4-2.

Peter Pollard is the owner of Pollard's Laboratory. The accounts in his ledger are: Cash; Accounts Receivable; Office Equipment; Laboratory Equipment; Accounts Payable; Peter Pollard, Capital; Peter Pollard, Drawing; Laboratory Fees; and Operating Expenses.

On September 1 of the current year Dr. Pollard's account balances were as follows:

Cash	$1,800	Laboratory Equipment	$5,200
Accounts Receivable	1,300	Peter Pollard, Capital	9,400
Office Equipment	1,100		

Instructions: (1) Set up "T" accounts for all of Mr. Pollard's accounts listed above.

(2) Record the beginning balances in the appropriate accounts. Identify the balances in the accounts by writing "Bal." to the left of the amount.

During the month of September the following transactions were completed:

(a) Paid office rent for September, $250.
(b) Purchased office equipment for cash, $50.
(c) Received cash from debtors on account, $900.
(d). Purchased laboratory equipment on account, $500.
(e) Withdrew cash for personal use, $800.
(f) Received cash in payment of laboratory services rendered during September, $1,200.
(g) Paid cash for miscellaneous operating expenses, $65.
(h) Paid cash to creditors on account, $250.
(i) Paid salaries of assistant and secretary, $520.
(j) Sent bills to patients for services rendered during September, $850, charging Accounts Receivable.

Instructions: (3) Record the transactions in "T" accounts. Identify each debit and each credit by the letter given for that transaction.

(4) Take a trial balance as of September 30 of the current year.

Problem 4-B

This problem may be completed in the workbook in the space provided for Problem 4-3.

On June 1 of the current year Paul Mason acquired the Gayland Amusement Park. The following accounts are to be used in recording the transactions for his business enterprise: Cash; Supplies; Prepaid Insurance; Amusement Equipment; Office Equipment; Buildings; Land; Accounts Payable; Mortgage Payable; Paul Mason, Capital; Paul Mason, Drawing; Admissions Income; Concession Income; Wages Expense; Maintenance Expense; Advertising Expense; Utilities Expense; Miscellaneous Expense.

The following transactions were completed during the month:

(a) Deposited cash in a bank account for use in the business, $30,000.
(b) Purchased the Gayland Amusement Park, including Amusement Equipment, $8,000, Buildings, $35,000, and Land, $6,000, making a down payment of $24,000 and giving a mortgage for the balance.
(c) Purchased supplies on account, $540.
(d) Paid premiums for property and casualty insurance policies, $1,200.
(e) Cash receipts from admissions for the week, $2,000.
(f) Paid wages for the week, $375.
(g) Granted concession for sale of popcorn, candy, soft drinks, etc. for 10% of sales, with a minimum of $300 per month collectible in advance. Received $225 cash as advance payment for remainder of November.
(h) Paid for newspaper advertising, $350.
(i) Purchased office equipment on account, $600.
(j) Cash receipts from admissions for the week, $2,150.
(k) Paid wages for the week, $375.
(l) Paid miscellaneous expenses, $85.
(m) Paid cash to creditors on account, $270.
(n) Cash receipts from admissions for the week, $2,500.
(o) Paid wages for the week, $375.
(p) Purchased supplies for cash, $30.
(q) Withdrew cash for personal use, $600.
(r) Paid wages for the week, $375.
(s) Paid utilities expenses, $280.
(t) Cash receipts from admissions for remainder of the month, $2,900.
(u) Paid for advertising, $250.
(v) Paid maintenance expenses, $3,400.
(w) Paid creditors on account, $600.
(x) Received concession income, $20.

Instructions: (1) Set up "T" accounts for all of the accounts listed above.

(2) Record the transactions for June in the accounts, identifying each entry by the letter given for that transaction.

(3) Prepare a trial balance as of June 30 of the current year.

CHAPTER 5

Problem 5-A

This problem may be completed in the workbook in the space provided for Problem 5-2.

Mary Fenton operates the Fenton Stenographic Service. The trial balance of her ledger on January 31 of the current year follows:

MARY FENTON
TRIAL BALANCE
JANUARY 31, 19--

Cash	11	$1,450	
Accounts Receivable	12	950	
Office Supplies	14	23	
Prepaid Insurance	15	75	
Automobile	17	2,500	
Office Equipment	18	600	
Accounts Payable	21		$ 120
Mary Fenton, Capital	31		5,146
Mary Fenton, Drawing	32	500	
Fees	41		1,355
Salary Expense	51	300	
Rent Expense	52	125	
Automobile Expense	53	29	
Advertising Expense	54	25	
Miscellaneous Expense	59	44	
		$6,621	$6,621

During the month of February, Miss Fenton completed the following transactions:

Feb. 1. Paid rent for month, $125.
2. Paid advertising, $42.
5. Collected accounts receivable, $465.
7. Purchased a typewriter on account, $160.
10. Purchased office supplies on account, $18.
14. Billed fees for first half of month, $915.
14. Paid salaries, $160.
16. Discovered that the entry for the transaction on February 2 was incorrectly recorded. The amount paid for advertising was $46 rather than $42.
19. Paid premium on property insurance, $25.
21. Collected accounts receivable, $845.
23. Paid $120 to creditors on account.
24. Purchased office equipment for cash, $35.
28. Paid automobile expense, $33, and miscellaneous expense, $15.
28. Billed fees for second half of month, $740.
28. Paid salaries, $160.
28. Withdrew cash for personal use, $450.

Instructions: (1) Open an account in the ledger for each item listed in the trial balance of January 31.

(2) Record the balance in each account under the date of Feb. 1, write the word "Bal." in the items column, and place a check mark in the posting reference column.

(3) Record the transactions for February in a two-column general journal.

(4) Post to the ledger.

(5) An error is discovered in billing the fees for the second half of the month. The amount is $790 instead of $740. Journalize the correcting entry and post.

(6) Take a trial balance of the ledger.

Problem 5-B

This problem may be completed in the workbook in the space provided for Problem 5-3.

James Stevens owns a 24-hour cash-and-carry dry cleaning establishment known as Jiffy Cleaners. The accounts in his ledger on July 1 of the current year, together with the balances of the asset, liability, and capital accounts, are as follows: 11, Cash, $1,703.67; 12, Dry Cleaning Supplies, $255.70; 13, Office Supplies, $30.00; 14, Prepaid Insurance, $36.90; 15, Prepaid Rent; 16, Dry Cleaning Equipment, $7,600.00; 17, Office Equipment, $615.00; 21, Notes Payable, $1,350.00; 22, Accounts Payable, $491.27; 31, James Stevens, Capital, $8,400.00; 32, James Stevens, Drawing; 41, Sales; 51, Sales Salary Expense; 59, Miscellaneous Selling Expense; 61, Office Salary Expense; 62, Power Expense; 69, Miscellaneous General Expense.

During the month of July Mr. Stevens completed the following transactions:

July 1. Paid rent for four months, $400. (Debit Prepaid Rent.)
  . 3. Paid premium on property insurance, $77.50.
     5. Paid creditors on account, $245.
     6. Cash sales for the week, $560.07.
     9. Paid cash for office supplies, $55.64.
    11. Purchased dry cleaning equipment for $1,000, giving a note payable for $600 and paying the balance in cash.
    13. Paid cash, $650, for biweekly salaries as follows: sales salaries, $475; office salaries, $175.
    13. Cash sales for the week, $511.42.
    14. Purchased dry cleaning supplies on account, $492.85.
    17. Withdrew $200 for personal use.
    20. Paid creditors on account, $202.10.
    20. Cash sales for the week, $519.32.
    21. Purchased dry cleaning supplies on account, $215.57.
    25. Paid cash for miscellaneous selling expenses, $21.40.
    26. Purchased office equipment on account, $25.
    27. Paid cash, $650, for biweekly salaries as follows: sales salaries, $475; office salaries, $175.
    27. Cash sales for the week, $537.12.
    31. Withdrew $200 for personal use.
    31. Paid cash for miscellaneous general expenses for the month, $12.
    31. Paid cash for power expense for the month, $185.
    31. Cash sales for the balance of the month, $176.18.

Instructions: (1) Open an account in the ledger for each item listed.

(2) Record the balances in the accounts under the date of July 1, write "Bal." in the items column, and place a check mark in the posting reference column.

(3) Record the transactions for July in a four-column general journal similar to that illustrated on page 75.

(4) Total and rule the journal.

(5) Post to the ledger.

(6) Take a trial balance of the ledger.

CHAPTER 6

Problem 6-A

This problem may be completed in the workbook in the space provided for Problem 6-2.

The accounts and their balances in the ledger of Martha's Beauty Shoppe on December 31, the end of the current fiscal year, were as follows:

11 Cash................	$2,026.65	32 Martha Mills, Drawing $6,000.00
12 Beauty Supplies......	923.18	33 Profit and Loss Sum-
13 Office Supplies	85.26	mary.............. ....
14 Prepaid Insurance.....	258.50	41 Sales................ 19,653.00
17 Beauty Equipment....	6,250.00	51 Salary Expense....... 7,421.00
18 Furniture...........	1,020.60	52 Beauty Supplies Exp... ....
21 Notes Payable........	1,500.00	53 Rent Expense......... 1,200.00
22 Accounts Payable.....	392.35	54 Utilities Expense...... 439.43
23 Salaries Payable......	....	55 Advertising Expense... 361.27
24 Rent Payable........	....	56 Insurance Expense.... ....
31 Martha Mills, Capital.	4,736.69	57 Office Supplies Expense ....
		58 Miscellaneous Expense. 296.15

The data for the adjustments on December 31 were as follows:

(a) Inventory of beauty supplies $135.70

(b) Inventory of office supplies 32.00

(c) Insurance expired 138.50

(d) Salary payable 115.00

(e) Rent amounting to $100 a month has been paid throughout the year; but the lease provides that, at the end of the year, there will be an additional liability for rent amounting to 8% of all sales in excess of $15,000.

Instructions: (1) Open an account in the ledger for each account listed. Enter the balances in the appropriate accounts under date of December 31.

(2) Prepare a ten-column work sheet for the year ended December 31.

(3) Prepare a profit and loss statement, a balance sheet in report form, and a statement of proprietor's capital.

(4) Record the adjusting entries in a general journal and post to the ledger accounts.

(5) Record the closing entries and post to the ledger accounts.

(6) Balance and rule the accounts having more than one entry.

(7) Prepare a post-closing trial balance.

Problem 6-B

This problem may be completed in the workbook in the space provided for Problem 6-3.

The ledger of John L. Sanders as of June 30 of the current year is reproduced in the workbook correlating with this textbook.

Instructions: (1) Take a trial balance of the ledger as of June 30, using the trial balance columns of a ten-column work sheet.

(2) Complete the ten-column work sheet for the month ended June 30. The data for the adjustments at the end of June are:

Supplies on hand........ $320.80
Insurance expired........   12.45
Salaries payable..........   22.50

(3) Prepare a profit and loss statement and a balance sheet in report form.

(4) Record the adjusting and the closing entries in the general journal and post to the ledger.

(5) Rule the temporary accounts. Balance and rule the asset, liability, and proprietorship accounts that contain more than one entry.

(6) Take a post-closing trial balance.

CHAPTER 7

Problem 7-A

This problem may be completed in the workbook in the space provided for Problem 7-1.

During November of the current year Carl Jenkins, a wholesale toy merchant, completed the transactions given below. The terms of all sales were 2/10 eom.

Nov. 3. Sold merchandise on account to M. A. Parker, Sale No. 472, $270.
       4. Sold merchandise on account to Ann Wenzel, Sale No. 473, $315.
       5. Sold merchandise on account to the Kiddy Korner, Sale No. 474, $133.
       9. Issued Credit Memorandum No. 37 for $55 to M. A. Parker for damage to merchandise caused by faulty packing.
      10. Sold merchandise on account to Jane Clark, Sale No. 475, $202.
      11. Sold merchandise on account to Kent Gift Shop, Sale No. 476, $425.
      15. Sold merchandise on account to M. A. Parker, Sale No. 477, $180.
      18. Sold merchandise on account to David Nelson, Sale No. 478, $245.
      22. Sold merchandise on account to Ann Wenzel, Sale No. 479, $280.
      25. Issued Credit Memorandum No. 38 for $35 to David Nelson for merchandise returned by him.
      26. Sold merchandise on account to the Kiddy Korner, Sale No. 480, $360.
      29. Sold merchandise on account to Jane Clark, Sale No. 481, $430.
      30. Issued Credit Memorandum No. 39 for $70 to the Kiddy Korner for merchandise returned.
      30. Sold merchandise on account to Kent Gift Shop, Sale No. 482, $345.

Instructions: (1) Record the above transactions, using a sales journal similar to the one illustrated on page 112 of the textbook and a four-column general journal similar to the one illustrated on page 118.

(2) Open the following accounts in the general ledger, using the account

numbers indicated: Accounts Receivable, 112; Sales, 411; Sales Returns and Allowances, 412.

(3) Open the following accounts in the accounts receivable ledger: Jane Clark, 346 Fourth St.; Kent Gift Shop, 2048 Kent Road; Kiddy Korner, 1390 Taylor St.; David Nelson, 3130 Marshall Ave.; M. A. Parker, 2215 Grant Ave.; Ann Wenzel, 3602 Lake St.

(4) Post from the two journals to the accounts receivable ledger and the general ledger.

(5) (a) What is the sum of the balances of the subsidiary accounts?

(b) What is the balance of the controlling account?

Problem 7-B

This problem may be completed in the workbook in the space provided for Problem 7-2.

During August of the current year Edward Kirk, a furniture dealer, issued invoices and credit memorandums for the following charge sales and sales returns. The terms of all sales were 2/10 eom.

Aug. 2. Invoice No. 475, to N. E. Reed, $318.

4. Invoice No. 476, to Herbert Clark, $155.

5. Invoice No. 477, to T. L. Jackson, $485.

8. Invoice No. 478, to David Ott, $166.

9. Credit Memo No. 62, to T. L. Jackson, $43.

13. Invoice No. 479, to Robert Hayden, $229.

16. Invoice No. 480, to Herbert Clark, $340.

18. Invoice No. 481, to T. L. Jackson, $118.

19. Credit Memo No. 63, to Herbert Clark, $70.

22. Invoice No. 482, to H. W. Beck, $405.

23. Invoice No. 483, to N. E. Reed, $374.

25. Credit Memo No. 64, to H. W. Beck, $17.

26. Invoice No. 484, to David Ott, $310.

29. Credit Memo No. 65, to N. E. Reed, $32.

30. Invoice No. 485, to H. W. Beck, $80.

Instructions: (1) Record the foregoing transactions in a sales journal and a sales returns and allowances journal similar to the ones illustrated on pages 112 and 119.

(2) Open the following accounts in the general ledger, and enter the following balances as of August 1:

112 Accounts Receivable.................. $ 1,420

411 Sales............................. 35,625

412 Sales Returns and Allowances......... 1,692

(3) Open the following accounts in the accounts receivable ledger and enter the balances in the balance columns, as of August 1: H. W. Beck, 914 Euclid Ave., $400; Herbert Clark, 4774 Lee Rd.; Robert Hayden, 9300 Carnegie Ave.; T. L. Jackson, 207 Superior Ave., $350; David Ott, 347 Clifton Blvd.; N. E. Reed, 565 Union Ave., $670.

(4) Post from the two journals to the accounts receivable ledger and the general ledger.

(5) Submit answers to the following questions:

(a) What is the total amount due from customers on August 31, determined by adding the balances in the subsidiary ledger?

(b) What is the balance of the accounts receivable account in the general ledger of August 31?

(c) How much will Herbert Clark need to pay to discharge his obligation within the discount period?

CHAPTER 8

Problem 8-A

This problem may be completed in the workbook in the space provided for Problem 8-1.

During October of the current year, the Harvey Haberdashery completed the following transactions:

Oct. 1. Purchased merchandise on account from Collins Shirt Co., $316.80, invoice dated September 30.

　　 3. Purchased store equipment on account from Carlson Equipment Co., $150, invoice dated October 2.

　　 6. Purchased merchandise on account from Riverdale Mills, Inc., $375.21, invoice dated October 5.

　　 8. Purchased store supplies on account from Vance Supply Co., $56.90, invoice dated October 8.

　　 9. Received a credit memorandum for $48 from Collins Shirt Co. for merchandise returned.

　　 12. Purchased merchandise on account from Becker & Page, $525, invoice dated October 10.

　　 14. Received a credit memorandum for $10.50 from Vance Supply Co. for store supplies returned.

　　 15. Purchased office equipment on account from Carlson Equipment Co., $85, invoice dated October 15.

　　 16. Purchased merchandise on account from Southern Textile Co., $389.10, invoice dated October 14.

　　 19. Purchased merchandise on account from Handmaid Tie Co., $430, invoice dated October 18.

　　 20. Received a credit memorandum for $5 from Carlson Equipment Co. as an allowance for damage caused by defective packing of office equipment.

　　 21. Purchased office supplies on account from Moore Printing Co., $31.75, invoice dated October 21.

　　 23. Purchased merchandise on account from Wylie & Sons, $244, invoice dated October 22.

　　 24. Purchased merchandise on account from Riverdale Mills, Inc., $352.25, invoice dated October 23.

　　 26. Received a credit memorandum for $7.50 from Moore Printing Co. for office supplies returned.

　　 28. Purchased merchandise on account from Collins Shirt Co., $202, invoice dated October 26.

　　 30. Received a credit memorandum for $21.80 from Wylie & Sons for merchandise returned.

　　 31. Purchased store supplies on account from Vance Supply Co., $63.33, invoice dated October 30.

　　 31. Purchased merchandise on account from Southern Textile Co., $138.90, invoice dated October 29.

Instructions: (1) Record the above transactions, using a purchases journal similar to the one illustrated on pages 126 and 127 of the text and a two-column general journal.

(2) Open the following accounts in the general ledger, using the account numbers indicated:

114 Store Supplies
115 Office Supplies
121 Store Equipment
122 Office Equipment

211 Accounts Payable
511 Purchases
512 Purchases Returns and Allowances

(3) Open the following accounts in the accounts payable ledger: Becker & Page, Philadelphia; Carlson Equipment Co., Harrisburg; Collins Shirt Co., Hartford; Handmaid Tie Co., Pittsburgh; Moore Printing Co., Harrisburg; Riverdale Mills, Inc., Charleston; Southern Textile Co., Richmond; Vance Supply Co., Harrisburg; Wylie & Sons, Pittsburgh.

(4) Post from the two journals to the accounts payable ledger and the general ledger.

(5) (a) What is the sum of the balances of the subsidiary accounts?

(b) What is the balance of the controlling account?

Problem 8-B

This problem may be completed in the workbook in the space provided for Problem 8-2.

During April of the current year, the Queen City Appliance House completed the following transactions:

Apr. 2. Purchased merchandise on account from General Manufacturing Co., $1,340.50, invoice dated April 1.

4. Purchased store supplies on account from Lamb Supply Co., $56.35, invoice dated April 2.

7. Received a credit memorandum for $65 from General Manufacturing Co. as an allowance on defective merchandise.

8. Purchased merchandise on account from Johnson Electric Co., $410, invoice dated April 7.

11. Purchased office supplies on account from Preston Supply Co., $37.42, invoice dated April 9.

12. Purchased merchandise on account from Imperial Appliance Co., $792.78, invoice dated April 11.

14. Purchased store equipment on account from Allen Equipment Co., $175.61, invoice dated April 13.

16. Received a credit memorandum for $6.25 from Preston Supply Co. for return of office supplies.

18. Purchased store supplies on account from Lamb Supply Co., $25, invoice dated April 16.

20. Received a credit memorandum for $30 from Allen Equipment Co. for return of store equipment.

21. Purchased merchandise on account from Cole & Grimes, $1,843.85, invoice dated April 20.

22. Purchased merchandise on account from Lite-Glo Lamp Co., $650.39, invoice dated April 21.

25. Purchased office supplies on account from Preston Supply Co., $18, invoice dated April 23.

26. Purchased merchandise on account from General Manufacturing Co., $300, invoice dated April 25.

28. Purchased merchandise on account from Imperial Appliance Co., $515.92, invoice dated April 27.

29. Received a credit memorandum for $112.34 from Cole & Grimes for return of merchandise.

30. Purchased electric fans for use in the store on account from Johnson Electric Co., $120, invoice dated April 29.

Instructions: (1) Record the above transactions, using a purchases journal similar to the one illustrated on pages 126 and 127 of the text and a general journal with special columns for Accounts Payable Dr. and Purchases Returns and Allowances Cr. similar to the one illustrated on page 133 of the text.

(2) Open the following accounts in the general ledger and enter the balances as of April 1:

114 Store Supplies	$ 369.40	511 Purchases	$10,039.80
115 Office Supplies	113.95	512 Purchases Returns	
121 Store Equipment	3,815.20	and Allowances	398.50
211 Accounts Payable	1,031.13		

(3) Open the following accounts in the accounts payable ledger and enter the balances in the balance columns as of April 1: Allen Equipment Co., Denver; Cole & Grimes, Chicago, $331.83; General Manufacturing Co., St. Louis, $447.50; Imperial Appliance Co., Omaha; Johnson Electric Co., Chicago; Lamb Supply Co., Denver, $23.80; Lite-Glo Lamp Co., St. Louis, $228; Preston Supply Co., Denver.

(4) Post to the accounts payable ledger and the general ledger.

(5) (a) What is the sum of the balances of the accounts in the subsidiary ledger? (b) What is the balance of the controlling account?

Problem 8-C

This problem may be completed in the workbook in the space provided for Problem 8-3.

During June of the current year the Swan Stationery Store completed the following transactions:

June 2. Purchased store supplies on account from General Supply Co., $60.47, invoice dated June 1.

4. Purchased merchandise on account from Garden City Printing Co., $470.35, invoice dated June 3.

7. Purchased merchandise on account from Pearl Paper Co., $112.04, invoice dated June 6.

8. Received a credit memorandum for $20.20 from General Supply Co. for store supplies returned.

10. Purchased merchandise on account from Smith Paper Co., $573.86, invoice dated June 9.

11. Purchased office supplies on account from White and Walker, Inc., $32, invoice dated June 11.

13. Received a credit memorandum for $62.50 from Garden City Printing Co. for merchandise returned.

15. Purchased merchandise on account from Chapman Paper Co., $225.45, invoice dated June 14.

16. Purchased store supplies on account from General Supply Co., $42.25, invoice dated June 15.

18. Purchased merchandise on account from Vernon Novelty Co., $210.38, invoice dated June 17.

20. Purchased merchandise on account from Loomis Publishing Co., $407.50, invoice dated June 18.

22. Received a credit memorandum for $107.30 from Smith Paper Co. for merchandise returned.

23. Purchased store equipment on account from Jasper Manufacturing Co., $215, invoice dated June 22.

June 24. Purchased merchandise on account from Banner Printing Co., $132.70, invoice dated June 23.

27. Purchased store supplies on account from General Supply Co., $57.04, invoice dated June 27.

28. Purchased merchandise on account from Garden City Printing Co., $245.19, invoice dated June 27.

30. Received a credit memorandum for $35.00 from Jasper Manufacturing Co. for store equipment returned.

Instructions: (1) Record the foregoing transactions, using a single-column purchases journal similar to the one on page 132, a purchases returns and allowances journal similar to the one on page 134, and a two-column general journal.

(2) Open the following accounts in the general ledger, using the account numbers indicated:

114 Store Supplies	211 Accounts Payable
115 Office Supplies	511 Purchases
121 Store Equipment	512 Purchases Returns and Allowances

(3) Open the following accounts in the accounts payable ledger: Banner Printing Co., Glendale; Chapman Paper Co., Fresno; Garden City Printing Co., Sacramento; General Supply Co., Fresno; Jasper Manufacturing Co., Sacramento; Loomis Publishing Co., San Francisco; Pearl Paper Co., Fresno; Smith Paper Co., Sacramento; Vernon Novelty Co., Glendale; White and Walker, Inc., Glendale.

(4) Post to the accounts payable ledger and the general ledger.

(5) (a) What is the sum of the balances of the accounts in the subsidiary ledger? (b) What is the balance of the controlling account?

CHAPTER 9

Problem 9-A

This problem may be completed in the workbook in the space provided for Problem 9-3.

In this problem you are to record and post the transactions of David Baldwin for July, the first month in his current fiscal year.

Instructions: (1) Open the following accounts in the general ledger, entering the balances in the appropriate accounts under date of July 1:

111 Cash	$ 9,620	312 David Baldwin, Drawing
112 Accounts Receivable	3,121	411 Sales
113 Notes Receivable	1,200	412 Sales Returns and Allowances
114 Merchandise Inventory	15,423	511 Purchases
115 Store Supplies	352	512 Purchases Returns and Allow-
116 Office Supplies	76	ances
117 Prepaid Insurance	498	611 Sales Salaries
118 Prepaid Rent	900	612 Miscellaneous Selling Expense
121 Store Equipment	4,615	711 Office Salaries
122 Office Equipment	1,226	712 Miscellaneous General Expense
211 Accounts Payable	4,600	811 Purchases Discount
311 David Baldwin, Capital	32,431	911 Sales Discount

(2) Open the following accounts in the accounts receivable ledger, entering the balances in the balance columns under date of July 1: Frank Arnold, Hannibal, $1,509; Kenneth Kerr, Springfield, $912; Newkirk & Co., Kansas City; Walter Westmore, St. Louis, $700.

(3) Open the following accounts in the accounts payable ledger, entering the balances in the balance columns under date of July 1: Caldwell-Loomis Corp., Chicago, $2,700; W. B. Kizer & Co., Denver, $600; Pearce Manufacturing Co., St. Louis; Reed and Lane, Kansas City, $1,300; Whitney Supply Corp., St. Louis.

(4) Record the transactions listed below, using a purchases journal (as on pages 126 and 127), a sales journal (as on page 112), a cash receipts journal (as on page 141), a cash payments journal (as on page 146), and a four-column general journal (as on page 118). The terms of all sales on account are 2/15, n/60.

July 1. Issued Check No. 647 for a three-year insurance policy, $419.
    3. Purchased supplies on account from Whitney Supply Corp., invoice dated July 2, $94. The invoice total should be distributed as follows: store supplies, $65; office supplies, $29.
    3. Sold merchandise on account to Frank Arnold, Invoice No. 735, $850.
    5. Issued Check No. 648 to Caldwell-Loomis Corp. for balance due; no discount.
    5. Purchased merchandise on account from Pearce Manufacturing Co., invoice dated July 3, $1,475.
    6. Sold merchandise on account to Newkirk & Co., Invoice No. 736, $1,450.
    6. Received check from Kenneth Kerr for balance due, $912; no discount.
    Post from all journals to the accounts receivable ledger and the accounts payable ledger.
    8. Received credit memorandum from Pearce Manufacturing Co. for merchandise returned to them, $175.
    8. Received check from Walter Westmore for balance due, less 2% discount.
    9. Issued Check No. 649 in payment of miscellaneous selling expense, $93.
    9. Sold merchandise on account to Kenneth Kerr, Invoice No. 737, $1,710.
    10. Purchased merchandise on account from Caldwell-Loomis Corp., invoice dated July 9, $1,650.
    11. Issued Check No. 650 to W. B. Kizer & Co. for balance due, less 1% discount.
    12. Issued Credit Memo No. 63 to Kenneth Kerr for returned merchandise, $60.
    13. Purchased merchandise for cash, issuing Check No. 651 for $700.
    Post from all journals to the accounts receivable ledger and the accounts payable ledger.
    15. Received check from Frank Arnold for $1,509; no discount.
    15. Sold Walter Westmore merchandise on account, Invoice No. 738, $929.
    16. Purchased store equipment from Reed and Lane on account, invoice dated July 15, $425.
    16. Cash sales for July 1 through 16, $2,743.

July 17. Sent Check No. 652 to Pearce Manufacturing Co. for balance due, less 1% discount.

19. Received check from Kenneth Kerr for balance due, less 2% discount.

19. Issued Credit Memo No. 64 to Walter Westmore for damaged merchandise, $34.

20. Sold merchandise to Kenneth Kerr on account, Invoice No. 739, $1,515.

Post from all journals to the accounts receivable ledger and the accounts payable ledger.

22. Purchased merchandise on account from W. B. Kizer & Co., invoice dated July 20, $1,630.

23. Issued Check No. 653 to Reed and Lane for balance on July 1; no discount.

24. Received check from Frank Arnold for balance due, less 2% discount.

24. Issued Check No. 654 to Whitney Supply Corp. for balance due; no discount.

25. Received $60 cash for merchandise purchased for cash and later returned.

26. Purchased merchandise on account from Caldwell-Loomis Corp., invoice dated July 25, $1,270.

27. Sold merchandise on account to Newkirk & Co., Invoice No. 740, $1,126.

Post from all journals to the accounts receivable ledger and the accounts payable ledger.

30. Paid utility bills, Check No. 655, $130. (Charge Miscellaneous General Expense.)

30. Purchased store supplies on account from Whitney Supply Corp., invoice dated July 29, $62.

31. Cash sales for July 17 through 31, $2,642.

31. Withdrew $400 for personal use, Check No. 656.

31. Issued Check No. 657 for monthly salaries as follows: sales salaries, $700; office salaries, $275.

31. The reconciliation of the bank statement with the balance shown on the check stubs as of July 31 reveals the following transactions that have not been recorded on Baldwin's books:

    (a) A note receivable for $300 left with the bank for collection was collected by the bank in July and credited to Baldwin's account.

    (b) The bank debited Baldwin's account during July for a collection fee and service charges totaling $4. (Charge Miscellaneous General Expense.)

Post from all journals to the accounts receivable ledger and the accounts payable ledger.

Instructions: (5) Post from the five journals to the general ledger.

(6) Prepare a trial balance.

(7) Prepare a schedule of accounts receivable and a schedule of accounts payable.

Problem 9-B

This problem may be completed in the workbook in the space provided for Problem 9-4.

Robert L. Baker's bank statement for September of the current year indicates a balance of $3,683.24 on September 30. The bank balance according to his check stubs on that date is $2,844.82. A comparison of the bank statement, the canceled checks, and the memorandums with the check stubs reveals the following:

- (a) Checks outstanding: No. 392, $5.75; No. 426, $6.52; No. 436, $396.33; No. 438, $184.26; No. 439, $56.60.
- (b) A counter check for $75 included with the canceled checks had not been recorded in the check stubs or the cash payments journal. It was a personal withdrawal of cash by the proprietor.
- (c) A check for $125 drawn by Robert M. Baker was erroneously debited by the bank to Robert L. Baker's account and was included with the canceled checks.
- (d) A deposit of $620 on September 10 had not been recorded in the check stubs. The receipts included in the deposit had been properly recorded in the cash receipts journal.
- (e) A deposit of $428.80 had been made too late to appear on the bank statement. The cash receipts involved in the deposit had been recorded in the cash receipts journal and the deposit had been recorded in the check stubs as of September 30.
- (f) The bank had credited Baker's account for $200 for a note receivable left for collection. No entry had been made in Baker's books or check stubs.
- (g) The bank deducted $2.24 for service charges, which had not been recorded in the cash payments journal or the check stubs.

Instructions: (1) Prepare a reconciliation of the bank statement with the check stubs.

(2) Prepare, in general journal form, the entries necessary to bring the books into agreement with the facts disclosed by the reconciliation. The cash receipts and cash payments journals have been ruled and posted, but the books have not been closed.

CHAPTER 10

Problem 10-A

This problem may be completed in the workbook in the space provided for Problem 10-2.

The accounts and their balances in the ledger of Inland Mercantile Co. on March 31 of the current year are as follows:

111 Cash	$ 18,763	115 Office Supplies	$1,035
112 Accounts Receivable	27,955	116 Prepaid Insurance	2,400
113 Merchandise Inventory	31,500	121 Store Equipment	3,150
114 Store Supplies	1,166	122 Office Equipment	1,275

123	Building.............	$18,250	513	Purchases Returns and	
124	Land...............	12,700		Allowances..........	$ 4,309
211	Accounts Payable.....	17,816	611	Sales Salaries........	14,400
212	Salaries Payable......	————	612	Advertising Expense...	10,600
213	Taxes Payable........	————	613	Store Supplies Expense	————
221	Mortgage Payable....	15,000	614	Insurance Expense —	
311	Kenneth Thornton,			Selling..............	————
	Capital.............	71,745	619	Misc. Selling Expense..	314
312	Kenneth Thornton,		711	Office Salaries........	7,200
	Drawing............	5,400	712	Taxes Expense........	488
313	Profit and Loss Sum-		713	Insurance Expense —	
	mary...............	————		General.............	————
411	Sales...............	215,112	714	Office Supplies Expense	————
412	Sales Returns and		719	Misc. General Expense.	637
	Allowances..........	6,440	811	Purchases Discount....	1,870
511	Purchases...........	156,350	911	Sales Discount........	2,702
512	Freight In...........	3,127			

The data for year-end adjustments on March 31 are as follows:

Merchandise inventory on March 31................		$38,600
Inventories of supplies on March 31:		
Store Supplies...............................		540
Office Supplies...............................		710
Insurance expired during the year:		
Allocable as selling expense.............. ..	$330	
Allocable as general expense...............	600	930
Salaries payable on March 31:		
Sales Salaries............................	$160	
Office Salaries...........................	80	240
Taxes payable on March 31......................		90

Instructions: (1) Open an account in the ledger for each account listed, using the account numbers indicated. Enter the balances in the appropriate accounts under date of March 31.

(2) Prepare an eight-column work sheet for the yearly fiscal period.

(3) Prepare a balance sheet in the report form (Exhibit A), a statement of proprietor's capital (Exhibit B), and a profit and loss statement (Exhibit C).

(4) Record the adjusting entries in a general journal and post to the ledger accounts.

(5) Record the closing entries and post to the ledger accounts.

(6) Rule and balance the ledger accounts that have two or more entries.

(7) Prepare a post-closing trial balance.

(8) Record the reversing entries on April 1, post to the ledger, and rule the additional accounts that are now in balance.

Problem 10-B

This problem may be completed in the workbook in the space provided for Problem 10-3.

An audit of the accounts of Charles Turner for the current fiscal year ended June 30 revealed the following errors:

(a) The inventory of office supplies at the end of the current year was understated by $90.

(b) An adding machine purchased for store use at a cost of $180 was erroneously debited to Miscellaneous Selling Expense.

(c) In adjusting the prepaid rent account at the end of the current year, the amount transferred to Rent Expense was $120. The correct amount was $1,200.

(d) Store equipment costing $175 was erroneously debited to the office equipment account.

(e) The merchandise inventory at the end of the current year was overstated by $1,400.

(f) A payment of $230 for furniture purchased by Mr. Turner for his home was erroneously debited to Store Equipment.

(g) In adjusting the books at the end of the current year, no provision was made for accrued sales salaries of $350 and accrued office salaries of $100.

(h) A payment of $718 from M. L. Jewett on account was erroneously credited to M. R. Jewell.

(i) Two purchases returns and allowances totaling $412 were erroneously recorded as sales of merchandise.

Instructions: (1) Assuming that the above errors are discovered before the books are closed, present the necessary correcting entries in general journal form. Identify each entry by the letter given for the error in the list above.

(2) Assuming that the above errors are not discovered until after the books are closed, present the necessary correcting entries in general journal form. Identify each entry by the letter given for the error in the list above.

CHAPTER 11

Problem 11-A

This problem may be completed in the workbook in the space provided for Problem 11-1.

The Contractors Supply Company received the notes described below:

	DATE	TERM	INTEREST RATE	FACE AMOUNT
(a)	May 1	90 days	6%	$ 880
(b)	May 15	60 days	—	1,500
(c)	June 12	2 months	7%	430
(d)	June 24	30 days	4%	650
(e)	July 3	4 months	5%	1,000

Instructions: (1) Determine the due date and the amount of interest due on each note at maturity. In your solution identify each note by letter.

(2) Assuming that note (b) was discounted on June 8 at the rate of 6% and that note (d) was discounted on June 30 at the rate of 6%, determine for each the maturity value, the discount period, the amount of discount, and the proceeds. Identify the notes by letter.

Problem 11-B

This problem may be completed in the workbook in the space provided for Problem 11-2.

Charles Johnson completed the transactions listed below, among others, during a three-month period:

Oct. 2. Purchased merchandise on account from Wolford & Co., $1,200, invoice dated October 1.

6. Sold merchandise on account to J. Davis, Sale No. 214, $700.

11. Issued a 60-day, non-interest-bearing note payable for $3,000 to the First National Bank, receiving proceeds of $2,970.

13. Sold merchandise on account to D. Russell, Sale No. 240, $600.

16. Received cash from J. Davis for the invoice of October 6 less 1% discount.

23. Sold merchandise on account to A. Chapman, Sale No. 273, $1,000.

Nov. 4. Gave Wolford & Co. a 30-day, 4% note for $1,200 on account.

8. Purchased merchandise on account from Dean Mfg. Co., $650, invoice dated November 6.

11. Received from D. Russell on account a 30-day, 6% note for $600, dated November 11.

19. Issued Check No. 733 to Dean Mfg. Co. for the amount due on the invoice of November 6 less 2% discount.

22. Received from A. Chapman on account a 1-month, 5% note for $1,000, dated Nov. 22.

Dec. 1. Discounted D. Russell's $600 note, dated November 11, at the First National Bank, receiving proceeds of $601.99.

4. Issued Check No. 790 to Wolford & Co. for the amount owed on the note dated November 4: principal, $1,200; interest, $4.

10. Issued Check No. 805 to the First National Bank for the amount owed on the note payable dated October 11, $3,000.

22. Received payment from A. Chapman for the note dated November 22: principal, $1,000; interest, $4.17.

Instructions: Record the transactions, using a sales journal (one money column), a purchases journal (one money column), a cash receipts journal and a cash payments journal like those illustrated in this chapter, and a two-column general journal.

CHAPTER 12

Problem 12-A

This problem may be completed in the workbook in the space provided for Problem 12-1.

The following are some of the accounts, together with their unadjusted balances, that appear in the ledger of William Althouse on December 31, the end of the current fiscal year:

114	Interest Receivable......	$ —	612 Advertising Expense.....	$1,600
115	Store Supplies..........	800	613 Store Supplies Expense...	—
116	Office Supplies..........	300	614 Insurance Expense —	
117	Prepaid Insurance.......	1,600	Selling..............	—
118	Prepaid Advertising.....	—	711 Office Salary Expense....	6,700
119	Prepaid Interest........	—	713 Insurance Expense —	
213	Salaries Payable........	—	General.............	—
214	Interest Payable........	—	714 Office Supplies Expense..	—
215	Unearned Rent.........	—	811 Interest Income........	250
313	Profit and Loss Summary	—	812 Rent Income...........	1,800
611	Sales Salary Expense.....	19,500	911 Interest Expense........	400

The following information relating to adjustments on December 31 was obtained from physical inventories, the insurance register, and other sources:

(a) The inventory of store supplies totals $145.

(b) The inventory of office supplies totals $190.

(c) The insurance register indicates that $750 of insurance has expired during the year, of which $510 is allocable to selling expense and $240 is allocable to general expense.

(d) Included in the balance of the advertising expense account is a debit of $800 in October for space in a weekly publication. The agreement provides that the space be used in uniform amounts in 52 consecutive issues. As of December 31, advertisements had appeared in 13 issues.

(e) Included in the interest expense account is a debit of $100 for the discount on a 4-month, non-interest-bearing note payable for $5,000, dated November 1.

(f) In addition to the non-interest-bearing note described in (e), there is a 60-day, 6% note payable for $2,000 outstanding, dated November 16.

(g) Salaries accrued are as follows: sales salaries, $500; office salaries, $175.

(h) The following interest-bearing notes receivable from customers are on hand:
30-day, 6%, $1,000, dated December 7.
60-day, 6%, $1,500, dated November 21.

(i) The rent income of $1,800 was received for a 12-month lease that began on July 1.

Instructions: (1) Open the accounts listed, using the account numbers given. Record the balances in the accounts as of December 31, writing "Balance" in the items column.

(2) Prepare adjusting journal entries and post to the appropriate accounts after each entry. Write "Adjusting" in the items column of the accounts.

(3) Prepare a compound journal entry to close the income accounts and another compound entry to close the expense accounts.

(4) Post the closing entries, writing "Closing" in the items column of the income and expense accounts.

(5) Total and rule the income and expense accounts. (Since not all income and expense accounts are given in the problem, do not rule the profit and loss summary account.)

(6) Prepare the reversing journal entries that should be made on January 1 and post to the appropriate accounts after each entry. Write "Reversing" in the items columns of the accounts.

(7) Rule the additional accounts that are now in balance.

Problem 12-B

This problem may be completed in the workbook in the space provided for Problem 12-2.

The following information is obtained from a review of the accounts and other records of Ronald Artim for the current fiscal year ended December 31:

(a) Prepaid Advertising has a debit balance of $850 on December 31. Of this amount, $530 has been used during the year and $320 applies to the following year.

(b) Prepaid Insurance has a debit balance of $1,526 composed of the following:

Policies in force at the beginning of the year:

POLICY NO.	PREPAID PREMIUM AT JAN. 1	TERM FROM JAN. 1
7309B	$200	8 mo.
3917F	285	19 mo.
4719	375	15 mo.

Policy purchased during the year:

POLICY NO.	PREMIUM PAID	EFFECTIVE DATE	TERM
8081	$666	May 1	36 mo.

Insurance expired is to be recorded in one account, no allocation being made between selling expense and general expense.

(c) Included in Interest Expense is a debit of $120 for discount on Artim's 120-day, non-interest-bearing note for $6,000 dated October 2, discounted at the Merchants Bank at the rate of 6%.

(d) Salaries accrued for the period December 27–31 are as follows: sales salaries, $600; office salaries, $80.

(e) The unearned rent account had a credit balance of $360 on January 1, representing rent for the first three months of the year. On April 1, the rental agreement was renewed for one year at a monthly rental of $125, and a year's rent of $1,500, collected at that time, was credited to Unearned Rent.

(f) Store Supplies has a debit balance of $580. The inventory of store supplies on December 31 is $265.

(g) Of the notes received from customers during the year, the following three are on hand on December 31. All were accepted at face value.

DATE	FACE	TERM	INTEREST RATE
Oct. 26	$3,000	90 days	6%
Dec. 1	1,400	60 days	6%
Dec. 12	900	30 days	—

(h) Rent Expense has a debit balance of $3,900. Included in this amount is rent of $300 paid on December 31 that is applicable to the succeeding January.

(i) Tax expense of $275 has accrued but is not due until the succeeding February.

Instructions: (1) Prepare adjusting entries as of December 31 of the current fiscal year.

(2) Prepare the reversing entries that should be made as of January 1 of the succeeding fiscal year.

CHAPTER 13

Problem 13-A

This problem may be completed in the workbook in the space provided for Problem 13-1.

During a two-year period of operations, George Williams completed several transactions in connection with bad debts.

Instructions: (1) Open the following accounts in the ledger of George Williams, using the account numbers indicated: Allowance for Bad Debts, 114.1; Profit and Loss Summary, 313; Bad Debts Expense, 718.

(2) Enter a credit balance of $900 in Account No. 114.1 as of January 1, 1953.

(3) Record in general journal form the following transactions and adjusting and closing entries completed during 1953:

Feb. 19. Wrote off the account of Donald Lamb, $240, as uncollectible.

June 3. Received 20% of the $400 balance owed by Ralph Kerns, bankrupt, and wrote off the remainder as uncollectible.

Aug. 10. Wrote off the account of P. J. Anthony, $315, as uncollectible.

Dec. 31. Recorded the provision for bad debts expense at 1% of net charge sales of $104,000.

Dec. 31. Recorded the entry to close Bad Debts Expense.

Instructions: (4) Post the foregoing journal entries to the three accounts in the ledger.

(5) Balance and rule the allowance for bad debts account and rule the bad debts expense account.

(6) Record in general journal form the following transactions and adjusting and closing entries completed during 1954:

Apr. 27. Wrote off the account of Gerald Lander, $210, as uncollectible.

July 22. Received $150 from P. J. Anthony in partial payment of his account written off on August 10, 1953.

Sept. 7. Wrote off the account of Robert Babka, $470, as uncollectible.

Nov. 16. Received $21 from the receiver in bankruptcy for Gerald Lander, in payment of his account written off on April 27, 1954.

Dec. 12. Wrote off the account of Stanley Fram, $360, as uncollectible.

Dec. 31. Recorded the provision for bad debts expense at 1% of net charge sales of $108,000.

Dec. 31. Recorded the entry to close Bad Debts Expense.

Instructions: (7) Post the foregoing journal entries to the three accounts in the ledger.

(8) Balance and rule the allowance for bad debts account and rule the bad debts expense account.

(9) Assuming that the accounts receivable account at December 31, 1954, has a debit balance of $26,400, what is the net value of the accounts receivable?

Problem 13-B

This problem may be completed in the workbook in the space provided for Problem 13-2.

Ralph Sprague is the Ohio distributor of Nu-Way (tank type) and Sturdy (upright type) vacuum cleaners. His trial balance on December 31, the end of the current fiscal year, is as follows:

Cash..............................	111	$ 10,400	
Accounts Receivable.................	112	40,000	
Allowance for Bad Debts.............	112.1		$ 600
Merchandise Inventory..............	113	12,400	
Notes Payable......................	211		13,500
Accounts Payable...................	213		5,000
Ralph Sprague, Capital..............	311		29,385
Ralph Sprague, Drawing.............	312	10,000	
Sales..............................	411		145,000
Purchases..........................	511	85,000	
Operating Expenses (Control Account)...	611	35,000	
Interest Expense....................	811	685	
		$193,485	$193,485

Adjustment data:

(a) The merchandise inventory on December 31 is composed of the following items (use cost or market, whichever is lower):

150 Nu-Way cleaners; cost $45 each; replacement price on December 31, $50 each.

100 Sturdy cleaners; cost $40 each; replacement price on December 31, $37.50 each.

Miscellaneous repair parts; cost, $1,300; replacement price on December 31, $1,150.

(b) Upon the basis of an analysis of accounts receivable it is estimated that $1,800 will be uncollectible. (Debit Operating Expenses for the bad debts expense.)

(c) Prepaid interest on notes payable, $140.

(d) Interest accrued on notes payable, $45.

Instructions: (1) Prepare an eight-column work sheet for the year.

(2) Prepare a profit and loss statement and a balance sheet.

(3) Record adjusting, closing, and reversing entries.

CHAPTER 14

Problem 14-A

This problem may be completed in the workbook in the space provided for Problem 14-1.

Instructions: (1) Open the following accounts in the ledger of S. A. Framburg, using the account numbers indicated: Delivery Equipment, 121; Allowance for Depreciation — Delivery Equipment, 121.1; Profit and Loss

Summary, 313; Depreciation Expense — Delivery Equipment, 614; Loss or Gain on Disposal of Fixed Assets, 813.

(2) Record in general journal form the following transactions:

June 8, 1952. Purchased a used delivery truck for $950, paying cash.

June 13, 1952. Paid garage $140 for new tires and repairs to delivery truck.

Dec. 31, 1952. Made adjusting entry to record depreciation. The estimated life of the truck is 2 years, with a salvage value of $250. The straight-line method is to be used; the minimum unit of time to be considered is a month.

Dec. 31, 1952. Recorded the entry to close Depreciation Expense — Delivery Equipment.

Instructions: (3) Post the foregoing journal entries to the selected accounts in the ledger.

(4) Rule Account No. 614.

(5) Record in general journal form the following transactions:

Aug. 22, 1953. Traded in old truck for new one priced at $2,450. Received a trade-in allowance of $645, paying the balance in cash. (Record depreciation to date in 1953; use income tax method of recording the exchange.)

Dec. 31, 1953. Made adjusting entry to record depreciation. The estimated life of the new truck is 4 years, with a trade-in value of $450.

Dec. 31, 1953. Recorded the entry to close Depreciation Expense — Delivery Equipment.

Instructions: (6) Post the foregoing entries to the selected accounts in the ledger.

(7) Balance and rule Accounts No. 121 and 121.1; rule Account No. 614.

(8) Record in general journal form the following transactions:

Oct. 5, 1954. Framburg decides to use the services of a commercial delivery service in the future. He sells the truck for $1,700, receiving cash. (Record depreciation in 1954.)

Dec. 31, 1954. Recorded the entry to close Depreciation Expense — Delivery Equipment and Loss or Gain on Disposal of Fixed Assets.

Instructions: (9) Post the foregoing journal entries to the selected accounts in the ledger.

(10) Balance and rule Accounts No. 121 and 121.1; rule Accounts No. 614 and 813.

Problem 14-B

This problem may be completed in the workbook in the space provided for Problem 14-2.

The general ledger of the Lake Erie Insurance Company includes controlling accounts for Equipment and Allowance for Depreciation — Equipment. The details of each item of equipment are recorded in a subsidiary equipment ledger. The following transactions affecting equipment occurred during the three years ending December 31, 1953:

May 8, 1951. Purchased the following items of equipment from Reliance Equipment, Inc. for cash:

Director desk........ $210
Director chair........   75
Filing cabinet........ 108

July 22, 1951. Purchased a rug from Goodman's Furniture on account, $450.

July 25, 1951. Purchased a Stillman typewriter from Empire Typewriter Co. for cash, $197. Serial number 2435B.

July 30, 1951. Purchased a secretarial desk, $135, and chair, $48, from Reliance Equipment, Inc. for cash.

Oct. 18, 1952. Purchased a Morrow electric typewriter from Empire Typewriter Co. for cash, $310. Serial number 41953.

Oct. 23, 1952. Sold the Stillman typewriter for cash, $125.

Apr. 28, 1953. Traded in secretary's desk for a new one from Reliance Equipment, Inc. The price of the new desk was $125. The allowance granted on the old desk was $100, the balance being paid in cash. (Use the income tax method.)

Additional details necessary for determining depreciation are as follows:

ITEMS	TRADE-IN VALUE	ESTIMATED LIFE
Desks............................	none	12½ yrs.
Chairs...........................	none	12½ yrs.
Filing cabinet....................	none	15 yrs.
Typewriter — Stillman............	$50	5 yrs.
Morrow............	$70	5 yrs.
Rug..............................	none	10 yrs.

Instructions: (1) Open the following general ledger accounts: Equipment, 121; Allowance for Depreciation — Equipment, 121.1. Open an account in the subsidiary ledger, using the form illustrated on page 251, as each item of equipment is purchased.

(2) Record the transactions in general journal form, posting to the two controlling accounts and to the subsidiary ledger after each entry. Journalize and post annual depreciation entries on December 31 of each of the three years.

(3) Make a list of the balances in the subsidiary ledger accounts and compare the totals with the balances of the two controlling accounts.

Problem 14-C

This problem may be completed in the workbook in the space provided for Problem 14-4.

In each of the following unrelated cases it is assumed that subsidiary equipment ledgers are maintained, that depreciation is recorded annually except for items disposed of during the year, and that the fiscal year ends on December 31.

(a) February 10. Discarded a chair (store equipment), realizing no salvage. The following details are taken from the subsidiary account: cost, $75; accumulated allowance for depreciation on previous December 31, $75. Give the necessary general journal entry.

(b) April 21. Discarded a filing cabinet (office equipment), realizing no salvage. The subsidiary account reveals the following details: cost, $48; accumulated allowance for depreciation on previous December 31, $44; monthly depreciation, 20 cents. Give the necessary entries in general journal form.

(c) May 12. Sold a desk (office equipment) for cash, $150. The following details are taken from the subsidiary account: cost, $240; accumulated allowance for depreciation on previous December 31, $132; monthly depreciation, $2. Give the necessary entries in general journal form.

(d) July 28. Sold a rug (store equipment) for cash, $100. The following details are taken from the subsidiary account: cost, $800; accumulated allowance for depreciation on previous December 31, $576; monthly depreciation, $8. Give the necessary entries in general journal form.

(e) September 30. Traded in an old truck (delivery equipment) for a new one priced at $3,600. Received a trade-in allowance of $2,000, paying $1,600 cash. The subsidiary account shows the following details: cost, $3,000; accumulated allowance for depreciation on previous December 31, $720; monthly depreciation, $20. Give the necessary entries in general journal form to recognize the gain or the loss on the old truck and to record the new truck at $3,600.

(f) November 10. Traded in an old press (printing equipment) for a new one priced at $20,000. Received a trade-in allowance of $5,000, paying $15,000 cash. The subsidiary account shows the following: cost, $25,000; accumulated allowance for depreciation on previous December 31, $16,200; monthly depreciation, $150. Give the necessary entries in general journal form, using the income tax method.

CHAPTER 15

Problem 15-A

This problem may be completed in the workbook in the space provided for Problem 15-1.

The following transactions involving petty cash were completed by the Walters Fur Store during the month of November:

(a) Nov. 1. Drew Check No. 123 for $50 to establish a petty cash fund.
(b) The following amounts were paid from petty cash on the dates indicated:

Nov. 3. To Arrow Messenger Service to deliver garments, $7.50 (Miscellaneous Selling Expense).
6. Postage, $6 (Office Supplies).
9. Paid the charges on a telegram received, 85 cents (Miscellaneous General Expense).
12. Store supplies, $6.25.
15. Water bill, $2.15 (Miscellaneous General Expense).
19. Paid the charges for having a sales letter mimeographed, $3.50 (Miscellaneous Selling Expense).
23. To Arrow Messenger Service to deliver garments, $5.
26. Gas and electric bill, $10.05 (Miscellaneous General Expense).
29. Office supplies, $4.20.

(c) Nov. 30. Drew Check No. 178 to replenish the petty cash fund.

Instructions: (1) Record in a check register the check to establish the petty cash fund. Enter the amount of the fund in a petty cash book having the same form and columns as the book illustrated on page 269 of the text.

(2) Record the payments in the petty cash book.

(3) Total and rule the columns of the petty cash book and bring down the balance.

(4) Record the replenishing check in the check register and the petty cash book.

Problem 15-B

This problem may be completed in the workbook in the space provided for Problem 15-4.

Joseph Gerard began business on November 1 of the current year as the Gerard Appliance Company. The following transactions were completed during the month of November. Begin checks with No. 1.

Nov. 1. Invested cash, $10,000.
  1. Paid rent for the month, $300.
  1. Purchased merchandise on account from Todd & Lane, $5,400.
  2. Issued check to establish petty cash fund, $100.
  3. Sold merchandise on account to Peter Curry, $550.
  4. Purchased merchandise on account from McArthur, Inc., $1,800.
  7. Paid miscellaneous general expenses, $18.50.
  10. Sold merchandise on account to John Marlow, $250.
  11. Paid $5,292 to Todd & Lane for invoice of November 1 less 2% discount.
  13. Received $539 from Peter Curry for invoice of November 3 less 2% discount.
  14. Check No. 5 was spoiled and voided.
  15. Sold merchandise on account to William Keat, $600.
  16. Purchased merchandise on account from Todd & Lane, $2,400.
  18. Paid $1,782 to McArthur, Inc. for invoice of November 4 less 1% discount.
  20. Received a note for $250 from John Marlow covering invoice of November 10.
  21. Sold merchandise on account to Peter Curry, $360.
  22. Paid $27.50 for repairs to the office, which were charged to Miscellaneous General Expense.
  24. Received $588 from William Keat for invoice of November 15 less 2% discount.
  25. Gave our note for $2,400 to Todd & Lane covering November 16 purchase.
  27. Purchased merchandise on account from McArthur, Inc., $985.
  28. Sold merchandise on account to William Keat, $490.
  29. Reimbursed petty cash: Freight In, $55; Miscellaneous General Expense, $22.65.
  30. Paid salaries for the month, $600.
  30. Cash sales for the month, $3,500.

Instructions: (1) Record the transactions in a combined cash journal similar to the one illustrated on pages 276 and 277.

(2) Open the ledger accounts listed below and post to them.

General Ledger Accounts: Cash, 111; Petty Cash, 112; Notes Receivable, 113; Accounts Receivable, 115; Notes Payable, 211; Accounts Payable, 213; Joseph Gerard, Capital, 311; Sales, 411; Purchases, 511; Freight In, 512; Salary Expense, 611; Rent Expense, 612; Miscellaneous General Expense, 619; Purchases Discount, 711; Sales Discount, 811.

Accounts Receivable Ledger: Peter Curry, 684 Center St.; William Keat, 2124 High St.; John Marlow, 3064 Trimble Ave.

Accounts Payable Ledger: McArthur, Inc., St. Paul; Todd & Lane, Minneapolis.

(3) Prepare a trial balance.

Problem 15-C

This problem may be completed in the workbook in the space provided for Problem 15-5.

Thomas Strong's accounting records include a check register, a petty cash book, and an insurance policy register similar to those illustrated in this chapter, and a two-column general journal.

The following transactions were among those completed in August, 1953:

Aug. 1. Issued Check No. 638 to establish a petty cash fund, $50.
    1. Issued Check No. 639 to Lever Realty Co. for August rent, $300.
    1. Issued Check No. 640 to Myer Insurance Agency for two insurance policies. One policy, No. M98603, is with the Fidelity Fire Insurance Co., covers merchandise for $50,000, has a premium of $468, and is effective for 3 years from August 1, 1953. The second policy, No. F5464, is with the same company, covers equipment for $10,000, has a premium of $360, and is effective for 5 years from August 1, 1953.
    3. Issued Check No. 641 for $240 to Myer Insurance Agency for Policy No. 67931 with the Atlas Indemnity Co. The policy, dated August 1, 1953, and effective for one year, is a surety bond on Strong's employees and gives him protection of $10,000.
    4. Paid $4.75 from petty cash for express charges on a shipment of merchandise received (Freight In).
    8. Issued Check No. 642 for $3,000 in payment of a note payable to the Security National Bank.
  10. Paid $7.50 from petty cash for stamps (Office Supplies).
  13. Spoiled Check No. 643.
  13. Issued Check No. 644 to C-D Manufacturing Co. for invoice for $803.69 less 2% discount.
  15. Paid $1.50 from petty cash for messenger service (Miscellaneous Selling Expense).
  18. Paid $8.50 from petty cash for: repairs to office equipment, $5 (Miscellaneous General Expense); repairs to cash register, $3.50 (Miscellaneous Selling Expense).
  22. Issued Check No. 645 to C. F. Mason Co. for store equipment, $120.
  28. Paid $3.75 from petty cash for decorations for the store (Miscellaneous Selling Expense).
  29. Issued Check No. 646 to Thomas Strong for personal use, $500.
  31. Issued Check No. 647 for salaries and wages, $1,750.
  31. Issued Check No. 648 to replenish the petty cash fund.

Instructions: (1) Record the foregoing transactions. When petty cash is replenished, rule and balance the petty cash book.

(2) Enter and distribute insurance policy premiums for the balance of the year. Prepare a journal entry to adjust prepaid insurance on August 31.

(3) Rule and foot the check register.

(4) The bank statement for August shows an August 31 bank balance of $5,526. With the exception of Nos. 646 and 648, all checks were returned with the statement. The cash account has an August 31 balance of $5,000. Prepare a bank reconciliation.

CHAPTER 16

Problem 16-A

This problem may be completed in the workbook in the space provided for Problem 16-2.

Crosby, Inc. uses a voucher system. Vouchers issued during September and October that were unpaid on October 31 were:

VOUCHER No.	COMPANY	FOR	DATE OF INVOICE	AMOUNT
722	Garson Company	Merchandise	Sept. 8	$ 5,000
745	Goodwin & Parker	Merchandise	Oct. 19	3,050
754	Ladwig Mfg. Corp.	Merchandise	Oct. 24	4,200
				$12,250

The following transactions were completed during November:

Nov. 2. Issued Voucher No. 765 to Stern Realty Agency for November rent, $400; then issued Check No. 813 in payment of this voucher.

3. Issued Voucher No. 766 for $150 to establish a petty cash fund; then issued Check No. 814 in payment of this voucher.

4. Issued Check No. 815 to Ladwig Mfg. Corp. in payment of Voucher No. 754 less a 2% discount.

6. Issued Voucher No. 767 to Ives, Inc. for the purchase of merchandise, $895.

7. Gave Garson Company a 15-day, 6% note in payment of Voucher No. 722.

10. Received a credit memorandum for $350 from Goodwin & Parker for merchandise returned to them. Canceled Voucher No. 745 and issued Voucher No. 768 for the adjusted amount.

11. Issued Voucher No. 769 to Taylor Manufacturing Co. for the purchase of merchandise, $2,500.

12. Issued Voucher No. 770 to Miller Supply Co. for the purchase of supplies as follows: store supplies, $120; office supplies, $35; advertising circulars, $80.

13. Received a credit memorandum for $125 from Ives, Inc. for merchandise returned to it that was included in Voucher No. 767. Made a "red ink" entry to record the return.

13. Issued Voucher No. 771 to Bauer's Garage for gas, oil, and repairs. The tickets attached to the invoice indicate that delivery trucks used $125 (charge to Miscellaneous Delivery Expense) and salesmen's cars used $65 (charge to Miscellaneous Selling Expense). Issued Check No. 816 in payment of this voucher.

14. Issued Check No. 817 in payment of Voucher No. 767 less the return and less 2% discount.

17. Purchased new store equipment from National Equipment Co. for $2,500. Issued Voucher No. 772 for $500 for the down payment and Voucher No. 773 for the balance of $2,000 that is to be paid in 30 days if the equipment is satisfactory. (Charge Store Equipment.) Issued Check No. 818 in payment of Voucher No. 772.

18. Issued Check No. 819 to Goodwin & Parker in payment of Voucher No. 768.

Nov. 19. Issued Voucher No. 774 to Hamilton Products Corp. for the purchase of merchandise, $1,800.

21. Issued Check No. 820 to Miller Supply Co. in payment of Voucher No. 770 less 1% discount.

21. Issued Voucher No. 775 to Garson Company for the note of November 7 plus interest; then issued Check No. 821 in payment of this voucher.

25. Received a credit memorandum for $50 from Hamilton Products Corp. as an allowance on damaged merchandise that was included in Voucher No. 774. Made a "red ink" entry to record the allowance.

30. Issued Voucher No. 776 to replenish the petty cash fund. The charges were distributed as follows: Store Supplies, $28.50; Advertising Expense, $15; Miscellaneous Selling Expense, $30; Miscellaneous Delivery Expense, $20; Office Supplies, $12.75; Miscellaneous General Expense, $13. Issued Check No. 822 in payment of this voucher.

30. Issued vouchers as follows:

No. 777, City Power Co., electricity, $25.

No. 778, Bell Telephone Co., telephone services, $15.85.

30. Issued checks as follows:

No. 823 to City Power Co. in payment of Voucher No. 777.

No. 824 to Bell Telephone Co. in payment of Voucher No. 778.

Instructions: (1) Under date of the original purchase, enter the unpaid vouchers on October 31 in a voucher register like the one illustrated on pages 288 and 289; then rule double lines across all the amount columns of the voucher register so that the amounts just recorded will not be included in the columnar totals posted at the end of November.

(2) Record the November transactions in the voucher register, in a check register like the one illustrated on page 291, and in a two-column general journal.

(3) Total and rule the voucher register and the check register.

(4) Open the following general ledger accounts: Account No. 213, Accounts Payable; Account No. 512, Purchases Returns and Allowances.

(5) Enter in the accounts payable account the October 31 balance of $12,250. Post the general journal entries to the accounts payable account and to the purchases returns and allowances account. Post the debit and the credit totals of the accounts payable column in the voucher register and the total of the accounts payable column in the check register. Post to the purchases returns and allowances account the total of the returns and allowances shown in the purchases column of the voucher register.

(6) Prove the November 30 balance of the accounts payable account by preparing a schedule of unpaid vouchers as shown by the voucher register.

CHAPTER 17

Problem 17-A

This problem may be completed in the workbook in the space provided for Problem 17–1.

The Industrial Equipment Co. has nine employees. They are paid on an hourly basis, receiving time-and-one-half pay for all hours worked in excess of 40 a week. The record of time worked for the week ended Saturday, July 25, of the current year, together with other relevant information, is summarized below:

Name	No.	M	T	W	Th	F	S	Rate Per Hour	Bond Deduction	Income Tax Withheld
A	1	8	8	8	8	8	4	$1.60		$ 8.50
B	6	8	4	8	8	8	4	2.50	$1.25	13.80
C	8	8	8	8	8	8	5	2.80	3.75	16.90
D	3	8	0	8	8	8	8	2.00		12.30
E	5	8	6	8	6	8	4	2.70	3.75	10.10
F	7	4	4	4	4	4	0	1.50		3.20
G	2	8	8	8	8	8	0	2.20		6.80
H	4	8	4	8	4	8	8	2.10		8.40
I	9	8	8	8	8	8	4	2.80	2.50	18.30

Cumulative earnings paid (before deductions) prior to the current week were as follows: A, $2,135; B, $2,950; C, $3,530; D, $2,320; E, $3,500; F, $1,200; G, $2,800; H, $2,450; I, $3,700.

A, C, and F are office employees, the others are salesmen. A group insurance deduction of $.20 per week is made from each employee's earnings. The following tax rates apply: F.I.C.A., 1½%; state unemployment (employer only), 1.8%; federal unemployment, .3%.

Instructions: (1) Prepare a payroll record similar to that illustrated on pages 306 and 307.

(2) Journalize the entry to record the payroll for the week.

(3) The company uses a voucher system and a payroll bank account. Give the entries in *general journal form* to record the payroll voucher and the payment of the payroll. The payroll checks are issued in the order of the names on the payroll, beginning with Check No. 461.

(4) Journalize the entry to record the employer's payroll taxes for the week.

Problem 17-B

This problem may be completed in the workbook in the space provided for Problem 17-2.

The following accounts, with the balances indicated, appear in the ledger of Southeastern Sales Co., Inc. on December 1 of the current year:

214	Salaries Payable		—
215.1	F.I.C.A. Taxes Payable	$	63.14
215.2	Employees Income Taxes Payable		750.20
215.3	State Unemployment Taxes Payable		82.30
215.4	Federal Unemployment Taxes Payable		198.15
216.1	Bond Deductions Payable		221.50
216.2	Hospital Deductions Payable		58.00
611	Sales Salary Expense		59,950.20
711	Officers Salary Expense		25,800.00
712	Office Salary Expense		7,610.30
719	Payroll Tax Expense		2,514.38

The following transactions relating to payroll, payroll deductions, and payroll taxes occur during December:

Dec. 5. Prepared Voucher No. 831, payable to Security Bank, for $131.25 to purchase U. S. Savings Bonds (2 at $37.50 and 3 at $18.75) for employees.

5. Issued Check No. 825 in payment of Voucher No. 831.

12. Prepared Voucher No. 858, payable to Security Bank, for the amount of employees' income tax and F.I.C.A. tax due on December 15. (Pay balance of Accounts Nos. 215.1 and 215.2.)

12. Issued Check No. 850 in payment of Voucher No. 858.

14. Prepared a general journal entry to record the biweekly payroll for the period ending today. A summary of the payroll record follows:
Deductions: F.I.C.A. tax, $26.42; income taxes withheld, $370.50; bond deductions, $86.25; hospital deductions, $58.

Salary Distribution: officers salaries, $1,100; sales salaries, $2,715; office salaries, $350.

Cash Paid: $3,623.83

14. Prepared Voucher No. 864, payable to Payroll Bank Account, for the net amount of the biweekly payroll.

14. Issued Check No. 860 in payment of Voucher No. 864.

17. Prepared Voucher No. 868, payable to State Bank, for $93.75 to purchase U. S. Savings Bonds (5 at $18.75) for employees.

17. Prepared Voucher No. 869, payable to Miami Hospital, for $116 for contributions withheld from employees' earnings during the past two pay periods.

18. Issued Check No. 861 in payment of Voucher No. 868.

18. Issued Check No. 862 in payment of Voucher No. 869.

28. Prepared a general journal entry to record the biweekly payroll for the period ending today. A summary of the payroll record follows:
Deductions: F.I.C.A. tax, $22.12; income taxes withheld, $396.50; bond deductions, $86.25.

Salary Distribution: officers salaries, $1,100; sales salaries, $2,890; office salaries, $350.

Cash Paid: $3,835.13.

28. Prepared Voucher No. 898, payable to Payroll Bank Account, for the net amount of the biweekly payroll.

28. Issued Check No. 887 in payment of Voucher No. 898.

29. Prepared Voucher No. 900, payable to Security Bank, for $75 to purchase U. S. Savings Bonds (4 at $18.75) for employees.

29. Issued Check No. 890 in payment of Voucher No. 900.

29. Prepared a general journal entry to record the employer's payroll taxes on earnings paid in December. Taxable earnings for the two payrolls, according to the payroll records, are as follows: subject to F.I.C.A. tax, $3,236; subject to unemployment compensation tax, $2,010. The following rates apply: F.I.C.A., 1½%; state unemployment, 1.7%; federal unemployment, .3%.

Instructions: (1) Open the accounts listed, and enter the balances shown under date of December 1.

(2) Record the transactions, using a voucher register like the one on page 311, a check register like the one on page 311, and a general journal. After each entry, post all items affecting the accounts opened in the ledger.

(3) Journalize the adjusting entry on December 31 to record salaries and related payroll taxes for the incomplete payroll period. Salaries accrued are as follows: officers salaries, $220; sales salaries, $546; office salaries, $70. Compute the accrued taxes at the rates given above, applying them to the full amount of the salaries. Post to the accounts.

(4) Journalize the entry to close the salary expense and payroll tax expense accounts to Profit and Loss Summary. Post to the accounts.

(5) Rule the expense accounts; balance and rule the liability accounts.

(6) Journalize the entry on January 1 to reverse the adjustment of December 31. Post to the accounts.

(7) Assume that three vouchers are prepared on January 29 for the payment of the liabilities for payroll taxes shown at December 31. Identify the taxes, the period of time to which they apply, and the amount due. Arrange your answer as follows:

VOUCHER	NAME OF TAX	PERIOD	AMOUNT
1			
2			
3			

CHAPTER 18

Problem 18-A

This problem may be completed in the workbook in the space provided for Problem 18–1.

The Albers Motor Sales Company prepares interim statements at the end of each month and closes its books annually on December 31. On January 31 of the current year Mr. Albers estimates that the property taxes assessed against the business for the current year will be $1,080. The statement for property taxes, showing a liability of $1,140, is received on March 25. Half of this amount is paid on April 15 and half is paid on October 15.

Instructions: (1) Give all of the entries in chronological order, in general journal form, to record monthly adjusting entries for the first six months of the year, the tax liability upon receipt of the tax bill on March 25, and the payment of half of the tax on April 15.

(2) What items relative to property taxes should appear on the balance sheet of February 28? of March 31? of April 30? of June 30? of November 30? (Give account titles and amounts.)

Problem 18-B

This problem may be completed in the workbook in the space provided for Problem 18–4.

John G. Blake is married and has four dependent children. One of the children earned $700 during the current year, another earned $150, and the other two had no income. Both Mr. and Mrs. Blake are under 65 years of age and have good vision. Details of their receipts and expenditures, exclusive of nondeductible personal expenses, for the current year ended December 31 are as follows:

Receipts — Mr. Blake:

Salary as manager of King Department Store.........	$15,426.00
(Earnings, $18,000; income tax withheld, $2,520; F.I.C.A. tax withheld, $54)	
Reimbursement for travel expenses (travel for King)..	649.50
Rent from rental property owned...................	2,400.00
Dividends on corporation stocks...................	390.75

Receipts — Mrs. Blake:

Withdrawals from Foley Enterprises, a partnership in which she is a partner (distributive share of the net profit for the year, $4,000)......................	2,500.00
Dividends on corporation stocks...................	285.00
Interest on corporation bonds.....................	120.00
Interest on bonds of City of Hamilton..............	150.00

Expenditures — Mr. Blake:

Travel expenses on trips for King Department Store....	720.00
Rental property:	
Property taxes.................................	212.36
Insurance (one-year policies)....................	50.00
Painting and repairs............................	460.50
Interest on mortgage...........................	360.00
Building was acquired several years ago at a cost of $18,000 and is being depreciated at the rate of 4%.	
Charitable contributions...........................	650.00
Interest on mortgage on residence..................	150.00
Automobile license fee on family car...............	15.00
Real estate tax on residence.......................	198.65
Sales taxes on items purchased for personal or family use	75.00
Damages to family car resulting from an accident (no insurance).....................................	450.00
Payments during year on Declaration of Estimated Income Tax.....................................	2,000.00

Expenditures — Mrs. Blake:

Charitable contributions...........................	220.00

Instructions: Compute Mr. and Mrs. Blake's income tax (joint return), patterning your solution after the illustration on page 346. Use the table of tax rates appearing on page 343.

CHAPTER 19

Problem 19-A

This problem may be completed in the workbook in the space provided for Problem 19–1.

In contemplating the formation of a partnership, C. F. Fling and J. D. Paxton discussed the division of profits. Fling was to invest $50,000; Paxton, $25,000. Fling agreed to devote one half of his time to the business; Paxton, full time.

(a) Fling proposed that the profits be divided according to the original capital investments.

(b) Paxton felt that the profits should be divided in the ratio of time devoted to the business; namely, $\frac{1}{3}$ to Fling and $\frac{2}{3}$ to himself.

(c) Fling then suggested that profits be divided equally in order to offset his larger capital investment against Paxton's devoting his full time to the business.

(d) Paxton finally recommended that annual salaries should be allowed — $6,000 to Paxton and $3,000 to Fling — and that the remaining profit or loss should be divided equally.

(e) An accountant who was consulted recommended that plan (d) be followed but that, in addition, each partner should be allowed 4% interest on his original capital investment.

Instructions: Assuming a profit of $15,000, prepare a summary comparing the partners' shares in the profit under the five conditions mentioned above.

Problem 19-B

This problem may be completed in the workbook in the space provided for Problem 19–4.

On January 2, 1953, Helen Gardner and Mary Holt formed a partnership (Gardner and Holt) in order to open a stenographic service business. The partnership agreement provided that monthly salaries of $300 and $400 be allowed to Miss Gardner and Miss Holt respectively. Interest at 5% on the original investments was to be allowed, after which the profit or the loss was to be distributed equally. The adjusted trial balance on December 31, 1953, at the end of the first year of business was as follows (capital accounts represent the original investments):

Cash	$ 2,800	
Accounts Receivable	3,600	
Office Supplies	700	
Office Equipment	3,500	
Notes Payable		$ 1,000
Helen Gardner, Capital		3,000
Helen Gardner, Drawing	3,600	
Mary Holt, Capital		5,000
Mary Holt, Drawing	4,800	
Fees		27,000
Operating Expenses	17,000	
	$36,000	$36,000

Instructions: (1) Prepare a profit and loss statement including distribution of net profit to partners.

(2) Prepare a statement of partners' capital accounts.

(3) Prepare a balance sheet.

(4) What amounts do the partners report on their income tax returns?

Problem 19-C

This problem may be completed in the workbook in the space provided for Problem 19–5.

The capital accounts of L. A. Boyle and C. W. Reilly, partners, are shown below. The profit and loss summary account for the partnership, to which all income and expense accounts have been closed, is also given; the balance in this account has not been closed into the partners' drawing accounts.

L. A. BOYLE, CAPITAL   Acct. No. 311

1953					1953				
May	1		CP5	10,000	Jan.	1		J1	40,000
					Aug.	1		CR8	20,000

C. W. REILLY, CAPITAL   Acct. No. 313

					1953				
					Jan.	1		J1	30,000
					July	1		CR7	5,000
					Nov.	1		CR10	5,000

PROFIT AND LOSS SUMMARY   Acct. No. 315

1953					1953				
Dec.	31		J12	103,850	Dec.	31		J12	116,450

Instructions: (1) Give the general journal entry that would be required to close the profit and loss summary account under each of the following bases of distribution of profits:

(a) Profits are distributed equally.

(b) Profits are distributed 60% to Boyle and 40% to Reilly.

(c) Profits are distributed according to the balances in the capital accounts at the beginning of the year.

(d) Profits are distributed according to the average balances in the capital accounts.

(e) Profits are distributed 60% to Boyle and 40% to Reilly after salaries of $500 and $600 a month respectively have been allowed.

(f) Profits are distributed according to the average balances in the capital accounts after monthly salaries of $400 to Boyle and $500 to Reilly have been allowed.

(g) Profits are distributed equally after monthly salaries of $500 to Boyle and $400 to Reilly have been allowed and after 4% interest on the balances in the capital accounts at the beginning of the year has been allowed.

(h) Same as (g) except that the monthly salaries are respectively $300 and $400 and that the interest is 5%.

(2) Using the results obtained in (h), prepare the distribution section of the profit and loss statement and a statement of partners' capital accounts for the year ended December 31, 1953. Assume that the partners withdrew their salary allowances each month, that these withdrawals were charged to their drawing accounts, and that there were no other withdrawals charged to the drawing accounts during the year.

CHAPTER 20

Problem 20-A

This problem may be completed in the workbook in the space provided or Problem 20–1.

Moore and Haas are partners sharing profits $3/5$ and $2/5$ respectively. On June 30 their interests in the firm are as follows: Moore, $36,000, and Haas, $24,000. Duval is admitted as a partner upon the investment of $15,000 in cash.

Instructions: Record the investment of Duval in general journal form under each of the following conditions:

(1) Duval is given a one-fourth interest, goodwill being recorded.
(2) Duval is given a one-fourth interest, a bonus being allowed to the new partner.
(3) Duval is given credit for the actual investment made.
(4) Duval is given a one-sixth interest, goodwill being recorded.
(5) Duval is given a one-sixth interest, a bonus being allowed to the old partners.

Problem 20-B

This problem may be completed in the workbook in the space provided for Problem 20–2.

On May 31, Wilson is retiring from the partnership of Cane, Simpson, and Wilson, who share profits equally. The balance sheet on this date is given below:

CANE, SIMPSON, AND WILSON
BALANCE SHEET
MAY 31, 19 - -

Cash...............	$25,000	Liabilities..............	$15,000
Other Assets.........	50,000	Cane, Capital.........	15,000
		Simpson, Capital.......	25,000
		Wilson, Capital........	20,000
Total Assets..........	$75,000	Total Liab. and Prop....	$75,000

Instructions: Construct general journal entries for Wilson's withdrawal under the following circumstances:

(1) Wilson sells his interest to Cane; he receives Cane's personal note for $17,500.

(2) Wilson sells his interest to Harkness, whom Cane and Simpson have agreed to accept as a partner, for $25,000 cash.

(3) Wilson accepts $5,000 less than the book value of his interest and withdraws that amount in cash.

(4) Wilson withdraws $18,000 in cash and accepts a note from Cane and Simpson for the remainder, equal in total to his proprietorship.

(5) Wilson withdraws $15,000 in cash and $10,000 in other assets in exchange for his interest.

Problem 20-C

This problem may be completed in the workbook in the space provided for Problem 20–5.

The balance sheet of the firm of Porter, Sarnoff, and Elder just prior to liquidation is as follows:

PORTER, SARNOFF, AND ELDER
BALANCE SHEET
JULY 31, 19 --

Cash.................	$ 8,000	Notes Payable.........	$ 1,000
Accounts Receivable...	5,500	Accounts Payable......	2,000
Merchandise Inventory	15,000	Porter, Capital........	15,000
Supplies.............	500	Sarnoff, Capital........	10,000
Equipment..........	4,000	Elder, Capital..........	5,000
Total Assets.........	$33,000	Total Liab. and Prop....	$33,000

Porter, Sarnoff, and Elder share profits in the ratio of 3:2:1.

The following liquidation transactions were completed:

(a) Collected $5,200 in cash from customers' accounts; charged the remainder to Loss and Gain on Sale of Assets.

(b) Sold the merchandise for $12,000 cash.

(c) Sold the supplies for $400 cash.

(d) Sold the equipment for $5,000 cash.

(e) Distributed the loss on the sale of the assets to the partners' capital accounts.

(f) Paid notes payable in full.

(g) Paid accounts payable in full.

(h) Distributed the cash balance to the partners.

Instructions: (1) Enter the balances shown on the July 31 balance sheet in T accounts. Also set up an account entitled Loss and Gain on Sale of Assets.

(2) Prepare general journal entries to record the liquidation.

(3) Post the liquidation entries and rule the accounts.

CHAPTER 21

Problem 21-A

This problem may be completed in the workbook in the space provided for Problem 21–1.

The Lanson Corporation and the Fremont Corporation both received their charters and began business on January 2, 1944. Both corporations have since had the same outstanding stock: 2,000 shares of $4\frac{1}{2}\%$ cumulative preferred, par $100; and 2,000 shares of common, par $60. In each case, the board of directors declared dividends on preferred stock whenever, and to the extent that, there was a credit balance in the surplus account at the end of the year and declared dividends on common stock amounting to one half of the difference between the earnings in any year and the preferred dividends paid in that year.

The profits (after income taxes) and the losses for a period of ten years are as follows:

	LANSON CORPORATION	FREMONT CORPORATION
1944	$ 2,000 loss	$ 3,000 loss
1945	4,000 loss	8,000 loss
1946	6,000 loss	2,000 profit
1947	23,000 profit	6,000 loss
1948	21,000 profit	45,000 profit
1949	18,000 profit	49,000 profit
1950	22,000 profit	36,000 profit
1951	24,000 profit	51,000 profit
1952	12,000 profit	59,000 profit
1953	3,000 profit	33,000 profit

Instructions: (1) Show for each year the distribution of the profit (after income taxes) or the loss for each corporation. Use columns with the following headings: Year; Income; To Preferred Stock; Balance Due on Preferred Stock; To Common Stock; To Surplus; Surplus Balance. Indicate negative or minus items by encircling them.

(2) Total the two columns showing the amounts paid on preferred and common stock. What was the amount received per share on common and preferred stock for the ten-year period?

Problem 21-B

This problem may be completed in the workbook in the space provided for Problem 21–2.

James Barnes and Alan Williams, partners, wish to retire from active participation in their manufacturing business. They decide to form a corporation to take over the firm's assets and liabilities. The balance sheet of the partnership on May 1 is as follows:

BARNES AND WILLIAMS
BALANCE SHEET
MAY 1, 1954

Cash		$ 12,000	Notes Payable		$ 10,000
Notes Receivable		20,000	Accounts Payable		32,000
Accounts Receivable		54,000	Salaries Payable		1,500
Inventories		85,500	James Barnes, Capital		145,000
Machinery	$80,000		Alan Williams, Capital		72,000
Less Allowance	44,000	36,000			
Buildings	45,000				
Less Allowance	22,000	23,000			
Land		30,000			
Total Assets		$260,500	Total Liab. & Prop		$260,500

The partners, together with John Adams, who would like to join in the new enterprise, agree to the following plan:

(a) The corporation is to be known as the Adams Corporation, and its authorized stock is to consist of 5,000 shares of common stock, par value $100.

(b) The partners are to withdraw all of the cash from the firm, each partner to receive an equal amount. All of the other assets and liabilities are to be transferred to the corporation. The partners are to receive common stock at par value in payment for their interests in the partnership. In determining their interests, an allowance for bad debts of $2,000 is to be set up against accounts receivable, and the land is to be valued at $40,000. The profit-and-loss ratio of the partnership is 3:2 respectively for Barnes and Williams.

(c) Adams, who owns land that is desirable for expansion purposes, is to be given 200 shares of common stock upon transfer of his land to the corporation. Adams also agrees to purchase 350 shares of common stock at par upon the organization of the corporation.

The Adams Corporation is incorporated, and on May 1 the foregoing transactions take place.

Instructions: (1) Prepare general journal entries (a) to record the withdrawal of cash, (b) to revalue the assets as agreed, and (c) to close the books of the partnership.

(2) Prepare journal entries to open the books of the corporation.

(3) Prepare a balance sheet in report form for the new corporation.

(4) Assuming a profit for the succeeding year of $13,400 after income taxes, what dividends would each of the three men receive if 30% of the profits are to be distributed? What rate will be paid on common stock?

CHAPTER 22

Problem 22-A

This problem may be completed in the workbook in the space provided for Problem 22–2.

The following is the trial balance of the Franklin Corporation one month after its organization:

FRANKLIN CORPORATION
TRIAL BALANCE
MARCH 1, 1952

Cash	$269,500	
Preferred Stock Subscriptions Receivable	49,500	
Preferred Stock ($100 par, 6%)		$ 60,000
Preferred Stock Subscribed		90,000
Premium on Preferred Stock		11,500
Common Stock ($100 par)		150,000
Premium on Common Stock		7,500
	$319,000	$319,000

The following transactions occurred during the balance of 1952:

(a) Acquired the going business of the Chason Company. Issued 600 shares of common stock, with a market value of $108 a share, and 250 shares of preferred stock, with a market value of $115 a share, in exchange for the following assets: Machinery, $51,550; Buildings, $15,000; Land, $12,000; and Goodwill, $15,000.

(b) Received cash in payment of the balance of Preferred Stock Subscriptions Receivable. Issued all preferred stock that had been subscribed for but not previously issued.

(c) Made a profit of $50,000 (after income taxes) on the first year's operation (debit Cash for $56,200; credit Allowance for Depreciation of Machinery, $4,700; credit Allowance for Depreciation of Buildings, $1,500; and credit Profit and Loss Summary, $50,000).

(d) Closed Profit and Loss Summary to Earned Surplus.

The following transactions occurred during 1953:

(e) Received subscriptions for 300 shares of preferred stock at $109, 50% of the purchase price being paid in cash at the time of subscription.

(f) Purchased the going business of the Norton Co. for $240,000. Assets are valued as follows: Machinery, $95,000; Buildings, $52,500; Land, $77,500; Goodwill, $15,000.

(g) Purchased machinery on account, $25,000.

(h) Made a profit of $110,000 (after income taxes) for 1953 (debit Cash, $125,500; credit Allowance for Depreciation of Machinery, $9,250; credit Allowance for Depreciation of Buildings, $6,250; and credit Profit and Loss Summary, $110,000).

(i) Closed Profit and Loss Summary to Earned Surplus.

(j) A subscriber to 50 shares of preferred stock at $109 notified the company that he would be unable to meet the balance of his payment. The amount paid in is to be returned to the subscriber, less any expenses and losses on resale. The 50 shares are resold at $105.

Instructions: (1) Record the March 1 balances and the above transactions directly in "T" accounts. The accounts required are: Cash; Preferred Stock Subscriptions Receivable; Machinery; Allowance for Depreciation of Machinery; Buildings; Allowance for Depreciation of Buildings; Land; Goodwill; Accounts Payable; Payable to Subscriber; Preferred Stock; Preferred Stock Subscribed; Premium on Preferred Stock; Common Stock; Premium on Common Stock; Earned Surplus; Profit and Loss Summary.

(2) Prepare a balance sheet as of December 31, 1953.

Problem 22-B

This problem may be completed in the workbook in the space provided for Problem 22-3.

Universal, Inc. was organized by John Moore, Ron Bane, and Barry Porter on May 1, 1953, with authorized capital stock of 20,000 shares of common, $50 par, and 10,000 shares of preferred, $100 par. The transactions for the first month were as follows:

May 1. Issued 3,000 shares of common stock to Ron Bane in exchange for land valued at $25,000 and a building valued at $134,000.

1. Issued 1,000 shares of common stock to Barry Porter in exchange for land valued at $53,000.

1. Sold to John Moore for cash 2,000 shares of common stock at $53.

2. Received subscriptions for 4,000 shares of common stock at $54 and cash for 25% of the subscription price. Also received subscriptions for 1,750 shares of preferred stock at par and cash for 50% of the subscription price.

3. Received a donation from the organizers of 1,200 shares of common stock. The stock was recorded at a value of $54 per share.

5. Issued 3,500 shares of common stock to Donald Bragg in exchange for his business, which included: merchandise inventory, $130,000; equipment, $79,500; goodwill, $25,000; and notes payable, $42,000.

7. Received subscriptions for 2,250 shares of preferred stock at $102 and cash for 50% of the subscription price.

12. Received payments on stock subscribed for on May 2 as follows: 25% of the subscription price on the common stock; 25% of the subscription price on the preferred stock from all but one subscriber for 100 shares. The subscriber was unable to meet his installment, the down payment was returned to him, and the corporation immediately resold the shares for cash at $104.

15. Sold 800 shares of common treasury stock at $56.

17. Received 25% of the subscription price on the preferred stock subscribed for on May 7.

20. Purchased for $185,000 cash the assets of a business formerly operated by Gene Logan. The assets were valued as follows: mer-

chandise inventory, $42,500; equipment, $35,000; building, $95,000; and land, $12,500.

May 27. Received payments on stock subscribed for on May 2 as follows: 25% of the subscription price on the common stock; the balance due on the preferred stock. Issued the preferred stock.

Instructions: (1) Record the foregoing transactions in T accounts. The accounts required are: Cash; Common Stock Subscriptions Receivable; Preferred Stock Subscriptions Receivable; Merchandise Inventory; Equipment; Buildings; Land; Goodwill; Notes Payable; Common Stock; Common Stock Subscribed; Premium on Common Stock; Common Treasury Stock; Preferred Stock; Preferred Stock Subscribed; Premium on Preferred Stock; Donated Surplus; Treasury Stock Surplus.

(2) Prepare a balance sheet as of May 31.

CHAPTER 23

Problem 23-A

This problem may be completed in the workbook in the space provided for Problem 23-2.

The Angvire Company received its charter of incorporation on December 31, 1951. Its authorized capitalization was as follows: 4,000 shares of 6% cumulative preferred stock, $50 par, and 20,000 shares of common stock, $25 par. During its first three years of operation the following transactions occurred:

1952

Jan. 2. Received cash for 3,000 shares of preferred stock and 10,000 shares of common stock, both at a premium of 4%.

15. Received subscriptions for 1,000 shares of preferred stock and 5,000 shares of common stock at a premium of 5%.

15. Paid $300,000 cash for other assets.

Feb. 15. Received in cash one half of the subscription price for the preferred stock and the common stock subscribed for on January 15.

Mar. 15. Received in cash half of the balance due on the preferred stock subscribed. Received in cash the complete balance due on the common stock subscribed and issued the common stock.

Apr. 15. Received in cash the balance due on the preferred stock subscribed. Issued the stock.

25. The attorney who secured the charter and performed other legal services in connection with organization rendered his bill for $8,000. He was paid in cash.

Dec. 31. Net loss for the first year's operations was $10,000 (debit Profit and Loss Summary; credit Cash). Closed Profit and Loss Summary to Earned Surplus.

1953

Mar. 21. Paid $200,000 cash for other assets.

Dec. 31. Net profit for 1953 was $100,000 (debit Cash; credit Profit and Loss Summary). Made provision for income tax liability of $40,000 and closed the balance of Profit and Loss Summary to Earned Surplus.

31. Declared the preferred dividends for first two years.

31. Wrote off one fifth of organization costs.

1954

Jan. 15. Paid the preferred dividends declared in 1953.

Mar. 15. Paid the income tax liability for 1953.

Apr. 1. Purchased 1,000 shares of own common stock at $27 and appropriated surplus equal to the purchase price.

Oct. 6. Sold 500 shares of treasury stock at $30 and reduced surplus restriction accordingly.

Dec. 31. Net profit for 1954 was $130,000 (debit Cash; credit Profit and Loss Summary). Made provision for income tax liability of $52,000 and closed the balance of Profit and Loss Summary to Earned Surplus.

31. Declared preferred dividends for 1954 and a $1 per share dividend on the outstanding common stock (14,500 shares).

31. Set up a reserve for plant additions of $20,000.

31. Wrote off one fifth of organization costs.

Instructions: (1) Record the transactions directly in T accounts. The accounts required are: Cash; Preferred Stock Subscriptions Receivable; Common Stock Subscriptions Receivable; Other Assets; Organization Costs; Income Taxes Payable; Preferred Dividends Payable; Common Dividends Payable; Preferred Stock; Preferred Stock Subscribed; Premium on Preferred Stock; Common Stock; Common Stock Subscribed; Premium on Common Stock; Common Treasury Stock; Treasury Stock Surplus; Reserve for Treasury Stock; Reserve for Plant Additions; Earned Surplus; Profit and Loss Summary.

(2) Take a trial balance as of December 31, 1954.

(3) Prepare a balance sheet as of December 31, 1954.

(4) What additional dividend may be declared on the common stock on December 31, 1954?

(5) What is the book value of the common stock on December 31, 1954?

Problem 23-B

This problem may be completed in the workbook in the space provided for Problem 23-4.

The Hale Corporation has a stable earnings record and hence is able to pay regular quarterly dividends on its preferred and common stock. Dividends are declared on the last day of each calendar quarter and are paid on the 25th of the following month to stockholders of record as of the 10th of the month following the calendar quarter. The current annual dividend rate on common stock is $8 per share. The post-closing trial balance for the Hale Corporation on December 31, 1953, is shown below:

HALE CORPORATION
POST-CLOSING TRIAL BALANCE
DECEMBER 31, 1953

Cash.......................................	$ 40,000	
Accounts Receivable.......................	60,000	
Merchandise Inventory.....................	180,000	
Plant and Equipment.......................	500,000	
Allowance for Depreciation of Plant and Equipment................................		$ 50,000
Preferred Dividends Payable................		3,500
Common Dividends Payable.................		10,000
Other Current Liabilities...................		36,500
7% Preferred Stock, $100 par..............		200,000
Common Stock, 5,500 shares, no par........		435,000
Treasury Stock (500 shares of common at cost)..	55,000	
Earned Surplus............................		100,000
	$835,000	$835,000

The following transactions took place during 1954:

Feb. 2. Appropriated earned surplus of $10,000 for possible inventory losses.

May 10. Sold the treasury stock for $65,000.

June 3. It was discovered that merchandise inventory on December 31, 1953, was understated by $5,000.

3. A machine having a life of 5 years and no scrap value was purchased on April 1, 1952, for $10,000 and recorded in Purchases. No depreciation has ever been recorded on the machine.

Dec. 15. Issued common stock to the Little Manufacturing Company for an old plant. The Little Manufacturing Company accepted 1,500 shares of common stock having a current-market value of $140 per share.

31. The operations for 1954 resulted in a $90,000 increase in the company's net assets summarized as follows:

Cash.......................................	40,000	
Accounts Receivable.......................	20,000	
Plant and Equipment.......................	115,000	
Allowance for Depreciation..............		25,000
Income Taxes Payable....................		60,000
Profit and Loss Summary...............		90,000

31. Closed the balance in Profit and Loss Summary to Earned Surplus.

31. The old plant acquired from the Little Manufacturing Company was valued by professional appraisers at $260,000, the increased valuation being recorded in the accounts.

Instructions: (1) Journalize all transactions for the Hale Corporation during 1954 in chronological order starting with the payment of dividends on January 25. (For quarterly dividend declarations, determine carefully the number of shares actually outstanding on the record dates.)

(2) Open T accounts for the accounts listed in the post-closing trial balance and for Treasury Stock Surplus, Appraisal Surplus, Reserve for Possible Inventory Losses, and Profit and Loss Summary. Enter in these accounts the balances shown on the post-closing trial balance, and post to these accounts all the transactions recorded in (1).

(3) Prepare a balance sheet as of December 31, 1954.

(4) Prepare an earned surplus statement for 1954 similar to the one illustrated on page 456.

CHAPTER 24

Problem 24-A

This problem may be completed in the workbook in the space provided for Problem 24-1.

The following transactions were completed by the Ohio Equipment Company during 1953 and 1954.

1953

Nov. 1. Issued $500,000 of 10-year, 3% bonds, receiving $479,000 in cash. Interest is payable semiannually on May 1 and November 1.

Dec. 31. Recorded adjusting entry for interest payable.

31. Recorded amortization of discount on bonds.

1954

Jan. 1. Reversed adjusting entry for interest payable.

May 1. Paid semiannual interest on the bonds.

Nov. 1. Paid semiannual interest on the bonds.

Dec. 31. Recorded adjusting entry for interest payable.

31. Recorded amortization of discount on bonds.

Instructions: (1) Record the foregoing transactions in general journal form. (Entries for amortization of bond discount are to be made on December 31, the end of the fiscal year.)

(2) State the amount of the bond interest expense in (a) 1953 and (b) 1954.

Problem 24-B

This problem may be completed in the workbook in the space provided for Problem 24-2.

The following transactions were completed by The Marsh Corporation during the first three years of its operation, 1952, 1953, and 1954:

(a) Received subscriptions to 2,000 shares of 7% preferred stock at $65 (par value $50). Collected 50% of the subscription price.

(b) Exchanged 4,000 shares of common stock, par value $25, for plant and equipment valued at $115,000.

(c) Received cash in full payment of the preferred stock subscriptions and issued the stock.

(d) Made a net profit for the year of $30,000. (Debit Cash; credit Profit and Loss Summary.)

(e) Recorded estimated income taxes of 40% of net profit. Closed Profit and Loss Summary to Earned Surplus.

(f) Declared the annual preferred dividend and a $2 a share common dividend.

(g) Appropriated $10,000 as a reserve for plant additions.

(h) Sold $100,000 of 10-year, 6% bonds for $107,000.

(i) Paid $125,000 for new plant and equipment.

(j) Paid the common and preferred dividends declared in (f) and the income tax liability recorded in (e).

(k) Paid the annual interest on bonds and recorded the amortization.

(l) Made a net operating profit of $80,000. (Debit Cash and credit Profit and Loss Summary.) Closed Bond Interest Expense to Profit and Loss Summary.

(m) Recorded estimated income taxes of 40% of net profit. Closed Profit and Loss Summary to Earned Surplus.

(n) Declared the annual preferred dividend.

(o) Declared a stock dividend of 25% on common stock and issued the stock.

(p) Increased the reserve for plant additions by $10,000.

(q) Paid the preferred dividends declared in (n) and the income tax liability recorded in (m).

(r) Paid the annual interest on bonds and recorded the amortization.

(s) Made a net operating profit of $105,000. (Debit Cash and credit Profit and Loss Summary.) Closed Bond Interest Expense to Profit and Loss Summary.

(t) Recorded estimate income taxes of 45% of net profit. Closed Profit and Loss Summary.

(u) Declared the annual preferred dividend and a $2.50 a share dividend on common.

Instructions: (1) Record the transactions directly in T accounts. The accounts required are: Cash; Preferred Stock Subscriptions Receivable; Plant and Equipment; Income Taxes Payable; Cash Dividends Payable; Stock Dividends Payable; Bonds Payable; Premium on Bonds Payable; Preferred Stock; Preferred Stock Subscribed; Premium on Preferred Stock; Common Stock; Premium on Common Stock; Reserve for Plant Additions; Earned Surplus; Profit and Loss Summary; Bond Interest Expense.

(2) Prepare a balance sheet as of December 31, 1954.

CHAPTER 25

Problem 25-A

This problem may be completed in the workbook in the space provided for Problem 25-1.

The Jeffries Supply Co. has four sales departments: Fishing Equipment, Hunting Equipment, Camping Supplies, and Sportswear, and three service departments: Purchasing, Advertising, and General Office. The following pertinent information is taken from the books:

	FISHING EQUIPMENT	HUNTING EQUIPMENT	CAMPING SUPPLIES	SPORTSWEAR
Sales for the month of June	$40,000	$8,000	$32,000	$16,000
Purchases for the month of June	20,000	5,000	15,000	10,000
Inventory, June 1, 1953	12,000	4,000	6,000	3,000
Inventory, June 30, 1953	9,000	5,000	4,000	2,000

Direct operating expenses for the month are:

	ADVERTISING	SALARIES	SUPPLIES	INSURANCE
Fishing Equipment	$275	$2,600	$220	$237
Hunting Equipment	50	900	85	70
Camping Supplies	100	2,400	215	129
Sportswear	75	1,750	180	80
Purchasing		3,200	120	15
Advertising		2,100	270	21
General Office		7,200	130	11

The telephone expense is $5 per instrument:

Fishing Equipment	3 instruments	Purchasing	5 instruments
Hunting Equipment	1 instrument	Advertising	3 instruments
Camping Supplies	3 instruments	General Office	5 instruments
Sportswear	1 instrument		

The lighting charges of $800 are distributed according to the number of kilowatt-hours used:

Fishing Equipment	10,000 kwh.	Purchasing	4,000 kwh.
Hunting Equipment	5,000 kwh.	Advertising	2,000 kwh.
Camping Supplies	10,000 kwh.	General Office	4,000 kwh.
Sportswear	5,000 kwh.		

The monthly depreciation charges are $900, distributed as follows:

Fishing Equipment	24%	Sportswear	14%	Advertising	6%
Hunting Equipment	16%	Purchasing	10%	General Office	10%
Camping Supplies	20%				

The purchasing department expenses are to be distributed on the basis of purchases; the advertising department expenses, on the basis of direct advertising charges; and the general office department expenses, on the basis of sales.

Instructions: (1) Prepare an expense distribution sheet.

(2) Prepare one departmentalized profit and loss statement for all departments.

Problem 25-B

This problem may be completed in the workbook in the space provided for Problem 25-2.

The trial balance of the C. B. Rader Company at the end of the fiscal year on June 30, 1953, is given below:

C. B. RADER COMPANY

TRIAL BALANCE

JUNE 30, 1953

Cash...	$ 37,500	
Accounts Receivable..........................	110,400	
Allowance for Bad Debts.....................		$ 2,200
Merchandise Inventory, Department A.........	60,000	
Merchandise Inventory, Department B.........	45,000	
Store Supplies................................	26,000	
Store Equipment..............................	75,000	
Allowance for Depreciation of Store Equipment..		22,500
Capital Stock.................................		200,000
Surplus.......................................		80,000
Sales, Department A..........................		220,000
Sales, Department B..........................		110,000
Purchases, Department A......................	150,000	
Purchases, Department B......................	70,000	
Selling Expenses (control).....................	37,200	
General Expenses (control)....................	22,500	
Interest Income...............................		1,600
Interest Expense..............................	2,700	
	$636,300	$636,300

The following adjustments are to be made on June 30:

Merchandise inventory, Department A....................	$65,000
Merchandise inventory, Department B....................	50,000
Store supplies inventory................................	9,800

Allowance for bad debts, an additional ½% of sales.
Depreciation of store equipment, 12½%.
Estimated income taxes payable, 40%.

All selling and general expenses are to be distributed to the two departments, A and B, in proportion to sales.

Instructions: (1) Prepare a twelve-column work sheet with columns similar to those in the illustration on page 506 of the textbook. The work sheet is to show the net profit or loss of each department of the business and the net profit or loss of the entire business.

(2) Prepare a profit and loss statement for each department.

(3) Prepare a profit and loss statement showing the net profit or loss of the business. This statement should begin with the net profits or losses earned by the two departments.

CHAPTER 26

Problem 26-A

This problem may be completed in the workbook in the space provided for Problem 26-1.

The Varden Company, of Dallas, opened a branch office in Houston on January 1, 1954. Transactions and adjustments reflecting branch operations for the year ended December 31, 1954, were as follows:

(a) Cash advanced by the home office, $50,000.
(b) Store equipment purchased for cash by the branch, $40,000.
(c) Shipments of merchandise from the home office to the branch, $500,000.
(d) Sales on account, $364,500.
(e) Purchases by the branch (invoices paid by the home office), $33,000.
(f) Freight in on merchandise, paid by the branch, $1,200.
(g) Collections on accounts receivable, $302,000.
(h) Remittance to home office, $250,000.
(i) Selling expenses paid in cash by the branch, $31,360. (Charge Selling Expenses Control.)
(j) General expenses paid in cash by the branch, $15,150. (Charge General Expenses Control.)
(k) Branch merchandise inventory, December 31, 1954, $225,000.
(l) Depreciation rate: 10% a year. (Charge Selling Expenses Control.)
(m) Provision for bad debts expense, 1% of sales. (Charge General Expenses Control.)

Instructions: (1) Set up T accounts for the branch office as follows: Cash, Accounts Receivable, Allowance for Bad Debts, Merchandise Inventory, Store Equipment, Allowance for Depreciation of Store Equipment, Home Office, Profit and Loss Summary, Sales, Purchases, Shipments from Home Office, Freight In, Selling Expenses Control, General Expenses Control. Record the foregoing transactions and adjustments in these accounts.

(2) Set up T accounts for the home office as follows: Cash, Branch Office, Profit of Branch, and Shipments to Branch. Record the effect of the transactions on these accounts.

(3) Close the branch office income and expense accounts to Profit and Loss Summary and the balance of Profit and Loss Summary to Home Office. Record the branch profit in the home office T accounts.

(4) Prepare a profit and loss statement and a balance sheet for the branch.

Problem 26-B

This problem may be completed in the workbook in the space provided for Problem 26-2.

Instructions: (1) Prepare a profit and loss statement and a balance sheet for the branch.

(2) Prepare a profit and loss statement and a balance sheet for the home office.

(3) Prepare a work sheet for a consolidated profit and loss statement and a work sheet for a consolidated balance sheet.

(4) Prepare a consolidated profit and loss statement and a consolidated balance sheet.

The balances of the ledger accounts at the home and the branch of the Parker Corporation on May 31, 1954, the close of a monthly fiscal period, are given below:

	HOME OFFICE	BRANCH
Cash...............................	$100,000	$16,000
Accounts Receivable.................	30,000	5,000
Merchandise Inventory..............	125,000	60,000
Branch Office......................	75,000	
Accounts Payable..................	40,000	3,000
Home Office.......................		75,000
Capital Stock......................	150,000	
Surplus...........................	80,000	
Sales.............................	130,000	75,000
Shipments to Branch...............	50,000	
Purchases........................	80,000	15,000
Shipments from Home Office........		50,000
Operating Expenses Control.........	40,000	7,000

Merchandise inventory on May 31 is as follows: home office, $75,000; branch, $65,000.

CHAPTER 27

Problem 27-A

This problem may be completed in the workbook in the space provided for Problem 27-3.

The Bloom Manufacturing Company was incorporated on December 28, 1953, and began operations on January 2, 1954. The trial balance on December 31, 1954, was as follows:

Cash.................................	$ 161,000	
Factory Supplies.......................	18,000	
Machinery and Equipment...............	600,000	
Common Stock.........................		$ 600,000
Sales.................................		1,050,000
Raw Materials Purchases................	375,000	
Direct Labor..........................	296,250	
Indirect Labor.........................	19,750	
Rent of Factory Building................	37,500	
Sundry Factory Expense.................	22,500	
Selling Expenses (control)...............	90,000	
General Expenses (control)...............	30,000	
	$1,650,000	$1,650,000

Data for adjustments are:

(1) Inventories (overhead rate is 40% of direct labor):

(a) Finished goods: 3,000 units — material, $1.20; direct labor, $5.00.

(b) Work in process: 4,000 units — material, $1.00; direct labor, $4.50.

(c) Raw materials: Material A, 10,000 units at $0.80; Material B, 15,000 units at $0.40.

(2) Estimated depreciation of machinery and equipment....   5%

(3) Factory supplies inventory $8,000

(4) Accrued payroll:

     Direct labor $3,750

     Indirect labor   250

Income taxes are estimated at 40%.

Instructions: (1) Prepare a work sheet with manufacturing schedule columns.

(2) Prepare a profit and loss statement with a supporting cost of goods manufactured schedule.

(3) Prepare a balance sheet.

Problem 27-B

This problem may be completed in the workbook in the space provided for Problem 27-1.

A cost of goods manufactured schedule is shown below:

THE CRONIN CORPORATION
Cost of Goods Manufactured Schedule
For Year Ended December 31, 19--

Work in Process Inventory, January 1, 19--..			$ 80,000
Raw Materials:			
Inventory, January 1, 19--		$100,000	
Purchases...............................		290,000	
Total Cost of Materials Available for Use...		$390,000	
Less Inventory, December 31, 19--........		90,000	
Cost of Materials Consumed..............		$300,000	
Direct Labor.............................		200,000	
Manufacturing Expenses:			
Indirect Labor..........................	$75,000		
Maintenance and Repairs.................	7,000		
Heat, Light, and Power..................	23,000		
Depreciation Expense....................	25,000		
Sundry Manufacturing Expense...........	5,000		
Total Manufacturing Expenses..........		135,000	
Total Manufacturing Costs.................			635,000
Total Work in Process During Period.........			$715,000
Less Work in Process Inventory, December 31, 19--..................................			95,000
Cost of Goods Manufactured...............			$620,000

Instructions: (1) Prepare journal entries to adjust the raw materials inventory account and the work in process inventory account on December 31, 19 – –, the end of the fiscal year.

(2) Prepare the journal entry to close the purchases, the direct labor, and the manufacturing expense accounts to the manufacturing summary account.

(3) Prepare the journal entry to close the manufacturing summary account.

(4) Set up a manufacturing summary account and post the foregoing entries affecting it.

CHAPTER 28

Problem 28-A

This problem may be completed in the workbook in the space provided for Problem 28-2.

On June 1, the beginning of the sixth month of the current fiscal year, the following balances appeared in the accounts in the Laidlaw Manufacturing Company's general ledger and subsidiary ledgers:

Cash	$ 52,000	
Accounts Receivable	80,000	
Finished Goods — Commodity A, 1,000 units	30,000	
Work in Process — Job No. 212	2,000	
Raw Materials — Material 1	18,000	
Plant and Equipment	160,000	
Allowance for Depreciation of Plant and Equipment		$ 70,000
Accounts Payable		48,000
Wages Payable		3,000
Capital Stock		100,000
Surplus		58,000
Sales		380,000
Cost of Goods Sold	280,000	
Factory Overhead	2,000	
Selling and General Expenses	35,000	

The transactions completed during June are summarized as follows:

(a) Raw materials were purchased on account as follows:

Material 1	$12,000
Material 2	20,000
Material 3	4,000

(b) Raw materials were requisitioned from the stores clerk as follows:

Job No. 212: Mat. 1, $3,000; Mat. 2, $5,000	$ 8,000
Job No. 213: Mat. 1, $6,000; Mat. 2, $7,000	13,000
For general factory use: Mat. 3	2,000

(c) Time tickets for the month were chargeable as follows:

Job No. 212	$18,000
Job No. 213	15,000
Indirect labor	5,000

(d) Factory pay checks for $35,000 were issued.

(e) Cash of $90,000 was received on accounts receivable.

(f) Various factory maintenance charges of $7,000 were paid.

(g) Depreciation on factory equipment was recorded, $1,500.

(h) Miscellaneous factory expenses incurred on account, $6,000.

(i) Factory overhead was applied to jobs at the rate of ⅔ of direct labor cost.

(j) Selling and general expenses incurred on account, $9,000.

(k) Payments on account, $51,000.

(l) All job orders were completed during the month: Job Order No. 212 produced 1,600 units of Commodity B; Job Order No. 213 produced 1,900 units of Commodity C.

(m) Total sales on account, $125,000. The goods sold were as follows:
      800 units of Commodity A
      500 units of Commodity B
   1,900 units of Commodity C

Instructions: (1) Prepare T accounts for the general ledger, the raw materials ledger, the cost ledger, and the finished goods ledger. Record directly in these accounts the balances as of June 1 and the transactions completed during the month. Identify balances as "Bal." and transactions by letter.

(2) Take a trial balance.

(3) Prove the subsidiary ledgers with the controlling accounts in the general ledger.

(4) Prepare a profit and loss statement for the six months ended June 30.

Journal entries are not required, but the student may find the preparation of such entries to be helpful.

Problem 28-B

This problem may be completed in the workbook in the space provided for Problem 28-3.

The Grayson Manufacturing Company prepares financial statements at the end of each month but it closes its accounts only on December 31. On November 30 of the current year the accounts in the general ledger showed the following balances:

Cash	$ 73,000
Finished Goods	24,500
Work in Process	23,000
Raw Materials	25,000
Wages Payable	1,500
Common Stock	100,000
Retained Earnings	25,000
Sales	350,000
Cost of Goods Sold	300,000
Factory Overhead (dr.)	1,000
Operating Expenses	30,000

Operations for the month of December are summarized as follows:

(a) All sales were for cash:
Selling price.................................... $ 40,000
Cost of goods sold............................ 28,000

(b) Cash disbursements:
Wages payable............................... 25,000
Factory overhead expenses..................... 8,000
Operating expenses........................... 3,000
Raw materials purchases....................... 10,000

(c) Withdrawals of raw materials:
Chargeable to jobs directly.................... 15,000

(d) Factory labor:
Chargeable to jobs directly.................... 20,000
Chargeable to factory overhead................. 6,000

(e) Overhead rate applied to jobs, 80% of direct labor cost.

(f) Cost of goods completed......................... 36,000

Instructions: (1) Set up T accounts and record the balances as of December 1. Include an account for Profit and Loss Summary following the retained earnings account.

(2) Record the transactions directly in the accounts.

(3) Prepare a profit and loss statement and a balance sheet for the year ended December 31. Overabsorbed overhead is to be subtracted from Cost of Goods Sold.

(4) Record closing entries directly in the accounts. Balance and rule the accounts.

CHAPTER 29

Problem 29-A

This problem may be completed in the workbook in the space provided for Problem 29-3.

The condensed post-closing trial balance of the Barnes Manufacturing Company as of September 30, 1954, is shown below:

BARNES MANUFACTURING COMPANY
POST-CLOSING TRIAL BALANCE
SEPTEMBER 30, 1954

Other Assets (net)...........................	$ 99,600	
Raw Materials—700 units at $4...............	2,800	
Work in Process (Process B)—600 units ⅓ completed.....................................	3,610	
Product X Inventory—300 units at $10........	3,000	
Factory Supplies.............................	1,000	
Accounts Payable.............................		$ 20,600
Wages Payable...............................		410
Capital......................................		89,000
	$110,010	$110,010

The company has two productive processes, Process A and Process B. All material requirements are placed in Process A; after a certain point in the manufacturing operation is reached, the materials move on into Process B, where Product X results. The company uses the first-in, first-out method in charging out inventory items.

The company's operations for October are summarized as follows:

(a) Purchased for cash 1,000 units of raw materials at $4.50 per unit.

(b) Raw materials requisitioned for use in Process A, 1,500 units.

(c) Factory supplies purchased on account, $800.

(d) Factory charges for labor: Process A, $1,700; Process B, $7,400; Power Department, $700.

(e) Depreciation, insurance, and taxes charged to the factory: Process A, $200; Process B, $300; Power Department, $100.

(f) Factory supplies requisitioned: Process A, $400; Process B, $300.

(g) Amount of wages paid during October, $9,900.

(h) Power Department expenses are allocated to Process A and Process B on a 3:5 basis.

(i) All materials placed in Process A were transferred to Process B.

(j) During October, 1,600 units of Product X were completed. The 500 units remaining in process were on the average 60% complete as to processing costs and 100% complete as to materials.

(k) 1,500 units of Product X were sold at $18 per unit during the month (record sales and cost of sales).

Instructions: (1) Set up T accounts for Other Assets, Raw Materials, Process A, Process B, Product X Inventory, Factory Supplies, Accounts Payable, Wages Payable, Capital, Power Department, Sales, and Cost of Goods Sold. Enter the balances in the accounts.

(2) Record the foregoing operations for October directly in the accounts, identifying each entry by letter. Prepare separate schedules to show how amounts in transactions (b), (j), and (k) were determined.

(3) Balance and rule the accounts and take a trial balance as of October 31, 1954.

Problem 29-B

This problem may be completed in the workbook in the space provided for Problem 29-4.

Connolly, Inc. produces a single product by a continuous process in which materials are placed at the start of production. On December 1, 1953, the process account appeared as follows:

WORK IN PROCESS

Direct Materials (10,000 at $1.45)............ 14,500	
Direct Labor.......... 50,000	
Factory Overhead....... 22,480	
———	
86,980	

By December 31, 1953, 9,000 units were completed and transferred to Finished Goods. The 1,000 units still in process were estimated to be 60% completed.

During January of 1954, the following internal transactions were completed:

(a) 15,000 additional units of raw materials were placed into production at $1.60 per unit.

(b) Labor costs for the month were $82,000.

(c) Overhead amounted to $34,000.

(d) 13,000 units were transferred to Finished Goods, the remaining 3,000 being 70% completed as of January 31, 1954.

Instructions: (1) Complete the process account as of December 31, 1953.

(2) Enter the data for January in the process account and complete the account as of January 31, 1954.

(3) Prepare journal entries to record all internal transactions during December and January.

CHAPTER 30

Problem 30-A

This problem may be completed in the workbook in the space provided for Problem 30-1.

The executives of Abbott, Inc. require an estimated profit and loss statement for the fiscal year ending June 30, 1955. The following information is available:

Sales: The selling price, which has been $20 per unit, is to be reduced 10%. It is anticipated that this price reduction will result in a sales volume increase of 24,000 units.

Cost of Goods Sold: The unit cost is $12. Purchases plus the beginning inventory should equal the total yearly budgeted sales volume plus an ending inventory of the sales requirements for one and one-half months. (Assume that monthly sales will be distributed evenly throughout the year.)

Selling Expenses:
(a) Sales salaries will increase 10%.
(b) Advertising expense will increase by $10,000.
(c) Store supplies expense will increase 40%.
(d) Depreciation of store equipment will be the same as for the preceding year.
(e) Miscellaneous selling expense will increase 25%.

General Expenses:
(a) Officers salaries will increase by $5,000.
(b) Office salaries will increase 10%.
(c) Bad debts expense is estimated at $\frac{1}{2}$% of sales.
(d) Office supplies expense will increase by $500.
(e) Depreciation of office equipment will be the same as for the preceding year.
(f) The lease on the property now rented will expire on October 1, 1954. Upon the expiration of the lease, the company plans to exercise an

ABBOTT, INC.
Profit and Loss Statement
For Year Ended June 30, 1954

Sales...................................			$720,000
Cost of Goods Sold:			
Merchandise Inventory, July 1, 1953.......		$ 80,000	
Purchases.............................		452,000	
Merchandise Available for Sale............		$532,000	
Less Merchandise Inventory, June 30, 1954 .		100,000	
Cost of Goods Sold.....................			432,000
Gross Profit on Sales......................			$288,000
Operating Expenses:			
Selling Expenses:			
Sales Salaries.........	$80,000		
Advertising Expense.....	30,000		
Store Supplies Expense................	5,000		
Depreciation of Store Equipment........	6,000		
Miscellaneous Selling Expense..........	4,000		
Total Selling Expenses................		$125,000	
General Expenses:			
Officers Salaries......................	$30,000		
Office Salaries........................	20,000		
Bad Debts Expense....................	3,600		
Office Supplies Expense...............	2,500		
Depreciation of Office Equipment.......	2,000		
Rent Expense........................	24,000		
Miscellaneous General Expense.........	3,400		
Total General Expenses...............		85,500	
Total Operating Expenses...............			210,500
Net Profit from Operations.................			$ 77,500
Other Income:			
Purchases Discount.....................		$ 10,500	
Other Expense:			
Sales Discount.........................		8,000	
Net Addition.............................			2,500
Total Net Profit before Estimated Income Taxes			$ 80,000
Less Estimated Income Taxes.............			32,000
Net Profit after Estimated Income Taxes.....			$ 48,000

option to purchase the property for $315,000, of which $300,000 is allocable to the building and $15,000 to the land. The owner has been paying property taxes of $2,000 a year, for which the company will be liable beginning October 1. Depreciation on the building is to be computed at 4% a year. Building maintenance expenses are expected to be $5,000 for the period from October 1, 1954, to June 30, 1955.

(g) Miscellaneous general expense will increase by $3,100.

Other Income and Expenses: Cash discounts are to be estimated at 2% of purchases and at 1% of sales. Interest expense is estimated at $6,000.

Income Taxes: Income taxes are estimated at 40%.

Instructions: Prepare an estimated profit and loss statement for the year ending June 30, 1955.

CHAPTER 31

Problem 31-A

This problem may be completed in the workbook in the space provided for Problem 31-1.

The Horsfall Corporation reported the following comparative balance sheets for December 31, 1954, and December 31, 1953:

THE HORSFALL CORPORATION
COMPARATIVE BALANCE SHEETS
DECEMBER 31, 1954 AND 1953

ASSETS	1954	1953	Liab. and Capital	1954	1953
Cash	$135,000	$138,000	Notes Payable	$ 75,000	$ 15,000
Accounts Rec. (net)	105,000	102,000	Accounts Payable	45,000	120,000
Mdse. Inventory	180,000	120,000	Common Stock ($100 par)	369,000	300,000
Plant (net)	231,000	132,000			
Organization Costs	4,500	9,000	Earned Surplus	166,500	66,000
			Total Liab. and		
Total Assets	$655,500	$501,000	Capital	$655,500	$501,000

PROFIT AND LOSS DATA:

	1954	1953
Sales	$750,000	$900,000
Cost of Sales	600,000	675,000
Operating Expenses	90,000	135,000
Purchases Discounts	9,000	6,000
Sales Discounts	6,000	12,000
Interest Expense	3,000	750
Net Profit	60,000	83,250

OTHER DATA:

Merchandise Inventory, 1/1/53, $105,000.
Dividends paid in 1954, $30,000.
Write-up of plant during 1954, $75,000.
Notes given upon purchase of plant, $30,000.

Instructions: (1) Indicate whether or not conditions are improving for the company. Use the following ratios and other analyses:

(a) Current ratio.
(b) Acid-test ratio.
(c) Ratio of owned capital to borrowed capital (analyze surplus account first).
(d) Merchandise turnover.
(e) Relationship of notes payable, accounts payable, and purchases discounts.
(f) Relationship of accounts receivable, sales, and sales discounts.

(2) Express cost of sales, gross profit on sales, operating expenses, and net profit from operations as percentages of sales. Analyze them, assuming that volume (number of units sold) has remained constant.

Problem 31-B

This problem may be completed in the workbook in the space provided for Problem 31-2.

The following data were taken from the records of the Connolly Corporation:

BALANCE SHEETS, DECEMBER 31

ASSETS	1954	1953	1952	1951	1950
Cash	$ 6,250	$ 3,500	$ 5,000	$ 3,750	$ 1,500
Notes and Accounts Receivable (net)	75,000	50,000	30,000	11,250	5,000
Inventories	87,500	62,500	45,000	12,500	7,500
Plant (less allowance)	45,000	32,500	27,500	20,000	25,000
Total Assets	$213,750	$148,500	$107,500	$47,500	$39,000
LIABILITIES AND CAPITAL					
Notes and Accounts Payable	$100,000	$ 62,500	$35,000	$15,000	$10,000
Mortgage Notes Payable	25,000	18,750	16,250	12,500	10,000
Common Stock, stated value $10	63,750	50,000	50,000	20,000	18,750
Retained Earnings	25,000	17,250	6,250	——	250
Total Liabilities and Capital	$213,750	$148,500	$107,500	$47,500	$39,000

PROFIT AND LOSS DATA FOR YEARS ENDED DECEMBER 31

	1954	1953	1952	1951
Sales................................	$225,000	$200,000	$125,000	$75,000
Cost of Sales.......................	206,250	175,000	107,500	60,000
Expenses............................	11,250	14,000	7,500	10,000

Instructions: (1) Compute the following ratios for each year:

    (a) Current ratio.

    (b) Acid-test ratio.

    (c) Fixed ratio.

    (d) Owned capital to borrowed capital.

    (e) Merchandise turnover (4 years only).

(2) Express profit and loss data as a percentage of sales for each year.

(3) Analyze the trends shown in (1) and (2).

(4) Comment on proportionate increases in sales, receivables, and inventories.

CHAPTER 32

Problem 32-A

This problem may be completed in the workbook in the space provided for Problem 32-1.

The comparative balance sheets of the Grove Corporation for 1953 and 1954 are given below:

DEBITS	DECEMBER 31, 1953	DECEMBER 31, 1954
Cash..	$ 10,000	$ 12,000
Notes Receivable..............................	16,000	14,000
Accounts Receivable...........................	19,000	22,000
Merchandise Inventory.........................	35,500	40,500
Store Fixtures................................	18,000	21,000
Buildings.....................................	37,000	46,000
Land..	33,000	28,000
	$ 168,500	$ 183,500

CREDITS		
Allowance for Depreciation of Store Fixtures..	$ 5,500	$ 8,000
Allowance for Depreciation of Buildings.......	3,500	5,500
Accounts Payable..............................	51,000	45,000
Mortgage Note.................................	25,000	20,000
Common Stock..................................	50,000	65,000
Earned Surplus................................	33,500	40,000
	$ 168,500	$ 183,500

The earned surplus statement for 1954 appears as follows:

Balance, January 1, 1954.....................		$ 33,500
Net Profit for 1954 after Income Taxes........		15,500
		$ 49,000
Deduct: Cash Dividends....................	$ 4,000	
Stock Dividend...................	5,000	9,000
Balance, December 31, 1954................		$ 40,000

Depreciation was charged to operations as follows:

Store Fixtures...........................	$ 2,500	
Buildings...............................	2,000	$ 4,500

Instructions: (1) Prepare working papers for a statement of application of funds. (Leave two lines for Common Stock and for Earned Surplus.)

(2) Prepare a statement of application of funds with a supporting schedule of changes in working capital.

Problem 32-B

The tabulation of operating data for Lichter Products, Inc. is shown below. This tabulation covers the five-year period ended on December 31, 1954. On December 31, 1950, the corporation had outstanding 5,000 shares of common stock, each share having a par value of $100.

LICHTER PRODUCTS, INC.
TABULATION OF OPERATING DATA
FOR FIVE YEARS ENDED ON DECEMBER 31, 1954

YEAR	NET SALES	NET INCOME AFTER INCOME TAXES	RATIO OF INCOME TO SALES	DIVIDENDS DECLARED	INCOME REIN-VESTED	DIVIDEND RATE
1950	$ 600,000	$ 60,000	10%	$ 50,000	$10,000	10%
1951	750,000	90,000	x	x	x	15%
1952	900,000	x	10%	x	x	10%
1953*	900,000	135,000	x	130,000*	x	x
1954	900,000	x	15%	90,000	x	x
Totals	$4,050,000	x		x	x	

*The dividend for 1953 included a stock dividend of 20% declared in January of that year. All cash dividends declared in that year applied to the new stock as well as to the old.

Instructions: (1) Supply the data omitted in the tabulation and indicated by an x.

(2) During the five-year period the gross profit on sales amounted to $1,650,000, and the selling and administrative expenses were $800,000. Assuming that the average income tax rate was 40%, construct a cumulative income statement for the five-year period ended on December 31, 1954.

INDEX

A

Acceptance, 666; accounting for, 669; memorandum record of, 669; trade, 667
Accountancy, profession of, 11
Account form of balance sheet, 27
Accounting, accrual basis and cash basis of, 336; and bookkeeping, 61; branch, see Branch accounting; budgetary, 13; cost, see Cost accounting, 13; definition of, 4; departmental, see Departmental accounting, 495; for estimated future transactions, 595; for income tax, 335; for notes and interest, 187; for taxes, 327; governmental, 13; growth, 12; period, 34; private, 12; public, 11; purpose of, 3; specialized fields of, 13; study of, 1; systems, 13, 285; tax, 13
Accounting cycle, 44, 102; completion of, 83
Accounting Research Bulletin, No. 9, 4; No. 30, 20, 22; No. 34, 224; No. 39, 402; No. 41, 402
Accounts, and the balance sheet, 45; and the trial balance, 44; arrangement of, in the ledger, 50; balance sheet, 48; balancing, 98; classification of, 64; controlling, 113; four-column, 277; mixed, 83; nature of, 44; negative asset, 224; normal balances in, 50; profit and loss statement, 49; reciprocal, 515; relationship of controlling to subsidiary ledger, 116; ruling, 98; standard form of, 63; three-column, 114, 128, 277; temporary proprietorship, 49; valuation, 224
Accounts payable, 22; comparison of controlling account with subsidiary ledger, 147; ratio of notes payable to, 623; schedule of, 150, 171
Accounts payable ledger, 128; at end of month, 148; illustrated, 128
Accounts receivable, 19; and sales accounts in general ledger, 113; comparison of controlling account with subsidiary ledger, 142; schedule of, 145, 171
Accounts receivable ledger, 113; at end of month, 143; illustrated, 114
Accrual basis, 336
Accrued assets, 205, 215
Accrued expenses, 205
Accrued income, 205
Accrued liabilities, 22, 205, 213
Acid-test ratio, 622
Adjusted gross income, 338; deductions from, 340
Adjusted trial balance, 89
Adjusting entries, 84, 92, 93, 171, 172; departmental, 509; for merchandise inventory, 164; for payroll, 318; for payroll taxes, 318; manufacturing, 534; on the work sheet, 165, 166
Adjustments, on work sheet, 87, 88, 166, 167; illustrated, in accounts, 84
Admission of partner, 369; by investment, 370; by purchase of an interest, 369; determining the amount of goodwill on, 373; with bonus or allowance for goodwill to former partners, 371; with

bonus or allowance for goodwill to new partner, 374
Age of receivables, 632
Allowance for bad debts, 224; for depletion, 256; for depreciation, 242
Amortization of bond premium and bond discount, 468, 480
Analysis and interpretation of financial statements, necessity for, 617
Application of funds, 645; preparation of statement of, 641; statement of, 639, 644, 649; transactions affecting, 640; working papers for statement of, 642
Appraisal, of assets, 454; surplus, 441, 442
Appropriated earned surplus, 444
Assets, 5; see also Property; appraisal of, 454; classification of, 18; definition, 18; fixed, see Fixed assets, 241; intangible, 372, 531; negative, 224; quick, 622; revaluation of, 413
Auditing, 13
Authorized capital stock, 411
Average capital, 359; division of partnership profits according to, 359

B

Bad debts, allowance for, 224; direct write-off of, 229; estimate based on analysis of accounts receivable, 228; estimate based on sales, 227; expense, 224; on the financial statements, 225; provision for, 223; reserve for, 224
Balances, normal, in accounts, 50
Balance sheet, 17, 46, 48, 92, 169; account form of, 25; bond premium and discount on, 470; branch, 521; classified, 26; comparative, 625; comparison of corresponding items and ratios on different, 624; comparison of items on a particular, 621; corporation, 415, 474; form of, 17; estimated, 608; heading of, 25; illustrated and analyzed, 26; nature of, 8; of a manufacturing enterprise, 543; relationship of profit and loss statement to, 9, 40; report form of, 25, 28; simplified, 620; standard forms of, 25; surplus on, 446
Balancing and ruling accounts, 98
Bank account, depositor's, 151
Bank draft, 664, 672; illustrated, 673
Bank statement, 152, 153; reconciliation of, 153, 154
Bill of exchange, see Draft
Bill of lading, 674; order, 674; order, illustrated, 675; straight, 674
Bond discount, 466; amortization of, 468, 481; on the balance sheet, 470
Bond indenture, 465
Bond premium, 466; amortization of, 468, 480; on the balance sheet, 470
Bonds, 463; convertible, 466; income from investment in, 480; investment in, 477; redemption and conversion of, 472; registered

and coupon, 465; secured and unsecured, 465; serial, 466; term, 466
Bond sinking fund, 470; reserve for, 443, 472
Bonds payable, 23, 465
Bonus, admission of partner with, to former partners, 371; admission of partner with, to new partners, 374
Book value, of fixed assets, 243; of stock, 406
Bookkeeping cycle, 44, 83, 102
Book or perpetual inventories, 234, 546
Branch, analyses of internal operations of, 524; balance sheet, 521; consolidated statements, 521; office account, 515; profit and loss statement, 521; working fund, 515; work sheet for consolidated balance sheet, 523; work sheet for consolidated profit and loss statement, 522
Branch accounting, and branch operations, 514; for many branches, 524; illustration of, 517; methods of, 514; reciprocal accounts in, 515
Budget, 595; see also Master budget, cash, 595; importance of, to nonprofit organizations, 609; operating, 595; period, 595; report, 599
Budgetary accounting, 13
Budgetary control, advantages of, 609; essentials of, 597
Building, 21
Business papers, 659; and bookkeeping machines, 267
By-products, 579

C

Canceled checks, 152
Capital, 5; see also Proprietorship; and revenue charges, 531; average, 359; corporation, on the balance sheet, 405; division of partnership profits according to average, 359; gains and losses, 342; ratio of owned to borrowed, 624; surplus, 441; working, 27, 622
Capital accounts, statement of partners', 363
Capital stock, 24; accounting for subscriptions to, 422; authorized, 411; issuing, at a premium or a discount, 421; types of, 403
Cash, 19; accounting for, 139; basis, 335, 336; double record of, 139, 268, 291; nature of, 139; short and over, 156
Cashbook, 139
Cash discount, 110; on the profit and loss statement, 150
Cashier's check, 672
Cash journal, combined, 275-277
Cash payments journal, 145; entries based on bank reconciliation, 155; footing, ruling, and posting of, 146; illustrated, 146
Cash receipts, sources of, 139
Cash receipts journal, 139; entries based on bank reconciliation, 155; footing, ruling, and posting of, 140; illustrated, 141; types of columns in, 141